Get the eBook FREE!

(PDF, ePub, Kindle, and liveBook all included)

We believe that once you buy a book from us, you should be able to read it in any format we have available. To get electronic versions of this book at no additional cost to you, purchase and then register this book at the Manning website.

Go to https://www.manning.com/freebook and follow the instructions to complete your pBook registration.

That's it!
Thanks from Manning!

Deep Learning with JavaScript

Deep Learning with JavaScript

NEURAL NETWORKS IN TENSORFLOW.JS

SHANQING CAI
STANLEY BILESCHI
ERIC D. NIELSEN
WITH FRANÇOIS CHOLLET

FOREWORD BY NIKHIL THORAT
DANIEL SMILKOV

MANNING

SHELTER ISLAND

Manning Publications Co.
20 Baldwin Road
PO Box 761
Shelter Island, NY 11964

Development editor: Jenny Stout
Technical development editor: Marc-Phillipe Huget
Review editor: Ivan Martinovič
Project editor: Lori Weidert
Copy editor: Rebecca Deuel-Gallegos
Proofreader: Jason Everett
Technical proofreader: Karsten Strøbæck
Typesetter: Dottie Marsico
Cover designer: Marija Tudor

ISBN 9781617296178
Printed in the United States of America

brief contents

contents

foreword

When we started TensorFlow.js (TF.js), formerly called deeplearn.js, machine learning (ML) was done mostly in Python. As both JavaScript developers and ML practitioners on the Google Brain team, we quickly realized that there was an opportunity to bridge the two worlds. Today, TF.js has empowered a new set of developers from the extensive JavaScript community to build and deploy ML models and enabled new classes of on-device computation.

TF.js would not exist in its form today without Shanqing, Stan, and Eric. Their contributions to TensorFlow Python, including the TensorFlow Debugger, eager execution, and build and test infrastructure, uniquely positioned them to tie the Python and JavaScript worlds together. Early on in the development, their team realized the need for a library on top of deeplearn.js that would provide high-level building blocks to develop ML models. Shanqing, Stan, and Eric, among others, built TF.js Layers, allowing conversion of Keras models to JavaScript, which dramatically increased the wealth of available models in the TF.js ecosystem. When TF.js Layers was ready, we released TF.js to the world.

To investigate the motivations, hurdles, and desires of software developers, Carrie Cai and Philip Guo deployed a survey to the TF.js website. This book is in direct response to the study's summary: "Our analysis found that developers' desires for ML frameworks extended beyond simply wanting help with APIs: more fundamentally, they desired guidance on understanding and applying the conceptual underpinnings of ML itself."[1]

Deep Learning with JavaScript contains a mix of deep learning theory as well as real-world examples in JavaScript with TF.js. It is a great resource for JavaScript developers

---

[1] C. Cai and P. Guo, (2019) "Software Developers Learning Machine Learning: Motivations, Hurdles, and Desires," *IEEE Symposium on Visual Languages and Human-Centric Computing*, 2019.

with no ML experience or formal math background, as well as ML practitioners who would like to extend their work into the JavaScript ecosystem. This book follows the template of *Deep Learning with Python*, one of the most popular applied-ML texts, written by the Keras creator, François Chollet. Expanding on Chollet's work, *Deep Learning with JavaScript* does an amazing job building on the unique things that JavaScript has to offer: interactivity, portability, and on-device computation. It covers core ML concepts, but does not shy away from state-of-the-art ML topics, such as text translation, generative models, and reinforcement learning. It even gives pragmatic advice on deploying ML models into real-world applications written by practitioners who have extensive experience deploying ML to the real world. The examples in this book are backed by interactive demos that demonstrate the unique advantages of the JavaScript ecosystem. All the code is open-sourced, so you can interact with it and fork it online.

This book should serve as the authoritative source for readers who want to learn ML and use JavaScript as their main language. Sitting at the forefront of ML and JavaScript, we hope you find the concepts in this book useful and the journey in Java-Script ML a fruitful and exciting one.

—NIKHIL THORAT AND DANIEL SMILKOV,
inventors of deeplearn.js
and technical leads of TensorFlow.js

preface

The most significant event in the recent history of technology is perhaps the explosion in the power of neural networks since 2012. This was when the growth in labeled datasets, increases in computation power, and innovations in algorithms came together and reached a critical mass. Since then, deep neural networks have made previously unachievable tasks achievable and boosted the accuracies in other tasks, pushing them beyond academic research and into practical applications in domains such as speech recognition, image labeling, generative models, and recommendation systems, just to name a few.

It was against this backdrop that our team at Google Brain started developing TensorFlow.js. When the project started, many regarded "deep learning in JavaScript" as a novelty, perhaps a gimmick, fun for certain use cases, but not to be pursued with seriousness. While Python already had several well-established and powerful frameworks for deep learning, the JavaScript machine-learning landscape remained splintered and incomplete. Of the handful of JavaScript libraries available back then, most only supported deploying models pretrained in other languages (usually in Python). For the few that supported building and training models from scratch, the scope of supported model types was limited. Considering JavaScript's popular status and its ubiquity that straddles client and server sides, this was a strange situation.

TensorFlow.js is the first full-fledged industry-quality library for doing neural networks in JavaScript. The range of capabilities it provides spans multiple dimensions. First, it supports a wide range of neural-networks layers, suitable for various data types ranging from numeric to text, from audio to images. Second, it provides APIs for loading pretrained models for inference, fine-tuning pretrained models, and building and training models from scratch. Third, it provides both a high-level, Keras-like API for practitioners who opt to use well-established layer types, and a low-level, TensorFlow-like API for those who wish to implement more novel algorithms. Finally, it is designed to be runnable in a wide selection of environments and hardware types, including the web browser, server side (Node.js), mobile (e.g., React Native and WeChat), and desktop (electron). Adding to the multidimensional capability of TensorFlow.js is its status as a first-class integrated part of the larger TensorFlow/Keras ecosystem, specifically its API consistency and two-way model-format compatibility with the Python libraries.

The book you have in your hands will guide your grand tour through this multidimensional space of capabilities. We've chosen a path that primarily cuts through the first dimension (modeling tasks), enriched by excursions along the remaining dimensions. We start from the relatively simpler task of predicting numbers from numbers (regression) to the more complex ones such as predicting classes from images and sequences, ending our trip on the fascinating topics of using neural networks to generate new images and training agents to make decisions (reinforcement learning).

We wrote the book not just as a recipe for how to write code in TensorFlow.js, but as an introductory course in the foundations of machine learning in the native language of JavaScript and web developers. The field of deep learning is a fast-evolving one. It is our belief that a firm understanding of machine learning is possible without formal mathematical treatment, and this understanding will enable you to keep yourself up-to-date in future evolution of the techniques.

With this book you've made the first step in becoming a member of the growing community of JavaScript machine-learning practitioners, who've already brought about many impactful applications at the intersection between JavaScript and deep learning. It is our sincere hope that this book will kindle your own creativity and ingenuity in this space.

SHANQING CAI, STAN BILESCHI, AND ERIC NIELSEN
September 2019
Cambridge, MA

acknowledgments

This book owes *Deep Learning with Python* by François Chollet for its overall structure. Despite the fact that the code was rewritten in a different language and much new content was added for the JavaScript ecosystem and to reflect new developments in the field, neither this book nor the entire high-level API of TensorFlow.js would have been a reality without pioneer work on Keras led by François.

Our journey to the completion of this book and all the related code was made pleasant and fulfilling thanks to the incredible support from our colleagues on Google's TensorFlow.js Team. The seminal and foundational work by Daniel Smilkov and Nikhil Thorat on the low-level WebGL kernels and backpropagation forms a rock-solid foundation for model building and training. The work by Nick Kreeger on the Node.js binding to TensorFlow's C library is the main reason why we can run neural networks in the browser and Node.js with the same code. The TensorFlow.js data API by David Soergel and Kangyi Zhang makes chapter 6 of the book possible, while chapter 7 was enabled by the visualization work by Yannick Assogba. The performance optimization techniques described in chapter 11 wouldn't be possible without Ping Yu's work on op-level interface with TensorFlow. The speed of our examples wouldn't be nearly as fast as it is today without the focused performance optimization work by Ann Yuan. The leadership of Sarah Sirajuddin, Sandeep Gupta, and Brijesh Krishnaswami is critical to the overall long-term success of the TensorFlow.js project.

We would have fallen off the track without the support and encouragement of D. Sculley, who carefully reviewed all the chapters of the book. We're also immensely grateful for all the encouragement we received from Fernanda Viegas, Martin Wattenberg, Hal Abelson, and many other colleagues of ours at Google. Our writing and content were greatly improved as a result of the detailed review by François Chollet,

Nikhil Thorat, Daniel Smilkov, Jamie Smith, Brian K. Lee, and Augustus Odena, as well as by in-depth discussion with Suharsh Sivakumar.

One of the unique pleasures of working on a project such as TensorFlow.js is the opportunity to work alongside and interact with the worldwide open-source software community. TensorFlow.js was fortunate to have a group of talented and driven contributors including Manraj Singh, Kai Sasaki, Josh Gartman, Sasha Illarionov, David Sanders, syt123450@, and many many others, whose tireless work on the library expanded its capability and improved its quality. Manraj Singh also contributed the phishing-detection example used in chapter 3 of the book.

We are grateful to our editorial team at Manning Publications. The dedicated and tireless work by Brian Sawyer, Jennifer Stout, Rebecca Rinehart, and Mehmed Pasic, and many others made it possible for we authors to focus on writing the content. Marc-Philip Huget provided extensive and incisive technical review throughout the development process. Special thanks go to our reviewers, Alain Lompo, Andreas Refsgaard, Buu Nguyen, David DiMaria, Edin Kapic, Edwin Kwok, Eoghan O'Donnell, Evan Wallace, George thomas, Giuliano Bertoti, Jason Hales, Marcio Nicolau, Michael Wall, Paulo Nuin, Pietro Maffi, Polina Keselman, Prabhuti Prakash, Ryan Burrows, Satej Sahu, Suresh Rangarajulu, Ursin Stauss, and Vaijanath Rao, whose suggestions helped make this a better book.

We thank our MEAP readers for catching and pointing out quite a few typographical and technical errors.

Finally, none of this would be possible without the tremendous understanding and sacrifice on the part of our families. Shanqing Cai would like to express the deepest gratitude to his wife, Wei, as well as his parents and parents-in-law for their help and support during this book's year-long writing process. Stan Bileschi would like to thank his mother and father, as well as his step-mother and step-father, for providing a foundation and direction to build a successful career in science and engineering. He would also like to thank his wife, Constance, for her love and support. Eric Nielsen would like to say to his friends and family, thank you.

about this book

Who should read this book

This book is written for programmers who have a working knowledge of JavaScript, from prior experience with either web frontend development or Node.js-based back-end development, and wish to venture into the world of deep learning. It aims to satisfy the learning needs of the following two subgroups of readers:

- JavaScript programmers who aspire to go from little-to-no experience with machine learning or its mathematical background, to a decent knowledge of how deep learning works and a practical understanding of the deep-learning workflow that is sufficient for solving common data-science problems such as classification and regression
- Web or Node.js developers who are tasked with deploying pre-trained models in their web app or backend stack as new features

For the first group of readers, this book develops the basic concepts of machine learning and deep learning in a ground-up fashion, using JavaScript code examples that are fun and ready for fiddling and hacking. We use diagrams, pseudo-code, and concrete examples in lieu of formal mathematics to help you form an intuitive, yet firm, grasp of the foundations of how deep learning works.

For the second group of readers, we cover the key steps of converting existing models (e.g., from Python training libraries) into a web- and/or Node-compatible format suitable for deployment in the frontend or the Node stack. We emphasize practical aspects such as optimizing model size and performance, as well as considerations for various deployment environments ranging from a server to browser extensions and mobile apps.

This book provides in-depth coverage of the TensorFlow.js API for ingesting and formatting data, for building and loading models, and for running inference, evaluation, and training for all readers.

Finally, technically minded people who don't code regularly in JavaScript or any other language will also find this book useful as an introductory text for both basic and advanced neural networks.

How this book is organized: A roadmap

This book is organized into four parts. The first part, consisting of chapter 1 only, introduces you to the landscape of artificial intelligence, machine learning, and deep learning, and why it makes sense to practice deep learning in JavaScript.

The second part forms a gentle introduction to the most foundational and frequently encountered concepts in deep learning. In particular:

- Chapters 2 and 3 are your gentle on-ramp to machine learning. Chapter 2 works through a simple problem of predicting a single number from another number by fitting a straight line (linear regression) and uses it to illustrate how backpropagation (the engine of deep learning) works. Chapter 3 builds on chapter 2 by introducing nonlinearity, multi-layered networks, and classification tasks. From this chapter you will gain an understanding of what nonlinearity is, how it works, and why it gives deep neural networks their expressive power.
- Chapter 4 deals with image data and the neural-network architecture dedicated to solving image-related machine-learning problems: convolutional networks (convnets). We will also show you why convolution is a generic method that has uses beyond images by using audio inputs as an example.
- Chapter 5 continues the focus on convnets and image-like inputs, but shifts into the topic of transfer learning: how to train new models based on existing ones, instead of starting from scratch.

Part 3 of the book systematically covers more advanced topics in deep learning for users who wish to build an understanding of more cutting-edge techniques, with a focus on specific challenging areas of ML systems, and the TensorFlow.js tools to work with them:

- Chapter 6 discusses techniques for dealing with data in the context of deep learning.
- Chapter 7 shows the techniques for visualizing data and the models that process them, an important and indispensable step for any deep-learning workflow.
- Chapter 8 focuses on the important topics of underfitting and overfitting in deep learning, and techniques for analyzing and mitigating them. Through this discussion, we condense what we've learned in this book so far into a recipe referred to as "the universal workflow of machine learning." This chapter prepares you for the advanced neural-network architectures and problems in chapters 9–11.

- Chapter 9 is dedicated to deep neural networks that process sequential data and text inputs.
- Chapters 10 and 11 cover the advanced deep-learning areas of generative models (including generative adversarial networks) and reinforcement learning, respectively.

In the fourth and final part of the book, we cover techniques for testing, optimizing and deploying models trained or converted with TensorFlow.js (chapter 12) and wrap up the whole book by recapitulating the most important concepts and workflows (chapter 13).

Each chapter finishes with exercises to help you gauge your level of understanding and hone your deep-learning skills in TensorFlow.js in a hands-on fashion.

About the code

This book contains many examples of source code both in numbered listings and in line with normal text. In both cases, source code is formatted in a `fixed-width font like this` to separate it from ordinary text. Sometimes code is also **in bold** to highlight code that has changed from previous steps in the chapter, such as when a new feature adds to an existing line of code.

In many cases, the original source code has been reformatted; we've added line breaks and reworked indentation to accommodate the available page space in the book. In rare cases, even this was not enough, and listings include line-continuation markers (➥). Additionally, comments in the source code have often been removed from the listings when the code is described in the text. Code annotations accompany many of the listings, highlighting important concepts. The code for the examples in this book is available for download from GitHub at https://github.com/tensorflow/tfjs-examples.

liveBook discussion forum

Purchase of *Deep Learning with JavaScript* includes free access to a private web forum run by Manning Publications where you can make comments about the book, ask technical questions, and receive help from the author and from other users. To access the forum, go to https://livebook.manning.com/#!/book/deep-learning-with-javascript/discussion. You can also learn more about Manning's forums and the rules of conduct at https://livebook.manning.com/#!/discussion.

Manning's commitment to our readers is to provide a venue where a meaningful dialogue between individual readers and between readers and the author can take place. It is not a commitment to any specific amount of participation on the part of the author, whose contribution to the forum remains voluntary (and unpaid). We suggest you try asking the authors some challenging questions lest their interest stray! The forum and the archives of previous discussions will be accessible from the publisher's website as long as the book is in print.

about the authors

SHANQING CAI, STANLEY BILESCHI, AND ERIC NIELSEN are software engineers on the Google Brain team. They were the primary developers of the high-level API of Tensor-Flow.js, including the examples, the documentation, and the related tooling. They have applied TensorFlow.js-based deep learning to real-world problems such as alternative communication for people with disabilities. They each have advanced degrees from MIT.

about the cover illustration

The figure on the cover of *Deep Learning with JavaScript* is captioned "Finne Katschin," or a girl from the Katschin tribe. The illustration is taken from a collection of dress costumes from various countries by Jacques Grasset de Saint-Sauveur (1757-1810), titled *Costumes de Différents Pays,* published in France in 1797. Each illustration is finely drawn and colored by hand. The rich variety of Grasset de Saint-Sauveur's collection reminds us vividly of how culturally apart the world's towns and regions were just 200 years ago. Isolated from each other, people spoke different dialects and languages. In the streets or in the countryside, it was easy to identify where they lived and what their trade or station in life was just by their dress.

The way we dress has changed since then and the diversity by region, so rich at the time, has faded away. It is now hard to tell apart the inhabitants of different continents, let alone different towns, regions, or countries. Perhaps we have traded cultural diversity for a more varied personal life—certainly for a more varied and fast-paced technological life.

At a time when it is hard to tell one computer book from another, Manning celebrates the inventiveness and initiative of the computer business with book covers based on the rich diversity of regional life of two centuries ago, brought back to life by Grasset de Saint-Sauveur's pictures.

Part 1

Motivation and basic concepts

Part 1 consists of a single chapter that orients you to the basic concepts that will form the backdrop for the rest of the book. These include artificial intelligence, machine learning, and deep learning and the relations between them. Chapter 1 also addresses the value and potential of practicing deep learning in JavaScript.

Deep learning and JavaScript

1

This chapter covers

- What deep learning is and how it is related to artificial intelligence (AI) and machine learning
- What makes deep learning stand out among various machine-learning techniques, and the factors that led to the current "deep-learning revolution"
- The reasons for doing deep learning in JavaScript using TensorFlow.js
- The overall organization of this book

All the buzz around artificial intelligence (AI) is happening for a good reason: the deep-learning revolution, as it is sometimes called, has indeed happened. *Deep-learning revolution* refers to the rapid progress made in the speed and techniques of deep neural networks that started around 2012 and is still ongoing. Since then, deep neural networks have been applied to an increasingly wide range of problems, enabling machines to solve previously unsolvable problems in some cases and dramatically improving solution accuracy in others (see table 1.1 for examples). To experts in AI, many of these breakthroughs in neural networks were stunning.

To engineers who use neural networks, the opportunities this progress has created are galvanizing.

JavaScript is a language traditionally devoted to creating web browser UI and back-end business logic (with Node.js). As someone who expresses ideas and creativity in JavaScript, you may feel a little left out by the deep-learning revolution, which seems to be the exclusive territory of languages such as Python, R, and C++. This book aims at bringing deep learning and JavaScript together through the JavaScript deep-learning library called TensorFlow.js. We do this so that JavaScript developers like you can learn how to write deep neural networks without learning a new language; more importantly, we believe deep learning and JavaScript belong together.

The cross-pollination will create unique opportunities, ones unavailable in any other programming language. It goes both ways for JavaScript and deep learning. With JavaScript, deep-learning applications can run on more platforms, reach a wider audience, and become more visual and interactive. With deep learning, JavaScript developers can make their web apps more intelligent. We will describe how later in this chapter.

Table 1.1 lists some of the most exciting achievements of deep learning that we've seen in this deep-learning revolution so far. In this book, we have selected a number of these applications and created examples of how to implement them in TensorFlow.js, either in their full glory or in reduced form. These examples will be covered in depth in the coming chapters. Therefore, you will not stop at marveling at the breakthroughs: you can learn about them, understand them, and implement them all in JavaScript.

But before you dive into these exciting, hands-on deep-learning examples, we need to introduce the essential context around AI, deep learning, and neural networks.

Table 1.1   Examples of tasks in which accuracy improved significantly thanks to deep-learning techniques since the beginning of the deep-learning revolution around 2012. This list is by no means comprehensive. The pace of progress will undoubtedly continue in the coming months and years.

Machine-learning task	Representative deep-learning technology	Where we use TensorFlow.js to perform a similar task in this book
Categorizing the content of images	Deep convolutional neural networks (convnets) such as ResNet[a] and Inception[b] reduced the error rate in the ImageNet classification task from ~25% in 2011 to below 5% in 2017.[c]	Training convnets for MNIST (chapter 4); MobileNet inference and transfer learning (chapter 5)

a. Kaiming He et al., "Deep Residual Learning for Image Recognition," *Proc. IEEE Conference Computer Vision and Pattern Recognition* (CVPR), 2016, pp. 770–778, http://mng.bz/PO5P.
b. Christian Szegedy et al., "Going Deeper with Convolutions," *Proc. IEEE Conference Computer Vision and Pattern Recognition* (CVPR), 2015, pp. 1–9, http://mng.bz/JzGv.
c. Large Scale Visual Recognition Challenge 2017 (ILSVRC2017) results, http://image-net.org/challenges/LSVRC/2017/results.

Table 1.1 Examples of tasks in which accuracy improved significantly thanks to deep-learning techniques since the beginning of the deep-learning revolution around 2012. This list is by no means comprehensive. The pace of progress will undoubtedly continue in the coming months and years. *(continued)*

Machine-learning task	Representative deep-learning technology	Where we use TensorFlow.js to perform a similar task in this book
Localizing objects and images	Variants of deep convnets[d] reduced localization error from 0.33 in 2012 to 0.06 in 2017.	YOLO in TensorFlow.js (section 5.2)
Translating one natural language to another	Google's neural machine translation (GNMT) reduced translation error by ~60% compared to the best traditional machine-translation techniques.[e]	Long Short-Term Memory (LSTM)-based sequence-to-sequence models with attention mechanisms (chapter 9)
Recognizing large-vocabulary, continuous speech	An LSTM-based encoder-attention-decoder architecture achieves a lower word-error rate than the best non-deep-learning speech recognition system.[f]	Attention-based LSTM small-vocabulary continuous speech recognition (chapter 9)
Generating realistic-looking images	Generative adversarial networks (GANs) are now capable of generating realistic-looking images based on training data (see https://github.com/junyanz/CycleGAN).	Generating images using variational autoencoders (VAEs) and GANs (chapter 9)
Generating music	Recurrent neural networks (RNNs) and VAEs are helping create music scores and novel instrument sounds (see https://magenta.tensorflow.org/demos).	Training LSTMs to generate text (chapter 9)
Learning to play games	Deep learning combined with reinforcement learning (RL) lets machines learn to play simple Atari games using raw pixels as the only input.[g] Combining deep learning and Monte Carlo tree search, Alpha-Zero reached a super-human level of Go purely through self-play.[h]	Using RL to solve the cart-pole control problem and a snake video game (chapter 11)
Diagnosing diseases using medical images	Deep convnets were able to achieve specificity and sensitivity comparable to trained human ophthalmologists in diagnosing diabetic retinopathy based on images of patients' retinas.[i]	Transfer learning using a pre-trained MobileNet image model (chapter 5).

d. Yunpeng Chen et al., "Dual Path Networks," https://arxiv.org/pdf/1707.01629.pdf.
e. Yonghui Wu et al., "Google's Neural Machine Translation System: Bridging the Gap between Human and Machine Translation," submitted 26 Sept. 2016, https://arxiv.org/abs/1609.08144.
f. Chung-Cheng Chiu et al., "State-of-the-Art Speech Recognition with Sequence-to-Sequence Models," submitted 5 Dec. 2017, https://arxiv.org/abs/1712.01769.
g. Volodymyr Mnih et al., "Playing Atari with Deep Reinforcement Learning," NIPS Deep Learning Workshop 2013, https://arxiv.org/abs/1312.5602.
h. David Silver et al., "Mastering Chess and Shogi by Self-Play with a General Reinforcement Learning Algorithm," submitted 5 Dec. 2017, https://arxiv.org/abs/1712.01815.
i. Varun Gulshan et al., "Development and Validation of a Deep Learning Algorithm for Detection of Diabetic Retinopathy in Retinal Fundus Photographs," JAMA, vol. 316, no. 22, 2016, pp. 2402–2410, http://mng.bz/wIDQ.

1.1 *Artificial intelligence, machine learning, neural networks, and deep learning*

Phrases like *AI*, *machine learning*, *neural networks*, and *deep learning* mean related but different things. To orient yourself in the dazzling world of AI, you need to understand what they refer to. Let's define these terms and the relations among them.

1.1.1 *Artificial intelligence*

As the Venn diagram in figure 1.1 shows, AI is a broad field. A concise definition of the field would be as follows: *the effort to automate intellectual tasks normally performed by humans.* As such, AI encompasses machine learning, neural networks, and deep learning, but it also includes many approaches distinct from machine learning. Early chess programs, for instance, involved hard-coded rules crafted by programmers. Those didn't qualify as machine learning because the machines were programmed explicitly to solve the problems instead of being allowed to discover strategies for solving the problems by learning from the data. For a long time, many experts believed that

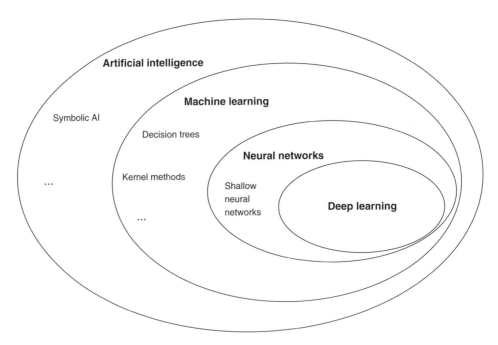

Figure 1.1   Relations between AI, machine learning, neural networks, and deep learning. As this Venn diagram shows, machine learning is a subfield of AI. Some areas of AI use approaches different from machine learning, such as symbolic AI. Neural networks are a subfield of machine learning. There exist non-neural-network machine-learning techniques, such as decision trees. Deep learning is the science and art of creating and applying "deep" neural networks—neural networks with multiple "layers"—versus "shallow" neural networks—neural networks with fewer layers.

human-level AI could be achieved through handcrafting a sufficiently large set of explicit rules for manipulating knowledge and making decisions. This approach is known as *symbolic AI*, and it was the dominant paradigm in AI from the 1950s to the late 1980s.[1]

1.1.2 Machine learning: How it differs from traditional programming

Machine learning, as a subfield of AI distinct from symbolic AI, arises from a question: Could a computer go beyond what a programmer knows how to program it to perform, and learn on its own how to perform a specific task? As you can see, the approach of machine learning is fundamentally different from that of symbolic AI. Whereas symbolic AI relies on hard-coding knowledge and rules, machine learning seeks to avoid this hard-coding. So, if a machine isn't explicitly instructed on how to perform a task, how would it learn how to do so? The answer is by learning from examples in the data.

This opened the door to a new programming paradigm (figure 1.2). To give an example of the machine-learning paradigm, let's suppose you are working on a web app that handles photos uploaded by users. A feature you want in the app is automatic classification of photos into ones that contain human faces and ones that don't. The app will take different actions on face images and no-face images. To this end, you want to create a program to output a binary face/no-face answer given any input image (made of an array of pixels).

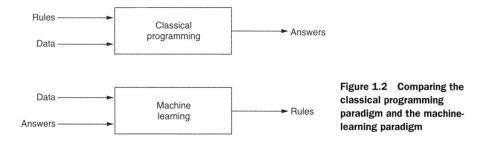

Figure 1.2 Comparing the classical programming paradigm and the machine-learning paradigm

We humans can perform this task in a split second: our brains' genetic hardwiring and life experience give us the ability to do so. However, it is hard for any programmer, no matter how smart and experienced, to write an explicit set of rules in a programming language (the only practical way for humans to communicate with a computer) on how to accurately decide whether an image contains a human face. You can spend days poring over code that does arithmetic on the RGB (red-green-blue) values of pixels to detect elliptic contours that look like faces, eyes, and mouths, as well as devising heuristic rules on the geometric relations between the contours. But you will soon realize that such effort is laden with arbitrary choices of logic and parameters that are

---

[1] An important type of symbolic AI is *expert systems*. See this Britannica article to learn about them: http://mng.bz/7zmy.

hard to justify. More importantly, it is hard to make it work well![2] Any heuristic you come up with is likely to fall short when facing the myriad variations that faces can present in real-life images, such as differences in the size, shape, and details of the face; facial expression; hairstyle; skin color; orientation; the presence or absence of partial obscuring; glasses; lighting conditions; objects in the background; and so on.

In the machine-learning paradigm, you recognize that handcrafting a set of rules for such a task is futile. Instead, you find a set of images, some with faces in them and some without. Then you enter the desired (that is, correct) face or no-face answer for each one. These answers are referred to as *labels*. This is a much more tractable (in fact, trivial) task. It may take some time to label all the images if there are a lot of them, but the labeling task can be divided among several humans and can proceed in parallel. Once you have the images labeled, you apply machine learning and let machines discover the set of rules on their own. If you use the correct machine-learning techniques, you will arrive at a trained set of rules capable of performing the face/no-face task with an accuracy > 99%—far better than anything you can hope to achieve with handcrafted rules.

From the previous example, we can see that machine learning is the process of automating the discovery of rules for solving complex problems. This automation is beneficial for problems like face detection, in which humans know the rules intuitively and can easily label the data. For other problems, the rules are not known intuitively. For example, consider the problem of predicting whether a user will click an ad displayed on a web page, given the page's and the ad's contents and other information, such as time and location. No human has a good sense about how to make accurate predictions for such problems in general. Even if one does, the pattern will probably change with time and with the appearance of new content and new ads. But the labeled training data is available from the ad service's history: it is available from the ad servers' logs. The availability of the data and labels alone makes machine learning a good fit for problems like this.

In figure 1.3, we take a closer look at the steps involved in machine learning. There are two important phases. The first is the *training phase*. This phase takes the data and answers, together referred to as the *training data*. Each pair of input data and the desired answer is called an *example*. With the help of the examples, the training process produces the automatically discovered *rules*. Although the rules are discovered automatically, they are not discovered entirely from scratch. In other words, machine-learning algorithms are not creative in coming up with rules. In particular, a human engineer provides a blueprint for the rules at the outset of training. The blueprint is encapsulated in a *model*, which forms a *hypothesis space* for the rules the machine may possibly learn. Without this hypothesis space, there is a completely unconstrained and infinite space of possible rules to search in, which is not conducive to finding good

---

[2] In fact, such approaches have indeed been attempted before and did not work very well. This survey paper provides good examples of handcrafting rules for face detection before the advent of deep learning: Erik Hjelmås and Boon Kee Low, "Face Detection: A Survey," *Computer Vision and Image Understanding*, Sept. 2001, pp. 236–274, http://mng.bz/m4d2.

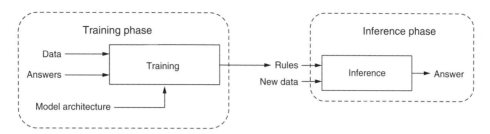

Figure 1.3   A more detailed view of the machine-learning paradigm than that in figure 1.2. The workflow of machine learning consists of two phases: training and inference. Training is the process of the machine automatically discovering the rules that convert the data into answers. The learned rules, encapsulated in a trained "model," are the fruit of the training phase and form the basis of the inference phase. Inference means using the model to obtain answers for new data.

rules in a limited amount of time. We will describe in great detail the kinds of models available and how to choose the best ones based on the problem at hand. For now, it suffices to say that in the context of deep learning, models vary in terms of how many layers the neural network consists of, what types of layers they are, and how they are wired together.

With the training data and the model architecture, the training process produces the learned rules, encapsulated in a trained model. This process takes the blueprint and alters (or tunes) it in ways that nudge the model's output closer and closer to the desired output. The training phase can take anywhere from milliseconds to days, depending on the amount of training data, the complexity of the model architecture, and how fast the hardware is. This style of machine learning—namely, using labeled examples to progressively reduce the error in a model's outputs—is known as *supervised learning.*[3] Most of the deep-learning algorithms we cover in this book are supervised learning. Once we have the trained model, we are ready to apply the learned rules on new data—data that the training process has never seen. This is the second phase, or *inference phase.* The inference phase is less computationally intensive than the training phase because 1) inference usually happens on one input (for instance, one image) at a time, whereas training involves going through all the training data; and 2) during inference, the model does not need to be altered.

LEARNING REPRESENTATIONS OF DATA

Machine learning is about learning from data. But *what* exactly is learned? The answer: a way to effectively transform the data or, in other words, to change the old representations of the data into a new one that gets us closer to solving the problem at hand.

---

[3] Another style of machine learning is *unsupervised learning,* in which unlabeled data is used. Examples of unsupervised learning are clustering (discovering distinct subsets of examples in a dataset) and anomaly detection (determining if a given example is sufficiently different from the examples in the training set).

Before we go any further, what is a representation? At its core, it is a way to look at the data. The same data can be looked at in different ways, leading to different representations. For example, a color image can have an RGB or HSV (hue-saturation-value) encoding. Here, the words *encoding* and *representation* mean essentially the same thing and can be used interchangeably. When encoded in these two different formats, the numerical values that represent the pixels are completely different, even though they are for the same image. Different representations are useful for solving different problems. For example, to find all the red parts of an image, the RGB representation is more useful; but to find color-saturated parts of the same image, the HSV representation is more useful. This is essentially what machine learning is all about: finding an appropriate transformation that turns the old representation of the input data into a new one—one that is amenable to solving the specific task at hand, such as detecting the location of cars in an image or deciding whether an image contains a cat and a dog.

To give a visual example, we have a collection of white points and several black points in a plane (figure 1.4). Let's say we want to develop an algorithm that can take the 2D (x, y) coordinates of a point and predict whether that point is black or white. In this case,

- The input data is the two-dimensional Cartesian coordinates (x and y) of a point.
- The output is the predicted color of the point (whether it's black or white).

The data shows a pattern in panel A of figure 1.4. How would the machine decide the color of a point given the x- and y-coordinates? It cannot simply compare x with a number, because the range of the x-coordinates of the white points overlaps with the range of the x-coordinates of the black ones! Similarly, the algorithm cannot rely on the y-coordinate. Therefore, we can see that the original representation of the points is not a good one for the black-white classification task.

What we need is a new representation that separates the two colors in a more straightforward way. Here, we transform the original Cartesian x-y representation into a polar-coordinate-system representation. In other words, we represent a point by 1) its angle—the angle formed by the x-axis and the line that connects the origin with the point (see the example in panel A of figure 1.4) and 2) its radius—its distance from the origin. After this transformation, we arrive at a new representation of the same set of data, as panel B of figure 1.4 shows. This representation is more amenable to our task, in that the angle values of the black and white points are now completely nonoverlapping. However, this new representation is still not an ideal one in that the black-white color classification cannot be made into a simple comparison with a threshold value (like zero).

Luckily, we can apply a second transformation to get us there. This transformation is based on the simple formula

```
(absolute value of angle) - 135 degrees
```

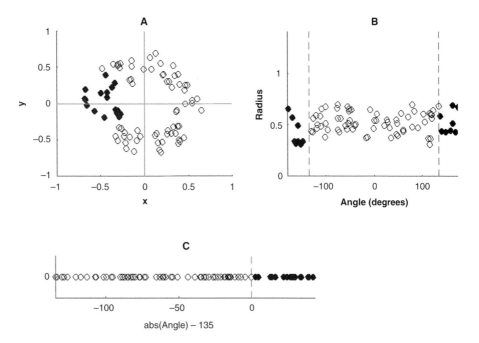

Figure 1.4 **A toy example of the representation transformations that machine learning is about. Panel A: the original representation of a dataset consisting of black and white points in a plane. Panels B and C: two successive transformation steps turn the original representation into one that is more amenable to the color-classification task.**

The resulting representation, as shown in panel C, is one-dimensional. Compared to the representation in panel B, it throws away the irrelevant information about the distance of the points to the origin. But it is a perfect representation in that it allows a completely straightforward decision process:

```
if the value < 0, the point is classified as white;
    else, the point is classified as black
```

In this example, we manually defined a two-step transform of the data representation. But if instead we tried automated searching for different possible coordinate transforms using feedback about the percentage of points classified correctly, then we would be doing machine learning. The number of transformation steps involved in solving real machine-learning problems is usually much greater than two, especially in deep learning, where it can reach hundreds. Also, the kind of representation transformations seen in real machine learning can be much more complex compared to those seen in this simple example. Ongoing research in deep learning keeps discovering more sophisticated and powerful transformations. But the example in figure 1.4 captures the essence of searching for better representations. This applies to all machine-learning algorithms, including neural networks, decision trees, kernel methods, and so forth.

1.1.3 *Neural networks and deep learning*

Neural networks are a subfield of machine learning, one in which the transformation of the data representation is done by a system with an architecture loosely inspired by how neurons are connected in human and animal brains. How are neurons connected to each other in brains? It varies among species and brain regions. But a frequently encountered theme of neuronal connection is the layer organization. Many parts of the mammalian brain are organized in a layered fashion. Examples include the retina, the cerebral cortex, and the cerebellar cortex.

At least on a superficial level, this pattern is somewhat similar to the general organization of *artificial neural networks* (simply called *neural networks* in the world of computing, where there is little risk of confusion), in which the data is processed in multiple separable stages, aptly named *layers*. These layers are usually stacked on top of each other, with connections only between adjacent ones. Figure 1.5 shows a simple (artificial) neural network with four layers. The input data (an image, in this case) feeds into the first layer (on the left side of the figure), then flows sequentially from one layer to the next. Each layer applies a new transformation on the representation of the data. As the data flows through the layers, the representation becomes increasingly different from the original and gets closer and closer to the goal of the neural network—namely, applying a correct label to the input image. The last layer (on the right side of the figure) emits the neural network's final output, which is the result of the image-classification task.

A layer of neural networks is similar to a mathematical function in that it is a mapping from an input value to an output value. However, neural network layers are different from pure mathematical functions in that they are generally *stateful*. In other words, they hold internal memory. A layer's memory is captured in its *weights*. What are weights? They are simply a set of numerical values that belong to the layer and govern the details of how each input representation is transformed by the layer into an output representation. For example, the frequently used *dense* layer transforms its input data by multiplying it with a matrix and adding a vector to the result of the matrix multiplication. The matrix and the vector are the dense layer's weights. When a neural network is trained through exposure to training data, the weights get altered systematically in a way that minimizes a certain value called the *loss function*, which we will cover in detail using concrete examples in chapters 2 and 3.

Although neural networks are inspired by the brain, we should be careful not to overly humanize them. The purpose of neural networks is *not* to study or mimic how the brain works. That is the realm of neuroscience, a separate academic discipline. Neural networks are about enabling machines to perform interesting practical tasks by learning from data. The fact that some neural networks show resemblance to some

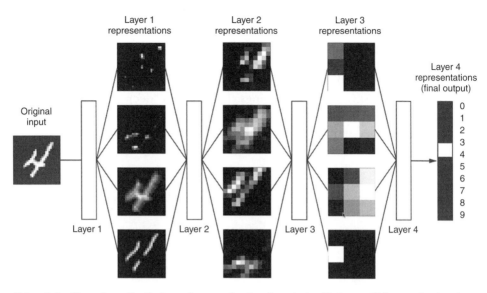

Figure 1.5   The schematic diagram of a neural network, organized in layers. This neural network classifies images of hand-written digits. In between the layers, you can see the intermediate representation of the original data. Reproduced with permission from François Chollet, *Deep Learning with Python*, Manning Publications, 2017.

parts of the biological brain, both in structure and in function,[4] is indeed remarkable. But whether this is a coincidence is beyond the scope of this book. In any case, the resemblance should not be overread. Importantly, there is no evidence that the brain learns through any form of gradient descent, the primary way in which neural networks are trained (covered in the next chapter). Many important techniques in neural networks that helped usher in the deep-learning revolution were invented and adopted not because they were backed by neuroscience, but instead because they helped neural networks solve practical learning tasks better and faster.

Now that you know what neural networks are, we can tell you what *deep learning* is. Deep learning is the study and application of *deep neural networks*, which are, quite simply, neural networks with *many layers* (typically, from a dozen to hundreds of layers). Here, the word *deep* refers to the idea of a large number of successive layers of representations. The number of layers that form a model of the data is called the model's *depth*. Other appropriate names for the field could have been "layered representation learning" or "hierarchical representation learning." Modern deep learning often involves tens or hundreds of successive layers of representations—and they are all learned automatically from exposure to training data. Meanwhile, other

---

[4]   For a compelling example of similarity in functions, see the inputs that maximally activate various layers of a convolutional neural network (see chapter 4), which closely resemble the neuronal receptive fields of various parts of the human visual system.

approaches to machine learning tend to focus on learning only one or two layers of representations of the data; hence, they are sometimes called *shallow learning*.

It is a misconception that the "deep" in deep learning is about any kind of deep understanding of data—that is, "deep" in the sense of understanding the meaning behind sentences like "freedom is not free" or savoring the contradictions and self-references in M.C. Escher's drawings. That kind of "deep" remains an elusive goal for AI researchers.[5] In the future, deep learning may bring us closer to this sort of depth, but that will certainly be harder to quantify and achieve than adding layers to neural networks.

INFO BOX 1.1 Not just neural networks: Other popular machine-learning techniques

We went directly from the "machine learning" circle of the Venn diagram in figure 1.1 to the "neural network" circle inside. However, it is worthwhile for us to briefly visit the machine-learning techniques that are not neural networks, not only because doing so will give us a better historical context but also because you may run into some of the techniques in existing code.

The *Naive Bayes classifier* is one of the earliest forms of machine learning. Put simply, Bayes' theorem is about how to estimate the probability of an event given 1) the a priori belief of how likely the event is and 2) the observed facts (called *features*) relating to the event. This theorem can be used to classify observed data points into one of many known categories by choosing the category with the highest probability (likelihood) given the observed facts. Naive Bayes is based on the assumption that the observed facts are mutually independent (a strong and naive assumption, hence the name).

Logistic regression (or *logreg*) is also a classification technique. Thanks to its simple and versatile nature, it is still popular and often the first thing a data scientist will try in order to get a feel for the classification task at hand.

Kernel methods, of which support vector machines (SVMs) are the best-known examples, tackle binary (that is, two-class) classification problems by mapping the original data into spaces of higher dimensionality and finding a transformation that maximizes a distance (called a *margin*) between two classes of examples.

Decision trees are flowchart-like structures that let you classify input data points or predict output values given inputs. At each step of the flowchart, you answer a simple yes/no question, such as, "Is feature X greater than a certain threshold?" Depending on whether the answer is yes or no, you advance to one of two possible next questions, which is just another yes/no question, and so forth. Once you reach the end of the flowchart, you will get the final answer. As such, decision trees are easy for humans to visualize and iterpret.

---

[5] Douglas Hofstadter, "The Shallowness of Google Translate," *The Atlantic*, 30 Jan. 2018, http://mng.bz/5AE1.

Random forests and gradient-boosted machines increase the accuracy of decision trees by forming an ensemble of a large number of specialized, individual decision trees. *Ensembling*, also known as *ensemble learning*, is the technique of training a collection (that is, an ensemble) of individual machine-learning models and using an aggregate of their outputs during inference. Today, gradient boosting may be one of the best algorithms, if not the best, for dealing with nonperceptual data (for example, credit card fraud detection). Alongside deep learning, it is one of the most commonly used techniques in data science competitions, such as those on Kaggle.

THE RISE, FALL, AND RISE OF NEURAL NETWORKS, AND THE REASONS BEHIND THEM

The core ideas of neural networks were formed as early as the 1950s. The key techniques for training neural networks, including backpropagation, were invented in the 1980s. However, for a long period of time between the 1980s and the 2010s, neural networks were almost completely shunned by the research community, partly because of the popularity of competing methods such as SVMs and partly because of the lack of an ability to train deep (many-layered) neural networks. But around 2010, a number of people still working on neural networks started to make important breakthroughs: the groups of Geoffrey Hinton at the University of Toronto, Yoshua Bengio at the University of Montreal, and Yann LeCun at New York University, as well as researchers at the Dalle Molle Institute for Artificial Intelligence Research (IDSIA) in Switzerland. These groups achieved important milestones, including the first practical implementations of deep neural networks on graphics processing units (GPUs) and driving the error rate from about 25% down to less than 5% in the ImageNet computer vision challenge.

Since 2012, deep *convolutional neural networks* (convnets) have become the go-to algorithm for all computer-vision tasks; more generally, they work on all perceptual tasks. Examples of non-computer-vision perceptual tasks include speech recognition. At major computer vision conferences in 2015 and 2016, it was nearly impossible to find presentations that didn't involve convnets in some form. At the same time, deep learning has also found applications in many other types of problems, such as natural language processing. It has completely replaced SVMs and decision trees in a wide range of applications. For instance, for several years, the European Organization for Nuclear Research, CERN, used decision-tree-based methods to analyze particle data from the ATLAS detector at the Large Hadron Collider; but CERN eventually switched to deep neural networks due to their higher performance and ease of training on large datasets.

So, what makes deep learning stand out from the range of available machine-learning algorithms? (See info box 1.1 for a list of some popular machine-learning techniques that are not deep neural networks.) The primary reason deep learning took off so quickly is that it offered better performance on many problems. But that's not the only reason. Deep learning also makes problem-solving much easier because it automates what used to be the most crucial and difficult step in a machine-learning workflow: *feature engineering*.

Previous machine-learning techniques—shallow learning—only involved transforming the input data into one or two successive representation spaces, usually via simple transformations such as high-dimensional nonlinear projections (kernel methods) or decision trees. But the refined representations required by complex problems generally can't be attained by such techniques. As such, human engineers had to go to great lengths to make the initial input data more amenable to processing by these methods: they had to manually engineer good layers of representations for their data. This is called *feature engineering*. Deep learning, on the other hand, automates this step: with deep learning, you learn all features in one pass rather than having to engineer them yourself. This has greatly simplified machine-learning workflows, often replacing sophisticated multistage pipelines with a single, simple, end-to-end deep-learning model. Through automating feature engineering, deep learning makes machine learning less labor-intensive and more robust—two birds with one stone.

These are the two essential characteristics of how deep learning learns from data: the incremental, layer-by-layer way in which increasingly complex representations are developed; and the fact that these intermediate incremental representations are learned jointly, each layer being updated to follow both the representational needs of the layer above and the needs of the layer below. Together, these two properties have made deep learning vastly more successful than previous approaches to machine learning.

1.1.4 Why deep learning? Why now?

If basic ideas and core techniques for neural networks already existed as early as the 1980s, why did the deep-learning revolution start to happen only after 2012? What changed in the two decades in between? In general, three technical forces drive advances in machine learning:

- Hardware
- Datasets and benchmarks
- Algorithmic advances

Let's visit these factors one by one.

HARDWARE

Deep learning is an engineering science guided by experimental findings rather than by theory. Algorithmic advances become possible only when appropriate hardware are available to try new ideas (or to scale up old ideas, as is often the case). Typical deep-learning models used in computer vision or speech recognition require orders of magnitude more computational power than what your laptop can deliver.

Throughout the 2000s, companies like NVIDIA and AMD invested billions of dollars in developing fast, massively parallel chips (GPUs) to power the graphics of increasingly photorealistic video games—cheap, single-purpose supercomputers designed to render complex 3D scenes on your screen in real time. This investment came to benefit the scientific community when, in 2007, NVIDIA launched CUDA (short for Compute Unified Device Architecture), a general-purpose programming interface for its line of GPUs. A small number of GPUs started replacing massive clusters of CPUs in various highly parallelizable applications, beginning with physics modeling. Deep neural networks, consisting mostly of many matrix multiplications and additions, are also highly parallelizable.

Around 2011, some researchers began to write CUDA implementations of neural nets—Dan Ciresan and Alex Krizhevsky were among the first. Today, high-end GPUs can deliver hundreds of times more parallel computation power when training deep neural networks than what a typical CPU is capable of. Without the sheer computational power of modern GPUs, it would be impossible to train many state-of-the-art deep neural networks.

DATA AND BENCHMARKS

If hardware and algorithms are the steam engine of the deep-learning revolution, then data is its coal: the raw material that powers our intelligent machines, without which nothing would be possible. When it comes to data, in addition to the exponential progress in storage hardware over the past 20 years (following Moore's law), the game changer has been the rise of the internet, which has made it feasible to collect and distribute very large datasets for machine learning. Today, large companies work with image datasets, video datasets, and natural language datasets that couldn't have been collected without the internet. User-generated image tags on Flickr, for instance, have been a treasure trove of data for computer vision. So are YouTube videos. And Wikipedia is a key dataset for natural language processing.

If there's one dataset that has been a catalyst for the rise of deep learning, it's Image-Net, which consists of 1.4 million images that have been hand annotated with 1,000 image categories. What makes ImageNet special isn't just its large size; it is also the yearly competition associated with it. As ImageNet and Kaggle have been demonstrating since 2010, public competitions are an excellent way to motivate researchers and engineers to push the envelope. Having common benchmarks that researchers compete to beat has greatly helped the recent rise of deep learning.

ALGORITHMIC ADVANCES

In addition to hardware and data, until the late 2000s, we were missing a reliable way to train very deep neural networks. As a result, neural networks were still fairly shallow, using only one or two layers of representations; thus, they couldn't shine against more refined shallow methods such as SVMs and random forests. The key issue was that of gradient propagation through deep stacks of layers. The feedback signal used to train neural networks would fade away as the number of layers increased.

This changed around 2009 to 2010 with the advent of several simple but important algorithmic improvements that allowed for better gradient propagation:

- Better activation functions for neural network layers (such as the rectified linear unit, or relu)

- Better weight-initialization schemes (for example, Glorot initialization)
- Better optimization schemes (for example, RMSProp and ADAM optimizers)

Only when these improvements began to allow for training models with 10 or more layers did deep learning start to shine. Finally, in 2014, 2015, and 2016, even more advanced ways to help gradient propagation were discovered, such as batch normalization, residual connections, and depthwise separable convolutions. Today we can train from scratch models that are thousands of layers deep.

1.2   *Why combine JavaScript and machine learning?*

Machine learning, like other branches of AI and data science, is usually done with traditionally backend-focused languages, such as Python and R, running on servers or workstations outside the web browser.[6] This status quo is not surprising. The training of deep neural networks often requires the kind of multicore and GPU-accelerated computation not directly available in a browser tab; the enormous amount of data that it sometimes takes to train such models is most conveniently ingested in the backend: for example, from a native file system of virtually unlimited size. Until recently, many regarded "deep learning in JavaScript" as a novelty. In this section, we will present reasons why, for many kinds of applications, performing deep learning in the browser environment with JavaScript is a wise choice, and explain how combining the power of deep learning and the web browser creates unique opportunities, especially with the help of TensorFlow.js.

First, once a machine-learning model is trained, it must be deployed somewhere in order to make predictions on real data (such as classifying images and text, detecting events in audio or video streams, and so on). Without deployment, training a model is just a waste of compute power. It is often desirable or imperative that the "somewhere" is a web frontend. Readers of this book are likely to appreciate the overall importance of the web browser. On desktops and laptops, the web browser is the dominant means through which users access content and services on the internet. It is how desktop and laptop users spend most of their time using those devices, exceeding the second place by a large margin. It is how users get vast amounts of their daily work done, stay connected, and entertain themselves. The wide range of applications that run in the web browser provide rich opportunities for applying client-side machine learning. For the mobile frontend, the web browser trails behind native mobile apps in terms of user engagement and time spent. But mobile browsers are nonetheless a force to be reckoned with because of their broader reach, instant access, and faster development cycles.[7] In fact, because of their flexibility and ease of use, many mobile apps, such as Twitter and Facebook, drop into a JavaScript-enabled web view for certain types of content.

---

[6] Srishti Deoras, "Top 10 Programming Languages for Data Scientists to Learn in 2018," *Analytics India Magazine*, 25 Jan. 2018, http://mng.bz/6wrD.

[7] Rishabh Borde, "Internet Time Spend in Mobile Apps, 2017–19: It's 8x than Mobile Web," DazeInfo, 12 Apr. 2017, http://mng.bz/omDr.

Due to this broad reach, the web browser is a logical choice for deploying deep-learning models, as long as the kinds of data the models expect are available in the browser. But what kinds of data are available in the browser? The answer is, many! Take, for example, the most popular applications of deep learning: classifying and detecting objects in images and videos, transcribing speech, translating languages, and analyzing text content. Web browsers are equipped with arguably the most comprehensive technologies and APIs for presenting (and, with user permission, for capturing) textual, image, audio, and video data. As a result, powerful machine-learning models can be directly used in the browser, for example, with TensorFlow.js and straightforward conversion processes. In the later chapters of this book, we will cover many concrete examples of deploying deep-learning models in the browser. For example, once you have captured images from a webcam, you can use TensorFlow.js to run MobileNet to label objects, run YOLO2 to put bounding boxes around detected objects, run Lipnet to do lipreading, or run a CNN-LSTM network to apply captions to images.

Once you have captured audio from the microphone using the browser's WebAudio API, TensorFlow.js can run models to perform real-time spoken-word recognition. There are exciting applications with textual data as well, such as assigning sentiment scores to user text like movie reviews (chapter 9). Beyond these data modalities, the modern web browser can access a range of sensors on mobile devices. For example, HTML5 provides API access to geolocation (latitude and longitude), motion (device orientation and acceleration), and ambient light (see http://mobilehtml5.org). Combined with deep learning and other data modalities, data from such sensors opens doors to many exciting new applications.

Browser-based application of deep learning comes with five additional benefits: reduced server cost, lowered inference latency, data privacy, instant GPU acceleration, and instant access:

- *Server cost* is often an important consideration when designing and scaling web services. The computation required to run deep-learning models in a timely manner is often significant, necessitating the use of GPU acceleration. If models are not deployed to the client side, they need to be deployed on GPU-backed machines, such as virtual machines with CUDA GPUs from Google Cloud or Amazon Web Services. Such cloud GPU machines are often costly. Even the most basic GPU machines presently cost in the neighborhood of $0.5–1 per hour (see https://www.ec2instances.info and https://cloud.google.com/ gpu). With increasing traffic, the cost of running a fleet of cloud GPU machines gets higher, not to mention the challenge of scalability and the added complexity of your server stack. All these concerns can be eliminated by deploying the model to the client. The overhead of client-side downloading of the model (which is often several megabytes or more) can be alleviated by the browser's caching and local storage capabilities (chapter 2).
- *Lowered inference latency*—For certain types of applications, the requirement for latency is so stringent that the deep-learning models must be run on the client

side. Any applications that involve real-time audio, image, and video data fall into this category. Consider what will happen if image frames need to be transferred to the server for inference. Suppose images are captured from a webcam at a modest size of 400 × 400 pixels with three color channels (RGB) and an 8-bit depth per color channel at a rate of 10 frames per second. Even with JPEG compression, each image has a size of about 150 Kb. On a typical mobile network with an approximately 300-Kbps upload bandwidth, it can take more than 500 milliseconds to upload each image, leading to a latency that is noticeable and perhaps unacceptable for certain applications (for example, games). This calculation doesn't take into account the fluctuation in (and possible loss of) network connectivity, the additional time it takes to download the inference results, and the vast amount of mobile data usage, each of which can be a showstopper.

Client-side inference addresses these potential latency and connectivity concerns by keeping the data and the computation on the device. It is impossible to run real-time machine-learning applications such as labeling objects and detecting poses in webcam images without the model running purely on the client. Even for applications without latency requirements, the reduction in model inference latency can lead to greater responsiveness and hence an improved user experience.

- *Data privacy*—Another benefit of leaving the training and inference data on the client is the protection of users' privacy. The topic of data privacy is becoming increasingly important today. For certain types of applications, data privacy is an absolute requirement. Applications related to health and medical data are a prominent example. Consider a "skin disease diagnosis aid" that collects images of a patient's skin from their webcam and uses deep learning to generate possible diagnoses of the skin condition. Health information privacy regulations in many countries will not allow the images to be transferred to a centralized server for inference. By running the model inference in the browser, no data needs to ever leave the user's phone or be stored anywhere, ensuring the privacy of the user's health data.

  Consider another browser-based application that uses deep learning to provide users with suggestions on how to improve the text they write in the application. Some users may use this application to write sensitive content such as legal documents and will not be comfortable with the data being transferred to a remote server via the public internet. Running the model purely in client-side browser JavaScript is an effective way to address this concern.

- *Instant WebGL acceleration*—In addition to the availability of data, another prerequisite for running machine-learning models in the web browser is sufficient compute power through GPU acceleration. As mentioned earlier, many state-of-the-art deep-learning models are so computationally intensive that acceleration through parallel computation on the GPU is a must (unless you are willing to let users wait for minutes for a single inference result, which rarely happens in real applications). Fortunately, modern web browsers come equipped with the WebGL API, which, even though it was originally designed for accelerated rendering of 2D and 3D graphics, can be ingeniously leveraged for the kind of parallel computation required for accelerating neural networks. The authors of TensorFlow.js painstakingly wrapped WebGL-based acceleration of the deep-learning components in the library, so the acceleration is available to you through a single line of JavaScript import.

WebGL-based acceleration of neural networks may not be perfectly on par with native, tailored GPU acceleration such as NVIDIA's CUDA and CuDNN (used by Python deep-learning libraries such as TensorFlow and PyTorch), but it still leads to orders of magnitude speedup of neural networks and enables real-time inference such as what PoseNet extraction of a human-body pose offers.

If performing inference on pretrained models is expensive, performing training or transfer learning on such models is even more so. Training and transfer learning enable exciting applications such as personalization of deep-learning models, frontend visualization of deep learning, and federated learning (training the same model on many devices, then aggregating the results of the training to obtain a good model). The WebGL acceleration of TensorFlow.js makes it possible to train or fine-tune neural networks with sufficient speed, purely inside the web browser.

- *Instant access*—Generally speaking, applications that run in the browser have the natural advantage of "zero install:" all it takes to access the app is typing a URL or clicking a link. This forgoes any potentially tedious and error-prone installation steps, along with possibly risky access control when installing new software. In the context of deep learning in the browser, the WebGL-based neural network acceleration that TensorFlow.js provides does not require special kinds of graphics cards or installation of drivers for such cards, which is often a nontrivial process. Most reasonably up-to-date desktop, laptop, and mobile devices come with graphics cards available to the browser and WebGL. Such devices, as long as they have a TensorFlow.js-compatible web browser installed (a low bar), are automatically ready to run WebGL-accelerated neural networks. This is an especially attractive feature in places where ease of access is vital—for example, the education of deep learning.

INFO BOX 1.2 Accelerating computation using GPU and WebGL

It takes a massive number of math operations to train machine-learning models and use them for inference. For example, the widely used "dense" neural network layers involve multiplying a large matrix with a vector and adding the result to another vector. A typical operation of this sort involves thousands or millions of floating-point operations. An important fact about such operations is that they are often *parallelizable*.

(continued)
For instance, adding two vectors can be divided into many smaller operations, such as adding two individual numbers. These smaller operations do not depend on each other. For example, you don't need to know the sum of the two elements of the two vectors at index 0 to compute the sum of the two elements at index 1. As a result, the smaller operations can be performed at the same time, instead of one at a time, no matter how large the vectors are. Serial computation, such as a naive CPU implementation of vector addition, is known as Single Instruction Single Data (SISD). Parallel computation on the GPU is known as Single Instruction Multiple Data (SIMD). It typically takes the CPU less time to compute each individual addition than a GPU takes. But the total cost over this large amount of data leads the GPU's SIMD to outperform the CPU's SISD. A deep neural network can contain millions of parameters. For a given input, it might take billions of element-by-element math operations to run (if not more). The massively parallel computation that GPUs are capable of really shines at this scale.

Task: Add two vectors, element by element:

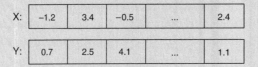

Computation on a CPU

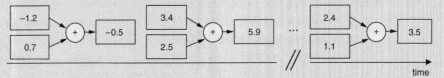

Computation on a GPU

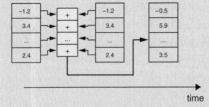

How WebGL acceleration leverages a GPU's parallel computation capability to achieve faster vector operation than a CPU

To be precise, modern CPUs are capable of certain levels of SIMD instructions, too. However, a GPU comes with a much greater number of processing units (on the order of hundreds or thousands) and can execute instructions on many slices of the input data at the same time. Vector addition is a relatively simple SIMD task in that each step of computation looks at only a single index, and the results at different indices are independent of each other. Other SIMD tasks seen in machine learning are more complex. For example, in matrix multiplication, each step of computation uses data from multiple indices, and there are dependencies between the indices. But the basic idea of acceleration through parallelization remains the same.

It is interesting to note that GPUs were not originally designed for accelerating neural networks. This can be seen in the name: *graphics processing unit*. The primary purpose of GPUs is processing 2D and 3D graphics. In many graphical applications, such as 3D gaming, it is critical that the processing be done in as little time as possible so that the images on the screen can be updated at a sufficiently high frame rate for smooth gaming experiences. This was the original motivation when the creators of the GPU exploited SIMD parallelization. But, as a pleasant surprise, the kind of parallel computing GPUs are capable of also suits the needs of machine learning.

The WebGL library TensorFlow.js uses for GPU acceleration was originally designed for tasks such as rendering textures (surface patterns) on 3D objects in the web browser. But textures are just arrays of numbers! Hence, we can pretend that the numbers are neural network weights or activations and repurpose WebGL's SIMD texture operations to run neural networks. This is exactly how TensorFlow.js accelerates neural networks in the browser.

In addition to the advantages we have described, web-based machine-learning applications enjoy the same benefits as generic web applications that do not involve machine learning:

- Unlike native app development, the JavaScript application you write with TensorFlow.js will work on many families of devices, ranging from Mac, Windows, and Linux desktops to Android and iOS devices.
- With its optimized 2D and 3D graphical capabilities, the web browser is the richest and most mature environment for data visualization and interactivity. In places where people would like to present the behavior and internals of neural networks to humans, it is hard to think of any environment that beats the browser. Take TensorFlow Playground, for example (https://playground .tensorflow.org). It is a highly popular web app in which you can interactively solve classification problems with neural networks. You can tune the structure and hyperparameters of the neural network and observe how its hidden layers and outputs change as a result (see figure 1.6). If you have not played with it before, we highly recommend you give it a try. Many have expressed the view that this is among the most instructive and delightful educational materials they've seen on the topic of neural networks. TensorFlow Playground is, in fact, an important forebearer of TensorFlow.js. As an offspring of the Playground, TensorFlow.js is powered by a far wider range of deep-learning capabilities and far more optimized performance. In addition, it is equipped with a dedicated component for visualization of deep-learning models (covered in chapter 7 in

detail). No matter whether you want to build basic educational applications along the lines of TensorFlow Playground or present your cutting-edge deep-learning research in a visually appealing and intuitive fashion, TensorFlow.js will help you go a long way toward your goals (see examples such as real-time tSNE embedding visualization[8]).

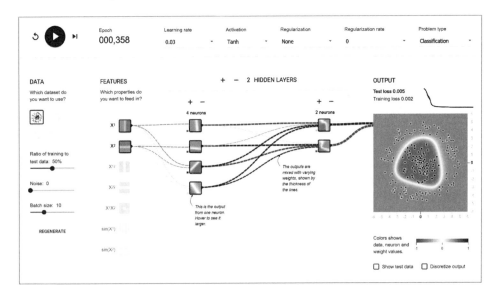

Figure 1.6   A screenshot of TensorFlow Playground (https://playground.tensorflow.org), a popular browser-based UI for teaching how neural networks work from Daniel Smilkov and his colleagues at Google. TensorFlow Playground was also an important precursor of the later TensorFlow.js project.

1.2.1   Deep learning with Node.js

For security and performance reasons, the web browser is designed to be a resource-constrained environment in terms of limited memory and storage quota. This means that the browser is not an ideal environment for training large machine-learning models with large amounts of data, despite the fact that it is ideal for many types of inference, small-scale training, and transfer-learning tasks, which require fewer resources. However, Node.js alters the equation entirely. Node.js enables JavaScript to be run outside the web browser, thus granting it access to all the native resources, such as RAM and the file system. TensorFlow.js comes with a Node.js version, called *tfjs-node*. It binds directly to the native TensorFlow libraries compiled from C++ and CUDA code, and so enables users to use the same parallelized CPU and GPU operation kernels as used under the hood by TensorFlow (in Python). As can be shown empirically, the speed of model training in tfjs-node is on par with the speed of Keras in Python. So, tfjs-node is

---

[8]   See Nicola Pezzotti, "Realtime tSNE Visualizations with TensorFlow.js," *googblogs*, http://mng.bz/nvDg.

an appropriate environment for training large machine-learning models with large amounts of data. In this book, you will see examples in which we use tfjs-node to train the kind of large models that are beyond the browser's capability (for example, the word recognizer in chapter 5 and the text-sentiment analyzer in chapter 9).

But what are the possible reasons to choose Node.js over the more established Python environment for training machine-learning models? The answers are 1) performance and 2) compatibility with existing stack and developer skill sets. First, in terms of performance, the state-of-the-art JavaScript interpreters, such as the V8 engine Node.js uses, perform just-in-time (JIT) compilation of JavaScript code, leading to superior performance over Python. As a result, it is often faster to train models in tfjs-node than in Keras (Python), as long as the model is small enough for the language interpreter performance to be the determining factor.

Second, Node.js is a very popular environment for building server-side applications. If your backend is already written in Node.js, and you would like to add machine learning to your stack, using tfjs-node is usually a better choice than using Python. By keeping code in a single language, you can directly reuse large portions of your code base, including those bits for loading and formatting the data. This will help you set up the model-training pipeline faster. By not adding a new language to your stack, you also keep its complexity and maintenance costs down, possibly saving the time and cost of hiring a Python programmer.

Finally, the machine-learning code written in TensorFlow.js will work in both the browser environment and Node.js, with the possible exception of data-related code that relies on browser-only or Node-only APIs. Most of the code examples you will encounter in this book will work in both environments. We have made efforts to separate the environment-independent, machine-learning-centric part of the code from the environment-specific data-ingestion and UI code. The added benefit is that you get the ability to do deep learning on both the server and client sides by learning only one library.

1.2.2 *The JavaScript ecosystem*

When assessing the suitability of JavaScript for a certain type of application such as deep learning, we should not ignore the factor that JavaScript is a language with an exceptionally strong ecosystem. For years, JavaScript has been consistently ranked number one among a few dozen programming languages in terms of repository count and pull activities on GitHub (see http://githut.info). On npm, the de facto public repository of JavaScript packages, there are more than 600,000 packages as of July 2018. This more than quadruples the number of packages in PyPI, the de facto public repository of Python packages (www.modulecounts.com). Despite the fact that Python and R have a better-established community for machine learning and data science, the JavaScript community is building up support for machine-learning-related data pipelines as well.

Want to ingest data from cloud storage and databases? Both Google Cloud and Amazon Web Services provide Node.js APIs. Most popular database systems today, such as MongoDB and RethinkDB, have first-class support for Node.js drivers. Want to wrangle data in JavaScript? We recommend the book *Data Wrangling with Java-Script* by Ashley Davis (Manning Publications, 2018, www.manning.com/books/data-wrangling-with-javascript). Want to visualize your data? There are mature and powerful libraries such as d3.js, vega.js, and plotly.js that outshine Python visualization libraries in many regards. Once you have your input data ready, TensorFlow.js, the main topic of this book, will take it from there and help you create, train, and execute your deep-learning models, as well as save, load, and visualize them.

Finally, the JavaScript ecosystem is still constantly evolving in exciting ways. Its reach is being extended from its traditional strongholds—namely, the web browser and Node.js backend environments—to new territories such as desktop applications (for example, Electron) and native mobile applications (for instance, React Native and Ionic). It is often easier to write UIs and apps for such frameworks than to use myriad platform-specific app creation tools. JavaScript is a language that has the potential to bring the power of deep learning to all major platforms. We summarize the main benefits of combining JavaScript and deep learning in table 1.2.

Table 1.2 A brief summary of the benefits of doing deep learning in JavaScript

Consideration	Examples
Reasons related to the client side	• Reduced inference and training latency due to the locality of data • Ability to run models when the client is offline • Privacy protection (data never leaves the browser) • Reduced server cost • Simplified deployment stack
Reasons related to the web browser	• Availability of multiple modalities of data (HTML5 video, audio, and sensor APIs) for inference and training • The zero-install user experience • The zero-install access to parallel computation via the WebGL API on a wide range of GPUs • Cross-platform support • Ideal environment for visualization and interactivity • Inherently interconnected environment opens direct access to various sources of machine-learning data and resources
Reasons related to Java-Script	• JavaScript is the most popular open source programming language by many measures, so there is an abundance of JavaScript talent and enthusiasm. • JavaScript has a vibrant ecosystem and wide applications at both client and server sides. • Node.js allows applications to run on the server side without the resource constraints of the browser. • The V8 engine makes JavaScript code run fast.

1.3 *Why TensorFlow.js?*

To do deep learning in JavaScript, you need to select a library. TensorFlow.js is our choice for this book. In this section, we will describe what TensorFlow.js is and the reasons we selected it.

1.3.1 *A brief history of TensorFlow, Keras, and TensorFlow.js*

TensorFlow.js is a library that enables you to do deep learning in JavaScript. As its name suggests, TensorFlow.js is designed to be consistent and compatible with TensorFlow, the Python framework for deep learning. To understand TensorFlow.js, we need to briefly examine the history of TensorFlow.

TensorFlow was made open source in November 2015 by a team of engineers working on deep learning at Google. The authors of this book are members of this team. Since its open source debut, TensorFlow has gained immense popularity. It is now being used for a wide range of industrial applications and research projects both at Google and in the larger technical community. The name "TensorFlow" was coined to reflect what happens inside a typical program written with the framework: data representations called *tensors* flow through layers and other data-processing nodes, allowing inference and training to happen on machine-learning models.

First off, what is a tensor? It is just a computer scientist's way of saying "multidimensional array" concisely. In neural networks and deep learning, every piece of data and every computation result is represented as a tensor. For example, a grayscale image can be represented as a 2D array of numbers—a 2D tensor; a color image is usually represented as a 3D tensor, with the extra dimension being the color channels. Sounds, videos, text, and any other types of data can all be represented as tensors. Each tensor has two basic properties: the data type (such as float32 or int32) and the shape. Shape describes the size of the tensor along all its dimensions. For instance, a 2D tensor may have the shape [128, 256], and a 3D tensor may have the shape [10, 20, 128]. Once data is turned into a tensor of a given data type and shape, it can be fed into any type of layer that accepts that data type and shape, regardless of the data's original meaning. Therefore, the tensor is the lingua franca of deep-learning models.

But *why* tensors? In the previous section, we learned that the bulk of the computations involved in running a deep neural network are performed as massively parallelized operations, commonly on GPUs, which require performing the same computation on multiple pieces of data. Tensors are containers that organize our data into structures that can be processed efficiently in parallel. When we add tensor A with shape [128, 128] to tensor B with shape [128, 128], it is very clear that there are 128 * 128 independent additions that need to take place.

How about the "flow" part? Imagine a tensor as a kind of fluid that carries data. In TensorFlow, it flows through a *graph*—a data structure consisting of interconnected mathematical operations (called *nodes*). As figure 1.7 shows, the node can be successive layers in a neural network. Each node takes tensors as inputs and produces tensors as outputs. The "tensor fluid" gets transformed into different shapes and

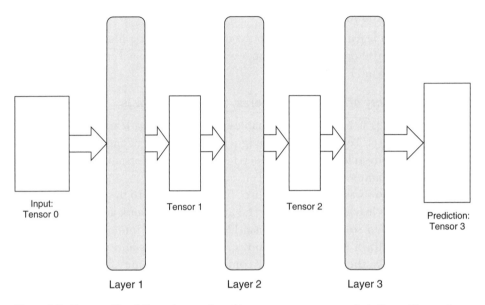

Figure 1.7   Tensors "flow" through a number of layers, a common scenario in TensorFlow and TensorFlow.js.

different values as it "flows" through the TensorFlow graph. This corresponds to the transformation of representations: that is, the crux of what neural networks do, as we have described in previous sections. Using TensorFlow, machine-learning engineers can write all kinds of neural networks, ranging from shallow ones to very deep ones, from convnets for computer vision to recurrent neural networks (RNNs) for sequence tasks. The graph data structure can be serialized and deployed to run many types of devices, from mainframes to mobile phones.

At its core, TensorFlow was designed to be very general and flexible: the operations can be any well-defined mathematical functions, not just layers of neural networks. For example, they can be low-level mathematical operations such as adding and multiplying two tensors—the kind of operations that happen *inside* a neural network layer. This gives deep-learning engineers and researchers great power to define arbitrary and novel operations for deep learning. However, for a large fraction of deep-learning practitioners, manipulating such low-level machinery is more trouble than it's worth. It leads to bloated and more error-prone code and longer development cycles. Most deep-learning engineers use a handful of fixed layer types (for instance, convolution, pooling, or dense, as you will learn in detail in later chapters). Rarely do they need to create new layer types. This is where the LEGO analogy is appropriate. With LEGOs, there are only a small number of block types. LEGO builders don't need to think about what it takes to make a LEGO block. This is different from a toy like, say, Play-Doh, which is analogous to TensorFlow's low-level API. Yet the ability to connect LEGO blocks leads to a combinatorially large number of possibilities and virtually infinite power. It is possible to build a toy house with either LEGOs or Play-Doh, but unless you have very special requirements for the house's size, shape, texture, or material, it is much easier and faster to build it with LEGOs. For most of us, the LEGO house we build will stand more stably and look nicer than the Play-Doh house we'd make.

In the world of TensorFlow, the LEGO equivalent is the high-level API called Keras.[9] Keras provides a set of the most frequently used types of neural network layers, each with configurable parameters. It also allows users to connect the layers together to form neural networks. Furthermore, Keras also comes with APIs for

- Specifying how the neural network will be trained (loss functions, metrics, and optimizers)
- Feeding data to train or evaluate the neural network or use the model for inference
- Monitoring the ongoing training process (callbacks)
- Saving and loading models
- Printing or plotting the architecture of models

With Keras, users can perform the full deep-learning workflow with very few lines of code. With the flexibility of the low-level API and the usability of the high-level API, TensorFlow and Keras form an ecosystem that leads the field of deep-learning frameworks in terms of industrial and academic adoption (see the tweet at http:// mng.bz/vlDJ). As a part of the ongoing deep-learning revolution, their role in making deep learning accessible to a wider audience should not be underestimated. Before frameworks such as TensorFlow and Keras, only those with CUDA programming skills and extensive experience in writing neural networks in C++ were able to do practical deep learning. With TensorFlow and Keras, it takes much less skill and effort to create GPU-accelerated deep neural networks. But there was one problem: it was not possible to run TensorFlow or Keras models in JavaScript or directly in the web browser. To serve trained deep-learning models in the browser, we had to do it via HTTP requests to a backend server. This is where TensorFlow.js comes into the picture. TensorFlow.js was an effort started by Nikhil Thorat and Daniel Smilkov, two experts in deep-learning-related data visualization and human-computer interaction[10] at Google. As we have mentioned, the highly popular TensorFlow Playground demo of a deep neural network planted the initial seed of the TensorFlow.js project. In September 2017, a library called deeplearn.js was released that has a low-level API analogous to the TensorFlow low-level API. Deeplearn.js championed WebGL-accelerated neural

---

[9] In fact, since the introduction of TensorFlow, a number of high-level APIs have emerged, some created by Google engineers and others by the open source community. Among the most popular ones are Keras, tf.Estimator, tf.contrib.slim, and TensorLayers. For the readers of this book, the most relevant high-level API to TensorFlow.js is Keras by far, because the high-level API of TensorFlow.js is modeled after Keras and because TensorFlow.js provides two-way compatibility in model saving and loading with Keras.

[10] As an interesting historical note, these authors also played key roles in creating TensorBoard, the popular visualization tool for TensorFlow models.

network operations, making it possible to run real neural networks with low inference latencies in the web browser.

Following the initial success of deeplearn.js, more members of the Google Brain team joined the project, and it was renamed TensorFlow.js. The JavaScript API underwent significant revamping, boosting API compatibility with TensorFlow. In addition, a Keras-like high-level API was built on top of the low-level core, making it much easier for users to define, train, and run deep-learning models in the JavaScript library. Today, what we said earlier about the power and usability of Keras is all true for TensorFlow.js as well. To further enhance interoperability, converters were built so that TensorFlow.js can import models saved from TensorFlow and Keras and export models to them. Since its debut at the worldwide TensorFlow Developer Summit and Google I/O in the spring of 2018 (see www.youtube.com/watch?v=YB-kfeNIPCE and www.youtube.com/watch?v=OmofOvMApTU), TensorFlow.js has quickly become a highly popular JavaScript deep-learning library, with currently the highest number of stars and forks among similar libraries on GitHub.

Figure 1.8 presents an overview of the TensorFlow.js architecture. The lowest level is responsible for parallel computing for fast mathematical operations. Although this layer is not visible to most users, it is critical that it have high performance so that model training and inference in higher levels of the API can be as fast as possible. In the browser, it leverages WebGL to achieve GPU acceleration (see info box 1.2). In Node.js, direct binding to the multicore CPU parallelization and CUDA GPU acceleration are both available. These are the same math backends used by TensorFlow and Keras in Python. Built on top of the lowest math level is the *Ops API*, which has good parity with the low-level API of TensorFlow and supports loading SavedModels from TensorFlow. On the highest level is the Keras-like *Layers API*. The Layers API is the right API choice for most programmers using TensorFlow.js and will be the main focus of this book. The Layers API also supports two-way model importing/exporting with Keras.

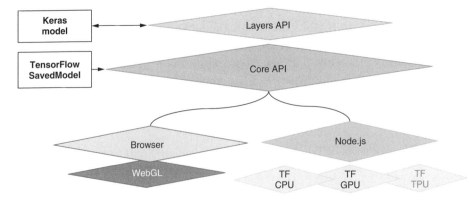

Figure 1.8 The architecture of TensorFlow.js at a glance. Its relationship to Python TensorFlow and Keras is also shown.

1.3.2 *Why TensorFlow.js: A brief comparison with similar libraries*

TensorFlow.js is not the only JavaScript library for deep learning; neither was it the first one to appear (for example, brain.js and ConvNetJS have a much longer history). So, why does TensorFlow.js stand out among similar libraries? The first reason is its comprehensiveness—TensorFlow.js is the only currently available library that supports all key parts of the production deep-learning workflow:

- Supports both inference and training
- Supports web browsers and Node.js
- Leverages GPU acceleration (WebGL in browsers and CUDA kernels in Node.js)
- Supports definition of neural network model architectures in JavaScript
- Supports serialization and deserialization of models
- Supports conversions to and from Python deep-learning frameworks
- Compatible in API with Python deep-learning frameworks
- Equipped with built-in support for data ingestion and with an API for visualization

The second reason is the ecosystem. Most JavaScript deep-learning libraries define their own unique API, whereas TensorFlow.js is tightly integrated with TensorFlow and Keras. You have a trained model from Python TensorFlow or Keras and want to use it in the browser? No problem. You have created a TensorFlow.js model in the browser and want to take it into Keras for access to faster accelerators such as Google TPUs? That works, too! Tight integration with non-JavaScript frameworks not only boosts interoperability but also makes it easier for developers to migrate between the worlds of programming languages and infrastructure stacks. For example, once you have mastered TensorFlow.js from reading this book, it will be smooth sailing if you want to start using Keras in Python. The reverse journey is as easy: someone with good knowledge of Keras should be able to learn TensorFlow.js quickly (assuming sufficient JavaScript skills). Last but not least, the popularity of TensorFlow.js and the strength of its community should not be overlooked. The developers of TensorFlow.js are committed to long-term maintenance and support of the library. From GitHub star and fork counts to number of external contributors, from the liveliness of the discussion to the number of questions and answers on Stack Overflow, TensorFlow.js is shadowed by none of the competing libraries.

1.3.3 *How is TensorFlow.js being used by the world?*

There is no more convincing testimony to the power and popularity of a library than the way in which it is used in real-world applications. A few noteworthy applications of TensorFlow.js include the following:

- Google's Project Magenta uses TensorFlow.js to run RNNs and other kinds of deep neural networks to generate musical scores and novel instrument sounds in the browser (https://magenta.tensorflow.org/demos/).

- Dan Shiffman and his colleagues at New York University built ML5.js, an easy-to-use, higher-level API for various out-of-the-box deep-learning models for the browser, such as object detection and image style transfer (https://ml5js.org).
- Abhishek Singh, an open source developer, created a browser-based interface that translates American Sign Language into speech to help people who can't speak or hear use smart speakers such as Amazon Echo.[11]
- Canvas Friends is a game-like web app based on TensorFlow.js that helps users improve their drawing and artistic skills (www.y8.com/games/canvas_friends).
- MetaCar, a self-driving car simulator that runs in the browser, uses TensorFlow.js to implement reinforcement learning algorithms that are critical to its simulations (www.metacar-project.com).
- Clinic doctor, a Node.js-based application that monitors the performance of server-side programs, implemented a Hidden Markov Model with TensorFlow.js and is using it to detect spikes in CPU usage.[12]
- See TensorFlow.js's gallery of other outstanding applications built by the open source community at https://github.com/tensorflow/tfjs/blob/master/GALLERY.md.

1.3.4   *What this book will and will not teach you about TensorFlow.js*

Through studying the materials in this book, you should be able to build applications like the following using TensorFlow.js:

- A website that classifies images uploaded by a user
- Deep neural networks that ingest image and audio data from browser-attached sensors and perform real-time machine-learning tasks, such as recognition and transfer learning, on them
- Client-side natural language AI such as a comment-sentiment classifier to assist with comment moderation
- A Node.js (backend) machine-learning model trainer that uses gigabyte-scale data and GPU acceleration
- A TensorFlow.js-powered reinforcement learner that can solve small-scale control and game problems
- A dashboard to illustrate the internals of trained models and the results of machine-learning experiments

Importantly, not only will you know how to build and run such applications, but you will also understand how they work. For instance, you will have practical knowledge of the strategies and constraints involved in creating deep-learning models for various

---

[11] Abhishek Singh, "Getting Alexa to Respond to Sign Language Using Your Webcam and TensorFlow.js," *Medium*, 8 Aug. 2018, http://mng.bz/4eEa.

[12] Andreas Madsen, "Clinic.js Doctor Just Got More Advanced with TensorFlow.js," *Clinic.js* blog, 22 Aug. 2018, http://mng.bz/Q06w.

types of problems, as well as the steps and gotchas in training and deploying such models.

Machine learning is a wide field; TensorFlow.js is a versatile library. Therefore, some applications are entirely doable with existing TensorFlow.js technology but are beyond what is covered in the book. Examples are:

- High-performance, distributed training of deep neural networks that involve a huge amount of data (on the order of terabytes) in the Node.js environment
- Non-neural-network techniques, such as SVMs, decision trees, and random forests
- Advanced deep-learning applications such as text-summarization engines that reduce large documents into a few representative sentences, image-to-text engines that generate text summary from input images, and generative image models that enhance the resolution of input images

This book will, however, give you foundational knowledge of deep learning with which you will be prepared to learn about the code and articles related to those advanced applications.

Like any other technology, TensorFlow.js has its limits. Some tasks are beyond what it can do. Even though these limits are likely to be pushed in the future, it is good to be aware of where the boundaries are at the time of writing:

- Running deep-learning models with memory requirements that exceed the RAM and WebGL limits in a browser tab. For in-browser inference, this typically means a model with a total weight size above ~100 MB. For training, more memory and compute power is required, so it is possible that even smaller models will be too slow to train in a browser tab. Model training also typically involves larger amounts of data than inference, which is another limiting factor that should be taken into account when assessing the feasibility of in-browser training.
- Creating a high-end reinforcement learner, such as the kind that can defeat human players at the game of Go.
- Training deep-learning models with a distributed (multimachine) setup using Node.js.

Exercises

1 Whether you are a frontend JavaScript developer or a Node.js developer, based on what you learned in this chapter, brainstorm a few possible cases in which you can apply machine learning to the system you are working on to make it more intelligent. For inspiration, refer to tables 1.1 and 1.2, as well as section 1.3.3. Some further examples include the following:
  a A fashion website that sells accessories such as sunglasses captures images of users' faces using the webcam and detects facial landmark points using a deep neural network running on TensorFlow.js. The detected landmarks are then used to synthesize an image of the sunglasses overlaid on the user's face

to simulate a try-on experience in the web page. The experience is realistic because the simulated try-on can run with low latency and at a high frame rate thanks to client-side inference. The user's data privacy is respected because the captured facial image never leaves the browser.

b   A mobile sports app written in React Native (a cross-platform JavaScript library for creating native mobile apps) tracks users' exercise. Using the HTML5 API, the app accesses real-time data from the phone's gyroscope and accelerometer. The data is run through a TensorFlow.js-powered model that automatically detects the user's current activity type (for example, resting versus walking versus jogging versus sprinting).

c   A browser extension automatically detects whether the person using the device is a child or an adult (by using images captured from the webcam at a frame rate of once per 5 seconds and a computer-vision model powered by TensorFlow.js) and uses the information to block or grant access to certain websites accordingly.

d   A browser-based programming environment uses a recurrent neural network implemented with TensorFlow.js to detect typos in code comments.

e   A Node.js-based server-side application that coordinates a cargo logistics service uses real-time signals such as carrier status, cargo type and quantity, date/time, and traffic information to predict the estimated time of arrival (ETA) for each transaction. The training and inference pipelines are all written in Node.js, using TensorFlow.js, simplifying the server stack.

Summary

- AI is the study of automating cognitive tasks. Machine learning is a subfield of AI in which rules for performing a task such as image classification are discovered automatically by learning from examples in the training data.

- A central problem in machine learning is how to transform the original representation of data into a representation more amenable to solving the task.

- Neural networks are an approach in machine learning wherein the transformation of data representation is performed by successive steps (or layers) of mathematical operations. The field of deep learning concerns deep neural networks—neural networks with many layers.

- Thanks to enhancements in hardware, increased availability of labeled data, and advances in algorithms, the field of deep learning has made astonishing progress since the early 2010s, solving previously unsolvable problems and creating exciting new opportunities.

- JavaScript and the web browser are a suitable environment for deploying and training deep neural networks.

- TensorFlow.js, the focus of this book, is a comprehensive, versatile, and powerful open source library for deep learning in JavaScript.

Part 2

A gentle introduction to TensorFlow.js

Having covered the foundations, in this part of the book we dive into machine learning in a hands-on fashion, armed with TensorFlow.js. We start in chapter 2 with a simple machine-learning task—regression (predicting a single number)—and work toward more sophisticated tasks such as binary and multi-class classification in chapters 3 and 4. In lockstep with task types, you'll also see a gentle progression from simple data (flat arrays of numbers) to more complex ones (images and sounds). The mathematical underpinning of methods such as backpropagation will be introduced alongside concrete problems and the code that solves them. We eschew formal math in favor of more intuitive explanations, diagrams, and pseudo-code. Chapter 5 discusses transfer learning, an efficient reuse of pretrained neural networks to adapt to new data, and presents an approach especially suited to the deep-learning browser environment.

Getting started: Simple linear regression in TensorFlow.js

This chapter covers

- A minimal example of a neural network for the simple machine-learning task of linear regression
- Tensors and tensor operations
- Basic neural network optimization

Nobody likes to wait, and it's especially annoying to wait when we don't know how long we'll have to wait for. Any user experience designer will tell you that if you can't hide the delay, then the next best thing is to give the user a reliable estimate of the wait time. Estimating expected delays is a prediction problem, and the TensorFlow.js library can be used to build an accurate download-time prediction, sensitive to the context and user, enabling us to build clear, reliable experiences that respect the user's time and attention.

In this chapter, using a simple download-time prediction problem as our motivating example, we will introduce the main components of a complete machine-learning model. We will cover tensors, modeling, and optimization from a practical point of view so that you can build intuitions about what they are, how they work, and how to use them appropriately.

A complete understanding of the internals of deep learning—the type a dedicated researcher would build over years of study—requires familiarity with many mathematical subjects. For the deep-learning practitioner, however, expertise with linear algebra, differential calculus, and the statistics of high-dimensional spaces is helpful but not necessary, even to build complex, high-performance systems. Our goal in this chapter, and throughout this book, is to introduce technical topics as necessary—using code, rather than mathematical notation, when possible. We aim to convey an intuitive understanding of the machinery and its purpose without requiring domain expertise.

2.1 Example 1: Predicting the duration of a download using TensorFlow.js

Let's jump right in! We will construct a bare-minimum neural network that uses the TensorFlow.js library (sometimes shortened to tfjs) to predict download times given the size of the download. Unless you already have experience with TensorFlow.js or similar libraries, you won't understand everything about this first example right away, and that's fine. Each subject introduced here will be covered in detail in the coming chapters, so don't worry if some parts look arbitrary or magical to you! We've got to start somewhere. We will begin by writing a short program that accepts a file size as input and outputs a predicted time to download the file.

2.1.1 Project overview: Duration prediction

When studying a machine-learning system for the first time, you may be intimidated by the variety of new concepts and lingo. Therefore, it's helpful to look at the entire workflow first. The general outline of this example is illustrated in figure 2.1, and it is a pattern that we will see repeated across our examples in this book.

First, we will access our training data. In machine learning, data can be read from disk, downloaded over the network, generated, or simply hard-coded. In this example, we take the last approach because it is convenient, and we are dealing with only a small amount of data. Second, we will convert the data into tensors, so they can be fed to our model. The next step is creating a model, which, as we saw in chapter 1, is akin to designing an appropriate trainable function: a function mapping input data to things we are trying to predict. In this case, the input data and the prediction targets are both numbers. Once our model and data are available, we will then train the model, monitoring its reported metrics as it goes. Finally, we will use the trained model to make predictions on data we haven't seen yet and measure the model's accuracy.

We will proceed through each of these phases with copy-and-paste runnable code snippets and explanations of both the theory and the tools.

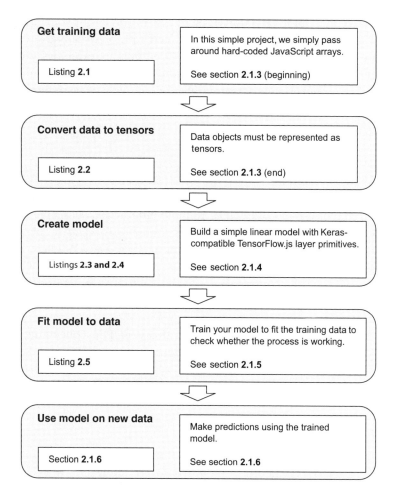

Figure 2.1   Overview of the major steps involved in the download-time prediction system, our first example

2.1.2   A note on code listings and console interactions

Code in this book will be presented in two formats. The first format, the code *listing*, presents structural code that you will find in the referenced code repositories. Each listing has a title and a number. For example, listing 2.1 contains a very short HTML snippet that you could copy verbatim into a file—for example, /tmp/tmp.html—on your computer and then open in your web browser at file:///tmp/tmp.html, though it won't do much by itself.

The second format of code is the *console interaction*. These more informal blocks are intended to convey example interactions at a JavaScript REPL,[1] such as the browser's

---

[1] Read-eval-print-loop, also known as an interactive interpreter or shell. The REPL allows us to interact actively with our code to interrogate variables and test functions.

JavaScript console (Cmd-Opt-J, Ctrl+Shift+J, or F12 in Chrome, but your browser/OS may be different). Console interactions are indicated with a preceding greater-than sign, like what we see in Chrome or Firefox, and their outputs are presented on the next line, just as in the console. For example, the following interaction creates an array and prints the value. The output you see at your JavaScript console may be slightly different, but the gist should be the same:

```
> let a = ['hello', 'world', 2 * 1009]
> a;
(3) ["hello", "world", 2018]
```

The best way to test, run, and learn from the code listings in this book is to clone the referenced repositories and then play with them. During the development of this book, we made frequent use of CodePen as a simple, interactive, shareable repository (http://codepen.io). For example, listing 2.1 is available for you to play with at codepen.io/tfjs-book/pen/VEVMbx. When you navigate to the CodePen, it should run automatically. You should be able to see output printed to the console. Click Console at bottom left to open the console. If the CodePen doesn't run automatically, try making a small, inconsequential change, such as adding a space to the end, to kickstart it.

The listings from this section are available in this CodePen collection: codepen .io/collection/Xzwavm/. CodePen works well where there is a single JavaScript file, but our larger and more structured examples are kept in GitHub repositories, which you will see in later examples. For this example, we recommend reading through this section and then playing with the associated CodePens in order.

2.1.3   Creating and formatting the data

Let's estimate how long it will take to download a file on a machine, given only its size in MB. We'll first use a pre-created dataset, but, if you're motivated, you can create a similar dataset, modeling your own system's network statistics.

Listing 2.1   Hard-coding the training and test data (from CodePen 2-a)

```
<script src='https://cdn.jsdelivr.net/npm/@tensorflow/tfjs@latest'></script>
<script>
const trainData = {
  sizeMB:  [0.080, 9.000, 0.001, 0.100, 8.000,
            5.000, 0.100, 6.000, 0.050, 0.500,
            0.002, 2.000, 0.005, 10.00, 0.010,
            7.000, 6.000, 5.000, 1.000, 1.000],
  timeSec: [0.135, 0.739, 0.067, 0.126, 0.646,
            0.435, 0.069, 0.497, 0.068, 0.116,
            0.070, 0.289, 0.076, 0.744, 0.083,
            0.560, 0.480, 0.399, 0.153, 0.149]
};
const testData = {
  sizeMB:  [5.000, 0.200, 0.001, 9.000, 0.002,
            0.020, 0.008, 4.000, 0.001, 1.000,
            0.005, 0.080, 0.800, 0.200, 0.050,
            7.000, 0.005, 0.002, 8.000, 0.008],
```

```
  timeSec: [0.425, 0.098, 0.052, 0.686, 0.066,
            0.078, 0.070, 0.375, 0.058, 0.136,
            0.052, 0.063, 0.183, 0.087, 0.066,
            0.558, 0.066, 0.068, 0.610, 0.057]
};
</script>
```

In the previous HTML code listing, we've chosen to explicitly include the `<script>` tags, illustrating how to load the most recent version of the TensorFlow.js library using the `@latest` suffix (at the time of writing, this code ran with tfjs 0.13.5). We will go into more detail later about different ways to import TensorFlow.js into your application, but going forward, the `<script>` tags will be assumed. The first script loads the TensorFlow package and defines the symbol `tf`, which provides a way to refer to names in TensorFlow. For example, `tf.add()` refers to the TensorFlow add operation, which adds two tensors. Going forward, we will assume that the `tf` symbol is loaded and available in the global namespace by, for example, sourcing the TensorFlow.js script as previously.

Listing 2.1 creates two constants, `trainData` and `testData`, each representing 20 samples of how long it took to download a file (`timeSec`) and the size of that file (`sizeMB`). The elements in `sizeMB` and those in `timeSec` have one-to-one correspondence. For example, the first element of `sizeMB` in `trainData` is 0.080 MB, and downloading that file took 0.135 seconds—that is, the first element of `timeSec`—and so forth. Our goal in this example will be to estimate `timeSec`, given just `sizeMB`. In this first example, we are creating the data directly by hard-coding it in our code. This approach is expedient for this simple example but will become unwieldy very quickly when the size of the dataset grows. Future examples will illustrate how to stream data from external storage or over the network.

Back to the data. From the plot in figure 2.2, we can see that there is a very predictable, if imperfect, relationship between the size and download time. Data in real life is noisy, but it looks like we should be able to make a pretty good linear estimate of the duration given the file size. Judging by eye, the duration should be about 0.1 seconds when the file size is zero and then grow at about 0.07 seconds for each additional MB. Recall from chapter 1 that each input-output pair is sometimes called an *example*. The output is often referred to as the *target*, while the elements of the input are often called the *features*. In our case here, each of our 40 examples has exactly one feature, `sizeMB`, and a numeric target, `timeSec`.

In listing 2.1, you might have noticed that the data is split into two subsets, namely `trainData` and `testData`. `trainData` is the training set. It contains the examples the model will be trained on. `testData` is the test set. We will use it to judge how well the model is trained after the training is complete. If we trained and evaluated using the exact same data, it would be like taking a test after having already seen the answers. In the most extreme case, the model could theoretically memorize the `timeSec` value for each `sizeMB` in the training data—not a very good learning algorithm. The result would not be a good judge of future performance because it is unlikely that the values

File download duration

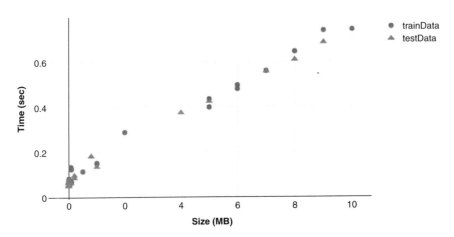

Figure 2.2 **Measured download duration versus file size. If you are interested, at this point, in how to create plots like this, the code is listed in CodePen codepen.io/tfjs-book/pen/ dgQVze.**

of the future input features will all be exactly the same as the ones the model has been trained on.

Therefore, the workflow will be as follows. First we'll fit the neural network on the training data to make accurate predictions of `timeSec` given `sizeMB`. Then, we'll ask the network to produce predictions for `sizeMB` using the testing data, and we'll measure how close those predictions are to `timeSec`. But first, we'll have to convert this data into a format that TensorFlow.js will understand, and this will be our first example usage of tensors. The code in listing 2.2 shows the first usage of functions under the `tf.*` namespace you will see in this book. Here, we see methods for converting data stored in raw JavaScript data structures into tensors.

Although the usage is pretty straightforward, those readers who wish to gain a firmer grounding in these APIs should read appendix B, which covers not only tensor-creation functions such as `tf.tensor2d()`, but also functions that perform operations transforming and combining tensors, and patterns of how common real-world data types, such as images and videos, are conventionally packed into tensors. We do not dive deeply into the low-level API in the main text because the material is somewhat dry and not tied to specific example problems.

Listing 2.2   Converting data into tensors (from CodePen 2-b)

```
const trainTensors = {
  sizeMB: tf.tensor2d(trainData.sizeMB, [20, 1]),
  timeSec: tf.tensor2d(trainData.timeSec, [20, 1])
};
const testTensors = {
```

The [20, 1] here is the tensor's "shape." More will be explained later, but here this shape means we want to interpret the list of numbers as 20 samples, where each sample is 1 number. If the shape is obvious from, for example, the structure of the data array, this argument can be left out.

```
  sizeMB: tf.tensor2d(testData.sizeMB, [20, 1]),
  timeSec: tf.tensor2d(testData.timeSec, [20, 1])
};
```

In general, all current machine-learning systems use tensors as their basic data structure. Tensors are fundamental to the field—so fundamental that TensorFlow and TensorFlow.js are named after them. A quick reminder from chapter 1: at its core, a tensor is a container for data—almost always numerical data. So, it can be thought of as a container for numbers. You may already be familiar with vectors and matrices, which are 1D and 2D tensors, respectively. Tensors are a generalization of matrices to an arbitrary number of dimensions. The number of dimensions and size of each dimension is called the tensor's *shape*. For instance, a 3 × 4 matrix is a tensor with shape [3, 4]. A vector of length 10 is a 1D tensor with shape [10].

In the context of tensors, a dimension is often called an *axis*. In TensorFlow.js, tensors are the common representation that lets components communicate and work with each other, whether on CPU, GPU, or other hardware. We will have more to say about tensors and their common use cases as the need arises, but for now, let's continue with our prediction project.

2.1.4 Defining a simple model

In the context of deep learning, the function from input features to targets is known as a *model*. The model function takes features, runs a computation, and produces predictions. The model we are building here is a function that takes a file size as input and outputs durations (see figure 2.2). In deep-learning parlance, sometimes we use *network* as a synonym for model. Our first model will be an implementation of *linear regression*.

Regression, in the context of machine learning, means that the model will output real-valued numbers and attempt to match the training targets; this is opposed to classification, which outputs choices from a set of options. In a regression task, a model that outputs numbers closer to the target is better than a model that outputs numbers farther away. If our model predicts that a 1 MB file will take about 0.15 seconds, that's better (as we can see from figure 2.2) than if our model predicts that a 1 MB file will take about 600 seconds.

Linear regression is a specific type of regression in which the output, as a function of the input, can be illustrated as a straight line (or, by analogy, a flat plane in a higher-dimensional space when there are multiple input features). An important property of models is that they are *tunable*. This means that the input-output computation can be adjusted. We use this property to tune the model to better "fit" the data. In the linear case, the model input-output relationship is always a straight line, but we can adjust the slope and y-intercept.

Let's build our first network to get a feel for this.

Listing 2.3 Constructing a linear regression model (from CodePen 2-c)

```
const model = tf.sequential();
model.add(tf.layers.dense({inputShape: [1], units: 1}));
```

The core building block of neural networks is the *layer*, a data-processing module that you can think of as a tunable function from tensors to tensors. Here, our network consists of a single dense layer. This layer has a constraint on the shape of the input tensor, as defined by the parameter `inputShape: [1]`. Here, it means that the layer is expecting input in the form of a 1D tensor with exactly one value. The output from the dense layer is always a 1D tensor for each example, but the size of that dimension is controlled by the `units` configuration parameter. In this case, we want just one output number because we are trying to predict exactly one number, namely the `timeSec`.

At its core, the dense layer is a tunable multiply-add between each input and each output. Since there is only one input and one output, this model is the simple `y = m * x + b` linear equation you may recall from high school math. The dense layer internally calls m the *kernel* and b the *bias*, as illustrated in figure 2.3. In this case, we have constructed a linear model for the relation between the input (`sizeMB`) and the output (`timeSec`):

        timeSec = **kernel** * sizeMB + **bias**

There are four terms in this equation. Two of them are fixed as far as model training is concerned: the values of `sizeMB` and `timeSec` are determined by the training data (see listing 2.1). The other two terms, the kernel and bias, are the model's parameters. Their values are randomly chosen when the model is created. Those random values will not give good predictions of download duration. In order for decent predictions to happen, we must search for good values of the kernel and bias by allowing the model to learn from data. This search is the *training process*.

To find a good setting for the kernel and bias (collectively, the *weights*) we need two things:

- A measure that tells us how well we are doing at a given setting of the weights
- A method to update the weights' values so that next time we will do better than we currently are doing, according to the measure previously mentioned

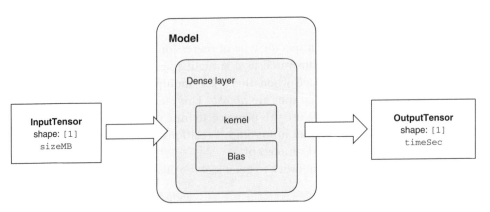

Figure 2.3   An illustration of our simple linear-regression model. The model has exactly one layer. The model's tunable parameters (or weights), the kernel and bias, are shown within the dense layer.

This brings us to the next step in solving the linear-regression problem. To make the network ready for training, we need to pick the measure and the update method, which correspond to the two required items listed previously. This is done as part of what TensorFlow.js calls the *model compilation* step, which takes

- A *loss function*—An error measurement. This is how the network measures its performance on the training data and steers itself in the right direction. Lower loss is better. As we train, we should be able to plot the loss over time and see it going down. If our model trains for a long while, and the loss is not decreasing, it could mean that our model is not learning to fit the data. Over the course of this book, you will learn to debug problems like this.
- An *optimizer*—The algorithm by which the network will update its weights (kernel and bias, in this case) based on the data and the loss function.

The exact purpose of the loss function and the optimizer, and how to make good choices for them, will be explored thoroughly throughout the next couple of chapters. But for now, the following choices will do.

> **Listing 2.4 Configuring training options: model compilation (from CodePen 2-c)**

```
model.compile({optimizer: 'sgd', loss: 'meanAbsoluteError'});
```

We call the `compile` method on our model, specifying `'sgd'` as our optimizer and `'meanAbsoluteError'` as our loss. `'meanAbsoluteError'` means that our loss function will calculate how far our predictions are from the targets, take their absolute values (making them all positive), and then return the average of those values:

```
meanAbsoluteError = average( absolute(modelOutput - targets) )
```

For example, given

```
modelOutput = [1.1, 2.2, 3.3, 3.6]
targets =     [1.0, 2.0, 3.0, 4.0]
```

then,

```
meanAbsoluteError = average([[|1.1 - 1.0|, |2.2 - 2.0|,
                              |3.3 - 3.0|, |3.6 - 4.0|])

                  = average([0.1, 0.2, 0.3, 0.4])

                  = 0.25
```

If our model makes very bad predictions that are very far from the targets, then the `meanAbsoluteError` will be very large. In contrast, the best we could possibly do is to get every prediction exactly right, in which case the difference between our model output and the targets would be zero, and therefore the loss (the `meanAbsolute-Error`) would be zero.

The `sgd` in listing 2.4 stands for *stochastic gradient descent*, which we will describe a bit more in section 2.2. Briefly, it means that we will use calculus to determine what adjustments we should make to the weights in order to reduce the loss; then we will make those adjustments and repeat the process.

Our model is now ready to be fit to our training data.

2.1.5   *Fitting the model to the training data*

Training a model in TensorFlow.js is done by calling the model's `fit()` method. We fit the model to the training data. Here, we pass in the `sizeMB` tensor as our input and the `timeSec` tensor as our desired output. We also pass in a configuration object with an `epochs` field that specifies that we would like to go through our training data exactly 10 times. In deep learning, each iteration through the complete training set is called an *epoch*.

Listing 2.5   Fitting a linear regression model (from CodePen 2-c)

```
(async function() {
  await model.fit(trainTensors.sizeMB,
                  trainTensors.timeSec,
                  {epochs: 10});
})();
```

The `fit()` method can often be long-running, lasting for seconds or minutes. Therefore, we utilize the *async/await* feature of ES2017/ES8 so that this function can be used in a way that does not block the main UI thread when running in the browser. This is similar to other potentially long-running functions in JavaScript, such as `async fetch`. Here, we wait for the `fit()` call to finish before going on, using the Immediately Invoked Async Function Expression[2] pattern, but future examples will train in the background while doing other work in the foreground thread.

Once our model has completed fitting, we will want to see whether it worked. Crucially, we will evaluate the model on data that was not used during training. This theme of separating test data from training data (and hence avoiding training on the test data) is something that will come up over and over in this book. It is an important part of the machine-learning workflow that you should internalize.

The model's `evaluate()` method calculates the loss function as applied to the provided example features and targets. It is similar to the `fit()` method in that it calculates the same loss, but `evaluate()` does not update the model's weights. We use `evaluate()` to estimate the quality of the model on the test data, so as to get an idea about how the model would perform in the future application:

```
> model.evaluate(testTensors.sizeMB, testTensors.timeSec).print();
Tensor
    0.31778740882873535
```

Here, we see that the loss, averaged across the test data, is about 0.318. Given that, by default, models are trained from a random initial state, you will get a different value.

---

[2] For more on Immediately Invoked Function Expressions, see http://mng.bz/RPOZ.

Another way to say the same thing is that the mean absolute error (MAE) of this model is just over 0.3 seconds. Is this good? Is it better than just estimating a constant? One good constant we could choose is the average delay. Let's see what kind of error that would get, using TensorFlow.js's support for mathematical operations on tensors. First, we'll compute the average download time, calculated over our training set:

```
> const avgDelaySec = tf.mean(trainData.timeSec);
> avgDelaySec.print();
Tensor
      0.2950500249862671
```

Next, let's calculate the `meanAbsoluteError` by hand. MAE is simply the average value of how far our prediction was from the actual value. We'll use `tf.sub()` to calculate the difference between the test targets and our (constant) prediction and `tf.abs()` to take the absolute value (since sometimes we'll be too low and other times too high), and then take the average with `tf.mean`:

```
> tf.mean(tf.abs(tf.sub(testData.timeSec, 0.295))).print();
Tensor
      0.22020000219345093
```

See info box 2.1 for how to perform the same computation using the concise chaining API.

INFO BOX 2.1   Tensor chaining API

In addition to the standard API, in which tensor functions are available under the `tf` namespace, most tensor functions are also available from the tensor objects themselves, allowing you to write in a chaining style if you prefer. The following code is functionally identical to the `meanAbsoluteError` computation in the main text:

```
// chaining API pattern
> testData.timeSec.sub(0.295).abs().mean().print();
Tensor
      0.22020000219345093
```

It seems that the average delay is about 0.295 seconds and that always guessing the average value gives a better estimate than our network does. This means our model's accuracy is even worse than that of a commonsense, trivial approach! Can we do better? It's possible that we haven't trained for enough epochs. Remember that during training, the values of the kernel and bias are updated step-by-step. In this case, each epoch is a step. If the model is trained only for a small number of epochs (steps), the parameter values may not have a chance to get close to the optimum. Let's train our model a few more cycles and evaluate again:

```
>  model.fit(trainTensors.sizeMB,
              trainTensors.timeSec,
              {epochs: 200});
```
Be sure to wait for the promise returned from model.fit to resolve before executing model.evaluate.

```
>  model.evaluate(testTensors.sizeMB, testTensors.timeSec).print();
```

```
Tensor
    0.04879039153456688
```

Much better! It seems we were previously *underfitting*, meaning our model hadn't been adapted enough to the training data. Now our estimates are within 0.05 seconds, on average. We are four times more accurate than naively guessing the mean. In this book, we will offer guidance about how to avoid underfitting, as well as the more insidious problem of *overfitting*, where the model is tuned *too much* to the training data and doesn't generalize well to data it hasn't seen!

2.1.6 *Using our trained model to make predictions*

OK, great! We now have a model that can make accurate predictions of download time given an input size, but how do we use it? The answer is the model's predict() method:

```
> const smallFileMB = 1;
> const bigFileMB = 100;
> const hugeFileMB = 10000;
> model.predict(tf.tensor2d([[smallFileMB], [bigFileMB],
    [hugeFileMB]])).print();
Tensor
    [[0.1373825 ],
     [7.2438402 ],
     [717.8896484]]
```

Here, we see that our model predicts that a 10,000 MB file download will take about 718 seconds. Note that we didn't have any examples in our training data near this size. In general, extrapolating to values well outside the training data is very risky, but with a problem this simple, it may be accurate . . . so long as we don't run into new complications with memory buffers, input-output connectivity, and so on. It would be better if we could collect more training data in this range.

We see also that we needed to wrap our input variables into an appropriately shaped tensor. In listing 2.3, we defined the inputShape to be [1], so the model expects each example to have that shape. Both fit() and predict() work with multiple examples at a time. To provide n samples, we stack them together into a single input tensor, which thus must have the shape [n, 1]. If we had forgotten, and instead provided a tensor with the wrong shape to the model, we would have gotten a shape error, like the following code:

```
> model.predict(tf.tensor1d([smallFileMB, bigFileMB, hugeFileMB])).print();
Uncaught Error: Error when checking : expected dense_Dense1_input to have 2
    dimension(s), but got array with shape [3]
```

Watch out for this type of shape mismatch because it is a very common type of error!

2.1.7   *Summary of our first example*

For this small example, it's possible to illustrate the model's result. Figure 2.4 shows the model's output (timeSec) as a function of the input (sizeMB) for the models at four points in the process, beginning with the underfit one at 10 epochs and the converged one. We see that the converged model closely fits the data. If you are interested, at this point, in exploring how to plot data like that in figure 2.4, please visit the CodePen at codepen.io/tfjs-book/pen/VEVMMd.

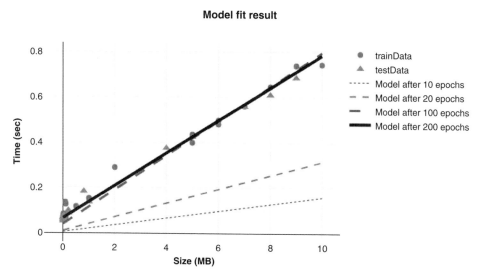

Figure 2.4   The linear model fit after training for 10, 20, 100, and 200 epochs

This concludes our first example. You just saw how you can build, train, and evaluate a TensorFlow.js model in very few lines of JavaScript code (see listing 2.6). In the next section, we'll go a bit deeper into what's going on inside of model.fit.

Listing 2.6   Model definition, training, evaluation, and prediction

```
const model = tf.sequential([tf.layers.dense({inputShape: [1], units: 1})]);
model.compile({optimizer: 'sgd', loss: 'meanAbsoluteError'});
(async () => await model.fit(trainTensors.sizeMB,
                             trainTensors.timeSec,
                             {epochs: 10}))();
model.evaluate(testTensors.sizeMB, testTensors.timeSec);
model.predict(tf.tensor2d([[7.8]])).print();
```

2.2   Inside Model.fit(): Dissecting gradient descent from example 1

In the previous section, we built a simple model and fit it to some training data, showing that we could make reasonably accurate predictions of download time given the file size. It isn't the most impressive neural network, but it works in precisely the same way as the larger, much more complicated systems we'll be building. We saw that fitting it for 10 epochs wasn't very good, but fitting it for 200 epochs produced a quality model.[3] Let's go into a bit more detail to understand exactly what happens under the hood when the model is trained.

2.2.1   The intuitions behind gradient-descent optimization

Recall that our simple, one-layer model is fitting a linear function f(input), defined as

output = **kernel** * input + **bias**

where the kernel and bias are tunable parameters (the weights) of the dense layer. These weights contain the information learned by the network from exposure to the training data.

Initially, these weights are filled with small random values (a step called *random initialization*). Of course, there's no reason to expect that kernel * input + bias will yield anything useful when the kernel and bias are random. Using our imagination, we can picture how the value of the MAE will change across different choices of these parameters. We expect that the loss will be low when they approximate the slope and intercept of the line we perceive in figure 2.4, and that the loss will get worse as the parameters describe very different lines. This concept—the loss as a function of all tunable parameters—is known as the *loss surface.*

Since this is a tiny example, and we just have two tunable parameters and a single target, it's possible to illustrate the loss surface as a 2D contour plot, as figure 2.5 shows. This loss surface has a nice bowl shape, with a global minimum at the bottom of the bowl representing the best parameter settings. In general, however, the loss surface of a deep-learning model is much more complex than this one. It will have many more than two dimensions and could have many local minima—that is, points that are lower than anything nearby but not the lowest overall.

We see that this loss surface is shaped like a bowl, with the best (lowest) value somewhere around {bias: 0.08, kernel: 0.07}. This fits the geometry of the line implied by our data, where the download time is about 0.10 seconds, even when the file size is near zero. Our model's random initialization starts us at a random parameter setting, analogous to a random location on this map, from which we calculate our initial loss. Next, we gradually adjust the parameters based on a feedback signal. This gradual adjustment, also called *training*, is the "learning" in "machine learning." This happens within a *training loop*—illustrated in figure 2.6.

---

[3] Note that for a simple linear model like this one, simple, efficient, closed-form solutions exist. However, this optimization method will continue to work even for the more complicated models we introduce later.

Loss surface

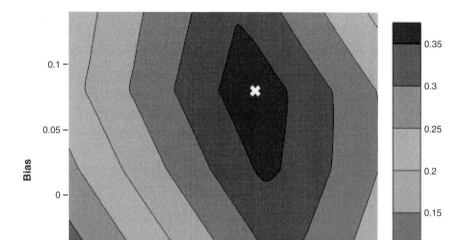

Figure 2.5 The loss surface illustrates loss, shown against the model's tunable parameters, as a contour plot. With this birds-eye view, we see that a choice of {bias: 0.08, kernel: 0.07} (marked with a white X) would be a reasonable choice for low loss. Rarely do we have the luxury of being able to test *all* the parameter settings to build a map like this, but if we did, optimization would be very easy; just pick the parameters corresponding to the lowest loss!

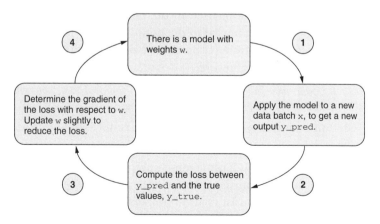

Figure 2.6 A flowchart illustrating the training loop, which updates the model via gradient descent

Figure 2.6 illustrates how the training loop iterates through these steps as long as necessary:

1   Draw a *batch* of training samples x and corresponding targets y_true. A batch is simply a number of input examples put together as a tensor. The number of examples in a batch is called the *batch size*. In practical deep learning, it is often set to be a power of 2, such as 128 or 256. Examples are batched together to take advantage of the GPU's parallel processing power and to make the calculated values of the gradients more stable (see section 2.2.2 for details).

2   Run the network on x (a step called the *forward pass*) to obtain predictions y_pred.

3   Compute the loss of the network on the batch, a measure of the mismatch between y_true and y_pred. Recall that the loss function is specified when model.compile() is called.

4   Update all the weights (parameters) in the network in a way that slightly reduces the loss on this batch. The detailed updates to the individual weights are managed by the optimizer, another option we specified during the model.compile() call.

If you can lower your loss at every step, you will eventually end up with a network with low loss on the training data. The network has "learned" to map its inputs to correct targets. From afar, it may look like magic, but when reduced to these elementary steps, it turns out to be simple.

The only difficult part is step 4: how can you determine which weights should be increased, which should be decreased, and by how much? We could simply guess and check, and only accept updates that actually reduce the loss. Such an algorithm might work for a simple problem like this one, but it would be very slow. For larger problems, when we are optimizing millions of weights, the likelihood of randomly selecting a good direction becomes vanishingly small. A much better approach is to take advantage of the fact that all operations used in the network are *differentiable* and to compute the *gradient* of the loss with regard to the network's parameters.

What is a gradient? Instead of defining it precisely (which requires some calculus), we can describe it intuitively as the following:

A direction such that if you move the weights by a tiny bit in that direction, you will increase the loss function the fastest, among all possible directions

Even though this definition is not overly technical, there is still a lot to unpack, so let's try to break it down:

■   First, the gradient is a vector. It has the same number of elements as the weights do. It represents a direction in the space of all choices of the weight values. If the weights of your model consist of two numbers, as is the case in our simple linear-regression network, then the gradient is a 2D vector. Deep-learning models often have thousands or millions of dimensions, and the gradients of these models are vectors (directions) with thousands or millions of elements.

- Second, the gradient depends on current weight values. In other words, different weight values will yield different gradients. This is clear from figure 2.5, in which the direction that descends most quickly depends on where you are on the loss surface. On the left edge, we must go right. Near the bottom, we must go up, and so on.

- Finally, the mathematical definition of a gradient specifies a direction along which the loss function *increases*. Of course, when training neural networks, we want the loss to *decrease*. This is why we must move the weights in the direction *opposite* the gradient.

Consider, by way of analogy, a hike in a mountain range. Imagine we wish to travel to a place with the lowest altitude. In this analogy, we can change our altitude by moving in any direction defined by the east-west and north-south axes. We should interpret the first bullet point as saying that the gradient of our altitude is the direction most steeply upward given the slope under our feet. The second bullet is somewhat obvious, stating that the direction most steeply upward depends on our current position. Finally, if we wish to go to a low altitude, we should take steps in the direction *opposite* the gradient.

This training process is aptly named *gradient descent*. Remember in listing 2.4, when we specified our model optimizer with the configuration `optimizer: 'sgd'`? The gradient-descent portion of stochastic gradient descent should now be clear. The "stochastic" part just means we draw random samples from the training data during each gradient-descent step for efficiency, as opposed to using every training data sample at every step. Stochastic gradient descent is simply a modification of gradient descent for computational efficiency.

We now have tools for a more complete explanation of how optimization works, and why 200 epochs were better than 10 for our download-time estimation model. Figure 2.7 illustrates how the gradient-descent algorithm follows a path down our loss surface to find a weight setting that fits our training data nicely. The contour plot in panel A of figure 2.7 shows the same loss surface as before, zoomed in a bit and now overlaid with the path followed by the gradient-descent algorithm. The path begins at the *random initialization*—a random place on the image. We have to pick somewhere random to start since we don't know the optimum beforehand! Several other points of interest are called out along the path, illustrating the positions corresponding to the underfit and the well-fit models. Panel B of figure 2.7 shows a plot of the model loss as a function of the step, highlighting the analogous points of interest. Panel C illustrates the models using the weights as snapshots at the steps highlighted in B.

Our simple linear-regression model is the only model in this book where we will have the luxury to visualize the gradient-descent process this vividly. But when we encounter more complex models later, keep in mind that the essence of gradient descent remains the same: it's just iteratively stepping down the slope of a complicated, high-dimensional surface, hoping that we will end up at a place with very low loss.

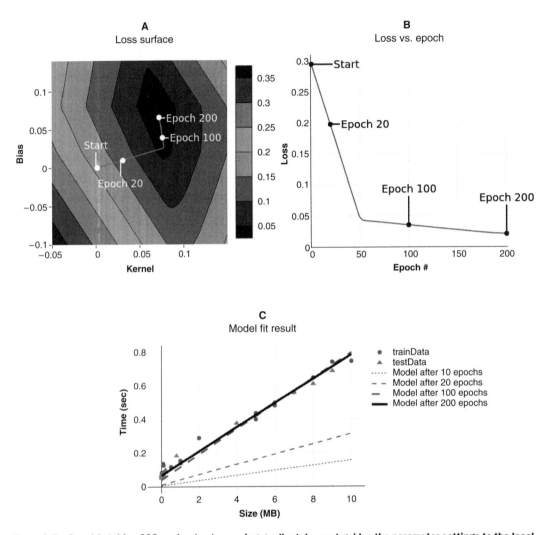

Figure 2.7   Panel A: taking 200 moderate steps using gradient descent guides the parameter settings to the local optimum. Annotations highlight the starting weights and values after 20, 100, and 200 epochs. Panel B: a plot of the loss as a function of the epoch, highlighting the loss at the same points. Panel C: the function from `sizeMB` to `timeSec`, embodied by the fitted model after 10, 20, 100, and 200 epochs of training, repeated here for you to easily compare the loss surface position and model output. See codepen.io/tfjs-book/pen/JmerMM to play with this code.

In our initial effort, we used the default step size (determined by the *default learning rate*), but in looping over our limited data only 10 times, there weren't enough steps to reach the optimum; 200 steps were enough. In general, how do you know how to set the learning rate, or how to know when training is done? There are some helpful rules of thumb, which we will cover over the course of this book, but there is no hard-and-fast rule that will always keep you out of trouble. If we use too small a learning rate and end up with *too small* a step, we won't reach the optimum parameters within a reasonable amount of time. Conversely, if we use too large a learning rate and therefore *too big* of a step, we will completely skip over the minimum and may even end up with higher loss than the place we left. This will cause our model's parameters to oscillate wildly around the optimum instead of approaching it quickly in a straightforward way. Figure 2.8 illustrates what happens when our gradient step is too large. In more extreme cases, large learning rates will cause the parameter values to diverge and go to infinity, which will in turn generate NaN (not-a-number) values in the weights, completely ruining your model.

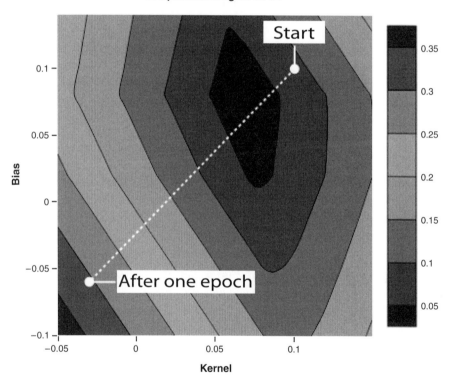

Figure 2.8 When the learning rate is too high, the gradient step will be too large, and the new parameters may be worse than the old ones. This could lead to oscillating behavior or some other instability resulting in infinities or NaNs. You can try increasing the learning rate in the CodePen code to 0.5 or higher to see this behavior.

2.2.2 Backpropagation: Inside gradient descent

In the previous section, we explained how the step size of weight updates affects the process of gradient descent. However, we haven't discussed how the *directions* of the updates are computed. The directions are critical to the neural network's learning process. They are determined by the gradients with respect to the weights, and the algorithm for computing the gradients is called *backpropagation*. Invented in the 1960s, backpropagation is one of the foundations of neural networks and deep learning. In this section, we will use a simple example to show how backpropagation works. Note that this section is for readers who wish to get an understanding of backpropagation. It is not necessary if you only wish to apply the algorithm using TensorFlow.js, because these mechanisms are all hidden nicely under the `tf.Model.fit()` API; you may skip this section and continue reading at section 2.3.

Consider the simple model linear model

```
y' = v * x,
```

where x is the input feature and y' is the predicted output, and v is the only weight parameter of the model to be updated during backpropagation. Suppose we are using the squared error as the loss function; we then have the following relation between loss, v, x, and y (the actual target value):

```
loss = square(y' - y) = square(v * x - y)
```

Let's assume the following concrete values: the two inputs are x = 2 and y = 5, and the weight value is v = 0. The loss can then be calculated as 25. This is shown step-by-step in figure 2.9. Each gray square in panel A represents an input (that is, the x and the y). Each white box is an operation. There are a total of three operations. The edges connecting the operations (and the one that connects the tunable weight v with the first operation) are labeled e_1, e_2, and e_3.

An important step of backpropagation is to determine the following quantity:

> *Assuming everything else (x and y in this case) stays the same, how much change in the loss value will we get if v is increased by a unit amount?*

This quantity is referred to as *the gradient of loss with respect to* v. Why do we need this gradient? Because once we have it, we can alter v in the direction *opposite* to it, so we can get a decrease in the loss value. Note that we do not need the gradient of loss with respect to x or y, because x and y don't need to be updated: they are the input data and are fixed.

This gradient is computed step-by-step, starting from the loss value and going back toward the variable v, as illustrated in panel B of figure 2.9. The direction in which the computation is carried out is the reason why this algorithm is called "backpropagation." Let's walk through the steps. Each of the following steps corresponds to an arrow in the figure:

- At the edge labeled `loss`, we start from a gradient value of 1. This is making the trivial point, "a unit increase in `loss` corresponds to a unit increase in `loss` itself."

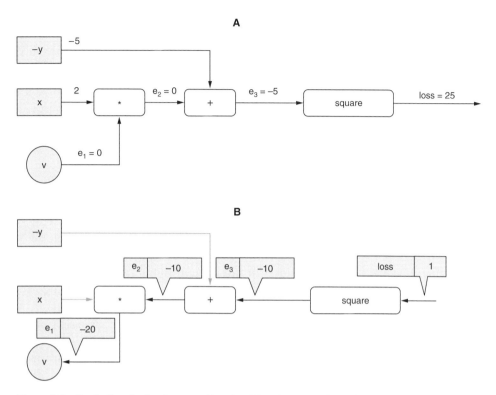

Figure 2.9 **Illustrating the backpropagation algorithm through a simple linear model with only one updatable weight (v). Panel A: forward pass on the model—the loss value is calculated from the weight (v) and the inputs (x and y). Panel B: backward pass—the gradient of loss with respect to v is calculated step-by-step, from the loss to v.**

- At the edge labeled e_3, we calculate the gradient of loss with respect to unit change of the current value at e_3. Because the intervening operation is a square, and from basic calculus we know that the derivative (gradient in the one-variable case) of $(e_3)^2$ with respect to e_3 is $2 * e_3$, we get a gradient value of $2 * -5 = -10$. The value -10 is multiplied with the gradient from before (that is, 1) to obtain the gradient on edge e_3: -10. This is the amount of increase in loss we'll get if e_3 is increased by 1. As you may have observed, the rule that we use to go from the gradient of the loss with respect to one edge to the one with respect to the next edge is to multiply the previous gradient with the gradient calculated locally at the current node. This rule is sometimes referred to as the *chain rule*.

- At edge e_2, we calculate the gradient of e_3 with respect to e_2. Because this is a simple add operation, the gradient is simply 1, regardless of the other input value ($-y$). Multiplying this 1 with the gradient on edge e_3, we get the gradient on edge e_2, that is, -10.

- At edge e_1, we calculate the gradient of e_2 with respect to e_1. The operation here is a multiplication between x and v, that is, x * v. So, the gradient of e_2 with respect to e_1 (that is, with respect to v) is x, or 2. The value of 2 is multiplied with the gradient on edge e_2 to get the final gradient: 2 * -10 = -20.

Up to this point, we have obtained the gradient of loss with respect to v: it is –20. In order to apply gradient descent, we need to multiply the negative of this gradient with the learning rate. Suppose the learning rate is 0.01. Then we get a gradient update of

```
-(-20) * 0.01 = 0.2
```

This is the update we will apply to v in this step of training:

```
v = 0 + 0.2 = 0.2
```

As you can see, because we have x = 2 and y = 5, and the function to be fit is y' = v * x, the optimal value of v is 5/2 = 2.5. After one step of training, the value of v changes from 0 to 0.2. In other words, the weight v gets a little closer to the desired value. It will get closer and closer in subsequent training steps (ignoring any noise in the training data), which will be based on the same backpropagation algorithm previously described.

The prior example is made intentionally simple so that it's easy to follow. Even though the example captures the essence of backpropagation, the backpropagation that happens in actual neural network training is different from it in the following aspects:

- Instead of providing a simple training example (x = 2 and y = 5, in our case), usually a batch of many input examples are provided simultaneously. The loss value used to derive the gradient is an arithmetic mean of the loss values for all the individual examples.
- The variables being updated generally have many more elements. So, instead of doing a simple, one-variable derivative as we just did, matrix calculus is often involved.
- Instead of having to calculate the gradient for only one variable, multiple variables are generally involved. Figure 2.10 shows an example, which is a slightly more complex linear model with two variables to optimize. In addition to k, the model has a bias term: y' = k * x + b. Here, there are two gradients to compute, one for k and one for b. Both paths of backpropagation start from the loss. They share some common edges and form a tree-like structure.

Our treatment of backpropagation in this section is a casual and high-level one. If you wish to gain a deeper understanding of the math and algorithms of backpropagation, refer to the links in info box 2.2.

At this point, you should have a pretty good understanding of what happens when fitting a simple model to training data, so let's put away our tiny download-time prediction problem and use TensorFlow.js to tackle something a bit more challenging. In

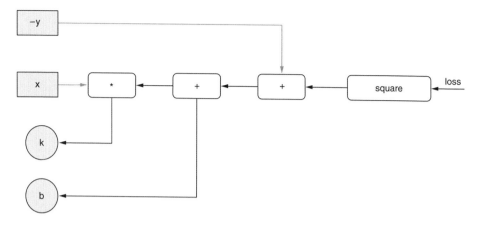

Figure 2.10 Schematic drawing showing backpropagation from loss to two updatable weights (k and b).

INFO BOX 2.2 Further reading on gradient descent and backpropagation

The differential calculus behind optimizing neural networks is definitely interesting and gives insight into how these algorithms behave; but beyond the basics, it is definitely *not* a requirement for the machine-learning practitioner, in the same way that understanding the intricacies of the TCP/IP protocol is useful but not critical to understanding how to build a modern web application. We invite the curious reader to explore the excellent resources here to build a deeper understanding of the mathematics of gradient-based optimization in networks:

- Backpropagation demo scrollytelling illustration: http://mng.bz/2J4g
- Stanford CS231 lecture 4 course notes on backpropagation: http://cs231n .github.io/optimization-2/
- Andrej Karpathy's "Hacker's Guide to Neural Nets:" http://karpathy.github .io/neuralnets/

---

the next section, we'll build a model to accurately predict the price of real estate from multiple input features simultaneously.

2.3 Linear regression with multiple input features

In our first example, we had just one input feature, `sizeMB`, with which to predict our target, `timeSec`. A much more common scenario is to have multiple input features, to not know exactly which ones are the most predictive and which are only loosely related to the target, and to use them all simultaneously and let the learning algorithm sort it out. In this section, we will tackle this more complicated problem.

By the end of this section, you will

- Understand how to build a model that takes in and learns from multiple input features.
- Use Yarn, Git, and the standard JavaScript project packaging structure to build and run a web app with machine learning.
- Know how to normalize data to stabilize the learning process.
- Get a feel for using `tf.Model.fit()` callbacks to update a web UI while training.

2.3.1 The Boston Housing Prices dataset

The Boston Housing Prices dataset[4] is a collection of 500 simple real-estate records collected in and around Boston, Massachusetts, in the late 1970s. It has been used as a standard dataset for introductory statistics and machine-learning problems for decades. Each independent record in the dataset includes numeric measurements of a Boston neighborhood, including, for example, the typical size of homes, how far the region is from the closest highway, whether the area has waterfront property, and so on. Table 2.1 provides the precise ordered list of features, along with the average value of each feature.

Table 2.1 Features of the Boston-housing dataset

Index	Feature short name	Feature description	Mean value	Range (max − min)
0	CRIM	Crime rate	3.62	88.9
1	ZN	Proportion of residential land zoned for lots over 25,000 sq. ft.	11.4	100
2	INDUS	Proportion of nonretail business acres (industry) in town	11.2	27.3
3	CHAS	Whether or not the area is next to the Charles River	0.0694	1
4	NOX	Nitric oxide concentration (parts per 10 million)	0.555	0.49
5	RM	Average number of rooms per dwelling	6.28	5.2
6	AGE	Portion of owner-occupied units built before 1940	68.6	97.1
7	DIS	Weighted distances to five Boston employment centers	3.80	11.0
8	RAD	Index of accessibility to radial highways	9.55	23.0

---

4 David Harrison and Daniel Rubinfeld, "Hedonic Housing Prices and the Demand for Clean Air," *Journal of Environmental Economics and Management*, vol. 5, 1978, pp. 81–102, http://mng.bz/1wvX.

Table 2.1 Features of the Boston-housing dataset *(continued)*

Index	Feature short name	Feature description	Mean value	Range (max – min)
9	TAX	Tax rate per US$10,000	408	524.0
10	PTRATIO	Pupil-teacher ratio	18.5	9.40
11	LSTAT	Percentage of working males without a high school education	12.7	36.2
12	MEDV	Median value of owner-occupied homes in units of $1,000	22.5	45

In this section, we will build, train, and evaluate a learning system to estimate the median value of the house prices in a neighborhood (MEDV) given all the input features from the neighborhood. You can imagine it as a system for estimating the price of real estate from measurable neighborhood properties.

2.3.2 *Getting and running the Boston-housing project from GitHub*

Because this problem is a bit larger than the download-time prediction example and has more moving pieces, we will begin by providing the solution in the form of a working code repository, and then guide you through it. If you are already an expert in the Git source-control workflow and npm/Yarn package management, you may want to just skim this subsection quickly. More about basic JavaScript project structure is provided in info box 2.3.

We will begin by cloning the project repository from its source on GitHub[5] to get a copy of the HTML, JavaScript, and configuration files required for the project. Except the simplest ones, which are hosted on CodePen, all the examples in this book are collected within one of two Git repositories and then separated by directory within the repository. The two repositories are tensorflow/tfjs-examples and tensorflow/tfjs-models, both hosted at GitHub. The following commands will clone the repository we need for this example locally and change the working directory to the Boston-housing prediction project:

```
git clone https://github.com/tensorflow/tfjs-examples.git
cd tfjs-examples/boston-housing
```

---

[5] The examples in this book are open source and are hosted at github.com and codepen.io. If you would like a refresher on how to use Git source-control tooling, GitHhub has a well-made tutorial beginning at https://help.github.com/articles/set-up-git. If you see a mistake or would like to help by clarifying something, you are welcome to send in fixes via GitHub pull requests.

INFO BOX 2.3   Basic JavaScript project structure of examples used in this book

The standard project structure we will be using for the examples in this book includes three important types of files. The first is HTML. The HTML files we will be using will be bare bones and serve mostly as a basic structure to hold a few components. Typically, there will be just one HTML file, titled index.html, which will include a few `div` tags, perhaps a few UI elements, and a source tag to pull in the JavaScript code, such as index.js.

The JavaScript code will usually be modularized into several files in order to promote good readability and style. In the case of this Boston-housing project, code dealing with updating visual elements resides in ui.js, and code for downloading the data is in data.js. Both are referenced via `import` statements from index.js.

The third important file type we will be working with is the metadata package .json file, a requirement from the npm package manager (www.npmjs.com). If you haven't worked with npm or Yarn before, we recommend skimming the npm "getting started" documentation at https://docs.npmjs.com/about-npm and becoming familiar enough to be able to build and run the example code. We will be using Yarn as our package manager (https://yarnpkg.com/en/), but you should be able to substitute npm for Yarn if it better suits your needs.

Inside the repository, take note of the following important files:

- *index.html*—The root HTML file, which provides the DOM root and calls to the JavaScript scripts
- *index.js*—The root JavaScript file, which loads the data, defines the model and the training loop, and specifies the UI elements
- *data.js*—Implementation of the structures necessary for downloading and accessing the Boston-housing dataset
- *ui.js*—Implementation of the UI hooks for connecting UI elements to actions; specification of the plot configuration
- *normalization.js*—Numeric routines for, for example, subtracting the mean from the data
- *package.json*—Standard npm package definition describing which dependencies are necessary for building and running this demo (such as TensorFlow.js!)

Note that we do not follow the standard practice of putting HTML files and JavaScript files in type-specific subdirectories. This pattern, while best practice for larger repositories, obscures more than it clarifies for smaller examples like we will be using for this book or those you can find at github.com/tensorflow/tfjs-examples.

To run the demo, use Yarn:

```
yarn && yarn watch
```

This should open a new tab in your browser pointing to a port on `localhost`, which will run the example. If your browser doesn't automatically react, you can navigate to the URL output on the command line. Clicking the button labeled Train Linear Regressor will trigger the routine to build a linear model and fit it to the Boston-housing data, and then output an animated graph of the loss on the training and testing datasets after each epoch, as figure 2.11 illustrates.

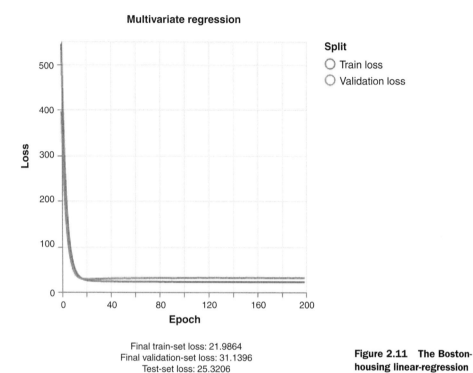

Final train-set loss: 21.9864
Final validation-set loss: 31.1396
Test-set loss: 25.3206
Baseline loss (meanSquaredError) is 85.58

Figure 2.11   The Boston-housing linear-regression example from tfjs-examples

The rest of this section will go through the important points in the construction of this Boston-housing linear-regression web app demo. We will first review how the data is collected and processed so as to work with TensorFlow.js. We will then focus on the construction, training, and evaluation of the model; and, finally, we will show how to use the model for live predictions on the web page.

2.3.3   *Accessing the Boston-housing data*

In our first project, in listing 2.1, we hard-coded our data as JavaScript arrays and converted it into tensors using the tf.tensor2d function. Hard-coding is fine for a little demo but clearly doesn't scale to larger applications. In general, JavaScript developers will find that their data is located in some serialized format at some URL (which may be local). For instance, the Boston-housing data is publicly and freely available in CSV format from the Google Cloud at the following URLs:

- https://storage.googleapis.com/tfjs-examples/multivariate-linear-regression/
  data/train-data.csv
- https://storage.googleapis.com/tfjs-examples/multivariate-linear-regression/
  data/train-target.csv
- https://storage.googleapis.com/tfjs-examples/multivariate-linear-regression/
  data/test-data.csv
- https://storage.googleapis.com/tfjs-examples/multivariate-linear-regression/
  data/test-target.csv

The data has been presplit by randomly assigning samples into training and testing portions. About two-thirds of the samples are in the training split, and the remaining one-third are reserved for independently evaluating the trained model. Additionally, for each split, the target feature has been separated into a CSV file apart from the other features, resulting in the four file names listed in table 2.2.

Table 2.2   File names by split and contents for the Boston-housing dataset

		Features (12 numbers)	Target (1 number)
Train-test split	Training	train-data.csv	train-target.csv
	Testing	test-data.csv	test-target.csv

In order to pull these into our application, we will need to be able to download this data and convert it into a tensor of the appropriate type and shape. The Boston-housing project defines a class `BostonHousingDataset` in data.js for this purpose. This class abstracts away the dataset streaming operation, providing an API to retrieve the raw data as numeric matrices. Internally, the class uses the public open source Papa Parse library (www.papaparse.com) to stream and parse the remote CSV files. Once the file has been loaded and parsed, the library returns an array of arrays of numbers. It is then converted into a tensor using the same API as in the first example, as per the following listing, a slightly trimmed-down sample from index.js focused on the relevant bits.

Listing 2.7   Converting the Boston-housing data to tensors in index.js

```
// Initialize a BostonHousingDataset object defined in data.js.
const bostonData = new BostonHousingDataset();
const tensors = {};

// Convert the loaded csv data, of type number[][] into 2d tensors.
export const arraysToTensors = () => {
  tensors.rawTrainFeatures = tf.tensor2d(bostonData.trainFeatures);
  tensors.trainTarget = tf.tensor2d(bostonData.trainTarget);
  tensors.rawTestFeatures = tf.tensor2d(bostonData.testFeatures);
  tensors.testTarget = tf.tensor2d(bostonData.testTarget);
}

// Trigger the data to load asynchronously once the page has loaded.
```

```
let tensors;
document.addEventListener('DOMContentLoaded', async () => {
  await bostonData.loadData();
  arraysToTensors();
}, false);
```

2.3.4 *Precisely defining the Boston-housing problem*

Now that we have access to our data in the form we want it, it is a good time to clarify our task more precisely. We said we would like to predict the MEDV from the other fields, but how will we decide if we're doing a good job? How can we distinguish a good model from an even better one?

The metric we used in our first example, meanAbsoluteError, counts all mistakes equally. If there were only 10 samples, and we made predictions for all 10, and we were exactly correct on 9 of them but off by 30 on the 10th sample, the meanAbsoluteError would be 3 (because 30/10 is 3). If, instead, our predictions were off by 3 on each and every sample, the meanAbsoluteError would still be 3. This "equality of mistakes" principle might seem like the only obviously correct choice, but there are good reasons for picking loss metrics other than meanAbsoluteError.

Another option is to weight large errors more than small errors. We could, instead of taking the average value of the absolute error, take the average value of the *squared* error.

Continuing the case study with the 10 samples, this mean squared error (MSE) approach sees a lower loss in being off by 3 on every example ($10 \times 3^2 = 90$) than being off by 30 on just one example ($1 \times 30^2 = 900$). Because of the sensitivity to large mistakes, squared error can be more sensitive to sample outliers than absolute error. An optimizer fitting models to minimize MSE will prefer models that systematically make small mistakes over models that occasionally give very bad estimates. Obviously, both error measures would prefer models that make no mistakes at all! However, if your application might be sensitive to very incorrect outliers, MSE could be a better choice than MAE. There are other technical reasons why you might select MSE or MAE, but they aren't important at this moment. In this example, we will use MSE for variety, but MAE would also suffice.

Before we continue, we should find a baseline estimate of the loss. If we don't know the error from a very simple estimate, then we are not equipped to evaluate it from a more complicated model. We will use the average real-estate price as a stand-in for our "best naive guess" and calculate what the error would be from always guessing that value.

Listing 2.8 Calculating baseline loss of guessing the mean price

```
export const computeBaseline = () => {                        Calculates the average price
  const avgPrice = tf.mean(tensors.trainTarget); ◁─┘
  console.log(`Average price: ${avgPrice.dataSync()[0]}`);

  const baseline =                                  Calculates the mean squared error
      tf.mean(tf.pow(tf.sub(                        on the test data. The sub(), pow, and
          tensors.testTarget, avgPrice), 2)); ◁─┘  mean() calls are the steps of
                                                    calculating the mean squared error.
```

```
console.log(
    `Baseline loss: ${baseline.dataSync()[0]}`);  ◁──────┐
};
```
Prints out the value of the loss

Because TensorFlow.js optimizes its computation by scheduling on the GPU, tensors might not always be accessible to the CPU. The calls to `dataSync` in listing 2.8 tell TensorFlow.js to finish computing the tensor and pull the value from the GPU into the CPU, so it can be printed out or otherwise shared with a non-TensorFlow operation.

When executed, the code in listing 2.8 yields the following at the console:

```
Average price: 22.768770217895508
Baseline loss: 85.58282470703125
```

This tells us that the naive error rate is approximately 85.58. If we were to build a model that always output 22.77, this model would achieve an MSE of 85.58 on the test data. Again, notice that we calculate the metric on the training data and evaluate it on the test data to avoid unfair bias.

The average *squared* error is 85.58, so we should take the square root to get the average error. The square root of 85.58 is about 9.25. Thus, we can say that we expect our (constant) estimate to be off (above or below) by about 9.25 on average. Since the values, as per table 2.1, are in thousands of US dollars, estimating a constant means we will be off by about US$9,250. If this were good enough for our application, we could stop here! The wise machine-learning practitioner knows when to avoid unnecessary complexity. Let's assume that our price estimator application needs to be closer than this. We will proceed by fitting a linear model to our data to see if we can achieve a better MSE than 85.58.

2.3.5   A slight diversion into data normalization

Looking at the Boston-housing features, we see a broad range of values. NOX ranges between 0.4 and 0.9, while TAX goes from 180 to 711. To fit a linear regression, the optimizer will be attempting to find a weight for each feature such that the sum of the features times the weights will approximately equal the housing price. Recall that to find these weights, the optimizer is hunting around, following a gradient in the weight space. If some features are scaled very differently from others, then certain weights will be much more sensitive than others. A very small move in one direction will change the output more than a very large move in a different direction. This can cause instability and makes it difficult to fit the model.

To counteract this, we will first *normalize* our data. This means that we will scale our features so that they have zero mean and unit standard deviation. This type of normalization is common and may also be referred to as *standard transformation* or *z-score normalization*. The algorithm for doing this is simple—we first calculate the mean of each feature and subtract it from the original value so that the feature has an average value of zero. We then calculate the feature's standard deviation with the mean value subtracted and do a division by that. In pseudo-code,

```
normalizedFeature = (feature - mean(feature)) / std(feature)
```

For instance, when the feature is `[10, 20, 30, 40]`, the normalized version would be approximately `[-1.3, -0.4, 0.4, 1.3]`, which clearly has a mean of zero; by eye, the standard deviation is about one. In the Boston-housing example, the normalization code is factored out into a separate file, normalization.js, the contents of which are in listing 2.9. Here, we see two functions, one to calculate the mean and standard deviation from a provided rank-2 tensor and the other to normalize a tensor given the provided precalculated mean and standard deviation.

> **Listing 2.9   Data normalization: zero mean, unit standard deviation**

```
/**

 * Calculates the mean and standard deviation of each column of an array.
 *
 * @param {Tensor2d} data Dataset from which to calculate the mean and
 *                        std of each column independently.
 *
 * @returns {Object} Contains the mean and std of each vector
 *                   column as 1d tensors.
 */
export function determineMeanAndStddev(data) {
  const dataMean = data.mean(0);
  const diffFromMean = data.sub(dataMean);
  const squaredDiffFromMean = diffFromMean.square();
  const variance = squaredDiffFromMean.mean(0);
  const std = variance.sqrt();
  return {mean, std};
}

/**
 * Given expected mean and standard deviation, normalizes a dataset by
 * subtracting the mean and dividing by the standard deviation.
 *
 * @param {Tensor2d} data: Data to normalize.
 *     Shape: [numSamples, numFeatures].
 * @param {Tensor1d} mean: Expected mean of the data. Shape [numFeatures].
 * @param {Tensor1d} std: Expected std of the data. Shape [numFeatures]
 *
 * @returns {Tensor2d}: Tensor the same shape as data, but each column
 * normalized to have zero mean and unit standard deviation.
 */
export function normalizeTensor(data, dataMean, dataStd) {
  return data.sub(dataMean).div(dataStd);
}
```

Let's dig into these functions a little. The function `determineMeanAndStddev` takes as input `data`, which is a rank-2 tensor. By convention, the first dimension is the *samples* dimension: each index corresponds to an independent, unique sample. The second dimension is the *feature* dimension: its 12 elements corresponds to the 12 input features (like CRIM, ZN, INDUS, and so on). Since we want to calculate the mean of each feature independently, we call

```
const dataMean = data.mean(0);
```

The 0 in this call means that the mean is to be taken over the 0th-index (first) dimension. Recall that data is a rank-2 tensor and thus has two dimensions (or axes). The first axis, the "batch" axis, is the sample dimension. As we move from the first to the second to the third element along that axis, we refer to different samples, or, in our case, different pieces of real estate. The second dimension is the feature dimension. As we move from the first to the second element in this dimension, we are referring to different features, such as CRIM, ZN, and INDUS, from table 2.1. When we take the mean along axis 0, we are taking the average over the sample direction. The result is a rank-1 tensor with only the features axis remaining. We have the mean of each feature. If, instead, we took the mean over axis 1, we would still get a rank-1 tensor, but the remaining axis would be the sample dimension. The values would correspond to the mean value of each piece of real estate, which wouldn't make sense for our application. Be careful when working with your axes that you are making your calculations in the right direction, as this is a common source of errors.

Sure enough, if we set a breakpoint[6] here, we can use the JavaScript console to explore the calculated mean values, and we see mean values pretty close to what we calculated for the entire dataset. This means that our training sample was representative:

```
> dataMean.shape
[12]
> dataMean.print();
    [3.3603415, 10.6891899, 11.2934837, 0.0600601, 0.5571442, 6.2656188,
    68.2264328, 3.7099338, 9.6336336, 409.2792969, 18.4480476, 12.5154343]
```

In the next line, we subtract (using tf.sub) the mean from our data to obtain a centered version of the data:

```
const diffFromMean = data.sub(dataMean);
```

If you weren't paying 100% attention, this line might have hidden a delightful little piece of magic. You see, data is a rank-2 tensor with shape [333, 12], while dataMean is a rank-1 tensor with shape [12]. In general, it is not possible to subtract two tensors with different shapes. However, in this case, TensorFlow uses broadcasting to expand the shape of the second tensor by, in effect, repeating it 333 times, doing exactly what the user intended without making them spell it out. This usability win comes in handy, but sometimes the rules for which shapes are compatible for broadcasting can be a little confusing. If you are interested in the details of broadcasting, dive right into info box 2.4.

The next few lines of the determineMeanAndStddev function hold no new surprises: tf.square() multiplies each element by itself, while tf.sqrt() takes the square root of the elements. The detailed API for each method is documented at the TensorFlow.js

---

[6] The instructions for setting a breakpoint in Chrome are here: http://mng.bz/rPQJ. If you need instructions for breakpoints in Firefox, Edge, or another browser, you may simply search for "how to set a breakpoint" using your favorite search engine.

Figure 2.12   The TensorFlow.js API documentation at js.tensorflow.org allows you to explore and interact with the TensorFlow API right within the documentation. This makes it simple and fast to understand functional uses and tricky edge cases.

API reference, https://js.tensorflow.org/api/latest/. The documentation page also has live, editable widgets that allow you to explore how the functions work with your own parameter values, as illustrated in figure 2.12.

In this example, we've written our code prioritizing the clarity of the exposition, but the `determineMeanAndStddev` function can be expressed much more concisely:

```
const std = data.sub(data.mean(0)).square().mean().sqrt();
```

You should be able to see that TensorFlow allows us to express quite a lot of numerical computation without much boilerplate code.

INFO BOX 2.4   Broadcasting

Consider a tensor operation like `C = tf.someOperation(A, B)`, where `A` and `B` are tensors. When possible, and if there's no ambiguity, the smaller tensor will be broadcast to match the shape of the larger tensor. Broadcasting consists of two steps:

1 Axes (called *broadcast axes*) are added to the smaller tensor to match the rank of the larger tensor.

2 The smaller tensor is repeated alongside these new axes to match the full shape of the larger tensor.

(continued)

In terms of implementation, no new tensor is actually created because that would be terribly inefficient. The repetition operation is entirely virtual—it happens at the algorithmic level rather than the memory level. But thinking of the smaller tensor being repeated along the new axis is a helpful mental model.

With broadcasting, you can generally apply two-tensor, element-wise operations if one tensor has shape (a, b, …, n, n + 1, … m) and the other has shape (n, n + 1, … , m). The broadcasting will then automatically happen for axis a through n - 1. For instance, the following example applies the element-wise maximum operation on two random tensors of different shapes via broadcasting:

```
x = tf.randomUniform([64, 3, 11, 9]);   ◁───  x is a random tensor with
                                               shape [64, 3, 11, 9].
y = tf.randomUniform([11, 9]);   ◁────── y is a random tensor with shape [11, 9].
z = tf.maximum(x, y);   ◁──── The output z has shape [64, 3, 11, 9] like x.
```

2.3.6 *Linear regression on the Boston-housing data*

Our data is normalized, and we have done the due diligence data work to calculate a reasonable baseline—the next step is to build and fit a model to see if we can outperform the baseline. In listing 2.10, we define a linear-regression model like we did in section 2.1 (from index.js). The code is remarkably similar; the only difference we see from the download-time prediction model is in the inputShape configuration, which now accepts vectors of length 12 instead of 1. The single dense layer still has units: 1, indicating that a single number is the output.

Listing 2.10 Defining a linear-regression model for Boston-housing

```
export const linearRegressionModel = () => {
  const model = tf.sequential();
  model.add(tf.layers.dense(
      {inputShape: [bostonData.numFeatures], units: 1}));
  return model;
};
```

Recall that after our model is defined, but before we begin training, we must specify the loss and optimizer via a call to model.compile. In listing 2.11, we see that the 'meanSquaredError' loss is specified and that the optimizer is using a customized learning rate. In our previous example, the optimizer parameter was set to the string 'sgd', but now it is tf.train.sgd(LEARNING_RATE). This factory function will return an object representing the stochastic gradient descent optimization algorithm, but parameterized with our custom learning rate. This is a common pattern in TensorFlow.js, borrowed from Keras, and you will see it adopted for many configurable options. For standard, well-known default parameters, a string sentinel value can substitute for the required object type, and TensorFlow.js will substitute the string for the required object with good default parameters. In this case, `'sgd'` would be replaced with `tf.train.sgd(0.01)`. When additional customizations are necessary, the user can build the object via the factory function and provide the required custom value. This allows code to be concise in most cases but allows the power user to override default behaviors when needed.

Listing 2.11 Model compilation for Boston-housing (from index.js)

```
const LEARNING_RATE = 0.01;
model.compile({
    optimizer: tf.train.sgd(LEARNING_RATE),
    loss: 'meanSquaredError'});
```

Now we can train our model with the training dataset. In listings 2.12 through 2.14, we'll use some additional features of the `model.fit()` call, but essentially it's doing the same thing as in figure 2.6. At each step, it selects a number of new samples from the features (`tensors.trainFeatures`) and targets (`tensors.trainTarget`), calculates the loss, and then updates the internal weights to reduce that loss. The process will repeat for `NUM_EPOCHS` complete passes through the training data and will select `BATCH_SIZE` samples at each step.

Listing 2.12 Training our model on the Boston-housing data

```
await model.fit(tensors.trainFeatures, tensors.trainTarget, {
  batchSize: BATCH_SIZE
  epochs: NUM_EPOCHS,
});
```

In the Boston-housing web app, we illustrate a graph of the training loss as the model trains. This requires using the `model.fit()` callback feature to update the UI. The `model.fit()` callback API allows the user to provide callback functions, which will be executed at specific events. The complete list of callback triggers, as of version 0.12.0, is `onTrainBegin`, `onTrainEnd`, `onEpochBegin`, `onEpochEnd`, `onBatchBegin`, and `onBatchEnd`.

Listing 2.13 Callbacks in `model.fit()`

```
let trainLoss;
await model.fit(tensors.trainFeatures, tensors.trainTarget, {
  batchSize: BATCH_SIZE,
  epochs: NUM_EPOCHS,
  callbacks: {
    onEpochEnd: async (epoch, logs) => {
      await ui.updateStatus(
          `Epoch ${epoch + 1} of ${NUM_EPOCHS} completed.`);
      trainLoss = logs.loss;
      await ui.plotData(epoch, trainLoss);
    }
  }
});
```

One last new customization introduced here is to make use of validation data. Validation is a machine-learning concept worth a bit of explanation. In the earlier downloading-time example, we separated our training data from our testing data because we wanted an unbiased estimate of how our model will perform on new, unseen data. Typically what happens, though, is that there is another split called *validation data*. Validation data is separate from both the training data and the testing data. What is validation data used for? The machine-learning engineer will see the result on the validation data and use that result to change certain configurations of the model[7] in order to improve the accuracy on the validation data. This is all well and good. However, if this cycle is done enough times, then we are in effect tuning on the validation data. If we use the same validation data to evaluate the model's final accuracy, the result of the final evaluation will no longer be generalizable, in the sense that the model has already seen the data, and the result of the evaluation isn't guaranteed to reflect how the model will perform on unseen data in the future. This is the purpose of separating validation out from testing data. The idea is that we will fit our model on the training data and adjust its hyperparameters based on assessments on the validation data. When we are all done and satisfied with the process, we will evaluate the model just one time on the testing data for a final, generalizable estimate of performance.

Let's summarize what the training, validation, and testing sets are and how to use them in TensorFlow.js. Not all projects will make use of all three types of data. Frequently, quick explorations or research projects will use only training and validation data and not reserve a set of "pure" data for the test. While less rigorous, this is sometimes the best use of limited resources:

- *Training data*—For fitting the model weights with gradient descent
  - *Usage in TensorFlow.js*: Typically, training data is employed using the main arguments (x and y) for calls to `Model.fit(x, y, config)`.
- *Validation data*—For selecting the model structure and hyperparameters
  - *Usage in TensorFlow.js*: `Model.fit()` has two ways of specifying validation data, both as parameters to the `config` argument. If you, the user, have explicit data to use for validation, this may be specified as `config.validationData`. If, instead, you wish the framework to split some of the training data off and use it as validation data, specify the fraction to use in `config.validationSplit`. The framework will take care to not use the validation data to train the model, so there is no overlap.
- *Testing data*—For a final, unbiased estimate of model performance
  - *Usage in TensorFlow.js*: Evaluation data is exposed to the system by passing it in as the x and y arguments to `Model.evaluate(x, y, config)`.

---

[7] Examples of those configurations include the number of layers in the model, the sizes of the layers, the type of optimizer and learning rate to use during training, and so forth. They are referred to as the model's *hyperparameters*, which we will cover in greater detail in section 3.1.2 of the next chapter.

In listing 2.14, validation loss is calculated along with training loss. The `validation-Split: 0.2` field instructs the `model.fit()` machinery to select the last 20% of the training data to use as validation data. This data will not be used for training (it does not affect gradient descent).

Listing 2.14 Including validation data in `model.fit()`

```
let trainLoss;
let valLoss;
await model.fit(tensors.trainFeatures, tensors.trainTarget, {
  batchSize: BATCH_SIZE,
  epochs: NUM_EPOCHS,
  validationSplit: 0.2,
  callbacks: {
    onEpochEnd: async (epoch, logs) => {
      await ui.updateStatus(
          `Epoch ${epoch + 1} of ${NUM_EPOCHS} completed.`);
      trainLoss = logs.loss;
      valLoss = logs.val_loss;
      await ui.plotData(epoch, trainLoss, valLoss);
    }
  }
});
```

Training this model to 200 epochs takes approximately 11 seconds in the browser on a modern laptop. We can now evaluate the model on our test set to see if it's any better than the baseline. The next listing shows how to use `model.evaluate()` to collect the performance of the model on our reserved test data and then call into our custom UI routines to update the view.

Listing 2.15 Evaluating our model on the test data and updating the UI (from index.js)

```
await ui.updateStatus('Running on test data...');
const result = model.evaluate(
    tensors.testFeatures, tensors.testTarget, {batchSize: BATCH_SIZE});
const testLoss = result.dataSync()[0];
await ui.updateStatus(
    `Final train-set loss: ${trainLoss.toFixed(4)}\n` +
    `Final validation-set loss: ${valLoss.toFixed(4)}\n` +
    `Test-set loss: ${testLoss.toFixed(4)}`);
```

Here, `model.evaluate()` returns a scalar (recall, a rank-0 tensor) containing the loss computed over the test set.

Because of the randomness involved in gradient descent, you might get different results, but the following results are typical:

- Final train-set loss: 21.9864
- Final validation-set loss: 31.1396
- Test-set loss: 25.3206
- Baseline loss: 85.58

We see from this that our final, unbiased estimate of our error is about 25.3, which is much better than our naive baseline of 85.6. Recall that our error is being calculated using meanSquaredError. Taking the square root, we see that the baseline estimate was typically off by more than 9.2, while the linear model is off by only about 5.0. Quite a large improvement! If we were the only ones in the world with access to this info, we could be the best Boston real-estate investors in 1978! Unless, somehow, someone were able to build an even more accurate estimate . . .

If you have let your curiosity get ahead of you and clicked Train Neural Network Regressor, you already know that *much* better estimates are possible. In the next chapter, we will introduce nonlinear deep models to show how such feats are possible.

2.4 *How to interpret your model*

Now that we've trained our model, and it's able to make reasonable predictions, it's natural to wonder what it has learned. Is there any way to peek inside the model to see how it understands the data? When the model predicts a specific price for an input, is it possible for you to find an understandable explanation for why it comes up with that value? For the general case of large deep networks, model understanding—also known as model interpretability—is still an area of active research, filling many posters and talks at academic conferences. But for this simple linear-regression model, it is quite simple.

By the end of this section, you will

- Be able to extract the learned weights from a model.
- Be able to interpret those weights and weigh them against your intuitions for what the weights *should* be.

2.4.1 *Extracting meaning from learned weights*

The simple linear model we built in section 2.3 contains 13 learned parameters, contained in a kernel and a bias, just like our first linear model in section 2.1.3:

output = **kernel** · features + **bias**

The values of the kernel and bias are both learned while fitting the model. In contrast to the *scalar* linear function learned in section 2.1.3, here, the features and the kernel are both *vectors*, and the "·" sign indicates the *inner product*, a generalization of scalar multiplication to vectors. The inner product, also known as the *dot product*, is simply the sum of the products of the matching elements. The pseudo-code in listing 2.16 defines the inner product more precisely.

We should take from this that there is a relationship between the elements of the features and the elements of the kernel. For each individual feature element, such as "Crime rate" and "Nitric oxide concentration," as listed in table 2.1, there is an associated learned number in the kernel. Each value tells us something about what the model has learned about this feature and how the feature influences the output.

Listing 2.16 Inner product pseudo-code

```
function innerProduct(a, b) {
    output = 0;
    for (let i = 0 ; i < a.length ; i++) {
        output += a[i] * b[i];
    }
    return output;
}
```

For instance, if the model learns that `kernel[i]` is positive, it means that the output will be larger if the `feature[i]` value is larger. Vice versa, if the model learns that `kernel[j]` is negative, then a larger value of `feature[j]` reduces the predicted output. A learned value that is very small in magnitude indicates that the model believes the associated feature has little impact on the prediction, whereas a learned value with a large magnitude indicates that the model places a heavy emphasis on the feature, and small changes in the feature value will have a comparatively large impact on the prediction.[8]

To make this concrete, the top five feature values, by absolute value, are printed in figure 2.13 for one run in the output area of the Boston-housing example. Subsequent runs may learn different values due to the randomness of the initialization. We can see that the values are negative for features we would expect to reflect negatively on the price of real estate, such as the rate at which local residents drop out of school and the distance of the real estate to desirable working locations. Learned weights are positive for features we would expect to correlate directly with the price, such as the number of rooms in the property.

School drop-out rate	−3.8119
Distance to commute	−3.7278
Number of rooms per house	2.8451
Distance to highway	2.2949
Nitric oxide concentration	−2.1190

Figure 2.13 Ranked by absolute value, these are the top five weights learned in one run of the linear model on the Boston-housing prediction problem. Note the negative values for features that you would expect to reflect negatively on the price of housing.

2.4.2 Extracting internal weights from the model

The modular structure of the learned model makes it easy to extract the relevant weights; we can access them directly, but there are a few API levels that need to be reached through in order to get the raw values. It's important to keep in mind that, since the value may be on the GPU, and interdevice communication is costly, requesting such values is asynchronous. The boldface code in listing 2.17 is an addition to the

---

[8] Note that comparing magnitudes in this way is only possible if the features have been normalized, as we have done for the Boston-housing dataset.

`model.fit` callbacks, extending listing 2.14 to illustrate the learned weights after each epoch. We will walk through the API calls step-by-step.

Given the model, we first wish to access the correct layer. This is easy because there is only one layer in this model, so we can get a handle to it at `model.layers[0]`. Now that we have the layer, we can access the internal weights with `getWeights()`, which returns an array of the weights. For the case of a dense layer, this will always contain two weights, the kernel and the bias, in that order. Thus, we can access the correct tensor at

```
> model.layers[0].getWeights()[0]
```

Now that we have the right tensor, we can access its contents with a call to its `data()` method. Due to the asynchronous nature of GPU ↔ CPU communication, `data()` is asynchronous and returns a promise of the tensor's value, not the actual value. In listing 2.17, a callback passed to the `then()` method of the promise binds the tensor values to a variable called `kernelAsArr`. If the `console.log()` statement is uncommented, statements like the following, listing the values of the kernel, are logged to the console once per each epoch:

```
> Float32Array(12) [-0.44015952944755554, 0.8829045295715332,
    0.11802537739276886, 0.9555914402008057, -1.6466193199157715,
    3.386948347091675, -0.36070501804351807, -3.0381457805633545,
    1.4347705841064453, -1.3844640254974365, -1.4223048686981201,
    -3.795234441757202]
```

Listing 2.17   Accessing internal model values

```
let trainLoss;
let valLoss;
await model.fit(tensors.trainFeatures, tensors.trainTarget, {
  batchSize: BATCH_SIZE,
  epochs: NUM_EPOCHS,
  validationSplit: 0.2,
  callbacks: {
    onEpochEnd: async (epoch, logs) => {
      await ui.updateStatus(
          `Epoch ${epoch + 1} of ${NUM_EPOCHS} completed.`);
      trainLoss = logs.loss;
        valLoss = logs.val_loss;
      await ui.plotData(epoch, trainLoss, valLoss);
      model.layers[0].getWeights()[0].data().then(kernelAsArr => {
        // console.log(kernelAsArr);
        const weightsList = describeKerenelElements(kernelAsArr);
        ui.updateWeightDescription(weightsList);
      });
    }
  }
});
```

2.4.3 *Caveats on interpretability*

The weights in figure 2.13 tell a story. As a human reader, you might look at this and say that the model has learned that the "Number of rooms per house" feature positively correlates with the price output or that the real-estate AGE feature, which is not listed due to its lower absolute magnitude, is of lower importance than those first five features. Because of the way our minds like to tell stories, it is common to take this too far and imagine these numbers say more than the evidence supports. For instance, one way that this sort of analysis can fail is if two input features are strongly correlated.

Consider a hypothetical example in which the same feature is included twice, perhaps by accident. Call them FEAT1 and FEAT2. Imagine the weights learned for the two features are 10 and –5. You might be inclined to say that increasing FEAT1 leads to larger outputs, while FEAT2 does the opposite. However, since the features are equivalent, the model would output the exact same values if the weights were reversed.

Another caveat to be aware of is the difference between correlation and causality. Imagine a simple model in which we wish to predict how hard it is raining outside from how wet our roof is. If we had a measure of roof wetness, we could probably make a prediction of how much rain there had been in the past hour. We could not, however, splash water on the sensor to make it rain!

Exercises

1. The hard-coded time estimation problem in section 2.1 was selected because the data is roughly linear. Other datasets will have different loss surfaces and dynamics during fitting. You may want to try substituting your own data here to explore how the model reacts. You may need to play with the learning rate, initialization, or normalization to get the model to converge to something interesting.

2. In section 2.3.5, we spent some time describing why normalization is important and how to normalize the input data to have zero mean and unit variance. You should be able to modify the example to remove the normalization and see that the model no longer trains. You should also be able to modify the normalization routine to have, for example, a mean of something other than 0 or a standard deviation that is lower, but not as low. Some normalizations will work, and some will lead to a model that never converges.

3. It is well known that some features of the Boston Housing Prices dataset are more *predictive* of the target than others. Some of the features are merely noise in the sense that they don't carry useful information for predicting housing prices. If we were to remove all but one feature, which feature should we keep? What if we were to keep two features: how can we select which ones? Play with the code in the Boston-housing example to explore this.

4. Describe how gradient descent allows for the optimization of a model by updating weights in a better-than-random way.

5 The Boston-housing example prints out the top five weights by absolute magnitude. Try modifying the code to print out the features associated with small weights. Can you imagine why those weights are small? If someone were to ask you why those weights were what they were, what could you tell them? What sorts of cautions would you tell that person about how to interpret the values?

Summary

- It is simple to build, train, and evaluate a simple machine-learning model in five lines of JavaScript using TensorFlow.js.
- Gradient descent, the basic algorithm structure behind deep learning, is conceptually simple and really just means repeatedly updating model parameters in small steps in the calculated direction that would most improve the model fit.
- A model's loss surface illustrates how well the model fits for a grid of parameter values. The loss surface is not generally calculable because of the high-dimensionality of the parameter space, but it's illustrative to think about and gives intuition to how machine learning works.
- A single dense layer is sufficient to solve some simple problems and can achieve reasonable performance on a real-estate pricing problem.

3

Adding nonlinearity: Beyond weighted sums

This chapter covers

- What nonlinearity is and how nonlinearity in hidden layers of a neural network enhances the network's capacity and leads to better prediction accuracies
- What hyperparameters are and methods for tuning them
- Binary classification through nonlinearity at the output layer, introduced with the phishing-website-detection example
- Multiclass classification and how it differs from binary classification, introduced with the iris-flower example

In this chapter, you'll build on the groundwork laid in chapter 2 to allow your neural networks to learn more complicated mappings, from features to labels. The primary enhancement we will introduce is *nonlinearity*—a mapping between input and output that isn't a simple weighted sum of the input's elements. Nonlinearity enhances the representational power of neural networks and, when used correctly, improves the prediction accuracy in many problems. We will illustrate this point by continuing to use the Boston-housing dataset. In addition, this chapter will introduce a deeper look at *over-* and *underfitting* to help you train models that not only perform well on the training data but also achieve good accuracy on data that the models haven't seen during training, which is what ultimately counts in terms of models' quality.

3.1   *Nonlinearity: What it is and what it is good for*

Let's pick up where we left off with the Boston-housing example from the last chapter. Using a single dense layer, you saw trained models leading to MSEs corresponding to misestimates of roughly US$5,000. Can we do better? The answer is yes. To make a better model for the Boston-housing data, we add one more dense layer to it, as shown by the following code listing (from index.js of the Boston-housing example).

> **Listing 3.1   Defining a two-layer neural network for the Boston-housing problem**

```
export function multiLayerPerceptronRegressionModel1Hidden() {
  const model = tf.sequential();
  model.add(tf.layers.dense({
    inputShape: [bostonData.numFeatures],
    units: 50,
    activation: 'sigmoid',
    kernelInitializer: 'leCunNormal'
  }));
  model.add(tf.layers.dense({units: 1}));

  model.summary();
  return model;
};
```

Specifies how the kernel values should be initialized; see section 3.1.2 for a discussion of how this is chosen through hyperparameter optimization.

Adds a hidden layer

Prints a text summary of the model's topology

To see this model in action, first run the `yarn && yarn watch` command as mentioned in chapter 2. Once the web page is open, click the Train Neural Network Regressor (1 Hidden Layer) button in the UI in order to start the model's training.

The model is a two-layer network. The first layer is a dense layer with 50 units. It is also configured to have custom activation and a kernel initializer, which we will discuss in section 3.1.2. This layer is a *hidden* layer because its output is not directly seen from outside the model. The second layer is a dense layer with the default activation (the linear activation) and is structurally the same layer we used in the pure linear model from chapter 2. This layer is an *output* layer because its output is the model's final output and is what's returned by the model's `predict()` method. You may have noticed that the function name in the code refers to the model as a *multilayer perceptron* (MLP). This is an oft-used term that describes neural networks that 1) have a simple topology without loops (what's referred to as *feedforward neural networks*) and 2) have at least one hidden layer. All the models you will see in this chapter meet this definition.

The `model.summary()` call in listing 3.1 is new. It is a diagnostic/reporting tool that prints the topology of TensorFlow.js models to the console (either in the browser's developer tool or to the standard output in Node.js). Here's what the two-layer model generated:

```
Layer (type)                    Output shape              Param #
=================================================================
dense_Dense1 (Dense)            [null,50]                 650
_____
dense_Dense2 (Dense)            [null,1]                  51
=================================================================
Total params: 701
Trainable params: 701
Non-trainable params: 0
```

The key information in the summary includes

- The names and types of the layers (first column).
- The output shape for each layer (second column). These shapes almost always contain a null dimension as the first (batch) dimension, representing undetermined and variable batch size.
- The number of weight parameters for each layer (third column). This is a count of all the individual numbers that make up the layer's weights. For layers with more than one weight, this is a sum across all the weights. For instance, the first dense layer in this example contains two weights: a kernel of shape [12, 50] and a bias of shape [50], leading to 12 * 50 + 50 = 650 parameters.
- The total number of the model's weight parameters (at the bottom of the summary), followed by a breakdown of how many of the parameters are trainable and how many are nontrainable. The models we've seen so far contain only trainable parameters, which belong to the model weights that are updated when tf.Model.fit() is called. We will discuss nontrainable weights when we talk about transfer learning and model fine-tuning in chapter 5.

The model.summary() output of the purely linear model from chapter 2 is as follows. Compared with the linear model, our two-layer model contains about 54 times as many weight parameters. Most of the additional weights come from the added hidden layer:

```
Layer (type)                    Output shape              Param #
=================================================================
dense_Dense3 (Dense)            [null,1]                  13
=================================================================
Total params: 13
Trainable params: 13
Non-trainable params: 0
```

Because the two-layer model contains more layers and weight parameters, its training and inference consumes more computation resources and time. Is this added cost worth the gain in accuracy? When we train this model for 200 epochs, we end up with final MSEs on the test set that fall into the range of 14–15 (variability due to randomness of initialization), as compared to a test-set loss of approximately 25 from the linear model. Our new model ends up with a misestimate of US$3,700–$3,900 versus the approximately \$5,000 misestimates we saw with the purely linear attempts. This is a significant improvement.

3.1.1 Building the intuition for nonlinearity in neural networks

Why does the accuracy improve? The key is the model's enhanced complexity, as figure 3.1 shows. First, there is an additional layer of neurons, which is the hidden layer. Second, the hidden layer contains a nonlinear *activation function* (as specified by `activation: 'sigmoid'` in the code), which is represented by the square boxes in panel B of figure 3.1. An activation function[1] is an element-by-element transform. The sigmoid function is a "squashing" nonlinearity, in the sense that it "squashes" all real values from –infinity to +infinity into a much smaller range (0 to +1, in this case). Its mathematical equation and plot are shown in figure 3.2. Let's take the hidden dense layer as an example. Suppose the result of the matrix multiplication and addition with the bias is a 2D tensor consisting of the following array of random values:

```
[[1.0], [0.5], …, [0.0]],
```

The final output of the dense layer is then obtained by calling the sigmoid (`S`) function on each of the 50 elements individually, giving

```
[[S(1.0)], [S(0.5)], …, [S(0.0)]] = [[0.731], [0.622], …, [0.0]]
```

Why is this function called *nonlinear*? Intuitively, the plot of the activation function is not a straight line. For example, sigmoid is a curve (figure 3.2, left panel), and relu is a concatenation of two line segments (figure 3.2, right panel). Even though sigmoid and relu are nonlinear, one of their properties is that they are smooth and differentiable at every point, which makes it possible to perform backpropagation[2] through them. Without this property, it wouldn't be possible to train a model with layers that contain this activation.

Apart from the sigmoid function, a few other types of differentiable nonlinear functions are used frequently in deep learning. These include relu and hyperbolic tangent (or tanh). We will describe them in detail when we encounter them in subsequent examples.

---

[1] The term *activation function* originated from the study of biological neurons, which communicate with each other through *action potentials* (voltage spikes on their cell membranes). A typical biological neuron receives inputs from a number of upstream neurons via contact points called *synapses*. The upstream neurons fire action potentials at different rates, which leads to the release of neurotransmitters and opening or closing of ion channels at the synapses. This in turn leads to variation in the voltage on the recipient neuron's membrane. This is not unlike the kind of weighted sum seen for a unit in the dense layer. Only when the potential exceeds a certain threshold will the recipient neuron actually produce action potentials (that is, be "activated") and thereby affect the state of downstream neurons. In this sense, the activation function of a typical biological neuron is somewhat similar to the relu function (figure 3.2, right panel), which consists of a "dead zone" below a certain threshold of the input and increases linearly with the input above the threshold (at least up to a certain saturation level, which is not captured by the relu function).

[2] See section 2.2.2 if you need a refresher on backpropagation.

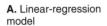

A. Linear-regression model

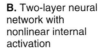

B. Two-layer neural network with nonlinear internal activation

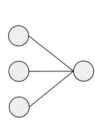

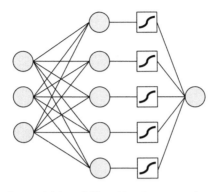

Figure 3.1 The linear-regression model (panel A) and two-layer neural network (panel B) created for the Boston-housing dataset. For the sake of clarity, we reduced the number of input features from 12 to 3 and the number of the hidden layer's units from 50 to 5 in panel B. Each model has only a single output unit because the models solve a univariate (one-target-number) regression problem. Panel B illustrates the nonlinear (sigmoid) activation of the model's hidden layer.

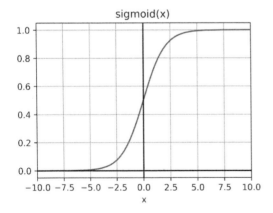

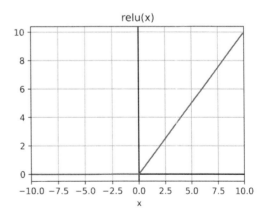

Figure 3.2 Two frequently used nonlinear activation functions for deep neural networks. Left: the sigmoid function `S(x) = 1 / (1 + e ^ -x)`. Right: the rectified linear unit (relu) function `relu(x) = {0:x < 0, x:x >= 0}`

NONLINEARITY AND MODEL CAPACITY

Why does nonlinearity improve the accuracy of our model? Nonlinear functions allow us to represent a more diverse family of input-output relations. Many relations in the real world are approximately linear, such as the download-time problem we saw in the last chapter. But many others are not. It is easy to conceive examples of nonlinear relations. Consider the relation between a person's height and their age. Height varies roughly linearly with age only up to a certain point, where it bends and plateaus. As another totally reasonable scenario, house prices can vary in a negative fashion with the neighborhood crime rate only if the crime rate is within a certain range. A purely linear model, like the one we developed in the last chapter, cannot accurately model this type of relation, while sigmoid nonlinearity is much better suited to model this relation. Of course, the crime-rate-house-price relation is more like an inverted (decreasing) sigmoid function than the original, increasing one in the left panel of figure 3.2. But our neural network has no issue modeling this relation because the sigmoid activation is preceded and followed by linear functions with tunable weights.

But by replacing the linear activation with a nonlinear one like sigmoid, do we lose the ability to learn any linear relations that might be present in the data? Luckily, the answer is no. This is because part of the sigmoid function (the part close to the center) is fairly close to being a straight line. Other frequently used nonlinear activations, such as tanh and relu, also contain linear or close-to-linear parts. If the relations between certain elements of the input and those of the output are approximately linear, it is entirely possible for a dense layer with a nonlinear activation to learn the proper weights and biases to utilize the near-linear parts of the activation function. Hence, adding nonlinear activation to a dense layer leads to a net gain in the breadth of input-output relations it can learn.

Furthermore, nonlinear functions are different from linear ones in that cascading nonlinear functions lead to richer sets of nonlinear functions. Here, *cascading* refers to passing the output of one function as the input to another. Suppose there are two linear functions,

```
f(x) = k1 * x + b1
```

and

```
g(x) = k2 * x + b2
```

Cascading the two functions amounts to defining a new function h:

```
h(x) = g(f(x)) = k2 * (k1 * x + b1) + b2 = (k2 * k1) * x + (k2 * b1 + b2)
```

As you can see, h is still a linear function. It just has a different kernel (slope) and a different bias (intercept) from those of `f1` and `f2`. The slope is now `(k2 * k1)`, and the bias is now `(k2 * b1 + b2)`. Cascading any number of linear functions always results in a linear function.

However, consider a frequently used nonlinear activation function: relu. In the bottom part of figure 3.3, we illustrate what happens when you cascade two relu functions with linear scaling. By cascading two scaled relu functions, we get a function that doesn't look like relu at all. It has a new shape (something of a downward slope flanked by two flat sections in this case). Further cascading the step function with other relu functions will give an even more diverse set of functions, such as a "window" function, a function consisting of multiple windows, functions with windows stacked on top of wider windows, and so on (not shown in figure 3.3). There is a remarkably rich range of function shapes that you can create by cascading nonlinearities such as relu (one of the most commonly used activation functions). But what does this have to do with neural networks? In essence, neural networks are cascaded functions. Each layer of a neural network can be viewed as a function, and the stacking of layers amounts to cascading these functions to form a more complex function that is the neural network itself. This should make it clear why including nonlinear activation functions increases the range of input-output relations the model is capable of learning. This also gives you an intuitive understanding behind the oft-used trick of "adding more layers to a deep neural network" and why it often (but not always!) leads to models that can fit the dataset better.

Cascading linear functions

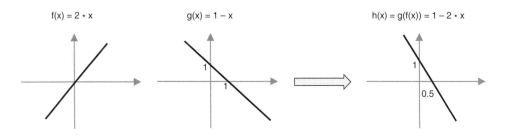

Cascading relu functions

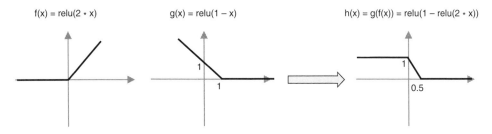

Figure 3.3   Cascading linear functions (top) and nonlinear functions (bottom). Cascading linear functions always leads to linear functions, albeit with new slopes and intercepts. Cascading nonlinear functions (such as relu in this example) leads to nonlinear functions with novel shapes, such as the "downward step" function in this example. This exemplifies why nonlinear activations and the cascading of them in neural networks leads to enhanced representational power (that is, capacity).

The range of input-output relations a machine-learning model is capable of learning is often referred to as the model's *capacity*. From the prior discussion about nonlinearity, we can see that a neural network with hidden layers and nonlinear activation functions has a greater capacity compared to a linear regressor. This explains why our two-layer network achieves a superior test-set accuracy compared to the linear-regression model.

You might ask, since cascading nonlinear activation functions leads to greater capacity (as in the bottom part of figure 3.3), can we get a better model for the Boston-housing problem by adding more hidden layers to the neural network? The `multi-LayerPerceptronRegressionModel2Hidden()` function in index.js, which is wired to the button titled Train Neural Network Regressor (2 Hidden Layers), does exactly that. See the following code excerpt (from index.js of the Boston-housing example).

Listing 3.2   Defining a three-layer neural network for the Boston-housing problem

```
export function multiLayerPerceptronRegressionModel2Hidden() {
  const model = tf.sequential();
  model.add(tf.layers.dense({
    inputShape: [bostonData.numFeatures],        Adds the first
    units: 50,                                    hidden layer
    activation: 'sigmoid',
    kernelInitializer: 'leCunNormal'
  }));
  model.add(tf.layers.dense({
    units: 50,                                    Adds another
    activation: 'sigmoid',                        hidden layer
    kernelInitializer: 'leCunNormal'
  }));
  model.add(tf.layers.dense({units: 1}));

  model.summary();          Prints a text summary of
  return model;             the model's topology
};
```

In the `summary()` printout (not shown), you can see that the model contains three layers—that is, one more than the model in listing 3.1. It also has a significantly larger number of parameters: 3,251 as compared to 701 in the two-layer model. The extra 2,550 weight parameters are due to the inclusion of the second hidden layer, which consists of a kernel of shape [50, 50] and a bias of shape [50].

Repeating the model training a number of times, we can get a sense of the range of the final test-set (that is, evaluation) MSE of the three-layer networks: roughly 10.8–13.4. This corresponds to a misestimate of $3,280–$3,660, which beats that of the two-layer network ($3,700–$3,900). So, we have again improved the prediction accuracy of our model by adding nonlinear hidden layers and thereby enhancing its capacity.

AVOIDING THE FALLACY OF STACKING LAYERS WITHOUT NONLINEARITY
Another way to see the importance of the nonlinear activation for the improved Boston-housing model is to remove it from the model. Listing 3.3 is the same as listing 3.1, except that the line that specifies the sigmoid activation function is commented

out. Removing the custom activation causes the layer to have the default linear activation. Other aspects of the model, including the number of layers and weight parameters, don't change.

Listing 3.3 A two-layer neural network without nonlinear activation

```
export function multiLayerPerceptronRegressionModel1Hidden() {
  const model = tf.sequential();
  model.add(tf.layers.dense({
    inputShape: [bostonData.numFeatures],
    units: 50,
    // activation: 'sigmoid',      ⊲—————— Disables the nonlinear activation function
    kernelInitializer: 'leCunNormal'
  }));
  model.add(tf.layers.dense({units: 1}));

  model.summary();
  return model;
};
```

How does this change affect the model's learning? As you can find out by clicking the Train Neural Network Regressor (1 Hidden Layer) button again in the UI, the MSE on the test goes up to about 25, as compared with the 14–15 range when the sigmoid activation was included. In other words, the two-layer model without the sigmoid activation performs about the same as the one-layer linear regressor!

This confirms our reasoning about cascading linear functions. By removing the nonlinear activation from the first layer, we end up with a model that is a cascade of two linear functions. As we have demonstrated before, the result is another linear function without any increase in the model's capacity. Thus, it is no surprise that we end up with about the same accuracy as the linear model. This brings up a common "gotcha" in building multilayer neural networks: *be sure to include nonlinear activations in the hidden layers*. Failing to do so results in wasted computation resources and time, with potential increases in numerical instability (observe the wigglier loss curves in panel B of figure 3.4). Later, we will see that this applies not only to dense but also to other layer types, such as convolutional layers.

NONLINEARITY AND MODEL INTERPRETABILITY

In chapter 2, we showed that once a linear model was trained on the Boston-housing dataset, we could examine its weights and interpret its individual parameters in a reasonably meaningful way. For example, the weight that corresponds to the "average number of rooms per dwelling" feature had a positive value, and the weight that corresponds to the "crime rate" feature had a negative value. The signs of such weights reflect the expected positive or negative relation between house price and the respective features. Their magnitudes also hint at the relative importance assigned to the various features by the model. Given what you just learned in this chapter, a natural question is: with a nonlinear model containing one or more hidden layers, is it still possible to come up with an understandable and intuitive interpretation of its weight values?

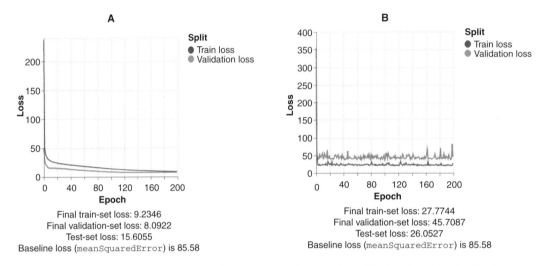

Final train-set loss: 9.2346
Final validation-set loss: 8.0922
Test-set loss: 15.6055
Baseline loss (meanSquaredError) is 85.58

Final train-set loss: 27.7744
Final validation-set loss: 45.7087
Test-set loss: 26.0527
Baseline loss (meanSquaredError) is 85.58

Figure 3.4   Comparing the training results with (panel A) and without (panel B) the sigmoid activation. Notice that removing the sigmoid activation leads to higher final loss values on the training, validation, and evaluation sets (a level comparable to the purely linear model from before) and to less smooth loss curves. Note that the y-axis scales are different between the two plots.

The API for accessing weight values is exactly the same between a nonlinear model and a linear model: you just use the getWeights() method on the model object or its constituent layer objects. Take the MLP in listing 3.1, for example—you can insert the following line after the model training is done (right after the model.fit() call):

```
model.layers[0].getWeights()[0].print();
```

This line prints the value of the kernel of the first layer (that is, the hidden layer). This is one of the four weight tensors in the model, the other three being the hidden layer's bias and the output layer's kernel and bias. One thing to notice about the printout is that it has a larger size than the kernel we saw when printing the kernel of the linear model:

```
Tensor
    [[-0.5701274, -0.1643915, -0.0009151, ..., 0.313205  , -0.3253246],
     [-0.4400523, -0.0081632, -0.2673715, ..., 0.1735748 , 0.0864024 ],
     [0.6294659 , 0.1240944 , -0.2472516, ..., 0.2181769 , 0.1706504 ],
     [0.9084488 , 0.0130388 , -0.3142847, ..., 0.4063887 , 0.2205501 ],
     [0.431214  , -0.5040522, 0.1784604 , ..., 0.3022115 , -0.1997144],
     [-0.9726604, -0.173905 , 0.8167523 , ..., -0.0406454, -0.4347956],
     [-0.2426955, 0.3274118 , -0.3496988, ..., 0.5623314 , 0.2339328 ],
     [-1.6335299, -1.1270424, 0.618491  , ..., -0.0868887, -0.4149215],
     [-0.1577617, 0.4981289 , -0.1368523, ..., 0.3636355 , -0.0784487],
     [-0.5824679, -0.1883982, -0.4883655, ..., 0.0026836 , -0.0549298],
     [-0.6993552, -0.1317919, -0.4666585, ..., 0.2831602 , -0.2487895],
     [0.0448515 , -0.6925298, 0.4945385 , ..., -0.3133179, -0.0241681]]
```

This is because the hidden layer consists of 50 units, which leads to a weight size of `[18, 50]`. This kernel has 900 individual weight parameters, as compared to the `12 + 1 = 13` parameters in the linear model's kernel. Can we assign a meaning to each of the individual weight parameters? In general, the answer is no. This is because there is no easily identifiable meaning to any of the 50 outputs from the hidden layer. These are the dimensions of high-dimensional space created so that the model can learn (automatically discover) nonlinear relations in it. The human mind is not very good at keeping track of nonlinear relations in such high-dimensional spaces. In general, it is very difficult to write down a few sentences in layman's terms to describe what each of the hidden layer's units does or to explain how it contributes to the final prediction of the deep neural network.

Also, realize that the model here has only one hidden layer. The relations become even more obscure and harder to describe when there are multiple hidden layers stacked on top of each other (as is the case in the model defined in listing 3.2). Even though there are research efforts to find better ways to interpret the meaning of deep neural networks' hidden layers,[3] and progress is being made for some classes of models,[4] it is fair to say that deep neural networks are harder to interpret compared to shallow neural networks and certain types of nonneural network machine-learning models (such as decision trees). By choosing a deep model over a shallow one, we are essentially trading some interpretability for greater model capacity.

3.1.2 *Hyperparameters and hyperparameter optimization*

Our discussion of the hidden layers in listings 3.1 and 3.2 has been focusing on the nonlinear activation (sigmoid). However, other configuration parameters for this layer are also important for ensuring a good training result from this model. These include the number of units (50) and the kernel's `'leCunNormal'` initialization. The latter is a special way to generate the random numbers that go into the kernel's initial value based on the size of the input. It is distinct from the default kernel initializer (`'glorotNormal'`), which uses the sizes of both the input and output. Natural questions to ask are: Why use this particular custom kernel initializer instead of the default one? Why use 50 units (instead of, say, 30)? These choices are made to ensure a best-possible or close-to-best-possible good model quality through trying out various combinations of parameters repeatedly.

Parameters such as number of units, kernel initializers, and activation are *hyperparameters* of the model. The name "hyperparameters" signifies the fact that these parameters are distinct from the model's weight parameters, which are updated automatically through backpropagation during training (that is, `Model.fit()` calls). Once

[3] Marco Tulio Ribeiro, Sameer Singh, and Carlos Guestrin, "Local Interpretable Model-Agnostic Explanations (LIME): An Introduction," O'Reilly, 12 Aug. 2016, http://mng.bz/j5vP.
[4] Chris Olah et al., "The Building Blocks of Interpretability," Distill, 6 Mar. 2018, https://distill.pub/2018/building-blocks/.

the hyperparameters have been selected for a model, they do not change during the training process. They often determine the number and size of the weight parameters (for instance, consider the `units` field for a dense layer), the initial values of the weight parameters (consider the `kernelInitializer` field), and how they are updated during training (consider the `optimizer` field passed to `Model.compile()`). Therefore, they are on a level higher than the weight parameters. Hence the name "hyperparameter."

Apart from the sizes of the layers and the type of weight initializers, there are many other types of hyperparameters for a model and its training, such as

- The number of dense layers in a model, like the ones in listings 3.1 and 3.2
- What type of initializer to use for the kernel of a dense layer
- Whether to use any weight regularization (see section 8.1) and, if so, the regularization factor
- Whether to include any dropout layers (see section 4.3.2, for example) and, if so, the dropout rate
- The type of optimizer used for training (such as `'sgd'` versus `'adam'`; see info box 3.1)
- How many epochs to train the model for
- The learning rate of the optimizer
- Whether the learning rate of the optimizer should be decreased gradually as training progresses and, if so, at what rate
- The batch size for training

The last five examples listed are somewhat special in that they are not related to the architecture of the model per se; instead, they are configurations of the model's training process. Nonetheless, they affect the outcome of the training and hence are treated as hyperparameters. For models consisting of more diverse types of layers (such as convolutional and recurrent layers, discussed in chapters 4, 5, and 9), there are even more potentially tunable hyperparameters. Therefore, it is clear why even a simple deep-learning model may have dozens of tunable hyperparameters.

The process of selecting good hyperparameter values is referred to as *hyperparameter optimization* or *hyperparameter tuning*. The goal of hyperparameter optimization is to find a set of parameters that leads to the lowest validation loss after training. Unfortunately, there is currently no definitive algorithm that can determine the best hyperparameters given a dataset and the machine-learning task involved. The difficulty lies in the fact that many of the hyperparameters are discrete, so the validation loss value is not differentiable with respect to them. For example, the number of units in a dense layer and the number of dense layers in a model are integers; the type of optimizer is a categorical parameter. Even for the hyperparameters that are continuous and against which the validation loss is differentiable (for example, regularization factors), it is usually too computationally expensive to keep track of the gradients with respect to those hyperparameters during training, so it is not really feasible to perform gradient descent in the space of such hyperparameters. Hyperparameter optimization remains an active area of research, one which deep-learning practitioners should pay attention to.

Given the lack of a standard, out-of-the-box methodology or tool for hyperparameter optimization, deep-learning practitioners often use the following three approaches. First, if the problem at hand is similar to a well-studied problem (say, any of the examples you can find in this book), you can start with applying a similar model on your problem and "inherit" the hyperparameters. Later, you can search in a relatively small hyperparameter space around that starting point.

Second, practitioners with sufficient experience might have intuition and educated guesses about what may be reasonably good hyperparameters for a given problem. Even such subjective choices are almost never optimal—they form good starting points and can facilitate subsequent fine-tuning.

Third, for cases in which there are only a small number of hyperparameters to optimize (for example, fewer than four), we can use grid search—that is, exhaustively iterating over a number of hyperparameter combinations, training a model to completion for each of them, recording the validation loss, and taking the hyperparameter combination that yields the lowest validation loss. For example, suppose the only two hyperparameters to tune are 1) the number of units in a dense layer and 2) the learning rate; you might select a set of units (`{10, 20, 50, 100, 200}`) and a set of learning rates (`{1e-5, 1e-4, 1e-3, 1e-2}`) and perform a cross of the two sets, which leads to a total of 5 * 4 = 20 hyperparameter combinations to search over. If you were to implement the grid search yourself, the pseudo-code might look something like the following listing.

> **Listing 3.4 Pseudo-code for a simple hyperparameter grid search**

```
function hyperparameterGridSearch():
  for units of [10, 20, 50, 100, 200]:
    for learningRate  of [1e-5, 1e-4, 1e-3, 1e-2]:
      Create a model using whose dense layer consists of `units` units
      Train the model with an optimizer with `learningRate`
      Calculate final validation loss as validationLoss
      if validationLoss < minValidationLoss
        minValidationLoss := validationLoss
        bestUnits := units
        bestLearningRate := learningRate

  return [bestUnits, bestLearningRate]
```

How are the ranges of these hyperparameters selected? Well, there is another place deep learning cannot provide a formal answer. These ranges are usually based on the experience and intuition of the deep-learning practitioner. They may also be constrained by computation resources. For example, a dense layer with too many units may cause the model to be too slow to train or to run during inference.

Oftentimes, there are a larger number of hyperparameters to optimize over, to the extent that it becomes computationally too expensive to search over the exponentially increasing number of hyperparameter combinations. In such cases, you should use more sophisticated methods than grid search, such as random search[5] and Bayesian[6] methods.

3.2 *Nonlinearity at output: Models for classification*

The two examples we've seen so far have both been regression tasks in which we try to predict a numeric value (such as the download time or the average house price). However, another common task in machine learning is classification. Some classification tasks are *binary classification*, wherein the target is the answer to a yes/no question. The tech world is full of this type of problem, including

- Whether a given email is or isn't spam
- Whether a given credit-card transaction is legitimate or fraudulent
- Whether a given one-second-long audio sample contains a specific spoken word
- Whether two fingerprint images match each other (come from the same person's same finger)

Another type of classification problem is a *multiclass-classification* task, for which examples also abound:

- Whether a news article is about sports, weather, gaming, politics, or other general topics
- Whether a picture is a cat, dog, shovel, and so on
- Given stroke data from an electronic stylus, determining what a handwritten character is
- In the scenario of using machine learning to play a simple Atari-like video game, determining in which of the four possible directions (up, down, left, and right) the game character should go next, given the current state of the game

3.2.1 *What is binary classification?*

We'll start with a simple case of binary classification. Given some data, we want a yes/no decision. For our motivating example, we'll talk about the Phishing Website dataset.[7] The task is, given a collection of features about a web page and its URL, predicting whether the web page is used for *phishing* (masquerading as another site with the aim to steal users' sensitive information).

The dataset contains 30 features, all of which are binary (represented as the values –1 and 1) or ternary (represented as –1, 0, and 1). Rather than listing all the individual

---

[5] James Bergstra and Yoshua Bengio, "Random Search for Hyper-Parameter Optimization," *Journal of Machine Learning Research*, vol. 13, 2012, pp. 281–305, http://mng.bz/WOg1.

[6] Will Koehrsen, "A Conceptual Explanation of Bayesian Hyperparameter Optimization for Machine Learning, *Towards Data Science*, 24 June 2018, http://mng.bz/8zQw.

[7] Rami M. Mohammad, Fadi Thabtah, and Lee McCluskey, "Phishing Websites Features," http://mng.bz/E1KO.

features like we did for the Boston-housing dataset, here we present a few representative features:

- HAVING_IP_ADDRESS—Whether an IP address is used as an alternative to a domain name (binary value: {-1, 1})
- SHORTENING_SERVICE—Whether it is using a URL shortening service or not (binary value: {1, -1})
- SSLFINAL_STATE—Whether 1) the URL uses HTTPS and the issuer is trusted, 2) it uses HTTPS but the issuer is not trusted, or 3) no HTTPS is used (ternary value: {-1, 0, 1})

The dataset consists of approximately 5,500 training examples and an equal number of test examples. In the training set, approximately 45% of the examples are positive (truly phishing web pages). The percentage of positive examples is about the same in the test set.

This is just about the easiest type of dataset to work with—the features in the data are already in a consistent range, so there is no need to normalize their means and standard deviations as we did for the Boston-housing dataset. Additionally, we have a large number of training examples relative to both the number of features and the number of possible predictions (two—yes or no). Taken as a whole, this is a good sanity check that it's a dataset we can work with. If we wanted to spend more time investigating our data, we might do pairwise feature-correlation checks to know if we have redundant information; however, this is something our model can tolerate.

Since our data looks similar to what we used (post-normalization) for Boston-housing, our starting model is based on the same structure. The example code for this problem is available in the website-phishing folder of the tfjs-examples repo. You can check out and run the example as follows:

```
git clone https://github.com/tensorflow/tfjs-examples.git
cd tfjs-examples/website-phishing
yarn && yarn watch
```

Listing 3.5 Defining a binary-classification model for phishing detection (from index.js)

```
const model = tf.sequential();
model.add(tf.layers.dense({
  inputShape: [data.numFeatures],
  units: 100,
  activation: 'sigmoid'
}));
model.add(tf.layers.dense({units: 100, activation: 'sigmoid'}));
model.add(tf.layers.dense({units: 1, activation: 'sigmoid'}));
model.compile({
  optimizer: 'adam',
  loss: 'binaryCrossentropy',
  metrics: ['accuracy']
});
```

This model has a lot of similarities to the multilayer network we built for the Boston-housing problem. It starts with two hidden layers, and both of them use the sigmoid activation. The last (output) has exactly 1 unit, which means the model outputs a single number for each input example. However, a key difference here is that the last layer of our model for phishing detection has a sigmoid activation instead of the default linear activation as in the model for Boston-housing. This means that our model is constrained to output numbers between only 0 and 1, which is unlike the Boston-housing model, which might output any float number.

Previously, we have seen sigmoid activations for hidden layers help increase model capacity. But why do we use sigmoid activation at the output of this new model? This has to do with the binary-classification nature of the problem we have at hand. For binary classification, we generally want the model to produce a guess of the probability for the positive class—that is, how likely it is that the model "thinks" a given example belongs to the positive class. As you may recall from high school math, a probability is always a number between 0 and 1. By having the model always output an estimated probability value, we get two benefits:

- It captures the degree of support for the assigned classification. A sigmoid value of 0.5 indicates complete uncertainty, wherein either classification is equally supported. A value of 0.6 indicates that while the system predicts the positive classification, it's only weakly supported. A value of 0.99 means the model is quite certain that the example belongs to the positive class, and so forth. Hence, we make it easy and straightforward to convert the model's output into a final answer (for instance, just threshold the output at a given value, say 0.5). Now imagine how hard it would be to find such a threshold if the range of the model's output may vary widely.
- We also make it easier to come up with a differentiable loss function, which, given the model's output and the true binary target labels, produces a number that is a measure of how much the model missed the mark. For the latter point, we will elaborate more when we examine the actual binary cross entropy used by this model.

However, the question is how to force the output of the neural network into the range of [0, 1]. The last layer of a neural network, which is often a dense layer, performs matrix multiplication (matMul) and bias addition (biasAdd) operations with its input. There are no intrinsic constraints in either the matMul or the biasAdd operation that guarantee a [0, 1] range in the result. Adding a squashing nonlinearity like sigmoid to the result of matMul and biasAdd is a natural way to achieve the [0, 1] range.

Another aspect of the code in listing 3.5 that's new to you is the type of optimizer: 'adam', which is different from the 'sgd' optimizer used in previous examples. How is adam different from sgd? As you may recall from section 2.2.2 in the last chapter, the sgd optimizer always multiplies the gradients obtained through backpropagation with a fixed number (its learning rate times –1) in order to calculate the updates to the model's weights. This approach has some drawbacks, including slow convergence toward the loss minimum when a small learning rate is chosen and "zigzag" paths in the weight space when the shape of the loss (hyper)surface has certain special properties. The adam optimizer aims at addressing these shortcomings of sgd by using a multiplication factor that varies with the history of the gradients (from earlier training iterations) in a smart way. Moreover, it uses different multiplication factors for different model weight parameters. As a result, adam usually leads to better convergence and less dependence on the choice of learning rate compared to sgd over a range of deep-learning model types; hence it is a popular choice of optimizer. The Tensor-Flow.js library provides a number of other optimizer types, some of which are also popular (such as rmsprop). The table in info box 3.1 gives a brief overview of them.

INFO BOX 3.1   Optimizers supported by TensorFlow.js

The following table summarizes the APIs of the most frequently used types of optimizers in TensorFlow.js, along with a simple, intuitive explanation for each of them.

Commonly used optimizers and their APIs in TensorFlow.js

Name	API (string)	API (function)	Description
Stochastic gradient descent (SGD)	'sgd'	tf.train.sgd	The simplest optimizer, always using the learning rate as the multiplier for gradients
Momentum	'momentum'	tf.train.momentum	Accumulates past gradients in a way such that the update to a weight parameter gets faster when past gradients for the parameter line up more in the same direction and gets slower when they change a lot in direction
RMSProp	'rmsprop'	tf.train.rmsprop	Scales the multiplication factor differently for different weight parameters of the model by keeping track of a recent history of each weight gradient's root-mean-square (RMS) value; hence its name
AdaDelta	'adadelta'	tf.train.adadelta	Scales the learning rate for each individual weight parameter in a way similar to RMSProp
ADAM	'adam'	tf.train.adam	Can be understood as a combination of the adaptive learning rate approach of AdaDelta and the momentum method
AdaMax	'adamax'	tf.train.adamax	Similar to ADAM, but keeps track of the magnitudes of gradients using a slightly different algorithm

(continued)
An obvious question is which optimizer you should use given the machine-learning problem and model you are working on. Unfortunately, there is no consensus in the field of deep learning yet (which is why TensorFlow.js provides all the optimizers listed in the previous table!). In practice, you should start with the popular ones, including `adam` and `rmsprop`. Given sufficient time and computation resources, you can also treat the optimizer as a hyperparameter and find the choice that gives you the best training result through hyperparameter tuning (see section 3.1.2).

3.2.2 Measuring the quality of binary classifiers: Precision, recall, accuracy, and ROC curves

In a binary-classification problem, we emit one of two values—0/1, yes/no, and so on. In a more abstract sense, we'll talk about the positives and negatives. When our network makes a guess, it is either right or wrong, so we have four possible scenarios for the actual label of the input example and the output of the network, as table 3.1 shows.

Table 3.1 The four types of classification results in a binary classification problem

		Prediction	
		Positive	Negative
Truth	Positive	True positive (TP)	False negative (FN)
	Negative	False positive (FP)	True negative (TN)

The true positives (TPs) and true negatives (TNs) are where the model predicted the correct answer; the false positives (FPs) and false negatives (FNs) are where the model got it wrong. If we fill in the four cells with counts, we get a *confusion matrix*; table 3.2 shows a hypothetical one for our phishing-detection problem.

Table 3.2 The confusion matrix from a hypothetical binary classification problem

		Prediction	
		Positive	Negative
Truth	Positive	4	2
	Negative	1	93

In our hypothetical results from our phishing examples, we see that we correctly identified four phishing web pages, missed two, and had one false alarm. Let's now look at the different common metrics for expressing this performance.

Accuracy is the simplest metric. It quantifies what percentage of the examples are classified correctly:

```
Accuracy = (#TP + #TN) / #examples = (#TP + #TN) / (#TP + #TN + #FP + #FN)
```

In our particular example,

```
Accuracy = (4 + 93) / 100 = 97%
```

Accuracy is an easy-to-communicate and easy-to-understand concept. However, it can be misleading—often in a binary-classification task, we don't have equal distributions of positive and negative examples. We're often in a situation where there are considerably fewer positive examples than there are negative ones (for example, most links aren't phishing, most parts aren't defective, and so on). If only 5 in 100 links are phishing, our network could always predict false and get 95% accuracy! Put that way, accuracy seems like a very bad measure for our system. High accuracy always sounds good but is often misleading. It's a good thing to monitor but would be a very bad thing to use as a loss function.

The next pair of metrics attempts to capture the subtlety missing in accuracy—*precision* and *recall*. In the discussion that follows, we're also typically thinking about problems in which a positive implies further action is required—a link is highlighted, a post is flagged for manual review—while a negative indicates the status quo. These metrics focus on the different types of "wrong" that our prediction could be.

Precision is the ratio of positive predictions made by the model that are actually positive:

```
precision = #TP / (#TP + #FP)
```

With our numbers from the confusion matrix, we'd calculate

```
precision = 4 / (4 + 1) = 80%
```

Like accuracy, it is usually possible to game precision. You can make your model very conservative in emitting positive predictions, for example, by labeling only the input examples with very high sigmoid output (say >0.95, instead of the default >0.5) as positive. This will usually cause the precision to go up, but doing so will likely cause the model to miss many actual positive examples (labeling them as negative). The last cost is captured by the metric that often goes with and complements precision, namely recall.

Recall is the ratio of actual positive examples that are classified by the model as positive:

```
recall = #TP / (#TP + #FN)
```

With the example data, we get a result of

```
recall = 4 / (4 + 2) = 66.7%
```

Of all the positives in the sample set, how many did the model find? It will normally be a conscious decision to accept a higher false alarm rate to lower the chance of missing something. To game this metric, you'd simply declare all examples as positives; because false positives don't enter into the equation, you can score 100% recall at the cost of decreased precision.

As we can see, it's fairly easy to craft a system that scores very well on accuracy, recall, or precision. In real-world binary-classification problems, it's often difficult to get both good precision and recall at the same time. (If it were easy to do so, you'd have a simple problem and probably wouldn't need to use machine learning in the first place.) Precision and recall are about tuning the model in the tricky places where there is a fundamental uncertainty about what the correct answer should be. You'll see more nuanced and combined metrics, such as *Precision at X% Recall*, X being something like 90%—what is the precision if we're tuned to find at least X% of the positives? For example, in figure 3.5, we see that after 400 epochs of training, our phishing-detection model is able to achieve a precision of 96.8% and a recall of 92.9% when the model's probability output is thresholded at 0.5.

As we have briefly alluded to, an important realization is that the threshold applied on the sigmoid output to pick out positive predictions doesn't have to be exactly 0.5. In fact, depending on the circumstances, it might be better to set it to a value above 0.5 (but below 1) or to one below 0.5 (but above 0). Lowering the threshold makes

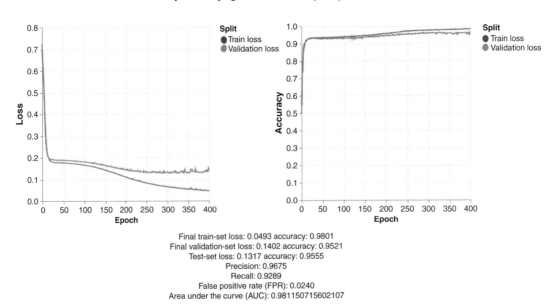

Figure 3.5   An example result from a round of training the model for phishing web page detection. Pay attention to the various metrics at the bottom: precision, recall, and FPR. The area under the curve (AUC) is discussed in section 3.2.3.

the model more liberal in labeling inputs as positive, which leads to higher recall but likely lower precision. On the other hand, raising the threshold causes the model to be more cautious in labeling inputs as positive, which usually leads to higher precision but likely lower recall. So, we can see that there is a trade-off between precision and recall, and this trade-off is hard to quantify with any one of the metrics we've talked about so far. Luckily, the rich history of research into binary classification has given us better ways to quantify and visualize this trade-off relation. The ROC curve that we will discuss next is a frequently used tool of this sort.

3.2.3 *The ROC curve: Showing trade-offs in binary classification*

ROC curves are used in a wide range of engineering problems that involve binary classification or the detection of certain types of events. The full name, *receiver operating characteristic*, is a term from the early age of radar. Nowadays, you'll almost never see the expanded name. Figure 3.6 is a sample ROC curve for our application.

As you may have noticed in the axis labels in figure 3.6, ROC curves are not exactly made by plotting the precision and recall metrics against each other. Instead, they are based on two slightly different metrics. The horizontal axis of an ROC curve is a *false positive rate* (FPR), defined as

```
FPR = #FP / (#FP + #TN)
```

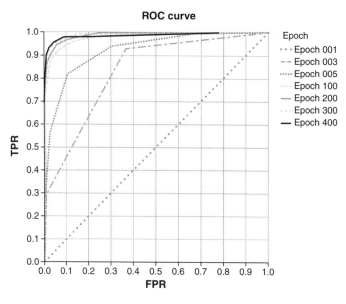

Figure 3.6   A set of sample ROCs plotted during the training of the phishing-detection model. Each curve is for a different epoch number. The curves show gradual improvement in the quality of the binary-classification model as the training progresses.

The vertical axis of an ROC curve is the *true positive rate* (TPR), defined as

```
TPR = #TP / (#TP + #FN) = recall
```

TPR has exactly the same definition as recall; it is just a different name for the same metric. However, FPR is something new. Its denominator is a count of all the cases in which the actual class of the example is negative; its numerator is a count of all false positive cases. In other words, FPR is the ratio of actually negative examples that are erroneously classified as positive, which is the probability of something commonly referred to as a *false alarm*. Table 3.3 summarizes the most common metrics you will encounter in a binary-classification problem.

Table 3.3   **Commonly seen metrics for a binary-classification problem**

Name of metric	Definition	How it is used in ROCs or precision/recall curves
Accuracy	`(#TP + #TN) / (#TP + #TN + # FP + #FN)`	(Not used by ROCs)
Precision	`#TP / (#TP + #FP)`	The vertical axis of a precision/recall curve
Recall/sensitivity/true positive rate (TPR)	`#TP / (#TP + #FN)`	The vertical axis of an ROC curve (as in figure 3.6), or the horizontal axis of a precision/recall curve
False positive rate (FPR)	`#FP / (#FP + #TN)`	The horizontal axis of an ROC curve (see figure 3.6)
Area under the curve (AUC)	Calculated through numerical integration under the ROC curve; see listing 3.7 for an example	(Not used by ROCs but is instead calculated from ROCs)

The seven ROC curves in figure 3.6 are made at the beginning of seven different training epochs, from the first epoch (epoch 001) to the last (epoch 400). Each one of them is created based on the model's predictions on the test data (not the training data). Listing 3.6 shows the details of how this is done with the onEpochBegin callback of the Model.fit() API. This approach allows you to perform interesting analysis and visualization on the model in the midst of a training call without needing to write a for loop or use multiple Model.fit() calls.

Listing 3.6   Using callback to render ROC curves in the middle of model training

```
await model.fit(trainData.data, trainData.target, {
  batchSize,
  epochs,
  validationSplit: 0.2,
  callbacks: {
  onEpochBegin: async (epoch) => {
      if ((epoch + 1)% 100 === 0 ||
```

```
        epoch === 0 || epoch === 2 || epoch === 4) {
                                    ◁———————— Draws ROC every few epochs
        const probs = model.predict(testData.data);
        drawROC(testData.target, probs, epoch);
      }
    },
    onEpochEnd: async (epoch, logs) => {
      await ui.updateStatus(
              `Epoch ${epoch + 1} of ${epochs} completed.`);
      trainLogs.push(logs);
      ui.plotLosses(trainLogs);
      ui.plotAccuracies(trainLogs);
    }
  }
});
```

The body of the function `drawROC()` contains the details of how an ROC is made (see listing 3.7). It does the following:

- Varies the threshold on the sigmoid output (probabilities) of the neural network to get different sets of classification results
- For each classification result, uses it in conjunction with the actual labels (targets) to calculate the TPR and FPR
- Plots the TPRs against the FPRs to form the ROC curve

As figure 3.6 shows, in the beginning of the training (epoch 001), as the model's weights are initialized randomly, the ROC curve is very close to a diagonal line connecting the point (0, 0) with the point (1, 1). This is what random guessing looks like. As the training progresses, the ROC curves are pushed up more and more toward the top-left corner—a place where the FPR is close to 0, and the TPR is close to 1. If we focus on any given level of FPR, such as 0.1, we see a monotonic increase in the corresponding TPR value as we move further along in the training. In plain words, this means that as the training goes on, we can achieve a higher and higher level of recall (TPR) if we are pinned to a fixed level of false alarm (FPR).

The "ideal" ROC is a curve bent so much toward the top-left corner that it becomes a γ[8] shape. In this scenario, you can get 100% TPR and 0% FPR, which is the "Holy Grail" for any binary classifier. However, with real problems, we can only improve the model to push the ROC curve ever closer to the top-left corner—the theoretical ideal at the top-left can never be achieved.

Based on this discussion of the shape of the ROC curve and its implications, we can see that it is possible to quantify how good an ROC curve is by looking at the area under it—that is, how much of the space in the unit square is enclosed by the ROC curve and the x-axis. This is called the *area under the curve* (AUC) and is computed by the code in listing 3.7 as well. This metric is better than precision, recall, and accuracy in the sense that it takes into account the trade-off between false positives and false

---

[8] The Greek letter gamma.

negatives. The ROC for random guessing (the diagonal line) has an AUC of 0.5, while the γ-shaped ideal ROC has an AUC of 1.0. Our phishing-detection model reaches an AUC of 0.981 after training.

Listing 3.7   The code for calculating and rendering an ROC curve and the AUC

```
function drawROC(targets, probs, epoch) {
  return tf.tidy(() => {
    const thresholds = [
      0.0, 0.05, 0.1, 0.15, 0.2, 0.25, 0.3, 0.35, 0.4, 0.45,      A manually
      0.5, 0.55, 0.6, 0.65, 0.7, 0.75, 0.8, 0.85,                 selected set of
      0.9, 0.92, 0.94, 0.96, 0.98, 1.0                            probability
    ];                                                            thresholds
    const tprs = [];  // True positive rates.
    const fprs = [];  // False positive rates.
    let area = 0;                                                 falsePositiveRate()
    for (let i = 0; i < thresholds.length; ++i) {                 calculates the false
        const threshold = thresholds[i];                         positive rate by
      const threshPredictions =                                  comparing the
              utils.binarize(probs, threshold).as1D();           predictions and actual
      const fpr = falsePositiveRate(                             targets. It is defined in
          targets,                                               the same file.
      threshPredictions).arraySync();
      const tpr = tf.metrics.recall(targets, threshPredictions).arraySync();
      fprs.push(fpr);
      tprs.push(tpr);

      if (i > 0) {
        area += (tprs[i] + tprs[i - 1]) * (fprs[i - 1] - fprs[i]) / 2;
      }
    }
    ui.plotROC(fprs, tprs, epoch);
    return area;                                        Accumulates to area
  });                                                   for AUC calculation
}
```

Converts the probability into predictions through thresholding

---

Apart from visualizing the characteristics of a binary classifier, the ROC also helps us make sensible decisions about how to select the probability threshold in real-world situations. For example, imagine that we are a commercial company developing the phishing detector as a service. Do we want to do one of the following?

- Make the threshold relatively low because missing a real phishing website will cost us a lot in terms of liability or lost contracts.
- Make the threshold relatively high because we are more averse to the complaints filed by users whose normal websites are blocked because the model classifies them as phishy.

Each threshold value corresponds to a point on the ROC curve. When we increase the threshold gradually from 0 to 1, we move from the top-right corner of the plot (where FPR and TPR are both 1) to the bottom-left corner of the plot (where FPR and TPR are both 0). In real engineering problems, the decision of which point to pick on the

ROC curve is always based on weighing opposing real-life costs of this sort, and it may vary for different clients and at different stages of business development.

Apart from the ROC curve, another commonly used visualization of binary classification is the *precision-recall curve* (sometimes called a P/R curve, mentioned briefly in table 3.3). Unlike the ROC curve, a precision-recall plots precision against recall. Since precision-recall curves are conceptually similar to ROC curves, we won't delve into them here.

One thing worth pointing out in listing 3.7 is the use of `tf.tidy()`. This function ensures that the tensors created within the anonymous function passed to it as arguments are disposed of properly, so they won't continue to occupy WebGL memory. In the browser, TensorFlow.js can't manage the memory of tensors created by the user, primarily due to a lack of object finalization in JavaScript and a lack of garbage collection for the WebGL textures that underlie TensorFlow.js tensors. If such intermediate tensors are not cleaned up properly, a WebGL memory leak will happen. If such memory leaks are allowed to continue long enough, they will eventually result in WebGL out-of-memory errors. Section 1.3 of appendix B contains a detailed tutorial on memory management in TensorFlow.js. There are also exercises on this topic in section 1.5 of appendix B. If you plan to define custom functions by composing TensorFlow.js functions, you should study these sections carefully.

3.2.4 *Binary cross entropy: The loss function for binary classification*

So far, we have talked about a few different metrics that quantify different aspects of how well a binary classifier is performing, such as accuracy, precision, and recall (table 3.3). But we haven't talked about an important metric, one that is differentiable and can generate gradients that support the model's gradient-descent training. This is the `binaryCrossentropy` that we saw briefly in listing 3.5 and haven't explained yet:

```
model.compile({
  optimizer: 'adam',
  loss: 'binaryCrossentropy',
  metrics: ['accuracy']
});
```

First off, you might ask, why can't we simply take accuracy, precision, recall, or perhaps even AUC and use it as the loss function? After all, these metrics are understandable. Also, in the regression problems we've seen previously, we used MSE, a fairly understandable metric, as the loss function for training directly. The answer is that none of these binary classification metrics can produce the gradients we need for training. Take the accuracy metric, for example: to see why it is not gradient-friendly, realize the fact that calculating accuracy requires determining which of the model's predictions are positive and which are negative (see the first row in table 3.3). In order to do that, it is necessary to apply a *thresholding function*, which converts the model's sigmoid output into binary predictions. Here is the crux of the problem: although the thresholding function (or *step function* in more technical terms) is differentiable almost everywhere ("almost" because it is not differentiable at the "jumping point" at 0.5), the derivative is always exactly zero (see figure 3.7)! What happens if you try to do backpropagation through this thresholding function? Your gradients will end up being all zeros because at some point, upstream gradient values need to be multiplied with these all-zero derivatives from the step function. Put more simply, if accuracy (or precision, recall, AUC, and so on) is chosen as the loss, the flat sections of the underlying step function make it impossible for the training procedure to know where to move in the weight space to decrease the loss value.

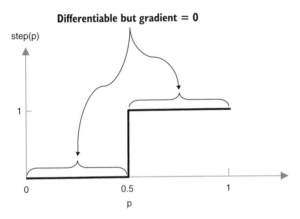

Figure 3.7   The step function used to convert the probability output of a binary-classification model is differentiable almost everywhere. Unfortunately, the gradient (derivative) at every differentiable point is exactly zero.

Therefore, using accuracy as the loss function doesn't allow us to calculate useful gradients and hence prevents us from getting meaningful updates to the weights of the model. The same limitation applies to metrics including precision, recall, FPR, and AUC. While these metrics are useful for humans to understand the behavior of a binary classifier, they are useless for these models' training process.

The loss function that we use for a binary classification task is *binary cross entropy*, which corresponds to the 'binaryCrossentropy' configuration in our phishing-detection model code (listings 3.5 and 3.6). Algorithmically, we can define binary cross entropy with the following pseudo-code.

> **Listing 3.8   The pseudo-code for the binary cross-entropy loss function[9]**

```
function binaryCrossentropy(truthLabel, prob):
  if truthLabel is 1:
      return -log(prob)
  else:
    return -log(1 - prob)
```

---

[9] The actual code for binaryCrossentropy needs to guard against cases in which prob or 1 - prob is exactly zero, which would lead to infinity if the value is passed directly to the log function. This is done by adding a very small positive number (such as 1e-6, commonly referred to as "epsilon" or a "fudge factor") to prob and 1 - prob before passing them to the log function.

In this pseudo-code, `truthLabel` is a number that takes the 0–1 values and indicates whether the input example has a negative (0) or positive (1) label in reality. `prob` is the probability of the example belonging to the positive class, as predicted by the model. Note that unlike `truthLabel`, `prob` is expected to be a real number that can take any value between 0 and 1. `log` is the natural logarithm, with e (2.718) as the base, which you may recall from high school math. The body of the `binaryCross-entropy` function contains an if-else logical branching, which performs different calculations depending on whether `truthLabel` is 0 or 1. Figure 3.8 plots the two cases in the same plot.

When looking at the plots in figure 3.8, remember that lower values are better because this is a loss function. The important things to note about the loss function are as follows:

- If `truthLabel` is 1, a value of `prob` closer to 1.0 leads to a lower loss-function value. This makes sense because when the example is actually positive, we want the model to output a probability as close to 1.0 as possible. And vice versa: if the `truthLabel` is 0, the loss value is lower when the probability value is closer to 0. This also makes sense because in that case, we want the model to output a probability as close to 0 as possible.
- Unlike the binary-thresholding function shown in figure 3.7, these curves have nonzero slopes at every point, leading to nonzero gradients. This is why it is suitable for backpropagation-based model training.

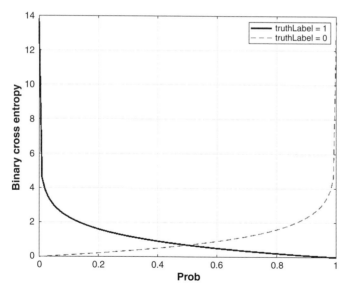

Figure 3.8 The binary cross-entropy loss function. The two cases (`truthLabel = 1` and `truthLabel = 0`) are plotted separately, reflecting the if-else logical branching in listing 3.8.

One question you might ask is, why not repeat what we did for the regression model— just pretend that the 0–1 values are regression targets and use MSE as the loss function? After all, MSE is differentiable, and calculating the MSE between the truth label and the probability would yield nonzero derivatives just like `binaryCrossentropy`. The answer has to do with the fact that MSE has "diminishing returns" at the boundaries. For example, in table 3.4, we list the `binaryCrossentropy` and MSE loss values for a number of `prob` values when `truthLabel` is 1. As `prob` gets closer to 1 (the desired value), the MSE decreases more and more slowly compared to `binaryCrossentropy`. As a result, it is not as good at "encouraging" the model to produce a higher (closer to 1) `prob` value when `prob` is already fairly close to 1 (for instance, 0.9). Likewise, when `truthLabel` is 0, MSE is not as good as `binaryCrossentropy` in generating gradients that push the model's `prob` output toward 0 either.

This shows another aspect in which binary-classification problems are different from regression problems: for a binary-classification problem, the loss (`binaryCrossentropy`) and metrics (accuracy, precision, and so on) are different, while they are usually the same for a regression problem (for example, `meanSquaredError`). As we will see in the next section, multiclass-classification problems also involve different loss functions and metrics.

Table 3.4 Comparing values of binary cross entropy and MSE for hypothetical binary classification results

truthLabel	prob	Binary cross entropy	MSE
1	0.1	2.302	0.81
1	0.5	0.693	0.25
1	0.9	0.100	0.01
1	0.99	0.010	0.0001
1	0.999	0.001	0.000001
1	1	0	0

3.3 *Multiclass classification*

In section 3.2, we explored how to structure a binary-classification problem; now we'll do a quick aside into how to handle *nonbinary classification*—that is, classification tasks involving three or more classes.[10] The dataset we will use to illustrate multiclass classification is

---

[10] It is important not to confuse *multiclass* classification with *multilabel* classification. In multilabel classification, an individual input example may correspond to multiple output classes. An example is detecting the presence of various types of objects in an input image. One image may include only a person; another image may include a person, a car, and an animal. A multilabel classifier is required to generate an output that represents all the classes that are applicable to the input example, no matter whether there is one or more than one such class. This section is not concerned with multilabel classification. Instead, we focus on the simpler single-label, multiclass classification, in which every input example corresponds to exactly one output class among >2 possible classes.

the *iris-flower dataset*, a famous dataset with its origin in the field of statistics (see https://en.wikipedia.org/wiki/Iris_flower_data_set). This dataset focuses on three species of the iris flower, called *iris setosa*, *iris versicolor*, and *iris virginica*. These three species can be distinguished from one another on the basis of their shapes and sizes. In the early 20th century, Ronald Fisher, a British statistician, measured the length and width of the petals and sepals (different parts of the flower) of 150 samples of iris. This dataset is balanced: there are exactly 50 samples for each target label.

In this problem, our model takes as input four numeric features—petal length, petal width, sepal length, and sepal width—and tries to predict a target label (one of the three species). The example is available in the iris folder of tfjs-examples, which you can check out and run with these commands:

```
git clone https://github.com/tensorflow/tfjs-examples.git
cd tfjs-examples/iris
yarn && yarn watch
```

3.3.1 One-hot encoding of categorical data

Before studying the model that solves the iris-classification problem, we need to highlight the way in which the categorical target (species) is represented in this multiclass-classification task. All the machine-learning examples we've seen in this book so far involve simpler representation of targets, such as the single number in the download-time prediction problem and that in the Boston-housing problem, as well as the 0–1 representation of binary targets in the phishing-detection problem. However, in the iris problem, the three species of flowers are represented in a slightly less familiar way called *one-hot encoding*. Open data.js, and you will notice this line:

```
const ys = tf.oneHot(tf.tensor1d(shuffledTargets).toInt(), IRIS_NUM_CLASSES);
```

Here, shuffledTargets is a plain JavaScript array consisting of the integer labels for the examples in a shuffled order. Its elements all have values 0, 1, and 2, reflecting the three iris species in the dataset. It is converted into a int32-type 1D tensor through the tf.tensor1d(shuffledTargets).toInt() call. The resultant 1D tensor is then passed into the tf.oneHot() function, which returns a 2D tensor of the shape [numExamples, IRIS_NUM_CLASSES]. numExamples is the number of examples that targets contains, and IRIS_NUM_CLASSES is simply the constant 3. You can examine the actual values of targets and ys by adding some printing lines right below the previously cited line— that is, something like

```
const ys = tf.oneHot(tf.tensor1d(shuffledTargets).toInt(), IRIS_NUM_CLASSES);
// Added lines for printing the values of `targets` and `ys`.
console.log('Value of targets:', targets);
ys.print();[11]
```

---

[11] Unlike target, ys is not a plain JavaScript array. Instead, it is a tensor object backed by GPU memory. Therefore, the regular console.log won't show its value. The print() method is specifically for retrieving the values from the GPU, formatting them in a shape-aware and human-friendly way, and logging them to the console.

Once you have made these changes, the parcel bundler process that has been started by the Yarn `watch` command in your terminal will automatically rebuild the web files. Then you can open the devtool in the browser tab being used to watch this demo and refresh the page. The printed messages from the `console.log()` and `print()` calls will be logged into the console of the devtool. The printed messages you will see will look something like this:

```
Value of targets: (50) [0, 0, 0, 0, 0, 0, 0, 0, 0, 0, 0, 0, 0, 0, 0, 0, 0, 0,
       0, 0, 0, 0, 0, 0, 0, 0, 0, 0, 0, 0, 0, 0, 0, 0, 0, 0, 0, 0, 0, 0, 0,
       0, 0, 0, 0, 0, 0, 0]

Tensor
    [[1, 0, 0],
     [1, 0, 0],
     [1, 0, 0],
     ...,
     [1, 0, 0],
     [1, 0, 0],
     [1, 0, 0]]
```

or

```
Value of targets: (50) [1, 1, 1, 1, 1, 1, 1, 1, 1, 1, 1, 1, 1, 1, 1, 1, 1,
       1, 1, 1, 1, 1, 1, 1, 1, 1, 1, 1, 1, 1, 1, 1, 1, 1, 1, 1, 1, 1, 1,
       1, 1, 1, 1, 1, 1, 1, 1]

Tensor
    [[0, 1, 0],
     [0, 1, 0],
     [0, 1, 0],
     ...,
     [0, 1, 0],
     [0, 1, 0],
     [0, 1, 0]]
```

and so forth. To describe this in words, for an example with the integer label 0, you get a row of values [1, 0, 0]; for an example with integer label 1, you get a row of values [0, 1, 0], and so forth. This is a simple and clear example of one-hot encoding: it turns an integer label into a vector consisting of all-zero values except at the index that corresponds to the label, where the value is 1. The length of the vector equals the number of all possible categories. The fact that there is a single 1 value in the vector is precisely the reason why this encoding scheme is called "one-hot."

This encoding may look unnecessarily complicated to you. Why use three numbers to represent a category when a single number could do the job? Why do we choose this over the simpler and more economical single-integer-index encoding? This can be understood from two different angles.

First, it is much easier for a neural network to output a continuous, float-type value than an integer one. It is not elegant to apply rounding on float-type output, either. A much more elegant and natural approach is for the last layer of the neural network to output a few separate float-type numbers, each constrained to be in the [0, 1] interval through a carefully chosen activation function similar to the sigmoid activation function we used for binary classification. In this approach, each number is the model's estimate of the probability of the input example belonging to the corresponding class. This is exactly what one-hot encoding is for: it is the "correct answer" for the probability scores, which the model should aim to fit through its training process.

Second, by encoding a category as an integer, we implicitly create an ordering among the classes. For example, we may label *iris setosa* as 0, *iris versicolor* as 1, and *iris virginica* as 2. But ordering schemes like this are often artificial and unjustified. For example, this numbering scheme implies that *setosa* is "closer" to *versicolor* than to *virginica*, which may not be true. Neural networks operate on real numbers and are based on mathematical operations such as multiplication and addition. Hence, they are sensitive to the magnitude of numbers and their ordering. If the categories are encoded as a single number, it becomes an extra, nonlinear relation that the neural network must learn. By contrast, one-hot-encoded categories don't involve any implied ordering and hence don't tax the learning capability of a neural network in this fashion.

As we will see in chapter 9, one-hot encoding not only is used for output targets of neural networks but also is applicable when categorical data form the inputs to neural networks.

3.3.2 Softmax activation

With an understanding of how the input features and output target are represented, we are now ready to look at the code that defines our model (from iris/index.js).

Listing 3.9 The multilayer neural network for iris-flower classification

```
const model = tf.sequential();
model.add(tf.layers.dense(
    {units: 10, activation: 'sigmoid', inputShape: [xTrain.shape[1]]}));
model.add(tf.layers.dense({units: 3, activation: 'softmax'}));
model.summary();

const optimizer = tf.train.adam(params.learningRate);
model.compile({
  optimizer: optimizer,
  loss: 'categoricalCrossentropy',
  metrics: ['accuracy'],
});
```

The model defined in listing 3.9 leads to the following summary:

Layer (type)	Output shape	Param #
dense_Dense1 (Dense)	[null,10]	50
dense_Dense2 (Dense)	[null,3]	33

```
Total params: 83
Trainable params: 83
Non-trainable params:
```

As can be seen from the printed summary, this is a fairly simple model with a relatively small (83) number of weight parameters. The output shape [null, 3] corresponds to the one-hot encoding of the categorical target. The activation used for the last layer, namely *softmax*, is designed specifically for the multiclass classification problem. The mathematical definition of softmax can be written as the following pseudo-code:

```
softmax([x1, x2, …, xn]) =
    [exp(x1) / (exp(x1) + exp(x2) + … + exp(xn)),
     exp(x2) / (exp(x1) + exp(x2) + … + exp(xn)),
     …,
     exp(xn) / (exp(x1) + exp(x2) + … + exp(xn))]
```

Unlike the sigmoid activation function we've seen, the softmax activation function is not element-by-element because each element of the input vector is transformed in a way that depends on all other elements. Specifically, each element of the input is converted to its natural exponential (the exp function, with $e = 2.718$ as the base). Then the exponential is divided by the sum of all elements' exponentials. What does this do? First, it ensures that every number is in the interval between 0 and 1. Second, it is guaranteed that all the elements of the output vector sum to 1. This is a desirable property because 1) the outputs can be interpreted as probability scores assigned to the classes, and 2) in order to be compatible with the categorical cross-entropy loss function, the outputs must satisfy this property. Third, the definition ensures that a larger element in the input vector maps to a larger element in the output vector. To give a concrete example, suppose the matrix multiplication and bias addition in the last dense layer produces a vector of

```
[-3, 0, -8]
```

Its length is 3 because the dense layer is configured to have 3 units. Note that the elements are float numbers unconstrained to any particular range. The softmax activation will convert the vector into

```
[0.0474107, 0.9522698, 0.0003195]
```

You can verify this yourself by running the following TensorFlow.js code (for example, in the devtool console when the page is pointing at js.tensorflow.org):

```
const x = tf.tensor1d([-3, 0, -8]);
tf.softmax(x).print();
```

The three elements of the softmax function's output 1) are all in the [0, 1] interval, 2) sum to 1, and 3) are ordered in a way that matches the ordering in the input vector. As a result of these properties, the output can be interpreted as the probability values assigned (by the model) to all the possible classes. In the previous code snippet, the second category is assigned the highest probability while the first is assigned the lowest.

As a consequence, when using an output from a multiclass classifier of this sort, you can choose the index of the highest softmax element as the final decision—that is, a decision on what class the input belongs to. This can be achieved by using the method `argMax()`. For example, this is an excerpt from index.js:

```
const predictOut = model.predict(input);
const winner = data.IRIS_CLASSES[predictOut.argMax(-1).dataSync()[0]];
```

`predictOut` is a 2D tensor of shape `[numExamples, 3]`. Calling its `argMax0` method causes the shape to be reduced to `[numExample]`. The argument value –1 indicates that `argMax()` should look for maximum values along the last dimension and return their indices. For instance, suppose `predictOut` has the following value:

```
[[0  , 0.6, 0.4],
 [0.8, 0  , 0.2]]
```

Then, `argMax(-1)` will return a tensor that indicates the maximum values along the last (second) dimension are found at indices 1 and 0 for the first and second examples, respectively:

```
[1, 0]
```

3.3.3 *Categorical cross entropy: The loss function for multiclass classification*

In the binary classification example, we saw how binary cross entropy was used as the loss function and why other, more human-interpretable metrics such as accuracy and recall couldn't be used as the loss function. The situation for multiclass classification is quite analogous. There exists a straightforward metric—accuracy—that is the fraction of examples that are classified correctly by the model. This metric is important for humans to understand how well the model is performing and is used in this code snippet in listing 3.9:

```
model.compile({
  optimizer: optimizer,
  loss: 'categoricalCrossentropy',
  metrics: ['accuracy'],
});
```

However, accuracy is a bad choice for loss function because it suffers from the same zero-gradient issue as the accuracy in binary classification. Therefore, people have devised a special loss function for multiclass classification: *categorical cross entropy*. It is simply a generalization of binary cross entropy into the cases where there are more than two categories.

> **Listing 3.10 Pseudo-code for categorical cross-entropy loss**

```
function categoricalCrossentropy(oneHotTruth, probs):
  for i in (0 to length of oneHotTruth)
    if oneHotTruth(i) is equal to 1
      return -log(probs[i]);
```

In the pseudo-code in the previous listing, `oneHotTruth` is the one-hot encoding of the input example's actual class. `probs` is the softmax probability output from the model. The key takeaway from this pseudo-code is that as far as categorical cross entropy is concerned, only one element of `probs` matters, and that is the element whose indices correspond to the actual class. The other elements of `probs` may vary all they like, but as long as they don't change the element for the actual class, it won't affect the categorical cross entropy. For that particular element of `probs`, the closer it gets to 1, the lower the value of the cross entropy will be. Like binary cross entropy, categorical cross entropy is directly available as a function under the `tf.metrics` namespace, and you can use it to calculate the categorical cross entropy of simple but illustrating examples. For example, with the following code, you can create a hypothetical, one-hot-encoded truth label and a hypothetical `probs` vector and compute the corresponding categorical cross-entropy value:

```
const oneHotTruth = tf.tensor1d([0, 1, 0]);
const probs = tf.tensor1d([0.2, 0.5, 0.3]);
tf.metrics.categoricalCrossentropy(oneHotTruth, probs).print();
```

This gives you an answer of approximately 0.693. This means that when the probability assigned by the model to the actual class is 0.5, `categoricalCrossentropy` has a value of 0.693. You can verify it against the pseudo-code in listing 3.10. You may also try raising or lowering the value from 0.5 to see how `categoricalCrossentropy` changes (for instance, see table 3.5). The table also includes a column that shows the MSE between the one-hot truth label and the `probs` vector.

Table 3.5 The values of categorical cross entropy under different probability outputs. Without loss of generality, all the examples (row) are based on a case in which there are three classes (as is the case in the iris-flower dataset), and the actual class is the second one.

One-hot truth label	probs (softmax output)	Categorical cross entropy	MSE
[0, 1, 0]	[0.2, 0.5, 0.3]	0.693	0.127
[0, 1, 0]	[0.0, 0.5, 0.5]	0.693	0.167
[0, 1, 0]	[0.0, 0.9, 0.1]	0.105	0.006
[0, 1, 0]	[0.1, 0.9, 0.0]	0.105	0.006
[0, 1, 0]	[0.0, 0.99, 0.01]	0.010	0.00006

By comparing rows 1 and 2 or comparing rows 3 and 4 in this table, it should be clear that changing the elements of `probs` that don't correspond to the actual class doesn't alter the binary cross entropy, even though it may alter the MSE between the one-hot truth label and `probs`. Also, like in binary cross entropy, MSE shows diminished return when the `probs` value for the actual class approaches 1, and hence is not good at encouraging the probability value of the correct class to go up as categorical entropy in this regime. These are the reasons why categorical cross entropy is more suitable as the loss function than MSE for multiclass-classification problems.

3.3.4 Confusion matrix: Fine-grained analysis of multiclass classification

By clicking the Train Model from Scratch button on the example's web page, you can get a trained model in a few seconds. As figure 3.9 shows, the model reaches nearly perfect accuracy after 40 epochs of training. This reflects the fact that the iris dataset is a small one with relatively well-defined boundaries between the classes in the feature space.

The bottom part of figure 3.9 shows an additional way of characterizing the behavior of a multiclass classifier, called a *confusion matrix*. A confusion matrix breaks down the results of a multiclass classifier according to their actual classes and the model's predicted classes. It is a square matrix of shape [numClasses, numClasses]. The element at indices [i, j] (row i and column j) is the number of examples that belong to class i and are predicted as class j by the model. Therefore, the diagonal elements of a confusion matrix correspond to correctly classified examples. A perfect multiclass classifier should produce a confusion matrix with no nonzero elements outside the diagonal. This is exactly the case for the confusion matrix in figure 3.9.

In addition to showing the final confusion matrix, the iris example also draws the confusion matrix at the end of every training epoch, using the onTrainEnd() callback.

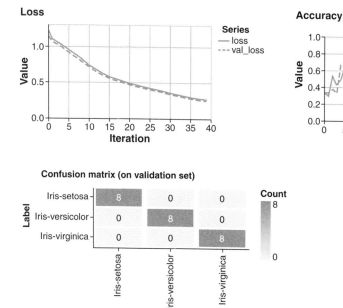

Figure 3.9 A typical result from training the iris model for 40 epochs. Top left: the loss function plotted against epochs of training. Top right: the accuracy plotted against epochs of training. Bottom: the confusion matrix.

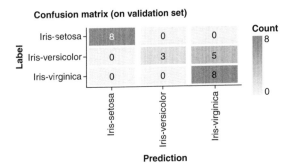

Figure 3.10   An example of an "imperfect" confusion matrix, in which there are nonzero elements off the diagonal. This confusion matrix is generated after only 2 epochs, before the training converged.

In early epochs, you may see a less perfect confusion matrix than the one in figure 3.9. The confusion matrix in figure 3.10 shows that 8 out of the 24 input examples were misclassified, which corresponds to an accuracy of 66.7%. However, the confusion matrix tells us about more than just a single number: it shows which classes involve the most mistakes and which involve fewer. In this particular example, all flowers from the second class are misclassified (either as the first or the third class), while the flowers from the first and third classes are always classified correctly. Therefore, you can see that in multiclass classification, a confusion matrix is a more informative measurement than simply the accuracy, just like precision and recall together form a more comprehensive measurement than accuracy in binary classification. Confusion matrices can provide information that aids decision-making related to the model and the training process. For example, making some types of mistakes may be more costly than confusing other pairs of classes. Perhaps mistaking a sports site for a gaming site is less of a problem than confusing a sports site for a phishing scam. In those cases, you can adjust the model's hyperparameters to minimize the costliest mistakes.

The models we've seen so far all take an array of numbers as inputs. In other words, each input example is represented as a simple list of numbers, of which the length is fixed, and the ordering of the elements doesn't matter as long as they are consistent for all examples fed to the model. While this type of model covers a large subset of important and practical machine-learning problems, it is far from the only kind. In the coming chapters, we will look at more complex input data types, including images and sequences. In chapter 4, we'll start from images, a ubiquitous and widely useful type of input data for which powerful neural network structures have been developed to push the accuracy of machine-learning models to superhuman levels.

Exercises

1   When creating neural networks for the Boston-housing problem, we stopped at a model with two hidden layers. Given what we said about cascading nonlinear functions leading to enhanced capacity of models, will adding more hidden layers to the model lead to improved evaluation accuracy? Try this out by modifying index.js and rerunning the training and evaluation.

a What is the factor that prevents more hidden layers from improving the evaluation accuracy?

b What makes you reach this conclusion? (Hint: look at the error on the training set.)

2 Look at how the code in listing 3.6 uses the `onEpochBegin` callback to calculate and draw an ROC curve at the beginning of every training epoch. Can you follow this pattern and make some modifications to the body of the callback function so that you can print the precision and recall values (calculated on the test set) at the beginning of every epoch? Describe how these values change as the training progresses.

3 Study the code in listing 3.7 and understand how it computes the ROC curve. Can you follow this example and write a new function, called `drawPrecision-RecallCurve()`, which, as its name indicates, computes and renders a precision-recall curve? Once you are done writing the function, call it from the `onEpoch-Begin` callback so that a precision-recall curve can be plotted alongside the ROC curve at the beginning of every training epoch. You may need to make some changes or additions to ui.js.

4 Suppose you are told the FPR and TPR of a binary classifier's results. With those two numbers, is it possible for you to calculate the overall accuracy? If not, what extra piece(s) of information do you require?

5 The definitions of binary cross entropy (section 3.2.4) and categorical cross entropy (section 3.3.3) are both based on the natural logarithm (the log of base e). What if we change the definition so that they use the log of base 10? How would that affect the training and inference of binary and multiclass classifiers?

6 Turn the pseudo-code for the hyperparameter grid search in listing 3.4 into actual JavaScript code, and use the code to perform hyperparameter optimization for the two-layer Boston-housing model in listing 3.1. Specifically, tune the number of units of the hidden layer and the learning rate. Feel free to decide on the ranges of units and learning rate to search over. Note that machine-learning engineers generally use approximately geometric sequences (that is, logarithmic) spacing for these searches (for example, units = 2, 5, 10, 20, 50, 100, 200, . . .).

Summary

- Classification tasks are different from regression tasks in that they involve making discrete predictions.
- There are two types of classification: binary and multiclass. In binary classification, there are two possible classes for a given input, whereas in multiclass classification, there are three or more.
- Binary classification can usually be viewed as detecting a certain type of event or object of significance, called positives, among all the input examples. When

viewed this way, we can use metrics such as precision, recall, and FPR, in addition to accuracy, to quantify various aspects of a binary classifier's behavior.

- The trade-off between the need to catch all positive examples and the need to minimize false positives (false alarms) is common in binary-classification tasks. The ROC curve, along with the associated AUC metric, is a technique that helps us quantify and visualize this relation.

- A neural network created for binary classification should use the sigmoid activation in its last (output) layer and use binary cross entropy as the loss function during training.

- To create a neural network for multiclass classification, the output target is usually represented by one-hot encoding. The neural network ought to use softmax activation in its output layer and be trained using the categorical cross-entropy loss function.

- For multiclass classification, confusion matrices can provide more fine-grained information regarding the mistakes made by the model than accuracy can.

- Table 3.6 summarizes recommended methodologies for the most common types of machine-learning problems we have seen so far (regression, binary classification, and multiclass classification).

- Hyperparameters are configurations concerning a machine-learning model's structure, properties of its layer, and its training process. They are distinct from the model's weight parameters in that 1) they do not change during the model's training process, and 2) they are often discrete. Hyperparameter optimization is the process in which values of the hyperparameters are sought in order to minimize a loss on the validation dataset. Hyperparameter optimization is still an active area of research. Currently, the most frequently used methods include grid search, random search, and Bayesian methods.

Table 3.6   An overview of the most common types of machine-learning tasks, their suitable last-layer activation function and loss function, as well as the metrics that help quantify the model quality

Type of task	Activation of output layer	Loss function	Suitable metrics supported during Model.fit() calls	Additional metrics
Regression	`'linear'` (default)	`'meanSquaredError'` or `'meanAbsoluteError'`	(same as loss)	
Binary classification	`'sigmoid'`	`'binaryCrossentropy'`	`'accuracy'`	Precision, recall, precision-recall curve, ROC curve, AUC
Single-label, multiclass classification	`'softmax'`	`'categoricalCrossentropy'`	`'accuracy'`	Confusion matrix

Recognizing images and sounds using convnets

This chapter covers

- How images and other perceptual data, such as audio, are represented as multidimensional tensors

- What convnets are, how they work, and why they are especially suitable for machine-learning tasks involving images

- How to write and train a convnet in TensorFlow.js to solve the task of classifying hand-written digits

- How to train models in Node.js to achieve faster training speeds

- How to use convnets on audio data for spoken-word recognition

The ongoing deep-learning revolution started with breakthroughs in image-recognition tasks such as the ImageNet competition. There is a wide range of useful and technically interesting problems that involve images, from recognizing the contents of images to segmenting images into meaningful parts, and from localizing objects in images to synthesizing images. This subarea of machine learning is sometimes referred to as *computer vision.*[1] Computer-vision techniques are often transplanted to areas that have nothing to do with vision or images (such as natural language processing), which is one more reason why it is important to study deep learning for computer vision.[2] But before delving into computer-vision problems, we need to discuss the ways in which images are represented in deep learning.

4.1   *From vectors to tensors: Representing images*

In the previous two chapters, we looked at machine-learning tasks involving numerical inputs. For example, the download-duration prediction problem in chapter 2 took a single number (file size) as the input. The input in the Boston-housing problem was an array of 12 numbers (number of rooms, crime rate, and so on). What these problems have in common is the fact that each input example can be represented as a flat (non-nested) array of numbers, which corresponds to a 1D tensor in TensorFlow.js. Images are represented differently in deep learning.

To represent an image, we use a 3D tensor. The first two dimensions of the tensor are the familiar height and width dimensions. The third one is the color channel. For example, color is often encoded as RGB values. In this case, each of the three colors is a channel, which leads to a size of 3 along the third dimension. If we have an RGB-encoded color image of size 224 × 224 pixels, we can represent it as a 3D tensor of size [224, 224, 3]. The images in some computer-vision problems are noncolor (for example, grayscale). In those cases, there is only one channel, which, if represented as a 3D tensor, will lead to a tensor shape of [height, width, 1] (see figure 4.1 for an example).[3]

This mode of encoding an image is referred to as *height-width-channel (HWC)*. To perform deep learning on images, we often combine a set of images into a batch for efficient parallelized computation. When batching images, the dimension of individual images is always the first dimension. This is similar to how we combined 1D tensors into a batched 2D tensor in chapters 2 and 3. Therefore, a batch of images is a 4D tensor, with the four dimensions being image number (N), height (H), width (W), and color channel (C), respectively. This format is referred to as *NHWC*. There is an alternative format, resulting from a different ordering of the four dimensions. It is called *NCHW*. As its name suggests, NCHW puts the channel dimension ahead of the height and width dimensions. TensorFlow.js can handle both the NHWC and NCHW formats. But we will only use the default NHWC format in this book, for consistency.

---

[1] Note that computer vision is itself a broad field, some parts of which use non-machine-learning techniques beyond the scope of this book.

[2] Readers who are especially interested in deep learning in computer vision and want to dive deeper into the topic can check out Mohamed Elgendy's, *Grokking Deep Learning for Computer Vision*, Manning Publications, in press.

[3] An alternative is to "flatten" all the pixels of the image and their associated color values into a 1D tensor (a flat array of numbers). But doing so makes it hard to exploit the association between the color channels of each pixel and the 2D spatial relations between pixels.

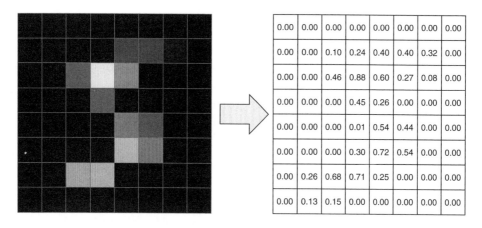

0.00	0.00	0.00	0.00	0.00	0.00	0.00	0.00
0.00	0.00	0.10	0.24	0.40	0.40	0.32	0.00
0.00	0.00	0.46	0.88	0.60	0.27	0.08	0.00
0.00	0.00	0.00	0.45	0.26	0.00	0.00	0.00
0.00	0.00	0.00	0.01	0.54	0.44	0.00	0.00
0.00	0.00	0.00	0.30	0.72	0.54	0.00	0.00
0.00	0.26	0.68	0.71	0.25	0.00	0.00	0.00
0.00	0.13	0.15	0.00	0.00	0.00	0.00	0.00

Figure 4.1   Representing an MNIST image as tensors in deep learning. For the sake of visualization, we downsized the MNIST image from 28 × 28 to 8 × 8. The image is a grayscale one, which leads to a height-width-channel (HWC) shape of `[8, 8, 1]`. The single color channel along the last dimension is omitted in this diagram.

4.1.1   The MNIST dataset

The computer-vision problem we will focus on in this chapter is the MNIST[4] handwritten-digit dataset. This is such an important and frequently used dataset that it is often referred to as the "hello world" for computer vision and deep learning. The MNIST dataset is older and smaller than most datasets you will find in deep learning. Yet it is good to be familiar with it because it is widely used as an example and often serves as a first test for novel deep-learning techniques.

Each example in the MNIST dataset is a 28 × 28 grayscale image (see figure 4.1 for an example). These images were converted from real handwriting of the 10 digits 0 through 9. The image size of 28 × 28 is sufficient for reliable recognition of these simple shapes, although it is smaller than the image sizes seen in typical computer-vision problems. Each image is accompanied by a definitive label, which indicates which of the 10 possible digits the image actually is. As we have seen in the download-time prediction and Boston-housing datasets, the data is divided into a training set and a test set. The training set consists of 60,000 images, while the test contains 10,000 images. The MNIST dataset[5] is approximately balanced, meaning that there are approximately equal numbers of examples for the 10 categories (that is, the 10 digits).

---

[4]   MNIST stands for Modified NIST. The "NIST" part of the name comes from the fact that the dataset originated from the US National Institute of Standards and Technology around 1995. The "modified" part of the name reflects the modification made to the original NIST dataset, which included 1) normalizing images into the same uniform 28 × 28 pixel raster with anti-aliasing to make the training and test subsets more homogeneous and 2) making sure that the sets of writers are disjoint between the training and test subsets. These modifications made the dataset easier to work with and more amenable to objective evaluation of model accuracy.

[5]   See Yann LeCun, Corinna Cortes, and Christopher J.C. Burges, "The MNIST Database of Handwritten Digits," http://yann.lecun.com/exdb/mnist/.

4.2   *Your first convnet*

Given the representation of the image data and the labels, we know what kind of input a neural network that solves the MNIST dataset should take and what kind of output it should generate. The input to the neural network is a tensor of the NHWC-format shape [null, 28, 28, 1]. The output is a tensor of shape [null, 10], where the second dimension corresponds to the 10 possible digits. This is the canonical one-hot encoding of multiclass-classification targets. It is the same as the one-hot encoding of the species of iris flowers we saw in the iris example in chapter 3. With this knowledge, we can dive into the details of convnets (which, as a reminder, is short for convolutional networks), the method of choice for image-classification tasks such as MNIST. The "convolutional" part of the name may sound scary. It is just a type of mathematical operation, and we will explain it in detail.

The code is in the mnist folder of tfjs-examples. Like the previous examples, you can access and run the code as follows:

```
git clone https://github.com/tensorflow/tfjs-examples.git
cd tfjs-examples/mnist
yarn && yarn watch
```

Listing 4.1 is an excerpt from the main index.js code file in the mnist example. It is a function that creates the convnet we use to solve the MNIST problem. The number of layers in this sequential model (seven) is significantly greater than in the examples we have seen so far (between one and three layers).

Listing 4.1   Defining a convolutional model for the MNIST dataset

```
function createConvModel() {
  const model = tf.sequential();

  model.add(tf.layers.conv2d({
    inputShape: [IMAGE_H, IMAGE_W, 1],
    kernelSize: 3,                              First conv2d layer
    filters: 16,
    activation: 'relu'
  }));
  model.add(tf.layers.maxPooling2d({
    poolSize: 2,
      strides: 2                          Pooling after convolution
  }));

  model.add(tf.layers.conv2d({                       Repeating "motif" of
    kernelSize: 3, filters: 32, activation: 'relu'}));   conv2d-maxPooling2d
  model.add(tf.layers.maxPooling2d({poolSize: 2, strides: 2}));

  model.add(tf.layers.flatten());   ◁——— Flattens tensor to prepare for dense layers
  model.add(tf.layers.dense({
    units: 64,                                  Uses softmax activation for
    activation:'relu'                      multiclass classification problem
  }));
  model.add(tf.layers.dense({units: 10, activation: 'softmax'}));   ◁———
```

```
model.summary();    <⎯⎯⎯    Prints a text summary of model
return model;
}
```

The sequential model constructed by the code in listing 4.1 consists of seven layers, created one by one through the add() method calls. Before we examine the detailed operations performed by each layer, let's look at the model's overall architecture, which is shown in figure 4.2. As the diagram shows, the model's first five layers include a repeating pattern of conv2d-maxPooling2d layer groups, followed by a flatten layer. The groups of conv2d-maxPooling2d layers are the working horse of feature extraction. Each of the layers transforms an input image into an output one. A conv2d layer operates through a *convolutional kernel*, which is "slid" over the height and width dimensions of the input image. At each sliding position, it is multiplied with the input pixels, and the products are summed and fed through a nonlinearity. This yields a pixel in the output image. The maxPooling2d layers operate in a similar fashion but without a kernel. By passing the input image data through the successive layers of convolution and pooling, we get tensors that become smaller and smaller in size and more and more abstract in the feature space. The output of the last pooling layer is transformed into a 1D tensor through flattening. The flattened 1D tensor then goes into the dense layer (not shown in the diagram).

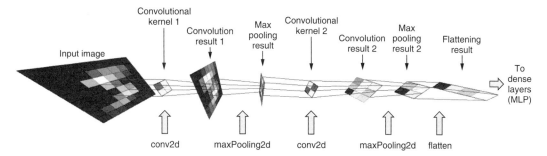

Figure 4.2 **A high-level overview of the architecture of a simple convnet of the kind constructed by the code in listing 4.1. In this figure, the sizes of the images and intermediate tensors are made smaller than the actual sizes in the model defined by listing 4.1 for illustration's sake. So are the sizes of the convolutional kernels. Also note that this diagram shows a single channel in each intermediate 4D tensor, whereas the intermediate tensors in the actual model have multiple channels.**

You can think of the convnet as an MLP built on top of convolutional and pooling preprocessing. The MLP is exactly the same type as what we've seen in the Boston-housing and phishing-detection problems: it's simply made of dense layers with non-linear activations. What's different in the convnet here is that the input to the MLP is the output of the cascaded conv2d and maxPooling2d layers. These layers are specifically designed for image inputs to extract useful features from them. This architecture was discovered through years of research in neural networks: it leads to an accuracy significantly better than feeding the pixel values of the images directly into an MLP.

With this high-level understanding of the MNIST convnet, let's now dive deeper into the internal workings of the model's layers.

4.2.1   conv2d layer

The first layer is a conv2d layer, which performs 2D convolution. This is the first convolutional layer you see in this book. What does it do? conv2d is an image-to-image transform—it transforms a 4D (NHWC) image tensor into another 4D image tensor, possibly with a different height, width, and number of channels. (It may seem strange that conv2d operates on 4D tensors, but keep in mind that there are two extra dimensions, one for batch examples and one for channels.) Intuitively, it can be understood as a group of simple "Photoshop filters"[6] that lead to image effects such as blurring and sharpening. These effects are done with 2D convolution, which involves sliding a small patch of pixels (the *convolutional kernel*, or simply *kernel*) over the input image. At each sliding position, the kernel is multiplied with the small patch of the input image that it overlaps with, pixel by pixel. Then the pixel-by-pixel products are summed to form pixels in the resulting image.

Compared to a dense layer, a conv2d layer has more configuration parameters. kernelSize and filters are two key parameters of the conv2d layer. To understand their meaning, we need to describe how 2D convolution works on a conceptual level.

Figure 4.3 illustrates 2D convolution in greater detail. Here, we suppose the input image (top left) tensor consists of a simple example so that we can draw it easily on paper. We suppose the conv2d operation is configured as kernelSize = 3 and filters = 3. Due to the fact that the input image has two color channels (a somewhat unusual number of channels just for illustration purposes), the kernel is a 3D tensor of shape [3, 3, 2, 3]. The first two numbers (3 and 3) are the height and width of the kernel, determined by kernelSize. The third dimension (2) is the number of input channels. What is the fourth dimension (3)? It is the number of filters, which equals the last dimension of conv2d's output tensor.

If the output is regarded as an image tensor (a totally valid way of looking at this!), then filters can be understood as the number of channels in the output. Unlike the input image, the channels in the output tensor don't actually have to do with colors. Instead, they represent different visual features of the input image, learned from the training data. For example, some filters may be sensitive to straight-line boundaries between bright and dark regions at a certain orientation, while others may be sensitive to corners formed by a brown color, and so forth. More on that later.

The "sliding" action mentioned previously is represented as extracting small patches from the input image. Each patch has height and width equal to kernelSize (3 in this case). Since the input image has a height of 4, there are only two possible sliding positions along the height dimension because we need to make sure that the

---

[6]   We owe this analogy to Ashi Krishnan's talk titled "Deep Learning in JS" at JSConf EU 2018: http://mng.bz/VPa0.

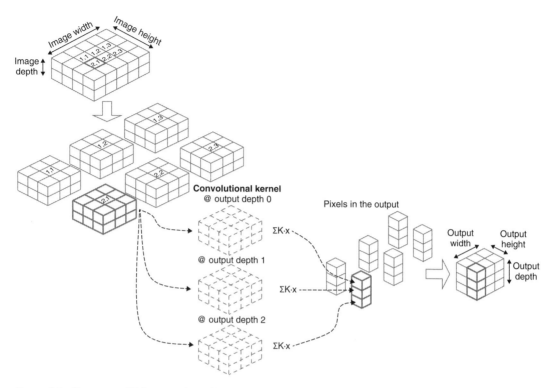

Figure 4.3 How a conv2D layer works, with an example. For simplicity, it is assumed that the input tensor (top left) contains only one image and is therefore a 3D tensor. Its dimensions are height, width, and depth (color channels). The batch dimension is omitted for simplicity. The depth of the input image tensor is set as 2 for simplicity. Note that the height and width of the image (4 and 5) are much smaller than those of a typical real image. The depth (2) is less than the more typical value of 3 or 4 (for example, for RGB or RGBA). Assuming that the `filters` property (the number of filters) of the conv2D layer is 3, `kernelSize` is `[3, 3]`, and `strides` is `[1, 1]`, the first step in performing the 2D convolution is to slide through the height and width dimensions and extract small patches of the original image. Each patch has a height of 3 and a width of 3, matching the layer's `filterSize`; it also has the same depth as the original image. In the second step, a dot product is calculated between every 3 × 3 × 2 patch and the convolutional kernel (that is, "filters"). Figure 4.4 gives more details on each dot-product operation. The kernel is a 4D tensor and consists of three 3D filters. The dot product between the image patch with the filter occurs separately for the three filters. The image patch is multiplied with the filter pixel-by-pixel, and the products are summed, which leads to a pixel in the output tensor. Because there are three filters in the kernel, each image patch is converted to a stack of three pixels. This dot-product operation is performed over all image patches, and the resulting stacks of three pixels are merged as the output tensor, which has a shape of `[2, 3, 3]` in this case.

3 × 3 window does not fall outside the bounds of the input image. Similarly, the width (5) of the input image gives us three possible sliding positions along the width dimension. Hence, we end up with 2 × 3 = 6 image patches extracted.

At each sliding-window position, a dot-product operation occurs. Recall that the convolutional kernel has a shape of `[3, 3, 2, 3]`. We can break up the 4D tensor along the last dimension into three separate 3D tensors, each of which has a shape of `[3, 3, 2]`, as shown by the hash lines in figure 4.3. We take the image patch and one of the 3D tensors, multiply them together pixel-by-pixel, and sum all the $3 * 3 * 2 = 18$ values to get a pixel in the output tensor. Figure 4.4 illustrates the dot-product step in greater detail. It is not a coincidence that the image patch and the slice of the convolutional kernel have exactly the same shape—we extracted the image patches based on the kernel's shape! This multiply-and-add operation is repeated for all three slices of the kernel, which gives a set of three numbers. Then this dot-product operation is repeated for the remaining image patches, which gives the six columns of three cubes in the figure. These columns are finally combined to form the output, which has an HWC shape of [2, 3, 3].

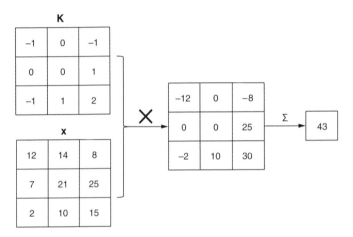

Figure 4.4   An illustration of the dot-product (that is, multiply-and-add) operation in the 2D convolution operation, a step in the full workflow outlined in figure 4.3. For the sake of illustration, it is assumed that the image patch (x) contains only one color channel. The image patch has a shape of [3, 3, 1], that is, the same as the size of the convolutional kernel slice (K). The first step is element-by-element multiplication, which yields another [3, 3, 1] tensor. The elements of the new tensor are added together (represented by the Σ), and the sum is the result.

Like a dense layer, a conv2d layer has a bias term, which is added to the result of the convolution. Also, a conv2d layer is usually configured to have a nonlinear activation function. In this example, we use relu. Recall that in the chapter 3 section "Avoiding the fallacy of stacking layers without nonlinearity," we warned that stacking two dense layers without nonlinearity is mathematically equivalent to using a single dense layer. A similar cautionary note applies to conv2d layers: stacking two such layers without a nonlinear activation is mathematically equivalent to using a single conv2d layer with a larger kernel and is hence an inefficient way of constructing a convnet that should be avoided.

Whew! That's it for the details of how conv2d layers work. Let's take a step back and look at what conv2d actually achieves. In a nutshell, it is a special way to transform an input image into an output image. The output image will usually have smaller height and width compared to the input. The reduction in size is dependent on the `kernel-Size` configuration. The output image may have fewer, more, or the same channels than the input, which is determined by the `filters` configuration.

So conv2d is an image-to-image transformation. Two key features of the conv2d transformation are locality and parameter sharing:

- *Locality* refers to the property that the value of a given pixel in the output image is affected by only a small patch of the input image, instead of all the pixels in the input image. The size of that patch is `kernelSize`. This is what makes conv2d distinct from dense layers: in a dense layer, every output element is affected by every input element. In other words, the input elements and output elements are "densely connected" in a dense layer (hence its name). So, we can say that a conv2d layer is "sparsely connected." While dense layers learn global patterns in the input, convolutional layers learn local patterns—patterns within the small window of the kernel.
- *Parameter sharing* refers to the property that the way in which output pixel A is affected by its small input patch is exactly the same as the way in which output pixel B is affected by its input patch. This is because the dot product at every sliding position uses the same convolutional kernel (figure 4.3).

Due to locality and parameter sharing, a conv2d layer is a highly efficient, image-to-image transform in terms of the number of parameters required. In particular, the size of the convolutional kernel does not change with the height or width of the input image. Coming back to the first conv2d layer in listing 4.1, the kernel has a shape of `[kernelSize, kernelSize, 1, filter]` (that is, `[5, 5, 1, 8]`), and therefore a total of $5 * 5 * 1 * 8 = 200$ parameters, regardless of whether the input MNIST images are 28×28 or much larger. The output of the first conv2d layer has a shape of `[24, 24, 8]` (omitting the batch dimension). So, the conv2d layer transforms a tensor consisting of $28 * 28 * 1 = 784$ elements into another tensor of $24 * 24 * 8 = 4,608$ elements. If we were to implement this transform with a dense layer, how many parameters will be involved? The answer is $784 * 4,608 = 3,612,672$ (not including the bias), which is about 18 thousand times more than the conv2d layer! This thought experiment shows the efficiency of convolutional layers.

The beauty of conv2d's locality and parameter sharing is not only in its efficiency, but also in the fact that it mimics (in a loose fashion) how biological visual systems work. Consider neurons in the retina. Each neuron is affected by only a small patch in the eye's field of view, called the *receptive field*. Two neurons located at different locations of the retina respond to light patterns in their respective receptive fields in pretty much the same way, which is analogous to the parameter sharing in a conv2d layer. What's more, conv2d layers prove to work well for computer-vision problems, as we will soon appreciate in this MNIST example. conv2d is a neat neural network layer that has it all: efficiency, accuracy, and relevance to biology. No wonder it is so widely used in deep learning.

4.2.2 *maxPooling2d layer*

Having examined the conv2d layer, let's look at the next layer in the sequential model—a maxPooling2d layer. Like conv2d, maxPooling2d is a kind of image-to-image transform. But the maxPooling2d transform is simpler compared to conv2d. As figure 4.5 shows, it simply calculates the maximum pixel values in small image patches and uses them as the pixel values in the output. The code that defines and adds the maxPooling2d layer is

```
model.add(tf.layers.maxPooling2d({poolSize: 2, strides: 2}));
```

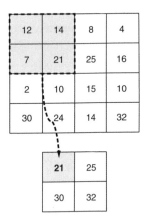

Figure 4.5 An example of how a maxPooling2D layer works. This example uses a tiny 4 × 4 image and assumes that the maxPooling2D layer is configured to have a poolSize of [2, 2] and strides of [2, 2]. The depth dimension is not shown, but the max-pooling operation occurs independently over the dimensions.

In this particular case, the image patches have a height and width of 2 × 2 because of the specified poolSize value of [2, 2]. The patches are extracted every two pixels, along both dimensions. This spacing between patches results from the strides value we use here: [2, 2]. As a result, the output image, with an HWC shape of [12, 12, 8], is half the height and half the width of the input image (shape [24, 24, 8]) but has the same number of channels.

A maxPooling2d layer serves two main purposes in a convnet. First, it makes the convnet less sensitive to the exact location of key features in the input image. For example, we want to be able to recognize the digit "8" regardless of whether it has shifted to the left or the right from the center in the 28 × 28 input image (or shifted up or down, for that matter), a property called *positional invariance*. To understand how the maxPooling2d layer enhances positional invariance, realize the fact that within each image patch that maxPooling2d operates on, it doesn't matter where the brightest pixel is, as long as it falls into that patch. Admittedly, a single maxPooling2d layer can do only so much in making the convnet insensitive to shifts because its pooling window is limited. However, when multiple maxPooling2d layers are used in the same convnet, they work together to achieve considerably greater positional invariance. This is exactly what is done in our MNIST model—as well as in virtually all practical convnets—which contains two maxPooling2d layers.

As a thought experiment, consider what happens when two conv2d layers (called conv2d_1 and conv2d_2) are stacked directly on top of each other without an intermediate maxPooling2d layer. Suppose each of the two conv2d layers has a `kernelSize` of 3; then each pixel in conv2d_2's output tensor is a function of a 5×5 region in the original input to conv2d_1. We can say that each "neuron" of the conv2d_2 layer has a receptive field of size 5×5. What happens when there is an intervening maxPooling2d layer between the two conv2d layers (as is the case in our MNIST convnet)? The receptive field of conv2d_2's neurons becomes larger: 11×11. This is due to the pooling operation, of course. When multiple maxPooling2d layers are present in a convnet, layers at higher levels can have broad receptive fields and positional invariance. In short, they can see wider!

Second, a maxPooling2d layer also shrinks the size of the height and width dimensions of the input tensor, significantly reducing the amount of compute required in subsequent layers and in the entire convnet overall. For example, the output from the first conv2d layer has an output tensor of shape `[26, 26, 16]`. After passing through the maxPooling2d layer, the tensor shape becomes `[13, 13, 16]`, which reduces the number of tensor elements by a factor of 4. The convnet contains another maxPooling2d layer, which further shrinks the size of the weights in subsequent layers and the number of elementwise mathematical operations in those layers.

4.2.3 *Repeating motifs of convolution and pooling*

Having examined the first maxPooling2d layer, let's focus our attention on the next two layers of the convnet, defined by these lines in listing 4.1:

```
model.add(tf.layers.conv2d(
    {kernelSize: 3, filters: 32, activation: 'relu'}));
model.add(tf.layers.maxPooling2d({poolSize: 2, strides: 2}));
```

These two layers are an exact repeat of the previous two layers (except that the conv2d layer has a larger value in its `filters` configuration and does not possess an `inputShape` field). This type of an almost-repeating "motif" consisting of a convolutional layer and a pooling layer is seen frequently in convnets. It performs a critical role: hierarchical extraction of features. To understand what it means, consider a convnet trained for the task of classifying animals in images. At early stages of the convnet, the filters (that is, channels) in a convolutional layer may encode low-level geometric features, such as straight lines, curved lines, and corners. These low-level features are transformed into more complex features, such as a cat's eye, nose, and ear (see figure 4.6). At the top level of the convnet, a layer may have filters that encode the presence of a whole cat. The higher the level, the more abstract the representation and the more removed from the pixel-level values the features are. But those abstract features are exactly what is required to achieve good accuracy on the convnet's task—for instance, detecting a cat when it is present in the image. Moreover, these features are not handcrafted but are instead extracted from the data in an automatic fashion through supervised learning. This is a quintessential example of the kind of layer-by-layer representational transformation that we described as the essence of deep learning in chapter 1.

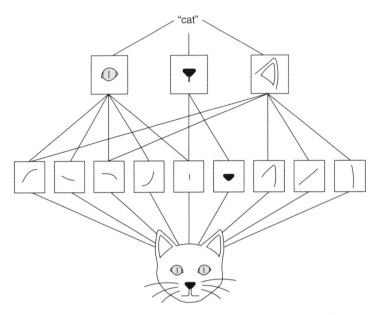

Figure 4.6   Hierarchical extraction of features from an input image by a convnet, using a cat image as an example. Note that in this example, the input to the neural network is at the bottom, and the output is at the top.

4.2.4   *Flatten and dense layers*

After the input tensor has passed through the two groups of conv2d-maxPooling2d transformations, it becomes a tensor of the HWC shape [4, 4, 16] (without the batch dimension). The next layer in the convnet is a flatten layer. This layer forms a bridge between the previous conv2d-maxPooling2d layers and the following layers of the sequential model.

The code for the flatten layer is simple, as the constructor doesn't require any configuration parameters:

```
model.add(tf.layers.flatten());
```

A flatten layer "squashes" a multidimensional tensor into a 1D tensor, preserving the total number of elements. In our case, the 3D tensor of shape [3, 3, 32] is flattened into a 1D tensor [288] (without the batch dimension). An obvious question for the squashing operation is how to order the elements, because there is no intrinsic order in the original 3D space. The answer is, we order the elements such that if you go down the elements in the flattened 1D tensor and look at how their original indices (from the 3D tensor) change, the last index changes the fastest, the second-to-last index changes the second fastest, and so forth, while the first index changes the slowest. This is illustrated in figure 4.7.

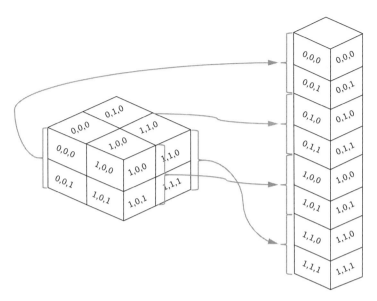

Figure 4.7   How a flatten layer works. A 3D tensor input is assumed. For the sake of simplicity, we let each dimension have a small size of 2. The indices of the elements are shown on the "faces" of the cubes that represent the elements. The flatten layer transforms the 3D tensor into a 1D tensor while preserving the total number of elements. The ordering of the elements in the flattened 1D tensor is such that when you go down the elements of the output 1D tensor and examine their original indices in the input tensor, the last dimension is the one that changes the fastest.

What purpose does the flatten layer serve in our convnet? It sets the stage for the subsequent dense layers. As we learned in chapters 2 and 3, a dense layer usually takes a 1D tensor (excluding the batch dimension) as its input due to how a dense layer works (section 2.1.4).

The next two lines of the code in listing 4.1 add two dense layers to the convnet:

```
model.add(tf.layers.dense({units: 64, activation: 'relu'}));
model.add(tf.layers.dense({units: 10, activation: 'softmax'}));
```

Why two dense layers and not just one? The same reason as in the Boston-housing example and phishing-URL-detection example we saw in chapter 3: adding layers with nonlinear activation increases the network's capacity. In fact, you can think of the convnet as consisting of two models stacked on top of each other:

- A model that contains conv2d, maxPooling2d, and flatten layers, which extracts visual features from the input images
- An MLP with two dense layers that uses the extracted features to make digit-class predictions—this is essentially what the two dense layers are for

In deep learning, many models show this pattern of feature-extraction layers followed by MLPs for final predictions. We will see more examples like this throughout the rest of this book, in models ranging from audio-signal classifiers to natural language processing.

4.2.5 Training the convnet

Now that we've successfully defined the topology of the convnet, the next step is to train it and evaluate the result of the training. This is what the code in the next listing is for.

Listing 4.2   Training and evaluating the MNIST convnet

```
const optimizer = 'rmsprop';
model.compile({
  optimizer,
  loss: 'categoricalCrossentropy',
  metrics: ['accuracy']
});

const batchSize = 320;
const validationSplit = 0.15;
await model.fit(trainData.xs, trainData.labels, {
  batchSize,
  validationSplit,
  epochs: trainEpochs,
  callbacks: {                                             Uses callbacks to plot accuracy
    onBatchEnd: async (batch, logs) => {                   and loss during training
      trainBatchCount++;
      ui.logStatus(
        `Training... (` +
        `${(trainBatchCount / totalNumBatches * 100).toFixed(1)}%` +
        ` complete). To stop training, refresh or close page.`);
      ui.plotLoss(trainBatchCount, logs.loss, 'train');
      ui.plotAccuracy(trainBatchCount, logs.acc, 'train');
    },
    onEpochEnd: async (epoch, logs) => {
      valAcc = logs.val_acc;
      ui.plotLoss(trainBatchCount, logs.val_loss, 'validation');
      ui.plotAccuracy(trainBatchCount, logs.val_acc, 'validation');
    }
  }
});

const testResult = model.evaluate(                         Evaluates the model's accuracy
    testData.xs, testData.labels);                         using data the model hasn't seen
```

Much of the code here is about updating the UI as the training progresses, for instance, to plot how the loss and accuracy values change. This is useful for monitoring the training process but not strictly essential for model training. Let's highlight the parts essential for training:

- `trainData.xs` (the first argument to `model.fit()`) contains the input MNIST images represented as a tensor of NHWC shape `[N, 28, 28, 1]`

- `trainData.labels` (the second argument to `model.fit()`). This includes the input labels, represented as a one-hot encoded 2D tensor of shape `[N, 10]`.
- The loss function used in the `model.compile()` call, `categoricalCross-entropy`, which is appropriate for multiclass-classification problems like MNIST. Recall that we used the same loss function for the iris-flower-classification problem in chapter 3.
- The metric function specified in the `model.compile()` call: `'accuracy'`. This function measures what fraction of the examples are classified correctly, given that the prediction is made based on the largest element among the 10 elements of the convnet's output. Again, this is exactly the same metric we used for the newswire problem. Recall the difference between the cross-entropy loss and the accuracy metric: cross-entropy is differentiable and hence makes backprop-agation-based training possible, whereas the accuracy metric is not differentiable but is more easily interpretable.
- The `batchSize` parameter specified for the `model.fit()` call. In general, the benefit of using larger batch sizes is that it produces a more consistent and less variable gradient update to the model's weights than a smaller batch size. But the larger the batch size, the more memory is required during training. You should also keep in mind that given the same amount of training data, a larger batch size leads to a small number of gradient updates per epoch. So, if you use a larger batch size, be sure to increase the number of epochs accordingly so you don't inadvertently decrease the number of weight updates during training. Thus, there is a trade-off. Here, we use a relatively small batch size of 64 because we need to make sure that this example works on a wide range of hardware. Like other parameters, you can modify the source code and refresh the page so as to experiment with the effect of using different batch sizes.
- The `validationSplit` used in the `model.fit()` call. This lets the training process leave out the last 15% of `trainData.xs` and `trainData.labels` for validation during training. As you learned with the previous nonimage models, monitoring validation loss and accuracy is important during training. It gives you an idea of whether and when the model is *overfitting*. What is overfitting? Put simply, it is a state in which the model pays too much attention to the fine details of the data it has seen during training—so much so that its prediction accuracy on data not seen during training is negatively affected. It is a critical concept in supervised machine learning. Later in the book (chapter 8), we will devote an entire chapter to how to spot and counteract overfitting.

`model.fit()` is an async function, so we need to use `await` on it if subsequent actions depend on the completion of the `fit()` call. This is exactly what's done here, as we need to perform an evaluation on the model using a test dataset after the model is trained. The evaluation is performed using the `model.evaluate()` method, which is synchronous. The data fed to `model.evaluate()` is testData, which has the same format as the `trainData` mentioned earlier, but has a smaller number of examples. These examples were never seen by the model during the `fit()` call, ensuring that the test dataset does not leak into the evaluation result and that the result of the evaluation is an objective assessment of the model's quality.

With this code, we let the model train 10 epochs (specified in the input box), which gives us the loss and accuracy curves in figure 4.8. As shown by the plots, the loss converges toward the end of the training epochs, and so does the accuracy. The validation loss and accuracy values do not deviate from their training counterparts too much, which indicates that there is no significant overfitting in this case. The final `model.evaluate()` call gives an accuracy in the neighborhood of 99.0% (the actual value you get will vary slightly from run to run, owing to the random initialization of weights and the implicit random shuffling of examples during training).

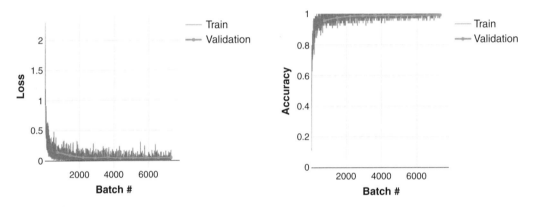

Figure 4.8   The MNIST convnet's training curves. Ten epochs of training are performed, with each epoch consisting of approximately 800 batches. Left: loss value. Right: accuracy value. The values from the training and validation sets are shown by the different colors, line widths, and marker symbols. The validation curves contain fewer data points than the training ones because, unlike the training batches, validation is performed only at the end of every epoch.

How good is 99.0%? It is passable from a practical point of view, but it is certainly not the state of the art. With more convolutional layers, it is possible to achieve an accuracy reaching 99.5% by increasing the number of convolutional and pooling layers and the number of filters in the model. However, training those larger convnets take significantly longer in the browser—so long that it makes sense to do the training in a less resource-constrained environment like Node.js. We will show you exactly how to do that in section 4.3.

From a theoretical point of view, remember MNIST is a 10-way classification problem. So, the chance-level (pure guessing) accuracy is 10%; 99.0% is way better than that. But chance level is not a very high bar. How do we show the value of the conv2d and maxPooling2d layers in the model? Would we have done as well if we stuck with the good old dense layers?

To answer these questions, we can do an experiment. The code in index.js contains another function for model creation called `createDenseModel()`. Unlike the `create-ConvModel()` function we saw in listing 4.1, `createDenseModel()` creates a sequential model made of only flatten and dense layers, that is, without using the new layer types we learned in this chapter. `createDenseModel()` makes sure that the total number of parameters is approximately equal between the dense model it creates and the convnet we just trained—approximately 33,000, so it will be a fairer comparison.

> **Listing 4.3 A flatten-and-dense-only model for MNIST, for comparison with convnet**

```
function createDenseModel() {
  const model = tf.sequential();
  model.add(tf.layers.flatten({inputShape: [IMAGE_H, IMAGE_W, 1]}));
  model.add(tf.layers.dense({units: 42, activation: 'relu'}));
  model.add(tf.layers.dense({units: 10, activation: 'softmax'}));
  model.summary();
  return model;
}
```

The summary of the model defined in listing 4.3 is as follows:

```
Layer (type)                Output shape            Param #
=================================================================
flatten_Flatten1 (Flatten)  [null,784]              0
_____
dense_Dense1 (Dense)        [null,42]               32970
_____
dense_Dense2 (Dense)        [null,10]               430
=================================================================
Total params: 33400
Trainable params: 33400
Non-trainable params: 0
_____
```

Using the same training configuration, we obtain training results as shown in figure 4.9 from the nonconvolutional model. The final evaluation accuracy we get after 10 training epochs is about 97.0%. The difference of two percentage points may seem small, but in terms of error rate, the nonconvolutional model is three times worse than the convnet. As a hands-on exercise, try increasing the size of the nonconvolutional model by increasing the `units` parameter of the hidden (first) dense layer in the `createDenseModel()` function. You will see that even with greater sizes, it is impossible for the dense-only model to achieve an accuracy on par with the convnet. This shows you the power of a convnet: through parameter sharing and exploiting the locality of visual features, convnets can achieve superior accuracy on computer-vision tasks with an equal or fewer number of parameters than nonconvolutional neural networks.

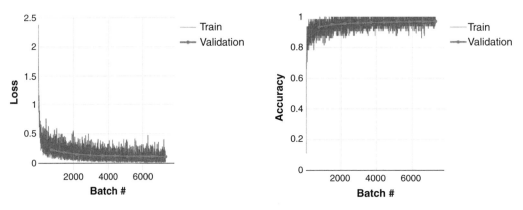

Figure 4.9   Same as figure 4.8, but for a nonconvolutional model for the MNIST problem, created by the `createDenseModel()` function in listing 4.3

4.2.6   *Using a convnet to make predictions*

Now we have a trained convnet. How do we use it to actually classify images of hand-written digits? First, you need to get hold of the image data. There are a number of ways through which image data can be made available to TensorFlow.js models. We will list them and describe when they are applicable.

CREATING IMAGE TENSORS FROM TYPEDARRAYS

In some cases, the image data you want are already stored as JavaScript `TypedArrays`. This is the case in the tfjs-example/mnist example we are focusing on. The details are in the data.js file, and we will not elaborate on the detailed machinery. Given a `Float32Array` representing an MNIST of the correct length (say, a variable named `imageDataArray`), we can convert it into a 4D tensor of the shape expected by our model with[7]

```
let x = tf.tensor4d(imageDataArray, [1, 28, 28, 1]);
```

The second argument in the `tf.tensor4d()` call specifies the shape of the tensor to be created. It is necessary because a `Float32Array` (or a `TypedArray` in general) is a flat structure with no information regarding the image's dimensions. The size of the first dimension is 1 because we are dealing with a single image in `imageDataArray`. As in previous examples, the model always expects a batch dimension during training, evaluation, and inference, no matter whether there is only one image or more than one. If the `Float32Array` contains a batch of multiple images, it can also be converted into a single tensor, where the size of the first dimension equals the number of images:

```
let x = tf.tensor4d(imageDataArray, [numImages, 28, 28, 1]);
```

---

[7] See appendix B for a more comprehensive tutorial on how to create tensors using the low-level API in TensorFlow.js.

TF.BROWSER.FROMPIXELS: GETTING IMAGE TENSORS FROM HTML IMG, CANVAS, OR VIDEO ELEMENTS

The second way to get image tensors in the browser is to use the TensorFlow.js function `tf.browser.fromPixels()` on HTML elements that contain image data—this includes `img`, `canvas`, and `video` elements.

For example, suppose a web page contains an `img` element defined as

```
<img id="my-image" src="foo.jpg"></img>
```

You can obtain the image data displayed in the `img` element with one line:

```
let x = tf.browser.fromPixels(
        document.getElementById('my-image')).asType('float32');
```

This generates a tensor of shape `[height, width, 3]`, where the three channels are for RGB color encoding. The `asType0` call at the end is necessary because `tf.browser.fromPixels()` returns a int32-type tensor, but the convnet expects float32-type tensors as inputs. The height and width are determined by the size of the `img` element. If it doesn't match the height and width expected by the model, you can either change the height and width attributes of the `img` element (if that doesn't make the UI look bad, of course) or resize the tensor from `tf.browser.fromPixels()` by using one of the two image-resizing methods provided by TensorFlow.js, `tf.image.resizeBilinear()` or `tf.image.resizeNearestNeigbor()`:

```
x = tf.image.resizeBilinear(x, [newHeight, newWidth]);
```

`tf.image.resizeBilinear()` and `tf.image.resizeNearestNeighbor()` have the same syntax, but they perform image resizing with two different algorithms. The former uses bilinear interpolation to form pixel values in the new tensor, while the latter performs nearest-neighbor sampling and is usually less computationally intensive than bilinear interpolation.

Note that the tensor created by `tf.browser.fromPixels()` does not include a batch dimension. So, if the tensor is to be fed into a TensorFlow.js model, it must be dimension-expanded first; for example,

```
x = x.expandDims();
```

`expandDims()` takes a dimension argument in general. But in this case, the argument can be omitted because we are expanding the first dimension, which is the default for that argument.

In addition to `img` elements, `tf.browser.fromPixels()` works on `canvas` and `video` elements in the same way. Applying `tf.browser.fromPixels()` on `canvas` elements is useful for cases in which the user can interactively alter the content of a canvas before the content is used by a TensorFlow.js model. For example, imagine an online handwriting-recognition app or an online hand-drawn-shape-recognition app. Apart from static images, applying `tf.browser.fromPixels()` on `video` elements is useful for obtaining frame-by-frame image data from a webcam. This is exactly what's done in the Pac-Man demo that Nikhil Thorat and Daniel Smilkov gave during the initial TensorFlow.js announcement (see http://mng.bz/xl0e), the PoseNet demo,[8] and many other TensorFlow.js-based web apps that use a webcam. You can read the source code on GitHub at http://mng.bz/ANYK.

As we have seen in the previous chapters, great care should be taken to avoid *skew* (that is, mismatch) between the training data and the inference data. In this case, our MNIST convnet is trained with image tensors normalized to the range between 0 and 1. Therefore, if the data in the x tensor has a different range, say 0–255, as is common in HTML-based image data, we should normalize the data:

```
x = x.div(255);
```

With the data at hand, we are now ready to call model.predict() to get the predictions. See the following listing.

Listing 4.4   Using the trained convnet for inference

```
const testExamples = 100;
const examples = data.getTestData(testExamples);

tf.tidy(() => {                                    ◁─────  Uses tf.tidy() to prevent
  const output = model.predict(examples.xs);               WebGL memory leaks

  const axis = 1;
  const labels = Array.from(examples.labels.argMax(axis).dataSync());
  const predictions = Array.from(
      output.argMax(axis).dataSync());       ◁─────  Calls argMax() to get
                                                      the class with the
  ui.showTestResults(examples, predictions, labels);      largest probability
});
```

The code is written with the assumption that the batch of images for prediction is already available in a single tensor, namely, examples.xs. It has a shape of [100, 28, 28, 1] (including the batch dimension), where the first dimension reflects the fact that there are 100 images we are running a prediction on. model.predict() returns an output 2D tensor of shape [100, 10]. The first dimension of the output corresponds to the examples, while the second dimension corresponds to the 10 possible digits. Every row of the output tensor includes the probability values assigned to the 10 digits for a given image input. To determine the prediction, we need to find out the indices of the maximum probability values, image by image. This is done with the lines

```
const axis = 1;
const labels = Array.from(examples.labels.argMax(axis).dataSync());
```

The argMax() function returns the indices of the maximum values along a given axis. In this case, this axis is the second dimension, const axis = 1. The return value of argMax() is a tensor of shape [100, 1]. By calling dataSync(), we convert the [100, 1]-shaped tensor into a length-100 Float32Array. Then Array.from() converts the

---

[8] Dan Oved, "Real-time Human Pose Estimation in the Browser with TensorFlow.js," Medium, 7 May 2018, http://mng.bz/ZeOO.

Float32Array into an ordinary JavaScript array consisting of 100 integers between 0 and 9. This predictions array has a very straightforward meaning: it is the classification results made by the model for the 100 input images. In the MNIST dataset, the target labels happen to match the output index exactly. Therefore, we don't even need to convert the array into string labels. The predictions array is consumed by the next line, which calls a UI function that renders the results of the classification alongside the test images (see figure 4.10).

Figure 4.10   A few examples of predictions made by the model after training, shown alongside the input MNIST images

4.3 *Beyond browsers: Training models faster using Node.js*

In the previous section, we trained a convnet in the browser, and it reached a test accuracy of 99.0%. In this section, we will create a more powerful convnet that will give us a higher test accuracy: around 99.5%. The improved accuracy comes at a cost, though: a greater amount of memory and computation consumed by the model during both training and inference. The increase in cost is more pronounced during training because training involves backpropagation, which is more computationally intensive compared to the forward runs that inference entails. The larger convnet will be too heavy and too slow to train in most web browser environments.

4.3.1 *Dependencies and imports for using tfjs-node*

Enter the Node.js version of TensorFlow.js! It runs in a backend environment, unhindered by any resource restriction like that of a browser tab. The CPU version of Node.js of TensorFlow (*tfjs-node* for short hereafter) directly uses the multithreaded math operations written in C++ and used by the main Python version of TensorFlow. If you have a CUDA-enabled GPU installed on your machine, tfjs-node can also use the GPU-accelerated math kernels written in CUDA, achieving even greater gains in speed.

The code for our enhanced MNIST convnet is in the mnist-node directory of tfjs-examples. As in the examples we have seen, you can use the following commands to access the code:

```
git clone https://github.com/tensorflow/tfjs-examples.git
cd tfjs-examples/mnist-node
```

What's different from the previous examples is that the mnist-node example will run in a terminal instead of a web browser. To download the dependencies, use the yarn command.

If you examine the package.json file, you can see the dependency @tensorflow/ tfjs-node. With @tensorflow/tfjs-node declared as a dependency, yarn will automatically download the C++ shared library (with the name libtensorflow.so, libtensorflw .dylib, or libtensorflow.dll on Linux, Mac, or Windows systems, respectively) into your node_ modules directory for use by TensorFlow.js.

Once the yarn command has finished running, you can kick off the model training with

```
node main.js
```

We assume that the node binary is available on your path since you have already installed yarn (see appendix A if you need more information on this).

The workflow just described will allow you to train the enhanced convnet on your CPU. If your workstation and laptop have a CUDA-enabled GPU inside, you can also train the model on your GPU. The steps involved are as follows:

1 Install the correct versions of the NVIDIA driver for your GPU.
2 Install the NVIDIA CUDA toolkit. This is the library that enables general-purpose parallel computing on NVIDIA's line of GPUs.
3 Install CuDNN, NVIDIA's library for high-performance, deep-learning algorithms built on top of CUDA (see appendix A for more details on steps 1–3).
4 In package.json, replace the @tensorflow/tfjs-node dependency with @tensorflow/tfjs-node-gpu, but keep the same version number because the two packages have synchronized releases.
5 Run yarn again, which will download the shared library that contains the CUDA math operations for TensorFlow.js use.
6 In main.js, replace the line

```
require('@tensorflow/tfjs-node');
```

with

```
require('@tensorflow/tfjs-node-gpu');
```

7 Start the training again with

```
node main.js
```

If the steps are done correctly, your model will be roaring ahead on your CUDA GPU, training at a speed that is typically five times the speed you can get with the CPU version (tfjs-node). Training with either the CPU or GPU version of tfjs-node is significantly faster compared to training the same model in the browser.

TRAINING AN ENHANCED CONVNET FOR MNIST IN TFJS-NODE

Once the training is complete in 20 epochs, the model should show a final test (or evaluation) accuracy of approximately 99.6%, which beats the previous result of 99.0% we achieved in section 4.2. So, what are the differences between this node-based model and the browser-based model that lead to this boost in accuracy? After all, if you train the same model in tfjs-node and the browser version of TensorFlow.js using the training data, you should get the same results (except the effects or random weights initialization.) To answer this question, let's look at the definition of the node-based model. The model is constructed in the file model.js, which is imported by main.js.

Listing 4.5 Defining a larger convnet for MNIST in Node.js

```
const model = tf.sequential();
model.add(tf.layers.conv2d({
  inputShape: [28, 28, 1],
  filters: 32,
  kernelSize: 3,
  activation: 'relu',
}));
model.add(tf.layers.conv2d({
  filters: 32,
  kernelSize: 3,
  activation: 'relu',
}));
model.add(tf.layers.maxPooling2d({poolSize: [2, 2]}));
model.add(tf.layers.conv2d({
  filters: 64,
  kernelSize: 3,
  activation: 'relu',
}));
model.add(tf.layers.conv2d({
  filters: 64,
  kernelSize: 3,
  activation: 'relu',
}));
model.add(tf.layers.maxPooling2d({poolSize: [2, 2]}));
model.add(tf.layers.flatten());
model.add(tf.layers.dropout({rate: 0.25}));          ◁——————  Adds dropout layers
model.add(tf.layers.dense({units: 512, activation: 'relu'}));    to reduce overfitting
model.add(tf.layers.dropout({rate: 0.5}));
model.add(tf.layers.dense({units: 10, activation: 'softmax'}));

model.summary();
model.compile({
  optimizer: 'rmsprop',
  loss: 'categoricalCrossentropy',
  metrics: ['accuracy'],
});
```

The summary of the model is as follows:

Layer (type)	Output shape	Param #
conv2d_Conv2D1 (Conv2D)	[null,26,26,32]	320
conv2d_Conv2D2 (Conv2D)	[null,24,24,32]	9248

max_pooling2d_MaxPooling2D1	[null,12,12,32]	0
conv2d_Conv2D3 (Conv2D)	[null,10,10,64]	18496
conv2d_Conv2D4 (Conv2D)	[null,8,8,64]	36928
max_pooling2d_MaxPooling2D2	[null,4,4,64]	0
flatten_Flatten1 (Flatten)	[null,1024]	0
dropout_Dropout1 (Dropout)	[null,1024]	0
dense_Dense1 (Dense)	[null,512]	524800
dropout_Dropout2 (Dropout)	[null,512]	0
dense_Dense2 (Dense)	[null,10]	5130

```
=================================================================
Total params: 594922
Trainable params: 594922
Non-trainable params: 0
```

These are the key differences between our tfjs-node model and the browser-based model:

- The node-based model has four conv2d layers, one more compared to the browser-based model.
- The hidden dense layer in the node-based model has more units (512) compared to the counterpart in the browser-based model (100).
- Overall, the node-based model has about 18 times as many weight parameters as the browser-based model.
- The node-based model has two *dropout* layers inserted between the flatten and dense layers.

The first three differences in this list give the node-based model a higher capacity than the browser-based model. They are also what make the node-based model too memory- and computation-intensive to be trained with acceptable speed in the browser. As we learned in chapter 3, with greater model capacity comes a greater risk of overfitting. The increased risk of overfitting is ameliorated by the fourth difference, namely, the inclusion of dropout layers.

REDUCING OVERFITTING WITH DROPOUT LAYERS

Dropout is yet another new TensorFlow.js layer type you have encountered in this chapter. It is one of the most effective and widely used ways to reduce overfitting in deep neural networks. Its functionality can be described simply:

- During the training phase (during Model.fit() calls), it randomly sets a fraction of the elements in the input tensor as zero (or "dropped"), and the result is the output tensor of the dropout layer. For the purpose of this example, a dropout layer has only one configuration parameter: the dropout rate (for example, the two `rate` fields as shown in listing 4.5). For example, suppose a dropout layer is configured to have a dropout rate of 0.25, and the input tensor is a 1D tensor of value `[0.7, -0.3, 0.8, -0.4]`; the output tensor may be `[0.7, -0.3, 0.0, 0.4]`—with 25% of the input tensor's elements selected at random and set to the value 0. During backpropagation, the gradient tensor on a dropout layer is affected similarly by this random zeroing-out.

- During the inference phase (during `Model.predict()` and `Model.evaluate()` calls), a dropout layer does *not* randomly zero-out elements in the input tensor. Instead, the input is simply passed through as the output without change (that is, an identity mapping).

Figure 4.11 shows an example of how a dropout layer with a 2D input tensor works at training time and testing time.

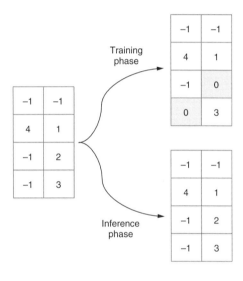

Figure 4.11   An example of how a dropout layer works. In this example, the input tensor is 2D and has a shape of `[4, 2]`. The dropout layer has its rate configured as 0.25, which leads to 25% (that is, two out of eight) elements of the input tensor being randomly selected and set to zero during the training phase. During the inference phase, the layer acts as a trivial passthrough.

It might seem strange that such a simple algorithm is one of the most effective ways of fighting overfitting. Why does it work? Geoff Hinton, the inventor of the dropout algorithm (among many other things in neural networks) says he was inspired by a mechanism used by some banks to prevent fraud by employees. In his own words,

> *I went to my bank. The tellers kept changing, and I asked one of them why. He said he didn't know, but they got moved around a lot. I figured it must be because it would require cooperation between employees to successfully defraud the bank. This made me realize that randomly removing a different subset of neurons on each example would prevent conspiracies and thus reduce overfitting.*

To put this into the lingo of deep learning, introducing noise in the output values of a layer breaks up happenstance patterns that aren't significant with regard to the true patterns in the data (what Hinton refers to as "conspiracies"). In exercise 3 at the end of this chapter, you should try removing the two dropout layers from the node-based convnet in model.js, train the model again, and see how the training, validation, and evaluation accuracies change as a result.

Listing 4.6 shows the key code we use to train and evaluate the enhanced convnet. If you compare the code here with that in listing 4.2, you can appreciate the similarity between the two chunks of code. Both are centered around `Model.fit()` and `Model.evaluate()` calls. The syntax and style are identical, except with regard to how the loss value, accuracy value, and training progress are rendered or displayed on different user interfaces (terminal versus browser).

This shows an important feature of TensorFlow.js, a JavaScript deep-learning framework that straddles the frontend and the backend:

As far as the creation and training of models is concerned, the code you write in TensorFlow.js is the same regardless of whether you are working with the web browser or with Node.js.

Listing 4.6 Training and evaluating the enhanced convnet in tfjs-node

```
await model.fit(trainImages, trainLabels, {
  epochs,
  batchSize,
  validationSplit
});

const {images: testImages, labels: testLabels} = data.getTestData();
const evalOutput = model.evaluate         ⟵  Evaluates the model using
    testImages, testLabels);                  data the model hasn't seen
console.log('\nEvaluation result:');
console.log(
    `   Loss = ${evalOutput[0].dataSync()[0].toFixed(3)}; ` +
    `Accuracy = ${evalOutput[1].dataSync()[0].toFixed(3)}`);
```

4.3.2 *Saving the model from Node.js and loading it in the browser*

Training your model consumes CPU and GPU resources and takes some time. You don't want to throw away the fruit of training. Without saving the model, you would have to start from scratch the next time you run main.js. This section shows how to save the model after training and export the saved model as files on the disk (called a *checkpoint* or an *artifact*). We will also show you how to import the checkpoint in the browser, reconstitute it as a model, and use it for inference. The final part of the main() function in main.js consists of the model-saving code in the following listing.

Listing 4.7 Saving the trained model to the file system in tfjs-node

```
if (modelSavePath != null) {
  await model.save(`file://${modelSavePath}`);
  console.log(`Saved model to path: ${modelSavePath}`);
}
```

The `save()` method of the `model` object is used to save the model to a directory on your file system. The method takes a single argument, which is a URL string that begins with the scheme file://. Note that it is possible to save the model on the file system because we are using tfjs-node. The browser version of TensorFlow.js also provides the `model.save()` API but cannot access the machine's native file system directly because the browser forbids that for security reasons. Non-file-system saving destinations (such as the browser's local storage and IndexedDB) will have to be used if we are using TensorFlow.js in the browser. Those correspond to URL schemes other than file://.

`model.save()` is an asynchronous function because it involves file or network input-output in general. Therefore, we use await on the `save()` call. Suppose `model-SavePath` has a value /tmp/tfjs-node-mnist; after the `model.save()` call completes, you can examine the content of the directory,

```
ls -lh /tmp/tfjs-node-mnist
```

which may print a list of files like the following:

```
-rw-r--r-- 1 user group 4.6K Aug 14 10:38 model.json
    -rw-r--r-- 1 user group 2.3M Aug 14 10:38 weights.bin
```

There, you can see two files:

- model.json is a JSON file that contains the model's saved topology. What's referred to as "topology" here includes the types of layers that form the model, their respective configuration parameters (such as `filters` for a conv2d layer and `rate` for a dropout layer), as well as the way in which the layers connect to each other. The connections are simple for the MNIST convnet because it is a sequential model. We will see models with less trivial connection patterns, which can also be saved to disk with `model.save()`.
- In addition to the model topology, model.json also contains a manifest of the model's weights. That part lists the names, shapes, and data types of all the model's weights, in addition to the locations at which the weight values are stored. This brings us to the second file: weights.bin.

  As its name indicates, weights.bin is a binary file that stores all the model's weight values. It is a flat binary stream without demarcation of where the individual weights begin and end. That "metainformation" is available in the weights-manifest part of the JSON object in model.json.

To load the model using tfjs-node, you can use the `tf.loadLayersModel()` method, pointing to the location of the model.json file (not shown in the example code):

```
const loadedModel = await tf.loadLayersModel('file:///tmp/tfjs-node-mnist');
```

`tf.loadLayersModel()` reconstitutes the model by deserializing the saved topology data in model.json. Then, `tf.loadLayersModel()` reads the binary weight values in weights.bin using the manifest in model.json and force-sets the model's weight to those values. Like `model.save()`, `tf.loadLayersModel()` is asynchronous, so we use await when calling it here. Once the call returns, the `loadedModel` object is, for all intents and purposes, equivalent to the model created and trained using the JavaScript code in listings 4.5 and 4.6. You can print a summary of the model by calling its `summary()` method, use it to perform inference by calling its `predict()` method, evaluate its accuracy by using the `evaluate()` method, or even retrain it using the `fit()` method. If so desired, the model can also be saved again. The workflow of retraining and resaving a loaded model will be relevant when we talk about transfer learning in chapter 5.

What's said in the previous paragraph applies to the browser environment as well. The files you saved can be used to reconstitute the model in a web page. The reconstituted model supports the full `tf.LayersModel()` workflow, with the caveat that, if you retrain the entire model, it will be especially slow and inefficient due to the large size of the enhanced convnet. The only thing that's fundamentally different between loading a model in tfjs-node and in the browser is that you should use a URL scheme other than file:// in the browser. Typically, you can put the model.json and weights.bin files as static asset files on an HTTP server. Suppose your hostname is localhost and your files are seen under the server path my/models/; you can use the following line to load the model in the browser:

```
const loadedModel =
    await tf.loadLayersModel('http:///localhost/my/models/model.json');
```

When handling HTTP-based model loading in the browser, `tf.loadLayersModel()` calls the browser's built-in fetch function under the hood. Therefore, it has the following features and properties:

- Both http:// and https:// are supported.
- Relative server paths are supported. In fact, if a relative path is used, the http:// or https:// part of the URL can be omitted. For example, if your web page is at the server path my/index.html, and your model's JSON file is at my/models/model.json, you can use the relative path model/model.json:

  ```
  const loadedModel = await tf.loadLayersModel('models/model.json');
  ```

- To specify additional options for the HTTP/HTTPS requests, the `tf.io.browserHTTPRequest()` method should be used in lieu of the string argument. For example, to include credentials and headers during model loading, you can do something like

  ```
  const loadedModel = await tf.loadLayersModel(tf.io.browserHTTPRequest(
      'http://foo.bar/path/to/model.json',
      {credentials: 'include', headers: {'key_1': 'value_1'}}));
  ```

4.4   *Spoken-word recognition: Applying convnets on audio data*

So far, we have shown you how to use convnets to perform computer-vision tasks. But human perception is not just vision. Audio is an important modality of perceptual data and is accessible via browser APIs. How to recognize the content and meaning of speech and other kinds of sounds? Remarkably, convnets not only work for computer vision, but also help audio-related machine learning in a significant way.

In this section, you will see how we can solve a relatively simple audio task with a convnet similar to the one we built for MNIST. The task is to classify short snippets of speech recordings into 20 or so word categories. This task is simpler than the kind of speech recognition you may see in devices such as Amazon Echo and Google Home. In particular, those speech-recognition systems involve larger vocabularies than the one used in this example. Also, they process connected speech consisting of multiple words spoken in succession, whereas our example deals with words spoken one at a time. Therefore, our example doesn't qualify as a "speech recognizer;" instead, it is more accurately described as a "word recognizer" or "speech-command recognizer." However, our example still has practical uses (such as hands-free UIs and accessibility features). Also, the deep-learning techniques embodied in this example actually form the basis of more advanced speech-recognition systems.[9]

4.4.1 Spectrograms: Representing sounds as images

As in any deep-learning application, if you want to understand how the model works, you need to understand the data first. To understand how audio convnets work, we need to first look at how sound is represented as tensors. Recall from high school physics that sounds are patterns of air-pressure changes. A microphone picks up the air-pressure changes and converts them to electrical signals, which can in turn be digitized by a computer's sound card. Modern web browsers feature the *WebAudio* API, which talks to the sound card and provides real-time access to the digitized audio signals (with permission granted by the user). So, from a JavaScript programmer's point of view, sounds are arrays of real-valued numbers. In deep learning, such arrays of numbers are usually represented as 1D tensors.

You might be wondering, how can the kinds of convnets we have seen so far work on 1D tensors? Aren't they supposed to operate on tensors that are at least 2D? The key layers of a convnet, including conv2d and maxPooling2d, exploit spatial relations in 2D spaces. It turns out that sounds *can* be represented as special types of images called *spectrograms*. Spectrograms not only make it possible to apply convnets on sounds but also have theoretical justifications beyond deep learning.

As figure 4.12 shows, a spectrogram is a 2D array of numbers, which can be shown as grayscale images pretty much in the same way as MNIST images. The horizontal dimension is time, and the vertical one is frequency. Each vertical slice of a spectrogram is the *spectrum* of the sound inside a short time window. A spectrum is a decomposition of a sound into different frequency components, which can be roughly understood as different "pitches." Just as light can be divided by a prism into multiple colors, sound can be decomposed by a mathematical operation called *Fourier transform* into multiple frequencies. In a nutshell, a spectrogram describes how the frequency content of sound changes over a number of successive, short time windows (usually on the order of 20 milliseconds).

---

[9] Ronan Collobert, Christian Puhrsch, and Gabriel Synnaeve, "Wav2Letter: An End-to-End ConvNet-based Speech Recognition System," submitted 13 Sept. 2016, https://arxiv.org/abs/1609.03193.

Spectrograms are a suitable representation of sound for the following reasons. First, they save space: the number of float numbers in a spectrogram is usually a few times less than the number of float values in the raw waveform. Second, in a loose sense, spectrograms correspond to how hearing works in biology. An anatomical structure inside the inner ear called the cochlea essentially performs the biological version of Fourier transform. It decomposes sounds into different frequencies, which are then picked up by different sets of auditory neurons. Third, spectrogram representation of speech sounds makes different types of speech sounds easier to distinguish from each other. This is shown by the example speech spectrograms in figure 4.12: vowels and consonants all have different defining patterns in their spectrograms. Decades ago, prior to the wide adoption of machine learning, people working on speech recognition actually tried to handcraft rules that detect different vowels and consonants from spectrograms. Deep learning saves us the trouble and tears of such handcrafting.

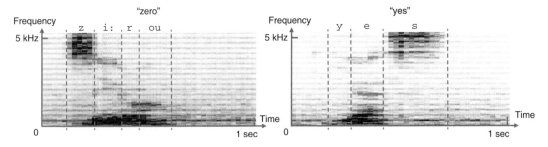

Figure 4.12   Example spectrograms of the isolated spoken words "zero" and "yes." A spectrogram is a joint time-frequency representation of sound. You can think of a spectrogram as a sound represented as an image. Each slice along the time axis (a column of the image) is a short moment (frame) in time; each slice along the frequency axis (a row of the image) corresponds to a particular narrow range of frequency (pitch). The value at each pixel of the image represents the relative energy of the sound in the given frequency bin at a given moment in time. The spectrograms in this figure are rendered such that a darker shade of gray corresponds to a higher amount of energy. Different speech sounds have different defining features. For example, sibilant consonants like "z" and "s" are characterized by a quasi-steady-state energy concentrated at frequencies above 2–3 kHz; vowel sounds like "e" and "o" are characterized by horizontal stripes (energy peaks) in the low end of the spectrum (< 3 kHz). These energy peaks are called *formants* in acoustics. Different vowels have different formant frequencies. All these distinctive features of different speech sounds can be used by a deep convnet for word recognition.

Let's stop and think for a moment. Looking at the MNIST images in figure 4.1 and the speech spectrograms in figure 4.12, you should be able to appreciate the similarity between the two datasets. Both datasets contain patterns in a 2D feature space, which a pair of trained eyes should be able to distinguish. Both datasets show some randomness in the detailed location, size, and details of the features. Finally, both are multi-category classification tasks. While MNIST contains 10 possible classes, our speech-commands dataset contains 20 (the 10 digits from 0 to 9, "up," "down," "left," "right," "go," "stop," "yes," and "no," in addition to the category of "unknown" words and background noise). It is exactly these similarities in the essence of the datasets that make convnets suitable for the speech-command-recognition task.

But there are also some noticeable differences between the two datasets. First, the audio recordings in the speech-command dataset are somewhat noisy, as you can see from the speckles of dark pixels that don't belong to the speech sound in the example spectrograms in figure 4.12. Second, every spectrogram in the speech-command dataset has a size of 43 × 232, which is significantly larger compared to the 28 × 28 size of the individual MNIST images. The size of the spectrogram is asymmetric between the time and frequency dimensions. These differences will be reflected by the convnet we will use on the audio dataset.

The code that defines and trains the speech-commands convnet lives in the tfjs-models repo. You can access the code with the following commands:

```
git clone https://github.com/tensorflow/tfjs-models.git
cd speech-commands/training/browser-fft
```

The creation and compilation of the model is encapsulated in the `createModel()` function in model.ts.

> **Listing 4.8   Convnet for classifying spectrograms of speech commands**

```
function createModel(inputShape: tf.Shape, numClasses: number) {
  const model = tf.sequential();
  model.add(tf.layers.conv2d({              ←—— Repeating motifs of
    filters: 8,                                  conv2d + maxPooling2d
    kernelSize: [2, 8],
    activation: 'relu',
    inputShape
  }));
  model.add(tf.layers.maxPooling2d({poolSize: [2, 2], strides: [2, 2]}));
  model.add(          tf.layers.conv2d({
        filters: 32,
        kernelSize: [2, 4],
        activation: 'relu'
      }));
  model.add(tf.layers.maxPooling2d({poolSize: [2, 2], strides: [2, 2]}));
  model.add(
      tf.layers.conv2d({
        filters: 32,
        kernelSize: [2, 4],
        activation: 'relu'
      }));
  model.add(tf.layers.maxPooling2d({poolSize: [2, 2], strides: [2, 2]}));
  model.add(
      tf.layers.conv2d({
        filters: 32,
        kernelSize: [2, 4],
        activation: 'relu'
      }));
  model.add(tf.layers.maxPooling2d({poolSize: [2, 2], strides: [1, 2]}));
  model.add(tf.layers.flatten());
  model.add(tf.layers.dropout({rate: 0.25}));   ←——
  model.add(tf.layers.dense({units: 2000, activation: 'relu'}));       Uses dropout to
  model.add(tf.layers.dropout({rate: 0.5}));                           reduce overfitting
```

Multilayer perceptron begins (points to `model.add(tf.layers.flatten());`)

```
model.add(tf.layers.dense({units: numClasses, activation: 'softmax'}));

model.compile({                      ◁──────────    Configures loss and metric for
  loss: 'categoricalCrossentropy',                  multicategory classification
  optimizer: tf.train.sgd(0.01),
  metrics: ['accuracy']
});
model.summary();
return model;
}
```

The topology of our audio convnet looks a lot like the MNIST convnets. The sequential model begins with several repeating motifs of conv2d layers paired with max-Pooling2d layers. The convolution-pooling part of the model ends at a flatten layer, on top of which an MLP is added. The MLP has two dense layers. The hidden dense layer has a relu activation, and the final (output) one has a softmax activation that suits the classification task. The model is compiled to use categoricalCrossentropy as the loss function and emit the accuracy metric during training and evaluation. This is exactly the same as the MNIST convnets because both datasets involve multicategory classification. The audio convnet also shows some interesting differences from the MNIST one. In particular, the kernelSize properties of the conv2d layers are rectangular (for instance, [2, 8]) instead of square-shaped. These values are selected to match the nonsquare shape of the spectrograms, which have a larger frequency dimension than the temporal dimension.

To train the model, you need to download the speech-command dataset first. The dataset originated from the speech-commands dataset collected by Pete Warden, an engineer on the Google Brain team (see www.tensorflow.org/tutorials/sequences/audio_recognition). It has been converted to a browser-specific spectrogram format:

```
curl -fSsL https://storage.googleapis.com/learnjs-data/speech-
    commands/speech-commands-data- v0.02-browser.tar.gz  -o speech-commands-
    data-v0.02-browser.tar.gz &&
tar xzvf speech-commands-data-v0.02-browser.tar.gz
```

These commands will download and extract the browser version of the speech-command dataset. Once the data has been extracted, you can kick off the training process with this command:

```
yarn
yarn train \
    speech-commands-data-browser/ \
    /tmp/speech-commands-model/
```

The first argument to the yarn train command points at the location of the training data. The following arguments specify the path at which the model's JSON file will be saved, together with the weight file and the metadata JSON file. Just like when we trained the enhanced MNIST convnet, the training of the audio convnet happens in tfjs-node, with the potential to utilize GPUs. Because the sizes of the dataset and the model are larger than the MNIST convnet, the training will take longer (on the order of a few hours). You can get a significant speedup of the training if you have a CUDA GPU and change the command slightly to use tfjs-node-gpu instead of the default tfjs-node (which runs on a CPU only). To do that, just add the flag `--gpu` to the previous command:

```
yarn train \
  --gpu \
  speech-commands-data-browser/ \
  /tmp/speech-commands-model/
```

When the training ends, the model should achieve a final evaluation (test) accuracy of approximately 94%.

The trained model is saved at the path specified by the flag in the previous command. Like the MNIST convnet we trained with tfjs-node, the saved model can be loaded in the browser for serving. However, you need to be familiar with the Web-Audio API to be able to acquire data from the microphone and preprocess it into a format that can be used by the model. For your convenience, we wrote a wrapper class that not only loads a trained audio convnet, but also takes care of the data ingestion and preprocessing. If you are interested in the mechanisms of the audio data input pipeline, you can study the underlying code in the tfjs-model Git repository, in the folder speech-commands/src. The wrapper is available via npm under the name @tensorflow-models/speech-commands. Listing 4.9 shows a minimal example of how the wrapper class can be used to perform online recognition of speech-command words in the browser.

In the speech-commands/demo folder of the tfjs-models repo, you can find a less barebones example of how to use the package. To clone and run the demo, run the following commands under the speech-commands directory:

```
git clone https://github.com/tensorflow/tfjs-models.git
cd tfjs-models/speech-commands
yarn && yarn publish-local
cd demo
yarn && yarn link-local && yarn watch
```

The `yarn watch` command will automatically open a new tab in your default web browser. In order to see the speech-command recognizer in action, make sure your machine has a microphone ready (which most laptops do). Each time a word within the vocabulary is recognized, it will be displayed on the screen along with the one-second-long spectrogram that contains the word. So, this is browser-based, single-word recognition in action, powered by the WebAudio API and a deep convnet. Surely it doesn't have the ability to recognize connected speech with grammar? That will require help from other types of neural network building blocks capable of processing sequential information. We will visit those in chapter 8.

> **Listing 4.9 Example usage of the @tensorflow-models/speech-commands module**

Imports the speech-commands module. Make sure it is listed as a dependency in package.json.

Creates an instance of the speech-command recognizer that uses the browser's built-in fast Fourier transform (FFT)

```
import * as SpeechCommands from
    '@tensorflow-models/speech-commands';

const recognizer =
    SpeechCommands.create('BROWSER_FFT');

console.log(recognizer.wordLabels());
```

You can examine what word labels (including the "background-noise" and "unknown" labels) the model is capable of recognizing.

```
recognizer.listen(result => {
    let maxIndex;
    let maxScore = -Infinity;
    result.scores.forEach((score, i) => {
        if (score > maxScore) {
            maxIndex = i;
            maxScore = score;
        }
    });
    console.log(`Detected word ${recognizer.wordLabels()[maxIndex]}`);
}, {
    probabilityThreshold: 0.75
});

setTimeout(() => recognizer.stopStreaming(), 10e3);
```

result.scores contains the probability scores that correspond to recognizer.wordLabels().

Finds the index of the word with the highest score

Stops the online streaming recognition in 10 seconds

Starts online streaming recognition. The first argument is a callback, which will be invoked anytime a non-background-noise, non-unknown word is recognized with a probability above the threshold (0.75 in this case).

Exercises

1 The convnet for classifying MNIST images in the browser (listing 4.1) has two groups of conv2d and maxPooling2d layers. Modify the code to reduce the number to only one group. Answer the following questions:

   a How does that affect the total number of trainable parameters of the convnet?

   b How does that affect the training speed?

   c How does that affect the final accuracy obtained by the convnet after training?

2 This exercise is similar to exercise 1. But instead of playing with the number of conv2d-maxPooling2d layer groups, experiment with the number of dense layers in the MLP part of the convnet in listing 4.1. How do the total number of parameters, training speed, and final accuracy change if you remove the first dense layer and keep only the second (output) one?

3 Remove dropout from the convnet in mnist-node (listing 4.5), and see what happens to the training process and the final test accuracy. Why does that happen? What does that show?

4 As practice using the `tf.browser.fromPixels()` method to pull image data from image- and video-related elements of a web page, try the following:

   a Use `tf.browser.fromPixels()` to get a tensor representing a color JPG image by using an `img` tag.

      – What are the height and width of the image tensor returned by `tf.browser.fromPixels()`? What determines the height and width?

      – Resize the image to a fixed dimension of 100 × 100 (height × width) using `tf.image.resizeBilinear()`.

      – Repeat the previous step, but using the alternative resizing function `tf.image.resizeNearestNeighbor()` instead. Can you spot any differences between the results of these two resizing functions?

   b Create an HTML canvas and draw some arbitrary shapes in it using functions such as `rect()`. Or, if you wish, you can use more advanced libraries such as d3.js or three.js to draw more complicated 2D and 3D shapes in it. Then, get the image tensor data from the canvas using `tf.browser.fromPixels()`.

Summary

- Convnets extract 2D spatial features from input images with a hierarchy of stacked conv2d and maxPooling2d layers.
- conv2d layers are multichannel, tunable spatial filters. They have the properties of locality and parameter sharing, which make them powerful feature extractors and efficient representational transforms.
- maxPooling2d layers reduce the size of the input image tensor by calculating the maximum within fixed-size windows, achieving better positional invariance.
- The conv2d-maxPooling2d "tower" of a convnet usually ends in a flatten layer, which is followed by an MLP made of dense layers for classification or regression tasks.
- With its restricted resources, the browser is only suitable for training small models. To train larger models, it is recommended you use tfjs-node, the Node.js version of TensorFlow.js; tfjs-node can use the same CPU- and GPU-parallelized kernels used by the Python version of TensorFlow.
- With greater model capacities comes greater risks of overfitting. Overfitting can be ameliorated by adding dropout layers in a convnet. Dropout layers randomly zero-out a given fraction of the input elements during training.
- Convnets are useful not only for computer vision tasks. When audio signals are represented as spectrograms, convnets can be applied on them to achieve good classification accuracies as well.

Transfer learning: Reusing pretrained neural networks

In chapter 4, we saw how to train convnets to classify images. Now consider the following scenario. Our convnet for classifying handwritten digits performs poorly for a user because their handwriting is very different from the original training data. Can we improve the model to serve the user better by using a small amount of data (say, 50 examples) we can collect from them? Consider another scenario:

an e-commerce website wishes to automatically classify pictures of commodity items uploaded by users. But none of the publicly available convnets (such as MobileNet[1]) are trained on such domain-specific images. Is it possible to use a publicly available image model to address the custom classification problem, given a modest number (say, a few hundred) of labeled pictures?

Fortunately, a technique called *transfer learning*, the main focus of this chapter, can help solve tasks like these.

5.1 Introduction to transfer learning: Reusing pretrained models

In essence, transfer learning is about speeding up a new learning task by reusing the results of previous learning. It involves using a model already trained on a dataset to perform a *different but related* machine-learning task. The already-trained model is referred to as the *base model*. Transfer learning sometimes involves retraining the base model and sometimes involves creating a new model on top of the base model. We refer to the new model as the *transfer model*. As figure 5.1 shows, the amount of data used for this retraining process is usually much smaller compared to the data that went into training the base model (as with the two examples given at the beginning of this chapter). As such, transfer learning is often much less time- and resource-consuming compared to the base model's training process. This makes it feasible to perform transfer learning in a resource-restricted environment like the browser using TensorFlow.js. And thus transfer learning is an important topic for TensorFlow.js learners.

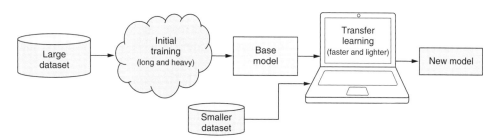

Figure 5.1   The general workflow of transfer learning. A large dataset goes into the training of the base model. This initial training process is often long and computationally heavy. The base model is then retrained, possibly by becoming part of a new model. The retraining process usually involves a dataset much smaller than the original one. The computation involved in the retraining is significantly less than the initial training and can happen on an edge device, such as a laptop or a phone running TensorFlow.js.

---

[1]   Andrew G. Howard et al., "MobileNets: Efficient Convolutional Neural Networks for Mobile Vision Applications," submitted 17 Apr. 2017, https://arxiv.org/abs/1704.04861.

The key phrase "different but related" in the description of transfer learning can mean different things in different cases:

- The first scenario mentioned at the beginning of this chapter involves adapting a model to the data from a specific user. Although the data is different from the original training set, the task is exactly the same—classifying an image into the 10 digits. This type of transfer learning is referred to as *model adaptation.*
- Other transfer-learning problems involve targets (labels) that are different from the original ones. The commodity image-classification scenario mentioned at the beginning of this chapter belongs to this category.

What is the advantage of transfer learning over training a new model from scratch? The answer is two-fold:

- Transfer learning is more efficient in terms of both the amount of data it requires and the amount of computation it takes.
- It builds on the gains of previous training by reusing the feature-extracting power of the base model.

These points are valid regardless of the type of problem (for instance, classification and regression). On the first point, transfer learning uses the trained weights from the base model (or a subset of them). As a result, it requires less training data and training time to converge to a given level of accuracy compared to training a new model from scratch. In this regard, transfer learning is analogous to how humans learn new tasks: once you have mastered a task (playing a card game, for example), learning similar tasks (such as playing similar card games) becomes significantly easier and faster in the future. The saved cost of training time may seem relatively small for a neural network like the convnet we built for MNIST. However, for larger models trained on larger datasets (such as industrial-scale convnets trained on terabytes of image data), the savings can be substantial.

On the second point, the core idea of transfer learning is reusing previous training results. Through learning from a very large dataset, the original neural network has become very good at extracting useful features from the original input data. These features will be useful for the new task as long as the new data in the transfer-learning task is not too different from the original data. Researchers have assembled very large datasets for common machine-learning domains. In computer vision, there is Image-Net,[2] which contains millions of labeled images from about a thousand categories. Deep-learning researchers have trained deep convnets using the ImageNet dataset, including ResNet, Inception, and MobileNet (the last of which we will soon lay our hands on). Due to the large number and diversity of the images in ImageNet, convnets trained on it are good feature extractors for general types of images. These feature extractors will be useful for working with small datasets like those in the aforementioned scenarios, but training such effective feature extractors is impossible with small

---

[2] Don't be confused by the name. "ImageNet" refers to a dataset, not a neural network.

datasets like those. Opportunities for transfer learning exist in other domains as well. For example, in natural language processing, people have trained word embeddings (that is, vector representation of all common words in a language) on large text corpora consisting of billions of words. These embeddings are useful for language-understanding tasks where much smaller text datasets are available. Without further ado, let's see how transfer learning works in practice through an example.

5.1.1 *Transfer learning based on compatible output shapes: Freezing layers*

Let's start by looking at a relatively simple example. We will train a convnet on only the first five digits of the MNIST dataset (0 through 4). We will then use the resulting model to recognize the remaining five digits (5 through 9), which the model never saw during the original training. Although this example is somewhat contrived, it illustrates the basic workflow of transfer learning. The example can be checked out and run with the following commands:

```
git clone https://github.com/tensorflow/tfjs-examples.git
cd tfjs-examples/mnist-transfer-cnn
yarn && yarn watch
```

In the demo web page that opens, start the transfer learning process by clicking the Retrain button. You can see the process reach an accuracy of about 96% on the new set of five digits (5 through 9), which takes about 30 seconds on a reasonably powerful laptop. As we will show, this is significantly faster than the non-transfer-learning alternative (namely, training a new model from scratch). Let's see how this is done, step-by-step.

Our example loads the pretrained base model from an HTTP server instead of training it from scratch so as not to obscure the workflow's key parts. Recall from section 4.3.3 that TensorFlow.js provides the tf.loadLayersModel() method for loading pretrained models. This is called in the loader.js file:

```
const model = await tf.loadLayersModel(url);
model.summary();
```

The printed summary of the model looks like figure 5.2. As you can see, this model consists of 12 layers.[3] All its 600,000 or so weight parameters are trainable, just like all the TensorFlow.js models we have seen so far. Note that loadLayersModel() loads not only the model's topology but also all its weight values. As a result, the loaded model is ready to predict the class of digits 0 through 4. However, this is not how we will use the model. Instead, we will train the model to recognize new digits (5 through 9).

---

[3] You may not have seen the *activation* layer type in this model. Activation layers are simple layers that perform only an activation function (such as relu and softmax) on the input. Suppose you have a dense layer with the default (linear) activation; stacking an activation layer on top of it is equivalent to using a dense layer with the nondefault activation included. The latter is what we did for the examples in chapter 4. But the former style is also sometimes seen. In TensorFlow.js, you can get such a model topology by using code like the following: const model = tf.sequential(); model.add(tf.layers.dense({untis: 5, inputShape})); model.add(tf.layers.activation({activation: 'relu'}).

Layer (type)	Output shape	Param #
conv2d_1 (Conv2D)	[null,26,26,32]	320
activation_1 (Activation)	[null,26,26,32]	0
conv2d_2 (Conv2D)	[null,24,24,32]	9248
activation_2 (Activation)	[null,24,24,32]	0
max_pooling2d_1 (MaxPooling2	[null,12,12,32]	0
dropout_1 (Dropout)	[null,12,12,32]	0
flatten_1 (Flatten)	[null,4608]	0
dense_1 (Dense)	[null,128]	589952
activation_3 (Activation)	[null,128]	0
dropout_2 (Dropout)	[null,128]	0
dense_2 (Dense)	[null,5]	645
activation_4 (Activation)	[null,5]	0

Will be set as untrainable (frozen) during transfer learning

```
Total params: 600165
Trainable params: 600165
Non-trainable params: 0
```

Figure 5.2   A printed summary of the convnet for recognition of MNIST images and transfer learning

Looking at the callback function for the Retrain button (in the `retrainModel()` function of index.js), you will notice a few lines of code that set the `trainable` property of the first seven layers of the model to `false` if the option Freeze Feature Layers is selected (it is selected by default).

What does that do? By default, the `trainable` property of each of the model's layers is `true` after the model is loaded via the `loadLayersModel()` method or created from scratch. The `trainable` property is used during training (that is, calls to the `fit()` or `fitDataset()` method). It tells the optimizer whether the layer's weights should be updated. By default, the weights of all layers of a model are updated during training. But if you set the property to `false` for some of the model's layers, the weights of those layers will *not* be updated during training. In TensorFlow.js terminology, those layers become *untrainable*, or *frozen*. The code in listing 5.1 freezes the first seven layers of the model, from the input conv2d layer to the flatten layer, while leaving the last several layers (the dense layers) trainable.

Listing 5.1   "Freezing" the first several layers of the convnet for transfer learning

```
const trainingMode = ui.getTrainingMode();
if (trainingMode === 'freeze-feature-layers') {
  console.log('Freezing feature layers of the model.');
  for (let i = 0; i < 7; ++i) {
```

```
    this.model.layers[i].trainable = false;   ⟵————— Freezes the layer
  }
} else if (trainingMode === 'reinitialize-weights') {
  const returnString = false ;
  this.model = await tf.models.modelFromJSON({
    modelTopology: this.model.toJSON(null, returnString)
  });

}
this.model.compile({                    ⟵————————
  loss: 'categoricalCrossentropy',
  optimizer: tf.train.adam(0.01),
  metrics: ['acc'],
});

this.model.summary();    ⟵———
```

Makes a new model with the same topology as the old one, but with reinitialized weight values

The freezing will not take effect during fit() calls unless you compile the model first.

Prints the model summary again after compile(). You should see that a number of the model's weights have become nontrainable.

However, setting the layers' `trainable` property alone is not enough: if you just modify the `trainable` property and call the model's `fit()` method right away, you will see the weights of those layers still get updated during the `fit()` call. You need to call `Model.compile()` before calling `Model.fit()` in order for the `trainable` property changes to take effect, as is done in listing 5.1. We mentioned previously that the `compile()` call configures the optimizer, loss function, and metrics. However, the method also lets the model refresh the list of weight variables to be updated during those calls. After the `compile()` call, we call `summary()` again to print a new summary of the model. As you can see by comparing the new summary with the old one in figure 5.2, some of the model's weights become nontrainable:

```
Total params: 600165
Trainable params: 590597
Non-trainable params: 9568
```

You can verify that the number of nontrainable parameters, 9,568, is the sum of weight parameters in the two frozen layers with weights (the two conv2d layers). Note that some of the layers we've frozen contain no weights (such as the maxPooling2d layer and the flatten layer) and therefore don't contribute to the count of nontrainable parameters when they are frozen.

The actual transfer-learning code is shown in listing 5.2. Here, we use the same `fit()` method that we've used to train models from scratch. In this call, we use the `validationData` field to get a measure of how accurate the model is doing on data it hasn't seen during training. In addition, we connect two callbacks to the `fit()` call, one for updating the progress bar in the UI and the other for plotting the loss and accuracy curves using the tfjs-vis module (more details coming in chapter 7). This shows an aspect of the `fit()` API that we haven't mentioned before: you can give a callback or an array of multiple callbacks to a `fit()` call. In the latter case, all the callbacks will be invoked (in the order they are specified in the array) during training.

Listing 5.2   Using `Model.fit()` to perform transfer learning

```
await this.model.fit(this.gte5TrainData.x, this.gte5TrainData.y, {
  batchSize: batchSize,
  epochs: epochs,
  validationData: [this.gte5TestData.x, this.gte5TestData.y],
  callbacks: [
    ui.getProgressBarCallbackConfig(epochs),

    tfVis.show.fitCallbacks(surfaceInfo, ['val_loss', 'val_acc'], {
      zoomToFit: true,
      zoomToFitAccuracy: true,
      height: 200,
      callbacks: ['onEpochEnd'],
    }),
  ]
});
```

Giving multiple callbacks to a fit() call is allowed.

Uses tfjs-vis to plot the validation loss and accuracy during transfer learning

How does the result of the transfer learning turn out? As you can see in panel A of figure 5.3, it reaches an accuracy of around 0.968 after 10 epochs of training, which takes roughly 15 seconds on a relatively up-to-date laptop—not bad. But how does this compare to training a model from scratch? One way in which we can demonstrate the value of starting from a pretrained model over starting from scratch is to do an experiment in which we randomly reinitialize the weights of the pretrained model right before the fit() call. This is what happens if you select the Reinitialize Weights option from the Training Mode drop-down menu before clicking the Retrain button. The result is shown in panel B of the same figure.

As you can see by comparing panel B with panel A, the random reinitialization of the model weights causes the loss to start at a significantly higher value (0.36 versus 0.30) and the accuracy to start from a significantly lower value (0.88 versus 0.91). The reinitialized model also ends up with a lower final validation accuracy (~0.954) than the model that reuses weights from the base model (~0.968). These differences reflect the advantage of transfer learning: by reusing weights in the early layers (the feature-extracting layers) of the model, the model gets a nice head start relative to learning everything from scratch. This is because the data encountered in the transfer-learning task is similar to the data used to train the original model. The images of digits 5 through 9 have a lot in common with those of digits 0 through 4: they are all grayscale images with a black background; they have similar visual patterns (strokes of comparable widths and curvatures). So, the features the model learned how to extract from digits 0 through 4 turn out to be useful for learning to classifying the new digits (5 through 9), too.

What if we don't freeze the weights of the feature layers? The Don't Freeze Feature Layers option of the Training Mode drop-down menu allows you to perform this experiment. The result is shown in panel C of figure 5.3. There are a few noteworthy differences from the results in panel A:

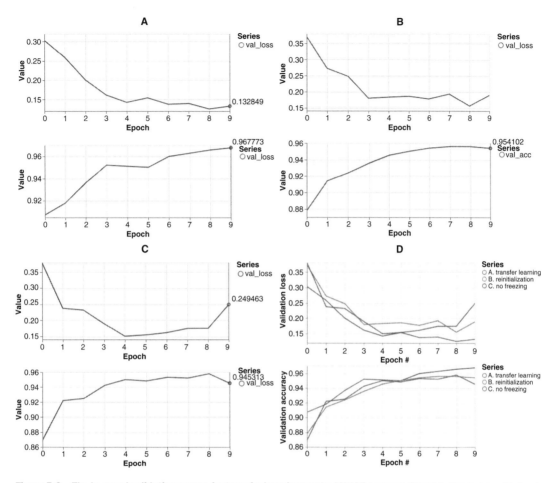

Figure 5.3 **The loss and validation curves for transfer learning on the MNIST convnet. Panel A: the curves obtained with the first seven layers of the pretrained model frozen. Panel B: the curves obtained with all the weights of the model reinitialized randomly. Panel C: the curves obtained without freezing any layers of the pretrained model. Note that the y-axes differ among the three panels. Panel D: a multiseries plot that shows the loss and accuracy curves from panels A–C on the same axes to facilitate comparison.**

- With no feature-layer freezing, the loss value starts off higher (for instance, after the first epoch: 0.37 versus 0.27); the accuracy starts off lower (0.87 versus 0.91). Why is this the case? When the pretrained model is first starting to be trained on the new dataset, the predictions will contain a large number of errors because the pretrained weights generate essentially random predictions for the five new digits. As a result, the loss function will have very high values and steep slopes. This causes the gradients calculated in the early phases of the training to be very large, which in turn leads to large fluctuations in all the model's weights. As a result, all layers' weights will undergo a period of large fluctuations, which leads to the higher initial loss seen in panel C. In the normal transfer-learning approach (panel A), the model's first few layers are frozen and are therefore "shielded" from these large initial weight perturbations.

- Partly due to these large initial perturbations, the final accuracy achieved by the no-freezing approach (~0.945, panel C) is *not* appreciably higher compared to that from the normal transfer-learning approach with layer freezing (~0.968, panel A).

- The training takes much longer when none of the model's layers are frozen. For example, on one of the laptops that we use, training the model with frozen feature layers takes about 30 seconds, whereas training the model without any layer freezing takes approximately twice as long (60 seconds). Figure 5.4 illustrates the reason behind this in a schematic way. The frozen layers are taken out from the equation during backpropagation, which causes each batch of the `fit()` call to go much faster.

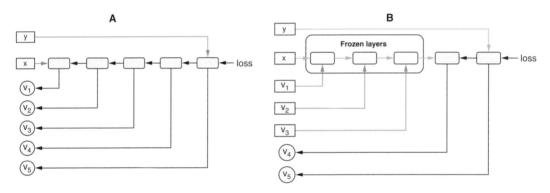

Figure 5.4 A schematic explanation for why freezing some layers of a model speeds up training. In this figure, the backpropagation path is shown by the black arrows pointing to the left. Panel A: when no layer is frozen, all the model's weights (v_1–v_5) need to be updated during each training step (each batch) and hence will be involved in backpropagation, represented by the black arrows. Note that the features (x) and targets (y) are never included in backpropagation because their values don't need to be updated. Panel B: by freezing the first few layers of the model, a subset of the weights (v_1–v_3) are no longer a part of backpropagation. Instead, they become analogous to x and y, which are just treated as constants that factor into the computation of the loss. As a result, the amount of computation it takes to perform the backpropagation decreases, and the training speed increases.

These points provide justification for the layer-freezing approach of transfer learning: it leverages the feature-extracting layers from the base model and protects them from large weight perturbations during the early phases of the new training, thereby achieving a higher accuracy in a shorter training period.

Two final remarks before we move on to the next section. First, model adaptation—the process of retraining a model to make it work better on the input data from a particular user—uses techniques very similar to the ones shown here, that is, freezing the base layers while letting the weights of the top few layers be altered through training on the user-specific data. This is despite the fact that the problem we solved in this section didn't involve data from a different user, but rather involved data with different labels. Second, you might wonder how to verify that a weight of a frozen layer (the conv2d layers, in this case) is indeed the same before and after a `fit()` call. It is not very hard to do this verification. We leave it as an exercise for you (see exercise 2 at the end of this chapter).

5.1.2 *Transfer learning on incompatible output shapes: Creating a new model using outputs from the base model*

In the example of transfer learning seen in the previous section, the base model had the same output shape as the new output shape. This property doesn't hold in many other transfer-learning cases (see figure 5.5). For example, if you want to use the base model trained initially on the five digits to classify *four* new digits, the approach previously described will not work. A more common scenario is the following: given a deep convnet that has been trained on the ImageNet classification dataset consisting of 1,000 output classes, you have an image-classification task at hand that involves a much smaller number of output classes (case B in figure 5.5). Perhaps it is a binary-classification problem—whether the image contains a human face or not—or perhaps it is a multiclass-classification problem with only a handful of classes—what kind of commodity item a picture contains (recall the example at the beginning of this chapter). In such cases, the base model's output shape doesn't work for the new problem.

In some cases, even the *type* of machine-learning task is different from the one the base model has been trained on. For instance, you can perform a regression task (predict a number, as in case C in figure 5.5) by applying transfer learning on the base model trained on a classification task. In section 5.2, you will see a still more intriguing use of transfer learning—predicting an array of numbers, instead of a single one, for the purpose of detecting and localizing objects in images.

These cases all involve a desired output shape that differs from that of the base model. This makes it necessary to construct a new model. But because we are doing transfer learning, the new model will not be created from scratch. Instead, it will use the base model. We will illustrate how to do this in the webcam-transfer-learning example in the tfjs-examples repository.

To see this example in action, make sure your machine has a front-facing camera—the example will collect the data for transfer learning from the camera. Most laptops and tablet computers come with a built-in front-facing camera nowadays. If you are using a desktop computer, however, you may need to find a webcam and attach it to the machine. Similar to the previous examples, you can use the following commands to check out and run the demo:

```
git clone https://github.com/tensorflow/tfjs-examples.git
cd tfjs-examples/webcam-transfer-learning
```

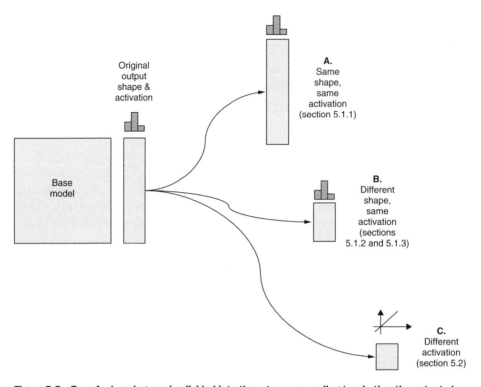

Figure 5.5   Transfer learning can be divided into three types according to whether the output shape and activation of the new model are the same as or different from those of the original model. Case A: the output shape and the activation function of the new model match those of the base model. The transfer of the MNIST model onto new digits in section 5.1.1 is an example of this type of transfer learning. Case B: the new model has the same activation type as the base model because the original task and the new task are of the same type (for example, both are multiclass classification). However, the output shapes are different (for instance, the new task involves a different number of classes). Examples of this type of transfer learning can be found in section 5.1.2 (controlling a video game in the style of Pac-Man™ [4] through a webcam) and 5.1.3 (recognizing a new set of spoken words). Case C: the new task is of a different type from the original one (such as regression versus classification). The object-detection model based on MobileNet is an example of this type.

This fun demo turns your webcam into a game controller by applying transfer learning on a TensorFlow.js implementation of MobileNet, and lets you play the Pac-Man game with it. Let's walk through the three steps it takes to run the demo: data collection, model transfer learning, and playing.

The data for transfer learning is collected from your webcam. Once the demo is running in your browser, you will see four black squares in the bottom-right part of the page. They are arranged in a way similar to the four direction buttons on a Nintendo Family Computer controller. They correspond to the four classes that the model will be trained to recognize in real time. These four classes correspond to the

---

[4]   Pac-Man is a trademark of Bandai Namco Entertainment Inc.

four directions in which Pac-Man will go. When you click and hold one of them, images will be collected via the webcam at a rate of 20–30 frames per second. A number beneath the square tells you how many images have been collected for this controller direction so far.

For the best transfer-learning quality, make sure you 1) collect at least 50 images per class, and 2) move and wiggle your head and face around a little bit during the data collection so that the training images contain more diversity, which benefits the robustness of the model you'll get from the transfer learning. In this demo, most people turn their heads in the four directions (up, down, left, and right; see figure 5.6) to indicate which way Pac-Man should go. But you can use any head positions, facial expressions, or even hand gestures that you desire as the input images, as long as the inputs are sufficiently visually distinct from one class to another.

Figure 5.6   The UI of the webcam-transfer-learning example[5]

After collecting the training images, click the Train Model button, which will start the transfer-learning process. Transfer learning should take only a few seconds. As it progresses, you should see the loss value displayed on the screen get smaller and smaller until it reaches a very small positive value (such as 0.00010) and stops changing. At this point, the transfer-learning model has been trained, and you can use it to play the game. To start the game, just click the Play button and wait for game state to settle. The model will then start performing real-time inference on the stream of images from the webcam. At each video frame, the winning class (the class with the highest probability score assigned by the transfer-learning model) will be indicated in the bottom-right part of the UI with bright yellow highlighting. In addition, it will cause Pac-Man to move in the corresponding direction (unless blocked by a wall).

---

[5] The UI of this webcam-transfer-learning example is the work of Jimbo Wilson and Shan Carter. A video recording of this fun example in action is available at https://youtu.be/YB-kfeNIPCE?t=941.

This demo might look like magic to those unfamiliar with machine learning, but it is based on nothing more than a transfer-learning algorithm that uses MobileNet to perform a four-class classification task. The algorithm uses the small amount of image data collected through the webcam. Those images are conveniently labeled through the click-and-hold action you performed while collecting the images. Thanks to the power of transfer learning, this process doesn't need much data or much training time (it even works on a smartphone). So, that is how this demo works in a nutshell. If you wish to understand the technical details, dive deep with us into the underlying TensorFlow.js code in the next section.

DEEP DIVE INTO WEBCAM TRANSFER LEARNING

The code in listing 5.3 (from webcam-transfer-learning/index.js) is responsible for loading the base model. In particular, we load a version of MobileNet that can run efficiently in TensorFlow.js. Info box 5.1 describes how this model is converted from the Keras deep-learning library in Python. As soon as the model is loaded, we use the `getLayer()` method to get hold of one of its layers. `getLayer()` allows you to specify a layer by its name (`'conv_pw_13_relu'` in this case). You may recall another way to access a model's layers from section 2.4.2—that is, by indexing into the model's `layers` attribute, which holds all the model's layers as a JavaScript array. This approach is easy to use only when the model consists of a small number of layers. The MobileNet model we are dealing with here has 93 layers, which makes that approach fragile (for example, what if more layers get added to the model in the future?). Therefore, the name-based `getLayer()` approach is more reliable, if we assume the authors of MobileNet will keep the names of the key layers unchanged when they release new versions of the model.

Listing 5.3   Loading MobileNet and creating a "truncated" model from it

```
async function loadTruncatedMobileNet() {
  const mobilenet = await tf.loadLayersModel(
    'https://storage.googleapis.com/' +
      'tfjs-models/tfjs/mobilenet_v1_0.25_224/model.json');

  const layer = mobilenet.getLayer(
    'conv_pw_13_relu');
  return tf.model({
    inputs: mobilenet.inputs,
    outputs: layer.output
  });
}
```

URLs under storage.google.com/tfjs-models are designed to be permanent and stable.

Gets an intermediate layer of the MobileNet. This layer contains features useful for the custom image-classification task.

Creates a new model that is the same as MobileNet except that it ends at the 'conv_pw_l3_relu' layer, that is, with the last few layers (referred to as the "head") truncated

INFO BOX 5.1 Converting models from Python Keras into the TensorFlow .js format

TensorFlow.js features a high degree of compatibility and interoperability with Keras, one of the most popular Python deep-learning libraries. One of the benefits that stems from this compatibility is that you can utilize many of the so-called "applications" from Keras. These applications are a set of pretrained deep convnets (see https://keras.io/applications/). The authors of Keras have painstakingly trained these convnets on large datasets such as ImageNet and made them available via the library so that they are ready for reuse, including inference and transfer learning, as we are doing here. For those who use Keras in Python, importing an application takes just one line of code. Due to the interoperability previously mentioned, it is also easy for a TensorFlow.js user to use these applications. Here are the steps it takes:

1 Make sure that the Python package called `tensorflowjs` is installed. The easiest way to install it is via the `pip` command:

```
pip install tensorflowjs
```

2 Run the following code through a Python source file or in an interactive Python REPL such as ipython:

```
import keras
import tensorflowjs as tfjs
model = keras.applications.mobilenet.MobileNet(alpha=0.25)
tfjs.converters.save_keras_model(model, '/tmp/mobilnet_0.25')
```

The first two lines import the required `keras` and `tensorflowjs` modules. The third line loads MobileNet into a Python object (`model`). You can, in fact, print a summary of the model in pretty much the same way as you print the summary of a Tensor-Flow.js model: that is, `model.summary()`. You can see that the last layer of the model (the model's output) indeed has a shape of (`None, 1000`) (equivalent to [`null, 1000`] in JavaScript), reflecting the 1,000-class ImageNet classification task that the MobileNet model was trained on. The keyword argument `alpha=0.25` that we specified for this constructor call chooses a version of MobileNet that is smaller in size. You may choose larger values of `alpha` (such as `0.75, 1`), and the same conversion code will continue to work.

The last line in the previous code snippet saves the model to the specified directory on the disk using a method from the tensorflowjs module. After the line finishes running, there will be a new directory at /tmp/mobilenet_0.25, with content that looks like

```
group1-shard1of6
    group1-shard2of6
    ...
    group1-shard6of6
    model.json
```

(continued)

This is exactly the same format as the one we saw in section 4.3.3, when we showed how to save a trained TensorFlow.js model to disk using its `save()` method in the Node.js version of TensorFlow.js. Therefore, to the TensorFlow.js-based programs that load this converted model from disk, the saved format is identical to a model created and trained in TensorFlow.js: it can simply call the `tf.loadLayersModel()` method and point at the path to the model.json file (either in the browser or in Node.js), which is exactly what happens in listing 5.3.

The loaded MobileNet model is ready to perform the machine-learning task that the model was originally trained on—classify input images into the 1,000 classes of the ImageNet dataset. Note that this particular dataset has a heavy emphasis on animals, especially various breeds of cats and dogs (which is probably related to the abundance of such images on the internet!). For those interested in this particular usage, the MobileNet example in the tfjs-example repository illustrates how to do that (https://github.com/tensorflow/tfjs-examples/tree/master/mobilenet). However, this direct usage of MobileNet is not what we focus on in this chapter; instead, we explore how to use the loaded MobileNet to perform transfer learning.

The `tfjs.converters.save_keras_model()` method shown previously is capable of converting and saving not only MobileNet but also other Keras applications, such as DenseNet and NasNet. In exercise 3 at the end of this chapter, you will practice converting another Keras application (MobileNetV2) into the TensorFlow.js format and loading it in the browser. Furthermore, it should be pointed out that `tfjs.converters` `.save_keras_model()` is generally applicable to any model objects you have created or trained in Keras, not just models from `keras.applications`.

What do we do with the `conv_pw_13_relu` layer once we get hold of it? We create a new model that contains the layers of the original MobiletNet model from its first (input) layer to the `conv_pw_13_relu` layer. This is the first time you see this kind of model construction in this book, so it requires some careful explanation. For that, we need to introduce the concept of a *symbolic tensor* first.

Creating models from symbolic tensors

You have seen tensors so far. `Tensor` is the basic data type (also abbreviated as *dtype*) in TensorFlow.js. A tensor object carries concrete numeric values of a given shape and dtype, backed by storage on WebGL textures (if in a WebGL-enabled browser) or CPU/GPU memory (if in Node.js). However, `SymbolicTensor` is another important class in TensorFlow.js. Instead of holding concrete values, a symbolic tensor specifies only a shape and a dtype. A symbolic tensor can be thought of as a "slot" or a "placeholder," into which an actual tensor value may be inserted later, given that the tensor value has a compatible shape and dtype. In TensorFlow.js, a layer or model object takes one or more inputs (so far, you've only seen cases of one input), and those are represented as one or more symbolic tensors.

Let's use an analogy that might help you understand a symbolic tensor. Consider a function in a programming language like Java or TypeScript (or any other statically typed language you are familiar with). The function takes one or more input arguments. Each argument of a function has a type, which stipulates what kind of variables may be passed in as the argument. However, the argument *itself* doesn't hold any concrete values. By itself, the argument is just a placeholder. A symbolic tensor is analogous to a function argument: it specifies what kind (combination of shape[6] and dtype) of tensors may be used in that slot. By parallel, a function in a statically typed language has a return type. This is comparable to the output symbolic tensor of a model or layer object. It is a "blueprint" for the shape and dtype of the actual tensor values that the model or layer object will output.

In TensorFlow.js, two important attributes of a model object are its inputs and outputs. Each of these is an array of symbolic tensors. For a model with exactly one input and exactly one output, both arrays have a length of 1. Similarly, a layer object has two attributes: input and output, each of which is a symbolic tensor. Symbolic tensors can be used to create a new model. This is a new way of creating models in TensorFlow.js, which is different from the approach you've seen before: namely, creating sequential models with `tf.sequential()` and subsequent calls to the `add()` method. In the new approach, we use the `tf.model()` function, which takes a configuration object with two mandatory fields: `inputs` and `outputs`. The `inputs` field is required to be a symbolic tensor (or, alternatively, an array of symbolic tensors), and likewise for the `outputs` field. Therefore, we can obtain the symbolic tensors from the original MobileNet model and feed them to a `tf.model()` call. The result is a new model that consists of a part of the original MobileNet.

This process is illustrated schematically in figure 5.7. (Note that the figure reduces the number of layers from the actual MobileNet model for the sake of a simple-looking diagram.) The important thing to realize is that the symbolic tensors taken from the original model and handed to the `tf.model()` call are *not* isolated objects. Instead, they carry information about what layers they belong to and how the layers are connected to each other. For readers familiar with graphs in data structure, the original model is a graph of symbolic tensors, with the connecting edges being the layers. By specifying the inputs and outputs of the new model as symbolic tensors in the original model, we are extracting a subgraph of the original MobileNet graph. The subgraph, which becomes the new model, contains the first few (in particular, the first 87) layers of MobileNet, while the last 6 layers are left out. The last few layers of a deep convnet are sometimes referred to as the *head*. What we are doing with the `tf.model()` call can be referred to as *truncating* the model. The truncated MobileNet preserves the feature-extracting layers while discarding the head. Why does the head contain *six* layers? This is because those layers are specific to the 1,000-class classification task that the MobileNet was originally trained on. The layers are not useful for the four-class classification task we are facing.

---

[6] A difference between a tensor's shape and a symbolic tensor's shape is that the former always has fully specified dimensions (such as `[8, 32, 20]`), while the latter may have undetermined dimensions (such as `[null, null, 20]`). You have already seen this in the "Output shape" column of the model summaries.

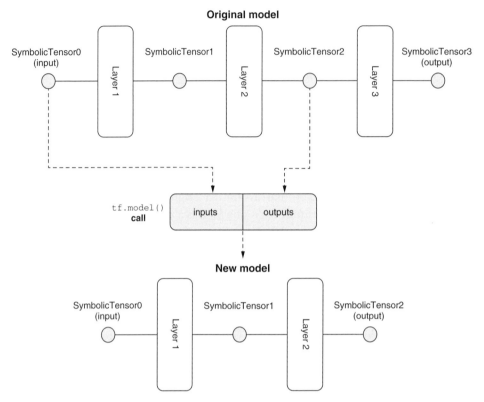

Figure 5.7 A schematic drawing that explains how the new ("truncated") model is created from MobileNet. See the `tf.model()` call in listing 5.3 for the corresponding code. Each layer has an input and an output, both of which are `SymbolicTensor` instances. In the original model, SymbolicTensor0 is the input of the first layer and the input of the entire model. It is used as the input symbolic tensor of the new model. In addition, we take the output symbolic tensor of an intermediate layer (equivalent to `conv_pw_13_relu`) as the output tensor of the new model. Hence, we get a model that consists of the first two layers of the original model, shown in the bottom part of the diagram. The last layer of the original model, which is the output layer and sometimes referred to as the model's head, is discarded. This is why approaches like this are sometimes referred to as *truncating* a model. Note that this diagram depicts models with small numbers of layers for the sake of clarity. What actually happens with the code in listing 5.3 involves a model with many more (93) layers compared to the one shown in this diagram.

Transfer learning based on embeddings

The output of the truncated MobileNet is the activation of an intermediate layer of the original MobileNet.[7] But how is intermediate-layer activation from MobileNet useful to us? The answer can be seen in the function that handles the events of clicking and holding each of the four black squares (listing 5.4.) Every time an input image is available from the webcam (via the `capture()` method), we call the `predict()` method of

---

[7] A frequently asked question about TensorFlow.js models is how to obtain the activations of intermediate layers. The approach we showed here is the answer.

the truncated MobileNet and save the output in an object called `controllerDataset`, which will be used for transfer learning later.

But how to interpret the output of the truncated MobileNet? For every image input, it is a tensor of shape [1, 7, 7, 256]. It is not the probabilities for any classification problem, nor is it the values predicted for any regression problem. It is a representation of the input image in a certain high-dimensional space. This space has 7 * 7 * 256, or approximately 12.5k, dimensions. Although the space has a lot of dimensions, it is lower-dimensional compared to the original image, which, due to the 224 × 224 image dimensions and three color channels, has 224 * 224 * 3 ≈ 150k dimensions. So, the output from the truncated MobileNet can be viewed as an efficient representation of the image. This kind of lower-dimension representation of inputs is often referred to as an *embedding*. Our transfer learning will be based on the embeddings of the four sets of images collected from the webcam.

Listing 5.4   Obtaining image embeddings using a truncated MobileNet

```
ui.setExampleHandler(label => {
  tf.tidy(() => {                          ◁──────────    Uses tf.tidy() to clean up
    const img = webcam.capture();                         intermediate tensors such as img.
    controllerDataset.addExample(                         See appendix B, section B.3 for a
      truncatedMobileNet.predict(img),  ◁────────         tutorial on TensorFlow.js memory
      label);                                             management in the browser.

    ui.drawThumb(img, label);
  });                                                     Gets MobileNet's internal
});                                                       activation for the input image
```

Now that we have a way to get the embeddings of the webcam images, how do we use them to predict what direction a given image corresponds to? For this, we need a new model, one that takes the embedding as its input and outputs the probability values for the four direction classes. The code in the following listing (from index.js) creates such a model.

Listing 5.5   Predicting controller direction using image embeddings

```
model = tf.sequential({
  layers: [
    tf.layers.flatten({
      inputShape: truncatedMobileNet.outputs[0].shape.slice(1)
    }),
    tf.layers.dense({
      units: ui.getDenseUnits(),
      activation: 'relu',
      kernelInitializer: 'varianceScaling',
      useBias: true
    }),
    tf.layers.dense({
      units: NUM_CLASSES,
      kernelInitializer: 'varianceScaling',
      useBias: false,
```

A first (hidden) dense layer with nonlinear (relu) activation

Flattens the [7, 7, 256] embedding from the truncated MobileNet. The slice(1) operation discards the first (batch) dimension, which is present in the output shape but unwanted by the inputShape attribute of the layer's factory method, so it can be used with a dense layer.

The number of units of the last layer should correspond to the number of classes we want to predict.

```
    activation: 'softmax'
  })
 ]
});
```

The number of units of the last layer should correspond to the number of classes we want to predict.

Compared to the truncated MobileNet, the new model created in listing 5.5 has a much smaller size. It consists of only three layers:

- The input layer is a flatten layer. It transforms the 3D embedding from the truncated model into a 1D tensor that subsequent dense layers can take. We have seen similar uses of flatten layers in the MNIST convnets in chapter 4. We let its `inputShape` match the output shape of the truncated MobileNet (without the batch dimension) because the new model will be fed embeddings that come out of the truncated MobileNet.

- The second layer is a hidden layer. It is hidden because it is neither the input layer nor the output layer of the model. Instead, it is sandwiched between two other layers in order to enhance the model's capacity. This is very similar to the MLPs you encountered in chapter 3. It is a hidden dense layer with a relu activation. Recall that in the chapter 3 section "Avoiding the fallacy of stacking layers without nonlinearity," we discussed the importance of using a nonlinear activation for hidden layers like this.

- The third layer is the final (output) layer of the new model. It has a softmax activation that suits the multiclass classification problem we are facing (that is, four classes: one for each Pac-Man direction).

Therefore, we have essentially built an MLP on top of MobileNet's feature-extraction layers. The MLP can be thought of as a new head for MobileNet, even though the feature extractor (the truncated MobileNet) and the head are two separate models in this case (see figure 5.8). As a result of the two-model setup, it is not possible to train the new head directly using the image tensors (of the shape [numExamples, 224, 224, 3]). Instead, the new head must be trained on the embeddings of the images—the output of the truncated MobileNet. Luckily, we have already collected those embedding tensors (listing 5.4). All we need to do to train the new head is call its `fit()` method on the embedding tensors. The code that does that inside the `train()` function in index.js is straightforward, and we won't elaborate on that further.

Once the transfer learning has finished, the truncated model and the new head will be used together to obtain probability scores from input images from the webcam. You can find the code in the `predict()` function in index.js, shown in listing 5.6. In particular, two `predict()` calls are involved. The first call converts the image tensor into its embedding using the truncated MobileNet; the second one converts the embedding into the probability scores for the four directions using the new head trained with transfer learning. Subsequent code in listing 5.6 obtains the winning index (the index that corresponds to the maximum probability score among the four directions) and uses it to steer the Pac-Man and update UI states. As in the previous

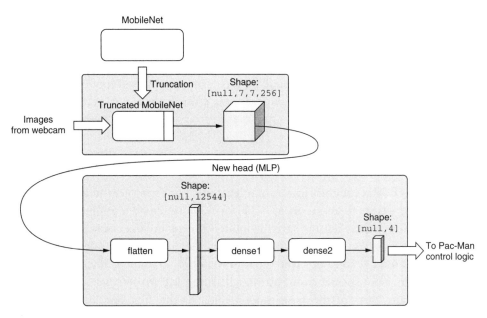

Figure 5.8   A schematic of the transfer-learning algorithm that underlies the webcam-transfer-learning example

examples, we don't cover the UI part of the example because it is not central to the machine-learning algorithms. You may study and play with the UI code at your own pleasure using the code in the next listing.

Listing 5.6   Getting the prediction from a webcam input image after transfer learning

```
async function predict() {
  ui.isPredicting();
  while (isPredicting) {
    const predictedClass = tf.tidy(() => {
      const img = webcam.capture();              ◄─── Captures a frame from the webcam

      const embedding = truncatedMobileNet.predict(
          img);                                  Gets the embedding from the truncatedMobileNet
      const predictions = model.predict(activation);  ◄─── Converts the embedding into the probability scores of the four directions using the new head model
      return predictions.as1D().argMax();        ◄─── Gets the index of the maximum probability score
    });

    const classId = (await predictedClass.data())[0];  ◄─── Downloads the index from GPU to CPU
    predictedClass.dispose();
    ui.predictClass(classId);  ◄───
    await tf.nextFrame();              Updates the UI according to the
  }                                    winning direction: steers the Pac-Man
  ui.donePredicting();                 and updates other UI states, such as
}                                      the highlighting of the corresponding
                                       "button" on the controller
```

This concludes our discussion of the part of the webcam-transfer-learning example relevant to the transfer-learning algorithm. One interesting aspect of the method we used in this example is that the training and inference process involves two separate model objects. This is good for our educational purpose of illustrating how to get embeddings from the intermediate layers of a pretrained model. Another advantage of this approach is that it exposes the embeddings and makes it easier to apply machine-learning techniques that make direct use of these embeddings. An example of such techniques is *k-nearest neighbors* (kNN, discussed in info box 5.2). However, exposing the embeddings directly may also be viewed as a shortcoming for the following reasons:

- It leads to slightly more complex code. For example, the inference requires two `predict()` calls in order to perform inference on a single image.
- Suppose we want to save the models for use in later sessions or for conversion to a non-TensorFlow.js library. Then the truncated model and the new head model need to be saved separately, as two separate artifacts.
- In some special cases, transfer learning will involve backpropagation over certain parts of the base model (such as the first few layers of the truncated MobileNet). This is not possible when the base and the head are two separate objects.

In the next section, we will show a way to overcome these limitations by forming a single model object for transfer learning. It will be an end-to-end model in the sense that it can transform input data in the original format into the final desired output.

INFO BOX 5.2   k-nearest neighbors classification based on embeddings

There are non-neural network approaches to solving classification problems in machine learning. One of the most famous is the k-nearest neighbors (kNN) algorithm. Unlike neural networks, the kNN algorithm doesn't involve a training step and is easier to understand.

We can describe how the kNN classification works in a few sentences:

1 You pick a positive integer k (for instance, 3).
2 You collect a number of reference examples, each labeled with the true class. Usually the number of reference examples collected is at least several times larger than k. Each example is represented as a series of real-valued numbers, or a *vector*. This step is similar to the collection of training examples in the neural network approach.
3 In order to predict the class of a new input, you compute the distances between the vector representation of the new input and those of all the reference examples. You then sort the distances. By doing so, you can find the k reference examples that are the closest to the input in the vector space. These are called the "k nearest neighbors" of the input (the namesake of the algorithm).

4 You look at the classes of the k nearest neighbors and use the most common class among them as the prediction for the input. In other words, you let the k nearest neighbors "vote" on the predicted class.

An example of this algorithm is shown in the following figure.

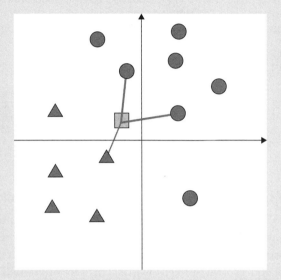

An example of kNN classification in a 2D embedding space. In this case, $k = 3$, and there are two classes (triangles and circles). There are five reference examples for the triangle class and seven for the circle class. The input example is represented as a square. The three nearest neighbors to the input are indicated by the line segments that connect them with the input. Because two of the three nearest neighbors are circles, the predicted class for the input example will be a circle.

As you can see from the previous description, one of the key requirements of the kNN algorithm is that every input example is represented as a vector. Embeddings like the one we obtained from the truncated MobileNet are good candidates for such vector representations for two reasons. First, they often have a lower dimensionality compared to the original inputs and hence reduce the amount of storage and computation required by the distance calculation. Second, the embeddings usually capture more important features in the input (such as important geometric features in images; see figure 4.5) and ignore less important ones (for example, brightness and size) owing to the fact that they have been trained on a large classification dataset. In some cases, embeddings give us vector representations for things that are not even originally represented as numbers (such as the word embeddings in chapter 9).

Compared to the neural network approach, kNN doesn't require any training. In cases where the number of reference examples is not too large, and the dimensionality of the input is not too high, using kNN can be computationally more efficient than training a neural network and running it for inference.

(continued)
However, kNN inference doesn't scale well with the amount of data. In particular, given N reference examples, a kNN classifier must compute N distances in order to make a prediction for every input.[a] When N gets large, the amount of computation can get intractable. By contrast, the inference with a neural network doesn't change with the amount of training data. Once the network has been trained, it doesn't matter how many examples went into the training. The amount of computation that the forward pass on the network takes is only a function of the network's topology.

If you are interested in using kNN for your applications, check out the WebGL-accelerated kNN library built on top of TensorFlow.js: http://mng.bz/2Jp8.

[a] But see research efforts to design algorithms that approximate the kNN algorithm but run faster and scale better than kNN: Gal Yona, "Fast Near-Duplicate Image Search Using Locality Sensitive Hashing," Towards Data Science, 5 May 2018, http://mng.bz/1wm1.

5.1.3   *Getting the most out of transfer learning through fine-tuning: An audio example*

In the previous sections, the examples of transfer learning dealt with visual inputs. In this example, we will show that transfer learning works on audio data represented as spectrogram images as well. Recall that we introduced the convnet for recognizing speech commands (isolated, short spoken words) in section 4.4. The speech-command recognizer we built was capable of recognizing only 18 different words (such as "one," "two," "up," and "down"). What if you want to train a recognizer for other words? Perhaps your particular application requires the user to say specific words such as "red" or "blue," or even words that are picked by the users themselves; or perhaps your application is intended for users who speak languages other than English. This is a classic example of transfer learning: with the small amount of data at hand, you *could* try to train a model entirely from scratch, but using a pretrained model as the base allows you to spend a smaller amount of time and computation resources while getting a higher degree of accuracy.

HOW TO DO TRANSFER LEARNING IN THE SPEECH-COMMAND EXAMPLE APP

Before we describe how transfer learning works in this example, it will be good for you to get familiar with how to use the transfer-learning feature through the UI. To use the UI, make sure your machine has an audio-input device (a microphone) attached and that the audio-input volume is set to a nonzero value in your system settings. To download the code of the demo and run it, do the following (the same procedure as in section 4.4.1):

```
git clone https://github.com/tensorflow/tfjs-models.git
cd tfjs-models/speech-commands
yarn && yarn publish-local
```

```
cd demo
yarn && yarn link-local && yarn watch
```

When the UI starts up, answer Yes to the browser's request for your permission to access the microphone. Figure 5.9 shows an example screenshot of the demo. When it starts up, the demo page will automatically load a pretrained speech-commands model from the internet, using the `tf.loadLayersModel()` method pointing to an HTTPS URL. After the model is loaded, the Start and Enter Transfer Words buttons will be enabled. If you click the Start button, the demo will enter an inference mode in which it detects the 18 basic words (as displayed on the screen) in a continuous fashion. Each time a word is detected, the corresponding word box will light up on the screen. However, if you click the Enter Transfer Words button, a number of additional buttons will appear on the screen. These buttons are created from the comma-separated words in the text-input box to the right. The default words are "noise," "red," and "green." These are the words that the transfer-learning model will be trained to recognize. But you are free to modify the content of the input box if you want to train a transfer model for other words, as long as you preserve the "noise" item. The "noise" item is a special one, for which you should collect background noise samples—that is, samples without any speech sound in them. This allows the transfer model to tell moments in which a word is spoken from moments of silence (background noise). When you click these buttons, the demo will record a 1-second audio snippet from the microphone and display its spectrogram next to the button. The

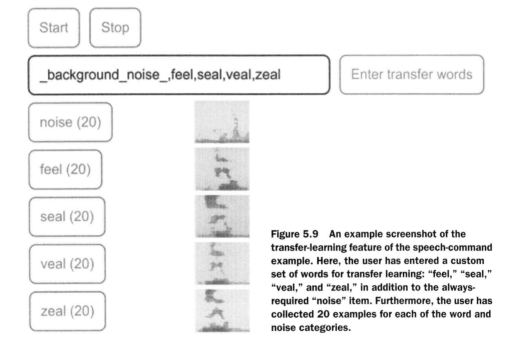

Figure 5.9   An example screenshot of the transfer-learning feature of the speech-command example. Here, the user has entered a custom set of words for transfer learning: "feel," "seal," "veal," and "zeal," in addition to the always-required "noise" item. Furthermore, the user has collected 20 examples for each of the word and noise categories.

number in the word button keeps track of how many examples you have collected for the particular word so far.

As is the general case in machine-learning problems, the more data you can collect (as permitted by the time and resources available), the better the trained model will turn out. The example app requires at least eight examples for every word. If you don't want to or cannot collect sound samples yourself, you can download a precollected dataset from http://mng.bz/POGY (file size: 9 MB) and upload it by using the Upload button in the Dataset IO section of the UI.

Once the dataset is ready, through either file uploading or your own sample collection, the Start Transfer Learning button will become enabled. You can click the button to kick off the training of the transfer model. The app performs a 3:1 split on the audio spectrograms you have collected so that a randomly selected 75% of them will be used for training, while the remaining 25% will be used for validation.[8] The app displays the training-set loss and accuracy values along with the validation-set values as the transfer learning happens. Once the training is complete, you can click the Start button to let the demo start a continuous recognition of the transfer words, during which time you can assess the accuracy of the transfer model empirically.

You should experiment with different sets of words and see how they affect the accuracy you can get after doing transfer learning on them. In the default set, "red" and "green," the words are fairly distinct from each other in terms of their phonemic content. For example, their onset consonants are two very distinct sounds, "r" and "g." Their vowels also sound fairly distinct ("e" versus "ee"); so do their ending consonants ("d" versus "n"). Therefore, you should be able to get near-perfect validation accuracy at the end of the transfer training, as long as the number of examples you collect for each word is not too small (say >= 8), and you don't use an epoch number that's too small (which leads to underfitting) or too large (which leads to overfitting; see chapter 8).

To make the transfer-learning task more challenging for the model, use a set consisting of 1) more confusable words and 2) a larger vocabulary. This is what we did for the screenshot in figure 5.9. There, a set of four words that sound similar to each other are used: "feel," "seal," "veal," and "zeal." These words have identical vowel and ending consonants, as well as four similar-sounding onset consonants. They might even confuse a human listener not paying attention or someone listening over a bad phone line. From the accuracy curve at the bottom-right part of the figure, you can see that it is not an easy task for the model to reach an accuracy higher than 90%, for which an initial phase of transfer learning has to be supplemented by an additional phase of *fine-tuning*—that is, a transfer-learning trick.

---

[8] This is the reason why the demo requires you to collect at least eight samples per word. With fewer words, the number of samples for each word will be small in the validation set, leading to potentially unreliable loss and accuracy estimates.

DEEP DIVE INTO FINE-TUNING IN TRANSFER LEARNING

Fine-tuning is a technique that helps you reach levels of accuracy not achievable just by training the new head of the transfer model. If you wish to understand how fine-tuning works, this section explains it in greater detail. There will be a few technical points to digest. But the deepened understanding of transfer learning and the related TensorFlow.js implementation that you'll get out of it will be worth the effort.

Constructing a single model for transfer learning

First, we need to understand how the speech transfer-learning app creates the model for transfer learning. The code in listing 5.7 (from speech-commands/src/browser_fft_recognizer.ts) creates a model from the base speech-command model (the one you learned in section 4.4.1). It first finds the penultimate (the second-last) dense layer of the model and gets its output symbolic tensor (truncatedBaseOutput in the code). It then creates a new head model consisting of only one dense layer. The input shape of this new head matches the shape of the truncatedBaseOutput symbolic tensor, and its output shape matches the number of words in the transfer dataset (five, in the case of figure 5.9). The dense layer is configured to use the softmax activation, which suits the multiclass-classification task. (Note that unlike most of the other code listings in the book, the following code is written in TypeScript. If you're unfamiliar with TypeScript, you can simply ignore the type notations such as void and tf.SymbolicTensor.)

> **Listing 5.7   Creating the transfer-learning model as a single tf.Model object[9]**

```
private createTransferModelFromBaseModel(): void {
  const layers = this.baseModel.layers;
  let layerIndex = layers.length - 2;
  while (layerIndex >= 0) {
    if (layers[layerIndex].getClassName().toLowerCase() === 'dense') {
      break;
    }
    layerIndex--;
  }
  if (layerIndex < 0) {
    throw new Error('Cannot find a hidden dense layer in the base model.');
  }
  this.secondLastBaseDenseLayer =
      layers[layerIndex];
  const truncatedBaseOutput = layers[layerIndex].output as
    tf.SymbolicTensor;

  this.transferHead = tf.layers.dense({
    units: this.words.length,
    activation: 'softmax',
```

Finds the second-last dense layer of the base model

Gets the layer that will be unfrozen during fine-tuning later (see listing 5.8)

Finds the symbolic tensor

Creates the new head of the model

---

[9] Two notes about this code listing: 1) The code is written in TypeScript because it is a part of the reusable @tensorflow-models/speech-commands library. 2) Some error-checking code has been removed from this code for the sake of simplicity.

```
    inputShape: truncatedBaseOutput.shape.slice(1)          Creates the new head
  }));                                                       of the model
  const transferOutput =
      this.transferHead.apply(truncatedBaseOutput) as tf.SymbolicTensor;
  this.model =
      tf.model({inputs: this.baseModel.inputs, outputs: transferOutput});
}
```

"Applies" the new head on the output of the truncated base model's output to get the final output of the new model as a symbolic tensor

Uses the tf.model() API to create a new model for transfer learning, specifying the original model's inputs as its input and the new symbolic tensor as the output

The new head is used in a novel way: its `apply()` method is called using the `truncatedBaseOutput` symbolic tensor as the input argument. `apply()` is a method that's available on every layer and model object in TensorFlow.js. What does the `apply()` method do? As its name suggests, it "applies" the new head model on an input and gives you an output. The important things to realize are as follows:

- Both the input and output involved here are symbolic—they are placeholders for concrete tensor values.
- Figure 5.10 shows a graphical illustration of this: the symbolic input (`truncated-BaseOutput`) is not an isolated entity; instead, it is the output of the second-last dense layer of the base model. The dense layer receives inputs from another layer, which in turn receives inputs from its upstream layer, and so forth. Therefore, `truncatedBaseOutput` carries with it a subgraph of the base model: namely, the subgraph between the base model's input and the second-last dense layer's output. In other words, it is the entire graph of the base model, minus the part after the second-last dense layer. As a result, the output of the `apply()` call carries a graph consisting of that subgraph plus the new dense layer. The output and the original input are used together in a call to the `tf.model()` function, which yields a new model. This new model is the same as the base model except that its head has been replaced with the new dense layer (see the bottom part of figure 5.10).

Note that the approach here is different from how we fused models in section 5.1.2. There, we created a truncated base and a new head model as two separate model instances. As a result, running inference on each input example involves two `predict()` calls. Here, the inputs expected by the new model are identical to the audio-spectrogram tensors expected by the base model. At the same time, the new model directly outputs the probability scores for the new words. Every inference takes only one `predict()` call and is therefore a more streamlined process. By encapsulating all the layers in a single model, our new approach has an additional advantage important for our application: it allows us to perform backpropagation through any of the layers involved in recognizing the new words. This enables us to perform the fine-tuning trick. This is what we will explore in the next section.

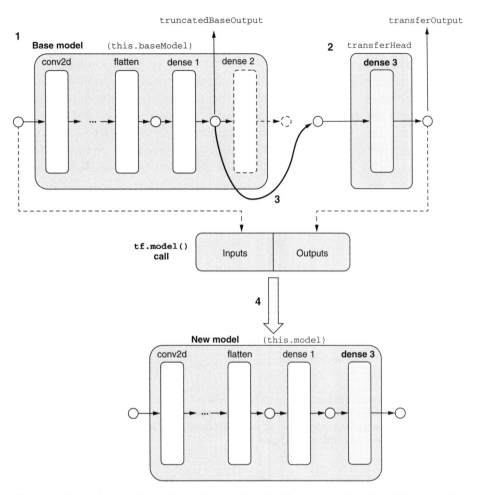

Figure 5.10 A schematic illustration of the way in which the new, end-to-end model is created for transfer learning. This figure should be read in conjunction with listing 5.7. Some parts of the figure that correspond to variables in listing 5.7 are labeled in fixed-width font. Step 1: the output symbolic tensor of the second-to-last dense layer of the original model is obtained (indicated by the thick arrow). It will later be used in step 3. Step 2: the new head model, consisting of a single output dense layer (labeled "dense 3") is created. Step 3: the `apply()` method of the new head model is invoked with the symbolic tensor from step 1 as the input argument. The call connects the input to the new head model with the truncated base model from step 1. Step 4: the return value of the `apply()` call is used in conjunction with the input symbolic tensor of the original model during a call to the `tf.model()` function. This call returns a new model that contains all the layers of the original model from the first layer to the second-last dense layer, in addition to the dense layer in the new head. In effect, this swaps the old head of the original model with the new head, setting the stage for subsequent training on the transfer data. Note that some (seven) layers of the actual speech-command model are omitted in this diagram for the sake of visual simplicity. In this figure, the tinted layers are trainable, while the white-colored layers are untrainable.

Fine-tuning through layer unfreezing

Fine-tuning is an optional step of transfer learning that follows an initial phase of model training. In the initial phase, all the layers from the base model were frozen (their `trainable` attribute was set to `false`), and weight updating happened only to the head layers. We have seen this type of initial training in the mnist-transfer-cnn and webcam-transfer-learning examples earlier in this chapter. During fine-tuning, some of the layers of the base model are unfrozen (their `trainable` attribute is set to `true`), and then the model is trained on the transfer data again. This layer unfreezing is shown schematically in figure 5.11. The code in listing 5.8 (from speech-commands/ src/browser_fft_recognizer.ts) shows how that's done in TensorFlow.js for the speech-command example.

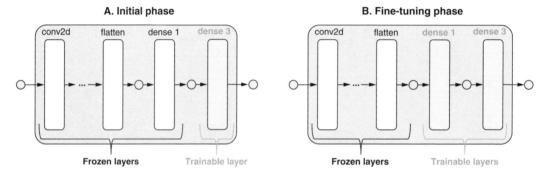

Figure 5.11 Illustrating frozen and unfrozen (that is, trainable) layers during the initial (panel A) and fine-tuning (panel B) phases of the transfer learning as done by the code in listing 5.8. Note that the reason dense1 is followed immediately by dense3 is that dense2 (the original output of the base model) has been truncated as the first step of the transfer learning (see figure 5.10).

Listing 5.8   Initial transfer learning, followed by fine-tuning[10]

```
async train(config?: TransferLearnConfig):
    Promise<tf.History|[tf.History, tf.History]> {
  if (config == null) {
    config = {};
  }
  if (this.model == null) {
    this.createTransferModelFromBaseModel();
  }

  this.secondLastBaseDenseLayer.trainable = false;
  this.model.compile({
    loss: 'categoricalCrossentropy',
    optimizer: config.optimizer || 'sgd',
    metrics: ['acc']
  });
```

> Makes sure all layers of the truncated base model, including the one that will be fine-tuned later, are frozen for the initial phase of transfer training

> Compiles the model for the initial transfer training

---

[10] Some error-checking code has been removed so as to focus on the key parts of the algorithm.

```
                    const {xs, ys} = this.collectTransferDataAsTensors();
                    let trainXs: tf.Tensor;
                    let trainYs: tf.Tensor;
                    let valData: [tf.Tensor, tf.Tensor];
                    try {
                      if (config.validationSplit != null) {
                        const splits = balancedTrainValSplit(
                            xs, ys, config.validationSplit);
                        trainXs = splits.trainXs;
                        trainYs = splits.trainYs;
                        valData = [splits.valXs, splits.valYs];
                      } else {
                        trainXs = xs;
                        trainYs = ys;
                      }
```

> **If validationSplit is required, splits the transfer data into a training set and a validation set in a balanced way**

```
                    const history = await this.model.fit(trainXs, trainYs, {
                      epochs: config.epochs == null ? 20 : config.epochs,
                      validationData: valData,
                      batchSize: config.batchSize,
                      callbacks: config.callback == null ? null : [config.callback]
                    });
```

> **Calls Model.fit() for initial transfer training**

```
                    if (config.fineTuningEpochs != null && config.fineTuningEpochs > 0) {
                      this.secondLastBaseDenseLayer.trainable =
                          true;
                      const fineTuningOptimizer: string|tf.Optimizer =
                          config.fineTuningOptimizer == null ? 'sgd' :
                                                        config.fineTuningOptimizer;
                    this.model.compile({
                      loss: 'categoricalCrossentropy',
                      optimizer: fineTuningOptimizer,
                      metrics: ['acc']
                    });
```

> **For fine-tuning, unfreezes the second-last dense layer of the base model (the last layer of the truncated base model)**

> **Recompiles the model after unfreezing the layer (or the unfreezing won't take effect)**

```
                    const fineTuningHistory = await this.model.fit(trainXs, trainYs, {
                      epochs: config.fineTuningEpochs,
                      validationData: valData,
                      batchSize: config.batchSize,
                      callbacks: config.fineTuningCallback == null ?
                          null :
                          [config.fineTuningCallback]
                    });
                    return [history, fineTuningHistory];
                  } else {
                    return history;
                  }
                } finally {
                  tf.dispose([xs, ys, trainXs, trainYs, valData]);
                }
              }
```

> **Calls Model.fit() for fine-tuning**

There are several important things to point out about the code in listing 5.8:

- Each time you freeze or unfreeze any layers by changing their `trainable` attribute, you need to call the `compile()` method of the model again in order for the change to take effect. We've already covered that when talking about the MNIST transfer-learning example in section 5.1.1.

- We reserve a fraction of the training data for validation. This ensures that the loss and accuracy we look at reflect how well the model works on inputs it hasn't seen during backpropagation. However, the way in which we split a fraction of the collected data out for validation is different from before and deserves some attention.

    In the MNIST convnet example (listing 4.2 in chapter 4), we used the `validationSplit` parameter to let the `Model.fit()` reserve the last 15–20% of the data for validation. The same approach won't work very well here. Why? Because we have a much smaller training set here compared to the size of the data in the earlier examples. As a result, blindly splitting the last several examples for validation may very well result in scenarios in which some words are underrepresented in the validation subset. For example, suppose you have collected eight examples for each of the four words "feel," "seal," "veal," and "zeal" and choose the last 25% of the 32 samples (8 examples) for validation. Then, on average, there will be only two examples for each word in the validation subset. Due to randomness, some of the words may end up having only one example in the validation subset, and others may have no example there at all! Obviously, if the validation set lacks certain words, it won't be a very good set to measure the model's accuracy on. This is why we use a custom function (`balancedTrainValSplit` in listing 5.8). This function takes into account the true word label of the examples and ensures that all the different words get fair representation in both the training and validation subsets. If you have a transfer-learning application involving a similarly small dataset, it is a good idea to do the same.

So, what does fine-tuning do for us? What added value does it provide on top of the initial phase of transfer learning? To illustrate that, we plot the loss and accuracy curves from the initial and fine-tuning phases concatenated as continuous curves in panel A of figure 5.12. The transfer dataset involved here consists of the same four words we saw in figure 5.9. The first 100 epochs of each curve correspond to the initial phase, while the last 300 epochs correspond to fine-tuning. You can see that toward the end of the 100 epochs of initial training, the loss and accuracy curves begin to flatten out and start to enter regimes of diminishing returns. The accuracy on the validation subset levels off around 84%. (Notice how misleading it would be to look at only the accuracy curve from the *training subset*, which easily approaches 100%.) However, unfreezing the dense layer in the base model, recompiling the model, and starting the fine-tuning phase of training, the validation accuracy gets unstuck and could go up to 90–92%, which is a very decent 6–8 percentage point gain in accuracy. A similar effect can be seen in the validation loss curve.

To illustrate the value of fine-tuning over transfer learning without fine-tuning, we show in panel B of figure 5.12 what happens if the transfer model is trained for an

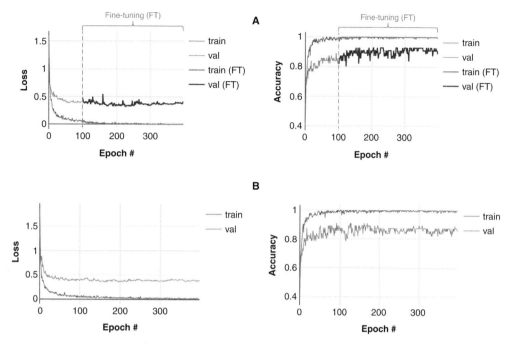

Figure 5.12   Panel A: example loss and accuracy curves from transfer learning and the subsequent fine-tuning (FT in the plot legends). Notice the inflection point at the junction between the initial and fine-tuning parts of the curves. Fine-tuning accelerates the reduction in the loss and gain in the accuracy, which is due to the unfreezing of the top few layers of the base model and the resulting increase in the model's capacity, and its adaptation toward the unique features in the transfer-learning data. Panel B: the loss and accuracy curves from training the transfer model an equal number of epochs (400 epochs) without fine-tuning. Notice that without the fine-tuning, the validation loss converges to a higher value and the validation accuracy to a lower value compared to panel A. Note that while the final accuracy reaches about 0.9 with fine-tuning (panel A), it gets stuck at about 0.85 without the fine-tuning but with the same number of total epochs (panel B).

equal number of (400) epochs without fine-tuning the top few layers of the base model. There is no "inflection point" in the loss or accuracy curves that happened in panel A at epoch 100 when the fine-tuning kicks in. Instead, the loss and accuracy curves level off and converge to worse values.

So why does fine-tuning help? It can be understood as an increase in the model capacity. By unfreezing some of the topmost layers of the base model, we allow the transfer model to minimize the loss function in a higher-dimensional parameter space than the initial phase. This is similar to adding hidden layers to a neural network. The weight parameters of the unfrozen dense layer have been optimized for the original dataset (the one consisting of words like "one," "two," "yes," and "no"), which may not be optimal for the transfer words. This is because the internal representations that help the model distinguish between those original words may not be the representations that make the transfer words easiest to distinguish from one another. By allowing those parameters to be optimized further (that is, fine-tuned) for the transfer words, we allow the representation to be optimized for the transfer words. Therefore, we get a boost in validation accuracy on the transfer words. Note that this boost is easier to see when the transfer-learning task is hard (as with the four confusable words: "feel," "seal," "veal," and "zeal"). With easier tasks (more distinct words like "red" and "green"), the validation accuracy may well reach 100% with only the initial transfer learning.

One question you might want to ask is, here we unfreeze only one layer in the base model, but will unfreezing more layers help? The short answer is, it depends, because unfreezing even more layers gives the model even higher capacity. But as we mentioned in chapter 4 and will discuss in greater detail in chapter 8, higher capacity leads to a higher risk of overfitting, especially when we are faced with a small dataset like the audio examples collected in the browser here. This is not to mention the additional computation load required to train more layers. You are encouraged to experiment with it yourself as a part of exercise 4 at the end of this chapter.

Let's wrap up this section on transfer learning in TensorFlow.js. We introduced three different ways to reuse a pretrained model on new tasks. In order to help you decide which approach to use in your future transfer-learning projects, we summarize the three approaches and their relative pros and cons in table 5.1.

Table 5.1 A summary of three approaches to transfer learning in TensorFlow.js and their relative advantages and shortcomings

Approach	Pros	Cons
Use the original model and freeze its first several (feature-extracting) layers (section 5.1.1).	• Simple and convenient	• Works only if the output shape and activation required by the transfer learning match those of the base model
Obtain internal activations from the original model as embeddings for the input example, and create a new model that takes the embedding as the input (section 5.1.2).	• Applicable to transfer-learning cases that require an output shape different from the original one • Embedding tensors are directly accessible, making methods such as k-nearest neighbors (kNN, see info box 5.2) classifiers possible	• Need to manage two separate model instances • Difficult to fine-tune layers of the original model
Create a new model that contains the feature-extracting layers of the original model and the layers of the new head (section 5.1.3).	• Applicable to transfer-learning cases that require an output shape different from the original one • Only a single model instance to manage • Enables fine-tuning of feature-extracting layers	• Internal activations (embeddings) that are not directly accessible

5.2 *Object detection through transfer learning on a convnet*

The examples of transfer learning you have seen in this chapter so far have a commonality: the nature of the machine-learning task stays the same after the transfer. In particular, they take a computer-vision model trained on a multiclass-classification task and apply it on another multiclass-classification task. In this section, we will show that this doesn't have to be the case. The base model can be used on a task very different from the original one—for example, when you want to use a base model trained on a classification task to perform regression (fitting a number). This type of cross-domain transfer is a good example of the versatility and reusability of deep learning, which is one of the main reasons behind the success of the field.

The new task we will use to illustrate this point is *object detection*, the first nonclassification computer-vision problem type you encounter in this book. Object detection involves detecting certain classes of objects in an image. How is it different from classification? In object detection, the detected object is reported in terms of not only its class (what type of object it is) but also some additional information regarding the location of the object inside the image (where the object is). The latter is a piece of information that a mere classifier doesn't provide. For example, in a typical object-detection system used by self-driving cars, a frame of input image is analyzed so that the system outputs not only the types of interesting objects that are present in the image (such as vehicles and pedestrians) but also the location, apparent size, and pose of such objects within the image's coordinate system.

The example code is in the simple-object-detection directory of the tfjs-examples repository. Note that this example is different from the ones you have seen so far in that it combines model training in Node.js with inference in the browser. Specifically, the model training happens with tfjs-node (or tfjs-node-gpu), and the trained model is saved to disk. A parcel server is then used to serve the saved model files, along with the static index.html and index.js, in order to showcase the inference on the model in the browser.

The sequence of commands you can use for running the example is as follows (with some comment strings that you don't need to include when entering the commands):

```
git clone https://github.com/tensorflow/tfjs-examples.git
cd tfjs-examples/simple-object-detection
yarn
# Optional step for training your own model using Node.js:
yarn train \
    --numExamples 20000 \
    --initialTransferEpochs 100 \
    --fineTuningEpochs 200
yarn watch  # Run object-detection inference in the browser.
```

The yarn train command performs model training on your machine and saves the model inside the ./dist folder when it's finished. Note that this is a long-running training job and is best handled if you have a CUDA-enabled GPU, which boosts the training speed by a factor of 3 to 4. To do this, you just need to add the `--gpu` flag to the yarn train command:

```
yarn train --gpu \
    --numExamples 20000 \
    --initialTransferEpochs 100 \
    --fineTuningEpochs 200
```

However, if you don't have the time or resources to train the model on your own machine, don't worry: you can just skip the `yarn train` command and proceed directly to `yarn watch`. The inference page that runs in the browser will allow you to load a model we've already trained for you from a centralized location via HTTP.

5.2.1   *A simple object-detection problem based on synthesized scenes*

State-of-the-art object-detection techniques involve many tricks that are not suitable for a beginning tutorial on the topic. Our goal here is to show the essence of how object detection works without being bogged down by too many technical details. To this end, we designed a simple object-detection problem that involves synthesized image scenes (see figure 5.13). These synthesized images have a dimension of 224 × 224 and color depth of 3 (RGB channels) and hence match the input specification of the MobileNet model that will form the base of our model. As the example in figure 5.13 shows, each scene has a white background. The object to detect is either an equilateral triangle or a rectangle. If the object is a triangle, its size and orientation are random; if the object is a rectangle, its height and width vary randomly. If the scene consisted of only the white background and the object of interest, the task would be too easy to show the power of our technique. To add to the difficulty of the task, a number of "noise objects" are randomly sprinkled in the scene. These include 10 circles and 10 line segments in every image. The locations and sizes of the circles are generated randomly, and so are the locations and lengths of the line segments. Some of the noise objects may lie on top of the target object, partially obscuring it. All the target and noise objects have randomly generated colors.

With the input data fully characterized, we can now define the task for the model we are about to create and train. The model will output five numbers, which are organized into two groups:

- The first group contains a single number, indicating whether the detected object is a triangle or a rectangle (regardless of its location, size, orientation, and color).
- The remaining four numbers form the second group. They are the coordinates of the bounding box around the detected object. Specifically, they are the left x-coordinate, right x-coordinate, top y-coordinate, and bottom y-coordinate of the bounding box, respectively. See figure 5.13 for an example.

The nice things about using synthesized data are 1) the true label values are automatically known, and 2) we can generate as much data as we want. Every time we generate

A
B

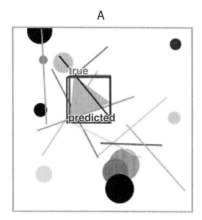
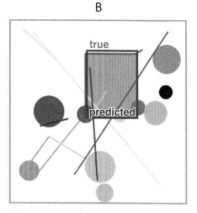

Inference time (ms): 36.7
True object class: **triangle**
Predicted object class: triangle

Inference time (ms): 26.0
True object class: **rectangle**
Predicted object class: rectangle

Figure 5.13 An example of the synthesized scenes used by simple object detection. Panel A: a rotated equilateral triangle as the target object. Panel B: a rectangle as the target object. The boxes labeled "true" are the true bounding box for the object of interest. Note that the object of interest can sometimes be partially obscured by some of the noise objects (line segments and circles).

a scene image, the type of the object and its bounding box are automatically available to us from the generation process. So, there is no need for any labor-intensive labeling of the training images. This very efficient process in which the input features and labels are synthesized together is used in many testing and prototyping environments for deep-learning models and is a technique you should be familiar with. However, training object-detection models meant for real-life image inputs requires manually labeled real scenes. Luckily, there are such labeled datasets available. The Common Object in Context (COCO) dataset is one of them (see http://cocodataset.org).

After the training completes, the model should be able to localize and classify the target objects with reasonably good accuracy (as shown by the examples in figure 5.13). To understand how the model learns this object-detection task, dive with us into the code in the next section.

5.2.2 *Deep dive into simple object detection*

Now let's build the neural network to solve the synthesized object-detection problem. As before, we build our model on the pretrained MobileNet model in order to use the powerful general visual feature extractor in the model's convolutional layers. This is what the `loadTruncatedBase()` method in listing 5.9 does. However, a new challenge our new model faces is how to predict two things at the same time: determining what shape the target object is and finding its coordinates in the image. We haven't seen this type of "dual-task prediction" before. The trick we use here is to let the model output a tensor that encapsulates both predictions, and we will design a new loss function that measures how well the model is doing in both tasks at once. We *could* train two separate models, one for classifying the shape and one for predicting the bounding box. But compared with using a single model to perform both tasks, running two models will involve more computation and more memory usage and doesn't leverage the fact that feature-extracting layers can be shared between the two tasks. (The following code is from simple-object-detection/train.js.)

Listing 5.9   Defining a model for simple object learning based on truncating MobileNet[11]

```
const topLayerGroupNames = [                          Sets what layers to
    'conv_pw_9', 'conv_pw_10', 'conv_pw_11'];         unfreeze for fine-tuning
const topLayerName =
    `${topLayerGroupNames[topLayerGroupNames.length - 1]}_relu`;

async function loadTruncatedBase() {
  const mobilenet = await tf.loadLayersModel(
      'https://storage.googleapis.com/' +
          'tfjs-models/tfjs/mobilenet_v1_0.25_224/model.json');

  const fineTuningLayers = [];
  const layer = mobilenet.getLayer(topLayerName);       Gets an intermediate
  const truncatedBase =                                 layer: the last feature-
      tf.model({                                        extraction layer
        inputs: mobilenet.inputs,
        outputs: layer.output
      });
  for (const layer of truncatedBase.layers) {
    layer.trainable = false;                            Freezes all feature-
    for (const groupName of topLayerGroupNames) {       extraction layers for
      if (layer.name.indexOf(groupName) === 0) {        the initial phase of
        fineTuningLayers.push(layer);                   transfer learning
        break;
      }                                                 Keeps track of layers
    }                                                   that will be unfrozen
  }                                                     during fine-tuning
  return {truncatedBase, fineTuningLayers};
}                                                       The length-5 output consists of a
                                                        length-1 shape indicator and a
function buildNewHead(inputShape) {                     length-4 bounding box (see figure 5.14).
  const newHead = tf.sequential();
  newHead.add(tf.layers.flatten({inputShape}));
  newHead.add(tf.layers.dense({units: 200, activation: 'relu'}));
  newHead.add(tf.layers.dense({units: 5}));
  return newHead;
}

async function buildObjectDetectionModel() {
  const {truncatedBase, fineTuningLayers} = await loadTruncatedBase();

  const newHead = buildNewHead(truncatedBase.outputs[0].shape.slice(1));
  const newOutput = newHead.apply(truncatedBase.outputs[0]);
  const model = tf.model({            Puts the new head model on top of the
                                      truncated MobileNet to form the
                                      entire model for object detection
```

Forms the truncated MobileNet

Builds the new head model for the simple object-detection task

---

[11] Some code for checking error conditions is removed for clarity.

```
        inputs: truncatedBase.inputs,
        outputs: newOutput
    });

    return {model, fineTuningLayers};
}
```

Puts the new head model on top of the truncated MobileNet to form the entire model for object detection

The key part of the "dual-task" model is built by the `buildNewHead()` method in listing 5.9. A schematic drawing of the model is shown in the left part of figure 5.14. The new head consists of three layers. A flatten layer shapes the output of the last convolutional layer of the truncated MobileNet base so that dense layers can be added later on. The first dense layer is a hidden one with a relu nonlinearity. The second dense layer is the final output of the head and hence the final output of the entire object-detection model. This layer has the default linear activation. It is the key to understanding how this model works and therefore needs to be looked at carefully.

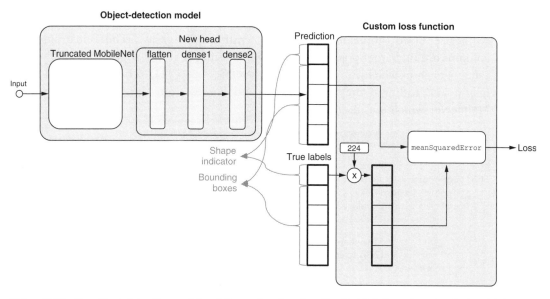

Figure 5.14 The object-detection model and the custom loss function that it is based on. See listing 5.9 for how the model (the left part) is constructed. See listing 5.10 for how the custom loss function is written.

As you can see from the code, the final dense layer has an output unit count of 5. What do the five numbers represent? They combine the shape prediction and the bounding-box prediction. Interestingly, what determines their meaning is not the model itself, but rather the loss function that will be used on it. Previously, you saw various types of loss functions that can be straightforward string names such as `"mean-SquaredError"` and are suitable to their respective machine-learning tasks (for example, see table 3.6 in chapter 3). However, this is only one of two ways to specify loss functions in TensorFlow.js. The other way, which is what we are using here, involves defining a custom JavaScript function that satisfies a certain signature. The signature is as follows:

- Two input arguments: 1) the true labels of the input examples and 2) the corresponding predictions of the model. Each of them is represented as a 2D tensor. The shape of the two tensors ought to be identical, with the first dimension of each tensor being the batch size.
- The return value is a scalar tensor (a tensor of shape `[]`) whose value is the mean loss of the examples in the batch.

Our custom loss function, written according to this signature, is shown in listing 5.10 and graphically illustrated in the right part of figure 5.14. The first input to `custom-LossFunction` (`yTrue`) is the true label tensor, which has a shape of `[batchSize, 5]`. The second input (`yPred`) is the model's output prediction, with exactly the same shape as `yTrue`. Of the five dimensions along the second axis of `yTrue` (the five columns, if we view it as a matrix), the first one is a 0–1 indicator for the shape of the target object (0 for triangle and 1 for rectangle). This is determined by how the data is synthesized (see simple-object-detection/synthetic_images.js). The remaining four columns are the target object's bounding box—that is, its left, right, top, and bottom values—each of which ranges from 0 to `CANVAS_SIZE` (224). The number 224 is the height and width of the input images and comes from the input image size to MobileNet, which our model is based on.

> **Listing 5.10   Defining the custom loss function for the object-detection task**

```
const labelMultiplier = tf.tensor1d([CANVAS_SIZE, 1, 1, 1, 1]);
function customLossFunction(yTrue, yPred) {
  return tf.tidy(() => {
    return tf.metrics.meanSquaredError(
        yTrue.mul(labelMultiplier), yPred);      ⟵
  });
}
```

The shape-indicator column of yTrue is scaled by CANVAS_SIZE (224) to ensure approximately equal contribution to the loss by shape prediction and bounding-box prediction.

The custom loss function takes `yTrue` and scales its first column (the 0–1 shape indicator) by `CANVAS_SIZE`, while leaving the other columns unchanged. It then calculates the MSE between `yPred` and the scaled `yTrue`. Why do we scale the 0–1 shape label in `yTrue`? We want the model to output a number that represents whether it predicts the shape to be a triangle or a rectangle. Specifically, it outputs a number close to 0 for triangle and a number close to `CANVAS_SIZE` (224) for rectangle. So, during inference time, we can just compare the first value in the model's output with `CANVAS_SIZE/2` (112) to get the model's prediction of whether the shape is more like a triangle or a rectangle. The question is then how to measure the accuracy of this shape prediction in order to come up with a loss function. Our answer is to compute the difference between this number and the 0–1 indicator, multiplied by `CANVAS_SIZE`.

Why do we do this instead of using binary cross entropy as we did for the phishing-detection example in chapter 3? We need to combine two metrics of accuracy here: one for the shape prediction and one for the bounding-box prediction. The latter task involves predicting continuous values and can be viewed as a regression task. Therefore, MSE is a natural metric for bounding boxes. In order to combine the metrics, we just "pretend" that the shape prediction is also a regression task. This trick allows us to use a single metric function (the `tf.metric.meanSquaredError()` call in listing 5.10) to encapsulate the loss for both predictions.

But why do we scale the 0–1 indicator by `CANVAS_SIZE`? Well, if we didn't do this scaling, our model would end up generating a number in the neighborhood of 0–1 as an indicator for whether it predicts the shape to be a triangle (close to 0) or a rectangle (close to 1). The difference between numbers around the `[0, 1]` interval would clearly be much smaller compared to the differences we get from comparing the true bounding box and the predicted ones, which are in the range of 0–224. As a result, the error signal from the shape prediction would be totally overshadowed by the error signal from the bounding-box prediction, which would not help us get accurate shape predictions. By scaling the 0–1 shape indicator, we make sure the shape prediction and bounding-box prediction contribute about equally to the final loss value (the return value of `customLossFunction()`), so that when the model is trained, it will optimize both types of predictions at once. In exercise 4 at the end of this chapter, you are encouraged to experiment with this scaling yourself.[12]

With the data prepared and the model and loss function defined, we are ready to train our model! The key parts of the model training code are shown in listing 5.11 (from simple-object-detection/train.js). Like the fine-tuning we've seen before (section 5.1.3), the training proceeds in two phases: an initial phase, during which only the new head layers are trained, and a fine-tuning phase, during which the new head layers are trained together with the top few layers of the truncated MobileNet base. It should be noted that the `compile()` method must be invoked (again) right before the fine-tuning `fit()` call in order for the changes to the `trainable` property of the layers to take effect. If you run the training on your own machine, it'll be easy to observe a significant downward jump in the loss values as soon as the fine-tuning phase starts, reflecting an increase in the capacity of the model and the adaptation of the unfrozen feature-extraction layers to the unique features in the object-detection data as a result of their unfreezing. The list of layers unfrozen during the fine-tuning is determined by the `fineTuningLayers` array, which is populated when we truncate the MobileNet

---

[12] An alternative to the scaling and `meanSquaredError`-based approach here is to take the first column of `yPred` as the shape probability score and compute the binary cross entropy with the first column of `yTrue`. Then the binary cross entropy value can be summed together with the MSE calculated on the remaining columns of `yTrue` and `yPred`. But in this alternative approach, the cross entropy needs to be scaled properly to ensure the balance with the bounding-box loss, just like in our current approach. The scaling involves a free parameter whose value needs to be carefully selected. In practice, it becomes an additional hyperparameter of the model and requires time and compute resources to tune, which is a downside of the approach. We opted against the approach in favor of our current approach for simplicity.

(see the `loadTruncatedBase()` function in listing 5.9). These are the top nine layers of the truncated MobileNet. In exercise 3 at the end of the chapter, you can experiment with unfreezing fewer or more top layers of the base and observe how they change the accuracy of the model produced by the training process.

Listing 5.11   Phase two of training the object-detection model

```
const {model, fineTuningLayers} = await buildObjectDetectionModel();
model.compile({
    loss: customLossFunction,
    optimizer: tf.train.rmsprop(5e-3)    Uses a relatively high learning
});                                       rate for the initial phase

await model.fit(images, targets, {
    epochs: args.initialTransferEpochs,
    batchSize: args.batchSize,            Performs the initial phase
    validationSplit: args.validationSplit of transfer learning
});

// Fine-tuning phase of transfer learning.

for (const layer of fineTuningLayers) {    ◁──── Fine-tuning phase starts
    layer.trainable = true;    ◁──── Unfreezes some layers for fine-tuning
}
model.compile({
    loss: customLossFunction,
    optimizer: tf.train.rmsprop(2e-3)    Uses a slightly lower learning
});                                       rate for the fine-tuning phase

await model.fit(images, targets, {
    epochs: args.fineTuningEpochs,        During the fine-tuning phase, we reduce
    batchSize: args.batchSize / 2,    ◁──── batchSize to avoid out-of-memory issues
    validationSplit: args.validationSplit caused by the fact that backpropagation
});    ◁──── Performs the fine-tuning phase involves more weights and consumes
                                          more memory than the initial phase.
```

After the fine-tuning ends, the model is saved to the disk and is then loaded during the in-browser inference step (started by the `yarn  watch` command). If you load a hosted model, or if you have spent the time and compute resources to train a reasonably good model on your own machine, the shape and bounding-box prediction you'll see in the inference page should be fairly good (validation loss at <100 after 100 epochs of initial training and 200 epochs of fine-tuning). The inference results are good but not perfect (see the examples in figure 5.13). When you examine the results, keep in mind that the in-browser evaluation is a fair one and reflects the model's true generalization power because the examples the trained model is tasked to solve in the browser are different from the training and validation examples that it has seen during the transfer-learning process.

To wrap up this section, we showed how a model trained previously on image classification can be applied successfully to a different task: object detection. In doing this, we demonstrated how to define a custom loss function to fit the "dual-task" (shape classification + bounding-box regression) nature of the object-detection problem and how to use the custom loss during model training. This example not only illustrates the basic principles behind object detection but also highlights the flexibility of transfer learning and the range of problems it may be used on. Object-detection models used in production applications are, of course, more complex and involve more tricks than the toy example we built using a synthesized dataset here. Info box 5.3 briefly presents some interesting facts about advanced object-detection models, and describes how they are different from the simple example you just saw and how you can use one of them through TensorFlow.js.

INFO BOX 5.3   Production object-detection models

An example object-detection result from the TensorFlow.js version of the Single-Shot Detection (SSD) model. Notice the multiple bounding boxes and their associated object class and confidence scores.

Object detection is an important task of interest to many types of applications, such as image understanding, industrial automation, and self-driving cars. The most well-known state-of-the-art object-detection models include the Single-Shot Detection[a] (SSD, for which an example inference result is shown in the figure) and You Only Look Once (YOLO).[b] These models are similar to the model we saw in our simple-object-detection example in the following regards:

- They predict both the class and location of objects.
- They are built on pretrained image-classification models such as MobileNet and VGG16[c] and are trained through transfer learning.

---

[a] Wei Liu et al., "SSD: Single Shot MultiBox Detector," *Lecture Notes in Computer Science* 9905, 2016, http://mng.bz/G4qD.

[b] Joseph Redmon et al., "You Only Look Once: Unified, Real-Time Object Detection," *Proceedings IEEE Conference on Computer Vision and Pattern Recognition* (CVPR), 2016, pp. 779–788, http://mng.bz/zlp1.

c Karen Simonyan and Andrew Zisserman, "Very Deep Convolutional Networks for Large-Scale Image Recognition," submitted 4 Sept. 2014, https://arxiv.org/abs/1409.1556.

(continued)
However, they are also different from our toy model in many regards:

- Real object-detection models predict many more classes of objects than our simple model (for example, the COCO dataset has 80 object categories; see http://cocodataset.org/#home).
- They are capable of detecting multiple objects in the same image (see the example figure).
- Their model architectures are more complex than the one in our simple model. For example, the SSD model adds multiple new heads on top of a truncated pretrained image model in order to predict the class confidence score and bounding boxes for multiple objects in the input image.
- Instead of using a single `meanSquaredError` metric as the loss function, the loss function of a real object-detection model is a weighted sum of two types of losses: 1) a softmax cross-entropy-like loss for the probability scores predicted for object classes and 2) a `meanSquaredError` or `meanAbsoluteError`-like loss for bounding boxes. The relative weight between the two types of loss values is carefully tuned to ensure balanced contributions from both sources of error.
- Real object-detection models produce a large number of candidate bounding boxes per input image. These bounding boxes are "pruned" so that the ones with the highest object-class probability scores are retained in the final output.
- Some real object-detection models incorporate "prior knowledge" about the location of object bounding boxes. These are educated guesses for where the bounding boxes are in the image, based on analysis of a larger number of labeled real images. The priors help speed up the training of the models by starting from a reasonable initial state instead of from complete random guesses (as is in our simple-object-detection example).

A few real object-detection models have been ported to TensorFlow.js. For example, one of the best ones you can play with is in the coco-ssd directory of the tfjs-models repository. To see it in action, do the following:

```
git clone https://github.com/tensorflow/tfjs-models.git
cd tfjs-models/coco-ssd/demo
yarn && yarn watch
```

If you are interested in learning more about real object-detection models, you can read the following blog posts. They are for the SSD model and YOLO model, respectively, which use different model architecture and postprocessing techniques:

- "Understanding SSD MultiBox—Real-Time Object Detection In Deep Learning" by Eddie Forson: http://mng.bz/07dJ.
- "Real-time Object Detection with YOLO, YOLOv2, and now YOLOv3" by Jonathan Hui: http://mng.bz/KEqX.

So far in this book, we've tackled machine-learning datasets that are handed to us and ready to be explored. They are well-formatted, having been cleaned up through the painstaking work by data scientists and machine-learning researchers before us, to the degree that we can focus on modeling without worrying too much about how to ingest the data and whether the data is correct. This is true for the MNIST and audio datasets used in this chapter; it's also certainly true for the phishing-website and iris-flower datasets we used in chapter 3.

We can safely say that this is *never* the case for real-world machine-learning problems you will encounter. Most of a machine-learning practitioner's time is in fact spent on acquiring, preprocessing, cleaning, verifying, and formatting the data.[13] In the next chapter, we'll teach you the tools available in TensorFlow.js to make these data-wrangling and ingestion workflows easier.

Exercises

1 When we visited the mnist-transfer-cnn example in section 5.1.1, we pointed out that setting the `trainable` property of a model's layers won't take effect during training, unless the model's `compile()` method is called before the training. Verify that by making some changes to the `retrainModel()` method in the index.js file of the example. Specifically,

   a Add a `this.model.summary()` call right before the line with `this.model` `.compile()`, and observe the numbers of trainable and nontrainable parameters. What do they show? How are they different from the numbers you get after the `compile()` call?

   b Independent from the previous item, move the `this.model.compile()` call to the part right before the setting of the `trainable` property of the feature layers. In other words, set the property of those layers after the `compile()` call. How does that change the training speed? Is the speed consistent with only the last several layers of the model being updated? Can you find other ways to confirm that, in this case, the weights of the first several layers of the models are updated during training?

2 During the transfer learning in section 5.1.1 (listing 5.1), we froze the first two conv2d layers by setting their `trainable` properties to `false` before starting the `fit()` call. Can you add some code to the index.js in the mnist-transfer-cnn example to verify that the weights of the conv2d layers are indeed unaltered by the `fit()` call? Another approach we experimented with in the same section was calling `fit()` without freezing the layers. Can you verify that the weight values of the layers are indeed altered by the `fit()` call in that case? (Hint: recall that in section 2.4.2 of chapter 2, we used the `layers` attribute of a model object and its `getWeights()` method to access the value of weights.)

---

[13] Gil Press, "Cleaning Big Data: Most Time-Consuming, Least Enjoyable Data Science Task, Survey Says," *Forbes*, 23 Mar. 2016, http://mng.bz/9wqj.

3 Convert the Keras MobileNetV2[14] (not MobileNetV1!—we already did that) application into the TensorFlow.js format, and load it into TensorFlow.js in the browser. Refer to info box 5.1 for detailed steps. Can you use the `summary()` method to examine the topology of MobileNetV2 and identify its main differences from MobileNetV1?

4 One of the important things about the fine-tuning code in listing 5.8 is that the `compile()` method of the model is called again after unfreezing the dense layer in the base model. Can you do the following?

a Use the same method from exercise 2 to verify that the weights (kernel and bias) of the dense layer are indeed not altered by the first `fit()` call (the one for the initial phase of transfer learning) and that they indeed are by the second `fit()` call (the one for the fine-tuning phase).

b Try commenting out the `compile()` call after the unfreezing line (the line that changes the value of the trainable attribute) and see how that affects the weight value changes you just observed. Convince yourself that the `compile()` call is indeed necessary for letting changes in the frozen/unfrozen states of the model take effect.

c Change the code and try unfreezing more weight-carrying layers of the base speech-command model (for instance, the conv2d layer before the second-last dense layer) and see how that affects the outcome of the fine-tuning.

5 In the custom loss function we defined for the simple object-detection task, we scaled the 0–1 shape label so the error signal from the shape prediction could match the error signal from the bounding-box prediction (see listing 5.10). Experiment with what happens if this scaling is not done by removing the `mul()` call in the code in listing 5.10. Convince yourself that this scaling is necessary for ensuring reasonably accurate shape predictions. This can also be done by simply replacing the instances of `customLossFunction` with `meanSquaredError` during the `compile()` call (see listing 5.11). Also note that removal of the scaling during training needs to be accompanied by a change in the thresholding during inference time: change the threshold from `CANVAS_SIZE/2` to `1/2` in the inference logic (in simple-object-detection/index.js).

6 The fine-tuning phase in the simple object-detection example involved unfreezing the nine top layers of the truncated MobileNet base (see how `fineTuning-Layers` is populated in listing 5.9). A natural question to ask is, why nine? In this exercise, change the number of unfrozen layers by including fewer or more layers in the `fineTuningLayers` array. What do you expect to see in the following quantities when you unfreeze fewer layers during fine-tuning: 1) the final loss value and 2) the time each epoch takes in the fine-tuning phase? Does the

---

[14] Mark Sandler et al., "MobileNetV2: Inverted Residuals and Linear Bottlenecks," revised 21 Mar. 2019, https://arxiv.org/abs/1801.04381.

experiment result match your expectations? How about unfreezing more layers during fine-tuning?

Summary

- Transfer learning is the process of reusing a pretrained model or a part of it on a learning task related to, but different from, the one that the model was originally trained for. This reusing speeds up the new learning task.

- In practical applications of transfer learning, people often reuse convnets that have been trained on very large classification datasets, such as MobileNet trained on the ImageNet dataset. Due to the sheer size of the original dataset and the diversity of the examples it contains, such pretrained models bring with them convolutional layers that are powerful, general-purpose feature extractors for a wide variety of compute-vision problems. Such layers are difficult, if not impossible, to train with the small amount of data that are available in typical transfer-learning problems.

- We discussed several general approaches of transfer learning in TensorFlow.js, which differ from each other in terms of 1) whether new layers are created as the "new head" for transfer learning and 2) whether the transfer learning is done with one model instance or two. Each approach has its pros and cons and is suited for different use cases (see table 5.1).

- By setting the `trainable` attribute of a model's layer, we can prevent its weights from being updated during training (`Model.fit()` calls). This is referred to as freezing and is used to "protect" the base model's feature-extraction layers during transfer learning.

- In some transfer-learning problems, we can boost the new model's performance by unfreezing a few top layers of the base model after an initial phase of training. This reflects the adaptation of the unfrozen layers to the unique features in the new dataset.

- Transfer learning is a versatile and flexible technique. The base model can help us solve problems that are different from the one that it is originally trained on. We illustrated this point by showing how to train an object-detection model based on MobileNet.

- Loss functions in TensorFlow.js can be defined as custom JavaScript functions that operate on tensor inputs and outputs. As we showed in the simple object-detection example, custom loss functions are often needed to solve practical machine-learning problems.

Part 3

Advanced deep learning with TensorFlow.js

After reading parts 1 and 2, you should now be familiar with how basic deep learning is done in TensorFlow.js. Part 3 is intended for users who want to develop a firmer grasp of the techniques and gain a broader understanding of deep learning. Chapter 6 covers techniques for ingesting, transforming, and using data for machine learning. Chapter 7 presents tools for visualizing data and models. Chapter 8 is concerned with the important phenomena of underfitting and overfitting and how to deal with them effectively. Based on this discussion, we introduce the universal workflow of machine learning. Chapters 9–11 are hands-on tours of three advanced areas: sequence-oriented models, generative models, and reinforcement learning, respectively. They will familiarize you with some of the most exciting frontiers of deep learning.

Working with data 6

This chapter covers

- How to use the `tf.data` API to train models using large datasets
- Exploring your data to find and fix potential issues
- How to use data augmentation to create new "pseudo-examples" to improve model quality

The wide availability of large volumes of data is a major factor leading to today's machine-learning revolution. Without easy access to large amounts of high-quality data, the dramatic rise in machine learning would not have happened. Datasets are now available all over the internet—freely shared on sites like Kaggle and OpenML, among others—as are benchmarks for state-of-the-art performance. Entire branches of machine learning have been propelled forward by the availability of "challenge" datasets, setting a bar and a common benchmark for the community.[1] If machine learning is our generation's Space Race, then data is clearly our rocket

---

[1] See how ImageNet propelled the field of object recognition or what the Netflix challenge did for collaborative filtering.

fuel;[2] it's potent, it's valuable, it's volatile, and it's absolutely critical to a working machine-learning system. Not to mention that polluted data, like tainted fuel, can quickly lead to systemic failure. This chapter is about data. We will cover best practices for organizing data, how to detect and clean out issues, and how to use it efficiently.

"But haven't we been working with data all along?" you might protest. It's true—in previous chapters we worked with all sorts of data sources. We've trained image models using both synthetic and webcam-image datasets. We've used transfer learning to build a spoken-word recognizer from a dataset of audio samples, and we accessed tabular datasets to predict prices. So what's left to discuss? Aren't we already proficient in handling data?

Recall in our previous examples the patterns of our data usage. We've typically needed to first download our data from a remote source. Then we (usually) applied some transformation to get our data into the correct format—for instance, by converting strings into one-hot vocabulary vectors or by normalizing the means and variances of tabular sources. We have then always needed to batch our data and convert it into a standard block of numbers represented as a tensor before connecting it to our model. All this before we even ran our first training step.

This download-transform-batch pattern is very common, and TensorFlow.js comes packaged with tooling to make these types of manipulations easier, more modular, and less error prone. This chapter will introduce the tools in the `tf.data` namespace: most importantly, `tf.data.Dataset`, which can be used to lazily stream data. The lazy-streaming approach allows for downloading, transforming, and accessing data on an as-needed basis rather than downloading the data source in its entirety and holding it in memory as it is accessed. Lazy streaming makes it much easier to work with data sources that are too large to fit in a single browser tab or even too large within the RAM of a single machine.

We will first introduce the `tf.data.Dataset` API and show how to configure it and connect it to a model. We will then introduce some theory and tooling to help you review and explore your data and resolve problems you might discover. The chapter wraps up by introducing data augmentation, a method for expanding a dataset to improve model quality by creating synthetic pseudo-examples.

6.1   *Using tf.data to manage data*

How would you train a spam filter if your email database were hundreds of gigabytes and required special credentials to access? How can you construct an image classifier if your database of training images is too large to fit on a single machine?

Accessing and manipulating large volumes of data is a key skill for the machine-learning engineer, but so far, we have been dealing with applications in which the data could conceivably fit within the memory available to our application. Many applications require working with large, cumbersome, and possibly privacy-sensitive data

---

[2] Credit for the analogy to Edd Dumbill, "Big Data Is Rocket Fuel," *Big Data*, vol. 1, no. 2, pp. 71–72.

sources that this technique is not suitable for. Large applications require technology for accessing data from a remote source, piece by piece, on demand.

TensorFlow.js comes packaged with an integrated library designed just for this sort of data management. It is built to enable users to ingest, preprocess, and route data in a concise and readable way, inspired by the `tf.data` API in the Python version of TensorFlow. Assuming your code imports TensorFlow.js using an import statement like

```
import * as tf from '@tensorflow/tfjs';
```

this functionality will be available under the `tf.data` namespace.

6.1.1 *The tf.data.Dataset object*

Most interaction with `tfjs-data` comes through a single object type called `Dataset`. The `tf.data.Dataset` object provides a simple, configurable, and performant way to iterate over and process large (possibly unlimited) lists of data elements.[3] In the coarsest abstraction, you can imagine a dataset as an iterable collection of arbitrary elements, not unlike the `Stream` in Node.js. Whenever the next element is requested from the dataset, the internal implementation will download it, access it, or execute a function to create it, as needed. This abstraction makes it easy for the model to train on more data than can conceivably be held in memory at once. It also makes it convenient to share and organize datasets as first-class objects when there is more than one dataset to keep track of. `Dataset` provides a memory benefit by streaming only the required bits of data, rather than accessing the whole thing monolithically. The `Dataset` API also provides performance optimizations over the naive implementation by prefetching values that are about to be needed.

6.1.2 *Creating a tf.data.Dataset*

As of TensorFlow.js version 1.2.7, there are three ways to connect up `tf.data .Dataset` to some data provider. We will go through each in some detail, but table 6.1 contains a brief summary.

CREATING A TF.DATA.DATASET FROM AN ARRAY

The simplest way to create a new `tf.data.Dataset` is to build one from a JavaScript array of elements. Given an array already in memory, you can create a dataset backed by the array using the `tf.data.array()` function. Of course, it won't bring any training speed or memory-usage benefit over using the array directly, but accessing an array via a dataset offers other important benefits. For instance, using datasets makes it easier to set up preprocessing and makes our training and evaluation easier through the simple `model.fitDataset()` and `model.evaluateDataset()` APIs, as we will see in

---

[3] In this chapter, we will use the term *elements* frequently to refer to the items in the `Dataset`. In most cases, *element* is synonymous with *example* or *datapoint*—that is, in the training dataset, each element is an (*x*, *y*) pair. When reading from a CSV source, each element is a row of the file. `Dataset` is flexible enough to handle heterogeneous types of elements, but this is not recommended.

Table 6.1   Creating a `tf.data.Dataset` object from a data source

How to get a new tf.data.Dataset	API	How to use it to build a dataset

From a JavaScript array of elements; also works for typed arrays like Float32Array	`tf.data.array(items)`	`const dataset =`
		`tf.data.array([1,2,3,4,5]);`
		See listing 6.1 for more.

From a (possibly remote) CSV file, where each row is an element	`tf.data.csv(`
	`    source,`
	`    csvConfig)`
		`const dataset =`
		`tf.data.csv("https://path/to/my.csv");`
		
		See listing 6.2 for more.
		
		The only required parameter is the URL from which to read the data. Additionally, `csvConfig` accepts an object with keys to help guide the parsing of the CSV file. For instance,
		
		• `columnNames`—A `string[]` can be provided to set the names of the columns manually if they don't exist in a header or need to be overridden.
		• `delimiter`—A single character string can be used to override the default comma delimiter.
		• `columnConfigs`—A map of string `columnName` to `columnConfig` objects can be provided to guide the parsing and return type of the dataset. The `columnConfig` will inform the parser of the element's type (string or int), or if the column is to be considered as the dataset label.
		• `configuredColumnsOnly`—Whether to return data for each column in the CSV or only those columns included in the `columnConfigs` object.
		
		More detail is available in the API docs at js.tensorflow.org.

From a generic generator function that yields elements	`tf.data.generator(`
	`    generatorFunction)`
		`function* countDownFrom10() {`
		`    for (let i=10; i>0; i--) {`
		`        yield(i);`
		`    }`
		`}`
		
		`const dataset =`
		`tf.data.generator(countDownFrom10);`
		See listing 6.3 for more.
		
		Note that the argument passed to `tf.data.generator()` when called with no arguments returns a `Generator` object.

section 6.2. In contrast to `model.fit(x, y)`, `model.fitDataset(myDataset)` does not immediately move all of the data into GPU memory, meaning that it is possible to work with datasets larger than the GPU can hold. Realize that the memory limit of the V8 JavaScript engine (1.4 GB on 64-bit systems) is usually larger than TensorFlow.js

can hold in WebGL memory at a time. Using the `tf.data` API is also good software engineering practice, as it makes it easy to swap in another type of data in a modular fashion without changing much code. Without the dataset abstraction, it is easy to let the details of the implementation of the dataset source leak into its usage in the training of the model, an entanglement that will need to be unwound as soon as a different implementation is used.

To build a dataset from an existing array, use `tf.data.array(itemsAsArray)`, as shown in the following listing.

Listing 6.1   Building a `tf.data.Dataset` from an array

```
const myArray = [{xs: [1, 0, 9], ys: 10},
                 {xs: [5, 1, 3], ys: 11},
                 {xs: [1, 1, 9], ys: 12}];
const myFirstDataset = tf.data.array(myArray);
await myFirstDataset.forEachAsync(
      e => console.log(e));

// Yields output like
// {xs: Array(3), ys: 10}
// {xs: Array(3), ys: 11}
// {xs: Array(3), ys: 12}
```

> Creates the tfjs-data dataset backed by an array. Note that this does not clone the array or its elements.

> Uses the forEachAsync() method to iterate on all values provided by the dataset. Note that forEachAsync() is an async function, and hence you should use await with it.

We iterate over the elements of the dataset using the `forEachAsync()` function, which yields each element in turn. See more details about the `Dataset.forEachAsync` function in section 6.1.3.

Elements of datasets may contain JavaScript primitives[4] (such as numbers and strings) as well as tuples, arrays, and nested objects of such structures, in addition to tensors. In this tiny example, the three elements of the dataset all have the same structure. They are all objects with the same keys and the same type of values at those keys. `tf.data.Dataset` can in general support a mixture of types of elements, but the common use case is that dataset elements are meaningful semantic units of the same type. Typically, they should represent examples of the same kind of thing. Thus, except in very unusual use cases, each element should have the same type and structure.

CREATING A TF.DATA.DATASET FROM A CSV FILE

A very common type of dataset element is a key-value object representing one row of a table, such as one row of a CSV file. The next listing shows a very simple program that will connect to and list out the Boston-housing dataset, the one we first used in chapter 2.

---

[4] If you are familiar with the Python TensorFlow implementation of `tf.data`, you may be surprised that `tf.data.Dataset` can contain JavaScript primitives in addition to tensors.

> **Listing 6.2 Building a `tf.data.Dataset` from a CSV file**

```
const myURL =
    "https://storage.googleapis.com/tfjs-examples/" +
        "multivariate-linear-regression/data/train-data.csv";
const myCSVDataset = tf.data.csv(myURL);
await myCSVDataset.forEachAsync(e => console.log(e));

// Yields output of 333 rows like
// {crim: 0.327, zn: 0, indus: 2.18, chas: 0, nox: 0.458, rm: 6.998,
// age: 45.8, tax: 222}
// ...
```

Creates the tfjs-data dataset backed by a remote CSV file

Uses the forEachAsync() method to iterate on all values provided by the dataset. Note that forEachAsync() is an async function.

…

Instead of `tf.data.array()`, here we use `tf.data.csv()` and point to a URL of a CSV file. This will create a dataset backed by the CSV file, and iterating over the dataset will iterate over the CSV rows. In Node.js, we can connect to a local CSV file by using a URL handle with the file:// prefix, like the following:

```
> const data = tf.data.csv(
    'file://./relative/fs/path/to/boston-housing-train.csv');
```

When iterating, we see that each CSV row is transformed into a JavaScript object. The elements returned from the dataset are objects with one property for each column of the CSV, and the properties are named according to the column names in the CSV file. This is convenient for interacting with the elements in that it is no longer necessary to remember the order of the fields. Section 6.3.1 will go into more detail describing how to work with CSVs and will go through an example.

CREATING A TF.DATA.DATASET FROM A GENERATOR FUNCTION

The third and most flexible way to create a `tf.data.Dataset` is to build one from a generator function. This is done using the `tf.data.generator()` method. `tf.data.generator()` takes a JavaScript *generator function* (or function*)[5] as its argument. If you are not familiar with generator functions, which are relatively new to JavaScript, you may wish to take a moment to read their documentation. The purpose of a generator function is to "yield" a sequence of values as they are needed, either forever or until the sequence is exhausted. The values that are yielded from the generator function flow through to become the values of the dataset. A very simple generator function might, for instance, yield random numbers or extract snapshots of data from a piece of attached hardware. A sophisticated generator may be integrated with a video game, yielding screen captures, scores, and control input-output. In the following listing, the very simple generator function yields samples of dice rolls.

---

[5] Learn more about ECMAscript generator functions at http://mng.bz/Q0rj.

Listing 6.3 Building a `tf.data.Dataset` for random dice rolls

```
let numPlaysSoFar = 0;              ◁─┐   numPlaysSoFar is closed over by rollTwoDice(),
                                      │   which allows us to calculate how many times
function rollTwoDice() {              │   the function is executed by the dataset.
  numPlaysSoFar++;
  return [Math.ceil(Math.random() * 6), Math.ceil(Math.random() * 6)];
}

function* rollTwoDiceGeneratorFn() {     Defines a generator function (using
  while(true) {                          function* syntax) that will yield the
    yield rollTwoDice();                 result of calling rollTwoDice() an
  }                                      unlimited number of times
}

const myGeneratorDataset = tf.data.generator(
    rollTwoDiceGeneratorFn);             The dataset is created here.
await myGeneratorDataset.take(1).forEachAsync(
    e => console.log(e));

// Prints to the console a value like     Takes a sample of exactly one element of
// [4, 2]                                  the dataset. The take() method will be
                                           described in section 6.1.4.
```

A couple of interesting notes regarding the game-simulation dataset created in listing 6.3. First, note that the dataset created here, `myGeneratorDataset`, is infinite. Since the generator function never returns, we could conceivably take samples from the dataset forever. If we were to execute `forEachAsync()` or `toArray()` (see section 6.1.3) on this dataset, it would never end and would probably crash our server or browser, so watch out for that. In order to work with such objects, we need to create some other dataset that is a limited sample of the unlimited one using `take(n)`. More on this in a moment.

Second, note that the dataset closes over a local variable. This is helpful for logging and debugging to determine how many times the generator function has been executed.

Third, note that the data does not exist until it is requested. In this case, we only ever access exactly one sample of the dataset, and this would be reflected in the value of `numPlaysSoFar`.

Generator datasets are powerful and tremendously flexible and allow developers to connect models to all sorts of data-providing APIs, such as data from a database query, from data downloaded piecemeal over the network, or from a piece of connected hardware. More details about the `tf.data.generator()` API are provided in info box 6.1.

INFO BOX 6.1   tf.data.generator() argument specification

The `tf.data.generator()` API is flexible and powerful, allowing the user to hook the model up to many sorts of data providers. The argument passed to `tf.data.generator()` must meet the following specifications:

- It must be callable with zero arguments.
- When called with zero arguments, it must return an object that conforms to the iterator and iterable protocol. This means that the returned object must have a method `next()`. When `next()` is called with no arguments, it should return a JavaScript object `{value: ELEMENT, done: false}` in order to pass forward the value `ELEMENT`. When there are no more values to return, it should return `{value: undefined, done: true}`.

JavaScript's generator functions return `Generator` objects, which meet this spec and are thus the easiest way to use `tf.data.generator()`. The function may close over local variables, access local hardware, connect to network resources, and so on.

Table 6.1 contains the following code illustrating how to use `tf.data.generator()`:

```
function* countDownFrom10() {
  for (let i = 10; i > 0; i--) {
    yield(i);
  }
}

const dataset = tf.data.generator(countDownFrom10);
```

If you wish to avoid using generator functions for some reason and would rather implement the iterable protocol directly, you can also write the previous code in the following, equivalent way:

```
function countDownFrom10Func() {
  let i = 10;
  return {
    next: () => {
      if (i > 0) {
        return {value: i--, done: false};
      } else {
        return {done: true};
      }
    }
  }
}

const dataset = tf.data.generator(countDownFrom10Func);
```

6.1.3 *Accessing the data in your dataset*

Once you have your data as a dataset, inevitably you are going to want to access the data in it. Data structures you can create but never read from are not really useful. There are two APIs to access the data from a dataset, but `tf.data` users should only need to use these infrequently. More typically, higher-level APIs will access the data within a dataset for you. For instance, when training a model, we use the `model.fit-Dataset()` API, described in section 6.2, which accesses the data in the dataset for us, and we, the users, never need to access the data directly. Nevertheless, when debugging, testing, and coming to understand how the `Dataset` object works, it's important to know how to peek into the contents.

The first way to access data from a dataset is to stream it all out into an array using `Dataset.toArray()`. This function does exactly what it sounds like. It iterates through the entire dataset, pushing all the elements into an array and returning that array to the user. The user should use caution when executing this function to not inadvertently produce an array that is too large for the JavaScript runtime. This mistake is easy to make if, for instance, the dataset is connected to a large remote data source or is an unlimited dataset reading from a sensor.

The second way to access data from a dataset is to execute a function on each example of the dataset using `dataset.forEachAsync(f)`. The argument provided to `forEachAsync()` will apply to each element in turn in a way similar to the `forEach()` construct in JavaScript arrays and sets—that is, the native `Array.forEach()` and `Set.forEach()`.

It is important to note that `Dataset.forEachAsync()` and `Dataset.toArray()` are both async functions. This is in contrast to `Array.forEach()`, which is synchronous, so it might be easy to make a mistake here. `Dataset.toArray()` returns a promise and will in general require `await` or `.then()` if synchronous behavior is required. Take care that if `await` is forgotten, the promise might not resolve in the order you expect, and bugs will arise. A typical bug is for the dataset to appear empty because the contents are iterated over before the promise resolves.

The reason why `Dataset.forEachAsync()` is asynchronous while `Array.forEach()` is not is that the data being accessed by the dataset might, in general, need to be created, calculated, or fetched from a remote source. Asynchronicity here allows us to make efficient use of the available computation while we wait. These methods are summarized in table 6.2.

Table 6.2   Methods that iterate over a dataset

Instance method of the tf.data.Dataset object	What it does	Example

`.toArray()`	Asynchronously iterates over the entire dataset and pushes each element into an array, which is returned	```const a = tf.data.array([1, 2, 3, 4, 5, 6]);```
		```const arr = await a.toArray();```
		```console.log(arr);```
		
		```// 1,2,3,4,5,6```

`.forEachAsync(f)`	Asynchronously iterates over all the elements of the dataset and executes `f` on each	```const a = tf.data.array([1, 2, 3]);```
		```await a.forEachAsync(e => console.log("hi " + e));```
		
		```// hi 1```
		```// hi 2```
		```// hi 3```

6.1.4   *Manipulating tfjs-data datasets*

It certainly is very nice when we can use data directly as it has been provided, without any cleanup or processing. But in the experience of the authors, this *almost never* happens outside of examples constructed for educational or benchmarking purposes. In the more common case, the data must be transformed in some way before it can be analyzed or used in a machine-learning task. For instance, often the source contains extra elements that must be filtered; or data at certain keys needs to be parsed, deserialized, or renamed; or the data was stored in sorted order and thus needs to be randomly shuffled before using it to train or evaluate a model. Perhaps the dataset must be split into nonoverlapping sets for training and testing. Preprocessing is nearly inevitable. If you come across a dataset that is clean and ready-to-use out of the box, chances are that someone already did the cleanup and preprocessing for you!

`tf.data.Dataset` provides a chainable API of methods to perform these sorts of operations, described in table 6.3. Each of these methods returns a new `Dataset` object, but don't be misled into thinking that all the elements of the dataset are copied or that all the elements are iterated over for each method call! The `tf.data.Dataset` API only loads and transforms elements in a lazy fashion. A dataset that was created by chaining together several of these methods can be thought of as a small program that will execute only once elements are requested from the end of the chain. It is only at that point that the `Dataset` instance crawls back up the chain of operations, possibly all the way to requesting data from the remote source.

Table 6.3 Chainable methods on the `tf.data.Dataset` object

Instance method of the tf.data.Dataset object	What it does	Example
`.filter(predicate)`	Returns a dataset containing only elements for which the predicate evaluates to `true`	`myDataset.filter(x => x < 10);` Returns a dataset containing only values from `myDataset` that are less than 10.
`.map(transform)`	Applies the provided function to every element in the dataset and returns a new dataset of the mapped elements	`myDataset.map(x => x * x);` Returns a dataset of the squared values of the original dataset.
`.mapAsync(` `    asyncTransform)`	Like `map`, but the provided function must be asynchronous	`myDataset.mapAsync(fetchAsync);` Assuming `fetchAsync` is an asynchronous function that yields the data fetched from a provided URL, will return a new dataset containing the data at each URL.

`.batch(`
`    batchSize,`
`    smallLastBatch?)`
	Bundles sequential spans of elements into single-element groups and converts primitive elements into tensors	`const a = tf.data.array(`
		`    [1, 2, 3, 4, 5, 6, 7, 8])`
		`    .batch(4);`
		`await a.forEach(e => e.print());`
		
		`// Prints:`
		`//     Tensor [1, 2, 3, 4]`
		`//     Tensor [5, 6, 7, 8]`

`.concatenate(` `    dataset)`	Concatenates the elements from two datasets together to form a new dataset	`myDataset1.concatenate(myDataset2)` Returns a dataset that will iterate over all the values of `myDataset1` first, and then over all the values of `myDataset2`.
`.repeat(count)`	Returns a dataset that will iterate over the original dataset multiple (possibly unlimited) times	`myDataset.repeat(NUM_EPOCHS)` Returns a dataset that will iterate over all the values of `myDataset` NUM_EPOCHS times. If NUM_EPOCHS is negative or undefined, the result will iterate an unlimited number of times.
`.take(count)`	Returns a dataset containing only the first `count` examples	`myDataset.take(10);` Returns a dataset containing only the first 10 elements of `myDataset`. If `myDataset` contains fewer than 10 elements, then there is no change.
`.skip(count)`	Returns a dataset that skips the first `count` examples	`myDataset.skip(10);` Returns a dataset that contains all the elements of `myDataset` except the first 10. If `myDataset` contains 10 or fewer elements, this returns an empty dataset.

Table 6.3 Chainable methods on the `tf.data.Dataset` object *(continued)*

Instance method of the tf.data.Dataset object	What it does	Example

`.shuffle(`
`    bufferSize,`
`    seed?`
`)`
	Produces a dataset that shuffles the elements of the original dataset
	
	Be aware: this shuffling is done by selecting randomly within a window of size `bufferSize`; thus, the ordering beyond the size of the window is preserved.
		`const a = tf.data.array(`
		`    [1, 2, 3, 4, 5, 6]).shuffle(3);`
		`await a.forEach(e => console.log(e));`
		`// prints, e.g., 2, 4, 1, 3, 6, 5`
		Prints the values 1 through 6 in a randomly shuffled order. The shuffle is partial, in that not all orders are possible since the window is smaller than the total data size. For example, it is not possible that the last element, 6, will now be the first in the new order, since the 6 would need to move back more than `bufferSize` (3) spaces.

These operations can be chained together to create simple but powerful processing pipelines. For instance, to split a dataset randomly into training and testing datasets, you can follow the recipe in the following listing (see tfjs-examples/iris-fitDataset/data.js).

Listing 6.4 Creating a train/test split using `tf.data.Dataset`

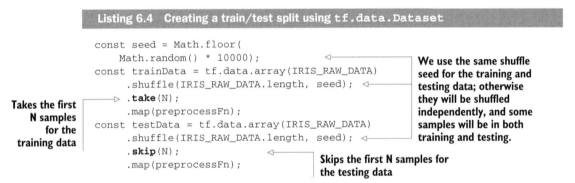

```
const seed = Math.floor(
    Math.random() * 10000);                              We use the same shuffle
const trainData = tf.data.array(IRIS_RAW_DATA)           seed for the training and
    .shuffle(IRIS_RAW_DATA.length, seed);                testing data; otherwise
    .take(N);                                            they will be shuffled
    .map(preprocessFn);                                  independently, and some
const testData = tf.data.array(IRIS_RAW_DATA)            samples will be in both
    .shuffle(IRIS_RAW_DATA.length, seed);                training and testing.
    .skip(N);
    .map(preprocessFn);
```

Takes the first N samples for the training data

Skips the first N samples for the testing data

There are some important considerations to attend to in this listing. We would like to randomly assign samples into the training and testing splits, and thus we shuffle the data first. We take the first N samples for the training data. For the testing data, we skip those samples, taking the rest. It is very important that the data is shuffled *the same way* when we are taking the samples, so we don't end up with the same example in both sets; thus we use the same random seed for both when sampling both pipelines.

It's also important to notice that we apply the map() function *after* the skip operation. It would also be possible to call .map(preprocessFn) *before* the skip, but then the preprocessFn would be executed even for examples we discard—a waste of computation. This behavior can be verified with the following listing.

Listing 6.5   Illustrating `Dataset.forEach skip()` and `map()` interactions

```
let count = 0;

// Identity function which also increments count.
function identityFn(x) {
  count += 1;
  return x;
}

console.log('skip before map');
await tf.data.array([1, 2, 3, 4, 5, 6])
    .skip(6)                          ◁──────────  Skips then maps
  .map(identityFn)
  .forEachAsync(x => undefined);
console.log(`count is ${count}`);

console.log('map before skip');
await tf.data.array([1, 2, 3, 4, 5, 6])
    .map(identityFn)                  ◁──────────  Maps then skips
  .skip(6)
  .forEachAsync(x => undefined);
console.log(`count is ${count}`);
```

```
// Prints:
// skip before map
// count is 0
// map before skip
// count is 6
```

Another common use for dataset.map() is to normalize our input data. We can imagine a scenario in which we wish to normalize our input to be zero mean, but we have an unlimited number of input samples. In order to subtract the mean, we would need to first calculate the mean of the distribution, but calculating the mean of an unlimited set is not tractable. We could also consider taking a representative sample and calculating the mean of that sample, but we could be making a mistake if we don't know what the right sample size is. Consider a distribution in which nearly all values are 0, but every ten-millionth example has a value of 1e9. This distribution has a mean value of 100, but if you calculate the mean on the first 1 million examples, you will be quite off.

We can perform a streaming normalization using the dataset API in the following way (listing 6.6). In this listing, we will keep a running tally of how many samples we've seen and what the sum of those samples has been. In this way, we can perform a streaming normalization. This listing operates on scalars (not tensors), but a version designed for tensors would have a similar structure.

Listing 6.6   Streaming normalization using `tf.data.map()`

```
function newStreamingZeroMeanFn() {    ◁─┐  Returns a unary function, which
  let samplesSoFar = 0;                   │  will return its input minus the
  let sumSoFar = 0;                       │  mean of all its input so far

  return (x) => {
```

```
      samplesSoFar += 1;
      sumSoFar += x;
      const estimatedMean = sumSoFar / samplesSoFar;
      return x - estimatedMean;
    }
  }
}
const normalizedDataset1 =
    unNormalizedDataset1.map(newStreamingZeroMeanFn());
const normalizedDataset2 =
    unNormalizedDataset2.map(newStreamingZeroMeanFn());
```

Note that we generate a new mapping function, which closes over its own copy of the
sample counter and accumulator. This is to allow for multiple datasets to be normalized
independently. Otherwise, both datasets would use the same variables to count invoca-
tions and sums. This solution is not without its own limitations, especially with the possi-
bility of numeric overflow in sumSoFar or samplesSoFar, so some care is warranted.

6.2   *Training models with model.fitDataset*

The streaming dataset API is nice, and we've seen that it allows us to do some elegant
data manipulation, but the main purpose of the tf.data API is to simplify connecting
data to our model for training and evaluation. How is tf.data going to help us here?

Ever since chapter 2, whenever we've wanted to train a model, we've used the
model.fit() API. Recall that model.fit() takes at least two mandatory arguments—
xs and ys. As a reminder, the xs variable must be a tensor that represents a collection
of input examples. The ys variable must be bound to a tensor that represents a corresponding collection of output targets. For example, in the previous chapter's listing
5.11, we trained and fine-tuned on our synthetic object-detection model with calls like

```
model.fit(images, targets, modelFitArgs)
```

where images was, by default, a rank-4 tensor of shape [2000, 224, 224, 3], representing a collection of 2,000 images. The modelFitArgs configuration object specified
the batch size for the optimizer, which was by default 128. Stepping back, we see that
TensorFlow.js was given an in-memory[6] collection of 2,000 examples, representing the
entirety of the data, and then looped through that data 128 examples at a time to
complete each epoch.

What if this wasn't enough data, and we wanted to train with a much larger dataset?
In this situation, we are faced with a pair of less than ideal options. Option 1 is to load
a much larger array and see if it works. At some point, however, TensorFlow.js is going
to run out of memory and emit a helpful error indicating that it was unable to allocate
the storage for the training data. Option 2 is for us to instead upload our data to the
GPU in separate chunks and call model.fit() on each chunk. We would need to perform our own orchestration of model.fit(), training our model on pieces of our
training data iteratively whenever it is ready. If we wanted to perform more than
one epoch, we would need to go back and re-download our chunks again in some

---

[6] In *GPU* memory, which is usually more limited than the system RAM!

(presumably shuffled) order. Not only is this orchestration cumbersome and error prone, but it also interferes with TensorFlow's own reporting of the epoch counter and reported metrics, which we will be forced to stitch back together ourselves.

Tensorflow.js provides us a much more convenient tool for this task using the `model.fitDataset()` API:

```
model.fitDataset(dataset, modelFitDatasetArgs)
```

`model.fitDataset()` accepts a dataset as its first argument, but the dataset must meet a certain pattern to work. Specifically, the dataset must yield objects with two properties. The first property is named `xs` and has a value of type `Tensor`, representing the features for a batch of examples; this is similar to the `xs` argument to `model.fit()`, but the dataset yields elements one batch at a time rather than the whole array at once. The second required property is named `ys` and contains the corresponding target tensor.[7] Compared to `model.fit()`, `model.fitDataset()` provides a number of advantages. Foremost, we don't need to write code to manage and orchestrate the downloading of pieces of our dataset—this is handled for us in an efficient, as-needed streaming manner. Caching structures built into the dataset allow for prefetching data that is anticipated to be needed, making efficient use of our computational resources. This API call is also more powerful, allowing us to train on much larger datasets than can fit on our GPU. In fact, the size of the dataset we can train on is now limited only by how much time we have because we can continue to train for as long as we are able to get new training examples. This behavior is illustrated in the data-generator example in the tfjs-examples repository.

In this example, we will train a model to learn how to estimate the likelihood of winning a simple game of chance. As usual, you can use the following commands to check out and run the demo:

```
git clone https://github.com/tensorflow/tfjs-examples.git
cd tfjs-examples/data-generator
yarn
yarn watch
```

The game used here is a simplified card game, somewhat like poker. Both players are given N cards, where N is a positive integer, and each card is represented by a random integer between 1 and 13. The rules of the game are as follows:

- The player with the largest group of same-valued cards wins. For example, if player 1 has three of a kind, and player 2 has only a pair, player 1 wins.
- If both players have the same-sized maximal group, then the player with the group with the largest face value wins. For example, a pair of 5s beats a pair of 4s.
- If neither player even has a pair, the player with the highest single card wins.
- Ties are settled randomly, 50/50.

---

[7] For models with multiple inputs, an array of tensors is expected instead of the individual feature tensors. The pattern is similar for models fitting multiple targets.

It should be easy to convince yourself that each player has an equal chance of winning. Thus, if we know nothing about our cards, we should only be able to guess whether we will win or not half of the time. We will build and train a model that takes as input player 1's cards and predicts whether that player will win. In the screenshot in figure 6.1, you should see that we were able to achieve approximately 75% accuracy on this problem after training on about 250,000 examples (50 epochs * 50 batches per epoch * 100 samples per batch). Five cards per hand were used in this simulation, but similar accuracies are achieved for other counts. Higher accuracies are achievable by running with larger batches and for more epochs, but even at 75%, our intelligent player has a significant advantage over the naive player at estimating the likelihood that they will win.

If we were to perform this operation using `model.fit()`, we would need to create and store a tensor of 250,000 examples just to represent the input features. The data

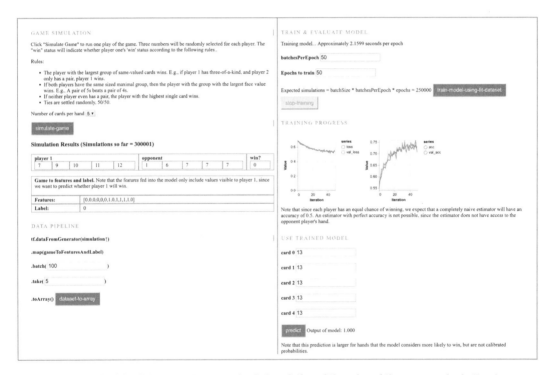

Figure 6.1 The UI of the data-generator example. A description of the rules of the game and a button to run simulations are at top-left. Below that are the generated features and the data pipeline. The Dataset-to-Array button runs the chained dataset operations that will simulate the game, generate features, batch samples together, take N such batches, convert them to an array, and print the array out. At top-right, there are affordances to train a model using this data pipeline. When the user clicks the Train-Model-Using-Fit-Dataset button, the `model.fitDataset()` operation takes over and pulls samples from the pipeline. Loss and accuracy curves are printed below this. At bottom-right, the user may enter values for player 1's hand and press a button to make predictions from the model. Larger predictions indicate that the model believes the hand is more likely to win. Values are drawn with replacement, so five of a kind can happen.

in this example are pretty small—only tens of floats per instance—but for our object-detection task in the previous chapter, 250,000 examples would have required 150 GB of GPU memory,[8] far beyond what is available in most browsers in 2019.

Let's take a dive into relevant portions of this example. First, let's look at how we generate our dataset. The code in the following listing (simplified from tfjs-examples/data-generator/index.js) is similar to the dice-rolling generator dataset in listing 6.3, with a bit more complexity since we are storing more information.

Listing 6.7 Building a `tf.data.Dataset` for our card game

```
import * as game from './game';          ◁────    The game library provides
                                                   randomHand() and compareHands(),
let numSimulationsSoFar = 0;                       functions to generate a hand from a
                                                   simplified poker-like card game and
function runOneGamePlay() {                        to compare two such hands to tell
  const player1Hand = game.randomHand();           which player has won.
  const player2Hand = game.randomHand();
  const player1Win = game.compareHands(      Simulates two players in a
      player1Hand, player2Hand);            simple, poker-like card game
  numSimulationsSoFar++;
  return {player1Hand, player2Hand, player1Win};   ◁─── Returns the two
}                                                         hands and who won

function* gameGeneratorFunction() {
  while (true) {
    yield runOneGamePlay();
  }
}

export const GAME_GENERATOR_DATASET =
    tf.data.generator(gameGeneratorFunction);

await GAME_GENERATOR_DATASET.take(1).forEach(
    e => console.log(e));
// Prints
// {player1Hand: [11, 9, 7, 8],
// player2Hand: [10, 9, 5, 1],
// player1Win: 1}
```

Calculates the winner of the game

Once we have our basic generator dataset connected up to the game logic, we want to format the data in a way that makes sense for our learning task. Specifically, our task is to attempt to predict the `player1Win` bit from the `player1Hand`. In order to do so, we are going to need to make our dataset return elements of the form `[batchOf-Features, batchOfTargets]`, where the features are calculated from player 1's hand. The following code is simplified from tfjs-examples/data-generator/index.js.

---

[8] numExamples × width × height × colorDepth × sizeOfInt32 = 250,000 × 224 × 224 × 3 × 4 bytes .

Listing 6.8   Building a dataset of player features

```
function gameToFeaturesAndLabel(gameState) {
  return tf.tidy(() => {
    const player1Hand = tf.tensor1d(gameState.player1Hand, 'int32');
    const handOneHot = tf.oneHot(
        tf.sub(player1Hand, tf.scalar(1, 'int32')),
        game.GAME_STATE.max_card_value);
    const features = tf.sum(handOneHot, 0);
    const label = tf.tensor1d([gameState.player1Win]);
    return {xs: features, ys: label};
  });
}

let BATCH_SIZE = 50;

export const TRAINING_DATASET =
  GAME_GENERATOR_DATASET.map(gameToFeaturesAndLabel)
                        .batch(BATCH_SIZE);

await TRAINING_DATASET.take(1).forEach(
    e => console.log([e.shape, e.shape]));
// Prints the shape of the tensors:
// [[50, 13], [50, 1]]
```

Takes the state of one complete game and returns a feature representation of player 1's hand and the win status

handOneHot has the shape [numCards, max_value_card]. This operation sums the number of each type of card, resulting in a tensor with the shape [max_value_card].

Groups together BATCH_SIZE consecutive elements into a single element. This would also convert the data from JavaScript arrays to tensors if they weren't already tensors.

Converts each element from the game output object format to an array of two tensors: one for the features and one for the target

Now that we have a dataset in the proper form, we can connect it to our model using model.fitDataset(), as shown in the following listing (simplified from tfjs-examples/data-generator/index.js).

Listing 6.9   Building and training a model on the dataset

This call launches the training.

How many batches constitutes an epoch. Since our dataset is unlimited, this needs to be defined to tell TensorFlow.js when to execute the epoch-end callback.

```
// Construct model.
model = tf.sequential();
model.add(tf.layers.dense({
  inputShape: [game.GAME_STATE.max_card_value],
  units: 20,
  activation: 'relu'
}));
model.add(tf.layers.dense({units: 20, activation: 'relu'}));
model.add(tf.layers.dense({units: 1, activation: 'sigmoid'}));

// Train model
await model.fitDataset(TRAINING_DATASET, {
  batchesPerEpoch: ui.getBatchesPerEpoch(),
  epochs: ui.getEpochsToTrain(),
  validationData: TRAINING_DATASET,
```

We are using the training data as validation data. Normally this is bad, since we will get a biased impression of how well we are doing. In this case, it is not a problem since the data used for training and the data used for validation are guaranteed to be independent by virtue of the generator.

```
    validationBatches: 10,
    callbacks: {
      onEpochEnd: async (epoch, logs) => {
        tfvis.show.history(
          ui.lossContainerElement, trainLogs, ['loss', 'val_loss'])
        tfvis.show.history(
          ui.accuracyContainerElement, trainLogs, ['acc', 'val_acc'],
          {zoomToFitAccuracy: true})
      },
    }
  }
```

> We need to tell TensorFlow.js how many samples to take from the validation dataset to constitute one evaluation.

> model.fitDataset() creates history that is compatible with tfvis, just like model.fit().

As we see in the previous listing, fitting a model to a dataset is just as simple as fitting a model to a pair of x, y tensors. As long as our dataset yields tensor values in the right format, everything just works, we get the benefit of streaming data from a possibly remote source, and we don't need to manage the orchestration on our own. Beyond passing in a dataset instead of a tensor pair, there are a few differences in the configuration object that merit discussion:

- batchesPerEpoch—As we saw in listing 6.9, the configuration for model.fit-Dataset() takes an optional field for specifying the number of batches that constitute an epoch. When we handed the entirety of the data to model.fit(), it was easy to calculate how many examples there are in the whole dataset. It's just data.shape[0]! When using fitDataset(), we can tell TensorFlow.js when an epoch ends in one of two ways. The first way is to use this configuration field, and fitDataset() will execute onEpochEnd and onEpochStart callbacks after that many batches. The second way is to have the dataset itself end as a signal that the dataset is exhausted. In listing 6.7, we could change

  ```
  while (true) { ... }
  ```

  to

  ```
  for (let i = 0; i<ui.getBatchesPerEpoch(); i++) { ... }
  ```

  to mimic this behavior.

- validationData—When using fitDataset(), the validationData may be a dataset also. But it doesn't have to be. You can continue to use tensors for validationData if you want to. The validation dataset needs to meet the same specification with respect to the format of returned elements as the training dataset does.

- validationBatches—If your validation data comes from a dataset, you need to tell TensorFlow.js how many samples to take from the dataset to constitute a complete evaluation. If no value is specified, then TensorFlow.js will continue to draw from the dataset until it returns a done signal. Because the code in listing 6.7 uses a never-ending generator to generate the dataset, this would never happen, and the program would hang.

The rest of the configuration is identical to that of the model.fit() API, so no changes are necessary.

6.3   *Common patterns for accessing data*

All developers need some solutions for connecting their data to their model. These connections range from common stock connections, to well-known experimental datasets like MNIST, to completely custom connections, to proprietary data formats within an enterprise. In this section, we will review how `tf.data` can help to make these connections simple and maintainable.

6.3.1   *Working with CSV format data*

Beyond working with common stock datasets, the most common way to access data involves loading prepared data stored in some file format. Data files are often stored in CSV (comma separated value) format[9] due to its simplicity, human readability, and broad support. Other formats have other advantages in storage efficiency and access speed, but CSV might be considered the *lingua franca* of datasets. In the JavaScript community, we typically want to be able to conveniently stream data from some HTTP endpoint. This is why TensorFlow.js provides native support for streaming and manip-ulating data from CSV files. In section 6.1.2, we briefly described how to construct a `tf.data.Dataset` backed by a CSV file. In this section, we will dive deeper into the CSV API to show how `tf.data` makes working with these data sources very easy. We will describe an example application that connects to remote CSV datasets, prints their schema, counts the elements of the dataset, and offers the user an affordance to select and print the individual examples. Check out the example using the familiar commands:

```
git clone https://github.com/tensorflow/tfjs-examples.git
cd tfjs-examples/data-csv
yarn && yarn watch
```

This should pop open a site that instructs us to enter the URL of a hosted CSV file or to use one of the suggested four URLs by clicking, for example, Boston Housing CSV. See figure 6.2 for an illustration. Underneath the URL entry input box, buttons are provided to perform three actions: 1) count the rows in the dataset, 2) retrieve the column names of the CSV, if they exist, and 3) access and print a specified sample row of the dataset. Let's go through how these work and how the `tf.data` API makes them very easy.

We saw earlier that creating a tfjs-data dataset from a remote CSV is very simple using a command like

```
const myData = tf.data.csv(url);
```

where `url` is either a string identifier using the http://, https://, or file:// protocol, or a `RequestInfo`. This call does *not* actually issue any requests to the URL to check whether, for example, the file exists or is accessible, because of the lazy iteration. In listing 6.10, the CSV is first fetched at the asynchronous `myData.forEach()` call. The

---

[9] As of January 2019, the data science and machine-learning challenge site kaggle.com/datasets boasts 13,971 public datasets, of which over two-thirds are hosted in the CSV format.

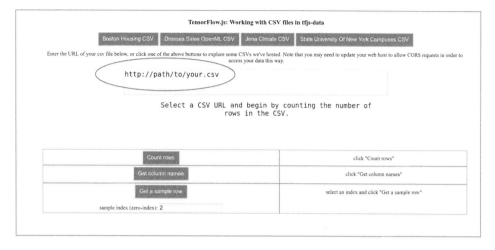

Figure 6.2 Web UI for our tfjs-data CSV example. Click one of the preset CSV buttons at the top or enter a path to your own hosted CSV, if you have one. Be sure to enable CORS access for your CSV if you go with your own hosted file.

function we call in the forEach() will simply stringify and print elements in the dataset, but we could imagine doing other things with this iterator, such as generating UI elements for every element in the set or computing statistics for a report.

Listing 6.10 Printing the first 10 records in a remote CSV file

```
const url = document.getElementById('queryURL').value;
const myData = tf.data.csv(url);          Creates the tfjs-data dataset by
await myData.take(10).forEach(            providing the URL to tf.data.csv()
    x => console.log(JSON.stringify(x))));

// Output is like
// {"crim":0.26169,"zn":0,"indus":9.9,"chas":0,"nox":0.544,"rm":6.023, ...
// ,"medv":19.4}
// {"crim":5.70818,"zn":0,"indus":18.1,"chas":0,"nox":0.532,"rm":6.75, ...
// ,"medv":23.7}
// ...
```

Creates a dataset consisting of the first 10 rows of the CSV dataset. Then, uses the forEach() method to iterate over all values provided by the dataset. Note that forEach() is an async function.

CSV datasets often use the first row as a metadata header containing the names associated with each column. By default, tf.data.csv() assumes this to be the case, but it can be controlled using the csvConfig object passed in as the second argument. If column names are not provided by the CSV file itself, they can be provided manually in the constructor like so:

```
const myData = tf.data.csv(url, {
    hasHeader: false,
    columnNames: ["firstName", "lastName", "id"]
});
```

If you provide a manual `columnNames` configuration to the CSV dataset, it will take precedence over the header row read from the data file. By default, the dataset will assume the first line is a header row. If the first row is not a header, the absence must be configured and `columnNames` provided manually.

Once the `CSVDataset` object exists, it is possible to query it for the column names using `dataset.columnNames()`, which returns an ordered string list of the column names. The `columnNames()` method is specific to the `CSVDataset` subclass and is not generally available from datasets built from other sources. The Get Column Names button in the example is connected to a handler that uses this API. Requesting the column names results in the `Dataset` object making a fetch call to the provided URL to access and parse the first row; thus the async call in the following listing (condensed from tfjs-examples/csv-data/index.js).

Listing 6.11 Accessing column names from a CSV

```
const url = document.getElementById('queryURL').value;
const myData = tf.data.csv(url);
    const columnNames = await myData.columnNames();     ◁─┐ Contacts the remote
console.log(columnNames);                                  │ CSV to collect and
// Outputs something like [                                │ parse the column
//     "crim", "zn", "indus", ..., "tax",                  │ headers
//     "ptratio", "lstat"] for Boston Housing
```

Now that we have the column names, let's get a row from our dataset. In listing 6.12, we show how the web app prints out a single selected row of the CSV file, where the user selects which row via an input element. In order to fulfill this request, we will first use the `Dataset.skip()` method to create a new dataset the same as the original one, but skipping the first n - 1 elements. We will then use the `Dataset.take()` method to create a dataset that ends after one element. Finally, we will use `Dataset.toArray()` to extract the data into a standard JavaScript array. If everything goes right, our request will produce an array that contains exactly one element at the specified position. This sequence is put together in the following listing (condensed from tfjs-examples/csv-data/index.js).

Listing 6.12 Accessing a selected row from a remote CSV

sampleIndex is a number   Creates the dataset myData, configured to read
returned by a UI element.   from url, but does not actually connect yet

```
const url = document.getElementById('queryURL').value;
const sampleIndex = document.getElementById(
    'whichSampleInput').valueAsNumber;
const myData = tf.data.csv(url);   ◁─────────────
const sample = await myData
                    .skip(sampleIndex)   ◁────────────
                    .take(1)   ◁───┐
              ┌─▷  .toArray();      │
```

Creates a new dataset but skips over the first sampleIndex values

Creates a new dataset, but only keeps the first 1 element

This is the call that actually causes the Dataset object to contact the URL and perform the fetch. Note that the return type is an array of objects, in this case, containing exactly one object, with keys corresponding to the header names and values associated with those columns.

```
console.log(sample);
// Outputs something like: [{crim: 0.3237, zn: 0, indus: 2.18, ..., tax:
// 222, ptratio: 18.7, lstat: 2.94}]
// for Boston Housing.
```

We can now take the output of the row, which—as you can see from the output of the console.log in listing 6.12 (repeated in a comment)—comes in the form of an object mapping the column name to the value, and styles it for insertion into our document. Something to watch out for: if we ask for a row that doesn't exist, perhaps the 400th element of a 300-element dataset, we will end up with an empty array.

It's pretty common when connecting to remote datasets to make a mistake and use a bad URL or improper credentials. In these circumstances, it's best to catch the error and provide the user with a reasonable error message. Since the Dataset object does not actually contact the remote resource until the data is needed, it's important to take care to write the error handling in the right place. The following listing shows a short snippet of how error handling is done in our CSV example web app (condensed from tfjs-examples/csv-data/index.js). For more details about how to connect to CSV files guarded by authentication, see info box 6.2.

Listing 6.13 Handling errors arising from failed connections

```
const url = 'http://some.bad.url';
const sampleIndex = document.getElementById(        Wrapping this line in a try block
    'whichSampleInput').valueAsNumber;              wouldn't help because the bad
const myData = tf.data.csv(url);           ◁────    URL is not fetched here.
let columnNames;
try {                                               The error from a bad connection
  columnNames = await myData.columnNames();  ◁────  will be thrown at this step.
} catch (e) {
  ui.updateColumnNamesMessage(`Could not connect to ${url}`);
}
```

In section 6.2, we learned how to use model.fitDataset(). We saw that the method requires a dataset that yields elements in a very particular form. Recall that the form is an object with two properties {xs, ys}, where xs is a tensor representing a batch of the input, and ys is a tensor representing a batch of the associated target. By default, the CSV dataset will return elements as JavaScript objects, but we can configure the dataset to instead return elements closer to what we need for training. For this, we will need to use the csvConfig.columnConfigs field of tf.data.csv(). Consider a CSV file about golf with three columns: "club," "strength," and "distance." If we wished to predict distance from club and strength, we could apply a map function on the raw output to arrange the fields into xs and ys; or, more easily, we could configure the CSV reader to do this for us. Table 6.4 shows how to configure the CSV dataset to separate the feature and label properties, and perform batching so that the output is suitable for entry into model.fitDataset().

Table 6.4   Configuring a CSV dataset to work with `model.fitDataset()`

How the dataset is built and configured	Code for building the dataset	Result of dataset.take(1).toArray()[0] (the first element returned from the dataset)
Raw CSV default	`dataset = tf.data.csv(csvURL)`	`{club: 1, strength: 45, distance: 200}`

CSV with label configured in `columnConfigs`	`columnConfigs =`
	`  {distance: {isLabel: true}};`
	`dataset = tf.data.csv(csvURL,`
	`  {columnConfigs});`
		`{xs: {club: 1, strength: 45},`
		`ys: {distance: 200}}`

CSV with `columnConfigs` and then batched	`columnConfigs =`
	`  {distance: {isLabel: true}};`
	`dataset = tf.data`
	`  .csv(csvURL,`
	`{columnConfigs})`
	`  .batch(128);`
		`[xs: {club: Tensor,`
		`  strength: Tensor},`
		`ys: {distance:Tensor}]`
		
		Each of these three tensors has shape = **[128]**.

CSV with `columnConfigs` and then batched and mapped from object to array	`columnConfigs = {distance:`
	`{isLabel: true}};`
	`dataset = tf.data`
	`  .csv(csvURL,`
	`{columnConfigs})`
	`    .map(({xs, ys}) =>`
	`        {`
	`            return`
	`{xs:Object.values(xs),`
	
	`ys:Object.values(ys)};`
	`        })`
	`    .batch(128);`
		`{xs: Tensor, ys: Tensor}`
		Note that the mapping function returned items of the form `{xs: [number, number], ys: [number]}`. The batch operation automatically converts numeric arrays to tensors. Thus, the first tensor (`xs`) has shape = `[128,2]`. The second tensor (`ys`) has shape = `[128, 1]`.

INFO BOX 6.2   Fetching CSV data guarded by authentication

In the previous examples, we have connected to data available from remote files by simply providing a URL. This works well both in Node.js and from the browser and is very easy, but sometimes our data is protected, and we need to provide `Request` parameters. The `tf.data.csv()` API allows us to provide `RequestInfo` in place of a raw string URL, as shown in the following code. Other than the additional authorization parameter, there is no change in the dataset:

```
> const url = 'http://path/to/your/private.csv'
> const requestInfo = new Request(url);
> const API_KEY = 'abcdef123456789'
> requestInfo.headers.append('Authorization', API_KEY);
> const myDataset = tf.data.csv(requestInfo);
```

6.3.2 Accessing video data using tf.data.webcam()

One of the most exciting applications for TensorFlow.js projects is to train and apply machine-learning models to the sensors directly available on mobile devices. Motion recognition using the mobile's onboard accelerometer? Sound or speech understanding using the onboard microphone? Visual assistance using the onboard camera? There are so many good ideas out there, and we've just begun.

In chapter 5, we explored working with the webcam and microphone in the context of transfer learning. We saw how to use the camera to control a game of Pac-Man, and we used the microphone to fine-tune a speech-understanding system. While not every modality is available as a convenient API call, tf.data does have a simple and easy API for working with the webcam. Let's explore how that works and how to use it to predict from trained models.

With the tf.data API, it is very simple to create a dataset iterator yielding a stream of images from the webcam. Listing 6.14 shows a basic example from the documentation. The first thing we notice is the call to the tf.data.webcam(). This constructor returns a webcam iterator by taking an optional HTML element as its input argument. The constructor works only in the browser environment. If the API is called in the Node.js environment, or if there is no available webcam, then the constructor will throw an exception indicating the source of the error. Furthermore, the browser will request permission from the user before opening the webcam. The constructor will throw an exception if the permission is denied. Responsible development should cover these cases with user-friendly messages.

> **Listing 6.14 Creating a dataset using `tf.data.webcam()` and an HTML element**

Element shows webcam video and determines tensor size

Constructor for the video Dataset object. The element will display content from the webcam. The element also configures the size of the created tensors.

```
const videoElement = document.createElement('video');
videoElement.width = 100;
videoElement.height = 100;

onst webcam = await tf.data.webcam(videoElement);
const img = await webcam.capture();
img.print();
webcam.stop();
```

Stops the video stream and pauses the webcam iterator

Takes one frame from the video stream and offers the value as a tensor

When creating a webcam iterator, it is important that the iterator knows the shape of the tensors to be produced. There are two ways to control this. The first way, shown in listing 6.14, uses the shape of the provided HTML element. If the shape needs to be different, or perhaps the video isn't to be shown at all, the desired shape can be provided via a configuration object, as shown in listing 6.15. Note that the provided

HTML element argument is undefined, meaning that the API will create a hidden element in the DOM to act as a handle to the video.

Listing 6.15 Creating a basic webcam dataset using a configuration object

```
const videoElement = undefined;
const webcamConfig = {
    facingMode: 'user',
    resizeWidth: 100,
   resizeHeight: 100};
const webcam = await tf.data.webcam(
    videoElement, webcamConfig);
```

Building a webcam dataset iterator using a configuration object instead of an HTML element. Here, we also specify which camera to use on a device featuring multiple cameras. 'user' refers to the camera facing the user; as an alternative to 'user,' 'environment' refers to the rear camera.

It is also possible to use the configuration object to crop and resize portions of the video stream. Using the HTML element and the configuration object in tandem, the API allows the caller to specify a location to crop from and a desired output size. The output tensor will be interpolated to the desired size. See the next listing for an example of selecting a rectangular portion of a square video and then reducing the size to fit a small model.

Listing 6.16 Cropping and resizing data from a webcam

```
const videoElement = document.createElement('video');
videoElement.width = 300;
videoElement.height = 300;

const webcamConfig = {
    resizeWidth: 150,
    resizeHeight: 100,
    centerCrop: true
};

const webcam = await tf.data.webcam(
    videoElement, webcamConfig);
```

Without the explicit configuration, the videoElement would control the output size, 300 × 300 here.

The user requests a 150 × 100 extraction from the video.

The extracted data will be from the center of the original video.

Data captured from this webcam iterator depends on both the HTML element and the webcamConfig.

It is important to point out some obvious differences between this type of dataset and the datasets we've been working with so far. For example, the values yielded from the webcam depend on when you extract them. Contrast this with the CSV dataset, which will yield the rows in order no matter how fast or slowly they are drawn. Furthermore, samples can be drawn from the webcam for as long as the user desires more. The API callers must explicitly tell the stream to end when they are done with it.

Data is accessed from the webcam iterator using the capture() method, which returns a tensor representing the most recent frame. API users should use this tensor for their machine-learning work, but must remember to dispose of it to prevent a memory leak. Because of the intricacies involved in asynchronous processing of the webcam data, it is better to apply necessary preprocessing functions directly to the captured frame rather than use the deferred map() functionality provided by tf.data.

That is to say, rather than processing data using `data.map()`,

```
// No:
    let webcam = await tfd.webcam(myElement)
    webcam = webcam.map(myProcessingFunction);
    const imgTensor = webcam.capture();
    // use imgTensor here.
    tf.dispose(imgTensor)
```

apply the function directly to the image:

```
// Yes:
    let webcam = await tfd.webcam(myElement);
    const imgTensor = myPreprocessingFunction(webcam.capture());
    // use imgTensor here.
    tf.dispose(imgTensor)
```

The `forEach()` and `toArray()` methods should not be used on a webcam iterator. For processing long sequences of frames from the device, users of the `tf.data.webcam()` API should define their own loop using, for example, `tf.nextFrame()` and call `capture()` at a reasonable frame rate. The reason is that if you were to call `forEach()` on your webcam, then the framework would draw frames as fast as the browser's JavaScript engine can possibly request them from the device. This will typically create tensors faster than the frame rate of the device, resulting in duplicate frames and wasted computation. For similar reasons, a webcam iterator should *not* be passed as an argument to the `model.fit()` method.

Listing 6.17 shows the abbreviated prediction loop from the webcam-transfer-learning (Pac-Man) example we saw in chapter 5. Note that the outer loop will continue for as long as `isPredicting` is true, which is controlled by a UI element. Internally, the rate of the loop is moderated by a call to `tf.nextFrame()`, which is pinned to the UI's refresh rate. The following code is from tfjs-examples/webcam-transfer-learning/index.js.

> **Listing 6.17 Using `tf.data.webcam()` in a prediction loop**

```
async function getImage() {          ◁─────────  Captures a frame from the webcam and
  return (await webcam.capture())   ◁────┐       normalizes it between –1 and 1. Returns
    .expandDims(0)                                a batched image (1-element batch) of
    .toFloat()                                    shape [1, w, h, c].
    .div(tf.scalar(127))
    .sub(tf.scalar(1));                    webcam here refers to an iterator
                                           returned from tfd.webcam; see init() in
while (isPredicting) {                      listing 6.18.
  const img = await getImage();      ◁──────────
                                                 Draws the next frame
  const predictedClass = tf.tidy(() => {         from the webcam iterator
    // Capture the frame from the webcam.

    // Process the image and make predictions...   Waits until the next animation
    ...                                            frame before performing another
                                                   prediction
    await tf.nextFrame();     ◁─────────────────
  }
```

One final note: when using the webcam, it is often a good idea to draw, process, and discard an image before making predictions on the feed. There are two good reasons for this. First, passing the image through the model ensures that the relevant model weights have been loaded to the GPU, preventing any stuttering slowness on startup. Second, this gives the webcam hardware time to warm up and begin sending actual frames. Depending on the hardware, sometimes webcams will send blank frames while the device is powering up. See the next listing for a snippet showing how this is done in the webcam-transfer-learning example (from webcam-transfer-learning/index.js).

Listing 6.18   Creating a video dataset from `tf.data.webcam()`

```
async function init() {
  try {
    webcam = await tfd.webcam(
        document.getElementById('webcam'));
  } catch (e) {
    console.log(e);
    document.getElementById('no-webcam').style.display = 'block';
  }
  truncatedMobileNet = await loadTruncatedMobileNet();

  ui.init();

  // Warm up the model. This uploads weights to the GPU and compiles the
  // WebGL programs so the first time we collect data from the webcam it
  // will be quick.
  const screenShot = await webcam.capture();
  truncatedMobileNet.predict(screenShot.expandDims(0));
  screenShot.dispose();
}
```

Constructor for the video dataset object. The 'webcam' element is a video element in the HTML document.

The value returned from webcam.capture() is a tensor. It must be disposed to prevent a leak.

Makes a prediction on the first frame returned from the webcam to make sure the model is completely loaded on the hardware

6.3.3   *Accessing audio data using tf.data.microphone()*

Along with image data, `tf.data` also includes specialized handling to collect audio data from the device microphone. Similar to the webcam API, the microphone API creates a lazy iterator allowing the caller to request frames as needed, packaged neatly as tensors suitable for consumption directly into a model. The typical use case here is to collect frames to be used for prediction. While it's technically possible to produce a training stream using this API, zipping it together with the labels would be challenging.

Listing 6.19 shows an example of how to collect one second of audio data using the `tf.data.microphone()` API. Note that executing this code will trigger the browser to request that the user grant access to the microphone.

Listing 6.19   Collecting one second of audio data using the `tf.data.microphone()` API

```
const mic = await tf.data.microphone({
  fftSize: 1024,
  columnTruncateLength: 232,
```

The microphone configuration allows the user to control some common audio parameters. We spell out some of these in the main text.

```
    numFramesPerSpectrogram: 43,
    sampleRateHz: 44100,
    smoothingTimeConstant: 0,
    includeSpectrogram: true,
    includeWaveform: true
});
const audioData = await mic.capture();
const spectrogramTensor = audioData.spectrogram;
const waveformTensor = audioData.waveform;
mic.stop();
```

Executes the capture of audio from the microphone

The audio spectrum data is returned as a tensor of shape [43, 232, 1].

Users should call stop() to end the audio stream and turn off the microphone.

In addition to the spectrogram data, it is also possible to retrieve the waveform data directly. The shape of this data will be [fftSize * numFramesPerSpectrogram, 1] = [44032, 1].

The microphone includes a number of configurable parameters to give users fine control over how the fast Fourier transform (FFT) is applied to the audio data. Users may want more or fewer frames of frequency-domain audio data per spectrogram, or they may be interested in only a certain frequency range of the audio spectrum, such as those frequencies necessary for audible speech. The fields in listing 6.19 have the following meaning:

- sampleRateHz: 44100
  - The sampling rate of the microphone waveform. This must be exactly 44,100 or 48,000 and must match the rate specified by the device itself. It will throw an error if the specified value doesn't match the value made available by the device.
- fftSize: 1024
  - Controls the number of samples used to compute each nonoverlapping "frame" of audio. Each frame undergoes an FFT, and larger frames give more frequency sensitivity but have less time resolution, as time information *within the frame* is lost.
  - Must be a power of 2 between 16 and 8,192, inclusive. Here, 1024 means that energy within a frequency band is calculated over a span of about 1,024 samples.
  - Note that the highest measurable frequency is equal to half the sample rate, or approximately 22 kHz.
- columnTruncateLength: 232
  - Controls how much frequency information is retained. By default, each audio frame contains fftSize points, or 1,024 in our case, covering the entire spectrum from 0 to maximum (22 kHz). However, we are typically interested in only the lower frequencies. Human speech is generally only up to 5 kHz, and thus we only keep the part of the data representing zero to 5 kHz.
  - Here, 232 = (5 kHz/22 kHz) * 1024.

- numFramesPerSpectrogram: 43
  - The FFT is calculated on a series of nonoverlapping windows (or frames) of the audio sample to create a spectrogram. This parameter controls how many are included in each returned spectrogram. The returned spectrogram will be of shape [numFramesPerSpectrogram, fftSize, 1], or [43, 232, 1] in our case.
  - The duration of each frame is equal to the sampleRate/fftSize. In our case, 44 kHz * 1,024 is about 0.023 seconds.
  - There is no delay between frames, so the entire spectrogram duration is about 43 * 0.023 = 0.98, or just about 1 second.
- smoothingTimeConstant: 0
  - How much to blend the previous frame's data with this frame. It must be between 0 and 1.
- includeSpectogram: True
  - If true, the spectrogram will be calculated and made available as a tensor. Set this to false if the application does not actually need to calculate the spectrogram. This can happen only if the waveform is needed.
- includeWaveform: True
  - If true, the waveform is kept and made available as a tensor. This can be set to false if the caller will not need the waveform. Note that at least one of includeSpectrogram and includeWaveform must be true. It is an error if they are both false. Here we have set them both to true to show that this is a valid option, but in a typical application, only one of the two will be necessary.

Similar to the video stream, the audio stream sometimes takes some time to start, and data from the device might be nonsense to begin with. Zeros and infinities are commonly encountered, but actual values and durations are platform dependent. The best solution is to "warm up" the microphone for a short amount of time by throwing away the first few samples until the data no longer is corrupted. Typically, 200 ms of data is enough to begin getting clean samples.

6.4   *Your data is likely flawed: Dealing with problems in your data*

It's nearly a guarantee that there are problems with your raw data. If you're using your own data source, and you haven't spent several hours with an expert combing through the individual features, their distributions, and their correlations, then there is a very high chance that there are flaws that will weaken or break your machine-learning model. We, the authors of this book, can say this with confidence because of our experience with mentoring the construction of many machine-learning systems in many domains and building some ourselves. The most common symptom is that some model is not converging, or is converging to an accuracy well below what is expected. Another related but even more nefarious and difficult-to-debug pattern is when the model converges and performs well on the validation and testing data but then fails to meet expectations in production. Sometimes there is a genuine modeling issue, or a bad hyperparameter, or just bad luck, but, by far, the most common root cause for these bugs is that there is a flaw in the data.

Behind the scenes, all the datasets we've used (such as MNIST, iris-flowers, and speech-commands) went through manual inspection, pruning of bad examples, formatting into a standard and suitable format, and other data science operations that we didn't talk about. Data issues can arise in many forms, including missing fields, correlated samples, and skewed distributions. There is such a richness and diversity of complexity in working with data, someone could write a book on it. In fact, please see *Data Wrangling with JavaScript* by Ashley Davis for a fuller exposition![10]

Data scientists and data managers have become full-time professional roles in many companies. The tools these professionals use and best practices they follow are diverse and often depend on the specific domain under scrutiny. In this section, we will touch on the basics and point to a few tools to help you avoid the heartbreak of long model debugging sessions only to find out that it was the data itself that was flawed. For a more thorough treatment of data science, we will offer references where you can learn more.

6.4.1 Theory of data

In order to know how to detect and fix *bad* data, we must first know what *good* data looks like. Much of the theory underpinning the field of machine learning rests on the premise that our data comes from a *probability distribution*. In this formulation, our training data consists of a collection of independent *samples*. Each sample is described as an (x, y) pair, where y is the part of the sample we wish to predict from the x part. Continuing this premise, our inference data consists of a collection of samples *from the exact same distribution as our training data*. The only important difference between the training data and the inference data is that at inference time, we do not get to see y. We are supposed to estimate the y part of the sample from the x part using the statistical relationships learned from the training data.

There are a number of ways that our real-life data can fail to live up to this platonic ideal. If, for instance, our training data and inference data are samples from *different* distributions, we say there is dataset *skew*. As a simple example, if you are estimating road traffic based on features like weather and time of day, and all of your training data comes from Mondays and Tuesdays while your test data comes from Saturdays and Sundays, you can expect that the model accuracy will be less than optimal. The distribution of auto traffic on weekdays is not the same as the distribution of traffic on weekends. As another example, imagine we are building a face-recognition system, and we train the system to recognize faces based on a collection of labeled data from our home country. We should not be surprised to find that the system struggles and fails when used in

---

[10] Available from Manning Publications, www.manning.com/books/data-wrangling-with-javascript.

locations with different demographics. Most data-skew issues you'll encounter in real machine-learning settings will be more subtle than these two examples.

Another way that skew can sneak into a dataset is if there was some shift during data collection. If, for instance, we are taking audio samples to learn speech signals, and then halfway through the construction of our training set, our microphone breaks, so we purchase an upgrade, we can expect that the second half of our training set will have a different noise and audio distribution than our first half. Presumably, at inference time, we will be testing using only the new microphone, so skew exists between the training and test set as well.

At some level, dataset skew is unavoidable. For many applications, our training data necessarily comes from the past, and the data we pass to our application necessarily comes from right now. The underlying distribution producing these samples is bound to change as cultures, interests, fashions, and other confounding factors change with the times. In such a situation, all we can do is understand the skew and minimize the impact. For this reason, many machine-learning models in production settings are constantly retrained using the freshest available training data in an attempt to keep up with continually shifting distributions.

Another way our data samples can fail to live up to the ideal is by failing to be independent. Our ideal states that the samples are *independent and identically distributed* (IID). But in some datasets, one sample gives clues to the likely value of the next. Samples from these datasets are not independent. The most common way that sample-to-sample dependence creeps into a dataset is by the phenomenon of sorting. For access speed and all sorts of other good reasons, we have been trained as computer scientists to organize our data. In fact, database systems often organize our data for us without us even trying. As a result, when you stream your data from some source, you have to be very careful that the results do not have some pattern in their order.

Consider the following hypothetical. We wish to build an estimate of the cost of housing in California for an application in real estate. We get a CSV dataset of housing prices[11] from around the state, along with relevant features, such as the number of rooms, the age of the development, and so on. We might be tempted to simply begin training a function from features to price right away since we have the data, and we know how to do it. But knowing that data often has flaws, we decide to take a look first. We begin by plotting some features versus their index in the array, using datasets and Plotly.js. See the plots in figure 6.3 for an illustration[12] and the following listing (summarized from https://codepen.io/tfjs-book/pen/MLQOem) for how the illustrations were made.

---

[11] A description of the California housing dataset used here is available from the Machine Learning Crash Course at http://mng.bz/Xpm6.

[12] The plots in figure 6.3 were made using the CodePen at https://codepen.io/tfjs-book/pen/MLQOem.

Listing 6.20   Building a plot of a feature vs. index using tfjs-data

```
const plottingData = {
  x: [],
  y: [],
  mode: 'markers',
  type: 'scatter',
  marker: {symbol: 'circle', size: 8}
};
const filename = 'https://storage.googleapis.com/learnjs-data/csv-
    datasets/california_housing_train.csv';
const dataset = tf.data.csv(filename);
await dataset.take(1000).forEachAsync(row => {        ◁──┐  Takes the first 1,000 samples
  plottingData.x.push(i++);                                and collects their values and
  plottingData.y.push(row['longitude']);                   their indices. Don't forget
});                                                         await, or your plot will
                                                           (probably) be empty!
Plotly.newPlot('plot', [plottingData], {
  width: 700,
  title: 'Longitude feature vs sample index',
  xaxis: {title: 'sample index'},
  yaxis: {title: 'longitude'}
});
```

Imagine we were to construct a train-test split with this dataset where we took the first 500 samples for training and the remainder for testing. What would happen? It appears from this analysis that we would be training with data from one geographic area and testing with data from another. The Longitude panel in figure 6.3 shows the crux of the problem: the first samples are from a higher longitude (more westerly) than any of the others. There is still probably plenty of signal in the features, and the model would "work" somewhat, but it would not be as accurate or high-quality as if our data were truly IID. If we didn't know better, we might spend days or weeks playing with different models and hyperparameters before we figured out what was wrong and looked at our data!

What can we do to clean this up? Fixing this particular issue is pretty simple. In order to remove the relationship between the data and the index, we can just shuffle our data into a random order. However, there is something we must watch out for here. TensorFlow.js datasets have a built-in shuffle routine, but it is a *streaming window* shuffle routine. This means that samples are randomly shuffled within a window of fixed size but no further. This is out of necessity because TensorFlow.js datasets stream data, and they may stream an unlimited number of samples. In order to completely shuffle a never-ending data source, you first need to wait until it is done.

So, can we make do with this streaming window shuffle for our longitude feature? Certainly if we know the size of the datasets (17,000 in this case), we can specify the window to be larger than the entire dataset, and we are all set. In the limit of very large window sizes, windowed shuffling and our normal exhaustive shuffling are identical. If we don't know how large our dataset is, or the size is prohibitively large (that is, we can't hold the whole thing at once in a memory cache), we may have to make do with less.

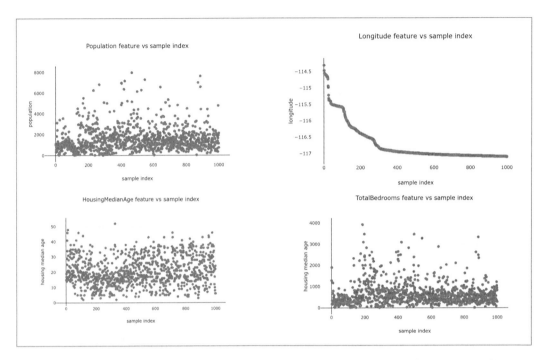

Figure 6.3   Plots of four dataset features vs. the sample index. Ideally, in a clean IID dataset, we would expect the sample index to give us no information about the feature value. We see that for some features, the distribution of y values clearly depends on x. Most egregiously, the "longitude" feature seems to be sorted by the sample index.

Figure 6.4, created with https://codepen.io/tfjs-book/pen/JxpMrj, illustrates what happens when we shuffle our data with four different window sizes using `tf.data` `.Dataset`'s `shuffle()` method:

```
for (let windowSize of [10, 50, 250, 6000]) {
    shuffledDataset = dataset.shuffle(windowSize);
    myPlot(shuffledDataset, windowSize)
}
```

We see that the structural relationship between the index and the feature value remains clear even for relatively large window sizes. It isn't until the window size is 6,000 that it looks to the naked eye like the data can now be treated as IID. So, is 6,000 the right window size? Was there a number between 250 and 6,000 that would have worked? Is 6,000 still not enough to catch distributional issues we aren't seeing in these illustrations? The right approach here is to shuffle the entire dataset by using a `windowSize` >= the number of samples in the dataset. For datasets where this is not possible due to memory limitations, time constraints, or possibly unlimited datasets, you must put on your data scientist hat and examine the distribution to determine an appropriate window size.

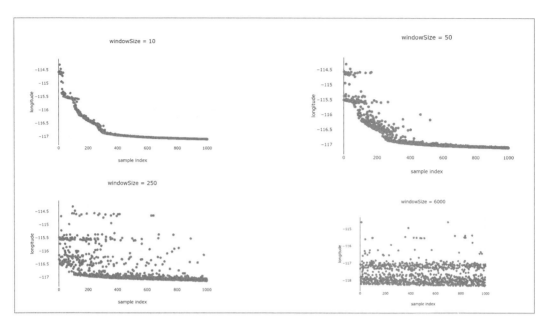

Figure 6.4 Four plots of longitude vs. the sample index for four shuffled datasets. The shuffle window size is different for each, increasing from 10 to 6,000 samples. We see that even at a window size of 250, there is still a strong relationship between the index and the feature value. There are more large values near the beginning. It isn't until we are using a shuffle window size almost as large as the dataset that the data's IID nature is nearly restored.

6.4.2 Detecting and cleaning problems with data

In the previous section, we went through how to detect and fix one type of data problem: sample-to-sample dependence. Of course, this is just one of the many types of problems that can arise in data. A full treatment of all the types of things that can go wrong is far beyond the scope of this book, because there are as many things that can go wrong with data as there are things that can go wrong with code. Let's go through a few here, though, so you will recognize the problems when you see them and know what terms to search for to find more information.

OUTLIERS

Outliers are samples in our dataset that are very unusual and somehow do not belong to the underlying distribution. For instance, if we were working with a dataset of health statistics, we might expect the typical adult's weight to be between roughly 40 and 130 kilograms. If, in our dataset, 99.9% of our samples were in this range, but every so often we encountered a nonsensical sample report of 145,000 kg, or 0 kg, or worse, NaN,[13] we would consider these samples as outliers. A quick online search reveals that there are many opinions about the right way to deal with outliers. Ideally, we would have very few outliers in our training data, and we would know how to find

---

[13] Ingesting a value of NaN in our input features would propagate that NaN throughout our model.

them. If we could write a program to reject outliers, we could remove them from our dataset and go on training without them. Of course, we would want to also trigger that same logic at inference time; otherwise we would introduce skew. In this case, we could use the same logic to inform the user that their sample constitutes an outlier to the system, and that they must try something different.

Another common way to deal with outliers at the feature level is to clamp values by providing a reasonable minimum and maximum. In our case, we might replace weight with

```
weight = Math.min(MAX_WEIGHT, Math.max(weight, MIN_WEIGHT));
```

In such circumstances, it is also a good idea to add a new feature, indicating that the outlier value has been replaced. This way, an original value of 40 kg can be distinguished from a value of –5 kg that was clamped to 40 kg, giving the network the opportunity to learn the relationship between the outlier status and the target, if such a relationship exists:

```
isOutlierWeight = weight > MAX_WEIGHT | weight < MIN_WEIGHT;
```

MISSING DATA

Frequently, we are confronted with situations in which some samples are missing some features. This can happen for any number of reasons. Sometimes the data comes from hand-entered forms, and some fields are just skipped. Sometimes sensors were broken or down at the time of data collection. For some samples, perhaps some features just don't make sense. For example, what is the most recent sale price of a home that has never been sold? Or what is the telephone number of a person without a telephone?

As with outliers, there are many ways to address the problem of missing data, and data scientists have different opinions about which techniques are appropriate in which situations. Which technique is best depends on a few considerations, including whether the likelihood of the feature to be missing depends on the value of the feature itself, or whether the "missingness" can be predicted from other features in the sample. Info box 6.3 outlines a glossary of categories of missing data.

INFO BOX 6.3   Categories of missing data

Missing at random (MAR):

- The likelihood of the feature to be missing does not depend on the hidden missing value, but it may depend on some other observed value.
- Example: If we had an automated visual system recording automobile traffic, it might record, among other things, license plate numbers and time of day. Sometimes, if it's dark, we are unable to read the license plate. The plate's presence does not depend on the license plate value, but it may depend on the (observed) time-of-day feature.

Missing completely at random (MCAR)

- The likelihood of the feature to be missing does not depend on the hidden missing value or any of the observed values.
- Example: Cosmic rays interfere with our equipment and sometimes corrupt values from our dataset. The likelihood of corruption does not depend on the value stored or on other values in the dataset.

Missing not at random (MNAR)

- The likelihood of the feature to be missing depends on the hidden value, given the observed data.
- Example: A personal weather station keeps track of all sorts of statistics, like air pressure, rainfall, and solar radiation. However, when it snows, the solar radiation meter does not take a signal.

When data is missing from our training set, we have to apply some corrections to be able to turn the data into a fixed-shape tensor, which requires a value in every cell. There are four important techniques for dealing with the missing data.

The simplest technique, if the training data is plentiful and the missing fields are rare, is to discard training samples that have missing data. However, be aware that this can introduce a bias in your trained model. To see this plainly, imagine a problem in which there is missing data much more commonly from the positive class than the negative class. You would end up learning an incorrect likelihood of the classes. Only if your missing data is MCAR are you completely safe to discard samples.

> **Listing 6.21 Handling missing features by removing the data**

```
const filteredDataset =
    tf.data.csv(csvFilename)
    .filter(e => e['featureName']);
```
Keeps only those elements whose value of 'featureName' is truthy: that is, not 0, null, undefined, NaN, or an empty string

Another technique for dealing with missing data is to fill the missing data in with some value, also known as *imputation*. Common imputation techniques include replacing missing numeric feature values with the mean, median, or mode value of that feature. Missing categorical features may be replaced with the most common value for that feature (also mode). More sophisticated techniques involve building predictors for the missing features from the available features and using those. In fact, using neural networks is one of the "sophisticated techniques" for the imputation of missing data. The downside of using imputation is that the learner is not aware that the feature was missing. If there is information in the missingness about the target variable, it will be lost in imputation.

Listing 6.22   Handling missing features with imputation

Function to calculate the value to use for
imputation. Remember to only include
valid values when computing the mean.

```
async function calculateMeanOfNonMissing(
    dataset, featureName) {
  let samplesSoFar = 0;
  let sumSoFar = 0;
  await dataset.forEachAsync(row => {
    const x = row[featureName];
    if (x != null) {        ◄
      samplesSoFar += 1;
      sumSoFar += x;
    }
  });
  return sumSoFar / samplesSoFar;   ◄
}

function replaceMissingWithImputed(
    row, featureName, imputedValue)) {
  const x = row[featureName];
  if (x == null) {
    return {...row, [featureName]: imputedValue};
  } else {
    return row;
  }
}

const rawDataset tf.data.csv(csvFilename);
const imputedValue = await calculateMeanOfNonMissing(
    rawDataset, 'myFeature');
const imputedDataset = rawDataset.map(
    row => replaceMissingWithImputed(
        row, 'myFeature', imputedValue));
```

Both undefined and null values are
considered to be missing here. Some
datasets might use sentinel values like
−1 or 0 to indicate missingness. Be
sure to look at your data!

Note that this will return NaN
when all the data is missing.

Function to conditionally
update a row if the value
at featureName is missing

Uses the tf.data.Dataset map()
method to map the replacement
over all the elements

Sometimes missing values are replaced with a *sentinel value*. For instance, a missing body weight value might be replaced with a −1, indicating that no weight was taken. If this appears to be the case with your data, take care to handle the sentinel value *before* clamping it as an outlier (for example, based on our prior example, replacing this −1 with 40 kg).

Conceivably, if there is a relationship between the missingness of the feature and the target to be predicted, the model may be able to use the sentinel value. In practice, the model will spend some of its computational resources learning to distinguish when the feature is used as a value and when it is used as an indicator.

Perhaps the most robust way to manage missing data is to both use imputation to fill in a value and add a second indicator feature to communicate to the model when that feature was missing. In this case, we would replace the missing body weight with a guess and also add a new feature `weight_missing`, which is 1 when weight was missing and 0 when it was provided. This allows the model to leverage the missingness, if valuable, and also to not conflate it with the actual value of the weight.

Listing 6.23 Adding a feature to indicate missingness

```
function addMissingness(row, featureName)) {
  const x = row[featureName];
  const isMissing = (x == null) ? 1 : 0;
  return {...row, [featureName + '_isMissing']: isMissing};
}

const rawDataset tf.data.csv(csvFilename);
const datasetWithIndicator = rawDataset.map(
    (row) => addMissingness(row, featureName);
```

Function to add a new feature to each row, which is 1 if the feature is missing and 0 otherwise

Uses the tf.data.Dataset map() method to map the additional feature into each row

SKEW

Earlier in this chapter, we described the concept of skew, a difference in distribution from one dataset to another. It is one of the major problems machine-learning practitioners face when deploying trained models to production. Detecting skew involves modeling the distributions of the datasets and comparing them to see if they match. A simple way to quickly look at the statistics of your dataset is to use a tool like Facets (https://pair-code.github.io/facets/). See figure 6.5 for a screenshot. Facets will analyze and summarize your datasets to allow you to look at per-feature distributions, which will help you to quickly suss out problems with different distributions between your datasets.

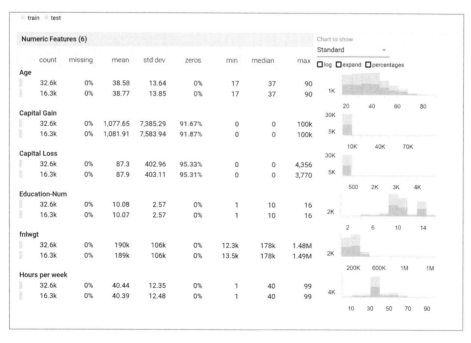

Figure 6.5 A screenshot of Facets showing per-feature value distributions for the training and test split of the UC Irvine Census Income datasets (see http://archive.ics.uci.edu/ml/datasets/ Census+ Income). This dataset is the default loaded at https://pair-code.github.io/facets/, but you can navigate to the site and upload your own CSVs to compare. This view is known as Facets Overview.

A simple, rudimentary skew-detection algorithm may calculate the mean, median, and variance of each feature and check whether any differences across datasets are within acceptable bounds. More sophisticated methods may attempt to predict, given samples, which dataset they are from. Ideally, this should not be possible since they are from the same distribution. If it is possible to predict whether a data point is from training or testing, this is a sign of skew.

BAD STRINGS

Very commonly, categorical data is provided as string-valued features. For instance, when users access your web page, you might keep logs of which browser was used with values like FIREFOX, SAFARI, and CHROME. Typically, before ingesting these values into a deep-learning model, the values are converted into integers (either through a known vocabulary or by hashing), which are then mapped into an *n*-dimensional vector space (See section 9.2.3 on word embeddings). A common problem is where the strings from one dataset have different formatting from the strings in a different dataset. For instance, the training data might have FIREFOX, while at service time, the model receives FIREFOX\n, with the newline character included, or "FIREFOX", with quotes. This is a particularly insidious form of skew and should be handled as such.

OTHER THINGS TO WATCH OUT FOR IN YOUR DATA

In addition to the problems called out in the previous sections, here are a few more things to be aware of when feeding your data to a machine-learning system:

- *Overly unbalanced data*—If there are some features that take the same value for nearly every sample in your dataset, you may consider getting rid of them. It is very easy to overfit with this type of signal, and deep-learning methods do not handle very sparse data well.

- *Numeric/categorical distinction*—Some datasets will use integers to represent elements of an enumerated set, and this can cause problems when the rank order of these integers is meaningless. For instance, if we have an enumerated set of music genres, like ROCK, CLASSICAL, and so on, and a vocabulary that mapped these values to integers, it is important that we handle the values like enumerated values when we pass them into the model. This means encoding the values using one-hot or embedding (see chapter 9). Otherwise, these numbers will be interpreted as floating-point values, suggesting spurious relationships between terms based on the numeric distance between their encodings.

- *Massive scale differences*—This was mentioned earlier, but it bears repeating in this section on what can go wrong with data. Watch out for numeric features that have large-scale differences. They can lead to instability in training. In general, it's best to z-normalize (normalize the mean and standard deviation of) your data before training. Just be sure to use the same preprocessing at serving time as you did during training. You can see an example of this in the tensorflow/tfjs-examples iris example, as we explored in chapter 3.

- *Bias, security, and privacy*—Obviously, there is much more to responsible machine-learning development than can be covered in a book chapter. It is critical, if you are developing machine-learning solutions, that you spend the time to familiarize yourself with at least the basics of the best practices for managing bias, security, and privacy. A good place to get started is the page on responsible AI practices at https://ai.google/education/responsible-ai-practices. Following these practices is just the right thing to do to be a good person and a responsible engineer—obviously important goals in and of themselves. In addition, paying careful attention to these issues is a wise choice from a purely selfish perspective, as even small failures of bias, security, or privacy can lead to embarrassing systemic failures that quickly lead customers to look elsewhere for more reliable solutions.

In general, you should aim to spend time convincing yourself that your data is as you expect it to be. There are many tools to help you do this, from notebooks like Observable, Jupyter, Kaggle Kernel, and Colab, to graphical UI tools like Facets. See figure 6.6

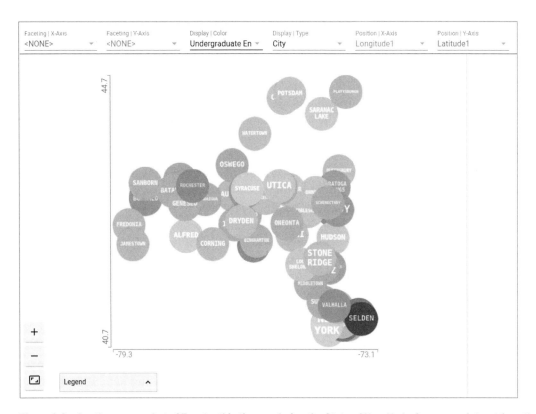

Figure 6.6 **Another screenshot of Facets, this time exploring the State of New York, Campuses dataset from the data-csv example. Here, we see the Facets Dive view that allows you to explore the relationships between different features of a dataset. Each point shown is a data point from the dataset, and here we have it configured so that the point's x-position is set to the Latitude1 feature, the y-position is the Longitude1 feature, the color is related to the Undergraduate Enrollment feature, and the words on the front are set to the City feature, which contains, for each data point, the name of the city the university campus is in. We can see from this visualization a rough outline of the state of New York, with Buffalo in the west and New York in the southeast. Apparently, the city of Selden contains one of the largest campuses by undergraduate enrollment.**

for another way to explore your data in Facets. Here, we use Facets' plotting feature, known as Facets Dive, to view points from the State Universities of New York (SUNY) dataset. Facets Dive allows the user to select columns from the data and visually express each field in a custom way. Here, we've used the drop-down menus to use the Longitude1 field as the x-position of the point, the Latitude1 field as the y-position of the point, the City string field as the name of the point, and the Undergraduate Enrollment as the color of the point. We expect the latitude and longitude, plotted on the 2D plane, to reveal a map of New York state, and indeed that's what we see. The correctness of the map can be verified by comparing it to SUNY's web page at www.suny .edu/attend/visit-us/campus-map/.

6.5   *Data augmentation*

So, we've collected our data, we've connected it to a `tf.data.Dataset` for easy manipulation, and we've scrutinized it and cleaned it of problems. What else can we do to help our model succeed?

Sometimes, the data you have isn't enough, and you wish to expand the dataset programmatically, creating new examples by making small changes to existing data. For instance, recall the MNIST hand-written digit-classification problem from chapter 4. MNIST contains 60,000 training images of 10 hand-written digits, or 6,000 per digit. Is that enough to learn all the types of flexibility we want for our digit classifier? What happens if someone draws a digit too large or small? Or rotated slightly? Or skewed? Or with a thicker or thinner pen? Will our model still understand?

If we take an MNIST sample digit and alter the image by moving the digit one pixel to the left, the semantic label of the digit doesn't change. The 9 shifted to the left is still a 9, but we have a new training example. This type of programmatically generated example, created from mutating an actual example, is known as a *pseudo-example*, and the process of adding pseudo-examples to the data is known as *data augmentation*.

Data augmentation takes the approach of generating more training data from existing training samples. In the case of image data, various transformations such as rotating, cropping, and scaling often yield believable-looking images. The purpose is to increase the diversity of the training data in order to benefit the generalization power of the trained model (in other words, to mitigate overfitting), which is especially useful when the size of the training dataset is small.

Figure 6.7 shows data augmentation applied to an input example consisting of an image of a cat, from a dataset of labeled images. The data is augmented by applying rotations and skew in such a way that the label of the example, that is, "CAT" does not change, but the input example changes significantly.

If you train a new network using this data-augmentation configuration, the network will never see the same input twice. But the inputs it sees are still heavily intercorrelated because they come from a small number of original images—you can't produce new information, you can only remix existing information. As such, this may not be enough

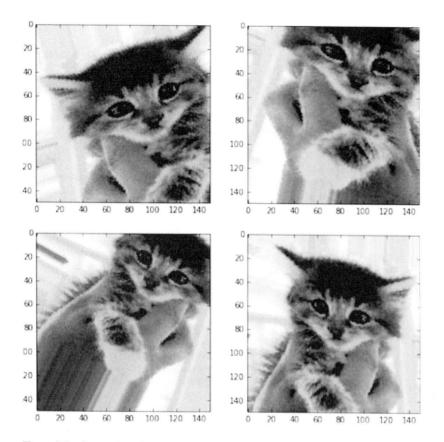

Figure 6.7   Generation of cat pictures via random data augmentation. A single labeled example can yield a whole family of training samples by providing random rotations, reflections, translations, and skews. Meow.

to completely get rid of overfitting. Another risk of using data augmentation is that the training data is now less likely to match the distribution of the inference data, introducing skew. Whether the benefits of the additional training pseudo-examples outweigh the costs of skew is application-dependent, and it's something you may just need to test and experiment with.

Listing 6.24 shows how you can include data augmentation as a `dataset.map()` function, injecting allowable transformations into your dataset. Note that augmentation should be applied per example. It's also important to see that augmentation should *not* be applied to the validation or testing set. If we test on augmented data, then we will have a biased measure of the power of our model because the augmentations will not be applied at inference time.

Listing 6.24   Training a model on a dataset with data augmentation

The augmentation function takes a sample in {image, label} format and returns a new, perturbed sample in the same format.

Assume that randomRotate, randomSkew, and randomMirror are defined elsewhere by some library. The amount to rotate, skew, and so on is generated randomly for each call. The augmentation should depend only on the features, not the label of the sample.

```
function augmentFn(sample) {
    const img = sample.image;
    const augmentedImg = randomRotate(
        randomSkew(randomMirror(img))));
    return {image: augmentedImg, label: sample.label};
}

const (trainingDataset, validationDataset} =
    getDatsetsFromSource();
augmentedDataset = trainingDataset
    .repeat().map(augmentFn).batch(BATCH_SIZE);

// Train model
await model.fitDataset(augmentedDataset, {
    batchesPerEpoch: ui.getBatchesPerEpoch(),
    epochs: ui.getEpochsToTrain(),
    validationData: validationDataset.repeat(),
    validationBatches: 10,
    callbacks: { ... },
    }
}
```

This function returns two tf.data.Datasets, each with element type {image, label}.

The augmentation is applied to the individual elements before batching.

We fit the model on the augmented dataset.

IMPORTANT! Do not apply augmentation to the validation set. Repeat is called on the validationData here since the data won't loop automatically. Only 10 batches are taken per validation measurement, as configured.

Hopefully, this chapter convinced you of the importance of understanding your data before throwing machine-learning models at it. We talked about out-of-the-box tools such as Facets, which you can use to examine your datasets and thereby deepen your understanding of them. However, when you need a more flexible and customized visualization of your data, it becomes necessary to write some code to do that job. In the next chapter, we will teach you the basics of tfjs-vis, a visualization module maintained by the authors of TensorFlow.js that can support such data-visualization use cases.

Exercises

1 Extend the simple-object-detection example from chapter 5 to use `tf.data .generator()` and `model.fitDataset()` instead of generating the full dataset up front. What advantages are there to this structure? Does performance meaningfully improve if the model is provided a much larger dataset of images to train from?

2 Add data augmentation to the MNIST example by adding small shifts, scales, and rotations to the examples. Does this help in performance? Does it make sense to validate and test on the data stream with augmentation, or is it more proper to test only on "real" natural examples?

3 Try plotting some of the features from some of the datasets we've used in other chapters using the techniques in section 6.4.1. Does the data meet the expectations of independence? Are there outliers? What about missing values?

4 Load some of the CSV datasets we've discussed here into the Facets tool. What features look like they could cause problems? Any surprises?

5 Consider some of the datasets we've used in earlier chapters. What sorts of data augmentation techniques would work for those?

Summary

- Data is a critical force powering the deep-learning revolution. Without access to large, well-organized datasets, most deep-learning applications could not happen.

- TensorFlow.js comes packaged with the `tf.data` API to make it easy to stream large datasets, transform data in various ways, and connect them to models for training and prediction.

- There are several ways to build a `tf.data.Dataset` object: from a JavaScript array, from a CSV file, or from a data-generating function. Building a dataset that streams from a remote CSV file can be done in one line of JavaScript.

- `tf.data.Dataset` objects have a chainable API that makes it easy and convenient to shuffle, filter, batch, map, and perform other operations commonly needed in a machine-learning application.

- `tf.data.Dataset` accesses data in a lazy streaming fashion. This makes working with large remote datasets simple and efficient but comes at the cost of working with asynchronous operations.

- `tf.Model` objects can be trained directly from a `tf.data.Dataset` using their `fitDataset()` method.

- Auditing and cleaning data requires time and care, but it is a required step for any machine-learning system you intend to put to practical use. Detecting and managing problems like skew, missing data, and outliers at the data-processing stage will end up saving debugging time during the modeling stage.

- Data augmentation can be used to expand the dataset to include programmatically generated pseudo-examples. This can help the model to cover known invariances that were underrepresented in the original dataset.

Visualizing data and models

This chapter covers
- How to use tfjs-vis to perform custom data visualization
- How to peek at the internal workings of models after they are trained and gain useful insights

Visualization is an important skill for machine-learning practitioners because it is involved in every phase of the machine-learning workflow. Before we build models, we examine our data by visualizing it; during model engineering and training, we monitor the training process through visualization; after the model is trained, we use visualization to get a sense about how it works.

In chapter 6, you learned the benefits of visualizing and understanding data before applying machine learning on it. We described how to use Facets, a browser-based tool that helps you get a quick, interactive look at your data. In this chapter, we will introduce a new tool, tfjs-vis, which helps you visualize your data in custom, programmatic ways. The benefit of doing so, versus just looking at the data in its raw format or using off-the-shelf tools such as Facets, is the more flexible and versatile visualization paradigm and the deeper understanding of data that it leads to.

In addition to the visualization of data, we will show how visualization can be used on deep-learning models *after* they are trained. We will use the fascinating examples of peeking into the "black boxes" of neural networks by visualizing their internal activations and computing the patterns that maximally "excite" layers of a convnet. This will complete the story of how visualization goes hand-in-hand with deep learning in each and every stage of it.

By the end of this chapter, you should know why visualization is an indispensable part of any machine-learning workflow. You should also be familiar with the standard ways in which data and models are visualized in the framework of TensorFlow.js and be able to apply them to your own machine-learning problems.

7.1 Data visualization

Let's start from the visualization of data, because that's the first thing a machine-learning practitioner does when laying hands on a new problem. We assume that the visualization task is more advanced than what can be covered by Facets (for instance, the data isn't in a small CSV file). For that, we will first introduce a basic charting API that helps you create simple and widely used types of plots, including line charts, scatter plots, bar charts, and histograms, in the browser. After we've covered the basic examples using hand-coded data, we will put things together by using an example involving the visualization of an interesting real dataset.

7.1.1 Visualizing data using tfjs-vis

tfjs-vis is a visualization library closely integrated with TensorFlow.js. Among its many features that this chapter will cover is a lightweight charting API under its `tfvis.render.*` namespace.[1] This simple and intuitive API allows you to make charts in the browser, with a focus on the types of charts most frequently used in machine learning. To help you get started with `tfvis.render`, we will give you a tour of the CodePen at https://codepen.io/tfjs-book/pen/BvzMZr, which showcases how to use `tfvis.render` to create various types of basic data plots.

BASICS OF TFJS-VIS
First, note that tfjs-vis is separate from the main TensorFlow.js library. You can see this from how the CodePen imports tfjs-vis with a `<script>` tag:

```
<script src="https://cdn.jsdelivr.net/npm/@tensorflow/tfjs-vis@latest">
</script>
```

This is different from how the main TensorFlow.js library is imported:

```
<script src="https://cdn.jsdelivr.net/npm/@tensorflow/tfjs@latest">
</script>
```

The same distinction applies to the npm packages of tfjs-vis and TensorFlow.js (`@tensorflow/tfjs-vis` and `@tensorflow/tfjs`, respectively). In a web page or JavaScript program that depends on both TensorFlow.js and tfjs-vis, the two dependencies must both be imported.

---

[1] This charting API is built on top of the Vega visualization library: https://vega.github.io/vega/.

Line charts

The most commonly used type of chart is perhaps the *line chart* (a curve that plots a quantity against an ordered quantity). A line chart has a horizontal axis and a vertical axis, which are often referred to as the *x-axis* and *y-axis*, respectively. This type of visualization is seen everywhere in life. For example, we can plot how the temperature changes over the course of a day with a line chart in which the horizontal axis is the time of day and the vertical axis is the reading of a thermometer. The horizontal axis of a line chart can also be something other than time. For instance, we can use a line chart to show the relation between the therapeutic effect of a high-blood-pressure medication (how much it reduces blood pressure) and the dose (how much of the medication is used per day). Such a plot is referred to as a *dose-response curve*. Another good example of a nontemporal line chart is the ROC curve we discussed in chapter 3. There, neither the x- nor y-axis has to do with time (they are the false and true positive rates of a binary classifier).

To create a line chart with `tfvis.render`, use the `linechart()` function. As the first example in the CodePen (also listing 7.1) shows, the function takes three arguments:

1 The first argument is the HTML element in which the chart will be drawn. An empty <div> element suffices.

2 The second argument is the values of the data points in the chart. This is a plain old JavaScript object (POJO) with the `value` field pointing to an array. The array consists of a number of x-y value pairs, each of which is represented by a POJO with fields named x and y. The x and y values are, of course, the x- and y-coordinates of the data points, respectively.

3 The third argument, which is optional, contains additional configuration fields for the line chart. In this example, we use the `width` field to specify the width of the resultant chart (in pixels). You will see more configuration fields in the coming examples.[2]

Listing 7.1 Making a simple line chart using `tfvis.render.linechart()`

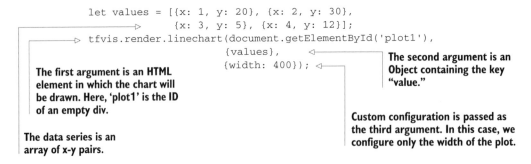

```
let values = [{x: 1, y: 20}, {x: 2, y: 30},
              {x: 3, y: 5}, {x: 4, y: 12}];
tfvis.render.linechart(document.getElementById('plot1'),
                       {values},
                       {width: 400});
```

The first argument is an HTML element in which the chart will be drawn. Here, 'plot1' is the ID of an empty div.

The data series is an array of x-y pairs.

The second argument is an Object containing the key "value."

Custom configuration is passed as the third argument. In this case, we configure only the width of the plot.

---

[2] https://js.tensorflow.org/api_vis/latest/ contains the full documentation of the tfjs-vis API, where you can find information about other configuration fields of this function.

The line chart created by the code in listing 7.1 is shown in the left panel of figure 7.1. This is a simple curve with only four data points. But the linechart() function can support curves with many more data points (for example, thousands). However, you will eventually run into the browser's resource restrictions if you try to plot too many data points at once. The limit is browser- and platform-dependent and should be discovered empirically. In general, it is good practice to limit the size of the data to be rendered in interactive visualizations for the sake of a smooth and responsive UI.

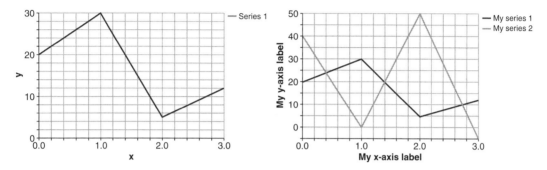

Figure 7.1 Line charts created using `tfvis.render.linechart()`. Left: a single series, made using the code in listing 7.1. Right: two series in the same axes, made using the code in listing 7.2.

Sometimes you want to plot two curves in the same chart in order to show the relation between them (for instance, to contrast them with each other). You can make these sorts of plots with `tfvis.render.linechart()`. An example is shown in the right panel of figure 7.1 and the code in listing 7.2.

These are known as *multiseries* charts, and each line is called a *series*. To create a multiseries chart, you must include an additional field, `series`, in the first argument to `linechart()`. The value of the field is an array of strings. The strings are the names given to the series and will be rendered as a legend in the resulting chart. In the example code, we call our series `'My series 1'` and `'My series 2'`.

The `value` field of the first argument also needs to be specified properly for a multiseries chart. For our first example, we provided an array of points, but for multiseries plots, we must provide an array of arrays. Each element of the nested array is the data points of a series and has the same format as the values array we saw in listing 7.1 when we plotted a single-series chart. Therefore, the length of the nested array must match the length of the `series` array, or an error will occur.

The chart created by listing 7.2 is shown in the right panel of figure 7.1. As you can see in the chart in electronic versions of this book, tfjs-vis has picked two different colors (blue and orange) to render the two curves in. This default coloring scheme works well in general because blue and orange are easy to tell apart. If there are more series to render, other new colors will be selected automatically.

The two series in this example chart are a little special in the sense that they have exactly the same set of x-coordinate values (1, 2, 3, and 4). However, in general, the x-coordinate values of different series in a multiseries chart don't have to be identical. You are encouraged to try this in exercise 1 at the end of this chapter. But, be aware that it is not always a good idea to plot two curves in the same chart. For example, if the two curves have very different and nonoverlapping y-value ranges, plotting them in the same line chart will make the variation in each curve harder to see. In such cases, it is better to plot them in separate line charts.

Another thing worth pointing out in listing 7.2 is the custom labels for the axes. We use the xLabel and yLabel fields in the configuration object (the third argument passed to linechart()) in order to label the x- and y-axis as custom strings of our choice. In general, it is good practice to always label your axes, as it makes the charts more self-explanatory. tfjs-vis will always label your axes as x and y if you don't specify xLabel and yLabel, which is what happened in listing 7.1 and the left panel of figure 7.1.

Listing 7.2   Making a line chart with two series using `tfvis.render.linechart()`

```
values = [
  [{x: 1, y: 20}, {x: 2, y: 30}, {x: 3, y: 5}, {x: 4, y: 12}],
  [{x: 1, y: 40}, {x: 2, y: 0}, {x: 3, y: 50}, {x: 4, y: -5}]
];
let series = ['My series 1', 'My series 2'];    ◁
tfvis.render.linechart(
        document.getElementById('plot2'), {values, series}, {
  width: 400,
  xLabel: 'My x-axis label',
  yLabel: 'My y-axis label'
});
```

Series names must be provided when plotting multiple series.

To show multiple series in the same axes, make values an array consisting of multiple arrays of x-y pairs.

Overrides the default x- and y-axis labels

Scatter plots

Scatter plots are another type of chart you can create with tfvis.render. The most salient difference between a scatter plot and a line chart is the fact that a scatter plot doesn't connect the data points with line segments. This makes scatter plots suitable for cases in which the ordering among data points is unimportant. For example, a scatter plot may plot the population of a few countries against their per-capita GDPs. In such a plot, the primary piece of information is the relation between the x- and y-values, not an ordering among the data points.

In tfvis.render, the function that lets you create scatter plots is scatterplot(). As the example in listing 7.3 shows, scatterplot() can render multiple series, just like linechart(). In fact, the APIs of scatterplot() and linechart() are practically identical, as you can see by comparing listing 7.2 with listing 7.3. The scatter plot created by listing 7.3 is shown in figure 7.2.

Listing 7.3   Making a scatter plot using `tfvis.render.scatterplot()`

```
values = [
  [{x: 20, y: 40}, {x: 32, y: 0}, {x: 5, y: 52}, {x: 12, y: -6}],
  [{x: 15, y: 35}, {x: 0, y: 9}, {x: 7, y: 28}, {x: 16, y: 8}]
];
series = ['My scatter series 1', 'My scatter series 2'];
tfvis.render.scatterplot(
    document.getElementById('plot4'),
  {values, series},
  {
    width: 400,
    xLabel: 'My x-values',
    yLabel: 'My y-values'
  });
```

As in linechart(), uses an array of x-y pair arrays to show multiple series in a scatter plot

Always remember to label your axes.

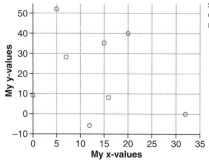

Figure 7.2   A scatter plot that contains two series, made with the code in listing 7.3.

Bar charts

As its name indicates, a *bar chart* uses bars to show the magnitude of quantities. Such bars usually start from zero at the bottom so that the ratios between the quantities can be read from the relative heights of the bars. Therefore, bar charts are a good choice when the ratio between quantities is of importance. For example, it is natural to use a bar chart to show the annual revenue of a company over a few years. In this case, the relative heights of the bars give the viewer an intuitive sense of how the revenue changes from one quarter to another in terms of the ratio between them. This makes bar charts distinct from line charts and scatter plots, in which the values are not necessarily "anchored" at zero.

To create a bar chart with `tfvis.render`, use `barchart()`. You can find an example in listing 7.4. The bar chart created by the code is shown in figure 7.3. The API of `barchart()` is similar to those of `linechart()` and `scatterplot()`. However, an important difference should be noted. The first argument passed to `barchart()` is not an object consisting of a `value` field. Instead, it is a simple array of index-value pairs. The horizontal values are not specified with a field called `x`, but are instead specified with a field called `index`. Similarly, the vertical values are not specified with a field called `y`, but are instead associated with a field called `value`. Why this difference? It is because the horizontal values of a bar in a bar chart don't have to have a number. Instead, they can be either strings or numbers, as is shown by our example in figure 7.3.

Listing 7.4   Creating a bar chart using `tfvis.render.barchart()`

```
const data = [
    {index: 'foo', value: 1},{index: 'bar', value: 7},
    {index: 3, value: 3},
    {index: 5, value: 6}];
 tfvis.render.barchart(document.getElementById('plot5'), data, {
    yLabel: 'My value',
    width: 400
 });
```

Notice how the index of a bar chart can be numeric or a string. Note that the order of the elements matters.

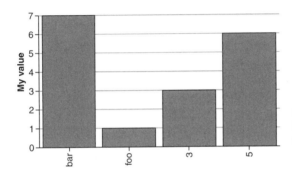

Figure 7.3   A bar chart consisting of both string- and numeric-named bars, made with the code in listing 7.4

Histograms

The three types of plots described previously let you plot the values of a certain quantity. Sometimes, the detailed quantitative values are not as important as the *distribution* of the values. For example, consider an economist looking at the annual household income data from the result of a national census. To the economist, the detailed income values are not the most interesting piece of information. They contain too much information (yes, sometimes too much information can be a bad thing!). Instead, the economist wants a more succinct summary of the income values. They're interested in how such values are distributed—that is, how many of them fall below US$20,000, how many of them are between $20,000 and $40,000, or between $40,000 and $60,000, and so forth. *Histograms* are a type of chart suited for such a visualization task.

A histogram assigns the values into *bins*. Each bin is simply a continuous range for the value, with a lower bound and an upper bound. The bins are chosen to be adjacent to each other so as to cover all possible values. In the prior example, the economist may use bins such as 0 ~ 20k, 20k ~ 40k, 40k ~ 60k, and so forth. Once such a set of N bins is chosen, you can write a program to count the number of individual data points that fall into each of the bins. Executing this program will give you *N* numbers (one for each bin). You can then plot the numbers using vertical bars. This gives you a histogram.

`tfvis.render.histogram()` does all these steps for you. This saves you the effort of determining the bounds of the bins and counting the examples by the bins. To invoke `histogram()`, simply pass an array of numbers, as shown in the following listing. These numbers don't need to be sorted in any order.

Listing 7.5 Visualizing a value distribution using `tfvis.render.histogram()`

```
const data = [1, 5, 5, 5, 5, 10, -3, -3];
tfvis.render.histogram(document.getElementById('plot6'), data, {
  width: 400
});                                              Uses automatically generated bins
// Histogram: with custom number of bins.
// Note that the data is the same as above.
tfvis.render.histogram(document.getElementById('plot7'), data, {
  maxBins: 3,          ◁──────── Specifies the number of bins explicitly
  width: 400
});
```

In listing 7.5, there are two slightly different `histogram()` calls. The first call doesn't specify any custom options beyond the width of the plot. In this case, `histogram()` uses its built-in heuristics to calculate the bins. This results in seven bins $-4 \sim -2, -2 \sim 0, 0 \sim 2, \ldots, 8 \sim 10$, as shown in the left panel of figure 7.4. When divided among these seven bins, the histogram shows the highest value in the bin $4 \sim 6$, which contains a count of 4 because four of the values in the data array are 5. Three bins of the histogram ($-2 \sim 0, 2 \sim 4,$ and $6 \sim 8$) have zero value because none of the elements of the data points falls into any of these three bins.

Hence, we can argue that the default heuristics end up with too many bins for our particular data points. If there are fewer bins, then it will be less likely that any of them will end up empty. You can use the configuration field `maxBins` to override the default binning heuristics and limit the number of bins. This is what's done by the second `histogram()` call in listing 7.5, the result of which is shown on the right in figure 7.4. You can see that by limiting the number of bins to three, all the bins become nonempty.

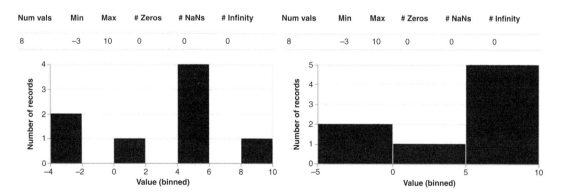

Figure 7.4 Histograms of the same data, plotted with the automatically calculated bins (left) and an explicitly specified number of bins (right). The code that generates these histograms is in listing 7.5.

Heatmaps

A *heatmap* displays a 2D array of numbers as a grid of colored cells. The color of each cell reflects the relative magnitude of the elements of the 2D array. Traditionally, "cooler" colors such as blue and green are used to represent lower values, while "warmer" colors such as orange and red are used to show higher ones. This is why these plots are called heatmaps. Perhaps the most frequently encountered examples of heatmaps in deep learning are confusion matrices (see the iris-flower example in chapter 3) and attention matrices (see the date-conversion example in chapter 9). tfjs-vis provides the function `tfvis.render.heatmap()` to support the rendering of this type of visualization.

Listing 7.6 shows how to make a heatmap to visualize a made-up confusion matrix involving three classes. The value of the confusion matrix is specified in the `values` field of the second input argument. The names of the classes, which are used to label the columns and rows of the heatmap, are specified as `xTickLabels` and `yTickLabels`. Do not confuse these tick labels with `xLabel` and `yLabel` in the third argument, which are for labeling the entire x- and y-axes. Figure 7.5 shows the resulting heatmap plot.

Listing 7.6   Visualizing 2D tensors using `tfvis.render.heatmap()`

```
tfvis.render.heatmap(document.getElementById('plot8'), {
  values: [[1, 0, 0], [0, 0.3, 0.7], [0, 0.7, 0.3]],
  xTickLabels: ['Apple', 'Orange', 'Tangerine'],
  yTickLabels: ['Apple', 'Orange', 'Tangerine']
}, {
  width: 500,
  height: 300,
  xLabel: 'Actual Fruit',
  yLabel: 'Recognized Fruit',
  colorMap: 'blues'
});
```

The values passed to heatmap() can be a nested JavaScript array (as shown here) or a 2D tf.Tensor.

xTickLabels is used to label the individual columns along the x-axis. Don't confuse it with xLabel. Likewise, yTickLabels is used to label the individual rows along the y-axis.

xLabel and yLabel are used to label the entire axes, unlike xTickLabel and yTickLabel.

Apart from the 'blues' color map shown here, there are also 'greyscale' and 'viridian'.

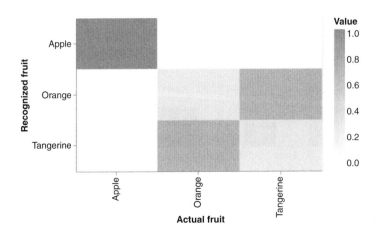

Figure 7.5   The heatmap rendered by the code in listing 7.6. It shows an imaginary confusion matrix involving three classes.

This concludes our quick tour of four major types of charts supported by `tfvis.render`. If your future work involves data visualization using tfjs-vis, odds are that you will use these charts a lot. Table 7.1 provides a brief summary of the chart types in order to help you decide which one to use for a given visualization task.

Table 7.1 A summary of the five major types of charts supported by tfjs-vis under the `tfvis.render` namespace

Name of chart	Corresponding function in tfjs-vis	Suitable visualization tasks and machine-learning examples
Line chart	`tfvis.render.linechart()`	A scalar (y-value) varying with another scalar (x-value) that has an intrinsic ordering (time, dose, and so on). Multiple series can be plotted in the same axes: for example, metrics from the training and validation sets, each of which is plotted against training-epoch number.
Scatter plot	`tfvis.render.scatterplot()`	x-y scalar value pairs that do not have an intrinsic ordering, such as the relation between two numeric columns of a CSV dataset. Multiple series can be plotted in the same axes.
Bar chart	`tfvis.render.barchart()`	A set of values belonging to a small number of categories, such as accuracies (as percent numbers) achieved by several models on the same classification problem.
Histogram	`tfvis.render.histogram()`	A set of values of which the distribution is of primary interest, such as the distribution of parameter values in the kernel of a dense layer.
Heatmap	`tfvis.render.heathmap()`	A 2D array of numbers to be visualized as a 2D grid of cells, each element of which is color-coded to reflect the magnitude of the corresponding value: for example, confusion matrix of a multiclass classifier (section 3.3); attention matrix of a sequence-to-sequence model (section 9.3).

7.1.2 *An integrative case study: Visualizing weather data with tfjs-vis*

The CodePen examples in the previous section used small, hand-coded data. In this section, we will show how to use the charting features of tfjs-vis on a much larger and more interesting real dataset. This will demonstrate the true power of the API and make a case for the value of such data visualization in the browser. This example will also highlight some of the nuances and gotchas you may run into when using the charting API on real problems.

The data we will use is the Jena-weather-archive dataset. It includes the measurements collected with a variety of meteorological instruments at a location in Jena, Germany, over a course of eight years (between 2009 and 2017). The dataset, which can be downloaded from the Kaggle page (see www.kaggle.com/pankrzysiu/weather-archive-jena), comes in a 42MB CSV file. It consists of 15 columns. The first column is a timestamp, while the remaining columns are weather data such as temperature (T deg(C)), air pressure (p (mbar)), relative humidity (rh (%s)), wind velocity (wv (m/s)), and so on. If you examine the timestamps, you can see that they have a 10-minute spacing, reflecting the fact that the measurements were made every 10 minutes. This is a rich dataset to visualize, explore, and try machine learning on. In the following sections, we will try making weather forecasts using various machine-learning models. In particular, we will predict the temperature of the next day using the weather data from the 10 preceding days. But before we embark on this exciting weather forecasting task, let's follow the principle of "always look at your data before trying machine learning on it" and see how tfjs-vis can be used to plot the data in a clear and intuitive fashion.

To download and run the Jena-weather example, use the following commands:

```
git clone https://github.com/tensorflow/tfjs-examples.git
cd tfjs-examples/jena-weather
yarn
yarn watch
```

LIMITING THE AMOUNT OF DATA FOR EFFICIENT AND EFFECTIVE VISUALIZATION

The Jena-weather dataset is quite large. At a file size of 42 MB, it is bigger than all the CSV or tabular datasets you've seen in this book so far. This leads to two challenges:

- The first challenge is for the computer: if you plot all the data from the eight years at once, the browser tab will run out of resources, become unresponsive, and probably crash. Even if you limit yourself to only 1 of the 14 columns, there are still about 420,000 data points to show. This is more than what tfjs-vis (or any JavaScript plotting library, for that matter) can safely render at a time.

- The second challenge is for the user: it is hard for a human to look at a large amount of data at once and make sense out of it. For instance, how is someone supposed to look at all 420,000 data points and extract useful information from them? Just like the computer, the human brain has limited information-processing bandwidth. The job of a visualization designer is to present the most relevant and informative aspects of the data in an efficient way.

We use three tricks to address these challenges:

- Instead of plotting the data from the whole eight years at once, we let the user choose what time range to plot using an interactive UI. This is the purpose of the Time Span drop-down menu in the UI (see the screenshots in figures 7.6 and 7.7). The time-span options include Day, Week, 10 Days, Month, Year, and Full. The last one corresponds to the whole eight years. For any of the other time spans, the UI allows the user to go back and forth in time. This is what the left-arrow and right-arrow buttons are for.

- For any time span longer than a week, we *downsample* the time series before plotting them on the screen. For example, consider the time span Month (30 days). The full data for this time span contains about 30 * 24 * 6 = 4.32k data points. In the code in listing 7.7, you can see that we only plot every sixth data point when showing the data from a month. This cuts the number of plotted data points down to 0.72k, a significant reduction in the rendering cost. But to human eyes, this six-fold reduction in the data-point count barely makes a difference.

- Similar to what we did with the Time Span drop-down menu, we include a drop-down menu in the UI so that the user can choose what weather data to plot at any given time. Notice the drop-down menus labeled Data Series 1 and Data Series 2. By using them, the user may plot any 1 or any 2 of the 14 columns as line charts on the screen, in the same axes.

Listing 7.7 shows the code responsible for making the charts like the ones in figure 7.6. Despite the fact that the code calls `tfvis.render.linechart()` just like the Code-Pen example in the previous section, it is much more abstract compared to the code in the previous listings. This is because in our web page, we need to defer the decision of what quantities to plot according to the UI state.

Listing 7.7 Weather data as a multiseries line chart (in jena-weather/index.js)

jenaWeatherData is an object that helps us organize and retrieve the weather data from the CSV file. See jena-weather/data.js.

```
function makeTimeSerieChart(
    series1, series2, timeSpan, normalize, chartContainer) {
  const values = [];
  const series = [];
  const includeTime = true;
  if (series1 !== 'None') {
    values.push(jenaWeatherData.getColumnData(      ← Chooses the appropriate stride (downsampling factor)
      series1, includeTime, normalize, currBeginIndex,
      TIME_SPAN_RANGE_MAP[timeSpan],     ← Specifies the time span for visualization
      TIME_SPAN_STRIDE_MAP[timeSpan]));     ←
    series.push(normalize ? `${series1} (normalized)` : series1);
  }
  if (series2 !== 'None') {      ← Takes advantage of the fact that tfjs-vis's line chart supports multiple series
    values.push(jenaWeatherData.getColumnData(
      series2, includeTime, normalize, currBeginIndex,
      TIME_SPAN_RANGE_MAP[timeSpan],
      TIME_SPAN_STRIDE_MAP[timeSpan]));
    series.push(normalize ? `${series2} (normalized)` : series2);
  }
  tfvis.render.linechart({values, series: series}, chartContainer, {
    width: chartContainer.offsetWidth * 0.95,
    height: chartContainer.offsetWidth * 0.3,
    xLabel: 'Time',      ← Always label the axes.
    yLabel: series.length === 1 ? series[0] : ''
  });
}
```

You are encouraged to explore the data-visualization UI. It contains a lot of interesting patterns you can discover about weather. For example, the top panel of figure 7.6 shows how the normalized temperature (T (degC)) and normalized air pressure (p (mbar)) vary over a time period of 10 days. In the temperature curve, you can see a clear daily cycle: the temperature tends to peak around the middle of the day and bottom out shortly after midnight. On top of the daily cycle, you can also see a more global trend (a gradual increase) over the 10-day period. By contrast, the air-pressure curve doesn't show a clear pattern. The bottom panel of the same figure shows the same measurements over the time span of a year. There, you can see the annual cycle of temperature: it peaks around August and reaches the bottom around January. The air pressure again shows a less clear-cut pattern than temperature at this time scale.

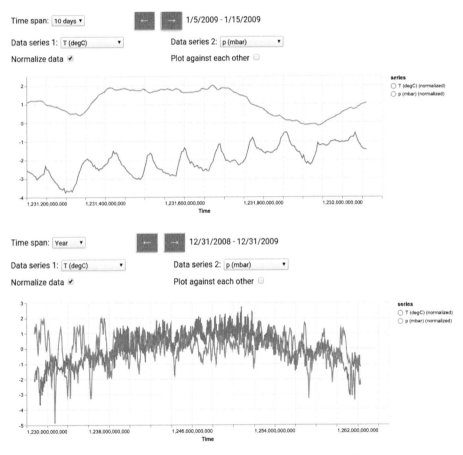

Figure 7.6   Line charts of temperature (T (degC)) and air pressure (p (mbar)) from the Jena-weather-archive dataset, plotted at two different time scales. Top: 10-day time span. Notice the daily cycle in the temperature curve. Bottom: 1-year time span. Notice the annual cycle in the temperature curve and the slight tendency for air pressure to be more stable during spring and summer than during other seasons.

The pressure can vary in a somewhat chaotic fashion over the entire year, although there appears to be a tendency for it to be less variable around summer than in winter. By looking at the same measurements at different time scales, we can notice various interesting patterns. All these patterns are nearly impossible to notice if we look at just the raw data in the numerical CSV format.

One thing you might have noticed in the charts in figure 7.6 is that they show normalized values of temperature and air pressure instead of their absolute values, which is due to the fact that the Normalize Data check box in the UI was checked when we made these plots. We briefly mentioned normalization when discussing the Boston-housing model back in chapter 2. The normalization there involved subtracting the mean and dividing the result by the standard deviation. We did this in order to improve model training. The normalization we performed here is exactly the same. However, it is not just for the accuracy of our machine-learning model (to be covered in the next section) but is also for visualization. Why? If you try unchecking the Normalize Data check box when the chart shows temperature and air pressure, you'll immediately see the reason. The temperature measurement varies in the range between –10 and 40 (on the Celsius scale), while the air pressure resides in the range between 980 and 1,000. When plotted in the same axes without normalization, the two quantities with vastly different ranges force the y-axis to expand to a very large range, causing both curves to look like basically flat lines with tiny variations. Normalization avoids this problem by mapping all measurements to a distribution of zero mean and unit standard deviation.

Figure 7.7 shows an example of plotting two weather measurements against each other as a scatter plot, a mode you can activate by checking the Plot Against Each Other check box and making sure that neither of the Data Series drop-down menus is set to None. The code for making such scatter plots is similar to the `make-TimeSerieChart()` function in listing 7.7 and is therefore omitted here for conciseness. You can study it in the same file (jena-weather/index.js) if you are interested in the details.

The example scatter plot shows the relation between the normalized air density (y-axis) and normalized temperature (x-axis). Here, you can spot a fairly strong negative correlation between the two quantities: the air density gets lower as the temperature increases. This example plot uses the 10-day time span, but you can verify that the trend largely holds at other time spans as well. This kind of correlation between variables is easy to visualize with scatter plots but much harder to discover by just looking at the text-format data. This is another example of the value afforded by data visualization.

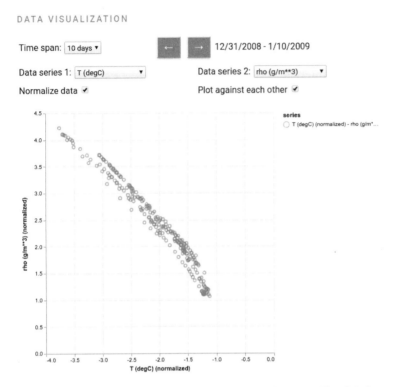

DATA VISUALIZATION

Time span: [10 days ▼]   [←] [→] 12/31/2008 - 1/10/2009

Data series 1: [T (degC)   ▼]   Data series 2: [rho (g/m**3)   ▼]

Normalize data ✔   Plot against each other ✔

Figure 7.7   An example scatter plot from the Jena-weather demo. The plot shows the relation between air density (rho, vertical axis) and temperature (T, horizontal) over a time period of 10 days, where a negative correlation can be seen.

7.2   *Visualizing models after training*

In the previous sections, we showed how visualization can be useful for data. In this section, we will show you how to visualize various aspects of models after they are trained in order to gain useful insight. To this end, we will focus primarily on convnets that take images as inputs, because they are used widely and produce interesting visualization results.

You may have heard the remark that deep neural networks are "black boxes." Don't let this remark mislead you into thinking that it's hard to get any information from the inside of a neural network during its inference or training. To the contrary, it is fairly easy to peek at what each layer is doing inside a model written in TensorFlow.js.[3]

---

[3] What that remark really means is that the large number of mathematical operations that occur in a deep neural network, even if they can be accessed, are harder to describe in layperson's terms as compared with certain other types of machine-learning algorithms, such as decision trees and logistic regression. For example, with a decision tree, you can walk down the branching points one by one and explain why a certain branch is chosen by verbalizing the reason as a simple sentence like "because factor X is greater than 0.35." That problem is referred to as *model interpretability* and is a different matter from what we are covering in this section.

Furthermore, as far as convnets are concerned, the internal representations they learn are highly amenable to visualization, in large part because they are representations of visual concepts. Since 2013, a wide array of techniques has been developed for visualizing and interpreting these representations. Since it's impractical to cover all the interesting techniques, we'll cover three of the most basic and useful ones:

- *Visualizing the outputs of intermediate layers (intermediate activations) of a convnet—* This is useful for understanding how successive convnet layers transform their inputs, and for getting a first idea of the visual features learned by individual convnet filters.
- *Visualizing convnet filters by finding input images that maximally activate them—*This is useful for understanding what visual pattern or concept each filter is sensitive to.
- *Visualizing heatmaps of class activation in an input image—*This helps in understanding which parts of an input image play the most important role in causing the convnet to generate the final classification result, which can also be useful for interpreting how a convnet reaches its output and for "debugging" incorrect outputs.

The code we will use to showcase these techniques is in the visualize-convnet example from the tfjs-examples repo. To run the example, use these commands:

```
git clone https://github.com/tensorflow/tfjs-examples.git
cd tfjs-examples/visualize-convnet
yarn && yarn visualize
```

The yarn visualize command is different from the yarn watch command you've seen in previous examples. In addition to building and launching the web page, it performs some additional steps outside the browser. First, it installs some required Python libraries, followed by downloading and converting the VGG16 model (a well-known and widely used deep convnet) into TensorFlow.js format. The VGG16 model has been pretrained on the large-scale ImageNet dataset and is available as a Keras application. Once the model conversion is complete, yarn visualize performs a series of analyses on the converted model in tfjs-node. Why are these steps carried out in Node.js instead of the browser? Because VGG16 is a relatively large convnet.[4] As a result, several of the steps are computationally heavy and run much faster in the less resource-restricted environment in Node.js. The computation can be further speeded up if you use tfjs-node-gpu instead of the default tfjs-node (this requires a CUDA-enabled GPU with the required driver and libraries installed; see appendix A):

```
yarn visualize --gpu
```

Once the computationally heavy steps are completed in Node.js, they will generate a set of image files in the dist/ folder. As its last step, yarn visualize will compile and

---

[4] To get an idea of how large VGG16 is, realize that its total weight size is 528 MB, as compared to the <10MB weight size of MobileNet.

launch a web server for a set of static web files including those images, in addition to opening the index page in your browser.

The `yarn visualize` command contains a few additional configurable flags. For example, by default, it performs computation and visualization on eight filters per convolutional layer of interest. You can change the number of filters by using the `--filters` flag: for example, `yarn visualize --filters 32`. Also, the default input image used by `yarn visualize` is the cat.jpg image that comes with the source code. You can use other image files by using the `--image` flag.[5] Now let's look at the visualization results based on the cat.jpg image and 32 filters.

7.2.1 Visualizing the internal activations of a convnet

Here, we compute and display the feature map generated by various convolutional layers of the VGG16 model given an input image. These feature maps are called *internal* activation because they are not the model's final output (the model's final output is a length-1,000 vector that represents the probability scores for the 1,000 ImageNet classes). Instead, they are the intermediate steps of the model's computation. These internal activations give us a view into how the input is decomposed into different features learned by the network.

Recall from chapter 4 that the output of a convolutional layer has the NHWC shape `[numExamples, height, width, channels]`. Here, we are dealing with a single input image, so `numExamples` is 1. We want to visualize the output of each convolutional layer along three remaining dimensions: height, width, and channels. The height and width of a convolutional layer's output are determined by its filter size, padding, and strides, as well as the height and width of the layer's input. In general, they get smaller and smaller as you go deeper into a convnet. On the other hand, the value of `channels` generally gets larger as you go deeper, as the convnet extracts a larger and larger number of features through successive layers of representation transformation. These channels of convolutional layers cannot be interpreted as different color components. Instead, they are the learned feature dimensions. This is why our visualization breaks them into separate panels and draws them in grayscale. Figure 7.8 shows the activations from five convolutional layers of VGG16 given the cat.jpg input image.

The first thing you may notice in the internal activations is that they look increasingly different from the original input as you go deeper in the network. The earlier layers (such as `block1_conv1`) appear to encode relatively simple visual features such as edges and colors. For example, the arrow labeled "A" points at an internal activation that seems to respond to the yellow and pink colors. The arrow labeled "B" points at an internal activation that seems to be about edges along certain orientations in the input image.

But the later layers (such as `block4_conv2` and `block5_conv3`) show activation patterns that are more and more removed from simple pixel-level features in the input

---

[5] Most common image formats, including JPEG and PNG, are supported.

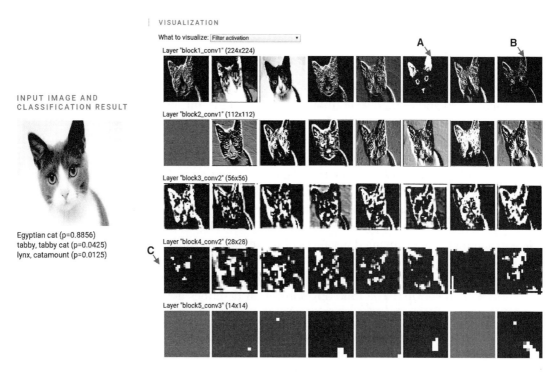

Figure 7.8 Internal activation from several convolutional layers of VGG16 performing inference on the cat.jpg image. The original input image is shown on the left, together with the top three classes output by the model and their associated probability scores. The five layers visualized are the layers named `block1_conv1`, `block2_conv1`, `block3_conv2`, `block4_conv2`, and `block5_conv3`. They are ordered by their depth in the VGG16 model from top to bottom. That is, `block1_conv1` is the closest to the input layer, while `block5_conv1` is the closest to the output layer. Note that all internal-activation images are scaled to the same size for visualization purposes, even though the activations have smaller sizes (lower resolution) in the later layers due to successive convolution and pooling. This can be seen in the coarse pixel patterns in the later layers.

image. For example, the arrow labeled "C" in figure 7.8 points at a filter in `block4_conv2` that seems to encode the cat's facial features, including the ears, eyes, and nose. This is a concrete example of the incremental feature extraction that we showed schematically in figure 4.6 of chapter 4. However, note that not all filters in later layers can be explained verbally in a straightforward way. Another interesting observation is that the "sparsity" of the activation maps also increases with the depth of the layer: in the first layer shown in figure 7.8, all filters are activated (show a nonconstant pixel pattern) by the input image; however, in the last layer, some of the layers become blank (constant pixel pattern; for example, see the last row in the right panel of figure 7.8). This means the features encoded by those blank filters are absent from this particular input image.

You just witnessed an important universal characteristic of the representations learned by deep convnets: the features extracted by a layer become increasingly more abstract with the depth of the layer. The activations of deeper layers carry less and less information about the details in the input, and more and more information about the target (in this case, which of the 1,000 ImageNet classes the image belongs to). So, a deep neural network effectively acts as an *information distillation pipeline*, with raw data going in and being repeatedly transformed so that aspects in the input that are irrelevant to the task are filtered out, and aspects that are useful for the task are gradually magnified and refined. Even though we showed this through a convnet example, this characteristic holds for other deep neural networks (such as MLPs) as well.

The aspects of input images that a convnet finds useful might be different from what the human visual system finds useful. The convnet training is driven by data and hence is prone to biases in the training data. For instance, the paper by Marco Ribeiro and colleagues listed in the "Materials for further reading and exploration" section at the end of the chapter points out a case in which the image of a dog got misclassified as a wolf due to the presence of snow in the background, presumably because the training images contained instances of wolves against snowy backgrounds but no dogs against similar backgrounds.

These are the useful insights we gained by visualizing the internal activation patterns of a deep convnet. The following subsection describes how to write code in TensorFlow.js to extract these internal activations.

DEEP DIVE INTO HOW INTERNAL ACTIVATIONS ARE EXTRACTED

The steps for extracting the internal activations are encapsulated in the `writeInternalActivationAndGetOutput()` function (listing 7.8). It takes as its input a TensorFlow.js model object that has already been constructed or loaded and the names of the layers in question (`layerNames`). The key step is creating a new model object (`compositeModel`) with multiple outputs, including the output of the specified layers and the output of the original model. `compositeModel` is constructed with the `tf.model()` API, as you saw in the Pac-Man and simple-object-detection examples in chapter 5. The nice thing about `compositeModel` is that its `predict()` method returns all the layers' activations, along with the model's final prediction (see the `const` named `outputs`). The rest of the code in listing 7.8 (from visualize-convnet/main.js) is about the more mundane task of splitting the layers' outputs into individual filters and writing them to files on disk.

Listing 7.8 Calculating the internal activation of a convnet in Node.js

```
async function writeInternalActivationAndGetOutput(
    model, layerNames, inputImage, numFilters, outputDir) {
  const layerName2FilePaths = {};
  const layerOutputs =
      layerNames.map(layerName => model.getLayer(layerName).output);
  const compositeModel = tf.model(            ◁──────
      {
        inputs: model.input,
       outputs: layerOutputs.concat(model.outputs[0])
      });
```

Constructs a model that returns all the desired internal activations, in addition to the final output of the original model

```
                const outputs = compositeModel.predict(inputImage);
```
> **outputs is an array of tf.Tensor's, including the internal activations and the final output.**

```
                for (let i = 0; i < outputs.length - 1; ++i) {
                  const layerName = layerNames[i];
                  const activationTensors =
```
Splits the activation of the convolutional layer by filter
```
                      tf.split(outputs[i],
                               outputs[i].shape[outputs[i].shape.length - 1],
                               -1);
                  const actualNumFilters = filters <= activationTensors.length ?
                      numFilters :
                      activationTensors.length;
                  const filePaths = [];
                  for (let j = 0; j < actualNumFilters; ++j) {
                    const imageTensor = tf.tidy(
                        () => deprocessImage(tf.tile(activationTensors[j],
                                             [1, 1, 1, 3])));
```
> **Formats activation tensors and writes them to disk**

```
                    const outputFilePath = path.join(
                        outputDir, `${layerName}_${j + 1}.png`);
                    filePaths.push(outputFilePath);
                    await utils.writeImageTensorToFile(imageTensor, outputFilePath);
                  }
                  layerName2FilePaths[layerName] = filePaths;
                  tf.dispose(activationTensors);
                }
                tf.dispose(outputs.slice(0, outputs.length - 1));
                return {modelOutput: outputs[outputs.length - 1], layerName2FilePaths};
              }
```

7.2.2 Visualizing what convolutional layers are sensitive to: Maximally activating images

Another way to illustrate what a convnet learns is by finding the input images that its various internal layers are sensitive to. What we mean by a filter being sensitive to a certain input image is a maximal activation in the filter's output (averaged across its output height and width dimensions) under the input image. By looking at such maximally activating inputs for various layers of the convnet, we can infer what each layer is trained to respond to.

The way in which we find the maximally activating images is through a trick that flips the "normal" neural network training process on its head. Panel A of figure 7.9 shows schematically what happens when we train a neural network with tf.Model.fit(). We freeze the input data and allow the weights of the model (such as the kernels and biases of all the trainable layers) to be updated from the loss function[6] via backpropagation. However, there is no reason why we can't swap the roles of the input and the weights: we can freeze the weights and allow the *input* to be updated through backpropagation. In the meantime, we tweak the loss function so that it causes the backpropagation to nudge the input in a way that maximizes the output of a certain convolutional filter when averaged across its height and width dimensions.

---

[6] This diagram can be viewed as a simplified version of figure 2.9, which we used to introduce backpropagation back in chapter 2.

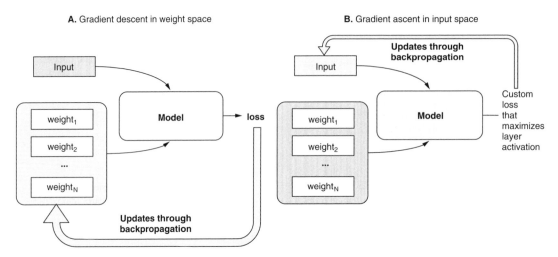

Figure 7.9   A schematic diagram showing the basic idea behind how the maximally activating image for a convolutional filter is found through gradient ascent in input space (panel B) and how that differs from the normal neural network training process based on gradient descent in weight space (panel A). Note that this figure differs from some of the model diagrams shown previously in that it breaks the weights out from the model. This is for highlighting the two sets of quantities that can be updated through backpropagation: the weights and the input.

This process is schematically shown in panel B of figure 7.9 and is called *gradient ascent in input space*, as opposed to the *gradient descent in weight space* that underlies typical model training. The code that implements gradient descent in input space is shown in the next subsection and can be studied by interested readers.

Figure 7.10 shows the result of performing the gradient-ascent-in-input-space process on four convolutional layers of the VGG16 model (the same model that we used to show internal activations). As in the previous illustration, the depth of the layers increases from the top to the bottom of the figure. A few interesting patterns can be gleaned from these maximally activating input images:

- First, these are color images instead of the grayscale internal activations like the ones in the previous section. This is because they are in the format of the convnet's actual input: an image consisting of three (RGB) channels. Hence, they can be displayed in color.
- The shallowest layer (block1_conv1) is sensitive to simple patterns such as global color values and edges with certain orientations.
- The intermediate-depth layers (such as block2_conv1) respond maximally to simple textures made from combining different edge patterns.
- The filters in deeper layers begin to respond to more complex patterns that show some resemblance to visual features in natural images (from the Image-Net training data, of course), such as grains, holes, colorful stripes, feathers, waves, and so forth.

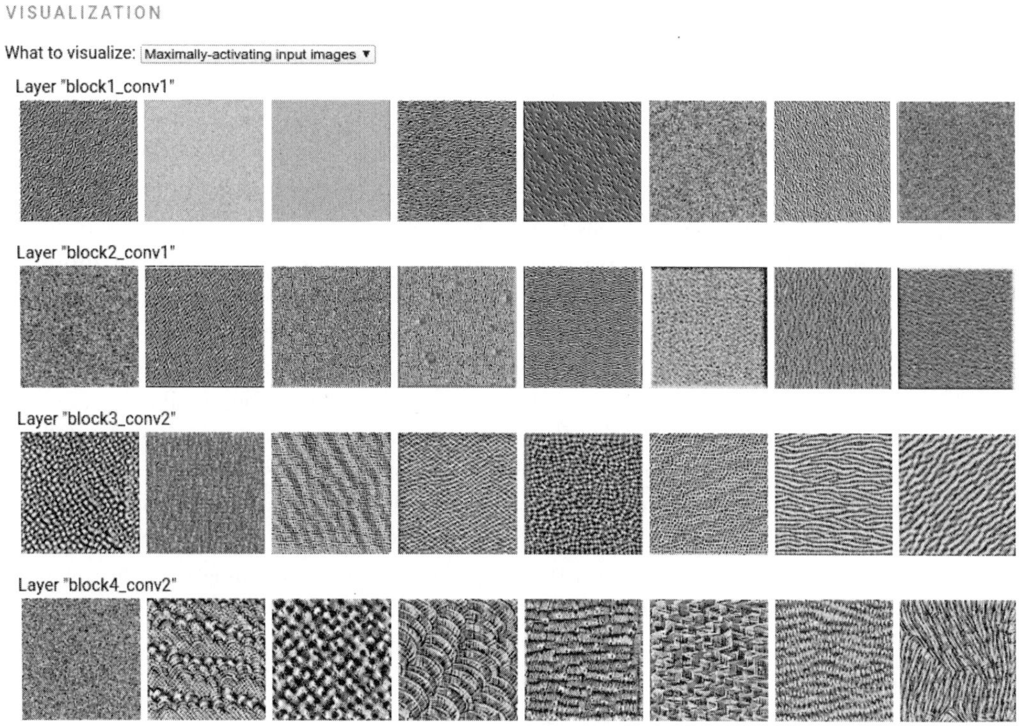

VISUALIZATION

What to visualize: Maximally-activating input images ▼

Layer "block1_conv1"

Layer "block2_conv1"

Layer "block3_conv2"

Layer "block4_conv2"

Figure 7.10   Maximally activating input images for four layers of the VGG16 deep convnet. These images are computed through 80 iterations of gradient ascent in input space.

In general, as the depth of the layer increases, the patterns get more and more removed from the pixel level and become more and more large-scale and complex. This reflects the layer-by-layer distillation of features by the deep convnet, composing patterns of patterns. Looking at the filters of the same layer, even though they share similar levels of abstraction, there is considerable variability in the detail patterns. This highlights the fact that each layer comes up with multiple representations of the same input in mutually complementary ways in order to capture the largest possible amount of useful information for solving the task that the network is trained to solve.

DEEP DIVE INTO GRADIENT ASCENT IN INPUT SPACE

In the visualize-convnet example, the core logic for gradient ascent in input space is in the inputGradientAscent() function in main.js and is shown in listing 7.9. The code runs in Node.js due to its time- and memory-consuming nature.[7] Note that even though the basic idea behind gradient ascent in input space is analogous to model training based on gradient descent in weight space (see figure 7.10), we cannot reuse

---

[7] For convnets smaller than VGG16 (such as MobileNet and MobileNetV2), it is possible to run this algorithm within a reasonable amount of time in the web browser.

`tf.Model.fit()` directly because that function is specialized to freeze the input and update the weights. Instead, we need to define a custom function that calculates a "loss" given an input image. This is the function defined by the line

```
const lossFunction = (input) =>
        auxModel.apply(input, {training: true}).gather([filterIndex], 3);
```

Here, `auxModel` is an auxiliary model object created with the familiar `tf.model()` function. It has the same input as the original model but outputs the activation of a given convolutional layer. We invoke the `apply()` method of the auxiliary model in order to obtain the value of the layer's activation. `apply()` is similar to `predict()` in that it executes a model's forward path. However, `apply()` provides finer-grained control, such as setting the `training` option to `true`, as is done in the prior line of code. Without setting `training` to `true`, backpropagation would not be possible because the forward pass disposes intermediate layer activations for memory efficiency by default. The `true` value in the `training` flag lets the `apply()` call preserve those internal activations and therefore enable backpropagation. The `gather()` call extracts a specific filter's activation. This is necessary because the maximally activating input is calculated on a filter-by-filter basis, and the results differ between filters even of the same layer (see the example results in figure 7.10).

Once we have the custom loss function, we pass it to `tf.grad()` in order to obtain a function that gives us the gradient of the loss with respect to the input:

```
const gradFunction = tf.grad(lossFunction);
```

The important thing to realize here is that `tf.grad()` doesn't give us the gradient values directly; instead, it gives us a function (`gradFunction` in the prior line) that will return the gradient values when invoked.

Once we have this gradient function, we invoke it in a loop. In each iteration, we use the gradient value it returns to update the input image. An important nonobvious trick here is to normalize the gradient values before adding them to the input image, which ensures that the update in each iteration has a consistent magnitude:

```
const norm = tf.sqrt(tf.mean(tf.square(grads))).add(EPSILON);
return grads.div(norm);
```

This iterative update to the input image is performed 80 times, giving us the results shown in figure 7.10.

Listing 7.9   Gradient ascent in input space (in Node.js, from visualize-convnet/main.js)

```
function inputGradientAscent(
    model, layerName, filterIndex, iterations = 80) {
  return tf.tidy(() => {
    const imageH = model.inputs[0].shape[1];
    const imageW = model.inputs[0].shape[2];
    const imageDepth = model.inputs[0].shape[3];

    const layerOutput = model.getLayer(layerName).output;
```

```
const auxModel = tf.model({        Creates an auxiliary model for which the input
    inputs: model.inputs,          is the same as the original model, but the
    outputs: layerOutput           output is the convolutional layer of interest
});

const lossFunction = (input) =>
    auxModel.apply(input, {training: true}).gather([filterIndex], 3);

const gradFunction = tf.grad(lossFunction);

let image = tf.randomUniform([1, imageH, imageW, imageDepth], 0, 1)
              .mul(20).add(128);

for (let i = 0; i < iterations; ++i) {
  const scaledGrads = tf.tidy(() => {
    const grads = gradFunction(image);
    const norm = tf.sqrt(tf.mean(tf.square(grads))).add(EPSILON);
    return grads.div(norm);
  });
  image = tf.clipByValue(
          image.add(scaledGrads), 0, 255);
}
return deprocessImage(image);
});
}
```

This function calculates the gradient of the convolutional filter's output with respect to the input image.

This function calculates the value of the convolutional layer's output at the designated filter index.

Performs one step of gradient ascent: updates the image along the direction of the gradient

Important trick: scales the gradient with the magnitude (norm) of the gradient

Generates a random image as the starting point of the gradient ascent

7.2.3 *Visual interpretation of a convnet's classification result*

The last post-training convnet visualization technique we will introduce is the *class activation map* (CAM) algorithm. The question that CAM aims to answer is "which parts of the input image play the most important roles in causing the convnet to output its top classification decision?" For instance, when the cat.jpg image was passed to the VGG16 network, we got a top class of "Egyptian cat" with a probability score of 0.89. But by looking at just the image input and the classification output, we can't tell which parts of the image are important for this decision. Surely some parts of the image (such as the cat's head) must have played a greater role than other parts (for example, the white background). But is there an objective way to quantify this for any input image?

The answer is yes! There are multiple ways of doing this, and CAM is one of them.[8] Given an input image and a classification result from a convnet, CAM gives you a heat map that assigns importance scores to different parts of the image. Figure 7.11 shows such CAM-generated heat maps overlaid on top of three input images: a cat, an owl,

---

[8] The CAM algorithm was first described in Bolei Zhou et al., "Learning Deep Features for Discriminative Localization," 2016, http://cnnlocalization.csail.mit.edu/. Another well-known method is Local Interpretable Model-Agnostic Explanations (LIME). See http://mng.bz/yzpq.

and two elephants. In the cat result, we see that the outline of the cat's head has the highest values in the heat map. We can make the post hoc observation that this is because the outline reveals the shape of the animal's head, which is a distinctive feature for a cat. The heat map for the owl image also meets our expectation because it highlights the head and wing of the animal. The result from the image with two elephants is interesting because the image differs from the other two images in that it contains two individual animals instead of one. The heat map generated by CAM assigns high importance scores to the head regions of both elephants in the image. There is a clear tendency for the heat map to focus on the trunks and ears of the animals, which may reflect the fact that the length of the trunk and the size of the ears are important in telling African elephants (the top class from the network) apart from Indian elephants (the third class from the network).

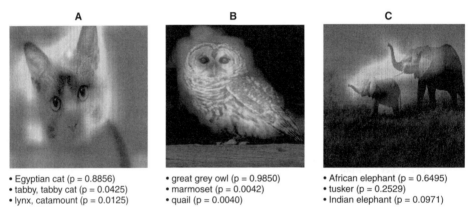

A	B	C

- Egyptian cat (p = 0.8856)
- tabby, tabby cat (p = 0.0425)
- lynx, catamount (p = 0.0125)

- great grey owl (p = 0.9850)
- marmoset (p = 0.0042)
- quail (p = 0.0040)

- African elephant (p = 0.6495)
- tusker (p = 0.2529)
- Indian elephant (p = 0.0971)

Figure 7.11   Class activation maps (CAMs) for three input images to the VGG16 deep convnet. The CAM heat maps are overlaid on the original input images.

TECHNICAL SIDE OF THE CAM ALGORITHM

As powerful as the CAM algorithm is, the idea behind it is actually not complicated. In a nutshell, each pixel in a CAM map shows how much the probability score of the winning class will change if the pixel value is increased by a unit amount. To go into the details a little more, the following steps are involved in CAM:

1 Find the last (that is, deepest) convolutional layer of the convnet. In VGG16, this layer is named `block5_conv3`.

2 Compute the gradient of the network's output probability for the winning class with respect to the output of the convolutional layer.

3 The gradient has a shape of `[1, h, w, numFilters]`, where h, w, and num-Filters are the layer's output height, width, and filter count, respectively. We then average the gradient across the example, height, and width dimensions, which gives us a tensor of shape `[numFilters]`. This is an array of importance scores, one for each filter of the convolutional layer.

4 Take the importance-score tensor (of shape [numFilters]), and multiply it with the actual output value of the convolutional layer (of shape [1, h, w, numFilters]), with broadcasting (see appendix B, section B.2.2). This gives us a new tensor of shape [1, h, w, numFilters] and is an "importance-scaled" version of the layer's output.

5 Finally, average the importance-scaled layer output across the last (filter) dimension and squeeze out the first (example) dimension, which yields a gray-scale image of shape [h, w]. The values in this image are a measure of how important each part of the image is for the winning classification result. However, this image contains negative values and is of smaller dimensions than the original input image (that is, 14×14 versus 224×224 in our VGG16 example). So, we zero out the negative values and up-sample the image before overlaying it on the input image.

The detailed code is in the function named gradClassActivationMap() in visualize-convnet/main.js. Although this function runs in Node.js by default, the amount of computation it involves is significantly less than the gradient-ascent-in-input-space algorithm that we saw in the previous section. So, you should be able to run the CAM algorithm using the same code in the browser with acceptable speed.

We talked about two things in this chapter: how to visualize data before it goes into training a machine-learning model and how to visualize a model after it's trained. We intentionally skipped the important step in between—that is, visualization of the model *while* it's being trained. This will be the focus of the next chapter. The reason why we single out the training process is that it is related to the concepts and phenomena of underfitting and overfitting, which are absolutely critical for any supervised-learning tasks and therefore deserve special treatment. Spotting and correcting underfitting and overfitting are made significantly easier by visualization. In the next chapter, we'll revisit the tfjs-vis library we introduced in the first part of the chapter and see that it can be useful for showing how a model-training process is progressing, in addition to its data-visualization power discussed in this chapter.

Materials for further reading and exploration

- Marco Tulio Ribeiro, Sameer Singh, and Carlos Guestrin, "Why Should I Trust You? Explaining the Predictions of Any Classifier," 2016, https://arxiv.org/pdf/1602.04938.pdf.
- TensorSpace (tensorspace.org) uses animated 3D graphics to visualize the topology and internal activations of convnets in the browser. It is built on top of TensorFlow.js, three.js, and tween.js.
- The TensorFlow.js tSNE library (github.com/tensorflow/tfjs-tsne) is an efficient implementation of the t-distributed Stochastic Neighbor Embedding (tSNE) algorithm based on WebGL. It can help you visualize high-dimensional datasets by projecting them to a 2D space while preserving the important structures in the data.

Exercises

1   Experiment with the following features of `tfjs.vis.linechart()`:

   a   Modify the code in listing 7.2 and see what happens when the two series being plotted have different sets of x-coordinate values. For example, try making the x-coordinate values 1, 3, 5, and 7 for the first series and 2, 4, 6, and 8 for the second series. You can fork and modify the CodePen from https://codepen.io/tfjs-book/pen/BvzMZr.

   b   The line charts in the example CodePen are all made with data series without duplicate x-coordinate values. Explore how the `linechart()` function handles data points with identical x-coordinate values. For example, in a data series, include two data points that both have x-value 0 but have different y-values (such as –5 and 5).

2   In the visualize-convnet example, use the `--image` flag to the `yarn visualize` command to specify your own input image. Since we used only animal images in section 7.2, explore other types of image content, such as people, vehicles, household items, and natural scenery. See what useful insights you can gain from the internal activations and CAMs.

3   In the example in which we calculated the CAM of VGG16, we computed the gradients of the probability score for the *winning* class with respect to the last convolutional layer's output. What if instead we compute the gradients for a *nonwinning* class (such as that of the lower probability)? We should expect the resulting CAM image to *not* highlight key parts that belong to the actual subject of the image. Confirm this by modifying the code of the visualize-convnet example and rerunning it. Specifically, the class index for which the gradients will be computed is specified as an argument to the function `gradClassActivation-Map()` in visualize-convnet/cam.js. The function is called in visualize-convnet/main.js.

Summary

- We studied the basic usage of tfjs-vis, a visualization library tightly integrated with TensorFlow.js. It can be used to render basic types of charts in the browser.
- Visualizing data is an indispensable part of machine learning. Efficient and effective presentation of data can reveal patterns and provide insights that are otherwise hard to obtain, as we showed by using the Jena-weather-archive data.
- Rich patterns and insights can be extracted from trained neural networks. We showed the steps and results of
   – Visualizing the internal-layer activations of a deep convnet.
   – Calculating what the layers are maximally responsive to.
   – Determining which parts of an input image are most relevant to the convnet's classification decision. These help us understand what is learned by the convnet and how it operates during inference.

Underfitting, overfitting, and the universal workflow of machine learning

This chapter covers

- Why it is important to visualize the model-training process and what the important things are to look for
- How to visualize and understand underfitting and overfitting
- The primary way of dealing with overfitting: regularization, and how to visualize its effect
- What the universal workflow of machine learning is, what steps it includes, and why it is an important recipe that guides all supervised machine-learning tasks

In the previous chapter, you learned how to use tfjs-vis to visualize data before you start designing and training machine-learning models for it. This chapter will start where that one left off and describe how tfjs-vis can be used to visualize the structure and metrics of models during their training. The most important goal in doing so is to spot the all-important phenomena of *underfitting* and *overfitting*. Once we can spot them, we'll delve into how to remedy them and how to verify that our remedying approaches are working using visualization.

8.1   *Formulation of the temperature-prediction problem*

To demonstrate underfitting and overfitting, we need a concrete machine-learning problem. The problem we'll use is predicting temperature based on the Jena-weather dataset you've just seen in the previous chapter. Section 7.1 showed the power of visualizing data in the browser and the benefits of doing so using the Jena-weather dataset. Hopefully, you've formed an intuition of the dataset through playing with the visualization UI in the previous section. We are now ready to start applying some machine learning to the dataset. But first, we need to define the problem.

The prediction task can be thought of as a toy weather-forecast problem. What we are trying to predict is the temperature 24 hours after a certain moment in time. We try to make this prediction using the 14 types of weather measurements taken in the 10-day period leading up to that moment.

Although the problem definition is straightforward, the way we generate the training data from the CSV file requires some careful explanation because it is different from the data-generation procedures in the problems seen in this book so far. In those problems, every row in the raw data file corresponded to a training example. That was how the iris-flower, Boston-housing, and phishing-detection examples worked (see chapters 2 and 3). However, in this problem, each example is formed by sampling and combining multiple rows from the CSV file. This is because a temperature prediction is made not just by looking at one moment in time, but instead by looking at the data over a time span. See figure 8.1 for a schematic illustration of the example-generation process.

To generate the features of a training example, we sample a set of rows over a time span of 10 days. Instead of using all the data rows from the 10 days, we sample every sixth row. Why? For two reasons. First, sampling all the rows would give us six times as much data and lead to a bigger model size and longer training time. Second, the data at a time scale of 1 hour has a lot of redundancy (the air pressure from 6 hours ago is usually close to that from 6 hours and 10 minutes ago). By throwing away five-sixths of the data, we get a more lightweight and performant model without sacrificing much predictive power. The sampled rows are combined into a 2D feature tensor of shape [timeSteps, numFeatures] for our training example (see figure 8.1). By default, timeSteps has a value of 240, which corresponds to the 240 sampling times evenly distributed across the 10-day period. numFeatures is 14, which corresponds to the 14 weather-instrument readings available in the CSV dataset.

Getting the target for the training example is easier: we just move forward a certain time delay from the last row that goes into the feature tensor and extract the value from the temperature column. Figure 8.1 shows how only a single training example is generated. To generate multiple training examples, we simply start from different rows of the CSV file.

You may have noticed something peculiar about the feature tensor for our temperature-prediction problem (see figure 8.1): in all the previous problems, the feature tensor of a single example was 1D, which led to a 2D tensor when multiple examples were batched. However, in this problem, the feature tensor of a single example is already

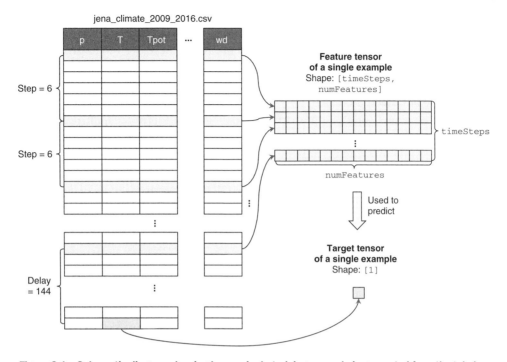

Figure 8.1 Schematic diagram showing how a single training example is generated from the tabular data. To generate the feature tensor of the example, the CSV file is sampled every `step` rows (for example, `step = 6`) up to `timeSteps` such rows (for example, `timeSteps = 240`). This forms a tensor of shape `[timeSteps, numFeatures]`, where `numFeatures` (default: 14) is the number of feature columns in the CSV file. To generate the target, sample the temperature (`T`) value at the row delay (for example, 144) step after the last row that went into the feature tensor. Other examples can be generated by starting from a different row in the CSV file, but they follow the same rule. This forms the temperature-prediction problem: given the 14 weather measurements for a certain period of time (such as 10 days) until now, predict the temperature a certain delay (such as 24 hours) from now. The code that does what's shown in this diagram is in the `getNextBatchFunction()` function in jena-weather/data.js.

2D, which means that we'll get a 3D tensor (of shape `[batchSize, timeSteps, numFeatures]`) when we combine multiple examples into a batch. This is an astute observation! The 2D feature-tensor shape originates from the fact that the features come from a *sequence* of events. In particular, they are the weather measurements taken at 240 points in time. This distinguishes this problem from all the other problems you've seen so far, in which the input features for a given example do not span multiple moments in time, be it the flower size measurements in the iris-flower problem or the 28 × 28 pixel values of an MNIST image.[1]

---

[1] The speech-command recognition problem in chapter 4 did, in fact, involve a sequence of events: namely, the successive frames of audio spectra that formed the spectrogram. However, our methodology treated the entire spectrogram as an image, thereby ignoring the temporal dimension of the problem by treating it as a spatial dimension.

This is the first time you encounter sequential input data in this book. In the next chapter, we will dive deeper into how to build specialized and more powerful models (RNNs) for sequential data in TensorFlow.js. But here, we will approach the problem using two types of models we already know: linear regressors and MLPs. This forms a buildup to our study of RNNs and gives us a baseline that can be compared with the more advanced models.

The actual code that performs the data-generation process illustrated in figure 8.1 is in jena-weather/data.js, under the function getNextBatchFunction(). This is an interesting function because instead of returning a concrete value, it returns an object with a function called next(). The next() function returns actual data values when it's called. The object with the next() function is referred to as an *iterator*. Why do we use this indirection instead of writing an iterator directly? First, this conforms to the generator/iterator specification of JavaScript.[2] We will soon pass it to the tf.data .generator() API in order to create a dataset object for model training. The API requires this function signature. Second, our iterator needs to be configurable; a function that returns the iterator is a good way to enable the configuration.

You can see the possible configuration options from the signature of getNext-BatchFunction():

```
getNextBatchFunction(
      shuffle, lookBack, delay, batchSize, step, minIndex, maxIndex,
           normalize,
      includeDateTime)
```

There are quite a few configurable parameters. For example, you can use the look-Back argument to specify how long a period to look back when making a temperature prediction. You can also use the delay argument to specify how far in the future the temperature prediction will be made for. The arguments minIndex and maxIndex allow you to specify the range of rows to draw data from, and so forth.

We convert the getNextBatchFunction() function into a tf.data.Dataset object by passing it to the tf.data.generator() function. As we described in chapter 6, a tf.data.Dataset object, when used in conjunction with the fitDataset() method of a tf.Model object, enables us to train the model even if the data is too large to fit into WebGL memory (or any applicable backing memory type) as a whole. The Dataset object will create a batch of training data on the GPU only when it is about to go into the training. This is exactly what we do for the temperature-prediction problem here. In fact, we wouldn't be able to train the model using the model's ordinary fit() method due to the large number and size of the examples. The fitDataset() call can be found in jena-weather/models.js and looks like the following listing.

---

[2] See "Iterators and Generators," MDN web docs, http://mng.bz/RPWK.

Listing 8.1 Visualizing the `fitDataset`-based model training with tfjs-vis

```
const trainShuffle = true;                              The first Dataset object will
const trainDataset = tf.data.generator(      ◁──┘       generate the training data.
    () => jenaWeatherData.getNextBatchFunction(
        trainShuffle, lookBack, delay, batchSize, step, TRAIN_MIN_ROW,
        TRAIN_MAX_ROW, normalize, includeDateTime)).prefetch(8);
const evalShuffle = false;
const valDataset = tf.data.generator(      ◁────────────────────────────┐
    () => jenaWeatherData.getNextBatchFunction(
        evalShuffle, lookBack, delay, batchSize, step, VAL_MIN_ROW,
        VAL_MAX_ROW, normalize, includeDateTime));

  await model.fitDataset(trainDataset, {                   The second Dataset
  batchesPerEpoch: 500,                                    object will generate
  epochs,                                                  the validation data.
  callbacks: customCallback,
  validationData: valDataset    ◁──┐  The validationData config for fitDataset()
});                                  │  accepts either a Dataset object or a set of
                                     │  tensors. Here, the first option is used.
```

The first two fields of the configuration object for `fitDataset()` specify how many epochs to train the model for and how many batches to draw for every epoch. As you learned in chapter 6, they are the standard configuration fields for a `fitDataset()` call. However, the third field (`callbacks: customCallback`) is something new. It is how we visualize the training process. Our `customCallback` takes different values depending on whether the model training occurs in the browser or, as we'll see in the next chapter, in Node.js.

In the browser, the function `tfvis.show.fitCallbacks()` provides the value of `customCallback`. The function helps us visualize the model training in the web page with just one line of JavaScript code. It not only saves us all the work of accessing and keeping track of batch-by-batch and epoch-by-epoch loss and metric values, but it also removes the need to manually create and maintain the HTML elements in which the plots will be rendered:

```
const trainingSurface =
    tfvis.visor().surface({tab: modelType, name: 'Model Training'});
const customCallback = tfvis.show.fitCallbacks(trainingSurface,
    ['loss', 'val_loss'], {
  callbacks: ['onBatchEnd', 'onEpochEnd']
}));
```

The first argument to `fitCallbacks()` specifies a rendering area created with the `tfvis.visor().surface()` method. It is called a *visor surface* in the terminology of tfjs-vis. A visor is a container that helps you conveniently organize all the visualization related to your in-browser machine-learning tasks. Structurally, a visor is organized on two levels of hierarchy. At the higher level, there can be one or more tabs that the user can navigate using clicks. At the lower level, every tab contains one or more *surfaces*.

The `tfvis.visor().surface()` method, with its `tab` and `name` configuration fields, lets you create a surface in a designated visor tab with a designated name. A visor surface is not limited to rendering loss and metric curves. In fact, all the basic charts we showed with the CodePen example in section 7.1 can be rendered on visor surfaces. We leave this as an exercise for you at the end of this chapter.

The second argument for `fitCallbacks()` specifies what losses and metrics will be rendered in the visor surface. In this case, we plot the loss from the training and validation datasets. The third argument contains a field that controls the frequency at which the plots are updated. By using both `onBatchEnd` and `onEpochEnd`, we will get updates at the end of every batch and every epoch. In the next section, we will examine the loss curves created by `fitCallbacks()` and use them to spot underfitting and overfitting.

8.2 Underfitting, overfitting, and countermeasures

During the training of a machine-learning model, we want to monitor how well our model is capturing the patterns in the training data. A model that doesn't capture the patterns very well is said to be *underfit*; a model that captures the patterns *too* well, to the extent that what it learns generalizes poorly to new data, is said to be *overfit*. An overfit model can be brought back on track through countermeasures such as regularization. In this section, we'll show how visualization can help us spot these model behaviors and the effects of the countermeasures.

8.2.1 Underfitting

To solve the temperature-prediction problem, let's first try the simplest possible machine-learning model: a linear regressor. The code in listing 8.2 (from jena-weather/index.js) creates such a model. It uses a dense layer with a single unit and the default linear activation to generate the prediction. However, compared with the linear regressor we built for the download-time prediction problem in chapter 2, this model has an extra flatten layer. This is because the shape of the feature tensor in this problem is 2D, which must be flattened into 1D to meet the requirement of the dense layer used for linear regression. This flattening process is illustrated in figure 8.2. It is important to note is that this flattening operation discards the information about the sequential (temporal) ordering in the data.

Listing 8.2   Creating a linear-regression model for the temperature-prediction problem

```
function buildLinearRegressionModel(inputShape) {
  const model = tf.sequential();
  model.add(tf.layers.flatten({inputShape}));
  model.add(tf.layers.dense({units: 1}));
  return model;
}
```

Flattens the [batchSize, timeSteps, numFeatures] input shape to [batchSize, timeSteps * numFeatures] in order to apply the dense layer

A single-unit dense layer with the default (linear) activation is a linear regressor.

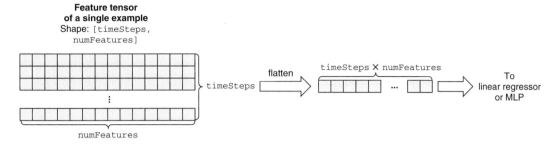

Figure 8.2   Flattening the 2D feature tensor of shape `[timeSteps, numFeatures]` into a 1D tensor of shape `[timeSteps × numFeatures]`, as done by both the linear regressor in listing 8.2 and the MLP model in listing 8.3

Once the model is constructed, we compile it for training with

```
model.compile({loss: 'meanAbsoluteError', optimizer: 'rmsprop'});
```

Here, we use the loss function `meanAbsoluteError` because our problem is predicting a continuous value (the normalized temperature). Unlike in some of the previous prob-lems, no separate metric is defined, because the MAE loss function itself serves as the human-interpretable metric. However, beware that since we are predicting the *normalized* temperature, the MAE loss has to be multiplied with the standard deviation of the temperature column (8.476 degrees Celsius) to be converted into a prediction error in absolute terms. For example, if we get an MAE of 0.5, it translates to 8.476 * 0.5 = 4.238 degrees Celsius of prediction error.

In the demo UI, choose Linear Regression in the Model Type drop-down menu and click Train Model to kick off the training of the linear regressor. Right after the training starts, you'll see a tabular summary of the model in a "card" that pops up on the right-hand side of the page (see the screenshot in figure 8.3). This model-summary table is

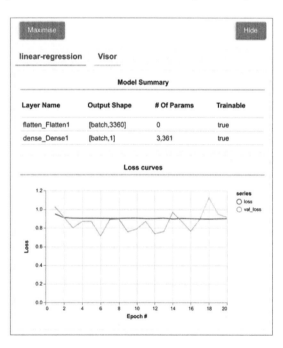

Figure 8.3   The tfjs-vis visor visualizing the training of a linear-regression model. Top: a summary table for the model. Bottom: the loss curves over 20 epochs of training. This chart is created with `tfvis.show .fitCallbacks()` (see jena-weather/index.js).

somewhat similar to the text output of a `model.summary()` call but is rendered graphically in HTML. The code that creates the table is as follows:

```
const surface = tfvis.visor().surface({name: 'Model Summary', tab});
tfvis.show.modelSummary(surface, model);
```

With the surface created, we draw a model-summary table in it by passing the surface to `tfvis.show.modelSummary()`, as in the second line of the previous code snippet.

Under the Model Summary part of the linear-regression tab is a plot that displays the loss curves from the model training (figure 8.3). It is created by the `fitCallbacks()` call that we described in the last section. From the plot, we can see how well the linear regressor does on the temperature-prediction problem. Both the training and validation losses end up oscillating around 0.9, which corresponds to 8.476 * 0.9 = 7.6 degrees Celsius in absolute terms (recall that 8.476 is the standard deviation of the temperature column in the CSV file). This means that after training, our linear regressor makes a prediction error of 7.6 degrees Celsius (or 13.7 degrees Fahrenheit) on average. These predictions are pretty bad. No one would want to trust the weather forecast based on this model! This is an example of *underfitting*.

Underfitting is usually a result of using an insufficient representational capacity (power) to model the feature-target relationship. In this example, our linear regressor is structurally too simple and hence is underpowered to capture the relation between the weather data of the previous 10 days and the temperature of the next day. To overcome underfitting, we usually increase the power of the model by making it bigger. Typical approaches include adding more layers (with nonlinear activations) to the model and increasing the size of the layers (such as the number of units in a dense layer). So, let's add a hidden layer to the linear regressor and see how much improvement we can get from the resultant MLP.

8.2.2 Overfitting

The function that creates MLP models is in listing 8.3 (from jena-weather/index.js). The MLP it creates includes two dense layers, one as the hidden layer and one as the output layer, in addition to a flatten layer that serves the same purpose as in the linear-regression model. You can see that the function has two more arguments compared to `buildLinearRegressionModel()` in listing 8.2. In particular, the `kernelRegularizer` and `dropoutRate` parameters are the ways in which we'll combat overfitting later. For now, let's see what prediction accuracy an MLP that doesn't use `kernelRegularizer` or `dropoutRate` is capable of achieving.

Listing 8.3   Creating an MLP for the temperature-prediction problem

```
function buildMLPModel(inputShape, kernelRegularizer, dropoutRate) {
  const model = tf.sequential();
  model.add(tf.layers.flatten({inputShape}));
  model.add(tf.layers.dense({
    units: 32,
    kernelRegularizer            ◁─────   If specified by the caller, add
    activation: 'relu',                   regularization to the kernel of
  }));                                     the hidden dense layer.
```

```
if (dropoutRate > 0) {
  model.add(tf.layers.dropout({rate: dropoutRate}));
}
model.add(tf.layers.dense({units: 1}));  ◁
return model;
}
```

If specified by the caller, add a dropout layer between the hidden dense layer and the output dense layer.

Panel A of figure 8.4 shows the loss curves from the MLP. Compared with the loss curves of the linear regressor, we can see a few important differences:

- The training and validation loss curves show a divergent pattern. This is different from the pattern in figure 8.3, where two loss curves show largely consistent trends.

- The training loss converges toward a much lower error than before. After 20 epochs of training, the training loss has a value of about 0.2, which corresponds to an error of 8.476 * 0.2 = 1.7 degrees Celsius—much better than the result from linear regression.

- However, the validation loss decreases briefly in the first two epochs and then starts to go back up slowly. At the end of epoch 20, it has a significantly higher value than the training loss (0.35, or about 3 degrees Celsius).

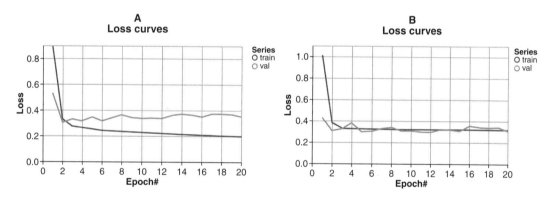

Figure 8.4   The loss curves from applying two different MLP models on the temperature-prediction problem. Panel A: from an MLP model without any regularization. Panel B: from an MLP model of the same layer size and count as the model in panel A, but with L2 regularization of the dense layers' kernels. Notice that the y-axis ranges differ slightly between the two panels.

The more than four-fold decrease in training loss relative to the previous result is due to the fact that our MLP has a higher power than the linear-regression model thanks to one more layer and several times more trainable weight parameters. However, the increased model power has a side effect: it causes the model to fit the training data significantly better than the validation data (data the model doesn't get to see during training). This is an example of *overfitting*. It is a case in which a model "pays too much attention" to the irrelevant details in the training data, to the extent that the model's predictions start to generalize poorly to unseen data.

8.2.3   *Reducing overfitting with weight regularization and visualizing it working*

In chapter 4, we reduced overfitting in a convnet by adding dropout layers to the model. Here, let's look at another frequently used overfitting-reduction approach: adding regularization to weights. In the Jena-weather demo UI, if you select the model type MLP with L2 Regularization, the underlying code will create an MLP by calling `buildMLPModel()` (listing 8.3) in the following manner:

```
model = buildMLPModel(inputShape, tf.regularizers.l2());
```

The second argument—the return value of `tf.regularizers.l2()`—is an *L2 regularizer*. By plugging the previous code into the `buildMLPModel()` function in listing 8.3, you can see that the L2 regularizer goes into the `kernelRegularizer` of the hidden dense layer's configuration. This attaches the L2 regularizer to the kernel of the dense layer. When a weight (such as the kernel of a dense layer) has an attached regularizer, we say that the weight is *regularized*. Similarly, when some or all of a model's weights are regularized, we say the model is regularized.

What does the regularizer do to the dense-layer kernel and the MLP that it belongs to? It adds an extra term to the loss function. Consider how the loss of the unregularized MLP is calculated: it's defined simply as the MAE between the targets and the model's predictions. In pseudo-code, it can be expressed as

```
loss = meanAbsoluteError(targets, predictions)
```

With a regularized weight, the loss of the model includes an extra term. In pseudo-code,

```
loss = meanAbsoluteError(targets, prediciton) + l2Rate * l2(kernel)
```

Here, `l2Rate * l2(kernel)` is the extra L2-regularization term of the loss function. Unlike the MAE, this term does *not* depend on the model's predictions. Instead, it depends only on the kernel (a weight of the layer) being regularized. Given the value of the kernel, it outputs a number associated only with the kernel's values. You can think of the number as a measure of how undesirable the current value of the kernel is.

Now let's look at the detailed definition of the L2-regularization function: `l2(kernel)`. It calculates the summed squares of all the weight values. For example, pretend our kernel has a small shape of `[2, 2]` for the sake of simplicity, and suppose its values are `[[0.1, 0.2], [-0.3, -0.4]]`; then,

```
l2(kernel) = 0.1^2 + 0.2^2 + (-0.3)^2 + (-0.4)^2 = 0.3
```

Therefore, `l2(kernel)` always returns a positive number that penalizes large weight values in `kernel`. With the term included in the total loss, it encourages all elements of `kernel` to be smaller in absolute value, everything else being equal.

Now the total loss includes two different terms: the target-prediction mismatch and a term related to `kernel`'s magnitudes. As a result, the training process will try to not only minimize the target-prediction mismatch but also reduce the sum of the squares of the kernel's elements. Oftentimes, the two goals will conflict with each other. For example, a reduction in the magnitude of the kernel's elements may reduce the second term but increase the first one (the MSE loss). How does the total loss balance the relative importance of the two conflicting terms? That's where the `l2Rate` multiplier comes into play. It quantifies the importance of the L2 term relative to the target-prediction-error term. The larger the value of `l2Rate`, the more the training process will tend to reduce the L2-regularization term at the cost of increased target-prediction error. This term, which defaults to `1e-3`, is a hyperparameter whose value can be tuned through hyperparameter optimization.

So how does the L2 regularizer help us? Panel B of figure 8.4 shows the loss curves from the regularized MLP. By comparing it with the curves from the unregularized MLP (panel A of the same figure), you can see that the regularized model yields less divergent training and validation loss curves. This means that the model is no longer "paying undue attention" to idiosyncratic patterns in the training dataset. Instead, the pattern it learns from the training set generalizes well to unseen examples in the validation set. In our regularized MLP, only the first dense layer incorporated a regularizer, while the second dense layer didn't. But that turned out to be sufficient to overcome the overfitting in this case. In the next section, we will look deeper at why smaller kernel values lead to less overfitting.

VISUALIZING THE EFFECT OF REGULARIZATION ON WEIGHT VALUES

Since the L2 regularizer works by encouraging the kernel of the hidden dense layer to have smaller values, we ought to be able to see that the post-training kernel values are smaller in the regularized MLP than in the unregularized one. How can we do that in TensorFlow.js? The `tfvis.show.layer()` function from tfjs-vis makes it possible to visualize a TensorFlow.js model's weights with one line of code. Listing 8.4 is a code excerpt that shows how this is done. The code is executed when the training of an MLP model ends. The `tfvis.show.layer()` call takes two arguments: the visor surface on which the rendering will happen and the layer being rendered.

> **Listing 8.4 Visualizing the weight distribution of layers (from jena-weather/index.js)**

```
function visualizeModelLayers(tab, layers, layerNames) {
  layers.forEach((layer, i) => {
    const surface = tfvis.visor().surface({name: layerNames[i], tab});
    tfvis.show.layer(surface, layer);
  });
}
```

The visualization made by this code is shown in figure 8.5. Panels A and B show the results from the unregularized and regularized MLPs, respectively. In each panel, `tfvis.show.layer()` displays a table of the layer's weights, with details about the names of the weights, their shape and parameter count, min/max of the parameter values, and counts of zero and NaN parameter values (the last of which can be useful for diagnosing problematic training runs). The layer visualization also contains Show

Figure 8.5 Distribution of the values in the kernel with (panel A) and without (panel B) L2 regularization. The visualization is created with `tfvis.show.layer()`. Note that the x-axes of the two histograms have different scales.

Values Distribution buttons for each of the layer's weights, which, when clicked, will create a histogram of the values in the weight.

Comparing the plots for the two flavors of MLP, you can see a clear difference: the values of the kernel are distributed over a considerably narrower range with the L2 regularization than without. This is reflected in both the min/max values (the first row) and in the value histogram. This is regularization at work!

But why do smaller kernel values result in reduced overfitting and improved generalization? An intuitive way to understand this is that L2 regularization enforces the principle of Occam's razor. Generally speaking, a larger magnitude in a weight parameter tends to cause the model to fit to fine-grained details in the training features that it sees, and a smaller magnitude tends to let the model ignore such details. In the extreme case, a kernel value of zero means the model doesn't attend to its corresponding input feature at all. The L2 regularization encourages the model to be more "economical" by avoiding large-magnitude weight values, and to retain those only when it is worth the cost (when the reduction in the target-prediction mismatch term outweighs the regularizer loss).

L2 regularization is but one of the weapons against overfitting in the machine-learning practitioner's arsenal. In chapter 4, we demonstrated the power of dropout layers. Dropout is a powerful countermeasure to overfitting in general. It helps us reduce overfitting in this temperature-prediction problem as well. You can see that yourself by choosing the model type MLP with Dropout in the demo UI. The quality of training you get from the dropout-enabled MLP is comparable to the one you get from the L2-regularized MLP. We discussed how and why dropout works in section 4.3.2 when we applied it to an MNIST convnet, so we won't repeat it here. However, table 8.1 provides a quick overview of the most widely used countermeasures to over-fitting. It includes an intuitive description of how each of them works and the corresponding API in TensorFlow.js. The question as to which countermeasure to use for a particular problem is usually answered through 1) following well-established models that solve similar problems and 2) treating the countermeasure as a hyperparameter and searching for it through hyperparameter optimization (section 3.1.2). In addition, each overfitting-reducing method itself contains tunable parameters that can also be determined through hyperparameter optimization (see the last column of table 8.1.)

Table 8.1 **An overview of commonly used methods for reducing overfitting in TensorFlow.js**

Name of method	How the method works	Corresponding API in TensorFlow.js	Main free parameter(s)
L2 regularizer	Assigns a positive loss (penalty) to the weight by calculating the summed squares of parameter values of the weight. It encourages the weight to have smaller parameter values.	`tf.regularizers.l2()` See the "Reducing overfitting with weight regularization" section, for example.	L2-regularization rate
L1 regularizer	Like L2 regularizers, encourages the weight parameters to be smaller. However, the loss it assigns to a weight is based on the summed *absolute values* of the parameters, instead of summed squares. This definition of regularization loss causes more weight parameters to become zero (that is, "sparser weights").	`tf.regularizers.l1()`	L1-regularization rate
Combined L1-L2 regularizer	A weighted sum of L1 and L2 regularization losses.	`tf.regularizers.l1l2()`	L1-regularization rate L2-regularization rate
Dropout	Randomly sets a fraction of the inputs to zero during training (but not during inference) in order to break spurious correlations (or "conspiracy" in Geoff Hinton's words) among weight parameters that emerge during training.	`tf.layers.dropout()` See section 4.3.2, for example.	Dropout rate

Table 8.1   An overview of commonly used methods for reducing overfitting in TensorFlow.js *(continued)*

Name of method	How the method works	Corresponding API in TensorFlow.js	Main free parameter(s)
Batch normalization	Learns the mean and standard deviation of its input values during training and uses the learned statistics to normalize the inputs to zero mean and unit standard deviation as its output.	`tf.layers` `.batchNormalization()`	Various (see https://js.tensorflow.org/api/latest/#layers.batchNormalization)
Early stopping of training based on validation-set loss	Stops model training as soon as the epoch-end loss value on the validation set stops decreasing.	`tf.callbacks` `.earlyStopping()`	`minDelta`: The threshold below which changes will be ignored `patience`: How many consecutive epochs of no improvement are tolerated at most

To wrap up this section on visualizing underfitting and overfitting, we provide a schematic diagram as a quick rule of thumb for spotting those states (figure 8.6). As panel A shows, underfitting is when the model achieves a suboptimal (high) loss value, regardless of whether it's on the training or validation set. In panel B, we see a typical pattern of overfitting, where the training loss looks fairly satisfactory (low), but the validation loss is worse (higher) in comparison. The validation loss can plateau and even start to edge up, even when the training-set loss continues to go down. Panel C is the state we want to be in—namely, a state where the loss value doesn't diverge too much between the training and validation sets so that the final validation loss is low. Be aware that the phrase "sufficiently low" can be relative, especially for problems that no existing models can solve perfectly. New models may come out in the future and lower the achievable loss relative to what we have in panel C. At that point, the pattern in panel C would become a case of underfitting, and we would need to adopt the new model type in order to fix it, possibly by going through the cycle of overfitting and regularization again.

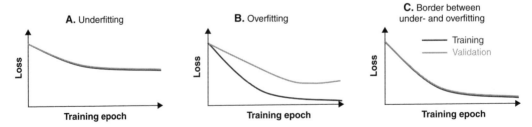

Figure 8.6   A schematic diagram showing the loss curves from simplified cases of underfitting (panel A), overfitting (panel B), and just-right fitting (panel C) in model training.

Finally, note that visualization of training is not limited to the losses. Other metrics are often visualized to aid in monitoring the training process as well. Examples of this are sprinkled throughout the book. For example, in chapter 3, we plotted the ROC curves when training a binary classifier for phishing websites. We also rendered the confusion matrix when training the iris-flower classifier. In chapter 9, we'll show an example of displaying machine-generated text during the training of a text generator. That example won't involve a GUI but will nonetheless provide useful and intuitive real-time information about the state of the model's training. Specifically, by looking at the text generated by the model, you can get an intuitive sense of how good the text generated by the model currently is.

8.3 *The universal workflow of machine learning*

Up to this point, you have seen all the important steps in designing and training a machine-learning model, including acquiring, formatting, visualizing, and ingesting data; choosing the appropriate model topology and loss function for the dataset; and training the model. You've also seen some of the most important failure modes that may appear during the training process: underfitting and overfitting. So, this is a good place for us to look back at what we've learned so far and reflect on what's common among the machine-learning model processes for different datasets. The resulting abstraction is what we refer to as *the universal workflow of machine learning*. We'll list the workflow step-by-step and expand on the key considerations in each step:

1 *Determine if machine learning is the right approach.* First, consider if machine learning is the right approach to your problem, and proceed to the next steps only if the answer is yes. In some cases, a non-machine-learning approach will work equally well or perhaps even better, at a lower cost. For example, given enough model-tuning efforts, you can train a neural network to "predict" the sum of two integers by taking the integers as text input data (for example, the addition-rnn example in the tfjs-examples repository). But this is far from the most efficient or reliable solution to this problem: the good old addition operation on the CPU suffices in this case.

2 *Define the machine-learning problem and what you are trying to predict using the data.* In this step, you need to answer two questions:
   - *What sort of data is available?* In supervised learning, you can only learn to predict something if you have labeled training data available. For example, the weather-prediction model we saw earlier in this chapter is possible only because the Jena-weather dataset is available. Data availability is usually a limiting factor in this stage. If the available data is insufficient, you may need to collect more data or hire people to manually label an unlabeled dataset.
   - *What type of problem are you facing?* Is it binary classification, multiclass classification, regression, or something else? Identifying the problem type will guide your choice of model architecture, loss function, and so forth.

You can't move on to the next step until you know what the inputs and outputs are and what data you'll use. Be aware of the hypotheses you've made implicitly at this stage:

– You hypothesize that the outputs can be predicted given the inputs (the input alone contains enough information for a model to predict the output for all possible examples in this problem).
– You hypothesize that the data available is sufficient for a model to learn this input-output relationship.

Until you have a working model, these are just hypotheses waiting to be validated or invalidated. Not all problems are solvable: just because you've assembled a large labeled dataset that maps from X to Y doesn't mean that X contains enough information for the value of Y. For instance, if you're trying to predict the future price of a stock based on the history of the stock's price, you'll likely fail because the price history doesn't contain enough predictive information about the future price.

One class of unsolvable problems you should be aware of is *nonstationary* problems, in which the input-output relation changes with time. Suppose you're trying to build a recommendation engine for clothes (given a user's clothes purchase history), and you're training your model on only one year's data. The big issue here is that people's tastes for clothes change with time. A model that works accurately on the validation data from last year isn't guaranteed to work equally accurately this year. Keep in mind that machine learning can only be used to learn patterns that are present in the training data. In this case, getting up-to-date data and continuously training new models will be a viable solution.

3   *Identify a way to reliably measure the success of a trained model on your goal.* For simple tasks, this may be just prediction accuracy, precision and recall, or the ROC curve and the AUC value (see chapter 3). But in many cases, it will require more sophisticated domain-specific metrics, such as customer retention rate and sales, which are better aligned with higher-level goals, such as the success of the business.

4   *Prepare the evaluation process.* Design the validation process that you'll use to evaluate your models. In particular, you should split your data into three homogeneous yet nonoverlapping sets: a training set, a validation set, and a test set. The validation- and test-set labels ought not to leak into the training data. For instance, with temporal prediction, the validation and test data should come from time intervals *after* the training data. Your data preprocessing code should be covered by tests to guard against bugs.

5   *Vectorize the data.* Turn the data into tensors, also known as *n*-dimensional arrays, the lingua franca of machine-learning models in frameworks such as TensorFlow.js and TensorFlow. Note the following guidelines for data vectorization:

- The numeric values taken by the tensors should usually be scaled to small and centered values: for example, within the [-1, 1] or [0, 1] interval.
- If different features (such as temperature and wind speed) take values in different ranges (heterogeneous data), then the data ought to be normalized, usually z-normalized to zero mean and unit standard deviation for each feature.

Once your tensors of input data and target (output) data are ready, you can begin to develop models.

6 *Develop a model that beats a commonsense baseline.* Develop a model that beats a non-machine-learning baseline (such as predicting the population average for a regression problem or predicting the last data point in a time-series prediction problem), thereby demonstrating that machine learning can truly add value to your solution. This may not always be the case (see step 1).

Assuming things are going well, you need to make three key choices to build your first baseline-beating, machine-learning model:

- *Last-layer activation*—This establishes useful constraints for the model's output. This activation should suit the type of problem you are solving. For example, the phishing-website classifier in chapter 3 used the sigmoid activation for its last (output) layer due to the binary-classification nature of the problem, and the temperature-prediction models in this chapter used the linear activation for the layer owing to the regression nature of the problem.
- *Loss function*—In a way similar to last-layer activation, the loss function should match the problem you're solving. For instance, use binaryCrossentropy for binary-classification problems, categoricalCrossentropy for multiclass-classification problems, and meanSquaredError for regression problems.
- *Optimizer configuration*—The optimizer is what drives the updates to the neural network's weights. What type of optimizer should be used? What should its learning rate be? These are generally questions answered by hyperparameter tuning. But in most cases, you can safely start with the rmsprop optimizer and its default learning rate.

7 *Develop a model with sufficient capacity and to overfit the training data.* Gradually scale up your model architecture by manually changing hyperparameters. You want to reach at a model that overfits the training set. Remember that the universal and central tension in supervised machine learning is between *optimization* (fitting the data seen during training) and *generalization* (being able to make accurate predictions for unseen data). The ideal model is one that stands right at the border between underfitting and overfitting: that is, between under-capacity and over-capacity. To figure out where this border is, you must first cross it.

In order to cross it, you must develop a model that overfits. This is usually fairly easy. You may

– Add more layers
– Make each layer bigger
– Train the model for more epochs

Always use visualization to monitor the training and validation losses, as well as any additional metrics that you care about (such as AUC) on both the training and validation sets. When you see the model's accuracy on the validation set begin to degrade (figure 8.6, panel B), you've achieved overfitting.

8 *Add regularization to your model and tune the hyperparameters.* The next step is to add regularization to your model and further tune its hyperparameters (usually in an automated way) to get as close as possible to the ideal model that neither underfits nor overfits. This step will take the most time, even though it can be automated. You'll repeatedly modify your model, train it, evaluate it on the validation set (not the test set at this point), modify it again, and repeat until the model is as good as it can get. These are the things you should try in terms of regularization:

– Add dropout layers with different dropout rates.
– Try L1 and/or L2 regularization.
– Try different architectures: add or remove a small number of layers.
– Change other hyperparameters (for example, the number of units of a dense layer).

Beware of validation-set overfitting when tuning hyperparameters. Because the hyperparameters are determined based on the performance on the validation set, their values will be overspecialized for the validation set and therefore may not generalize well to other data. It is the purpose of the test set to obtain an unbiased estimate of the model's accuracy after hyperparameter tuning. So, you shouldn't use the test set when tuning the hyperparameters.

This is the universal workflow of machine learning! In chapter 12, we'll add two more practically oriented steps to it (an evaluation step and a deployment step). But for now, this is a recipe for how to go from a vaguely defined machine-learning idea to a model that's trained and ready to make some useful predictions.

With this foundational knowledge, we'll start exploring more advanced types of neural networks in the upcoming part of the book. We'll start from models designed for sequential data in chapter 9.

Exercises

1 In the temperature-prediction problem, we found that the linear regressor significantly underfit the data and produced poor prediction results on both the training and validation sets. Would adding L2 regularization to the linear regressor help improve the accuracy of such an underfitting model? It should be easy to try it out yourself by modifying the `buildLinearRegressionModel()` function in the file jena-weather/models.js.

2 When predicting the temperature of the next day in the Jena-weather example, we used a look-back period of 10 days to produce the input features. A natural question is, what if we use a longer look-back period? Is including more data going to help us get more accurate predictions? You can find this out by modifying the const lookBack in jena-weather/index.js and running the training in the browser (for example, by using the MLP with L2 regularization). Of course, a longer look-back period will increase the size of the input features and lead to longer training time. So, the flip side of the question is, can we use a shorter look-back period without sacrificing the prediction accuracy significantly? Try this out as well.

Summary

- tfjs-vis can aid the visualization of a machine-learning model's training process in the browser. Specifically, we showed how tfjs-vis can be used to
  - Visualize the topology of TensorFlow.js models.
  - Plot loss and metrics curves during training.
  - Summarize weight distributions after training.

  We showed concrete examples of these visualization workflows.
- Underfitting and overfitting are fundamental behaviors of machine-learning models and should be monitored and understood in every machine-learning problem. They can both be seen by comparing the loss curves from the training and validation sets during training. The built-in tfvis.show.fitCallbacks() method helps you visualize these curves in the browser with ease.
- The universal workflow of machine learning is a list of common steps and best practices of different types of supervised learning tasks. It goes from deciding the nature of the problem and the requirements on the data to finding a model that sits nicely on the border between underfitting and overfitting.

Deep learning for
sequences and text

This chapter covers

- How sequential data differs from nonsequential data
- Which deep-learning techniques are suitable for problems that involve sequential data
- How to represent text data in deep learning, including with one-hot encoding, multi-hot encoding, and word embedding
- What RNNs are and why they are suitable for sequential problems
- What 1D convolution is and why it is an attractive alternative to RNNs
- The unique properties of sequence-to-sequence tasks and how to use the attention mechanism to solve them

This chapter focuses on problems involving sequential data. The essence of sequential data is the ordering of its elements. As you may have realized, we've dealt with sequential data before. Specifically, the Jena-weather data we introduced in chapter 7 is sequential. The data can be represented as an array of arrays of numbers.

Order certainly matters for the outer array because the measurements come in over time. If you reverse the order of the outer array—for instance, a rising air-pressure trend becomes a falling one—it has completely different implications if you are trying to predict future weather. Sequential data is everywhere in life: stock prices, electrocardiogram (ECG) readings, strings of characters in software code, consecutive frames of a video, and sequences of actions taken by a robot. Contrast those with nonsequential data such as the iris flowers in chapter 3: it doesn't matter if you alter the order of the four numeric features (sepal and petal length and width).[1]

The first part of the chapter will introduce a fascinating type of model we mentioned in chapter 1—RNNs, or recurrent neural networks, which are designed specifically to learn from sequential data. We will build the intuition for what special features of RNNs make these models sensitive to the ordering of elements and the information it bears.

The second part of the chapter will talk about a special kind of sequential data: text, which is perhaps the most ubiquitous sequential data (especially in the web environment!). We will start by examining how text is represented in deep learning and how to apply RNNs on such representations. We will then move on to 1D convnets and talk about why they are also powerful at processing text and how they can be attractive alternatives to RNNs for certain types of problems.

In the last part of the chapter, we will go a step further and explore sequence-based tasks that are slightly more complex than predicting a number or a class. In particular, we will venture into sequence-to-sequence tasks, which involve predicting an output sequence from an input one. We will use an example to illustrate how to solve basic sequence-to-sequence tasks with a new model architecture called the *attention mechanism*, which is becoming more and more important in the field of deep-learning-based natural language processing.

By the end of this chapter, you should be familiar with common types of sequential data in deep learning, how they are presented as tensors, and how to use TensorFlow.js to write basic RNNs, 1D convnets, and attention networks to solve machine-learning tasks involving sequential data.

The layers and models you will see in this chapter are among the most complex in this book. This is the cost that comes with their enhanced capacity for sequential-learning tasks. You may find some of them hard to grasp the first time you read about them, even though we strive to present them in a fashion that's as intuitive as possible, with the help of diagrams and pseudo-code. If that's the case, try playing with the example code and working through the exercises provided at the end of the chapter. In our experience, the hands-on experience makes it much easier to internalize complex concepts and architectures like the ones that appear in this chapter.

---

[1] Convince yourself that this is indeed the case in exercise 1 at the end of the chapter.

9.1   *Second attempt at weather prediction: Introducing RNNs*

The models we built for the Jena-weather problem in chapter 8 threw away the order information. In this section, we will tell you why that's the case and how we can bring the order information back by using RNNs. This will allow us to achieve superior prediction accuracies in the temperature-prediction task.

9.1.1   *Why dense layers fail to model sequential order*

Since we described the Jena-weather dataset in detail in the previous chapter, we will go over the dataset and the related machine-learning task only briefly here. The task involves predicting the temperature 24 hours from a certain moment in time by using readings from 14 weather instruments (such as temperature, air pressure, and wind speed) over a 10-day period leading up to the moment. The instrument readings are taken at regular intervals of 10 minutes, but we downsample them by a factor of 6 to once per hour for the sake of manageable model size and training time. So, each training example comes with a feature tensor of shape [240, 14], where 240 is the number of time steps over the 10-day period, and 14 is the number of different weather-instrument readings.

When we tried a linear-regression model and an MLP on the task in the previous chapter, we flattened the 2D input features to 1D by using a `tf.layers.flatten` layer (see listing 8.2 and figure 8.2). The flattening step was necessary because both the linear regressor and the MLP used dense layers to handle the input data, and dense layers require the input data to be 1D for each input example. This means that the information from all the time steps is mixed together in a way that erases the significance of which step comes first and which one next, which time step follows which other one, how far apart two time steps are, and so forth. In other words, it doesn't matter how we order the 240 time steps when we flatten the 2D tensor of shape [240, 14] into the 1D tensor of shape [3360] as long as we are consistent between training and inference. You can confirm this point experimentally in exercise 1 at the end of this chapter. But from a theoretical point of view, this lack of sensitivity to the order of data elements can be understood in the following way. At the core of a dense layer is a set of linear equations, each of which multiplies every input feature value $[x_1, x_2, ..., x_n]$ with a tunable coefficient from the kernel $[k_1, k_2, ..., k_n]$:

$$y = f(k_1 \cdot x_1 + k_2 \cdot x_2 + ... + k_n \cdot x_n) \qquad \textbf{(Equation 9.1)}$$

Figure 9.1 provides a visual representation of how a dense layer works: the paths leading from the input elements to the output of the layer are graphically symmetric with one another, reflecting the mathematical symmetry in equation 9.1. The symmetry is *undesirable* when we deal with sequential data because it renders the model blind to the order among the elements.

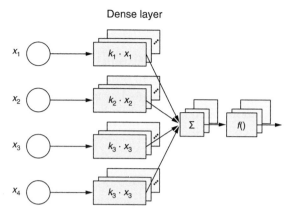

Dense layer

Figure 9.1　The internal architecture of a dense layer. The multiplication and addition performed by a dense layer is symmetric with respect to its inputs. Contrast this with a simpleRNN layer (figure 9.2), which breaks the symmetry by introducing step-by-step computation. Note that we assume the input has only four elements and omit the bias terms for simplicity. Also, we show the operations for only one output unit of the dense layer. The remaining units are represented as the stack of obscured boxes in the background.

In fact, there is an easy way to show that our dense-layer-based approach (the MLPs, even with regularization) did not provide a very good solution to the temperature-prediction problem: comparing its accuracy with the accuracy we can obtain from a commonsense, non-machine-learning approach.

What is the commonsense approach we are speaking of? Predict the temperature as the last temperature reading in the input features. To put this simply, just pretend that the temperature 24 hours from now will be the same as the temperature right now! This approach makes "gut sense" because we know from everyday experience that the temperature tomorrow tends to be close to the temperature today (that is, at exactly the same time of day). It is a very simple algorithm and gives a reasonable guess that should beat all other similarly simple algorithms (such as predicting the temperature as the temperature from 48 hours ago).

The jena-weather directory of tfjs-examples that we used in chapter 8 provides a command for you to assess the accuracy of this commonsense approach:

```
git clone https://github.com/tensorflow/tfjs-examples.git
cd tfjs-examples/jena-weather
yarn
yarn train-rnn --modelType baseline
```

The `yarn train-rnn` command calls the script train-rnn.js and performs computation in the Node.js-based backend environment.[2] We will come back to this mode of operation when we explore RNNs shortly. The command should give you the following screen output:

```
Commonsense baseline mean absolute error: 0.290331
```

So, the simple non-machine-learning approach yields a mean absolute prediction error of about 0.29 (in normalized terms), which is about equal to (if not slightly better

---

[2]　The code that implements this commonsense, non-machine-learning approach is in the function named `getBaselineMeanAbsoluteError()` in jena-weather/models.js. It uses the `forEachAsync()` method of the `Dataset` object to iterate through all batches of the validation subset, compute the MAE loss for each batch, and accumulate all the losses to obtain the final loss.

than) the best validation error we got from the MLP in chapter 8 (see figure 8.4). In other words, the MLP, with or without regularization, wasn't able to beat the accuracy from the commonsense baseline method reliably!

Such observations are not uncommon in machine learning: it's not always easy for machine learning to beat a commonsense approach. In order to beat it, the machine-learning model sometimes needs to be carefully designed or tuned through hyperparameter optimization. Our observation also underlines how important it is to create a non-machine-learning baseline for comparison when working on a machine-learning problem. We certainly want to avoid wasting all the effort on building a machine-learning algorithm that can't even beat a much simpler and computationally cheaper baseline! Can we beat the baseline in the temperature-prediction problem? The answer is yes, and we will rely on RNNs to do that. Let's now take a look at how RNNs capture and process sequential order.

9.1.2 How RNNs model sequential order

Panel A of figure 9.2 shows the internal structure of an RNN layer by using a short, four-item sequence. There are several variants of RNN layers out there, and the diagram shows the simplest variant, which is referred to as simpleRNN and is available in TensorFlow.js as the `tf.layers.simpleRNN()` factory function. We will talk about more complicated RNN variants later in this chapter, but for now we will focus on simpleRNN.

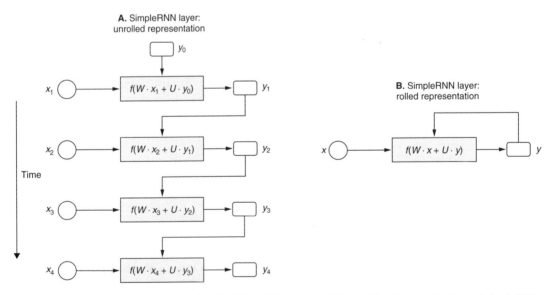

Figure 9.2   The "unrolled" (panel A) and "rolled" (panel B) representations of the internal structure of simpleRNN. The rolled view (panel B) represents the same algorithm as the unrolled one, albeit in a more succinct form. It illustrates simpleRNN's sequential processing of input data in a more concise fashion. In the rolled representation in panel B, the connection that goes back from output (*y*) into the model itself is the reason why such layers are called *recurrent*. As in figure 9.1, we display only four input elements and omit the bias terms for simplicity.

The diagram shows how the time slices of the input (x_1, x_2, x_3, ...) are processed step-by-step. At each step, x_i is processed by a function ($f()$), represented as the rectangular box at the center of the diagram. This yields an output (y_i) that gets combined with the next input slice (x_{i+1}) as the input to the $f()$ at the next step. It is important to note that even though the diagram shows four separate boxes with function definitions in them, they in fact represent the same function. This function ($f()$) is called the *cell* of the RNN layer. It is used in an iterative fashion during the invocation of the RNN layer. Therefore, an RNN layer can be viewed as "an RNN cell wrapped in a `for` loop."[3]

Comparing the structure of simpleRNN and that of the dense layer (figure 9.1), we can see two major differences:

- SimpleRNN processes the input elements (time steps) one step at a time. This reflects the sequential nature of the inputs, something a dense layer can't do.
- In simpleRNN, the processing at every input time step generates an output (y_i). The output from a previous time step (for example, y_1) is used by the layer when it processes the next time step (such as x_2). This is the reason behind the "recurrent" part of the name RNN: the output from previous time steps flows back and becomes an input for later time steps. Recurrence doesn't happen in layer types such as dense, conv2d, and maxPooling2d. Those layers don't involve output information flowing back and hence are referred to as *feedforward* layers.

Due to these unique features, simpleRNN breaks the symmetry between the input elements. It is sensitive to the order of the input elements. If you reorder the elements of a sequential input, the output will be altered as a result. This distinguishes simpleRNN from a dense layer.

Panel B of figure 9.2 is a more abstract representation of simpleRNN. It is referred to as a *rolled* RNN diagram, versus the *unrolled* diagram in panel A, because it "rolls" all time steps into a single loop. The rolled diagram corresponds nicely to a `for` loop in programming languages, which is actually how simpleRNN and other types of RNNs are implemented under the hood in TensorFlow.js. But instead of showing the real code, let's look at the much shorter pseudo-code for simpleRNN in the following listing, which you can view as the implementation of the simpleRNN architecture shown in figure 9.2. This will help you focus on the essence of how the RNN layer works.

> **Listing 9.1 Pseudo-code for the internal computation of simpleRNN**

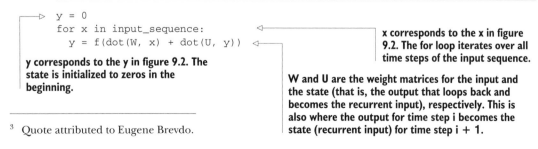

```
y = 0
for x in input_sequence:
    y = f(dot(W, x) + dot(U, y))
```

y corresponds to the y in figure 9.2. The state is initialized to zeros in the beginning.

x corresponds to the x in figure 9.2. The for loop iterates over all time steps of the input sequence.

W and U are the weight matrices for the input and the state (that is, the output that loops back and becomes the recurrent input), respectively. This is also where the output for time step i becomes the state (recurrent input) for time step i + 1.

---

[3] Quote attributed to Eugene Brevdo.

In listing 9.1, you can see that the output at time step i becomes the "state" for the next time step (next iteration). *State* is an important concept for RNNs. It is how an RNN "remembers" what happened in the steps of the input sequence it has already seen. In the for loop, this memory state gets combined with future input steps and becomes the new memory state. This gives the simpleRNN the ability to react to the same input element differently depending on what elements have appeared in the sequence before. This type of memory-based sensitivity is at the heart of sequential processing. As a simple example, if you are trying to decode Morse code (made of dots and dashes), the meaning of a dash depends on the sequence of dots and dashes that go before (and after) it. As another example, in English, the word *last* can have completely different meanings depending on what words go before it.

SimpleRNN is appropriately named because its output and state are the same thing. Later, we will explore more complex and powerful RNN architectures. Some of these have output and state as two separate things; others even have multiple states.

Another thing worth noting about RNNs is that the for loop enables them to process input sequences made of an arbitrary number of input steps. This is something that can't be done through flattening a sequential input and feeding it to a dense layer because a dense layer can only take a fixed input shape.

Furthermore, the for loop reflects another important property of RNNs: *parameter sharing*. What we mean by this is the fact that the same weight parameters (W and U) are used in all time steps. The alternative is to have a unique value of W (and U) for every time step. That would be undesirable because 1) it limits the number of time steps that can be processed by the RNN, and 2) it leads to a dramatic increase in the number of tunable parameters, which will increase the amount of computation and the likelihood of overfitting during training. Therefore, the RNN layers are similar to conv2d layers in convnets in that they use parameter sharing to achieve efficient computation and protect against overfitting—although the recurrent and conv2d layers achieve parameter sharing in different ways. While conv2d layers exploit the translational invariance along spatial dimensions, RNN layers exploit translational invariance along the *time* dimension.

Figure 9.2 shows what happens in a simpleRNN during inference time (the forward pass). It doesn't show how the weight parameters (W and U) are updated during training (the backward pass). However, the training of RNNs follows the same backpropagation rules that we introduced in section 2.2.2 (figure 2.8)—that is, starting from the loss, backtracking the list of operations, taking their derivatives, and accumulating gradient values through them. Mathematically, the backward pass on a recurrent network is basically the same as that on a feedforward one. The only difference is that the backward pass of an RNN layer goes backwards in time, on an unrolled graph like the one in panel A of figure 9.2. This is why the process of training RNNs is sometimes referred to as *backpropagation through time* (BPTT).

SIMPLERNN IN ACTION

That's enough abstract musing about simpleRNN and RNNs in general. Let's now look at how to create a simpleRNN layer and include it in a model object, so we can use it to predict temperatures more accurately than before. The code in listing 9.2 (excerpted from jena-weather/train-rnn.js) is how this is done. For all the internal complexity of the simpleRNN layer, the model itself is fairly simple. It has only two layers. The first one is simpleRNN, configured to have 32 units. The second one is a dense layer that uses the default linear activation to generate continuous numerical predictions for the temperature. Note that because the model starts with an RNN, it is no longer necessary to flatten the sequential input (compare this with listing 8.3 in the previous chapter, when we created MLPs for the same problem). In fact, if we put a flatten layer before the simpleRNN layer, an error would be thrown because RNN layers in TensorFlow.js expect their inputs to be at least 3D (including the batch dimension).

Listing 9.2   Creating a simpleRNN-based model for the temperature-prediction problem

```
function buildSimpleRNNModel(inputShape) {
  const model = tf.sequential();
  const rnnUnits = 32;           ◁
  model.add(tf.layers.simpleRNN({   ◁
    units: rnnUnits,
    inputShape
  }));
  model.add(tf.layers.dense({units: 1}));   ◁
  return model;
}
```

The hard-coded unit count of the simpleRNN layer is a value that works well, determined through hand-tuning of the hyperparameter.

The first layer of the model is a simpleRNN layer. There is no need to flatten the sequential input, which has a shape of [null, 240, 14].

We end the model with a dense layer with a single unit and the default linear activation for the regression problem.

To see the simpleRNN model in action, use the following command:

```
yarn train-rnn --modelType simpleRNN --logDir /tmp/
  jean-weather-simpleRNN-logs
```

The RNN model is trained in the backend environment using tfjs-node. Due to the amount of computation involved in the BPTT-based RNN training, it would be much harder and slower, if not impossible, to train the same model in the resource-restricted browser environment. If you have a CUDA environment set up properly, you can add the `--gpu` flag to the command to get a further boost in training speed.

The `--logDir` flag in the previous command causes the model-training process to log the loss values to the specified directory. You can load and plot the loss curves in the browser using a tool called TensorBoard. Figure 9.3 is a screenshot from Tensor-Board. At the level of JavaScript code, this is achieved by configuring the `tf.Layers-Model.fit()` call with a special callback that points to the log directory. Info box 9.1 contains further information on how this is done.

INFO BOX 9.1   Using the TensorBoard callbacks to monitor long-running model training in Node.js

In chapter 8, we introduced callbacks from the tfjs-vis library that help you monitor `tf.LayersModel.fit()` calls in the browser. However, tfjs-vis is a browser-only library and is not applicable to Node.js. By default, `tf.LayersModel.fit()` in tfjs-node (or tfjs-node-gpu) renders progress bars and displays loss and timing metrics in the terminal. While this is lightweight and informative, text and numbers are often a less intuitive and less visually appealing way to monitor long-running model training than a GUI. For example, small changes in the loss value over an extensive period of time, which is often what we are looking for during late stages of model training, are much easier to spot in a chart (with properly set scales and grids) than in a body of text.

Luckily, a tool called *TensorBoard* can help us in the backend environment. TensorBoard was originally designed for TensorFlow (Python), but tfjs-node and tfjs-node-gpu can write data in a compatible format that can be ingested by TensorBoard. To log loss and metric values to TensorBoard from a `tf.LayersModel.fit()` or `tf.LayersModel.fitDataset()` call, follow this pattern:

```
import * as tf from '@tensorflow/tfjs-node';
// Or '@tensorflow/tfjs-node-gpu'

    // ...
await model.fit(xs, ys, {
  epochs,
  callbacks: tf.node.tensorBoard('/path/to/my/logdir')
});

      // Or for fitDataset():
await model.fitDataset(dataset, {
  epochs,
  batchesPerEpoch,
  callbacks: tf.node.tensorBoard('/path/to/my/logdir')
});
```

These calls will write the loss values, along with any metrics configured during the `compile()` call, to the directory /path/to/my/logdir. To view the logs in the browser,

1 Open a separate terminal.
2 Install TensorBoard with the following command (unless it's already installed):
   `pip install tensorboard`
3 Start the backend server of TensorBoard, and point it to the log directory specified during the callback creation:
   `tensorboard --logdir /path/to/my/logdir`
4 In the web browser, navigate to the http:// URL displayed by the TensorBoard process. Then the loss and metric charts such as those shown in figures 9.3 and 9.5 will appear in the beautiful web UI of TensorBoard.

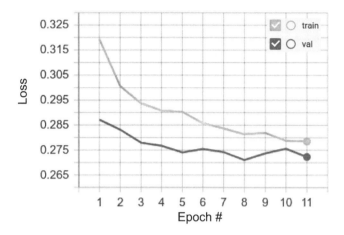

Figure 9.3 MAE loss curves from the simpleRNN model built for the Jena-temperature-prediction problem. This chart is a screenshot from TensorBoard serving the logs from the Node.js-based training of the simpleRNN model.

The text summary of the simpleRNN model created by listing 9.2 looks like the following:

```
Layer (type)                   Output shape              Param #
=================================================================
    simple_rnn_SimpleRNN1 (Simpl [null,32]                 1504
_____
    dense_Dense1 (Dense)           [null,1]                  33
=================================================================
Total params: 1537
    Trainable params: 1537
    Non-trainable params: 0
```

It has significantly fewer weight parameters than the MLP we used before (1,537 versus 107,585, or a reduction by a factor of 70), but it achieves a lower validation MAE loss (that is, more accurate predictions) than the MLP during training (0.271 versus 0.289). This small but solid reduction in the temperature-prediction error highlights the power of parameter sharing based on temporal invariance and the advantages of RNNs in learning from sequence data like the weather data we are dealing with.

You might have noticed that even though simpleRNN involves a relatively small number of weight parameters, its training and inference take much longer compared to feedforward models such as MLP. This is a major shortcoming of RNNs, one in which it is impossible to parallelize the operations over the time steps. Such parallelization is not achievable because subsequent steps depend on the state values computed in previous steps (see figure 9.2 and the pseudo-code in listing 9.1). If we use the Big-O notation, the forward pass on an RNN takes an $O(n)$ amount of time, where

n is the number of input time steps. The backward pass (BPTT) takes another $O(n)$ amount of time. The input future of the Jena-weather problem consists of a large number of (240) time steps, which leads to the slow training time seen previously. This is the main reason why we train the model in tfjs-node instead of in the browser.

This situation of RNNs is in contrast to feedforward layers such as dense and conv2d. In those layers, computation can be parallelized among the input elements because the operation on one element does not depend on the result from another input element. This allows such feedforward layers to take less than $O(n)$ time (in some cases close to $O(1)$) to execute their forward and backward passes with the help of GPU acceleration. In section 9.2, we will explore some more parallelizable sequential modeling approaches such as 1D convolution. However, it is still important to be familiar with RNNs because they are sensitive to sequential positions in a way that 1D convolution isn't (more on that later).

GATED RECURRENT UNIT: A MORE SOPHISTICATED TYPE OF RNN

SimpleRNN isn't the only recurrent layer available in TensorFlow.js. There are two others: Gated Recurrent Unit (GRU[4]) and LSTM (which you'll recall stands for Long Short-Term Memory[5]). In most practical use cases, you'll probably want to use one of these two. SimpleRNN is too simplistic for most real problems, despite the fact that it is computationally much cheaper and has an easier-to-understand internal mechanism than GRU and LSTM. There is a major issue with simpleRNN: although it is theoretically able to retain at time t information about inputs seen many time steps before, such long-term dependencies are hard to learn in practice.

This is due to the *vanishing-gradient problem,* an effect similar to what is observed in feedforward networks that are many layers deep: As you keep adding layers to a network, the size of the gradients backpropagated from the loss function to the early layers gets smaller and smaller. Henceforth, the updates to the weights get smaller and smaller, to the point where the network eventually becomes untrainable. For RNNs, the large number of time steps plays the role of the many layers in this problem. GRU and LSTM are RNNs designed to solve the vanishing-gradient problem, and GRU is the simpler of the two. Let's look at how GRU does that.

Compared to simpleRNN, GRU has a more complex internal structure. Figure 9.4 shows a rolled representation of a GRU's internal structure. Compared with the same rolled representation of simpleRNN (panel B of figure 9.2), it contains more nuts and bolts. The input (x) and the output/state (referred to as h by the convention in the RNN literature) pass through *four* equations to give rise to the new output/state. Compare this with simpleRNN, which involves only *one* equation. This complexity is also reflected in the pseudo-code in listing 9.3, which can be viewed as an implementation of the mechanisms of figure 9.4. We omit the bias terms in the pseudo-code for simplicity.

---

[4] Kyunghyun Cho et al., "Learning Phrase Representations using RNN Encoder-Decoder for Statistical Machine Translation," 2014, https://arxiv.org/abs/1406.1078.

[5] Sepp Hochreiter and Jürgen Schmidhuber, "Long Short-Term Memory," *Neural Computation*, vol. 9, no. 8, 1997, pp. 1735–1780.

GRU layer:
rolled representation

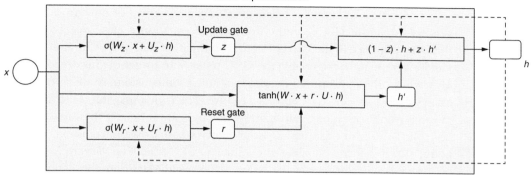

Figure 9.4   A rolled representation of the GRU cell, a more complex and powerful RNN layer type than simpleRNN. This is a rolled representation, comparable to panel B of figure 9.2. Note that we omit the bias terms in the equations for simplicity. The dashed lines indicate feedback connections from the output of the GRU cell (*h*) to the same cell in subsequent time steps.

Listing 9.3   Pseudo-code for a GRU layer

```
h = 0
for x_i in input_sequence:
    z = sigmoid(dot(W_z, x) + dot(U_z, h))          ◁───── z is called the update gate.
    r = sigmoid(dot(W_r, x) + dot(W_r, h))      ◁───── r is called the reset gate.
    h_prime = tanh(dot(W, x) + dot(r, dot(U, h)))   ◁─┐
    h = dot(1 - z, h) + dot(z, h_prime)   ◁─┐         │ h_prime is the temporary state
                                            │         │ of the current state.
This for loop iterates over all time        │
steps of the input sequence.                │
                                   h_prime (current temporary state)
                                   and h (previous state) are combined in
This is the h in figure 9.4. As in         a weighted fashion (z being the
simpleRNN, the state is initialized        weight) to form the new state.
to zero in the beginning.
```

Of all the internal details of GRU, we highlight the two most important ones:

1. GRU makes it easy to carry information across many time steps. This is achieved by the intermediate quantity z, which is referred to as the *update gate*. Because of the update gate, GRU can learn to carry the same state across many time steps with minimal changes. In particular, in the equation $(1 - z) \cdot h + z \cdot h'$, if the value of z is 0, then the state h will simply be copied from the current time step to the next. The ability to perform wholesale carrying like this is an important part of how GRU combats the vanishing-gradient problem. The reset gate z is calculated as a linear combination of the input x and the current state h, followed by a sigmoid nonlinearity.

2. In addition to the update gate z, another "gate" in GRU is the so-called *reset gate*, r. Like the update gate z, r is calculated as a sigmoid nonlinearity operating on a

linear combination of the input and the current state h. The reset gate controls how much of the current state to "forget." In particular, in the equation $\tanh(W \cdot x + r \cdot U \cdot h)$, if the value of r becomes 0, then the effect of the current state h gets erased; and if $(1 - z)$ in the downstream equation is close to zero as well, then the influence of the current state h on the next state will be minimized. So, r and z work together to enable the GRU to learn to forget the history, or a part of it, under the appropriate conditions. For instance, suppose we're trying to classify a movie review as positive or negative. The review may start by saying "this movie is pretty enjoyable," but halfway through the review, it then reads "however, the movie isn't as good as other movies based on similar ideas." At this point, the memory regarding the initial praise should be largely forgotten, because it is the later part of the review that should weigh more in determining the final sentiment-analysis result of this review.

So, that's a very rough and high-level outline of how GRU works. The important thing to remember is that the internal structure of GRU allows the RNN to learn when to carry over old state and when to update the state with information from the inputs. This learning is embodied by updates to the tunable weights, W_z, U_z, W_r, W_r, W, and U (in addition to the omitted bias terms).

Don't worry if you don't follow all the details right away. At the end of the day, the intuitive explanation for GRU we wrote in the last couple of paragraphs doesn't matter that much. It is not the human engineer's job to understand how a GRU processes sequential data at a very detailed level, just like it is not the human engineer's job to understand the fine-grained details of how a convnet converts an image input to output class probabilities. The details are found by the neural network in the hypothesis space delineated by the RNN's structure data through the data-driven training process.

To apply GRU on our temperature-prediction problem, we construct a TensorFlow.js model that contains a GRU layer. The code we use to do this (excerpted from jena-weather/train-rnn.js.) looks almost identical to what we used for the simpleRNN model (listing 9.2). The only difference is the type of the model's first layer (GRU versus simpleRNN).

Listing 9.4   Creating a GRU model for the Jena-temperature-prediction problem

```
function buildGRUModel(inputShape) {
  const model = tf.sequential();
  const rnnUnits = 32;
  model.add(tf.layers.gru({
    units: rnnUnits,
    inputShape
  }));
  model.add(tf.layers.dense({units: 1}));
  return model;
}
```

The hard-coded unit count is a number that works well, discovered through hand-tuning of the hyperparameter.

The first layer of the model is a GRU layer.

The model ends with a dense layer with a single unit and the default linear activation for the regression problem.

To start training the GRU model on the Jena-weather dataset, use

```
yarn train-rnn --modelType gru
```

Figure 9.5 shows the training and validation loss curves obtained with the GRU model. It gets a best validation error of approximately 0.266, which beats the one we got from the simpleRNN model in the previous section (0.271). This reflects the greater capacity of GRU in learning sequential patterns compared to simpleRNN. There are indeed sequential patterns hidden in the weather-instrument readings that can help improve the accuracy of predicting the temperature; this information is picked up by GRU but not simpleRNN. This comes at the cost of greater training time. For example, on one of our machines, the GRU model trains at a speed of 3,000 ms/batch, as compared to the simpleRNN's 950 ms/batch.[6] But if the goal is to predict temperature as accurately as possible, this cost will most likely be worth it.

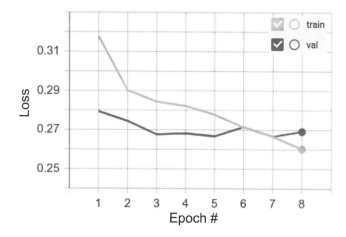

Figure 9.5 The loss curves from training a GRU model on the temperature-prediction problem. Compare this with the loss curves from the simpleRNN model (figure 9.3), and notice the small but real reduction in the best validation loss achieved by the GRU model.

9.2   *Building deep-learning models for text*

The weather-prediction problem we just studied dealt with sequential numerical data. But the most ubiquitous kinds of sequential data are probably text instead of numbers. In alphabet-based languages such as English, text can be viewed as either a sequence of characters or a sequence of words. The two approaches are suitable for different problems, and we will use both of them for different tasks in this section.

---

[6] These performance numbers are obtained from tfjs-node running on the CPU backend. If you use tfjs-node-gpu and the CUDA GPU backend, you'll get approximately proportionate speedups for both model types.

The deep-learning models for text data we'll introduce in the following sections can perform text-related tasks such as

- Assigning a sentiment score to a body of text (for instance, whether a product review is positive or negative)
- Classifying a body of text by its topic (for example, whether a news article is about politics, finance, sports, health, weather, or miscellaneous)
- Converting a text input into a text output (for instance, for standardization of format or machine translation)
- Predicting the upcoming parts of a text (for example, smart suggestion features of mobile input methods)

This list is just a very small subset of interesting machine-learning problems that involve text, which are systematically studied in the field of natural language processing. Although we will only scratch the surface of neural-network-based natural language processing techniques in this chapter, the concepts and examples introduced here should give you a good starting point for further exploration (see the "Materials for further reading" section at the end of this chapter).

Keep in mind that none of the deep neural networks in this chapter truly understand text or language in a human sense. Rather, these models can map the statistical structure of text to a certain target space, whether it is a continuous sentiment score, a multiclass-classification result, or a new sequence. This turns out to be sufficient for solving many practical, text-related tasks. Deep learning for natural language processing is nothing more than pattern recognition applied to characters and words, in much the same way that deep-learning-based computer vision (chapter 4) is pattern recognition applied to pixels.

Before we dive into the deep neural networks designed for text, we need to first understand how text is represented in machine learning.

9.2.1   *How text is represented in machine learning:*
One-hot and multi-hot encoding

Most of the input data we've encountered in this book so far is continuous. For example, the petal length of an iris flower varies continuously in a certain range; the weather-instrument readings in the Jena-weather dataset are all real numbers. These values are represented straightforwardly as float-type tensors (floating-point numbers). However, text is different. Text data comes in as a string of characters or words, not real numbers. Characters and words are discrete. For instance, there is no such thing as a letter between "j" and "k" in the same sense as there is a number between 0.13 and 0.14. In this sense, characters and words are similar to classes in multiclass classification (such as the three iris-flower species or the 1,000 output classes of MobileNet). Text data needs to be turned into vectors (arrays of numbers) before it can be fed into deep-learning models. This conversion process is called *text vectorization.*

There are multiple ways to vectorize text. *One-hot encoding* (as we've introduced in chapter 3) is one of the options. In English, depending on where you draw the line, there are about 10,000 most frequently used words. We can collect these 10,000 words and form a *vocabulary*. The unique words in the vocabulary may be sorted in a certain order (for example, descending order of frequency) so that any given word can be given an integer index.[7] Then every English word can be represented as a length-10,000 vector, in which only the element that corresponds to the index is 1, and all remaining elements are 0. This is the *one-hot vectorization* of the word. Panel A of figure 9.6 presents this graphically.

What if we have a sentence instead of a single word? We can get the one-hot vectors for all the words that make up the sentence and put them together to form a 2D

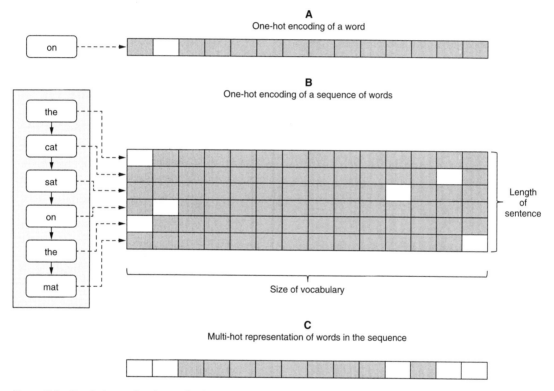

Figure 9.6 One-hot encoding (vectorization) of a word (panel A) and of a sentence as a sequence of words (panel B). Panel C shows a simplified, multi-hot encoding of the same sentence as in panel B. It is a more succinct and scalable representation of the sequence, but it discards the order information. For the sake of visualization, we assume that the size of the vocabulary is only 14. In reality, the vocabulary size of English words used in deep learning is much larger (on the order of thousands or tens of thousands, for example, 10,000).

---

[7] An obvious question is: what if we get a rare word that falls out of the 10,000-word vocabulary? This is a practical problem that any text-oriented deep-learning algorithm is faced with. In practice, we solve this problem by adding a special item called *OOV* to the vocabulary. OOV stands for *out-of-vocabulary*. So, all rare words that do not belong to the vocabulary are lumped together in that special item and will have the same one-hot encoding or embedding vector. More sophisticated techniques have multiple OOV buckets and use a hash function to assign rare words to those buckets.

representation of the words of the sentence (see panel B of figure 9.6). This approach is simple and unambiguous. It perfectly preserves the information about what words appear in the sentence and in what order.[8] However, when text gets long, the size of the vector may get so big that it is no longer manageable. For instance, a sentence in English contains about 18 words on average. Given that our vocabulary has a size of 10,000, it takes 180,000 numbers to represent just a single sentence, which already takes a much larger space than the sentence itself. This is not to mention that some text-related problems deal with paragraphs or whole articles, which have many more words and will cause the size of the representation and the amount of computation to explode.

One way to deal with this problem is to include all the words in a single vector so that each element in the vector represents whether the corresponding word has appeared in the text. Panel C of figure 9.6 illustrates. In this representation, multiple elements of the vector can have the value 1. This is why people sometimes refer to it as *multi-hot encoding*. Multi-hot encoding has a fixed length (the size of the vocabulary) regardless of how long the text is, so it solves the size-explosion problem. But this comes at the cost of losing the order information: we can't tell from the multi-hot vector which words come first and which words come next. For some problems, this might be okay; for others, this is unacceptable. There are more sophisticated representations that take care of the size-explosion problem while preserving the order information, which we will explore later in this chapter. But first, let's look at a concrete, text-related machine-learning problem that can be solved to a reasonable accuracy using the multi-hot approach.

9.2.2 *First attempt at the sentiment-analysis problem*

We will use the Internet Movie Database (IMDb) dataset in our first example of applying machine learning to text. The dataset is a collection of approximately 25,000 textual movie reviews on imdb.com, each of which has been labeled as positive or negative. The machine-learning task is binary classification: that is, whether a given movie review is positive or negative. The dataset is balanced (50% positive reviews and 50% negative ones). Just like what you expect from online reviews, the examples vary in word length. Some of them are as short as 10 words, while others can be as long as 2,000 words. The following is an example of what a typical review looks like. This example is labeled as negative. Punctuation is omitted in the dataset:

> *the mother in this movie is reckless with her children to the point of neglect i wish i wasn't so angry about her and her actions because i would have otherwise enjoyed the flick what a number she was take my advise and fast forward through everything you see her do until the end also is anyone else getting sick of watching movies that are filmed so dark anymore one can hardly see what is being filmed as an audience we are impossibly involved with the actions on the screen so then why the hell can't we have night vision*

---

[8] This assumes there are no OOV words.

The data is divided into a training set and an evaluation set, both of which are automatically downloaded from the web and written to your tmp directory when you issue a model-training command such as

```
git clone https://github.com/tensorflow/tfjs-examples.git
cd tfjs-examples/sentiment
yarn
yarn train multihot
```

If you examine sentiment/data.js carefully, you can see that the data files it downloads and reads do not contain the actual words as character strings. Instead, the words are represented as 32-bit integers in those files. Although we won't cover the data-loading code in that file in detail, it's worthwhile to call out a part that performs the multi-hot vectorization of the sentences, shown in the next listing.

> **Listing 9.5 Multi-hot vectorization of sentences from the `loadFeatures()` function**

```
const buffer = tf.buffer([sequences.length, numWords]);
    sequences.forEach((seq, i) => {
  seq.forEach(wordIndex => {
    if (wordIndex !== OOV_INDEX) {
      buffer.set(1, i, wordIndex);
    }
  });
});
```

Iterates over all examples, each of which is a sentence

Each sequence (sentence) is an array of integers.

Skips out-of-vocabulary (OOV) words for multi-hot encoding

Creates a TensorBuffer instead of a tensor because we will be setting its element values next. The buffer starts from all-zero.

Sets the corresponding index in the buffer to 1. Note that every index i may have multiple wordIndex values set to 1, hence the multi-hot encoding.

The multi-hot-encoded features are represented as a 2D tensor of shape [numExamples, numWords], where numWords is the size of the vocabulary (10,000 in this case). This shape isn't affected by the length of the individual sentences, which makes this a simple vectorization paradigm. The targets loaded from the data files have a shape of [numExamples, 1] and contain the negative and positive labels represented as 0s and 1s, respectively.

The model that we apply to the multi-hot data is an MLP. In fact, with the sequential information lost with the multi-hot encoding, there is no way to apply an RNN model to the data even if we wanted to. We will talk about RNN-based approaches in the next section. The code that creates the MLP model is from the buildModel() function in sentiment/train.js, with simplification, and looks like the following listing.

> **Listing 9.6 Building an MLP model for the multi-hot-encoded IMDb movie reviews**

```
const model = tf.sequential();
model.add(tf.layers.dense({
  units: 16,
  activation: 'relu',
```

Adds two hidden dense layers with relu activation to enhance the representational power

```
    inputShape: [vocabularySize]
}));
model.add(tf.layers.dense({
    units: 16,
    activation: 'relu'
}));
model.add(tf.layers.dense({
    units: 1,
    activation: 'sigmoid'
}));
```

> The input shape is the size of the vocabulary due to the multi-hot vectorization we are dealing with here.

> Uses sigmoid activation for the output layer to suit the binary-classification task

By running the `yarn train multihot --maxLen 500` command, you can see that the model achieves a best validation accuracy of approximately 0.89. This accuracy is okay, and is significantly higher than chance (0.5). This shows that it is possible to achieve a reasonable degree of accuracy in this sentiment-analysis problem by looking at just what words appear in the review. For example, words such as *enjoyable* and *sublime* are associated with positive reviews, and words such as *sucks* and *bland* are associated with negative ones with a relatively high degree of reliability. Of course, there are plenty of scenarios in which looking just at what words there are will be misleading. As a contrived example, understanding the true meaning of a sentence like "Don't get me wrong, I hardly disagree this is an excellent film" requires taking into account sequential information—not only what the words are but also in what order they appear. In the next section, we will show that by using a text vectorization that doesn't discard the sequential information and a model that can utilize the sequential information, we can beat this baseline accuracy. Let's now look at how word embeddings and 1D convnets work.

9.2.3 *A more efficient representation of text: Word embeddings*

What is *word embedding*? Just like one-hot encoding (figure 9.6), word embedding is a way to represent a word as a vector (a 1D tensor in TensorFlow.js). However, word embeddings allow the values of the vector's elements to be trained, instead of hard-coded according to a rigid rule such as the word-to-index map in one-hot encoding. In other words, when a text-oriented neural network uses word embedding, the embedding vectors become trainable weight parameters of the model. They are updated through the same backpropagation rule as all other weight parameters of the model.

This situation is illustrated schematically in figure 9.7. The layer type in Tensor-Flow.js that allows you to perform word embedding is `tf.layer.embedding()`. It contains a trainable weight matrix of shape `[vocabularySize, embeddingDims]`, where `vocabularySize` is the number of unique words in the vocabulary and `embeddingDims` is the user-selected dimensionality of the embedding vectors. Every time you are given a word, say *the*, you find the corresponding row in the embedding matrix using a word-to-index lookup table, and that row is the embedding vector for your word. Note that the word-to-index lookup table is not part of the embedding layer; it is maintained as a separate entity from the model (see listing 9.9, for example).

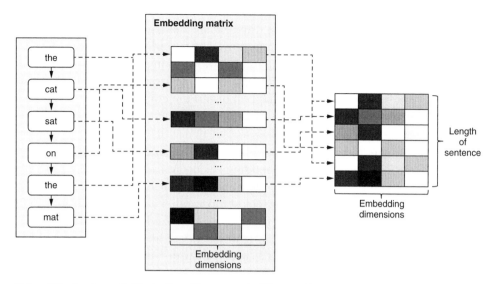

Figure 9.7 A schematic illustration of how an embedding matrix works. Each row of the embedding matrix corresponds to a word in the vocabulary, and each column is an embedding dimension. The values of the embedding matrix's elements, represented as shades of gray in the diagram, are chosen at random.

If you have a sequence of words, like a sentence as shown in figure 9.7, you repeat this lookup process for all the words in the correct sequential order and stack the resulting embedding vectors into a 2D tensor of shape [sequenceLength, embeddingDims], where sequenceLength is the number of words in the sentence.[9] What if there are repeating words in the sentence (such as the word *the* in the example in figure 9.7)? It doesn't matter: just let the same embedding vector appear repeatedly in the resulting 2D tensor.

Word embedding gives us the following benefits:

- It addresses the size problem with one-hot encodings. embeddingDims is usually much smaller than vocabularySize. For example, in the 1D convnet we are about to use on the IMDb dataset, vocabularySize is 10,000, and embedding-Dims is 128. So, with a 500-word review from the IMDb dataset, representing the example requires 500 * 128 = 64k float numbers, instead of 500 * 10,000 = 5M numbers, as in one-hot encoding—a much more economical vectorization.
- By not being opinionated about how to order the words in the vocabulary and by allowing the embedding matrix to be trained via backpropagation just like all other neural network weights, word embeddings can learn semantic relations between words. Words with similar meanings should have embedding vectors that are closer in the embedding space. For example, words with similar

---

[9] This multiword embedding lookup process can be done effectively using the tf.gather() method, which is how the embedding layer in TensorFlow.js is implemented under the hood.

meanings, such as *very* and *truly* should have vectors that are closer together than words that are more different in meaning, such as *very* and *barely*. Why should this be the case? An intuitive way to understand it is to realize the following: suppose you replace a number of words in a movie-review input with words with similar meaning; a well-trained network ought to output the same classification result. This could happen only if the embedding vectors for each pair of words, which are the input to the downstream part of the model, are close to each other.

- Also, the fact that the embedding space has multiple dimensions (for example, 128) should allow the embedding vectors to capture different aspects of words. For example, there can be a dimension that represents part of speech, along which an adjective like *fast* is closer to another adjective (such as *warm*) than to a noun (such as *house*). There might be another dimension that encodes the gender aspect of a word, one along which a word like *actress* is closer to another feminine-meaning word (such as *queen*) than to a masculine-meaning one (such as *actor*). In the next section (see info box 9.2), we will show you a way to visualize the word embeddings and explore their interesting structures after they emerge from training an embedding-based neural network on the IMDb dataset.

Table 9.1 gives a more succinct summary of the differences between one-/multi-hot encoding and word embedding, the two most frequently used paradigms for word vectorization.

Table 9.1 Comparing two paradigms of word vectorization: one-hot/multi-hot encoding and word embedding

	One-hot or multi-hot encoding	Word embedding
Hard-coded or learned?	Hard-coded.	Learned: the embedding matrix is a trainable weight parameter; the values often reflect the semantic structure of the vocabulary after training.
Sparse or dense?	Sparse: most elements are zero; some are one.	Dense: elements take continuously varying values.
Scalability	Not scalable to large vocabularies: the size of the vector is proportional to the size of the vocabulary.	Scalable to large vocabularies: the embedding size (number of embedding dimensions) doesn't have to increase with the number of words in the vocabulary.

9.2.4   1D convnets

In chapter 4, we showed the key role played by 2D convolutional layers in deep neural networks for image inputs. conv2d layers learn to represent local features in small 2D patches in images. The idea of convolution can be extended to sequences. The resulting algorithm is called *1D convolution* and is available through the `tf.layers.conv1d()` function in TensorFlow.js. The ideas underlying conv1d and conv2d are the same: they are both trainable extractors of translationally invariant local features. For instance, a conv2d layer may become sensitive to corner patterns of a certain orientation and of a certain color change after training on an image task, while a conv1d layer may become sensitive to a pattern of "a negative verb followed by a praising adjective" after training on a text-related task.[10]

Figure 9.8 illustrates how a conv1d layer works in greater detail. Recall from figure 4.3 in chapter 4 that a conv2d layer involves sliding a kernel over all possible locations in the input image. The 1D convolution algorithm also involves sliding a kernel, but is simpler because the sliding movement happens in only one dimension. At each sliding position, a slice of the input tensor is extracted. The slice has the length `kernel-Size` (a configuration field for the conv1d layer), and in the case of this example, it has a second dimension equal to the number of embedding dimensions. Then a *dot* (multiply-and-add) operation is performed between the input slice and the kernel of the conv1d layer, which yields a single slice of the output sequence. This operation is repeated for all valid sliding positions until the full output is generated. Like the input tensor of the conv1d layer, the full output is a sequence, albeit with a different length (determined by the input sequence length, the `kernelSize`, and other configurations of the conv1d layer) and a different number of feature dimensions (determined by the `filters` configuration of the conv1d layer). This makes it possible to stack multiple conv1d layers to form a deep 1D convnet, just as stacking multiple conv2d layers is a frequently used trick in 2D convnets.

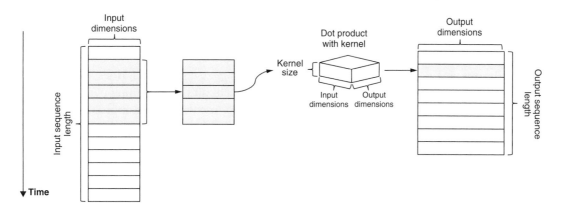

Figure 9.8   Schematic illustration of how 1D convolution (`tf.layers.conv1d()`) works. For the sake of simplicity, only one input example is shown (on the left side of the image). We suppose that the input sequence has a length of 12 and the conv1d layer has a kernel size of 5. At each sliding window position, a length-5 slice of the input sequence is extracted. The slice is dot-multiplied with the kernel of the conv1d layer, which generates one slide of the output sequence. This is repeated for all possible sliding-window positions, which gives rise to the output sequence (on the right side of the diagram).

---

[10] As you might have guessed, there is indeed 3D convolution, and it is useful for deep-learning tasks that involve 3D (volumetric) data, such as certain types of medical images and geological data.

Deep learning for sequences and text

SEQUENCE TRUNCATION AND PADDING

Now that we have conv1d in our arsenal for text-oriented machine learning, are we ready to train a 1D convnet on the IMDb data? Not quite yet. There is one more thing to explain: truncating and padding of sequences. Why do we need to do truncation and padding? TensorFlow.js models require the inputs to fit() to be a tensor, and a tensor must have a concrete shape. Therefore, although our movie reviews don't have a fixed length (recall that they vary between 10 and 2,400 words), we have to pick a specific length as the second dimension of the input feature tensor (maxLen), so that the full shape of the input tensor is [numExamples, maxLen]. No such problem existed when we used multi-hot encoding in the previous section because tensors from multi-hot encoding had a second tensor dimension unaffected by sequence length.

The considerations that go into choosing the value of maxLen are as follows:

- It should be long enough to capture the useful part of most of the reviews. If we choose maxLen to be 20, it will perhaps be so short that it will cut out the useful part for most reviews.
- It should not be so large that a majority of the reviews are much shorter than that length, because that would lead to a waste of memory and computation time.

The trade-off of the two leads us to pick a value of 500 words per review (at maximum) for this example. This is specified in the flag --maxLen in the command for training the 1D convnet:

```
yarn train --maxLen 500 cnn
```

Once the maxLen is chosen, all the review examples must be molded into this particular length. In particular, the ones that are longer are truncated; the ones that are shorter are padded. This is what the function padSequences() does (listing 9.7). There are two ways to truncate a long sequence: cut off the beginning part (the 'pre' option in listing 9.7) or the ending part. Here, we use the former approach, based on the reasoning that the ending part of a movie review is more likely to contain information relevant to the sentiment than the beginning part. Similarly, there are two ways to pad a short sequence to the desired length: adding the padding character (PAD_CHAR) before (the 'pre' option in listing 9.7) or after the sentence. Here, we arbitrarily choose the former option as well. The code in this listing is from sentiment/sequence_utils.js.

Listing 9.7 Truncating and padding a sequence as a step of loading text features

```
export function padSequences(
    sequences, maxLen,
        padding = 'pre',
        truncating = 'pre',
        value = PAD_CHAR) {
  return sequences.map(seq => {
    if (seq.length > maxLen) {
```

Loops over all the input sequences

This particular sequence is longer than the prescribed length (maxLen): truncate it to that length.

```
    if (truncating === 'pre') {
      seq.splice(0, seq.length - maxLen);
    } else {
      seq.splice(maxLen, seq.length - maxLen);
    }
  }
```

> There are two ways to truncate a sequence: cut off the beginning ('pre') or the end

```
  if (seq.length < maxLen) {
    const pad = [];
    for (let i = 0; i < maxLen - seq.length; ++i) {
      pad.push(value);
    }
    if (padding === 'pre') {
      seq = pad.concat(seq);
    } else {
      seq = seq.concat(pad);
    }
  }
  return seq;
});
}
```

> The sequence is shorter than the prescribed length: it needs to be padded.

> Generates the padding sequence

> Like truncation, there are two ways to pad the sublength sequence: from the beginning ('pre') or from behind.

> Note: if the length of seq is exactly maxLen, it will be returned without change.

BUILDING AND RUNNING A 1D CONVNET ON THE IMDB DATASET

Now we have all the pieces ready for the 1D convnet; let's put them together and see if we can get a higher accuracy on the IMDb sentiment-analysis task. The code in listing 9.8 creates our 1D convnet (excerpted from sentiment/train.js, with simplification). The summary of the resulting `tf.Model` object is shown after that.

Listing 9.8 Building a 1D convnet for the IMDb problem

```
const model = tf.sequential();
model.add(tf.layers.embedding({
  inputDim: vocabularySize,
  outputDim: embeddingSize,
  inputLength: maxLen
}));
model.add(tf.layers.dropout({rate: 0.5}));
model.add(tf.layers.conv1d({
  filters: 250,
  kernelSize: 5,
  strides: 1,
  padding: 'valid',
  activation: 'relu'
}));
model.add(tf.layers.globalMaxPool1d({}));
model.add(tf.layers.dense({
    units: 250,
    activation: 'relu'
  }));
model.add(tf.layers.dense({units: 1, activation: 'sigmoid'}));
```

> The model begins with an embedding layer, which turns the input integer indices into the corresponding word vectors.

> The embedding layer needs to know the size of the vocabulary. Without this, it can't determine the size of the embedding matrix.

> Adds a dropout layer to combat overfitting

> Here comes the conv1D layer.

> The globalMaxPool1d layer collapses the time dimension by extracting the maximum element value in each filter. The output is ready for the upcoming dense layers (MLP).

> Adds a two-layer MLP at the top of the model

```
Layer (type)                    Output shape               Param #
=================================================================
embedding_Embedding1 (Embedd  [null,500,128]               1280000
_____
dropout_Dropout1 (Dropout)     [null,500,128]              0
_____
conv1d_Conv1D1 (Conv1D)        [null,496,250]              160250
_____
global_max_pooling1d_GlobalM  [null,250]                   0
_____
dense_Dense1 (Dense)           [null,250]                   62750
_____
dense_Dense2 (Dense)           [null,1]                     251
=================================================================
Total params: 1503251
Trainable params: 1503251
Non-trainable params: 0
```

It is helpful to look at the JavaScript code and the text summary together. There are a few things worth calling out here:

- The model has a shape of [null, 500], where null is the undetermined batch dimension (the number of examples) and 500 is the maximally allowed word length of each review (maxLen). The input tensor contains the truncated and padded sequences of integer word indices.
- The first layer of the model is an embedding layer. It turns the word indices into their corresponding word vectors, which leads to a shape of [null, 500, 128]. As you can see, the sequence length (500) is preserved, and the embedding dimension (128) is reflected as the last element of the shape.
- The layer that follows the embedding layer is a conv1d layer—the core part of this model. It is configured to have a kernel size of 5, a default stride size of 1, and "valid" padding. As a result, there are $500 - 5 + 1 = 496$ possible sliding positions along the sequence dimension. This leads to a value of 496 in the second element of the output shape ([null, 496, 250]). The last element of the shape (250) reflects the number of filters the conv1d layer is configured to have.
- The globalMaxPool1d layer that follows the conv1d layer is somewhat similar to the maxPooling2d layer we've seen in image convnets. However, it does a more dramatic pooling, one in which all elements along the sequence dimension are collapsed to a single maximum value. This leads to the output shape of [null, 250].
- Now that the tensor has a 1D shape (ignoring the batch dimension), we can build two dense layers on top of it to form an MLP as the top of the entire model.

Start training the 1D convnet with the command `yarn train --maxLen 500 cnn`. After two to three training epochs, you can see the model reach a best validation accuracy of about 0.903, which is a small but solid gain relative to the accuracy we got from the MLP based on the multi-hot vectorization (0.890). This reflects the sequential order information that our 1D convnet managed to learn but that was impossible to learn by the multi-hot MLP.

So how does a 1D convnet capture sequential order? It does this through its convolutional kernel. The dot product of the kernel is sensitive to the ordering of the elements. For example, if an input consists of five words, *I like it so much*, the 1D convolution will output one particular value; however, if the order of the words is altered to be *much so I like it*, it will cause a different output from the 1D convolution, even though the set of elements is exactly the same.

However, it needs to be pointed out that a conv1d layer by itself is not able to learn sequential patterns beyond its kernel size. For instance, suppose the ordering of two far-apart words affects the meaning of the sentence; a conv1d layer with a kernel size smaller than the distance won't be able to learn the long-range interaction. This is an aspect in which RNNs such as GRU and LSTM outshine 1D convolution.

One way in which 1D convolution can ameliorate this shortcoming is to go deep—namely, stacking up multiple conv1d layers so that the "receptive field" of the higher-level conv1d layers is large enough to capture such long-range dependencies. However, in many text-related machine-learning problems, such long-range dependencies don't play important roles, so that using a 1D convnet with a small number of conv1d layers suffices. In the IMDb sentiment example, you can try training an LSTM-based model based on the same `maxLen` value and embedding dimensions as the 1D convnet:

```
yarn train --maxLen 500 lstm
```

Notice that the best validation accuracy from the LSTM (similar to but slightly more complex that GRU; see figure 9.4) is about the same as that from the 1D convnet. This is perhaps because long-range interactions between words and phrases don't matter a lot for this body of movie reviews and the sentiment-classification task.

So, you can see that 1D convnets are an attractive alternative to RNNs for this type of text problem. This is especially true considering the much lower computational cost of 1D convnets compared to that of RNNs. From the `cnn` and `lstm` commands, you can see that training the 1D convnet is about six times as fast as training the LSTM model. The slower performance of LSTM and RNNs is related to their step-by-step internal operations, which cannot be parallelized; convolutions are amenable to parallelization by design.

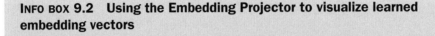

INFO BOX 9.2   Using the Embedding Projector to visualize learned embedding vectors

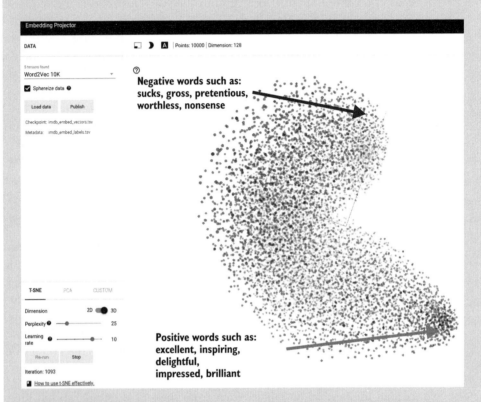

Visualizing the trained word embeddings from the 1D convnet using t-SNE dimension reduction in the Embedding Projector

Do any interesting structures emerge in the word embeddings of the 1D convnet after training? To find this out, you can use the optional flag `--embeddingFilesPrefix` of the `yarn train` command:

```
yarn train --maxLen 500 cnn --epochs 2 --embeddingFilesPrefix
            /tmp/imdb_embed
```

This command will generate two files:

- /tmp/imdb_embed_vectors.tsv—A tab-separated-values file for the numeric values of the word embeddings. Each line contains the embedding vector from a word. In our case, there are 10,000 lines (our vocabulary size), and each line contains 128 numbers (our embedding dimensions).
- /tmp/imdb_embed_labels.tsv—A file consisting of the word labels that correspond to the vectors in the previous file. Each line is a word.

These files can be uploaded to the Embedding Projector (https://projector.tensorflow .org) for visualization (see the previous figure). Because our embedding vectors reside in a high-dimensional (128D) space, it is necessary to reduce their dimensionality to three or fewer dimensions so that they can be understood by a human. The Embedding Projector tool provides two algorithms for dimension reduction: t-distributed stochastic neighbor embedding (t-SNE) and principal component analysis (PCA), which we won't discuss in detail. But briefly, these methods map the high-dimensional embedding vectors to 3D while ensuring minimal loss in the relations between the vectors. t-SNE is the more sophisticated and computationally more intensive method between the two. The visualization it produces is shown in the figure.

Each dot in the dot cloud corresponds to a word in our vocabulary. Move your mouse cursor around and hover it above the dots to see what words they correspond to. Our embedding vectors, trained on the smallish sentiment-analysis dataset, already show some interesting structure related to the semantics of the words. In particular, one end of the dot cloud contains a large proportion of words that appear frequently in positive movie reviews (such as *excellent*, *inspiring*, and *delightful*), while the opposite end contains many negative-sounding words (*sucks*, *gross*, and *pretentious*). More interesting structures may emerge from training larger models on larger text datasets, but this small example already gives you a hint of the power of the word-embedding method.

Because word embeddings are an important part of text-oriented deep neural networks, researchers have created pretrained word embeddings that machine-learning practitioners can use out-of-the-box, forgoing the need to train their own word embeddings as we did in our IMDb convnet example. One of the best known pretrained word-embedding sets is GloVe (for Global Vectors) by the Stanford Natural Language Processing Group (see https://nlp.stanford.edu/projects/glove/).

The advantage of using pretrained word embeddings such as GloVe is two-fold. First, it reduces the amount of computation during training because the embedding layer doesn't need to be trained further and hence can simply be frozen. Second, pretrained embeddings such as GloVe are trained from billions of words and hence are much higher-quality than what would be possible by training on a small dataset, such as the IMDb dataset here. In these senses, the role played by pretrained word embeddings in natural language processing problems is similar to the role of pretrained deep convnet bases (such as MobileNet, which we saw in chapter 5) in computer vision.

USING THE 1D CONVNET FOR INFERENCE IN A WEB PAGE

In sentiment/index.js, you can find the code that deploys the model trained in Node.js to use at the client side. To see the client-side app in action, run the command `yarn watch` just like in most other examples in this book. The command will compile the code, start a web server, and automatically pop open a browser tab to display the index.html page. In the page, you can click a button to load the trained model via HTTP requests and use the loaded model to perform sentiment analysis on movie reviews in a text box. The movie review sample in the text box is editable, so you can make arbitrary edits to it and observe how that affects the binary prediction in real time. The page comes with two stock example reviews (a positive one and a negative one) that you may use as the starting point of your fiddling. The loaded 1D convnet runs fast enough that it can generate the sentiment score on the fly as you type in the text box.

The core of the inference code is straightforward (see listing 9.9, from sentiment/index.js), but there are several interesting things to point out:

- The code converts all the input text to lowercase, discards punctuation, and erases extra whitespace before converting the text to word indices. This is because the vocabulary we use contains only lowercase words.
- Out-of-vocabulary words—words that fall outside the vocabulary—are represented with a special word index (OOV_INDEX). These include rare words and typos.
- The same padSequences() function that we used for training (see listing 9.7) is used here to make sure that the tensor input to the model has the correct length. This is achieved through truncation and padding, as we've seen previously. This is an example of a benefit of using TensorFlow.js for machine-learning tasks like this: you get to use the same data-preprocessing code for the backend training environment and the frontend serving environment, reducing the risk of data skew (see chapter 6 for a more in-depth discussion of the risks of skew).

> **Listing 9.9 Using the trained 1D convnet for inference in the frontend**

```
predict(text) {
  const inputText =
      text.trim().toLowerCase().replace(/(\.|\,|\!)/g, '').split(' ');   // Converts to lowercase; removes punctuation and extra whitespace from the input text
  const sequence = inputText.map(word => {
    let wordIndex =
            this.wordIndex[word] + this.indexFrom;   // Maps all the words to word indices. this.wordIndex has been loaded from a JSON file.
    if (wordIndex > this.vocabularySize) {
      wordIndex = OOV_INDEX;   // Words that fall out of the vocabulary are represented as a special word index: OOV_INDEX.
    }
    return wordIndex;
  });
  const paddedSequence =
          padSequences([sequence], this.maxLen);   // Truncates long reviews and pads short ones to the desired length
  const input = tf.tensor2d(
          paddedSequence, [1, this.maxLen]);   // Converts the data to a tensor representation, so it can be fed into the model
  const beginMs = performance.now();   // Keeps track of how much time is spent on the model's inference
  const predictOut = this.model.predict(input);   // The actual inference (forward pass on the model) happens here.
  const score = predictOut.dataSync()[0];
  predictOut.dispose();
  const endMs = performance.now();

  return {score: score, elapsed: (endMs - beginMs)};
}
```

9.3 *Sequence-to-sequence tasks with attention mechanism*

In the Jena-weather and IMDb sentiment examples, we showed how to predict a single number or a class from an input sequence. However, some of the most interesting sequential problems involve generating an *output sequence* based on an input one. These types of tasks are aptly named *sequence-to-sequence* (or seq2seq, for short) tasks. There is a great variety of seq2seq tasks, of which the following list is just a small subset:

- *Text summarization*—Given an article that may contain tens of thousands of words, generate a succinct summary of it (for example, in 100 or fewer words).
- *Machine translation*—Given a paragraph in one language (such as English), generate a translation of it in another (such as Japanese).
- *Word prediction for autocompletion*—Given a few first words in a sentence, predict what words will come after them. This is useful for autocompletion and suggestion in email apps and UIs for search engines.
- *Music composition*—Given a leading sequence of musical notes, generate a melody that begins with those notes.
- *Chat bots*—Given a sentence entered by a user, generate a response that fulfills some conversational goal (for instance, a certain type of customer support or simply chatting for fun).

The *attention mechanism*[11] is a powerful and popular method for seq2seq tasks. It is often used in conjunction with RNNs. In this section, we will show how we can use attention and LSTMs to solve a simple seq2seq task, namely, converting a myriad of calendar-date formats into a standard date format. Even though this is an intentionally simple example, the knowledge you'll gain from it applies to more complex seq2seq tasks like the ones listed previously. Let's first formulate the date-conversion problem.

9.3.1 *Formulation of the sequence-to-sequence task*

If you are like us, you have been confused (or even mildly annoyed) by the large number of possible ways to write calendar dates, especially if you have traveled to different countries. Some people prefer to use the month-day-year order, some adopt the day-month-year order, and still others use the year-month-day order. Even within the same order, there are variations with regard to whether the month is written as a word (January), an abbreviation (Jan), a number (1), or a zero-padded two-digit number (01). The options for the day include whether you prepad it with a zero and whether you write it as an ordinal number (4th versus 4). As for the year, you can write the full four digits or only the last two. What's more, the year, month, and day parts can be concatenated with spaces, commas, periods, or slashes, or they may be concatenated

---

[11] See Alex Graves, "Generating Sequences with Recurrent Neural Networks, submitted 4 Aug. 2013, https://arxiv.org/abs/1308.0850; and Dzmitry Bahdanau, Kyunghyun Cho, and Yoshua Bengio, "Neural Machine Translation by Jointly Learning to Align and Translate," submitted 1 Sept. 2014, https://arxiv.org/abs/1409.0473.

without any intervening characters at all! All these options come together in a combinatorial way, which gives rise to at least a few dozen ways to write the same date.

So, it will be nice to have an algorithm that can take a calendar-date string in these formats as the input, and output the corresponding date string in the ISO-8601 format (for instance, 2019-02-05). We could solve this problem in a non-machine-learning way by writing a traditional program. But given the large number of possible formats, this is a somewhat cumbersome and time-consuming task, and the resulting code can easily reach hundreds of lines. Let's try a deep-learning approach—in particular, with an LSTM-based attention encoder-decoder architecture.

To limit the scope of this example, we start from the 18 commonly seen date formats shown by the following examples. Note that all these are different ways to write the same date:

```
"23Jan2015", "012315", "01/23/15", "1/23/15",
"01/23/2015", "1/23/2015", "23-01-2015", "23-1-2015",
"JAN 23, 15", "Jan 23, 2015", "23.01.2015", "23.1.2015",
"2015.01.23", "2015.1.23", "20150123", "2015/01/23",
"2015-01-23", "2015-1-23"
```

Of course, there are other date formats.[12] But adding support for additional formats will basically be a repetitive task once the foundation of the model training and inference has been laid. We leave the part of adding more input date formats as an exercise for you at the end of this chapter (exercise 3).

First, let's get the example running. Like the sentiment-analysis example earlier, this example consists of a training part and an inference part. The training part runs in the backend environment using tfjs-node or tfjs-node-gpu. To kick off the training, use the following commands:

```
git clone https://github.com/tensorflow/tfjs-examples.git
cd tfjs-examples/sentiment
yarn
yarn train
```

To perform the training using a CUDA GPU, use the `--gpu` flag with the `yarn train` command:

```
yarn train --gpu
```

The training runs for two epochs by default, which should be sufficient to bring the loss value close to zero and the conversion accuracy close to perfect. In the sample inference results printed at the end of the training job, most, if not all, of the results should be correct. These inference samples are drawn from a test set that is non-overlapping with the training set. The trained model is saved to the relative path

---

[12] Another thing you might have noticed is that we use a set of date formats without any ambiguity. If we included both MM/DD/YYYY and DD/MM/YYYY in our set of formats, then there would be ambiguous date strings: that is, ones that can't be interpreted with certainty. For instance, the string "01/02/2019" can be interpreted as either as January 2, 2019 or February 1, 2019.

dist/model and will be used during the browser-based inference stage. To bring up the inference UI, use

```
yarn watch
```

In the web page that pops up, you can type dates into the Input Date String text box, hit Enter, and observe how the output date string changes accordingly. In addition, the heatmap with different shades displays the attention matrix used during the conversion (see figure 9.9). The attention matrix contains some interesting information and is central to this seq2seq model. It's especially amenable to interpretation by humans. You should get yourself familiar with it by playing with it.

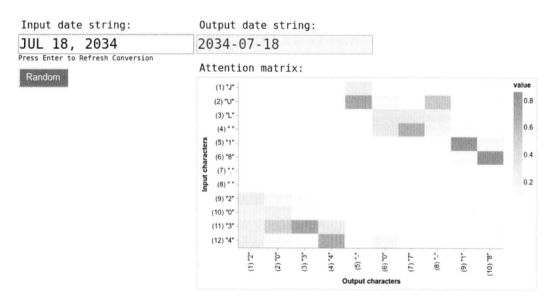

Figure 9.9   The attention-based encoder-decoder for date conversion at work, with the attention matrix for the particular input-output pair displayed at the bottom-right

Let's take the result shown in figure 9.9 as an example. The output of the model (`"2034-07-18"`) correctly translates the input date (`"JUL 18, 2034"`). The rows of the attention matrix correspond to the input characters (`"J"`, `"U"`, `"L"`, `" "`, and so forth), while the columns correspond to the output characters (`"2"`, `"0"`, `"3"`, and so forth). So, each element of the attention matrix indicates how much attention is paid to the corresponding input character when the corresponding output character is generated. The higher the element's value, the more attention is paid. For instance, look at the fourth column of the last row: that is, the one that corresponds to the last input character (`"4"`) and the fourth output character (`"4"`). It has a relatively high value, as indicated by the color scale. This makes sense because the last digit of the year part of the output should indeed depend primarily on the last digit of the year part in the input string. By contrast, other elements in that column have lower values, which indicates that the generation of the character "4" in the output string did not use much information from other characters of the input string. Similar patterns can be seen in the month and day parts of the output string. You are encouraged to experiment with other input date formats and see how the attention matrix changes.

9.3.2 The encoder-decoder architecture and the attention mechanism

This section helps you develop intuition for how the encoder-decoder architecture solves the seq2seq problem and what role the attention mechanism plays in it. An in-depth discussion of the mechanisms is presented alongside with the code in the following deep-dive section.

Up to this point, all the neural networks we've seen output a single item. For a regression network, the output is just a single number; for a classification network, it's a single probability distribution over a number of possible categories. But the date-conversion problem we are faced with is different: instead of predicting a single item, we need to predict a number of them. Specifically, we need to predict exactly 10 characters for the ISO-8601 date format. How should we achieve this using a neural network?

The solution is to create a network that outputs a sequence of items. In particular, since the output sequence is made of discrete symbols from an "alphabet" with exactly 11 items (0 through 9, as well as the hyphen), we let the output tensor shape of the network have a 3D shape: [numExamples, OUTPUT_LENGTH, OUTPUT_VOCAB_ SIZE]. The first dimension (numExamples) is the conventional example dimension that enables batch processing like all other networks we've seen in this book. OUTPUT_ LENGTH is 10—that is, the fixed length of the output date string in the ISO-8601 format. OUTPUT_VOCAB_SIZE is the size of the output vocabulary (or more accurately, "output alphabet"), which includes the digits 0 through 9 and the hyphen (-), in addition to a couple of characters with special meanings that we'll discuss later.

So that covers the model's output. How about the model's inputs? It turns out the model takes *two* inputs instead of one. The model can be divided roughly into two parts, the encoder and the decoder, as is shown schematically in figure 9.10. The first input of the model goes into the encoder part. It is the input date string itself, represented as a sequence of character indices of shape [numExamples, INPUT_LENGTH]. INPUT_LENGTH is the maximum possible length among the supported input date formats (which turns out to be 12). Inputs shorter than that length are padded with zeros at the end. The second input goes into the decoder part of the model. It is the conversion result shifted to the right by one time step, and it has a shape of [numExamples, OUTPUT_LENGTH].

Wait, the first input makes sense because it's the input date string, but why does the model take the conversion result as an additional input? Isn't that meant to be the *output* of the model? The key lies in the shifting of the conversion result. Note that the second input is *not* exactly the conversion result. Instead, it is a time-delayed version of the conversion result. The time delay is by exactly one step. For example, if during

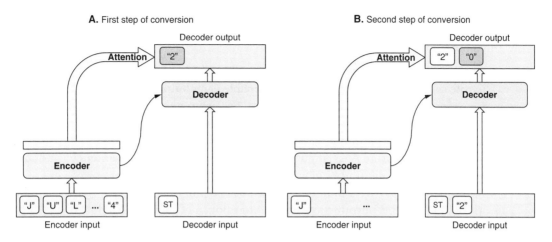

Figure 9.10   How the encoder-decoder architecture converts an input date string into an output one. ST is the special starting token for the decoder's input and output. Panels A and B show the first two steps of the conversion, respectively. After the first conversion step, the first character in the output ("2") is generated. After the second step, the second character ("0") is generated. The remaining steps follow the same pattern and are hence omitted.

training, the desired conversion result is "2034-07-18", then the second input to the model will be "<ST>2034-07-1", where <ST> is a special start-of-sequence symbol. This shifted input lets the decoder be aware of the output sequence that has been generated so far. It makes it easier for the decoder to keep track of where it is in the conversion process.

This is analogous to how humans speak. When you put a thought into words, your mental effort is spent on two things: the concept itself and what you've said so far. The latter part is important to ensure coherent, complete, and nonrepetitive speech. Our model works in a similar fashion: to generate every output character, it uses the information from both the input date string and the output characters that have been generated so far.

The time-delaying of the conversion result works during the training phase because we already know what the correct conversion result is. But how does it work during inference? The answer can be seen in the two panels of figure 9.10: we generate the output characters one by one.[13] As panel A of the figure shows, we start by sticking an ST symbol at the beginning of the decoder's input. Through one step of inference (one Model.predict() call), we obtain a new output item (the "2" in the panel). This new output item is then appended to the decoder input. Then the next step of conversion ensues. It sees the newly generated output character "2" in the decoder input (see panel B of figure 9.10). This step involves another Model.predict() call and generates a new output character ("0"), which is again appended to the decoder input.

---

[13] The code that implements the step-by-step conversion algorithm is the function runSeq2SeqInference() in date-conversion-attention/model.js.

This process repeats until the desired length of the output (10 in this case) is reached. Notice that the output doesn't include the ST item, so it can be used directly as the final output of the entire algorithm.

THE ROLE OF THE ATTENTION MECHANISM

The role of the attention mechanism is to enable each output character to "attend" to the correct characters in the input sequence. For example, the `"7"` part of the output string `"2034-07-18"` should attend to the `"JUL"` part of the input date string. This is again analogous to how humans generate language. For instance, when we translate a sentence from language A to language B, each word in the output sentence is usually determined by a small number of words from the input sentence.

This may seem like a no-brainer: it's hard to imagine what other approaches might work better. But the introduction of the attention mechanism introduced by deep-learning researchers around 2014–2015 was a major advancement in the field. To understand the historical reason behind this, look at the arrow that connects the Encoder box with the Decoder box in panel A of figure 9.10. This arrow represents the last output of an LSTM in the encoder part of the model, which is passed to an LSTM in the decoder part of the model as its initial state. Recall that the initial state of RNNs is typically all-zero (for example, the simpleRNN we used in section 9.1.2); however, TensorFlow.js allows you to set the initial state of an RNN to any given tensor value of the correct shape. This can be used as a way to pass upstream information to an LSTM. In this case, the encoder-to-decoder connection uses this mechanism to let the decoder LSTM access the encoded input sequence.

However, the initial state is an entire input sequence packed into a single vector. It turns out that this representation is a little too condensed for the decoder to unpack, especially for longer and more complex sequences (such as the sentences seen in typical machine-translation problems). This is where the attention mechanism comes into play.

The attention mechanism expands the "field of view" available to the decoder. Instead of using just the encoder's final output, the attention mechanism accesses the entire sequence of the encoder's output. At each step of the conversion process, the mechanism attends to specific time steps in the encoder's output sequence in order to decide what output character to generate. For example, the first conversion step may pay attention to the first two input characters, while the second conversion step pays attention to the second and third input characters, and so forth (see figure 9.10 for a concrete example of such an attention matrix). Just like all weight parameters of the neural network, an attention model *learns* the way in which it allocated attention, instead of hard-coding a policy. This makes the model flexible and powerful: it can learn to attend to different parts of the input sequence depending on both the input sequence itself and what has been generated in the output sequence so far.

This is as far as we can go in talking about the encoder-decoder mechanism without looking at the code or opening the black boxes that are the encoder, decoder, and attention mechanism. If this treatment sounds too high-level or too vague to you, read the next section, where we'll dive a little deeper into the nuts and bolts of the model. This is worth the mental effort for those who wish to get a deeper understanding of the attention-based encoder-decoder architecture. To motivate you to read it, realize that the same architecture underlies systems such as state-of-the-art machine-translation models (Google Neural Machine Translation, or GNMT), even though these production models employ more layers of LSTMs and are trained on much larger amounts of data than the simple date-conversion model we are dealing with here.

9.3.3 Deep dive into the attention-based encoder-decoder model

Figure 9.11 expands the boxes in figure 9.10 and provides a more detailed view of their internal structures. It is most illustrative to view it in conjunction with the code that builds the model: `createModel()` function in date-conversion-attention/model.js. We'll next walk through the important aspects of the code.

First, we define a couple of constants for the embedding and LSTM layers in the encoder and decoder:

```
const embeddingDims = 64;
const lstmUnits = 64;
```

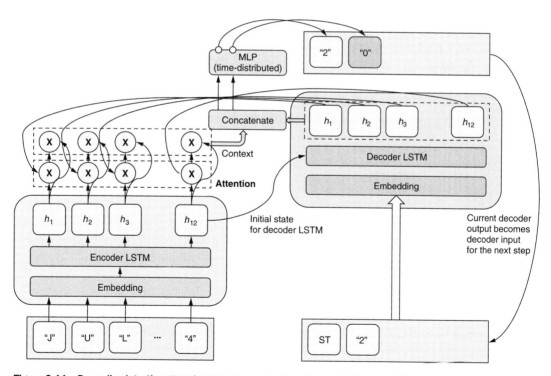

Figure 9.11 Deep dive into the attention-based encoder-decoder model. You can think of this figure as an expanded view of the encoder-decoder architecture outlined in figure 9.10, with finer-grained details depicted.

The model we will construct takes two inputs, so we must use the functional model API instead of the sequential API. We start from the model's symbolic inputs for the encoder input and the decoder input, respectively:

```
const encoderInput = tf.input({shape: [inputLength]});
const decoderInput = tf.input({shape: [outputLength]});
```

The encoder and decoder both apply an embedding layer on their respective input sequences. The code for the encoder looks like

```
let encoder = tf.layers.embedding({
  inputDim: inputVocabSize,
  outputDim: embeddingDims,
  inputLength,
  maskZero: true
}).apply(encoderInput);
```

This is similar to the embedding layers we used in the IMDb sentiment problem, but it embeds characters instead of words. This shows that the embedding method is not limited to words. In fact, it is flexible enough to be applied on any finite, discrete set, such as music genres, articles on a news website, airports in a country, and so forth. The `maskZero: true` configuration of the embedding layer instructs the downstream LSTM to skip steps with all-zero values. This saves unnecessary computation on sequences that have already ended.

LSTM is an RNN type we haven't covered in detail yet. We won't go into its internal structure here. It suffices to say that it is similar to GRU (figure 9.4) in that it addresses the vanishing-gradient problem by making it easier to carry a state over multiple time steps. Chris Olah's blog post "Understanding LSTM Networks," for which a pointer is provided in "Materials for further reading" at the end of the chapter, presents an excellent review and visualization of the structure and mechanisms of LSTMs. Our encoder LSTM is applied on the character-embedding vectors:

```
encoder = tf.layers.lstm({
  units: lstmUnits,
  returnSequences: true
}).apply(encoder);
```

The `returnSequences: true` configuration lets the output of the LSTM be a sequence of output vectors instead of the default output of a single vector that's the final output (as we did in the temperature-prediction and sentiment-analysis models). This step is required by the downstream attention mechanism.

The `GetLastTimestepLayer` layer that follows the encoder LSTM is a custom-defined layer:

```
const encoderLast = new GetLastTimestepLayer({
  name: 'encoderLast'
}).apply(encoder);
```

It simply slices the time-sequence tensor along the time dimension (the second dimension) and outputs the last time step. This allows us to send the final state of the encoder LSTM to the decoder LSTM as its initial state. This connection is one of the ways in which the decoder gets information about the input sequence. This is illustrated in figure 9.11 with the arrow that connects h_{12} in the green encoder block to the decoder LSTM layer in the blue decoder block.

The decoder part of the code begins with an embedding layer and an LSTM layer reminiscent of the encoder's topology:

```
let decoder = tf.layers.embedding({
  inputDim: outputVocabSize,
  outputDim: embeddingDims,
  inputLength: outputLength,
  maskZero: true
}).apply(decoderInput);
decoder = tf.layers.lstm({
  units: lstmUnits,
  returnSequences: true
}).apply(decoder, {initialState: [encoderLast, encoderLast]});
```

In the last line of this code snippet, notice how the final state of the encoder is used as the initial state of the decoder. In case you wonder why the symbolic tensor `encoderLast` is repeated in the last line of code here, it is because an LSTM layer contains two states, unlike the one-state structure we've seen in simpleRNN and GRU.

The additional, and more powerful, way in which the decoder gets a view at the input sequences is, of course, the attention mechanism. The attention is a dot product (element-by-element product) between the encoder LSTM's output and the decoder LSTM's output, followed by a softmax activation:

```
let attention = tf.layers.dot({axes: [2, 2]}).apply([decoder, encoder]);
attention = tf.layers.activation({
  activation: 'softmax',
  name: 'attention'
}).apply(attention);
```

The encoder LSTM's output has a shape of `[null, 12, 64]`, where 12 is the input sequence's length and 64 is the LSTM's size. The decoder LSTM's output has a shape of `[null, 10, 64]`, where 10 is the output sequence's length and 64 is the LSTM's size. A dot product between the two is performed along the last (LSTM features) dimension, which gives rise to a shape of `[null, 10, 12]` (that is, `[null, inputLength, outputLength]`). The softmax applied on the dot product turns the values into probability scores, which are guaranteed to be positive and sum to 1 along each column of the matrix. This is the attention matrix that's central to our model. Its value is what's visualized in the earlier figure 9.9.

The attention matrix is then applied on the sequential output from the encoder LSTM. This is how the conversion process learns to pay attention to different elements of the input sequence (in its encoded form) at each step. The result of applying the attention on the encoder's output is called the *context*:

```
const context = tf.layers.dot({
  axes: [2, 1],
```

```
  name: 'context'
}).apply([attention, encoder]);
```

The context has a shape of `[null, 10, 64]` (that is, `[null, outputLength, lstm-Units]`). It is concatenated with the decoder's output, which also has a shape of `[null, 10, 64]`. So, the result of the concatenation has a shape of `[null, 10, 128]`:

```
const decoderCombinedContext =
    tf.layers.concatenate().apply([context, decoder]);
```

`decoderCombinedContext` contains the feature vectors that go into the final stage of the model, namely, the stage that generates the output characters.

The output characters are generated using an MLP that contains one hidden layer and a softmax output layer:

```
let output = tf.layers.timeDistributed({
  layer: tf.layers.dense({
    units: lstmUnits,
    activation: 'tanh'
  })
}).apply(decoderCombinedContext);
output = tf.layers.timeDistributed({
  layer: tf.layers.dense({
    units: outputVocabSize,
    activation: 'softmax'
  })
}).apply(output);
```

Thanks to the `timeDistributed` layer, all steps share the same MLP. The `time-Distributed` layer takes a layer and calls it repeatedly over all steps along the time dimension (that is, the second dimension) of its input. This converts the input feature shape of `[null, 10, 128]` to `[null, 10, 13]`, where 13 corresponds to the 11 possible characters of the ISO-8601 date format, as well as the 2 special characters (padding and start-of-sequence).

With all the pieces in place, we assemble them together into a `tf.Model` object with two inputs and one output:

```
const model = tf.model({
  inputs: [encoderInput, decoderInput],
  outputs: output
});
```

To prepare for training, we call the `compile()` method with a categorical cross-entropy loss function. The choice of this loss function is based on the fact that the conversion problem is essentially a classification problem—at each time step, we choose a character from the set of all possible characters:

```
model.compile({
  loss: 'categoricalCrossentropy',
  optimizer: 'adam'
});
```

At inference time, an `argMax()` operation is applied on the model's output tensor to obtain the winning output character. At every step of the conversion, the winning output character is appended to the decoder's input, so the next conversion step can use it (see the arrow on the right end of figure 9.11). As we mentioned before, this iterative process eventually yields the entire output sequence.

Materials for further reading

- Chris Olah, "Understanding LSTM Networks," blog, 27 Aug. 2015, http://mng .bz/m4Wa.
- Chris Olah and Shan Carter, "Attention and Augmented Recurrent Neural Networks," Distill, 8 Sept. 2016, https://distill.pub/2016/augmented-rnns/.
- Andrej Karpathy, "The Unreasonable Effectiveness of Recurrent Neural Networks," blog, 21 May 2015, http://mng.bz/6wK6.
- Zafarali Ahmed, "How to Visualize Your Recurrent Neural Network with Attention in Keras," Medium, 29 June 2017, http://mng.bz/6w2e.
- In the date-conversion example, we described a decoding technique based on `argMax()`. This approach is often referred to as the *greedy decoding* technique because it extracts the output symbol of the highest probability at every step. A popular alternative to the greedy-decoding approach is *beam-search* decoding, which examines a larger range of possible output sequences in order to determine the best one. You can read more about it from Jason Brownlee, "How to Implement a Beam Search Decoder for Natural Language Processing," 5 Jan. 2018, https://machinelearningmastery.com/beam-search-decoder-natural-language-processing/.
- Stephan Raaijmakers, *Deep Learning for Natural Language Processing*, Manning Publications, in press, www.manning.com/books/deep-learning-for-natural-language-processing.

Exercises

1 Try rearranging the order of the data elements for various nonsequential data. Confirm that such reordering has no effect on the loss-metric values (for example, accuracy) of the modeling (beyond random fluctuation caused by random initialization of the weight parameters). You can do this for the following two problems:

   a In the iris-flower example (from chapter 3), rearrange the order of the four numeric features (petal length, petal width, sepal length, and sepal width) by making changes to the line

   ```
   shuffledData.push(data[indices[i]]);
   ```

   in the iris/data.js file of the tfjs-examples repo. In particular, alter the order of the four elements in `data[indices[i]]`. This can be done through calls to the `slice()` and `concat()` methods of the JavaScript array. Note that the order rearrangement ought to be the same for all examples. You may write a JavaScript function to perform the reordering.

b In the linear regressor and MLP that we developed for the Jena-weather problem, try reordering the 240 time steps *and* the 14 numeric features (weather-instrument measurements). Specifically, you can achieve this by modifying the `nextBatchFn()` function in jena-weather/data.js. The line where it is the easiest to implement the reordering is

```
samples.set(value, j, exampleRow, exampleCol++);
```

where you can map the index `exampleRow` to a new value using a function that performs a fixed permutation and map `exampleCol` in a similar manner.

2 The 1D convnet we built for the IMDb sentiment analysis consisted of only one conv1d layer (see listing 9.8). As we discussed, stacking more conv1d layers on top of it may give us a deeper 1D convnet capable of capturing order information over a longer span of words. In this exercise, practice modifying the code in the `buildModel()` function of sentiment/train.js. The goal is to add another conv1d layer after the existing one, retrain the model, and observe if there is any improvement in its classification accuracy. The new conv1d layer may use the same number of filters and kernel size as the existing one. Also, read the output shapes in the summary of the modified model and make sure you understand how the `filters` and `kernelSize` parameters lead to the output shape of the new conv1d layer.

3 In the date-conversion-attention example, try adding a couple more input date formats. Following are the new formats you can choose from, sorted in order of increasing coding difficulty. You can also come up with your own date formats:

a The YYYY-MMM-DD format: for example, "2012-MAR-08" or "2012-MAR-18." Depending on whether single-digit day numbers are prepadded with a zero (as in 12/03/2015), this can actually be two different formats. However, regardless of the padding, the maximum length of this format is less than 12, and all the possible characters are already in the `INPUT_VOCAB` in date-conversion-attention/date_format.js. Therefore, all it takes is to add a function or two to the file, and those functions can be modeled after existing ones, such as `dateTupleToMMMSpaceDDSpaceYY()`. Make sure you add the new function(s) to the `INPUT_FNS` array in the file, so they can be included in the training. As a best practice, you should also add unit tests for your new date-format functions to date-conversion-attention/date_format_test.js.

b A format with ordinal numbers as the day part, such as "Mar 8th, 2012." Note that this is the same as the existing `dateTupleToMMMSpaceDDComma-SpaceYYYY()` format, except that the day number is suffixed with the ordinal suffices (`"st"`, `"nd"`, and `"th"`). Your new function should include the logic to determine the suffix based on the day value. In addition, you need to revise the `INPUT_LENGTH` constant in date_format_test.js to a larger value because the maximum possible length of the date string in this format exceeds the current value of 12. Furthermore, the letters "t" and "h" need to be added to INPUT_VOCAB, as they do not appear in any of the three-letter month strings.

c Now consider a format with the full English name of the month spelled out, such as "March 8th, 2012." What is the maximum possible length of the input date string? How should you change INPUT_VOCAB in date_format.js accordingly?

Summary

- By virtue of being able to extract and learn information contained in the sequential order of things, RNNs can outperform feedforward models (for example, MLPs) in tasks that involve sequential input data. We see this through the example of applying simpleRNN and GRU to the temperature-prediction problem.

- There are three types of RNNs available from TensorFlow.js: simpleRNN, GRU, and LSTM. The latter two types are more sophisticated than simpleRNN in that they use a more complex internal structure to make it possible to carry memory state over many time steps, which mitigates the vanishing-gradient problem. GRU is computationally less intensive than LSTM. In most practical problems, you'll probably want to use GRU and LSTM.

- When building neural networks for text, the text inputs need to be represented as vectors of numbers first. This is called text vectorization. Most frequently used methods of text vectorization include one-hot and multi-hot encoding, as well as the more powerful embedding method.

- In word embedding, each word is represented as a nonsparse vector, of which the element values are learned through backpropagation, just like all other weight parameters of the neural network. The function in TensorFlow.js that performs embedding is `tf.layers.embedding()`.

- seq2seq problems are different from sequence-based regression and classification problems in that they involve generating a new sequence as the output. RNNs can be used (together with other layer types) to form an encoder-decoder architecture to solve seq2seq problems.

- In seq2seq problems, the attention mechanism enables different items of the output sequence to selectively depend on specific elements of the input sequence. We demonstrate how to train an attention-based encoder-decoder network to solve a simple date-conversion problem and visualize the attention matrix during inference.

$$10$$

Generative deep learning

This chapter covers

- What generative deep learning is, its applications, and how it differs from the deep-learning tasks we've seen so far
- How to generate text using an RNN
- What latent space is and how it can form the basis of generating novel images, through the example of variational autoencoders
- The basics of generative adversarial networks

Some of the most impressive tasks demonstrated by deep neural networks have involved generating images, sounds, and text that look or sound real. Nowadays, deep neural networks are capable of creating highly realistic human face images,[1] synthesizing natural-sounding speech,[2] and composing compellingly coherent

---

[1] Tero Karras, Samuli Laine, and Timo Aila, "A Style-Based Generator Architecture for Generative Adversarial Networks," submitted 12 Dec. 2018, https://arxiv.org/abs/1812.04948. See a live demo at https://thispersondoesnotexist.com/.

[2] Aäron van den Oord and Sander Dieleman, "WaveNet: A Generative Model for Raw Audio," blog, 8 Sept. 2016, http://mng.bz/MOrn.

text,[3] just to name a few achievements. Such *generative* models are useful for a number of reasons, including aiding artistic creation, conditionally modifying existing content, and augmenting existing datasets to support other deep-learning tasks.[4]

Apart from practical applications such as putting makeup on the selfie of a potential cosmetic customer, generative models are also worth studying for theoretical reasons. Generative and discriminative modeling are two fundamentally different types of models in machine learning. All the models we've studied in this book so far are *discriminative* models. Such models are designed to map an input into a discrete or continuous value without caring about the process through which the input is generated. Recall the classifiers for phishing websites, iris flowers, MNIST digits, and speech sounds, as well as the regressor for housing prices we've built. By contrast, generative models are designed to mathematically mimic the process through which the examples of different classes are generated. But once a generative model has learned this generative knowledge, it can perform discriminative tasks as well. So generative models can be said to "understand" the data better compared to discriminative models.

This section covers the foundations of deep generative models for text and images. By the end of the chapter, you should be familiar with the ideas behind RNN-based language models, image-oriented autoencoders, and generative adversarial networks. You should also be familiar with the pattern in which such models are implemented in TensorFlow.js and be capable of applying these models to your own dataset.

10.1 Generating text with LSTM

Let's start from text generation. To do that, we will use RNNs, which we introduced in the previous chapter. Although the technique you'll see here generates text, it is not limited to this particular output domain. The technique can be adapted to generate other types of sequences, such as music—given the ability to represent musical notes in a suitable way and find an adequate training dataset.[5] Similar ideas can be applied to generate pen strokes in sketching so that nice-looking sketches[6] or even realistic-looking Kanjis[7] can be generated.

10.1.1 Next-character predictor: A simple way to generate text

First, let's define the text-generation task. Suppose we have a corpus of text data of decent size (at least a few megabytes) as the training input, such as the complete works of Shakespeare (a very long string). We want to train a model to generate

---

[3] "Better Language Models and Their Implications," OpenAI, 2019, https://openai.com/blog/better-language-models/.

[4] Antreas Antoniou, Amos Storkey, and Harrison Edwards, "Data Augmentation Generative Adversarial Networks," submitted 12 Nov. 2017, https://arxiv.org/abs/1711.04340.

[5] For example, see Performance-RNN from Google's Magenta Project: https://magenta.tensorflow.org/performance-rnn.

[6] For example, see Sketch-RNN by David Ha and Douglas Eck: http://mng.bz/omyv.

[7] David Ha, "Recurrent Net Dreams Up Fake Chinese Characters in Vector Format with TensorFlow," blog, 28 Dec. 2015, http://mng.bz/nvX4.

new texts that *look like* the training data as much as possible. The key phrase here is, of course, "look like." For now, let's be content with not precisely defining what "look like" means. The meaning will become clearer after we show the method and the results.

Let's think about how to formulate this task in the paradigm of deep learning. In the date-conversion example covered in the previous chapter, we saw how a precisely formatted output sequence can be generated from a casually formatted input one. That text-to-text conversion task had a well-defined answer: the correct date string in the ISO-8601 format. However, the text-generation task here doesn't seem to fit this bill. There is no explicit input sequence, and the "correct" output is not well-defined; we just want to generate something that "looks real." What can we do?

A solution is to build a model to predict what character will come after a sequence of characters. This is called *next-character prediction*. For instance, a well-trained model on the Shakespeare dataset should predict the character "u" with a high probability when given the character string "Love looks not with the eyes, b" as the input. However, that generates only one character. How do we use the model to generate a sequence of characters? To do that, we simply form a new input sequence of the same length as before by shifting the previous input to the left by one character, discarding the first character, and sticking the newly generated character ("u") at the end. This gives us a new input for our next-character predictor, namely, "ove looks not with the eyes, bu" in this case. Given this new input sequence, the model should predict the character "t" with a high probability. This process, which is illustrated in figure 10.1, can be repeated as many times as necessary to generate a sequence as long as desired. Of course, we need an initial snippet of text as the starting point. For that, we can just sample randomly from the text corpus.

This formulation turns the sequence-generation task into a sequence-based classification problem. This problem is similar to what we saw in the IMDb sentiment-analysis problem in chapter 9, in which a binary class was predicted from an input of a fixed length. The model for text generation does essentially the same thing, although it is a multiclass-classification problem involving N possible classes, where N is the size of the character set—namely, the number of all unique characters in the text dataset.

This next-character-prediction formulation has a long history in natural language processing and computer science. Claude Shannon, the pioneer of information theory, conducted an experiment in which human participants were asked to guess the next letter after seeing a short snippet of English text.[8] Through this experiment, he was able to estimate the average amount of uncertainty in every letter of the typical English texts, given the context. This uncertainty, which turned out to be about 1.3 bits of entropy, tells us the average amount of information carried by every letter in English.

---

[8] The original 1951 paper is accessible at http://mng.bz/5AzB.

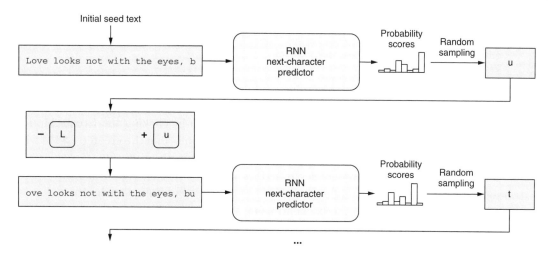

Figure 10.1 A schematic illustration of how an RNN-based next-character predictor can be used to generate a sequence of text from an initial input snippet of text as the seed. At each step, the RNN predicts the next character using the input text. Then, the input text is concatenated with the predicted next character and discards the first character. The result forms the input for the next step. At each step, the RNN outputs the probability scores for all possible characters in the character set. To determine the actual next character, a random sampling is carried out.

The 1.3 bits result is less than the number of bits if the 26 letters appeared in a completely random fashion, which would be $\log_2(26)$ = 4.7 bits. This matches our intuition because we know letters do not appear randomly in English. Instead, they follow patterns. At a lower level, only certain sequences of letters are valid English words. At a higher level, only a certain ordering of words satisfies English grammar. At an even higher level, only a subset of grammatically valid sentences actually make real sense.

If you think about it, this is what our text-generation task is fundamentally about: learning these patterns on all these levels. Realize that our model is essentially trained to do what Shannon's subjects did—that is, guess the next character. Let's now take a look at the example code and how it works. Keep Shannon's result of 1.3 bits in mind because we'll come back to it later.

10.1.2 *The LSTM-text-generation example*

The lstm-text-generation example in the tfjs-examples repository involves training an LSTM-based next-character predictor and using it to generate new text. The training and generation steps both happen in JavaScript using TensorFlow.js. You can run the example either in the browser or in the backend environment with Node.js. While the former approach provides a more visual and interactive interface, the latter gives you faster training speed.

To see the example running in the browser, use these commands:

```
git clone https://github.com/tensorflow/tfjs-examples.git
cd tfjs-examples/lstm-text-generation
yarn && yarn watch
```

In the page that pops up, you can select and load one of four provided text datasets to train the model on. We will use the Shakespeare dataset in the following discussion. Once the data is loaded, you can create a model for it by clicking the Create Model button. A text box allows you to adjust the number of units that the created LSTM will have. It is set to 128 by default. But you can experiment with other values, such as 64. If you enter multiple numbers separated by commas (for example, 128,128), the model created will contain multiple LSTM layers stacked on top of each other.

To perform training on the backend using tfjs-node or tfjs-node-gpu, use the command `yarn train` instead of `yarn watch`:

```
yarn train shakespeare \
    --lstmLayerSize 128,128 \
    --epochs 120 \
    --savePath ./my-shakespeare-model
```

If you have a CUDA-enabled GPU set up properly, you can add the `--gpu` flag to the command to let the training happen on your GPU, which will further increase the training speed. The flag `--lstmLayerSize` plays the same role as the LSTM-size text box in the browser version of the example. The previous command will create and train a model consisting of two LSTM layers, both with 128 units, stacked on top of each other.

The model being trained here has a stacked-LSTM architecture. What does *stacking* LSTM layers mean? It is conceptually similar to stacking multiple dense layers in an MLP, which increases the MLP's capacity. In a similar fashion, stacking multiple LSTMs allows an input sequence to go through multiple stages of seq2seq representational transformation before being converted into a final regression or classification output by the final LSTM layer. Figure 10.2 gives a schematic illustration of this architecture. One important thing to notice is the fact that the first LSTM has its `return-Sequence` property set to `true` and hence generates a sequence of output that includes the output for every single item of the input sequence. This makes it possible to feed the output of the first LSTM into the second one, as an LSTM layer expects a sequential input instead of a single-item input.

Listing 10.1 contains the code that builds next-character prediction models with the architecture shown in figure 10.2 (excerpted from lstm-text-generation/model.js). Notice that unlike the diagram, the code includes a dense layer as the model's final output. The dense layer has a softmax activation. Recall that the softmax activation normalizes the outputs so that they have values between 0 and 1 and sum to 1, like a probability distribution. So, the final dense layer's output represents the predicted probabilities of the unique characters.

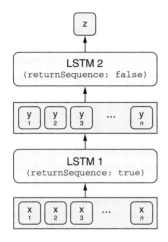

Figure 10.2 How stacking multiple LSTM layers works in a model. In this case, two LSTM layers are stacked together. The first one has its `returnSequence` property set to `true` and hence outputs a sequence of items. The sequential output of the first LSTM is received by the second LSTM as its input. The second LSTM outputs a single item instead of a sequence of items. The single item could be regression prediction or an array of softmax probabilities, which forms the final output of the model.

The `lstmLayerSize` argument of the `createModel()` function controls the number of LSTM layers and the size of each. The first LSTM layer has its input shape configured based on `sampleLen` (how many characters the model takes at a time) and `charSet-Size` (how many unique characters there are in the text data). For the browser-based example, `sampleLen` is hard-coded to 40; for the Node.js-based training script, it is adjustable via the `--sampleLen` flag. `charSetSize` has a value of 71 for the Shakespeare dataset. The character set includes the upper- and lowercase English letters, punctuation, the space, the line break, and several other special characters. Given these parameters, the model created by the function in listing 10.1 has an input shape of [40, 71] (ignoring the batch dimension). This shape corresponds to 40 one-hot-encoded characters. The model's output shape is [71] (again, ignoring the batch dimension), which is the softmax probability value for the 71 possible choices of the next character.

Listing 10.1 Building a multilayer LSTM model for next-character prediction

```
export function createModel(sampleLen,      ⟵  The length of the model's input sequence
                            charSetSize,    ⟵  The number of all possible unique characters
                            lstmLayerSizes) {   ⟵  Size of the LSTM layers of the
  if (!Array.isArray(lstmLayerSizes)) {            model, as a single number or an
    lstmLayerSizes = [lstmLayerSizes];             array of numbers
  }

  const model = tf.sequential();
  for (let i = 0; i < lstmLayerSizes.length; ++i) {
    const lstmLayerSize = lstmLayerSizes[i];       The model begins with
    model.add(tf.layers.lstm({      ⟵              a stack of LSTM layers.
      units: lstmLayerSize,
      returnSequences: i < lstmLayerSizes.length - 1,  ⟵  Sets returnSequences to
                                                          true so that multiple LSTM
                                                          layers can be stacked
```

```
    inputShape: i === 0 ?
        [sampleLen, charSetSize] : undefined
   }));
 }
 model.add(
    tf.layers.dense({
       units: charSetSize,
       activation: 'softmax'
   }));

   return model;
 }
```

> The first LSTM layer is special in that it needs to specify its input shape.

> The model ends with a dense layer with a softmax activation over all possible characters, reflecting the classification nature of the next-character prediction problem.

To prepare the model for training, we compile it with the categorical cross-entropy loss, as the model is essentially a 71-way classifier. For the optimizer, we use RMSProp, which is a popular choice for recurrent models:

```
const optimizer = tf.train.rmsprop(learningRate);
model.compile({optimizer: optimizer, loss: 'categoricalCrossentropy'});
```

The data that goes into the model's training consists of pairs of input text snippets and the characters that follow each of them, all encoded as one-hot vectors (see figure 10.1). The class TextData defined in lstm-text-generation/data.js contains the logic to generate such tensor data from the training text corpus. The code there is somewhat tedious, but the idea is simple: randomly sample snippets of fixed length from the very long string that is our text corpus, and convert them into one-hot tensor representations.

If you are using the web-based demo, the Model Training section of the page allows you to adjust hyperparameters such as the number of training epochs, the number of examples that go into each epoch, the learning rate, and so forth. Click the Train Model button to kick off the model-training process. For Node.js-based training, these hyperparameters are adjustable through the command-line flags. For details, you can get help messages by entering the yarn train --help command.

Depending on the number of training epochs you specified and the size of the model, the training should take anywhere between a few minutes to a couple of hours. The Node.js-based training job automatically prints a number of sample text snippets generated by the model after every training epoch (see table 10.1). As the training progresses, you should see the loss value go down continuously from the initial value of approximately 3.2 and converge in the range of 1.4–1.5. As the loss decreases after about 120 epochs, the quality of the generated text should improve, such that toward the end of the training, the text should look *somewhat* Shakespearean, and the validation loss should approach the neighborhood of 1.5—not too far from the 1.3 bits/character information uncertainty from Shannon's experiment. But note that given our training paradigm and model capacity, the generated text will never look like the actual Shakespeare's writing.

Table 10.1 Samples of text generated by the LSTM-based next-character prediction model. The generation is based on the seed text. Initial seed text: " in hourly synod about thy particular prosperity, and lo".[a] Actual text that follows the seed text (for comparison): "ve thee no worse than thy old father Menenius does! ...".

Epochs of training	Validation loss	T = 0	T = 0.25	T = 0.5	T = 0.75
5	2.44	"rle the the the the the the the the the the the the the the the the the the the the the the the "	"te ans and and and and and warl torle an at an yawl and tand and an an ind an an in thall ang ind an tord and and and wa"	"te toll nlatese ant ann, tomdenl, teurteeinlndti ng fall ald antetetell linde ing thathere taod winld mlinl theens tord y"	"p, af ane me pfleh; fove this? Iretltard efidestind ants anl het insethou loellr ard,
25	1.96	"ve tray the stanter an truent to the stanter to the stanter to the stanter to the stanter to the stanter "	"ve to the enter an truint to the surt an truin to me truent me the will tray mane but a bean to the stanter an trust tra"	"ve of marter at it not me shank to an him truece preater the beaty atweath and that marient shall me the manst on hath s"	"rd; not an an beilloters An bentest the like have bencest on it love gray to dreath avalace the lien I am sach me, m"
50	1.67	"rds the world the world the world the world the world the world the world the world the world the world the worl"	"ngs they are their shall the englents the world the world the stand the provicess their string shall the world I"	"nger of the hath the forgest as you for sear the device of thee shall, them at a hame, The now the would have bo"	"ngs, he coll, As heirs to me which upon to my light fronest prowirness foir. I be chall do vall twell. SIR C"
100	1.61	"nd the sough the sought That the more the man the forth and the strange as the sought That the more the man the "	"nd the sough as the sought In the consude the more of the princes and show her art the compont "	"rds as the manner. To the charit and the stranger and house a tarron. A tommern the bear you art this a contents, "	"nd their conswents That thou be three as me a thout thou do end, The longers and an heart and not strange. A G"

Table 10.1 Samples of text generated by the LSTM-based next-character prediction model. The generation is based on the seed text. Initial seed text: " in hourly synod about thy particular prosperity, and lo".[a] Actual text that follows the seed text (for comparison): "ve thee no worse than thy old father Menenius does! ...". *(continued)*

Epochs of training	Validation loss	T = 0	T = 0.25	T = 0.5	T = 0.75
120	1.49	"ve the strike the strike the strike the strike the strikes the strike And the strike the strike the strike A"	"ve the fair brother, And this in the strike my sort the strike, The strike the sound in the dear strike And "	"ve the stratter for soul. Monty to digning him your poising. This for his brother be this did fool. A mock'd"	"ve of his trusdum him. poins thinks him where sudy's such then you; And soul they will I would from in my than s"

a. From *Shakespeare's Coriolanus*, act 5, scene 2. Note that the sample includes line breaks and stops in the middle of a word (love).

Table 10.1 shows some texts sampled under four different *temperature values*, a parameter that controls the randomness of the generated text. In the samples of generated text, you may have noticed that lower temperature values are associated with more repetitive and mechanical-looking text, while higher values are associated with less-predictable text. The highest temperature value demonstrated by the Node.js-based training script is 0.75 by default, and it sometimes leads to character sequences that look like English but are not actually English words (such as "stratter" and "poins" in the samples in the table). In the next section, we'll examine how temperature works and why it is called temperature.

10.1.3 *Temperature: Adjustable randomness in the generated text*

The function `sample()` in listing 10.2 is responsible for determining which character will be chosen based on the model's output probabilities at each step of the text-generation process. As you can see, the algorithm is somewhat complex: it involves calls to three low-level TensorFlow.js operations: `tf.div()`, `tf.log()`, and `tf.multinomial()`. Why do we use this complicated algorithm instead of simply picking the choice with the highest probability score, which would take a single `argMax()` call?

If we did that, the output of the text-generation process would be *deterministic*. That is, it would give you exactly the same output if you ran it multiple times. The deep neural networks we've seen so far are all deterministic, in the sense that given an input tensor, the output tensor is completely determined by the network's topology and the values of its weights. If so desired, you can write a unit test to assert its output value (see chapter 12 for a discussion of testing machine-learning algorithms). This determinism is *not* ideal for our text-generation task. After all, writing is a creative process.

It is much more interesting to have some randomness in the generated text, even when the same seed text is given. This is what the tf.multinomial() operation and the temperature parameter are useful for. tf.multinomial() is the source of randomness, while temperature controls the degree of randomness.

Listing 10.2 The stochastic sampling function, with a temperature parameter

The dense layer of the model outputs normalized probability scores; we use log() to convert them to unnormalized logits before dividing them by the temperature.

```
export function sample(probs, temperature) {
  return tf.tidy(() => {
    const logPreds = tf.div(
      tf.log(probs),
      Math.max(temperature, 1e-6));
    const isNormalized = false;
    return tf.multinomial(logPreds, 1, null, isNormalized).dataSync()[0];
  });
}
```

We protect against division-by-zero errors with a small positive number. The result of the division is logits with adjusted uncertainty.

tf.multinomial() is a stochastic sampling function. It's like a multisided die with unequal per-side probabilities as determined by logPreds—the temperature-scaled logits.

The most important part of the sample() function in listing 10.2 is the following line:

```
const logPreds = tf.div(tf.log(probs),
                        Math.max(temperature, 1e-6));
```

It takes the probs (the probability outputs from the model) and converts them into logPreds, the logarithms of the probabilities scaled by a factor. What do the logarithm operation (tf.log()) and the scaling (tf.div()) do? We'll explain that through an example. For the sake of simplicity, let's assume there are only three choices (three characters in our character set). Suppose our next-character predictor yields the following three probability scores given a certain input sequence:

```
[0.1, 0.7, 0.2]
```

Let's see how two different temperature values alter these probabilities. First, let's look at a relatively lower temperature: 0.25. The scaled logits are

```
log([0.1, 0.7, 0.2]) / 0.25 = [-9.2103, -1.4267, -6.4378]
```

To understand what the logits mean, we convert them back to actual probability scores by using the softmax equation, which involves taking the exponential of the logits and normalizing them:

```
exp([-9.2103, -1.4267, -6.4378]) / sum(exp([-9.2103, -1.4267, -6.4378]))
= [0.0004, 0.9930, 0.0066]
```

As you can see, our logits from temperature = 0.25 correspond to a highly concentrated probability distribution in which the second choice has a much higher probability compared to the other two choices (see the second panel in figure 10.3).

What if we use a higher temperature, say 0.75? By repeating the same calculation, we get

```
log([0.1, 0.7, 0.2]) / 0.75 = [-3.0701, -0.4756, -2.1459]
exp([-3.0701, -0.4756, -2.1459]) / sum([-3.0701, -0.4756, -2.1459])
= [0.0591, 0.7919 0.1490]
```

This is a much less "peaked" distribution compared to the one from before, when the temperature was 0.25 (see the fourth panel in figure 10.3). But it is still more peaked compared to the original distribution. As you might have realized, a temperature of 1 will give you exactly the original probabilities (figure 10.3, fifth panel). A temperature higher than 1 leads to a more "equalized" probability distribution among the choices (figure 10.3, sixth panel), while the ranking among the choices always remains the same.

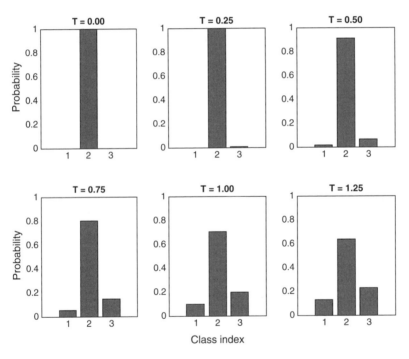

Figure 10.3   The probability scores after scaling by different values of temperature (T). A lower value of T leads to a more concentrated (less stochastic) distribution; a higher value of T causes the distribution to be more equal among the classes (more stochastic). A T-value of 1 corresponds to the original probabilities (no change). Note that the relative ranking of the three choices is always preserved regardless of the value of T.

These converted probabilities (or rather, the logarithms of them) are then fed to the `tf.multinomial()` function, which acts like a multifaced die, with unequal probabilities of the faces controlled by the input argument. This gives us the final choice of the next character.

So, this is how the temperature parameter controls the randomness of the generated text. The term *temperature* has its origin in thermodynamics, from which we know that a system with a higher temperature has a higher degree of chaos inside it. The analogy is appropriate here because when we increase the temperature value in our code, we get more chaotic-looking text. There is a "sweet medium" for the temperature value. Below it, the generated text looks too repetitive and mechanical; above it, the text looks too unpredictable and wacky.

This concludes our tour of the text-generating LSTM. Note that this methodology is very general and is applicable to many other sequences with proper modifications. For instance, if trained on a sufficiently large dataset of musical scores, an LSTM can be used to compose music by iteratively predicting the next musical note from the ones that come before it.[9]

10.2 Variational autoencoders: Finding an efficient and structured vector representation of images

The previous section gave you a quick tour of how deep learning can be used to generate sequential data such as text. In the remaining parts of this chapter, we will look at how to build neural networks to generate images. We will examine two types of models: variational autoencoder (VAE) and generative adversarial network (GAN). Compared to a GAN, the VAE has a longer history and is structurally simpler. So, it forms a good on-ramp for you to get into the fast-moving world of deep-learning-based image generation.

10.2.1 Classical autoencoder and VAE: Basic ideas

Figure 10.4 shows the overall architecture of an autoencoder schematically. At first glance, an autoencoder is a funny model because its input and output models are images of the same size. At the most basic level, the loss function of an autoencoder is the MSE between the input and output. This means that, if trained properly, an autoencoder will take an image and output an essentially identical image. What on earth would a model like that be useful for?

In fact, autoencoders are an important type of generative model and are far from useless. The answer to the prior question lies in the hourglass-shaped architecture (figure 10.4). The thinnest, middle part of an autoencoder is a vector with a much smaller number of elements compared to the input and output images. Hence, the image-to-image transformation performed by an autoencoder is nontrivial: it first

---

[9] Allen Huang and Raymond Wu, "Deep Learning for Music," submitted 15 June 2016, https://arxiv.org/abs/1606.04930.

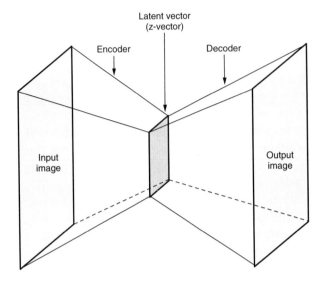

Figure 10.4   The architecture of a classical autoencoder

turns the input image into a highly compressed representation and then reconstructs the image from that representation without using any additional information. The efficient representation at the middle is referred to as the *latent vector*, or the *z-vector*. We will use these two terms interchangeably. The vector space in which these vectors reside is called the *latent space*, or the *z-space*. The part of the autoencoder that converts the input image to the latent vector can be called the *encoder*; the later part that converts the latent vector back to an image is called the *decoder*.

The latent vector can be hundreds of times smaller compared to the image itself, as we'll show through a concrete example shortly. Therefore, the encoder portion of a trained autoencoder is a remarkably efficient dimensionality reducer. Its summarization of the input image is highly succinct yet contains enough essential information to allow the decoder to reproduce the input image faithfully without using any extra bits of information. The fact that the decoder can do that is also remarkable.

We can also look at an autoencoder from an information-theory point of view. Let's say the input and output images each contain N bits of information. Naively, N is the number of pixels multiplied by the bit depth of each pixel. By contrast, the latent vector in the middle of the autoencoder can hold only a very small amount of information because of its small size (say, m bits). If m were smaller than N, it would be theoretically impossible to reconstruct the image from the latent vector. However, pixels in images are not completely random (an image made of completely random pixels looks like static noise). Instead, the pixels follow certain patterns, such as color continuity and characteristics of the type of real-world objects being depicted. This causes the value of N to be much smaller than the naive calculation based on the number and depth of the pixels. It is the autoencoder's job to learn this pattern; this is also the reason why autoencoders can work.

After an autoencoder is trained, its decoder part can be used without the encoder. Given any latent vector, it can generate an image that conforms to the patterns and styles of the training images. This fits the description of a generative model nicely. Furthermore, the latent space will hopefully contain some nice, interpretable structure. In particular, each dimension of the latent space may be associated with a meaningful aspect of the image. For instance, suppose we've trained an autoencoder on images of human faces; perhaps one of the latent space's dimensions will be associated with the degree of smiling. When you fix the values in all other dimensions of a latent vector and vary only the value on the "smile dimension," the images produced by the decoder will be exactly the same face but with varying degrees of smiling (see, for example, figure 10.5). This will enable interesting applications, such as changing the degree of smiling of an input face image while leaving all other aspects unchanged. This can be done through the following steps. First, obtain the latent vector of the input by applying the encoder. Then, modify only the "smile dimension" of the vector; finally, run the modified latent vector through the decoder.

Figure 10.5   The "smile dimension." An example of desired structure in latent spaces learned by autoencoders.

Unfortunately, *classical autoencoders* of the architecture shown in figure 10.4 don't lead to particularly useful or nicely structured latent spaces. They are not very good at compression, either. For these reasons, they largely fell out of fashion by 2013. VAEs—discovered almost simultaneously by Diederik Kingma and Max Welling in December 2013[10] and Danilo Rezende, Shakir Mohamed, and Daan Wiestra in January 2014[11]—augment autoencoders with a little bit of statistical magic, which forces the models to learn continuous and highly structured latent spaces. VAEs have turned out to be a powerful type of generative image model.

A VAE, instead of compressing its input image into a fixed vector in the latent space, turns the image into the parameters of a statistical distribution—specifically, those of a *Gaussian distribution*. As you may recall from high school math, a Gaussian distribution has two parameters: the mean and the variance (or, equivalently, the standard deviation). A VAE maps every input image into a mean. The only additional com-

[10] Diederik P. Kingma and Max Welling, "Auto-Encoding Variational Bayes," submitted 20 Dec. 2013, https://arxiv.org/abs/1312.6114.

[11] Danilo Jimenez Rezende, Shakir Mohamed, and Daan Wierstra, "Stochastic Backpropagation and Approximate Inference in Deep Generative Models," submitted 16 Jan. 2014, https://arxiv.org/abs/1401.4082.

plexity is that the mean and the variance can be higher than one-dimensional if the latent space is more than 1D, as we'll see in the following example. Essentially, we are assuming that the images are generated via a stochastic process and that the randomness of this process should be taken into account during encoding and decoding. The VAE then uses the mean and variance parameters to randomly sample one vector from the distribution and decode that element back to the size of the original input (see figure 10.6). This stochasticity is one of the key ways in which VAE improves robustness and forces the latent space to encode meaningful representations everywhere: every point sampled in the latent space should be a valid image output when decoded by the decoder.

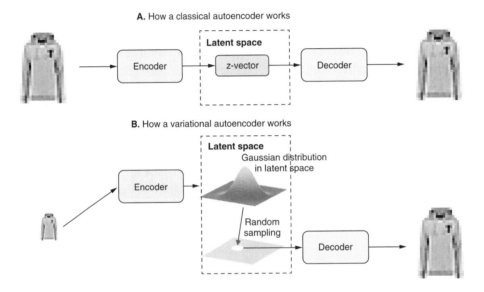

Figure 10.6   Comparing how a classical autoencoder (panel A) and a VAE (panel B) work. A classical autoencoder maps an input image to a fixed latent vector and performs decoding using that vector. By contrast, a VAE maps an input image to a distribution, described by a mean and a variance, draws a random latent vector from this distribution, and generates the decoded image using that random vector. The T-shirt image is an example from the Fashion-MNIST dataset.

Next, we will show you a VAE in action by using the Fashion-MNIST dataset. As its name indicates, Fashion-MNIST[12] is inspired by the MNIST hand-written digit dataset, but contains images of clothing and fashion items. Like the MNIST images, the Fashion-MNIST images are 28 × 28 grayscale images. There are exactly 10 classes of clothing and fashion items (such as T-shirt, pullover, shoe, and bag; see figure 10.6 for an example). However, the Fashion-MNIST dataset is slightly "harder" for machine-learning

---

[12] Han Xiao, Kashif Rasul, and Roland Vollgraf, "Fashion-MNIST: A Novel Image Dataset for Benchmarking Machine Learning Algorithms," submitted 25 Aug. 2017, https://arxiv.org/abs/1708.07747.

algorithms compared to the MNIST dataset, with the current state-of-the-art test-set accuracy standing at approximately 96.5%, much lower compared to the 99.75% state-of-the-art accuracy on the MNIST dataset.[13] We will use TensorFlow.js to build a VAE and train it on the Fashion-MNIST dataset. We'll then use the decoder of the VAE to sample from the 2D latent space and observe the structure inside that space.

10.2.2 A detailed example of VAE: The Fashion-MNIST example

To check out the fashion-mnist-vae example, use the following commands:

```
git clone https://github.com/tensorflow/tfjs-examples.git
cd tfjs-examples/fashion-mnist-vae
yarn
yarn download-data
```

This example consists of two parts: training the VAE in Node.js and using the VAE decoder to generate images in the browser. To start the training part, use

```
yarn train
```

If you have a CUDA-enabled GPU set up properly, you can use the `--gpu` flag to get a boost in the training speed:

```
yarn train --gpu
```

The training should take about five minutes on a reasonably update-to-date desktop equipped with a CUDA GPU, and under an hour without the GPU. Once the training is complete, use the following command to build and launch the browser frontend:

```
yarn watch
```

The frontend will load the VAE's decoder, generate a number of images by using a 2D grid of regularly spaced latent vectors, and display the images on the page. This will give you an appreciation of the structure of the latent space.

In technical terms, here is a how a VAE works:

1 The encoder turns the input samples into two parameters in a latent space: zMean and zLogVar, the mean and the logarithm of the variance (log variance), respectively. Each of the two vectors has the same length as the dimensionality of the latent space.[14] For example, our latent space will be 2D, so zMean and zLogVar will each be a length-2 vector. Why do we use log variance (zLogVar) instead of the variance itself? Because variances are by definition required to be nonnegative, but there is no easy way to enforce that sign requirement on a layer's output. By contrast, log variance is allowed to have any sign. By using the logarithm, we don't have to worry about the sign of the layers' outputs. Log

---

[13] Source: "State-of-the-Art Result for All Machine Learning Problems," GitHub, 2019, http://mng.bz/6w0o.

[14] Strictly speaking, the covariance matrix of the length-N latent vector is an $N \times N$ matrix. However, zLogVar is a length-N vector because we constrain the covariance matrix to be diagonal—that is, there is no correlation between two different elements of the latent vector.

variance can be easily converted to the corresponding variance through a simple exponentiation (`tf.exp()`) operation.

2   The VAE algorithm randomly samples a latent vector from the latent normal distribution by using a vector called `epsilon`—a random vector of the same length as `zMean` and `zLogVar`. In simple math equations, this step, which is referred to as *reparameterization* in the literature, looks like

```
z = zMean + exp(zLogVar * 0.5) * epsilon
```

The multiplication by 0.5 converts the variance to the standard deviation, which is based on the fact that the standard deviation is the square root of the variance. The equivalent JavaScript code is

```
z = zMean.add(zLogVar.mul(0.5).exp().mul(epsilon));
```

(See listing 10.3.) Then, z will be fed to the decoder portion of the VAE so that an output image can be generated.

In our implementation of VAE, the latent-vector-sampling step is performed by a custom layer called `ZLayer` (listing 10.3). We briefly saw a custom TensorFlow.js layer in chapter 9 (the `GetLastTimestepLayer` layer that we used in the attention-based date converter). The custom layer used by our VAE is slightly more complex and deserves some explanation.

The `ZLayer` class has two key methods: `computeOutputShape()` and `call()`. `computeOutputShape()` are used by TensorFlow.js to infer the output shape of the `Layer` instance given the shape(s) of the input. The `call()` method contains the actual math. It contains the equation line introduced previously. The following code is excerpted from fashion-mnist-vae/model.js.

> **Listing 10.3 Sampling from the latent space (z-space) with a custom layer**

```
class ZLayer extends tf.layers.Layer {
  constructor(config) {
    super(config);
  }

  computeOutputShape(inputShape) {
    tf.util.assert(inputShape.length === 2 && Array.isArray(inputShape[0]),
        () => `Expected exactly 2 input shapes. ` +          ◁─────  Checks to make sure that
            `But got: ${inputShape}`);                                 we have exactly two inputs:
    return inputShape[0];          ◁──────────────────┐               zMean and zLogVar
  }

  call(inputs, kwargs) {
    const [zMean, zLogVar] = inputs;          The shape of the output (z) will be
    const batch = zMean.shape[0];             the same as the shape of zMean.
    const dim = zMean.shape[1];

    const mean = 0;
    const std = 1.0;
    const epsilon = tf.randomNormal(          Gets a random batch of epsilon from
        [batch, dim], mean, std);             the unit Gaussian distribution
```

```
    return zMean.add(
        zLogVar.mul(0.5).exp().mul(epsilon));
    }

    static get ClassName() {
        return 'ZLayer';
    }
}
tf.serialization.registerClass(ZLayer);
```

This is where the sampling of z-vectors happens: zMean + standardDeviation * epsilon.

The static className property is set in case the layer is to be serialized.

Registers the class to support deserialization

As listing 10.4 shows, ZLayer is instantiated and gets used as a part of the encoder. The encoder is written as a functional model, instead of the simpler sequential model, because it has a nonlinear internal structure and produces three outputs: zMean, zLogVar, and z (see the schematic in figure 10.7). The encoder outputs z because it will get used by the decoder, but why does the encoder include zMean and zLogVar in the outputs? It's because they will be used to calculate the loss function of the VAE, as you will see shortly.

In addition to ZLayer, the encoder consists of two one-hidden-layer MLPs. They are used to convert the flattened input Fashion-MNIST images into the zMean and zLog-Var vectors, respectively. The two MLPs share the same hidden layer but use separate output layers. This branching model topology is also made possible by the fact that the encoder is a functional model.

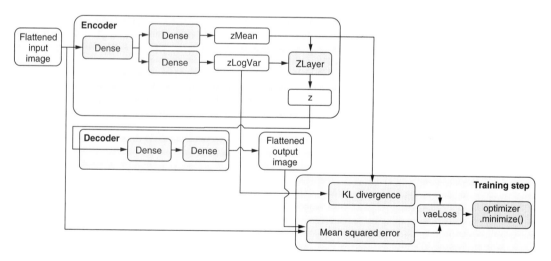

Figure 10.7 Schematic illustration of the TensorFlow.js implementation of VAE, including the internal details of the encoder and decoder parts and the custom loss function and optimizer that support VAE training.

Listing 10.4   The encoder part of our VAE (excerpt from fashion-mnist-vae/model.js)

```
function encoder(opts) {
  const {originalDim, intermediateDim, latentDim} = opts;

  const inputs = tf.input({shape: [originalDim], name: 'encoder_input'});
  const x = tf.layers.dense({units: intermediateDim, activation: 'relu'})
      .apply(inputs);
  const zMean = tf.layers.dense({units: latentDim, name: 'z_mean'}).apply(x);
  const zLogVar = tf.layers.dense({
      units: latentDim,
      name: 'z_log_var'
    }).apply(x);
  const z =
      new ZLayer({name: 'z', outputShape: [latentDim]}).apply([zMean,
    zLogVar]);

  const enc = tf.model({
    inputs: inputs,
    outputs: [zMean, zLogVar, z],
    name: 'encoder',
  })
  return enc;
}
```

Instantiates our custom ZLayer and uses it to draw random samples that follow the distribution specified by zMean and zLogVar

Unlike a normal MLP, we put two layers downstream from the hidden dense layer to predict zMean and zLogVar, respectively. This is also the reason why we use a functional model instead of the simpler sequential model type.

At the base of the encoder is a simple MLP with one hidden layer.

The code in listing 10.5 builds the decoder. Compared to the encoder, the decoder has a simpler topology. It uses an MLP to convert the input z-vector (that is, the latent vector) into an image of the same shape as the encoder's input. Note that the way in which our VAE handles images is somewhat simplistic and unusual in that it flattens the images into 1D vectors and hence discards the spatial information. Image-oriented VAEs typically use convolutional and pooling layers, but due to the simplicity of our images (their small size and the fact that there is only one color channel), the flattening approach works well enough for the purpose of this example.

Listing 10.5   The decoder part of our VAE (excerpt from fashion-mnist-vae/model.js)

```
function decoder(opts) {
  const {originalDim, intermediateDim, latentDim} = opts;

  const dec = tf.sequential({name: 'decoder'});
  dec.add(tf.layers.dense({
    units: intermediateDim,
    activation: 'relu',
    inputShape: [latentDim]
  }));
  dec.add(tf.layers.dense({
    units: originalDim,
    activation: 'sigmoid'
  }));
  return dec;
}
```

The decoder is a simple MLP that converts a latent (z) vector into a (flattened) image.

Sigmoid activation is a good choice for the output layer because it makes sure that the pixel values of the output image are bounded between 0 and 1.

To combine the encoder and decoder into a single `tf.LayerModel` object that is the VAE, the code in listing 10.6 extracts the third output (z-vector) of the encoder and runs it through the decoder. Then the combined model exposes the decoded image as its output, along with three additional outputs: the `zMean`, `zLogVar`, and z-vectors. This completes the definition of the VAE model's topology. In order to train the model, we need two more things: the loss function and an optimizer. The code in the following listing was excerpted from fashion-mnist-vae/model.js.

Listing 10.6   Putting the encoder and decoder together into the VAE

```
function vae(encoder, decoder) {
  const inputs = encoder.inputs;
  const encoderOutputs = encoder.apply(inputs);
  const encoded = encoderOutputs[2];
  const decoderOutput = decoder.apply(encoded);
  const v = tf.model({
    inputs: inputs,
    outputs: [decoderOutput, ...encoderOutputs],
    name: 'vae_mlp',
  })
  return v;
}
```

The input to the VAE is the same as the input to the encoder: the original input image.

Of all three outputs of the encoder, only the last one (z) goes into the decoder.

The output of the VAE model object includes the decoded image in addition to zMean, zLogVar, and z.

We use the functional model API due to the model's nonlinear topology.

When we were visiting the simple-object-detection model in chapter 5, we described the way in which custom loss functions can be defined in TensorFlow.js. Here, a custom loss function is needed to train the VAE. This is because the loss function will be the sum of two terms: one that quantifies the discrepancy between the input and output and one that quantifies the statistical properties of the latent space. This is reminiscent of the simple-object-detection model's custom loss function, which was a sum of a term for object classification and another for object localization.

As you can see from the code in listing 10.7 (excerpted from fashion-mnist-vae/model.js), defining the input-output discrepancy term is straightforward. We simply calculate the MSE between the original input and the decoder's output. However, the statistical term, called the *Kullbach-Liebler* (KL) divergence, is more mathematically involved. We will spare you the detailed math,[15] but on an intuitive level, the KL divergence term (`klLoss` in the code) encourages the distributions for different input images to be more evenly distributed around the center of the latent space, which makes it easier for the decoder to interpolate between the images. Therefore, the `klLoss` term can be thought of as a regularization term added on top of the main input-output discrepancy term of the VAE.

---

[15] This blog post by Irhum Shafkat includes a deeper discussion of the math behind the KL divergence: http://mng.bz/vlvr.

Listing 10.7   The loss function for the VAE

```
function vaeLoss(inputs, outputs) {
  const originalDim = inputs.shape[1];
  const decoderOutput = outputs[0];
  const zMean = outputs[1];
  const zLogVar = outputs[2];

  const reconstructionLoss =
      tf.losses.meanSquaredError(inputs, decoderOutput).mul(originalDim);

  let klLoss = zLogVar.add(1).sub(zMean.square()).sub(zLogVar.exp());
  klLoss = klLoss.sum(-1).mul(-0.5);
  return reconstructionLoss.add(klLoss).mean();
}
```

Computes a "reconstruction loss" term. The goal of minimizing this term is to make the model outputs match the input data.

Sums the image reconstruction loss and the KL-divergence loss into the final VAE loss

Computes the KL-divergence between zLogVar and zMean. Minimizing this term aims to make the distribution of the latent variable more normally distributed around the center of the latent space.

Another missing piece for our VAE training is the optimizer and the training step that uses it. The type of optimizer is the popular ADAM optimizer (`tf.train .adam()`). The training step for the VAE differs from all other models we've seen in this book in that it doesn't use the `fit()` or `fitDataset()` method of the model object. Instead, it calls the `minimize()` method of the optimizer (listing 10.8). This is because the KL-divergence term of the custom loss function uses two of the model's four outputs, but in TensorFlow.js, the `fit()` and `fitDataset()` methods work only if each of the model's outputs has a loss function that doesn't depend on any other output.

As listing 10.8 shows, the `minimize()` function is called with an arrow function as the only argument. This arrow function returns the loss under the current batch of flattened images (`reshaped` in the code), which is closed over by the function. `minimize()` calculates the gradient of the loss with respect to all the trainable weights of the VAE (including the encoder and decoder), adjusts them according to the ADAM algorithm, and then applies updates to the weights in directions opposite to the adjusted gradients. This completes a single step of training. This step is performed repeatedly, over all images in the Fashion-MNIST dataset, and constitutes an epoch of training. The `yarn train` command performs multiple epochs of training (default: 5 epochs), after which the loss value converges, and the decoder part of the VAE is saved to disk. The reason the encoder part isn't saved is that it won't be used in the following, browser-based demo step.

Listing 10.8   The training loop of the VAE (excerpt from fashion-mnist-vae/train.js)

```
for (let i = 0; i < epochs; i++) {
  console.log(`\nEpoch #${i} of ${epochs}\n`)
  for (let j = 0; j < batches.length; j++) {
    const currentBatchSize = batches[j].length
    const batchedImages = batchImages(batches[j]);
```

Gets a batch of (flattened) Fashion-MNIST images

```
const reshaped =
    batchedImages.reshape([currentBatchSize, vaeOpts.originalDim]);

optimizer.minimize(() => {
  const outputs = vaeModel.apply(reshaped);
  const loss = vaeLoss(reshaped, outputs, vaeOpts);
  process.stdout.write('.');
  if (j % 50 === 0) {
    console.log('\nLoss:', loss.dataSync()[0]);
  }
  return loss;
});
tf.dispose([batchedImages, reshaped]);
}
console.log('');
await generate(decoderModel, vaeOpts.latentDim);
}
```

A single step of VAE training: makes a prediction with the VAE and computes the loss so that optimizer.minimize can adjust all the trainable weights of the model

Since we are not using the stock fit() method, we cannot use the built-in progress bar and hence must print status updates to the console ourselves.

At the end of every training epoch, generates an image using the decoder and prints it to the console for preview

The web page brought up by the yarn watch command will load the saved decoder and use it to generate a grid of images similar to what's shown in figure 10.8. These images are obtained from a regular grid of latent vectors in the 2D latent space. The upper and lower limit along each of the two latent dimensions can be adjusted in the UI.

The grid of images shows a completely continuous distribution of different types of clothing from the Fashion-MNIST dataset, with one clothing type morphing gradually into another type as you follow a continuous path through the latent space (for example, pullover to T-shirt, T-shirt to pants, boots to shoes). Specific directions in the latent space have a meaning inside a subdomain of the latent space. For example, near the top section of the latent space, the horizontal dimension appears to represent

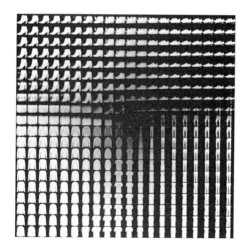

Figure 10.8 Sampling the latent space of the VAE after training. This figure shows a 20 × 20 grid of decoder outputs. This grid corresponds to a regularly spaced grid of 20 × 20 2D latent vectors, of which each dimension is in the interval of [–4, 4].

"bootness versus shoeness;" around the bottom-right corner of the latent space, the horizontal dimension seems to represent "T-shirtness versus pantsness," and so forth.

In the next section, we will cover another major type of model for generating images: GANs.

10.3   *Image generation with GANs*

Since Ian Goodfellow and his colleagues introduced GANs in 2014,[16] the technique has seen rapid growth in interest and sophistication. Today, GANs have become a powerful tool for generating images and other modalities of data. They are capable of outputting high-resolution images that in some cases are indistinguishable from real ones to human eyes. See the human face images generated by NVIDIA's StyleGANs in figure 10.9.[17] If not for the occasional artifact spots on the face and the unnatural-looking scenes in the background, it would be virtually impossible for a human viewer to tell these generated images apart from real ones.

Figure 10.9   Example human-face images generated by NVIDIA's StyleGAN, sampled from https://thispersondoesnotexist.com in April 2019

Apart from generating compelling images "out of the blue," the images generated by GANs can be conditioned on certain input data or parameters, which leads to a variety of more task-specific and useful applications. For example, GANs can be used to generate a higher-resolution image from a low-resolution input (image super-resolution), fill in missing parts of an image (image inpainting), convert a black-and-white image into a color one (image colorization), generate an image given a text description, and generate the image of a person in a given pose given an input image of the same person in another pose. In addition, new types of GANs have been developed to generate nonimage outputs, such as music.[18] Apart from the obvious value of generating an unlimited amount of realistic-looking material, which is desired in domains such as

---

[16] Ian Goodfellow et al., "Generative Adversarial Nets," *NIPS Proceedings*, 2014, http://mng.bz/4ePv.

[17] Website at https://thispersondoesnotexist.com. For the academic paper, see Tero Karras, Samuli Laine, and Timo Aila, "A Style-Based Generator Architecture for Generative Adversarial Networks," submitted 12 Dec. 2018, https://arxiv.org/abs/1812.04948.

[18] See the MuseGAN project from Hao-Wen Dong et al.: https://salu133445.github.io/musegan/.

art, music production, and game design, GANs have other applications, such as assisting deep learning by generating training examples in cases where such examples are costly to acquire. For instance, GANs are being used to generate realistic-looking street scenes for training self-driving neural networks.[19]

Although VAEs and GANs are both generative models, they are based on different ideas. While VAEs ensure the quality of generated examples by using an MSE loss between the original input and the decoder output, a GAN makes sure its outputs are realistic by employing a *discriminator*, as we'll soon explain. In addition, many variants of GANs allow inputs to consist of not only the latent-space vector but also conditioning inputs, such as a desired image class. The ACGAN we'll explore next is a good example of this. In this type of GAN with mixed inputs, latent spaces are no longer even continuous with respect to the network inputs.

In this section, we will dive into a relatively simple type of GAN. Specifically, we will train an *auxiliary classifier* GAN (ACGAN)[20] on the familiar MNIST hand-written digit dataset. This will give us a model capable of generating digit images that look just like the real MNIST digits. At the same time, we will be able to control what digit class (0 through 9) each generated image belongs to, thanks to the "auxiliary classifier" part of ACGAN. In order to understand how ACGAN works, let's do it one step at a time. First, we will explain how the base "GAN" part of ACGAN works. Then, we will describe the additional mechanisms by which ACGAN makes the class identity controllable.

10.3.1 *The basic idea behind GANs*

How does a GAN learn to generate realistic-looking images? It achieves this through an interplay between two subparts that it comprises: a *generator* and a *discriminator*. Think of the generator as a counterfeiter whose goal is to create high-quality fake Picasso paintings; the discriminator is like an art dealer whose job is to tell fake Picasso paintings apart from real ones. The counterfeiter (generator) strives to create better and better fake paintings in order to fool the art dealer (the discriminator), while the art dealer's job is to become a better and better critiquer of the paintings so as *not* to be fooled by the counterfeiter. This antagonism between our two players is the reason behind the "adversarial" part of the name "GAN." Intriguingly, the counterfeiter and art dealer end up *helping* each other become better, despite apparently being adversaries.

In the beginning, the counterfeiter (generator) is bad at creating realistic-looking Picassos because its weights are initialized randomly. As a result, the art dealer (discriminator) quickly learns to tell real and fake Picassos apart. Here is an important part of how all of this works: every time the counterfeiter brings a new painting to the

---

[19] James Vincent, "Nvidia Uses AI to Make it Snow on Streets that Are Always Sunny," *The Verge*, 5 Dec. 2017, http://mng.bz/Q0oQ.

[20] Augustus Odena, Christopher Olah, and Jonathon Shlens, "Conditional Image Synthesis with Auxiliary Classifier GANs," submitted 30 Oct. 2016, https://arxiv.org/abs/1610.09585.

art dealer, they are provided with detailed feedback (from the art dealer) about which parts of the painting look wrong and how to change the painting to make it look more real. The counterfeiter learns and remembers this so that next time they come to the art dealer, their painting will look slightly better. This process repeats many times. It turns out, if all the parameters are set properly, we will end up with a skillful counterfeiter (generator). Of course, we will also get a skillful discriminator (art dealer), but we usually need only the generator after the GAN is trained.

Figure 10.10 provides a more detailed look at how the discriminator part of a generic GAN model is trained. In order to train the discriminator, we need a batch of generated images and a batch of real ones. The generated ones are generated by the generator. But the generator can't make images out of thin air. Instead, it needs to be given a random vector as the input. The latent vectors are conceptually similar to the ones we used for VAEs in section 10.2. For each image generated by the generator, the latent vector is a 1D tensor of shape [latentSize]. But like most training procedures in this book, we perform the step for a batch of images at a time. Therefore, the latent vector has a shape of [batchSize, latentSize]. The real images are directly drawn from the actual MNIST dataset. For symmetry, we draw batchSize real images (exactly the same number as the generated ones) for each step of training.

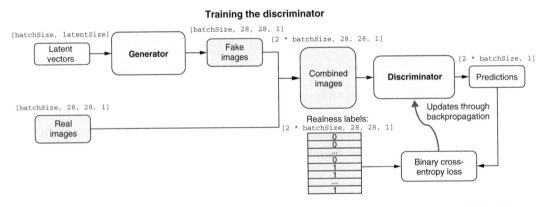

Figure 10.10   A schematic diagram illustrating the algorithm by which the discriminator part of a GAN is trained. Notice that this diagram omits the digit-class part of the ACGAN for the sake of simplicity. For a complete diagram of generator training in ACGAN, see figure 10.13.

The generated images and real ones are then concatenated into a single batch of images, represented as a tensor of shape [2 * batchSize, 28, 28, 1]. The discriminator is executed on this batch of combined images, which outputs predicted probability scores for whether each image is real. These probability scores can be easily tested against the ground truth (we know which ones are real and which ones are generated!) through the binary cross-entropy loss function. Then, the familiar backpropagation algorithm does its job, updating the weight parameters of the discriminator with the help of an optimizer (not shown in the figure). This step nudges the discriminator a bit toward making correct predictions. Notice that the generator merely participates in this training step by providing generated samples, but it's not updated by the backpropagation process. It is the next training step that updates the generator (figure 10.11).

Training the generator

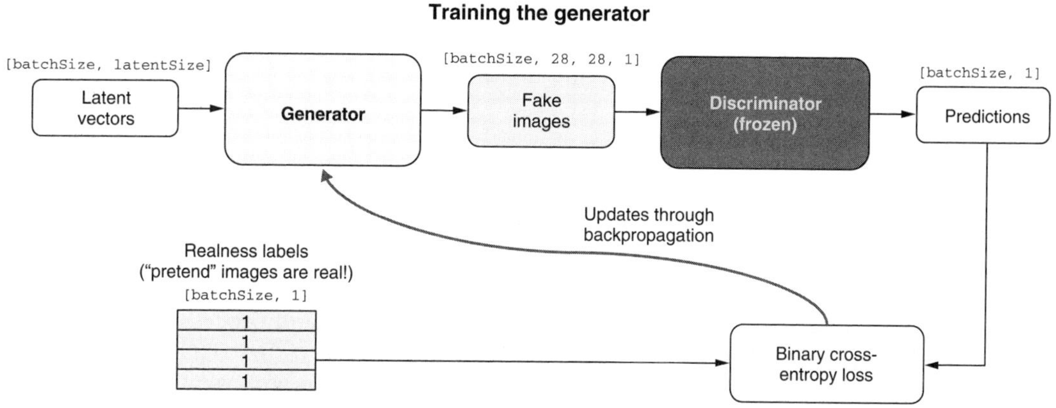

Figure 10.11 A schematic diagram illustrating the algorithm by which the generator part of a GAN is trained. Notice that this diagram omits the digit-class part of the ACGAN for the sake of simplicity. For a complete diagram of ACGAN's generator-training process, see figure 10.14.

Figure 10.11 illustrates the generator-training step. We let the generator make another batch of generated images. But unlike the discriminator-training step, we don't need any real MNIST images. The discriminator is given this batch of generated images along with a batch of binary realness labels. We *pretend* that the generated images are real by setting the realness labels to all 1s. Pause for a moment and let that sink in: this is the most important trick in GAN training. Of course the images are all generated (not real), but we let the realness label say they are real anyway. The discriminator may (correctly) assign low realness probabilities to some or all of the input images. But if it does so, the binary cross-entropy loss will end up with a large value, thanks to the bogus realness labels. This will cause the backpropagation to update the generator in a way that nudges the discriminator's realness scores a little higher. Note that the backpropagation updates *only* the generator. It leaves the discriminator untouched. This is another important trick: it ensures that the generator ends up making slightly more realistic-looking images, instead of the discriminator lowering its bar for what's real. This is achieved by freezing the discriminator part of the model, an operation we've used for transfer learning in chapter 5.

To summarize the generator-training step: we freeze the discriminator and feed an all-1 realness label to it, despite the fact that it is given generated images generated by the generator. As a result, the weight updates to the generator will cause it to generate images that look slightly more real to the discriminator. This way of training the generator will work only if the discriminator is reasonably good at telling what's real and what's generated. How do we ensure that? The answer is the discriminator-training step we already talked about. Therefore, you can see that the two training steps form an intricate yin-and-yang dynamic, in which the two parts of the GAN counter and help each other at the same time.

That concludes our high-level overview of generic GAN training. In the next section, we will look at the internal architecture of the discriminator and generator and how they incorporate the information about image class.

10.3.2 *The building blocks of ACGAN*

Listing 10.9 shows the TensorFlow.js code that creates the discriminator part of the MNIST ACGAN (excerpted from mnist-acgan/gan.js). At the core of the discriminator is a deep convnet similar to the ones we saw in chapter 4. Its input has the canonical shape of MNIST images, namely [28, 28, 1]. The input image passes through four 2D convolutional (conv2d) layers before being flattened and processed by two dense layers. One dense layer outputs a binary prediction for the realness of the input image, while the other outputs the softmax probabilities for the 10 digit classes. The discriminator is a functional model that has both dense layers' outputs. Panel A of figure 10.12 provides a schematic view of the discriminator's one-input-two-output topology.

Listing 10.9   Creating the discriminator part of ACGAN

```
function buildDiscriminator() {
  const cnn = tf.sequential();

  cnn.add(tf.layers.conv2d({
    filters: 32,
    kernelSize: 3,
    padding: 'same',
    strides: 2,
    inputShape: [IMAGE_SIZE, IMAGE_SIZE, 1]     ◁——  The discriminator takes only one
  }));                                                input: images in the MNIST format.
  cnn.add(tf.layers.leakyReLU({alpha: 0.2}));
  cnn.add(tf.layers.dropout({rate: 0.3}));      ◁——  Dropout layers are used to
                                                      counteract overfitting.
  cnn.add(tf.layers.conv2d(
      {filters: 64, kernelSize: 3, padding: 'same', strides: 1}));
  cnn.add(tf.layers.leakyReLU({alpha: 0.2}));
  cnn.add(tf.layers.dropout({rate: 0.3}));

  cnn.add(tf.layers.conv2d(
      {filters: 128, kernelSize: 3, padding: 'same', strides: 2}));
  cnn.add(tf.layers.leakyReLU({alpha: 0.2}));
  cnn.add(tf.layers.dropout({rate: 0.3}));

  cnn.add(tf.layers.conv2d(
      {filters: 256, kernelSize: 3, padding: 'same', strides: 1}));
  cnn.add(tf.layers.leakyReLU({alpha: 0.2}));
```

```
cnn.add(tf.layers.dropout({rate: 0.3}));

cnn.add(tf.layers.flatten());

const image = tf.input({shape: [IMAGE_SIZE, IMAGE_SIZE, 1]});
const features = cnn.apply(image);

const realnessScore =
    tf.layers.dense({units: 1, activation: 'sigmoid'}).apply(features);
const aux = tf.layers.dense({units: NUM_CLASSES, activation: 'softmax'})
                .apply(features);

return tf.model({inputs: image, outputs: [realnessScore, aux]});
}
```

The first of the discriminator's two outputs: the probability score from the binary realness classification

The second output is the softmax probabilities for the 10 MNIST digit classes.

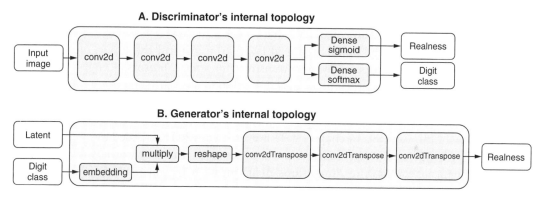

Figure 10.12 Schematic diagrams of the internal topology of the discriminator (panel A) and generator (panel B) parts of ACGAN. Certain details (the dropout layers in the discriminator) are omitted for simplicity. See listings 10.9 and 10.10 for the detailed code.

The code in listing 10.10 is responsible for creating the ACGAN generator. As we've alluded to before, the generator's generation process requires an input called a *latent vector* (named `latent` in the code). This is reflected in the `inputShape` parameter of its first dense layer. However, if you examine the code more carefully, you can see that the generator actually takes *two* inputs. This is illustrated in panel B of figure 10.12. In addition to the latent vector, which is a 1D tensor of shape `[latentSize]`, the generator requires an additional input, which is named `imageClass` and has a simple shape of `[1]`. This is the way in which we tell the model which MNIST digit class (0 to 9) it is commanded to generate. For example, if we want the model to generate an image for digit 8, we should feed a tensor value of `tf.tensor2d([[8]])` to the second input (remember that the model always expects batched tensors, even if there is only one example). Likewise, if we want the model to generate two images, one for the digit 8 and one for 9, then the fed tensor should be `tensor2d([[8], [9]])`.

As soon as the `imageClass` input enters the generator, an embedding layer transforms it into a tensor of the same shape as `latent` (`[latentSize]`). This step is mathematically similar to the embedding-lookup procedure we used in the sentiment-analysis and date-conversion models in chapter 9. The desired digit class is an integer quantity analogous to the word indices in the sentiment-analysis data and the character indices in the date-conversion data. It is transformed into a 1D vector in the same way that word and character indices were transformed into 1D vectors. However, we use embedding lookup on `imageClass` here for a different purpose: to merge it with the `latent` vector and form a single, combined vector (named h in listing 10.10.) This merging is done through a `multiply` layer, which performs element-by-element multiplication between the two vectors of identical shapes. The resultant tensor has the same shape as the inputs (`[latentSize]`) and goes into later parts of the generator.

The generator immediately applies a dense layer on the combined latent vector (h) and reshapes it into a 3D shape of `[3, 3, 384]`. This reshaping yields an image-like tensor, which can then be transformed by the following parts of the generator into an image that has the canonical MNIST shape (`[28, 28, 1]`).

Instead of using the familiar conv2d layers to transform the input, the generator uses the conv2dTranspose layer to transform its image tensors. Roughly speaking, conv2dTranspose performs the inverse operation to conv2d (sometimes referred to as *deconvolution*). The output of a conv2d layer generally has smaller height and width compared to its input (except for the rare cases in which the `kernelSize` is 1), as you can see in the convnets in chapter 4. However, a conv2dTranspose layer generally has a larger height and weight in its output than its input. In other words, while a conv2d layer typically *shrinks* the dimensions of its input, a typical conv2dTranspose layer *expands* them. This is why, in the generator, the first conv2dTranspose layer takes an input with height 3 and width 3, but the last conv2dTranspose layer outputs height 28 and width 28. This is how the generator turns an input latent vector and a digit index into an image in the standard MNIST image dimensions. The code in the following listing is excerpted from mnist-acgan/gan.js; some error-checking code is removed for clarity.

Listing 10.10 Creating the generator part of ACGAN

```
function buildGenerator(latentSize) {
  const cnn = tf.sequential();

  cnn.add(tf.layers.dense({
    units: 3 * 3 * 384,
    inputShape: [latentSize],
    activation: 'relu'
  }));
  cnn.add(tf.layers.reshape({targetShape: [3, 3, 384]}));

  cnn.add(tf.layers.conv2dTranspose({
    filters: 192,
    kernelSize: 5,
```

The number of units is chosen so that when the output is reshaped and fed through the subsequent conv2dTranspose layers, the tensor that comes out at the end has the exact shape that matches MNIST images (`[28, 28, 1]`).

Upsamples from [3, 3, ...] to [7, 7, ...]

```
    strides: 1,
    padding: 'valid',
    activation: 'relu',
    kernelInitializer: 'glorotNormal'
}));
cnn.add(tf.layers.batchNormalization());

cnn.add(tf.layers.conv2dTranspose({        ◁─────── Upsamples to [14, 14, ...]
    filters: 96,
    kernelSize: 5,
    strides: 2,
    padding: 'same',
    activation: 'relu',
    kernelInitializer: 'glorotNormal'
}));
cnn.add(tf.layers.batchNormalization());

cnn.add(tf.layers.conv2dTranspose({        ◁─────── Upsamples to [28, 28, ...]
    filters: 1,
    kernelSize: 5,
    strides: 2,
    padding: 'same',
    activation: 'tanh',
    kernelInitializer: 'glorotNormal'
}));

const latent = tf.input({shape: [latentSize]});   ◁───

const imageClass = tf.input({shape: [1]});    ◁───

const classEmbedding = tf.layers.embedding({  ◁───
    inputDim: NUM_CLASSES,
    outputDim: latentSize,
    embeddingsInitializer: 'glorotNormal'
}).apply(imageClass);

const h = tf.layers.multiply().apply(
    [latent, classEmbedding]);

const fakeImage = cnn.apply(h);
return tf.model({
    inputs: [latent, imageClass],
    outputs: fakeImage
});
}
```

This is the first of the two inputs of the generator: the latent (z-space) vector that is used as the "seed" of the fake-image generation.

The second input of the generator: class labels that control which of the 10 MNIST digit classes the generated images should belong to

Converts the desired label to a vector of length latentSize through embedding lookup

Combines the latent vector and the class conditional embedding through multiplication

The model is finally created, with the sequential convnet as its core.

10.3.3 *Diving deeper into the training of ACGAN*

The last section should have given you a better understanding of the internal structure of ACGAN's discriminator and generator and how they incorporate the digit-class information (the "AC" part of ACGAN's name). With this knowledge, we are ready to expand on figures 10.10 and 10.11 in order to form a thorough understanding of how ACGAN is trained.

Figure 10.13 is an expanded version of figure 10.10. It shows the training of ACGAN's discriminator part. Compared to before, this training step not only improves the discriminator's ability to tell real and generated (fake) images apart but also hones its ability to determine which digit class a given image (including real and generated) belongs to. To make it easier to compare with the simpler diagram from before, we grayed out the parts already seen in figure 10.10 and highlighted the new parts. First, note that the generator now has an additional input (Digit Class), which makes it possible to specify what digits the generator should generate. In addition, the discriminator outputs not only a realness prediction but also a digit-class prediction. As a result, both output heads of the discriminator need to be trained. The training of the realness-predicting part remains the same as before (figure 10.10); the training of the class-predicting part relies on the fact that we know what digit classes the generated and real images belong to. The two heads of the model are compiled with different loss functions, reflecting the different nature of the two predictions. For the realness prediction, we use the binary cross-entropy loss, but for the digit-class prediction, we use the sparse categorical cross-entropy loss. You can see this in the following line from mnist-acgan/gan.js:

```
discriminator.compile({
  optimizer: tf.train.adam(args.learningRate, args.adamBeta1),
  loss: ['binaryCrossentropy', 'sparseCategoricalCrossentropy']
});
```

As the two curved arrows in figure 10.13 show, the gradients backpropagated from both losses are added on top of each other when updating the discriminator's weights. Figure 10.14 is an expanded version of figure 10.11 and provides a detailed schematic view of how ACGAN's generator portion is trained. This diagram shows how the generator learns to generate correct images given a specified digit class, in addition to learning how to generate real-looking images. Similar to figure 10.13, the new parts are highlighted, while the parts that already exist in figure 10.11 are grayed out. From the highlighted parts, you can see that the labels we feed into the training step now include not only the realness labels but also the digit-class labels. As before, the realness labels are all intentionally bogus. But the newly added digit-class labels are more honest, in the sense that we indeed gave these class labels to the generator.

Previously, we've seen that any discrepancies between the bogus realness labels and the discriminator's realness probability output are used to update the generator of ACGAN in a way that makes it better at "fooling" the discriminator. Here, the digit-class prediction from the discriminator plays a similar role. For instance, if we tell the generator to generate an image for the digit 8, but the discriminator classifies the image as 9, the value of the sparse categorical cross entropy will be high, and the gradients associated with it will have large magnitudes. As a result, the updates to the generator's weights will cause the generator to generate an image that looks more like an 8 (according to the discriminator.) Obviously, this way of training the generator will work only if the discriminator is sufficiently good at classifying images into the 10 MNIST

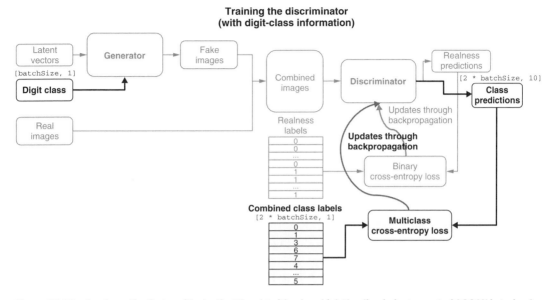

Figure 10.13 A schematic diagram illustrating the algorithm by which the discriminator part of ACGAN is trained. This diagram adds to the one in figure 10.10 by showing the parts that have to do with the digit class. The remaining parts of the diagram, which have already appeared in figure 10.10, are grayed out.

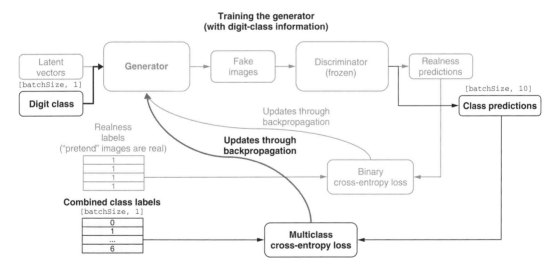

Figure 10.14 A schematic diagram illustrating the algorithm by which the generator part of ACGAN is trained. This diagram adds to the one in figure 10.11 by showing the parts that have to do with the digit class. The remaining parts of the diagram, which have already appeared in figure 10.11, are grayed out.

digit classes. This is what the previous discriminator training step helps to ensure. Again, we are seeing the yin-and-yang dynamics between the discriminator and generator portions at play during the training of ACGAN.

GAN TRAINING: A BAG OF TRICKS

The process of training and tuning GANs is notoriously difficult. The training scripts you see in the mnist-acgan example are the crystallization of a tremendous amount of trial-and-error by researchers. Like most things in deep learning, it's more like an art than an exact science: these tricks are heuristics, not backed by systematic theories. They are supported by a level of intuitive understanding of the phenomenon at hand, and they are known to work well empirically, although not necessarily in every situation.

The following is a list of noteworthy tricks used in the ACGAN in this section:

- We use tanh as the activation of the last conv2dTranspose layer in the generator. The tanh activation is seen less frequently in other types of models.
- Randomness is good for inducing robustness. Because GAN training may result in a dynamic equilibrium, GANs are prone to getting stuck in all sorts of ways. Introducing randomness during training helps prevent this. We introduce randomness in two ways: by using dropout in the discriminator and by using a "soft one" value (0.95) for the realness labels for the discriminator.
- Sparse gradients (gradients in which many values are zero) can hinder GAN training. In other types of deep learning, sparsity is often a desirable property, but not so in GANs. Two things can cause sparsity in gradients: the max pooling operation and relu activations. Instead of max pooling, strided convolutions are recommended for downsampling, which is exactly what's shown in the generator-creating code in listing 10.10. Instead of the usual relu activation, it's recommended to use the leakyReLU activation, of which the negative part has a small negative value, instead of strictly zero. This is also shown in listing 10.10.

10.3.4   Seeing the MNIST ACGAN training and generation

The mnist-acgan example can be checked out and prepared with the following commands:

```
git clone https://github.com/tensorflow/tfjs-examples.git
cd tfjs-examples/mnist-acganyarn
```

Running the example involves two stages: training in Node.js and generation in the browser. To start the training process, simply use the following command:

```
yarn train
```

The training uses tfjs-node by default. However, like in the examples involving convnets we've seen before, using tfjs-node-gpu can significantly improve the training speed. If you have a CUDA-enabled GPU set up properly on your machine, you can append the --gpu flag to the yarn train command to achieve that. Training the

ACGAN takes at least a couple of hours. For this long-running training job, you can monitor the progress with TensorBoard by using the `--logDir` flag:

```
yarn train --logDir /tmp/mnist-acgan-logs
```

Once the TensorBoard process has been brought up with the following command in a separate terminal,

```
tensorboard --logdir /tmp/mnist-acgan-logs
```

you can navigate to the TensorBoard URL (as printed out by the TensorBoard server process) in your browser to look at the loss curves. Figure 10.15 shows some example loss curves from the training process. One distinct feature of loss curves from GAN training is the fact that they don't always trend downward like the loss curves of most other types of neural networks. Instead, the losses from the discriminator (dLoss in the figure) and the generator (gLoss in the figure) both change in nonmonotonic ways and form an intricate dance with one another.

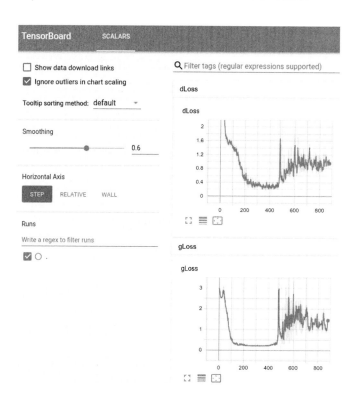

Figure 10.15   Sample loss curves from the ACGAN training job. dLoss is the loss from the discriminator training step. Specifically, it is the sum of the binary cross entropy from the realness prediction and the sparse categorical cross entropy from the digit-class prediction. gLoss is the loss from the generator training step. Like dLoss, gLoss is the sum of the losses from the binary realness classification and the multiclass digit classification.

Toward the end of the training, neither loss gets close to zero. Instead, they just level out (converge). At that point, the training process ends and saves the generator part of the model to the disk for serving during the in-browser generation step:

```
await generator.save(saveURL);
```

To run the in-browser generation demo, use the command `yarn watch`. It will compile mnist-acgan/index.js and the associated HTML and CSS assets, after which it will pop open a tab in your browser and show the demo page.[21]

The demo page loads the trained ACGAN generator saved from the previous stage. Since the discriminator is not really useful for this demo stage, it is neither saved nor loaded. With the generator loaded, we can construct a batch of latent vectors, along with a batch of desired digit-class indices, and call the generator's `predict()` with them. The code that does this is in mnist-acgan/index.js:

```
const latentVectors = getLatentVectors(10);
const sampledLabels = tf.tensor2d(
    [0, 1, 2, 3, 4, 5, 6, 7, 8, 9], [10, 1]);
const generatedImages =
    generator.predict([latentVectors, sampledLabels]).add(1).div(2);
```

Our batch of digit-class labels is always an ordered vector of 10 elements, from 0 to 9. This is why the batch of generated images is always an orderly array of images from 0 to 9. These images are stitched together with the `tf.concat()` function and rendered in a `div` element on the page (see the top image in figure 10.16). Compared with randomly sampled real MNIST images (see the bottom image in figure 10.16), these ACGAN-generated images look just like the real ones. In addition, their digit-class identities look correct. This shows that our ACGAN training was successful. If you want to see more outputs from the ACGAN generator, click the Generator button on the page. Each time the button is clicked, a new batch of 10 fake images will be generated and shown on the page. You can play with that and get an intuitive sense of the quality of the image generation.

Materials for further reading

- Ian Goodfellow, Yoshua Bengio, and Aaron Courville, "Deep Generative Models," *Deep Learning*, chapter 20, MIT Press, 2017.
- Jakub Langr and Vladimir Bok, *GANs in Action: Deep Learning with Generative Adversarial Networks*, Manning Publications, 2019.
- Andrej Karpathy, "The Unreasonable Effectiveness of Recurrent Neural Networks," blog, 21 May 2015, http://karpathy.github.io/2015/05/21/rnn-effectiveness/.

---

[21] You can also skip the training and building step entirely and directly navigate to the hosted demo page at http://mng.bz/4eGw.

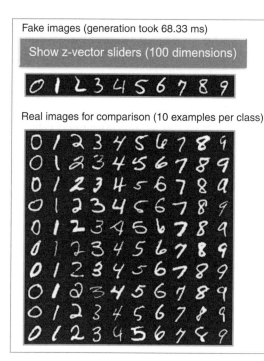

Fake images (generation took 68.33 ms)

Show z-vector sliders (100 dimensions)

Real images for comparison (10 examples per class)

Figure 10.16 Sample generated images (the 10 x 1 top panel) from the generator part of a trained ACGAN. The bottom panel, which contains a 10 x 10 grid of real MNIST images, is shown for comparison. By clicking the Show Z-vector Sliders button, you can open a section filled with 100 sliders. These sliders allow you to change the elements of the latent vector (the z-vector) and observe the effects on the generated MNIST images. Note that if you change the sliders one at a time, most of them will have tiny and unnoticeable effects on the images. But occasionally, you'll be able to find a slider with a larger and more noticeable effect.

- Jonathan Hui, "GAN—What is Generative Adversary Networks GAN?" Medium, 19 June 2018, http://mng.bz/Q0N6.
- GAN Lab, an interactive, web-based environment for understanding and exploring how GANs work, built using TensorFlow.js: Minsuk Kahng et al., https://poloclub.github.io/ganlab/.

Exercises

1 Apart from the Shakespeare text corpus, the lstm-text-generation example has a few other text datasets configured and ready for you to explore. Run the training on them, and observe the effects. For instance, use the unminified Tensor-Flow.js code as the training dataset. During and after the model's training, observe if the generated text exhibits the following patterns of JavaScript source code and how the temperature parameter affects the patterns:

   a Shorter-range patterns such as keywords (for example, "for" and "function")

   b Medium-range patterns such as the line-by-line organization of the code

   c Longer-range patterns such as pairing of parentheses and square brackets, and the fact that each "function" keyword must be followed by a pair of parentheses and a pair of curly braces

2 In the fashion-mnist-vae example, what happens if you take the KL divergence term out of the VAE's custom loss? Test that by modifying the `vaeLoss()` func-

tion in fashion-mnist-vae/model.js (listing 10.7). Do the sampled images from the latent space still look like the Fashion-MNIST images? Does the space still exhibit any interpretable patterns?

3 In the mnist-acgan example, try collapsing the 10 digit classes into 5 (0 and 1 will become the first class, 2 and 3 the second class, and so forth), and observe how that changes the output of the ACGAN after training. What do you expect to see in the generated images? For instance, what do you expect the ACGAN to generate when you specify that the first class is desired?

Hint: to make this change, you need to modify the `loadLabels()` function in mnist-acgan/data.js. The constant `NUM_CLASSES` in gan.js needs to be modified accordingly. In addition, the `sampledLabels` variable in the `generateAndVisualizeImages()` function (in index.js) also needs to be revised.

Summary

- Generative models are different from the discriminative ones we've studied throughout earlier chapters of this book in that they are designed to model the process in which examples of the training dataset are generated, along with their statistical distributions. Due to this design, they are capable of generating new examples that conform to the distributions and hence appear similar to the real training data.

- We introduce one way to model the structure of text datasets: next-character prediction. LSTMs can be used to perform this task in an iterative fashion to generate text of arbitrary length. The temperature parameter controls the stochasticity (how random and unpredictable) the generated text is.

- Autoencoders are a type of generative model that consists of an encoder and a decoder. First, the encoder compresses the input data into a concise representation called the latent vector, or z-vector. Then, the decoder tries to reconstruct the input data by using just the latent vector. Through the training process, the encoder becomes an efficient data summarizer, and the decoder is endowed with knowledge of the statistical distribution of the examples. A VAE adds some additional statistical constraints on the latent vectors so that the latent spaces comprising those vectors display continuously varying and interpretable structures after the VAE is trained.

- GANs are based on the idea of a simultaneous competition and cooperation between a discriminator and a generator. The discriminator tries to distinguish real data examples from the generated ones, while the generator aims at generating fake examples that "fool" the discriminator. Through joint training, the generator part will eventually become capable of generating realistic-looking examples. An ACGAN adds class information to the basic GAN architecture to make it possible to specify what class of examples to generate.

11

Basics of deep reinforcement learning

This chapter covers

- How reinforcement learning differs from the supervised learning discussed in the previous chapters
- The basic paradigm of reinforcement learning: agent, environment, action, and reward, and the interactions between them
- The general ideas behind two major approaches to solving reinforcement-learning problems: policy-based and value-based methods

Up to this point in this book, we have focused primarily on a type of machine learning called *supervised learning*. In supervised learning, we train a model to give us the correct answer given an input. Whether it's assigning a class label to an input image (chapter 4) or predicting future temperature based on past weather data (chapters 8 and 9), the paradigm is the same: mapping a static input to a static output. The sequence-generating models we visited in chapters 9 and 10 were slightly more complicated in that the output is a sequence of items instead of a single item. But those problems can still be reduced to one-input-one-output mapping by breaking the sequences into steps.

In this chapter, we will look at a very different type of machine learning called *reinforcement learning* (RL). In RL, our primary concern is not a static output; instead, we train a model (or an *agent* in RL parlance) to take actions in an environment with the goal of maximizing a metric of success called a *reward*. For example, RL can be used to train a robot to navigate the interior of a building and collect trash. In fact, the environment doesn't have to be a physical one; it can be any real or virtual space that an agent takes actions in. The chess board is the environment in which an agent can be trained to play chess; the stock market is the environment in which an agent can be trained to trade stocks. The generality of the RL paradigm makes it applicable to a wide range of real-world problems (figure 11.1). Also, some of the most spectacular advances in the deep-learning revolution involve combining the power of deep learning with RL. These include bots that can beat Atari games with superhuman skill and algorithms that can beat world champions at the games of Go and chess.[1]

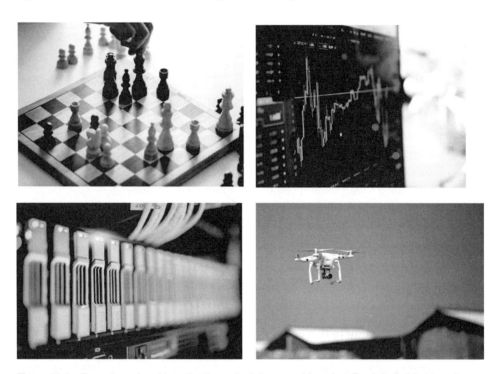

Figure 11.1 **Example real-world applications of reinforcement learning. Top left: Solving board games such as chess and Go. Top right: algorithmic trading of stocks. Bottom left: automated resource management in data centers. Bottom right: control and action planning in robotics. All images are free license and downloaded from www.pexels.com.**

[1] David Silver et al., "Mastering Chess and Shogi by Self-Play with a General Reinforcement Learning Algorithm," submitted 5 Dec. 2017, https://arxiv.org/abs/1712.01815.

The fascinating topic of RL differs from the supervised-learning problems we saw in the previous chapters in some fundamental ways. Unlike learning input-output mappings in supervised learning, RL is about discovering optimal decision-making processes by interacting with an environment. In RL, we are not given labeled training datasets; instead, we are given different types of environments to explore. In addition, time is an indispensable and foundational dimension in RL problems, unlike in many supervised-learning problems, which either lack a time dimension or treat time more or less like a spatial dimension. As a result of RL's unique characteristics, this chapter will involve a vocabulary and way of thinking very different from the previous chapters. But don't worry. We will use simple and concrete examples to illustrate the basic concepts and approaches. In addition, our old friends, deep neural networks and their implementations in TensorFlow.js, will still be with us. They will form an important pillar (albeit not the only one!) of the RL algorithms that we'll encounter in this chapter.

By the end of the chapter, you should be familiar with the basic formulation of RL problems, understand the basic ideas underlying two commonly used types of neural networks in RL (policy networks and Q-networks), and know how to train such networks using the API of TensorFlow.js.

11.1 The formulation of reinforcement-learning problems

Figure 11.2 lays out the major components of an RL problem. The agent is what we (the RL practitioners) have direct control over. The agent (such as a robot collecting trash in a building) interacts with the environment in three ways:

- At each step, the agent takes an *action*, which changes the state of the environment. In the context of our trash-collecting robot, for instance, the set of actions to choose from may be {go forward, go backward, turn left, turn right, grab trash, dump trash into container}.

- Once in a while, the environment provides the agent with a *reward*, which can be understood in anthropomorphic terms as a measurement of instantaneous pleasure or fulfillment. But in more abstract terms, a reward (or rather, a sum of rewards over time, as we'll see later) is a number that the agent tries to maximize. It is an important numeric value that guides RL algorithms in a way similar to how loss values guide supervised-learning algorithms. A reward can be positive or negative. In the example of our trash-collecting robot, a positive reward can be given when a bag of trash is dumped successfully into the robot's trash container. In addition, a negative reward should be given when the robot knocks over a trash can, bumps into people or furniture, or dumps trash outside its container.

- Apart from the reward, the agent can observe the state of the environment through another channel, namely, *observation*. This can be the full state of the environment or only the part of it visible to the agent, possibly distorted

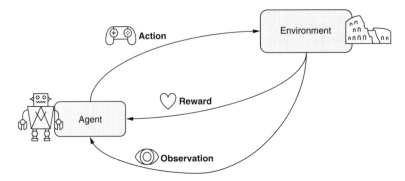

Figure 11.2   A schematic diagram of the basic formulation of RL problems. At each time step, an agent selects an action from the set of possible actions, which causes a change in the state of the environment. The environment provides the agent with a reward according to its current state and the action selected. The state of the environment is fully or partially observed by the agent, which will use that state to make decisions about future actions.

through a certain imperfect channel. For our trash-collecting robot, observations are the streams of images and signals from cameras and various types of sensors on its body.

The formulation just defined is somewhat abstract. Let's look at some concrete RL problems and get a sense of the range of possibilities the formulation encompasses. In this process, we will also glance at the taxonomy of all the RL problems out there. First let's consider actions. The space from which the agent can choose its actions can be discrete or continuous. For example, RL agents that play board games usually have discrete action spaces because in such problems, there are only a finite set of moves to choose from. However, an RL problem that involves controlling a virtual humanoid robot to walk bipedally[2] involves a continuous action space because torques on the joints are continuous-varying quantities. The example problems we'll cover in this chapter will be about discrete action spaces. Note that in some RL problems, continuous action spaces can be turned into discrete ones through discretization. For example, DeepMind's StarCraft II game agent divides the high-resolution 2D screen into coarser rectangles to determine where to move units or launch attacks.[3]

Rewards, which play a centric role in RL problems, also show variations. First, some RL problems involve only positive rewards. For example, as we'll see shortly, an RL agent whose goal is to balance a pole on a moving cart gets only positive rewards. It gets a small positive reward for every time step it keeps the pole standing. However, many RL problems involve a mix of positive and negative rewards. Negative rewards

---

[2]   See the Humanoid environment in OpenAI Gym: https://gym.openai.com/envs/Humanoid-v2/.

[3]   Oriol Vinyals et al., "StarCraft II: A New Challenge for Reinforcement Learning," submitted 16 Aug. 2017, https://arxiv.org/abs/1708.04782.

can be thought of as "penalties" or "punishment." For instance, an agent that learns to shoot a basketball at the hoop should receive positive rewards for goals and negative ones for misses.

Rewards can also vary in the frequency of occurrence. Some RL problems involve a continuous flow of rewards. Take the aforementioned cart-pole problem, for example: as long as the pole is still standing, the agent receives a (positive) reward at each and every time step. On the other hand, consider a chess-playing RL agent—the reward comes only at the end, when the outcome of the game (win, lose, or draw) is determined. There are also RL problems between these two extremes. For instance, our trash-collecting robot may receive no reward at all in the steps between two successful trash dumps—that is, when it's just moving from place A to place B. Also, an RL agent trained to play the Atari game Pong doesn't receive a reward at every step (frame) of the video game; instead, it is rewarded positively once every few steps, when the bat it controls hits the ball and bounces back toward the opponent. The example problems we'll visit in this chapter contain a mix of RL problems with high and low reward frequencies of occurrence.

Observation is another important factor in RL problems. It is a window through which the agent can glance at the state of the environment and form a basis on which to make decisions apart from any reward. Like actions, observations can be discrete (such as in a board or card game) or continuous (as in a physical environment). One question you might want to ask is why our RL formulation separates observation and reward into two entities, even though they can both be viewed as feedback provided by the environment to the agent. The answer is conceptual clarity and simplicity. Although the reward can be regarded as an observation, it is what the agent ultimately "cares" about. Observation may contain both relevant and irrelevant information, which the agent needs to learn to filter and make smart use of.

Some RL problems reveal the entire state of the environment to the agent through observation, while others make available only parts of their states. Examples of the first kind include board games such as chess and Go. For the latter kind, good examples are card games like poker, in which you cannot see your opponent's hand, as well as stock trading. Stock prices are determined by many factors, such as the internal operations of the companies and the mindset of other stock traders on the market. But very few of these states are directly observable by the agent. As a result, the agent's observations are limited to the moment-by-moment history of stock prices, perhaps in addition to publicly available information such as financial news.

This discussion sets up the playground in which RL happens. An interesting thing worth pointing out about this formulation is that the flow of information between the agent and the environment is bidirectional: the agent acts on the environment; the environment, in turn, provides the agent with rewards and state information. This distinguishes RL from supervised learning, in which the flow of information is largely unidirectional: the input contains enough information for an algorithm to predict the output, but the output doesn't act on the input in any significant way.

Another interesting and unique fact about RL problems is that they must happen along the time dimension in order for the agent-environment interaction to consist of multiple rounds or steps. Time can be either discrete or continuous. For instance, RL agents that solve board games usually operate on a discrete time axis because such games are played out in discrete turns. The same applies to video games. However, an RL agent that controls a physical robotic arm to manipulate objects is faced with a continuous time axis, even though it may still choose to take actions at discrete points in time. In this chapter, we will focus on discrete-time RL problems.

This theoretical discussion of RL should be enough for now. In the next section, we will start exploring some actual RL problems and algorithms hands-on.

11.2 Policy networks and policy gradients: The cart-pole example

The first RL problem we'll solve is a simulation of a physical system in which a cart carrying a pole moves on a one-dimensional track. Aptly named the *cart-pole* problem, it was first proposed by Andrew Barto, Richard Sutton, and Charles Anderson in 1983.[4] Since then, it has become a benchmark problem for control-systems engineering (somewhat analogous to the MNIST digit-recognition problem for supervised learning), owing to its simplicity and well-formulated physics and math, as well as to the fact that it is not entirely trivial to solve. In this problem, the agent's goal is to control the movement of a cart by exerting leftward or rightward forces in order to keep a pole standing in balance for as long as possible.

11.2.1 Cart-pole as a reinforcement-learning problem

Before going further, you should play with the cart-pole example to get an intuitive understanding of the problem. The cart-pole problem is simple and lightweight enough that we perform the simulation and training entirely in the browser. Figure 11.3 offers a visual depiction of the cart-pole problem, which you can find in the page opened by the yarn watch command. To checkout and run the example, use

```
git clone https://github.com/tensorflow/tfjs-examples.git
cd tfjs-examples/cart-pole
yarn && yarn watch
```

Click the Create Model button and then the Train button. You should then see an animation at the bottom of the page showing an untrained agent performing the cart-pole task. Since the agent's model has its weights initialize random values (more on the model later), it will perform quite poorly. All time steps from the beginning of a game to the end are sometimes referred to collectively as an *episode* in RL terminology. We will use the terms *game* and *episode* interchangeably here.

---

[4] Andrew G. Barto, Richard S. Sutton, and Charles W. Anderson, "Neuronlike Adaptive Elements that Can Solve Difficult Learning Control Problems," *IEEE Transactions on Systems, Man, and Cybernetics*, Sept./Oct. 1983, pp. 834–846, http://mng.bz/Q0rG.

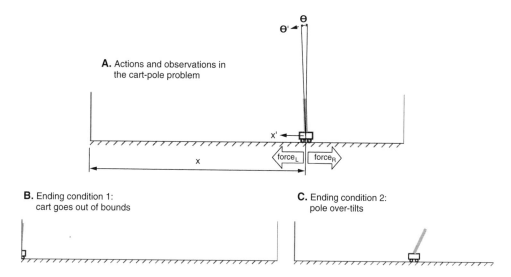

Figure 11.3 **Visual rendering of the cart-pole problem. Panel A: four physical quantities (cart position** *x*, **cart velocity** *x'*, **pole tilt angle** θ, **and pole angular velocity** θ') **make up the environment state and observation. At each time step, the agent may choose a leftward-force action or a rightward-force one, which will change the environment state accordingly. Panels B and C: the two conditions that will cause a game to end—either the cart goes too much to the left or to the right (B) or the pole tilts too much from the upright position (C).**

As panel A in figure 11.3 shows, the position of the cart along the track at any time step is captured by a variable called *x*. Its instantaneous velocity is denoted *x'*. In addition, the tilt angle of the pole is captured by another variable called θ. The angular velocity of the pole (how fast θ changes and in what direction) is denoted θ'. Together, the four physical quantities (*x*, *x'*, θ, and θ') are completely observed by the agent at every step and constitute the observation part of this RL problem.

The simulation ends when either of two conditions is met:

- The value of *x* goes out of a prespecified bound, or, in physical terms, the cart bumps into one of the walls on the two ends of the track (panel B in figure 11.3).
- The absolute value of θ exceeds a certain threshold, or, in physical terms, the pole tilts too much away from the upright position (panel C in figure 11.3).

The environment also terminates an episode after the 500th simulation step. This prevents the game from lasting too long (which can happen once the agent gets very good at the game through learning). This upper bound on the number of steps is adjustable in the UI. Until the game ends, the agent gets a reward of a unit (1) at every step of the simulation. Therefore, in order to achieve a higher cumulative reward, the agent needs to find a way to keep the pole standing. But how does the agent control the cart-pole system? This brings us to the action part of this RL problem.

As the Force arrows in panel A of figure 11.3 show, the agent is limited to two possible actions at every step: exerting a force to the left or to the right on the cart. The agent must choose one of the two force directions. The magnitude of the force is fixed. Once the force is exerted, the simulation will enact a set of mathematical equations to compute the next state (new values of x, x', θ, and θ') of the environment. The details involve familiar Newtonian mechanics. We won't cover the detailed equations, as understanding them is not essential here, but they are available in the cart-pole/cart_pole.js file under the cart-pole directory if you are interested.

Likewise, the code that renders the cart-pole system in an HTML canvas can be found in cart-pole/ui.js. This code underlines an advantage of writing RL algorithms in JavaScript (in particular, in TensorFlow.js): the UI and the learning algorithm can be conveniently written in the same language and be tightly integrated with each other. This facilitates the visualization and intuitive understanding of the problem and speeds up the development process. To summarize the cart-pole problem, we can describe it in the canonical RL formulation (see table 11.1).

Table 11.1   Describing the cart-pole problem in the canonical RL formulation

Abstract RL concept	Realization in the cart-pole problem
Environment	A cart carrying a pole and moving on a one-dimensional track.
Action	(Discrete) Binary choice between a leftward force and a rightward one at each step. The magnitude of the force is fixed.
Reward	(Frequent and positive-only) For each step of the game episode, the agent receives a fixed reward (1). The episode ends as soon as the cart hits a wall at one end of the track, or the pole tilts too much from the upright position.
Observation	(Complete state, continuous) At each step, the agent can access the full state of the cart-pole system, including the cart position (x) and velocity (x'), in addition to the pole tilt angle (θ) and angular velocity (θ').

11.2.2 Policy network

Now that the cart-pole RL problem is laid out, let's look at how to solve it. Historically, control theorists have devised ingenious solutions to this problem. Their solutions are based on the underlying physics of this system.[5] That's *not* how we will approach the problem in this book. In the context of this book, doing that would be somewhat analogous to writing heuristics to parse edges and corners in MNIST images in order to classify the digits. Instead, we will ignore the physics of the system and let our agent learn through repeated trial and error. This jibes with the spirit of the rest of this

---

[5] If you are interested in the traditional, non-RL approach to the cart-pole problem and are not scared of the math, you can read the open courseware of a control-theory course at MIT by Russ Tedrake: http://mng .bz/j5lp.

book: instead of hard-coding an algorithm or manually engineering features based on human knowledge, we design an algorithm that allows the model to learn on its own.

How can we let the agent decide the action (leftward versus rightward force) to take at each step? Given the observations available to the agent and the decision the agent has to make at every step, this problem can be reformulated as a simple input-output mapping problem like the ones in supervised learning. A natural solution is to build a neural network to select an action based on the observation. This is the basic idea behind the *policy network.*

This neural network takes a length-4 observation vector (x, x', θ, and θ') and outputs a number that can be translated into a left-versus-right decision. The network architecture is similar to the binary classifier we built for the phishing websites in chapter 3. Abstractly, at each step, we will look at the environment and use our network to decide which action to take. By letting our network play a number of rounds, we will collect some data with which to evaluate those decisions. Then, we will invent a way to assign quality to those decisions so that we can adjust the weights of our network so that it will make decisions more like the "good" ones and less like the "bad" ones in the future.

The details of this system are different from our previous classifier work in the following aspects:

- The model is invoked many times in the course of a game episode (at every time step).
- The model's output (the output from the Policy Network box in figure 11.4) is logits instead of probability scores. The logits are subsequently converted into probability scores through a sigmoid function. The reason we don't include the sigmoid nonlinearity directly in the last (output) layer of the policy network is that we need the logits for training, as we'll see shortly.

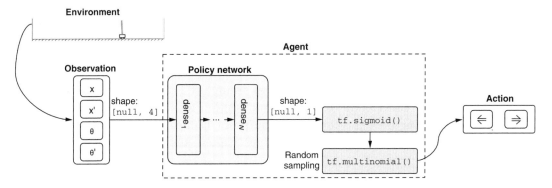

Figure 11.4 How the policy network fits into our solution to the cart-pole problem. The policy network is a TensorFlow.js model that outputs the probability of the leftward-force action by using the observation vector (x, x', θ, and θ') as the input. The probability is converted to an actual action through random sampling.

- The probability output by the sigmoid function must be converted to a concrete action (left versus right). This is done through the random-sampling `tf.multinomial()` function call. Recall that we used `tf.multinomial()` in the lstm-text-generation example in chapter 10, when we sampled the next character using softmax probabilities over letters of the alphabet to sample the next character. The situation here is slightly simpler because there are only two choices.

The last point has deeper implications. Consider the fact that we *could* convert the output of the `tf.sigmoid()` function directly into an action by applying a threshold (for example, selecting the left action when the network's output is greater than 0.5 and the right action otherwise). Why do we prefer the more complicated random-sampling approach with `tf.multinomial()` over this simpler approach? The answer is that we *want* the randomness that comes with `tf.multinomial()`. In the early phase of the training, the policy network is clueless about how to select the direction of the force because its weights are initialized randomly. By using random sampling, we encourage it to try random actions and see which ones work better. Some of the random trials will end up being bad, while others will give good results. Our algorithm will remember the good choices and make more of them in the future. But these good choices won't become available unless the agent is allowed to try randomly. If we had chosen the deterministic threshold approach, the model would be stuck with its initial choices.

This brings us to a classical and important topic in RL called *exploration versus exploitation*. *Exploration* refers to random tries; it is the basis on which good actions are discovered by the RL agent. *Exploitation* means making the optimal solutions that the agent has learned in order to maximize the reward. The two are incompatible with each other. Finding a good balance between them is critical to designing working RL algorithms. In the beginning, we want to explore a diverse array of possible strategies, but as we converge on better strategies, we want to fine-tune those strategies. So, there is generally a gradual ramping down of exploration with training in many algorithms. In the cart-pole problem, the ramping is implicit in the `tf.multinomial()` sampling function because it gives more and more deterministic outcomes when the model's confidence level increases with training.

Listing 11.1 (excerpted from cart-pole/index.js) shows the TensorFlow.js calls that create the policy network. The code in listing 11.2 (also excerpted from cart-pole/index.js) converts the policy network's output into the agent's action, in addition to returning the logits for training purposes. Compared to the supervised-learning models we encountered in the previous chapters, the model-related code here is not much different.

However, what's fundamentally different here is the fact that we don't have a set of labeled data that can be used to teach the model which action choices are good and which are bad. If we had such a dataset, we could simply call `fit()` or `fitDataset()` on the policy network in order to solve the problem, like we did for the models in the previous chapters. But the fact is that we don't, so the agent has to figure out which actions are good by playing the game and looking at the rewards it gets. In other words, it has to "learn swimming by swimming," a key feature of RL problems. Next, we'll look at how that's done in detail.

Listing 11.1 Policy network MLP: selecting actions based on observations

```
createModel(hiddenLayerSizes) {
    if (!Array.isArray(hiddenLayerSizes)) {
        hiddenLayerSizes = [hiddenLayerSizes];
    }
    this.model = tf.sequential();
    hiddenLayerSizes.forEach((hiddenLayerSize, i) => {
        this.model.add(tf.layers.dense({
            units: hiddenLayerSize,
            activation: 'elu',
            inputShape: i === 0 ? [4] : undefined
        }));
    });
    this.model.add(tf.layers.dense({units: 1}));
    }
}
```

hiddenLayerSize controls the sizes of all the policy network's layers except the last one (output layer).

inputShape is needed only for the first layer.

The last layer is hard-coded to have one unit. The single output number will be converted to a probability of selecting the leftward-force action.

Listing 11.2 Getting the logits and actions from the output of the policy network

```
getLogitsAndActions(inputs) {
    return tf.tidy(() => {
        const logits = this.policyNet.predict(inputs);

        const leftProb = tf.sigmoid(logits);
        const leftRightProbs = tf.concat(
            [leftProb, tf.sub(1, leftProb)], 1);
        const actions = tf.multinomial(
            leftRightProbs, 1, null, true);
        return [logits, actions];
    });
}
```

Converts the logits to the probability values of the leftward action

Calculates the probability values for both actions, as they are required by tf.multinomial()

Randomly samples actions based on the probability values. The four arguments are probability values, number of samples, random seed (unused), and a flag that indicates that the probability values are normalized.

11.2.3 Training the policy network: The REINFORCE algorithm

Now the key question becomes how to calculate which actions are good and which are bad. If we can answer this question, we'll be able to update the weights of the policy network to make it more likely to pick the good actions in the future, in a way similar to supervised learning. What quickly comes to mind is that we can use the reward to measure how good the actions are. But the cart-pole problem involves rewards that 1) always have a fixed value (1) and 2) happen at every step as long as the episode hasn't ended. So, we can't simply use the step-by-step reward as a metric, or we'll end up labeling all actions as equally good. We need to take into account how long each episode lasts.

A naive approach is to sum all the rewards in an episode, which gives us the length of the episode. But can the sum be a good assessment of the actions? It is not hard to realize that it won't work. The reason is the steps at the end of an episode. Suppose in a long episode, the agent balances the cart-pole system quite well all the way until near the end, when it makes a few bad choices that cause the episode to finally end. The naive summing approach will assign equally good assessment to the bad actions at the end and the good ones from before. Instead, we want to assign higher scores to the actions in the early and middle parts of the episode and assign lower ones to the actions near the end.

This brings us to the idea of *reward discounting*, a simple but important idea in RL that the value of a certain step should equal the immediate reward plus the reward that is expected for the future. The future reward may be equally as important as the immediate reward, or it may be less important. The relative balance can be quantified with a discounting factor called γ (gamma). γ is usually set to a value close to but slightly less than 1, such as 0.95 or 0.99. We write this in a mathematical equation as

$$v_i = r_i + \gamma \cdot r_{i+1} + \gamma^2 \cdot r_{i+2} + \ldots + \gamma^{N-i} \cdot r_N \qquad \textbf{(Equation 11.1)}$$

In equation 11.1, v_i is the total discounted reward of the state at step i, which can be understood as the value of that particular state. It is equal to the immediate reward given to the agent at that step (r_i), plus the reward from the next step (r_{i+1}) discounted by γ, plus a further discounted reward from two steps later, and so forth, up to the end of the episode (step N).

To illustrate reward discounting, we show how this equation transforms our original rewards to a more useful value metric in figure 11.5. The top plot in panel A displays the original rewards from all four steps from a short episode. The bottom plot shows the discounted rewards (based on equation 11.1). Panel B shows the original and discounted total rewards from a longer episode (length = 20) for comparison. From the two panels, we can see that the discounted total reward value is higher in the beginning and lower at the end, which makes sense because we want to assign lower values to actions toward the end of an episode, which causes the game to end. Also, the values at the beginning and middle parts of the longer episode (panel B) are higher than those at the beginning of the shorter one (panel A). This also makes intuitive sense because we want to assign higher values to the actions that lead to longer episodes.

The reward-discounting equation gives us a set of values that make more sense than the naive summing before. But we are still faced with the question of how to use these

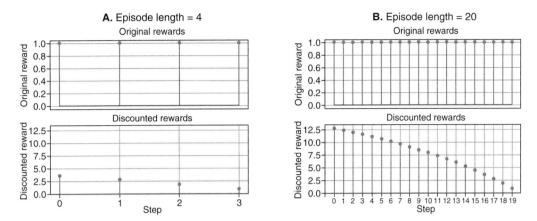

Figure 11.5   Panel A: applying reward discounting (equation 11.1) on rewards from an episode with four steps. Panel B: same as panel A, but from an episode with 20 steps (that is, five times longer than the one in panel A). As a result of the discounting, higher values are assigned to the actions in the beginning of each episode compared to the actions near the end.

discounted reward values to train the policy network. For that, we will use an algorithm called REINFORCE, invented by Ronald Williams in 1992.[6] The basic idea behind REINFORCE is to adjust the weights of the policy network to make it more likely to make good choices (choices assigned higher discounted rewards) and less likely to make bad choices (the ones assigned lower discounted rewards).

To this end, we need to calculate the direction in which to change the parameters to make an action more likely given the observation inputs. This is done with the code in listing 11.3 (excerpted from cart-pole/index.js). The function `getGradientsAndSaveActions()` is invoked at every step of the game. It compares the logits (unnormalized probability scores) and the actual action selected at the step and returns the gradient of the discrepancy between the two with respect to the policy network's weights. This may sound complicated, but intuitively, it's fairly straightforward. The returned gradient tells the policy network how to change its weights so as to make the choices more like the choices that were actually selected. The gradients, together with the rewards from the training episodes, form the basis of our RL method. This is why this method belongs to the family of RL algorithms called *policy gradients*.

Listing 11.3   Comparing logits and actual actions to obtain gradients for weights

```
getGradientsAndSaveActions(inputTensor) {
  const f = () => tf.tidy(() => {
    const [logits, actions] =
        this.getLogitsAndActions(inputTensor);
    this.currentActions_ = actions.dataSync();
```

getLogitsAndActions() is
defined in listing 11.2.

---

[6]   Ronald J. Williams, "Simple Statistical Gradient-Following Algorithms for Connectionist Reinforcement Learning," *Machine Learning*, vol. 8, nos. 3–4, pp. 229–256, http://mng.bz/WOyw.

```
const labels =
    tf.sub(1, tf.tensor2d(this.currentActions_, actions.shape));
return tf.losses.sigmoidCrossEntropy(
    labels, logits).asScalar();
});
return tf.variableGrads(f);   ⟵
}
```

The sigmoid cross-entropy loss quantifies the discrepancy between the actual action made during the game and the policy network's output logits.

Calculates the gradient of the loss with respect to the policy network's weights

During training, we let the agent play a number of games (say, *N* games) and collect all the discounted rewards according to equation 11.1, as well as the gradients from all the steps. Then, we combine the discounted rewards and gradients by multiplying the gradients with a normalized version of the discounted rewards. The reward normalization here is an important step. It linearly shifts and scales all the discounted rewards from the *N* games so that they have an overall mean value of 0 and overall standard deviation of 1. An example of applying this normalization on the discounted rewards is shown in figure 11.6. It illustrates the normalized, discounted rewards from a short episode (length = 4) and a longer one (length = 20). From this figure, it should be clear what steps are favored by the REINFORCE algorithm: they are the actions made in the early and middle parts of longer episodes. By contrast, all the steps from the shorter (length-4) episode are assigned *negative* values. What does a negative normalized reward mean? It means that when it is used to update the policy network's weights later, it will steer the network *away* from making a similar choice of actions

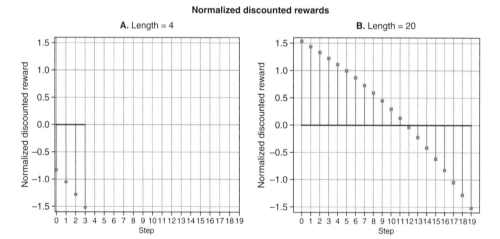

Figure 11.6   Normalizing the discounted rewards from the two episodes with lengths 4 (panel A) and 20 (panel B). We can see that the normalized, discounted rewards have the highest values at the beginning of the length-20 episode. The policy gradient method will use these discounted reward values to update the weights of the policy network, which will make the network less likely to make the action choices that resulted in the bad rewards in the first case (length = 4) and more likely to make the choices that resulted in the good rewards in the beginning part of the second case (length = 20) (given the same state inputs as before, that is).

given similar state inputs in the future. This is in contrast to a positive normalized reward, which will steer the policy network *toward* choosing similar actions given similar inputs in the future.

The code for the normalization of the discounted rewards, and using it to scale the gradients, is somewhat tedious but not complicated. It is in the scaleAndAverage-Gradients() function in cart-pole/index.js, which is not listed here for the sake of brevity. The scaled gradients are used to update the policy network's weights. With the weights updated, the policy network will output higher logits for the actions from the steps assigned higher discounted rewards and lower logits for the actions from the steps assigned lower ones.

That is basically how the REINFORCE algorithm works. The core training logic of the cart-pole example, which is based on REINFORCE, is shown in listing 11.4. It is a reiteration of the steps described previously:

1 Invoke the policy network to get logits based on current agent observation.
2 Randomly sample an action based on the logits.
3 Update the environment using the sampled action.
4 Remember the following for updating weights later (step 7): the logits and the selected action, as well as the gradients of the loss function with respect to the policy network's weights. These gradients are referred to as *policy gradients*.
5 Receive a reward from the environment, and remember it for later (step 7).
6 Repeat steps 1–5 until numGames episodes are completed.
7 Once all numGames episodes have ended, discount and normalize the rewards and use the results to scale the gradients from step 4. Then update the policy network's weights using the scaled gradients. (This is where the policy network's weights get updated.)
8 (Not shown in listing 11.4) Repeat steps 1–7 numIterations times.

Compare these steps with the code in the listing (excerpted from cart-pole/index.js) to make sure you can see the correspondence and follow the logic.

Listing 11.4 Cart-pole example's training loop implementing the REINFORCE algorithm

```
async train(
    cartPoleSystem, optimizer, discountRate, numGames, maxStepsPerGame) {
  const allGradients = [];
  const allRewards = [];
  const gameSteps = [];
  onGameEnd(0, numGames);
  for (let i = 0; i < numGames; ++i) {                      Loops over specified
    cartPoleSystem.setRandomState();                        number of episodes
    const gameRewards = [];                                 Randomly initializes
    const gameGradients = [];                               a game episode
    for (let j = 0; j < maxStepsPerGame; ++j) {
      const gradients = tf.tidy(() => {
        const inputTensor = cartPoleSystem.getStateTensor();
```

Loops over steps of the game

```
      return this.getGradientsAndSaveActions(
          inputTensor).grads;
    });

    this.pushGradients(gameGradients, gradients);
    const action = this.currentActions_[0];
    const isDone = cartPoleSystem.update(action);

    await maybeRenderDuringTraining(cartPoleSystem);

    if (isDone) {
      gameRewards.push(0);
      break;
    } else {
      gameRewards.push(1);
    }
  }
  onGameEnd(i + 1, numGames);
  gameSteps.push(gameRewards.length);
  this.pushGradients(allGradients, gameGradients);
  allRewards.push(gameRewards);
  await tf.nextFrame();
}

tf.tidy(() => {
  const normalizedRewards =
      discountAndNormalizeRewards(allRewards, discountRate);
  optimizer.applyGradients(
      scaleAndAverageGradients(allGradients, normalizedRewards));
});
tf.dispose(allGradients);
return gameSteps;
}
```

Keeps track of the gradients from every step for later REINFORCE training

The agent takes an action in the environment.

As long as the game hasn't ended, the agent receives a unit reward per step.

Discounts and normalizes the rewards (key step of REINFORCE)

Updates the policy network's weights using the scaled gradients from all steps

To see the REINFORCE algorithm in action, specify 25 epochs on the demo page and click the Train button. By default, the state of the environment is displayed in real time during training so that you can see repeated tries by the learning agent. To speed up the training, uncheck the Render During Training check box. Twenty-five epochs of training will take a few minutes on a reasonably up-to-date laptop and should be sufficient to achieve ceiling performance (500 steps per game episode in the default setting). Figure 11.7 shows a typical training curve, which plots the average episode length as a function of the training iteration. Notice that the training progress shows some dramatic fluctuation, with the mean number of steps changing in a nonmonotonic and highly noisy fashion over the iterations. This type of fluctuation is not uncommon in RL training jobs.

After the training completes, click the Test button, and you should see the agent do a good job keeping the cart-pole system balanced over many steps. Since the testing phase doesn't involve a maximum number of steps (500 by default), it is possible that the agent can keep the episode going for over 1,000 steps. If it continues too long, you can click the Stop button to terminate the simulation.

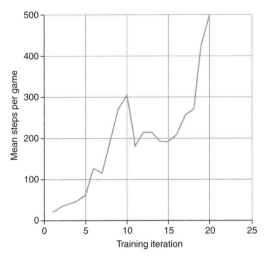

Figure 11.7 **A curve showing the average number of steps the agent survives in the cart-pole episodes as a function of the number of training iterations. The perfect score (500 steps in this case) is attained at around iteration 20. This result is obtained with a hidden layer size of 128. The highly nonmonotonic and fluctuating shape of the curve is not uncommon among RL problems.**

To wrap up this section, figure 11.8 recapitulates the formulation of the problem and the role of the REINFORCE policy-gradient algorithm. All major parts of the solution are depicted in this figure. At each step, the agent uses a neural network called the *policy network* to estimate the likelihood that the leftward action (or, equivalently, the rightward one) is the better choice. This likelihood is converted into an actual action through a random sampling process that encourages the agent to explore early on

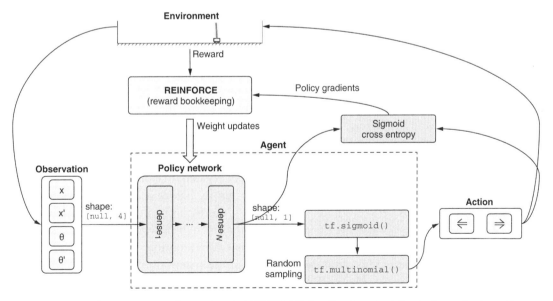

Figure 11.8 **A schematic diagram illustrating the REINFORCE algorithm-based solution to the cart-pole problem. This diagram is an expanded view of the diagram in figure 11.4.**

and obeys the certainty of the estimates later. The action drives the cart-pole system in the environment, which in turn provides the agent with rewards until the end of the episode. This process repeats a number of episodes, during which the REINFORCE algorithm remembers the reward, the action, and the policy network's estimate at every step. When it's time for REINFORCE to update the policy network, it distinguishes good estimates from the network from bad ones through reward discounting and normalization, and then uses the results to nudge the network's weights in the direction of making better estimates in the future. This process iterates a number of times until the end of the training (for instance, when the agent reaches a threshold performance).

All the elegant technical details aside, let's take a step back and look at the bigger picture of RL embodied in this example. The RL-based approach has clear advantages over non-machine-learning methods such as traditional control theory: the generality and the economy of human effort. In cases where the system has complex or unknown characteristics, the RL approach may be the only viable solution. If the characteristics of the system change over time, we won't have to derive new mathematical solutions from scratch: we can just re-run the RL algorithm and let the agent adapt itself to the new situation.

The disadvantage of the RL approach, which is still an unsolved question in the field of RL research, is that it requires many repeated trials in the environment. In the case of the cart-pole example, it took about 400 game episodes to reach the target level of proficiency. Some traditional, non-RL approaches may require no trial at all. Implement the control-theory-based algorithm, and the agent should be able to balance the pole from episode 1. For a problem like cart-pole, RL's hunger for repeated trials is not a major problem because the computer simulation of the environment is simple, fast, and cheap. However, in more realistic problems, such as self-driving cars and object-manipulating robot arms, this problem of RL becomes a more acute and pressing challenge. No one can afford crashing a car or breaking a robotic arm hundreds or thousands of times in order to train an agent, not to mention the prohibitively long time it would take to run the RL training algorithm in such real-world problems.

This concludes our first RL example. The cart-pole problem has some special characteristics that don't hold in other RL problems. For example, many RL environments don't provide a positive reward to the agent at every step. In some situations, the agent may need to make dozens of decisions, if not more, before it can be rewarded positively. In the gaps between the positive rewards, there may be no reward, or there may be only negative rewards (it can be argued that many real-world endeavors, such as studying, exercising, and investing, are like that!). In addition, the cart-pole system is "memoryless" in the sense that the dynamics of the system don't depend on what the agent did in the past. Many RL problems are more complex than that, in that the agent's action changes certain aspects of the environment. The RL problem we'll study in the next section will show both sparse positive rewards and an environment that changes with action history. To tackle the problem, we'll introduce another useful and popular RL algorithm, called *deep Q-learning*.

11.3 Value networks and Q-learning: The snake game example

We will use the classic action game called *snake* as our example problem to cover deep Q-learning. As we did in the last section, we'll first describe the RL problem and the challenge it poses. In doing so, we'll also discuss why policy gradients and REIN-FORCE won't be very effective on this problem.

11.3.1 Snake as a reinforcement-learning problem

First appearing in 1970s arcade games, snake has become a well-known video game genre. The snake-dqn directory in tfjs-examples contains a JavaScript implementation of a simple variant of it. You can check out the code with

```
git clone https://github.com/tensorflow/tfjs-examples.git
cd tfjs-examples/snake-dqn
yarn
yarn watch
```

In the web page opened by the `yarn watch` command, you can see a board of the snake game. You can load a pretrained and hosted deep Q-network (DQN) model and observe it play the game. Later, we'll talk about how you can train such a model from scratch. For now, you should be able to get an intuitive sense of how this game works through observing. In case you aren't already familiar with the snake game, its settings and rules can be summarized as follows.

First, all actions happen in a 9 × 9 grid world (see an example in figure 11.9). The world (or board) can made be larger, but 9 × 9 is the default size in our example. There are three types of squares on the board: the snake, the fruit, and the empty space. The snake is represented by blue squares, except the head, which is colored orange with a semicircle representing the snake's mouth. The fruit is represented by a green square with a circle inside. The empty squares are white. The game happens in steps—or, in video game terminology, *frames*. At each frame, the agent must choose from three possible actions for the snake: go straight, turn left, or turn right (staying put is not an option). The agent is rewarded positively when the head of the snake comes into contact with a fruit square, in which case the fruit square will disappear (get "eaten" by the snake), and the length of the snake will increase by one at the tail. A new fruit will appear in one of the empty squares. The agent will be rewarded negatively if it doesn't eat a fruit at a step. The game terminates (the snake "dies") when the head of the snake goes out of bounds (as in panel B of figure 11.9) or runs into its own body (as in panel C).

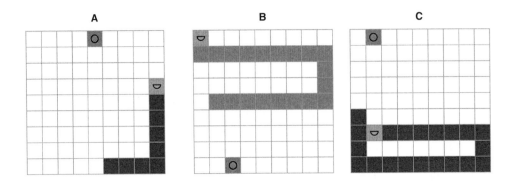

Figure 11.9   The snake game: a grid world in which the player controls a snake to eat fruit. The snake's "goal" is to eat as many fruits as possible through an efficient movement pattern (panel A). The length of the snake grows by 1 every time a fruit is eaten. The game ends (the snake "dies") as soon as the snake goes out of bounds (panel B) or bumps into its own body (panel C). Note that in panel B, the snake's head reaches the edge position, and then an upward motion (a go-straight action) ensues that causes the game to terminate. Simply reaching the edge squares with the snake's head won't result in termination. Eating every fruit leads to a large positive reward. Moving one square without eating a fruit incurs a negative reward that is smaller in magnitude. Game termination (the snake dying) also incurs a negative reward.

One key challenge in the snake game is the snake's growth. If not for this rule, the game would be much simpler. Simply navigate the snake to the fruit over and over, and there's no limit to the reward the agent can get. With the length-growth rule, however, the agent must learn to avoid bumping into its own body, which gets harder as the snake eats more fruit and grows longer. This is the nonstatic aspect of the snake RL problem that the cart-pole environment lacks, as we mentioned at the end of the last section.

Table 11.2 describes the snake problem in the canonical RL formulation. Compared with the formulation of the cart-pole problem (table 11.1), the biggest difference is in the reward structure. In the snake problem, the positive rewards (+10 for each fruit eaten) come infrequently—that is, only after a number of negative rewards due to the movement the snake needs to reach the fruit. Given the size of the board, two positive rewards may be spaced out by as much as 17 steps even if the snake moves in the most efficient manner. The small negative reward is a penalty that encourages the snake to move in a more straightforward path. Without this penalty, the snake can move in a meandering and indirect way and still receive the same rewards, which will make the gameplay and training process unnecessarily long. This sparse and complex reward structure is also the main reason why the policy gradient and REINFORCE method will not work well on this problem. The policy-gradient method works better when the rewards are frequent and simple, as in the cart-pole problem.

Table 11.2 Describing the snake-game problem in the canonical RL formulation

Abstract RL concept	Realization in the snake problem
Environment	A grid world that contains a moving snake and a self-replenishing fruit.
Action	(Discrete) Ternary choice: go straight, turn left, or turn right.
Reward	(Frequent, mixed positive negative rewards) • Eating fruit—Large positive reward (+10) • Moving without eating fruit—Small negative reward (–0.2) • Dying—Large negative reward (–10)
Observation	(Complete state, discrete) At each step, the agent can access the full state of the game: that is, what is in every square of the board.

THE JAVASCRIPT API OF SNAKE

Our JavaScript implementation of snake can be found in the file snake-dqn/snake_ game.js. We will describe only the API of the SnakeGame class and spare you the implementation details, which you can study at your own pleasure if they are of interest to you. The constructor of the SnakeGame class has the following syntax:

```
const game = new SnakeGame({height, width, numFruits, initLen});
```

Here, the size parameters of the board, height and width, have default values of 9. numFruits is the number of fruits present on the board at any given time; it has a default value of 1. initLen, the initial length of the snake, defaults to 2.

The step() method exposed by the game object allows the caller to play one step in the game:

```
const {state, reward, done, fruitEaten} = game.step(action);
```

The argument to the step() method represents the action: 0 for going straight, 1 for turning left, and 2 for turning right. The return of the step() value has the following fields:

- state—The new state of the board immediately after the action, represented as a plain JavaScript object with two fields:
  - s—The squares occupied by the snake, as an array of [x, y] coordinates. The elements of this array are ordered such that the first element corresponds to the head and the last element to the tail.
  - f—The [x, y] coordinates of the square(s) occupied by the fruit(s).

  Note that this representation of the game state is designed to be efficient, which is necessitated by the Q-learning algorithm's storage of a large number (for example, tens of thousands) of such state objects, as we will soon see. An alternative is to use an array or nested array to record the status of every square of the board, including the empty ones. This would be much less space-efficient.
- reward—The reward given to the snake at the step, immediately after the action takes place. This is a single number.

- `done`—A Boolean flag indicating whether the game is over immediately after the action takes place.
- `fruitEaten`—A Boolean flag indicating whether a fruit was eaten by the snake in the step as a result of the action. Note that this field is partly redundant with the `reward` field because we can infer from `reward` whether a fruit was eaten. It is included for simplicity and to decouple the exact values of the rewards (which may be tunable hyperparameters) from the binary event of fruit eaten versus fruit not eaten.

As we will see later, the first three fields (`state`, `reward`, and `done`) will play important roles in the Q-learning algorithm, while the last field (`fruitEaten`) is mainly for monitoring.

11.3.2 *Markov decision process and Q-values*

To explain the deep Q-learning algorithm we will apply on the snake problem, it is necessary to first go a little abstract. In particular, we will introduce the *Markov decision process* (MDP) and its underlying math at a basic level. Don't worry: we'll use simple and concrete examples and tie the concepts to the snake problem we have at hand.

From the viewpoint of MDP, the history of an RL environment is a sequence of transitions through a finite set of discrete states. In addition, the transitions between the states follow a particular type of rule:

> *The state of the environment at the next step is determined completely by the state and the action taken by the agent at the current step.*

The key is that the next state depends on *only* two things: the current state and the action taken, and nothing more. In other words, MDP assumes that your history (how you got to your current state) is irrelevant to deciding what you should do next. It is a powerful simplification that makes the problem more tractable. What is a *non-Markov decision process*? That would be a case in which the next state depends on not only the current state and the current action but also the states or actions at earlier steps, potentially going all the way back to the beginning of the episode. In the non-Markov scenario, the math would be much more complex, and a much greater amount of computational resources would be required to solve the math.

The MDP requirement makes intuitive sense for a lot of RL problems. A game of chess is a good example of this. At any step of the game, the board configuration (plus which player's turn it is) fully characterizes the game state and provides all the information the player needs for calculating the next move. In other words, it is possible to resume a chess game from the board configuration without knowing the previous moves. (Incidentally, this is why newspapers can post chess puzzles in a very space-efficient way.) Video games such as snake are also consistent with the MDP formulation. The positions of the snake and the fruit on the board fully characterize the game state and are all it takes to resume the game from that point or for the agent to decide the next action.

Even though problems such as chess and snake are fully compatible with MDP, they each involve an astronomical number of possible states. In order to present MDP in an intuitive and visual fashion, we need a simpler example. In figure 11.10, we show a very simple MDP problem in which there are only seven possible states and two possible agent actions. The transition between the states is governed by the following rules:

- The initial state is always s_1.
- From state s_1, if the agent takes action a_1, the environment will enter state s_2. If the agent takes action a_2, the environment will enter state s_3.
- From each of the states s_2 and s_3, the transition into the next state follows a similar set of bifurcating rules.
- States s_4, s_5, s_6, and s_7 are terminal states: if any of the states is reached, the episode ends.

So, each episode in this RL problem lasts exactly three steps. How should the agent in this RL problem decide what action to take at the first and second steps? Given that we are dealing with an RL problem, the question makes sense only if the rewards are considered. In MDP, each action not only causes a state transition but also leads to a reward. In figure 11.10, the rewards are depicted as the arrows that connect actions with the next states, labeled with r = <reward_value>. The agent's goal is, of course, to maximize the total reward (discounted by a factor). Now imagine we are the agent at the first step. Let's examine the thought process through which we'll decide which of a_1 or a_2 is the better choice. Let's suppose the reward discount factor (γ) has a value of 0.9.

The thought process goes like this. If we pick action a_1, we will get an immediate reward of –3 and transition to state s_2. If we pick action a_2, we will get an immediate reward of 3 and transition to state s_3. Does that mean a_2 is a better choice because 3 is greater than –3? The answer is no, because 3 and –3 are just the immediate rewards, and we haven't taken into account the rewards from the following steps. We should look at the *best possible* outcome from each of s_2 and s_3. What is the best outcome from s_2? It is the outcome engendered by action a_2, which gives a reward of 11. That leads to the best discounted reward we can expect if we take the action a_1 from state s_1:

Best reward from state s_1 taking action a_1	= immediate reward + discounted future reward = –3 + γ * 10 = –3 + 0.9 * 10 = 6

Similarly, the best outcome from state s_3 is if we take action a_1, which gives us a reward of –4. Therefore, if we take action a_2 from state s_1, the best discounted reward for us is

Best reward from state s_1 taking action a_2	= immediate reward + discounted future reward = 3 + γ * –4 = 3 + 0.9 * –4 = 0.6

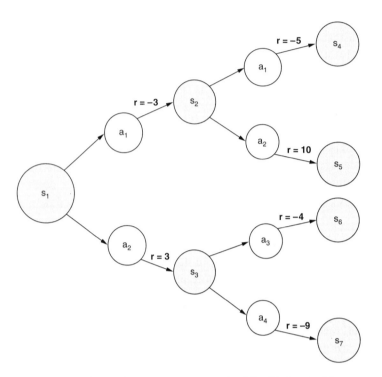

Figure 11.10   A very simple concrete example of the Markov decision process (MDP). States are represented as gray circles labeled with s_n, while actions are represented as gray circles labeled with a_m. The reward associated with each state transition caused by an action is labeled with *r = x.*

The discounted rewards we calculated here are examples of what we refer to as a *Q-values.* A Q-value is the expected total cumulative reward (with discounting) for an action at a given state. From these Q-values, it is clear that a_1 is the better choice at state s_1—a different conclusion from what we'd reach if we considered only the immediate reward caused by the first action. Exercise 3 at the end of the chapter guides you through the Q-value calculation for more realistic scenarios of MDP that involve stochasticity.

The example thought process described may seem trivial. But it leads us to an abstraction that plays a central role in Q-learning. A Q-value, denoted $Q(s, a)$, is a function of the current state (s) and the action (a). In other words, $Q(s, a)$ is a function that maps a state-action pair to the estimated value of taking the particular action at the particular state. This value is farsighted, in the sense that it accounts for best future rewards, under the assumption of optimal actions at all future steps.

Thanks to its farsightedness, $Q(s, a)$ is all we need to decide on the best action at any given state. In particular, given that we know what $Q(s, a)$ is, the best action is the one that gives us the highest Q-value among all possible actions:

The a_1 that gives us the maximum value among
$$Q(s_i, s_1), Q(s_i, a_2), \ldots, Q(s_i, a_N) \qquad \textbf{(Equation 11.2)}$$

where N is the number of all possible actions. If we have a good estimate of $Q(s, a)$, we can simply follow this decision process at every step, and we'll be guaranteed to get the highest possible cumulative reward. Therefore, the RL problem of finding the best decision-making process is reduced to learning the function $Q(s, a)$. This is why this learning algorithm is called Q-learning.

Let's stop for a moment and look at how Q-learning differs from the policy-gradient method we saw in the cart-pole problem. Policy gradient is about predicting the best action; Q-learning is about predicting the values of all possible actions (Q-values). While policy gradient tells us which action to choose directly, Q-learning requires an additional "pick-the-maximum" step and is hence slightly more indirect. The benefit afforded by this indirection is that it makes it easier to form a connection between the rewards and values of successive steps, which facilitates learning in problems that involve sparse positive rewards like snake.

What are the connections between rewards and values of successive steps? We have already gotten a glimpse of this when solving the simple MDP problem in figure 11.10. This connection can be written mathematically as

$$Q(s_i, a) = r + \gamma \cdot [\text{The maximum value among}$$
$$Q(s_{\text{next}}, a_1), Q(s_{\text{next}}, a_2), \ldots, Q(s_{\text{next}}, a_N)] \qquad \textbf{(Equation 11.3)}$$

where s_{next} is the state we'll reach after choosing action a from state s_i. This equation, known as the *Bellman equation*,[7] is an abstraction for how we got the numbers 6 and −0.6 for the actions a_1 and a_2 in the simple earlier example. In plain words, the equation says

> *The Q-value of taking action a at state s_i is a sum of two terms:*
>
> 1. *The immediate reward due to a, and*
> 2. *The best possible Q-value from that next state multiplied by a discounting factor ("best" in the sense of optimal choice of action at the next state)*

The Bellman equation is what makes Q-learning possible and is therefore important to understand. The programmer in you will immediately notice that the Bellman equation (equation 11.3) is recursive: all the Q-values on the right-hand side of the equation can be expanded further using the equation itself. The example in figure 11.10 we worked through ends after two steps, while real MDP problems usually involve a much larger number of steps and states, potentially even containing cycles in the state-action-transition graph. But the beauty and power of the Bellman equation is

---

[7] Attributed to American applied mathematician Richard E. Bellman (1920–1984). See his book *Dynamic Programming*, Princeton University Press, 1957.

that it allows us to turn the Q-learning problem into a supervised learning problem, even for large state spaces. We'll explain why that's the case in the next section.

11.3.3 Deep Q-network

Hand-crafting the function $Q(s, a)$ can be difficult, so we will instead let the function be a deep neural network (the DQN mentioned earlier in the section) and train its parameters. This DQN receives an input tensor that represents the complete state of the environment—that is, the snake board configuration—which is available to the agent as the observation. As figure 11.11 shows, the tensor has a shape `[9, 9, 2]` (excluding the batch dimension). The first two dimensions correspond to the height and width of the game board. Hence, the tensor can be viewed as a bitmap representation of all squares on the board. The last dimension (2) is two channels that represent the snake and the fruit, respectively. In particular, the snake is encoded in the first channel, with the head labeled as 2 and the body labeled as 1. The fruit is encoded in the second channel, with a value 1. In both channels, empty squares are represented by 0s. Note that these pixel values and the number of channels are more or less arbitrary. Other value arrangements (such as 100 for the snake's head and 50 for the snake's body, or separating the snake's head and body into two channels) will likely also work, as long as they keep the three types of entities (snake head, snake body, and fruit) distinct.

Note that this tensor representation of the game state is much less space-efficient than the JSON representation consisting of the fields `s` and `f` that we described in the previous section, because it always includes all the squares of the board regardless of how long the snake is. This inefficient representation is used only when we use

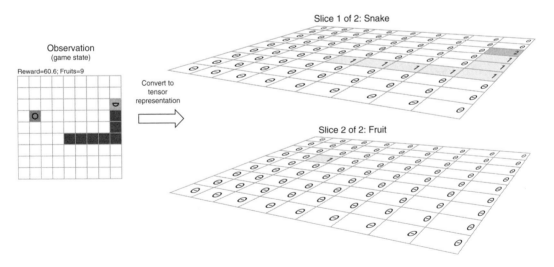

Figure 11.11   How the snake game's board state is represented as a 3D tensor of shape `[9, 9, 2]`

back-propagation to update the DQN's weights. In addition, only a small number (`batchSize`) of game states are present in this way at any given time, due to the batch-based training paradigm we will soon visit.

The code that converts an efficient representation of the board state into the kind of tensors illustrated in figure 11.11 can be found in the `getStateTensor()` function in snake-dqn/snake_game.js. This function will be used a lot during the DQN's training, but we omit its details here because it is just mechanically assigning values to the elements of a tensor buffer based on where the snake and fruit are.

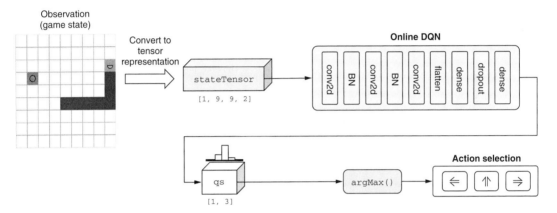

Figure 11.12 A schematic illustration of the DQN that we use as an approximation to the function Q(s, a) for the snake problem. In the "Online DQN" box, "BN" stands for BatchNormalization.

You might have noticed that this `[height, width, channel]` input format is exactly what convnets are designed to process. The DQN we use is of the familiar convnet architecture. The code that defines the topology of the DQN can be found in listing 11.5 (excerpted from snake-dqn/dqn.js, with some error-checking code removed for clarity). As the code and the diagram in figure 11.12 show, the network consists of a stack of conv2d layers followed by an MLP. Additional layers including batchNormalization and dropout are inserted to increase the generalization power of the DQN. The output of the DQN has a shape of `[3]` (excluding the batch dimension). The three elements of the output are the predicted Q-values of the corresponding actions (turn left, going straight, and turn right). Thus our model of $Q(s, a)$ is a neural network that takes a state as the input and outputs the Q-values for all possible actions given that state.

Listing 11.5 Creating the DQN for the snake problem

```
export function createDeepQNetwork(h, w, numActions) {
  const model = tf.sequential();
  model.add(tf.layers.conv2d({
    filters: 128,
    kernelSize: 3,
```

◁──── **The DQN has a typical convnet architecture: it begins with a stack of conv2d layers.**

```
      strides: 1,
      activation: 'relu',                    The input shape matches the tensor representation of
      inputShape: [h, w, 2]          ◁────── the agent's observation, as shown in figure 11.11.
    }));
    model.add(tf.layers.batchNormalization());  ◁────
    model.add(tf.layers.conv2d({                       batchNormalization layers are
      filters: 256,                                    added to counter overfitting
      kernelSize: 3,                                   and improve generalization
      strides: 1,
      activation: 'relu'
    }));
    model.add(tf.layers.batchNormalization());
    model.add(tf.layers.conv2d({
      filters: 256,
      kernelSize: 3,
      strides: 1,
      activation: 'relu'                       The MLP portion of the DQN
    }));                                        begins with a flatten layer.
    model.add(tf.layers.flatten());  ◁────
    model.add(tf.layers.dense({units: 100, activation: 'relu'}));
    model.add(tf.layers.dropout({rate: 0.25}));  ◁────  Like batchNormalization,
    model.add(tf.layers.dense({units: numActions}));    the dropout layer is added
    return model;                                        to counter overfitting.
}
```

Let's pause for a moment and think about why it makes sense to use a neural network as the function $Q(s, a)$ in this problem. The snake game has a discrete state space, unlike the continuous state space in the cart-pole problem, which consisted of four floating-point numbers. Therefore, the $Q(s, a)$ function could in principle be implemented as a lookup table—that is, one that maps every single possible combination of board configuration and action into a value of Q. So why do we prefer a DQN over such a lookup table? The reason: there are far too many possible board configurations with even the relatively small board size (9×9),[8] which leads to two major shortcomings of the lookup table approach. First, the system RAM is unable to hold such a huge lookup table. Second, even if we manage to build a system with sufficient RAM, it will take a prohibitively long time for the agent to visit all the states during RL. The DQN addresses the first (memory space) problem thanks to its moderate size (about 1 million parameters). It addresses the second (state-visit time) problem because of

---

[8] A back-of-the-envelope calculation leads to the rough estimate that the number of possible board configurations is on the order of at least 10^{15}, even if we limit the snake length to 20. For example, consider the particular snake length of 20. First, pick a location for the head of the snake, for which there are 9 * 9 = 81 possibilities. Then there are four possible locations for the first segment of the body, followed by three possible locations for the second segment, and so forth. Of course, in some body-pose configurations, there will be fewer than three possibilities, but that shouldn't significantly alter the order of magnitude. Hence, we can estimate the number of possible body configurations of a length-20 snake to be approximately $81 * 4 * 3^{18} \approx 10^{12}$. Considering that there are 61 possible fruit locations for each body configuration, the estimate for possible joint snake-fruit configurations goes up to 10^{14}. Similar estimations can be applied to shorter snake lengths, from 2 to 19. Summing all the estimated numbers from the lengths from 2 to 20 gives us the order of magnitude of 10^{15}. Video games such as Atari 2600 games involve a much larger number of pixels compared to the number of squares on our snake board, and are therefore even less amenable to the lookup-table approach. This is one of the reasons why DQNs are a suitable technique for solving such video games using RL, as demonstrated in the landmark 2015 paper by DeepMind's Volodymyr Mnih and colleagues.

neural networks' generalization power. As we've seen ample evidence for in the previous chapters, a neural network doesn't need to see all the possible inputs; it learns to interpolate between training examples through generalization. Therefore, by using DQN, we kill two birds with one stone.

11.3.4 *Training the deep Q-network*

Now we have a DQN that estimates the Q-values of all three possible actions at every step of the snake game. To achieve the greatest possible cumulative reward, all we have to do is run the DQN using the observation at every step and pick the action with the highest Q-value. Are we done yet? No, because the DQN is not trained yet! Without proper training, the DQN will contain only randomly initialized weights, and the actions it gives us will be no better than random guesses. Now the snake RL problem has been reduced to the question of how to train the DQN, a topic we'll cover in this section. The process is somewhat involved. But don't worry: we'll use plenty of diagrams, accompanied by code excerpts, to spell out the training algorithm step-by-step.

INTUITION BEHIND THE DEEP Q-NETWORK'S TRAINING

We will train our DQN by pressuring it to match the Bellman equation. If all goes well, this means that our DQN will reflect both the immediate rewards and the optimal discounted future rewards.

How can we do that? What we will need is many samples of input-output pairs, the input being the state and action actually taken and the output being the "correct" (target) value of Q. Computing samples of input requires the current state s_i and the action we took at that state, a_j, both of which are directly available in the game history. Computing the target value of Q requires the immediate reward r_i and the next state s_{i+1}, which are also available from game history. We can use r_i and s_{i+1} to compute the target Q-value by applying the Bellman equation, the details of which will be covered shortly. We will then calculate the difference between Q-value predicted by the DQN and the target Q-value from the Bellman equation and call that our loss. We will reduce the loss (in a least-squares sense) using standard backpropagation and gradient descent. The machinery making this possible and efficient is somewhat complicated, but the intuition is rather straightforward. We want an estimate of the Q function so we can make good decisions. We know our estimate of Q must match the environmental rewards and the Bellman equation, so we will use gradient descent to make it so. Simple!

REPLAY MEMORY: A ROLLING DATASET FOR THE DQN'S TRAINING

Our DQN is a familiar convnet implemented as an instance of `tf.LayersModel` in TensorFlow.js. With regard to how to train it, the first thing that comes to mind is to call its `fit()` or `fitDataset()` method. However, we can't use that usual approach here because we don't have a labeled dataset that contains observed states and the corresponding Q-values. Consider this: before the DQN is trained, there is no way to know the Q-values. If we had a method that gave us the true Q-values, we would just use it in our Markov decision process and be done with it. So, if we confine ourselves to the traditional supervised-learning approach, we will face a chicken-and-egg prob-lem: without a trained DQN, we can't estimate the Q-values; without a good estimate of Q-values, we can't train the DQN. The RL algorithm we are about to introduce will help us solve this chicken-and-egg problem.

Specifically, our method is to let the agent play the game randomly (at least ini-tially) and remember what happened at every step of the game. The random-play part is easily achieved using a random-number generator. The remembering part is achieved with a data structure known as *replay memory*. Figure 11.13 illustrates how the replay memory works. It stores five items for every step of the game:

1 s_i, observation of the current state at step i (the board configuration).

2 a_i, action actually performed at the current step (selected either by the DQN as depicted in figure 11.12 or through random selection).

3 r_i, the immediate reward received at this step.

4 d_i, a Boolean flag indicating whether the game ends immediately after the cur-rent step. From this, you can see the fact that the replay memory is not just for a single episode of the game. Instead, it concatenates the results from multiple game episodes. Once a previous game is over, the training algorithm simply starts a new one and keeps appending the new records to the replay memory.

5 s_{i+1}, the observation from the next step if d_i is false. (If d_i is true, a null is stored as the placeholder.)

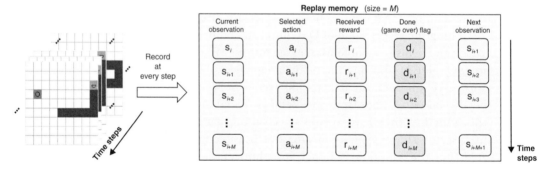

Figure 11.13   **The replay memory used during the training of the DQN. Five pieces of data are pushed to the end of the replay memory at every step. These data are sampled during the DQN's training.**

These pieces of data will go into the backpropagation-based training of the DQN. The replay memory can be thought of as a "dataset" for the DQN's training. However, it's different from the kind of datasets in supervised learning, in the sense that it keeps getting updated as the training goes on. The replay memory has a fixed length M ($M = 10,000$ by default in the example code). When a record (s_i, a_i, r_i, d_i, s_{i+1}) is pushed to its end after a new game step, an old record is popped out from its begin-ning, which maintains a fixed replay-memory length. This ensures that the replay memory keeps track of what happened in the most recent M steps of the training, in addition to avoiding out-of-memory problems. It is beneficial to always train the DQN using the latest game records. Why? Consider the following: once the DQN has been trained for a while and starts to "get the hang of" the game, we won't want to teach it using old game records like the ones from the beginning of the training because those may contain naive moves that are no longer relevant or conducive to the further training of the network.

The code that implements the replay memory is very simple and can be found in the file snake-dqn/replay_memory.js. We won't describe the details of the code, except its two public methods, append() and sample():

- append() allows the caller to push a new record to the end of the replay memory.
- sample(batchSize) selects batchSize records from the replay memory randomly. The records are sampled completely uniformly and will in general include records from multiple different episodes. The sample() method will be used to extract training batches during the calculation of the loss function and the subsequent backpropagation, as we will see shortly.

THE EPSILON-GREEDY ALGORITHM: BALANCING EXPLORATION AND EXPLOITATION

An agent that keeps trying random things will stumble onto some good moves (eat a fruit or two in a snake game) by pure luck. This is useful for kickstarting the agent's early learning process. In fact, it is the only way because the agent is never told the rules of the game. But if the agent keeps behaving randomly, it won't make it very far in the learning process, both because random choices lead to accidental deaths and because some advanced states can be achieved only through streaks of good moves.

This is the manifestation of the exploration-versus-exploitation dilemma in the snake game. We've seen this dilemma in the cart-pole example, where the policy-gradient method addresses the problem thanks to the gradual increase in the determinism of the multinomial sampling with training. In the snake game, we do not have this luxury because our action selection is based not on tf.multinomial() but on selecting the maximum Q-value among the actions. The way in which we address the dilemma is by parameterizing the randomness of the action-selection process and gradually reducing the parameter of randomness. In particular, we use the so-called *epsilon-greedy policy*. This policy can be expressed in pseudo-code as

```
x = Sample a random number uniformly between 0 and 1.
if x < epsilon:
  Choose an action randomly
else:
  qValues = DQN.predict(observation)
  Choose the action that corresponds to the maximum element of qValues
```

This logic is applied at every step of the training. The larger the value of epsilon (the closer it is to 1), the more likely the action will be chosen at random. Conversely, a smaller value of epsilon (closer to 0) leads to a higher probability of choosing the action based on the Q-values predicted by the DQN. Choosing actions at random can be viewed as exploring the environment ("epsilon" stands for "exploration"), while choosing actions to maximize the Q-value is referred to as *greedy*. Now you understand where the name *epsilon-greedy* comes from.

As shown in listing 11.6, the actual TensorFlow.js code that implements the epsilon-greedy algorithm in the snake-dqn example has a close one-to-one correspondence with the previous pseudo-code. This code is excerpted from snake-dqn/agent.js.

Listing 11.6   The part of snake-dqn code that implements the epsilon-greedy algorithm

```
let action;
const state = this.game.getState();
if (Math.random() < this.epsilon) {        Exploration: picks
  action = getRandomAction();        ◁———   actions randomly
} else {
  tf.tidy(() => {
    const stateTensor =
        getStateTensor(state,                Represents the game
                this.game.height,            state as a tensor
                this.game.width);
    action = ALL_ACTIONS[                          Greedy policy: gets predicted
        this.onlineNetwork.predict(                Q-values from the DQN and
            stateTensor).argMax(-1).dataSync()[0]];  finds the index of the action
  });                                                 that corresponds to the
}                                                      highest Q-value
```

The epsilon-greedy policy balances the early need for exploration and later need for stable behavior. It does so through gradually ramping down the value of epsilon from a relative large value to a value close to (but not exactly) zero. In our snake-dqn example, epsilon is ramped down in a linear fashion from 0.5 to 0.01 over the first 1×105 steps of the training. Note that we don't decrease the epsilon all the way to zero because we need a moderate degree of exploration even at advanced stages of the agent's training in order to help the agent discover smart new moves. In RL problems based on the epsilon-greedy policy, the initial and final values of epsilon are tunable hyperparameters, and so is the time course of epsilon's down-ramping.

With the backdrop of our deep Q-learning algorithm set by the epsilon-greedy policy, next let's examine the details of how the DQN is trained.

EXTRACTING PREDICTED Q-VALUES

Although we are using a new approach to attack the RL problem, we still want to mold our algorithm into supervised learning because that will allow us to use the familiar backpropagation approach to update the DQN's weights. Such a formulation requires three things:

- Predicted Q-values.
- "True" Q-values. Note that the word "true" is in quotes here because there isn't really a way to obtain the ground truths for Q-values. These values are merely the best estimates of $Q(s, a)$ that we can come up with at a given stage of the training algorithm. For this reason, we'll refer to them as the target Q-values instead.

- A loss function that takes the predicted and target Q-values and outputs a number that quantifies the mismatch between the two.

In this subsection, we'll look at how the predicted Q-values can be obtained from the replay memory. The following two subsections will talk about how to obtain the target Q-values and the loss function. Once we have all three, our snake RL problem will basically become a straightforward backpropagation problem.

Figure 11.14 illustrates how the predicted Q-values are extracted from the replay memory in a step of the DQN's training. The diagram should be viewed in conjunction with the implementing code in listing 11.7 to facilitate understanding.

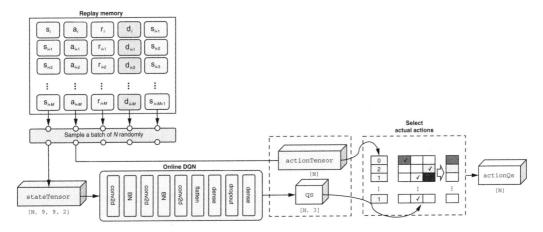

Figure 11.14 How the predicted Q-values are obtained from the replay memory and the online DQN. This is the first of the two parts that go into the supervised-learning portion of the DQN training algorithm. The result of this workflow, `actionQs`—that is, the Q-values predicted by the DQN—is one of the two arguments that will go into the calculation of the MSE loss together with `targetQs`. See figure 11.15 for the workflow in which `targetQs` is calculated.

In particular, we sample `batchSize` (N = 128 by default) records randomly from the replay memory. As described before, each record has five items. For the purpose of getting the predicted Q-values, we need only the first two. The first items, consisting of the N state observations, are converted together into a tensor. This batched observation tensor is processed by the online DQN, which gives the predicted Q-values (qs in both the diagram and the code). However, qs includes the Q-values for not only the actually selected actions but also the nonselected ones. For our training, we want to ignore the Q-values for the nonselected actions because there isn't a way to know their target Q-values. This is where the second replay-memory item comes in.

The second items contain the actually selected actions. They are formatted into a tensor representation (`actionTensor` in the diagram and code). `actionTensor` is then used to select the elements of qs that we want. This step, illustrated in the box labeled Select Actual Actions in the diagram, is achieved using three TensorFlow.js functions: `tf.oneHot()`, `mul()`, and `sum()` (see the last line in listing 11.7). This is slightly more complex than slicing a tensor because different actions can be selected at different game steps. The code in listing 11.7 is excerpted from the SnakeGameAgent.trainOn-ReplayBatch() method in snake-dqn/agent.js, with minor omissions for clarity.

Listing 11.7   Extracting a batch of predicted Q-values from the replay memory

Gets a batch of batchSize randomly chosen game records from the replay memory

The first element of every game record is the agent's state observation (see figure 11.13). It is converted from a JSON object into a tensor by the getStateTensor() function (see figure 11.11).

```
const batch = this.replayMemory.sample(batchSize);
const stateTensor = getStateTensor(
    batch.map(example => example[0]),
    this.game.height, this.game.width);
const actionTensor = tf.tensor1d(
    batch.map(example => example[1]),
    'int32');
const qs = this.onlineNetwork.apply(
    stateTensor, {training: true})
    .mul(tf.oneHot(actionTensor, NUM_ACTIONS)).sum(-1);
```

The second element of the game record is the actually selected action. It's represented as a tensor as well.

The apply() method is similar to the predict() method, but the "training: true" flag is specified explicitly to enable backpropagation.

We use tf.oneHot(), mul(), and sum() to isolate the Q-values for only the actually selected actions and discard the ones for the actions not selected.

These operations give us a tensor called actionQs, which has a shape of [N], N being the batch size. This is the predicted Q-value that we sought—that is, the predicted $Q(s, a)$ for the state *s* we were in and the action *a* we actually took. Next, we'll examine how the target Q-values are obtained.

EXTRACTING TARGET Q-VALUES: USING THE BELLMAN EQUATION

It is slightly more involved to obtain the target Q-values than the predicted ones. This is where the theoretical Bellman equation will be put to practical use. Recall that the Bellman equation describes the Q-value of a state-action pair in terms of two things: 1) the immediate reward and 2) the maximum Q-value available from the next step's state (discounted by a factor). The former is easy to obtain. It is directly available as the third item of the replay memory. The rewardTensor in figure 11.15 illustrates this schematically.

To calculate the latter (maximum next-step Q-value), we need the state observation from the next step. Luckily, the next-step observation is stored in the replay memory as the fifth item. We take the next-step observation of the randomly sampled batch, convert it to a tensor, and run it through a copy of the DQN called the *target DQN* (see figure 11.15). This gives us the estimated Q-values for the next-step states. Once we have these, we perform a max() call along the last (actions) dimension, which leads to the maximum Q-values achievable from the next-step state (represented as nextMax-QTensor in listing 11.8). Following the Bellman equation, this maximum value is mul-

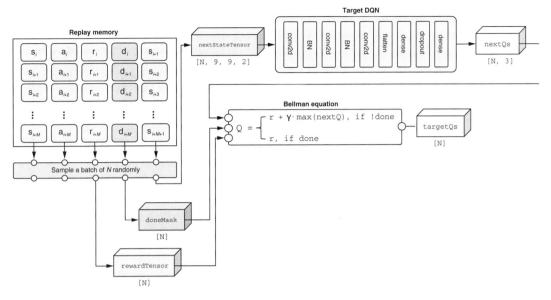

Figure 11.15 How the target Q-values (`targetQs`) are obtained from the replay memory and the target DQN. This figure shares the replay-memory and batch-sampling parts with figure 11.14. It should be examined in conjunction with the code in listing 11.8. This is the second of the two parts that goes into the supervised-learning portion of the DQN training algorithm. `targetQs` plays a role similar to the truth labels in supervised-learning problems seen in the previous chapters (for example, known true labels in the MNIST examples or known true future temperature values in the Jena-weather example). The Bellman equation plays a critical role in the calculation of `targetQs`. Together with the target DQN, the equation allows us to calculate the values of `targetQs` through forming a connection between the Q-values of the current step and the Q-values of the ensuing step.

tiplied by the discount factor (γ in figure 11.15 and `gamma` in listing 11.8) and combined with the immediate reward, which yields the target Q-values (`targetQs` in both the diagram and the code).

Note that the next-step Q-value exists only when the current step is not the last step of a game episode (that is, it doesn't cause the snake to die). If it is, then the right-hand side of the Bellman equation will include only the immediate-reward term, as shown in figure 11.15. This corresponds to the `doneMask` tensor in listing 11.8. The code in this listing is excerpted from the `SnakeGameAgent.trainOnReplayBatch()` method in snake-dqn/agent.js, with minor omissions for clarity.

Listing 11.8 Extracting a batch of target ("true") Q-values from the replay memory

```
const rewardTensor = tf.tensor1d(
    batch.map(example => example[2]));
const nextStateTensor = getStateTensor(
    batch.map(example => example[4]),
    this.game.height, this.game.width);
```

The third item of a replay record contains the immediate reward value.

The fifth item of a record contains the next-state observation. It's transformed into a tensor representation.

```
const nextMaxQTensor =
    this.targetNetwork.predict(nextStateTensor) ◁─┐
    ▷ .max(-1);
const doneMask = tf.scalar(1).sub(
    tf.tensor1d(batch.map(example => example[3]))
        .asType('float32'));    ◁┄┄┄┄┄┄┄┄┄┄┄┄┄┄
const targetQs =
    rewardTensor.add(nextMaxQTensor.mul(
        doneMask).mul(gamma));
```

The target DQN is used on the next-state tensor, which yields the Q-values for all actions at the next step.

Uses the max() function to extract the highest possible reward at the next step. This is on the right-hand side of the Bellman equation.

doneMask has the value 0 for the steps that terminate the game and 1 for other steps.

Uses the Bellman equation to calculate the target Q-values.

As you may have noticed, an important trick in the deep Q-learning algorithm here is the use of two instances of DQNs. They are called the *online* DQN and the *target* DQN, respectively. The online DQN is responsible for calculating the predicted Q-values (see figure 11.14 in the previous subsection). It is also the DQN that we use to choose the snake's action when the epsilon-greedy algorithm decides on the greedy (no-exploration) approach. This is why it's called the "online" network. By contrast, the target DQN is used only to calculate the target Q-values, as we've just seen. This is why it's called the "target" DQN. Why do we use two DQNs instead of one? To break up undesirable feedback loops, which can cause instabilities in the training process.

The online DQN and target DQN are created by the same `createDeepQNetwork()` function (listing 11.5). They are two deep convnets with identical topologies. Therefore, they have exactly the same set of layers and weights. The weight values are copied from the online DQN to the target one periodically (every 1,000 steps in the default setting of snake-dqn). This keeps the target DQN up-to-date with the online DQN. Without this synchronization, the target DQN will go out-of-date and hamper the training process by producing poor estimates of the best next-step Q-values in the Bellman equation.

LOSS FUNCTION FOR Q-VALUE PREDICTION AND BACKPROPAGATION

With both predicted and target Q-values at hand, we use the familiar `meanSquared-Error` loss function to compute the discrepancy between the two (figure 11.16). At this point, we've managed to turn our DQN training process into a regression problem, not unlike previous examples such as Boston-housing and Jena-weather. The error signal from the `meanSquareError` loss drives the backpropagation; the resulting weight updates are used to update the online DQN.

The schematic diagram in figure 11.16 includes parts we've already shown in figures 11.12 and 11.13. It puts those parts together and adds the new boxes and arrows for the `meanSquaredError` loss and the backpropagation based on it (see the bottom-right of the diagram). This completes the full picture of the deep Q-learning algorithm we use to train our snake-game agent.

The code in listing 11.9 has a close correspondence with the diagram in figure 11.16. It is the `trainOnReplayBatch()` method of the `SnakeGameAgent` class in snake-

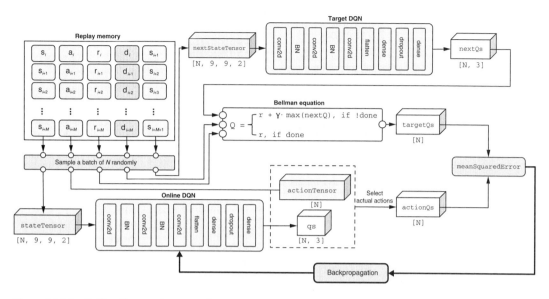

Figure 11.16 Putting the `actionQs` and `targetQs` together in order to calculate the online DQN's `meanSquaredError` prediction error and thereby use backpropagation to update its weights. Most parts of this diagram have already been shown in figures 11.12 and 11.13. The newly added parts are the `meanSquaredError` loss function and the backpropagation step based on it, located in the bottom-right part of the diagram.

dqn/agent.js, which plays a central role in our RL algorithm. The method defines a loss function that calculates the `meanSquaredError` between the predicted and target Q-values. It then calculates the gradients of the `meanSquaredError` with respect to the online DQN's weights using the `tf.variableGrads()` function (appendix B, section B.4 contains a detailed discussion of TensorFlow.js's gradient-computing functions such as `tf.variableGrads()`). The calculated gradients are used to update the DQN's weights with the help of an optimizer. This nudges the online DQN in the direction of making more accurate estimates of the Q-values. Repeated over millions of iterations, this leads to a DQN that can guide the snake to a decent performance. For the following listing, the part of the code responsible for calculating the target Q-values (`targetQs`) has already been shown in listing 11.8.

Listing 11.9 The core function that trains the DQN

```
trainOnReplayBatch(batchSize, gamma, optimizer) {
  const batch =
    this.replayMemory.sample(batchSize);
  const lossFunction = () => tf.tidy(() => {
    const stateTensor = getStateTensor(
      batch.map(example => example[0]),
               this.game.height,
               this.game.width);
```

Gets a random batch of examples from the replay buffer

lossFunction returns a scalar and will be used for backpropagation.

```
            const actionTensor = tf.tensor1d(
                batch.map(example => example[1]), 'int32');
            const qs = this.onlineNetwork
                .apply(stateTensor, {training: true})
                .mul(tf.oneHot(actionTensor, NUM_ACTIONS)).sum(-1);

            const rewardTensor = tf.tensor1d(batch.map(example => example[2]));
            const nextStateTensor = getStateTensor(
                batch.map(example => example[4]),
                        this.game.height, this.game.width);
            const nextMaxQTensor =
                this.targetNetwork.predict(nextStateTensor).max(-1);
            const doneMask = tf.scalar(1).sub(
                tf.tensor1d(batch.map(example => example[3])).asType('float32'));
            const targetQs =
                rewardTensor.add(nextMaxQTensor.mul(doneMask).mul(gamma));
            return tf.losses.meanSquaredError(targetQs, qs);
        });

        const grads = tf.variableGrads(
            lossFunction, this.onlineNetwork.getWeights());
        optimizer.applyGradients(grads.grads);
        tf.dispose(grads);
    }
```

The predicted Q-values → `const qs = this.onlineNetwork`

The target Q-values calculated by applying the Bellman equation

Uses MSE as a measure of the discrepancy between the predicted and target Q-values

Calculates the gradient of lossFunction with respect to weights of the online DQN

Updates the weights using the gradients through an optimizer

That's it for the internal details of the deep Q-learning algorithm. The training based on this algorithm can be started with the following command in the Node.js environment:

```
yarn train --logDir /tmp/snake_logs
```

Add the `--gpu` flag to the command to speed up the training if you have a CUDA-enabled GPU. This `--logDir` flag lets the command log the following metrics to the TensorBoard log directory during training: 1) the running average of the cumulative rewards from the 100 most recent game episodes (cumulativeReward100); 2) the running average of the number of fruits eaten in the 100 most recent episodes (eaten-100); 3) the value of the exploration parameter (epsilon); and 4) the training speed in number of steps per second (framesPerSecond). These logs can be viewed by launching TensorBoard with the following commands and navigating to the HTTP URL of the TensorBoard frontend (by default: http://localhost:6006):

```
pip install tensorboard tensorboard --logdir /tmp/snake_logs
```

Figure 11.17 shows a set of typical log curves from the training process. As seen frequently in RL training, the cumulativeReward100 and eaten100 curves both show fluctuation. After a few hours of training, the model is able to reach a best cumulativeReward100 of 70–80 and a best eaten100 of about 12.

The training script also saves the model to the relative path ./models/dqn every time a new best cumulativeReward100 value has been achieved. The saved model is served from the web frontend when the yarn watch command is invoked. The frontend

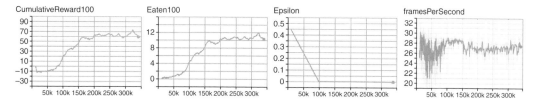

**Figure 11.17   Example logs from a snake-dqn training process in tfjs-node. The panels show
1) `cumulativeReward100`, a moving average of the cumulative reward obtained in the most recent
100 games; 2) `eaten100`, a moving average of the number of fruits eaten in the most recent 100 games;
3) `epsilon`, the value of epsilon, from which you can see the time course of the epsilon-greedy policy;
and 4) `framesPerSecond`, a measure of the training speed.**

displays the Q-values predicted by the DQN at every step of the game (see figure 11.18). The epsilon-greedy policy used during training is replaced with the "always-greedy" policy during the post-training gameplay. The action that corresponds to the highest Q-value (for example, 33.9 for going straight in figure 11.18) is always chosen as the snake's action. This gives you an intuitive understanding of how the trained DQN plays the game.

There are a couple of interesting observations from the snake's behavior. First, the number of fruits actually eaten by the snake in the frontend demo (~18) is on average greater than the `eaten100` curve from the training logs (~12). This is because of the removal of the epsilon-greedy policy, which abolishes random actions in the gameplay. Recall that epsilon is maintained as a small but nonzero value throughout the late stage of the DQN's training (see the third panel of figure 11.17). The random actions caused by this lead to premature deaths occasionally, and this is the cost of exploratory behavior. Second, the snake has developed an interesting strategy of going to the edges and corners of the board before approaching the fruit, even when the fruit is located near the center of the board. This strategy is effective in helping the snake reduce the likelihood of bumping into itself when its length is moderately large (for example, in the range of 10–18). This is not bad, but it is not perfect either because there are smarter strategies that the snake hasn't developed. For example, the snake frequently traps itself in a circle when its length gets above 20. This is as far as the algorithm in the snake-dqn can take us. To improve the snake agent further, we need to tweak the epsilon-greedy algorithm to encourage the snake to explore better moves when its length is long.[9] In the current algorithm, the

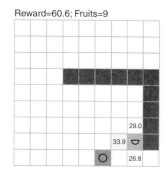

**Figure 11.18   The Q-values
estimated by a trained DQN are
displayed as numbers and overlaid
as different shades of green in the
game's frontend.**

9   For example, see https://github.com/carsonprindle/OpenAIExam2018.

degree of exploration is too low once the snake grows to a length that calls for skillful maneuvering around its own body.

This concludes our tour of the DQN technique for RL. Our algorithm is modeled after the 2015 paper "Human-Level Control through Deep Reinforcement Learning,"[10] in which researchers at DeepMind demonstrated for the first time that combining the power of deep neural networks and RL enables machines to solve many Atari 2600-style video games. The snake-dqn solution we've demonstrated is a simplified version of DeepMind's algorithm. For instance, our DQN looks at the observation from only the current step, while DeepMind's algorithm combines the current observation with observations from the previous several steps as the input to the DQN. But our example captures the essence of the groundbreaking technique—namely, using a deep convnet as a powerful function approximator to estimate the state-dependent values of actions, and training it using MDP and the Bellman equation. Subsequent feats by RL researchers, such as conquering the games of Go and chess, are based on a similar wedding between deep neural networks and traditional non-deep-learning RL methods.

Materials for further reading

- Richard S. Sutton and Andrew G. Barto, *Reinforcement Learning: An Introduction*, A Bradford Book, 2018.
- David Silver's lecture notes on reinforcement learning at University College London: http://www0.cs.ucl.ac.uk/staff/d.silver/web/Teaching.html.
- Alexander Zai and Brandon Brown, *Deep Reinforcement Learning in Action*, Manning Publications, in press, www.manning.com/books/deep-reinforcement-learning-in-action.
- Maxim Laplan, *Deep Reinforcement Learning Hands-On: Apply Modern RL Methods, with Deep Q-networks, Value Iteration, Policy Gradients, TRPO, AlphaGo Zero, and More*, Packt Publishing, 2018.

Exercises

1 In the cart-pole example, we used a policy network consisting of a hidden dense layer with 128 units, as it was the default setting. How does this hyperparameter affect the policy-gradient-based training? Try changing it to a small value such as 4 or 8 and comparing the resulting learning curve (mean steps per game versus iteration curve) with the one from the default hidden-layer size. What does that tell you about the relation between model capacity and its effectiveness in estimating the best action?

2 We mentioned that one of the advantages of using machine learning to solve a problem like cart-pole is the economy of human effort. Specifically, if the

---

[10] Volodymyr Mnih et al., "Human-Level Control through Deep Reinforcement Learning," *Nature*, vol. 518, 2015, pp. 529–533, www.nature.com/articles/nature14236/.

environment unexpectedly changes, we don't need to figure out *how* it has really changed and rework the physical equations. Instead, we can just let the agent re-learn the problem on its own. Prove to yourself that this is the case by following these steps. First, make sure that the cart-pole example is launched from source code and not the hosted web page. Train a working cart-pole policy network using the regular approach. Second, edit the value of `this`.`gravity` in cart-pole/cart_pole.js and change it to a new value (say, 12, if you want to pretend that we've moved the cart-pole setup to an exoplanet with a higher gravity than Earth!). Launch the page again, load the policy network you've trained in the first step, and test it. Can you confirm that it performs significantly worse than before, just because of the gravity change? Finally, train the policy network a few more iterations. Can you see the policy getting better at the game again (adapting to the new environment)?

3 (Exercise on MDP and Bellman equation) The example of MDP we presented in section 11.3.2 and figure 11.10 was simple in the sense that it was fully deterministic because there is no randomness in the state transitions and the associated rewards. But many real-world problems are better described as stochastic (random) MDPs. In a stochastic MDP, the state the agent will end up in and the reward it will get after taking an action follows a probabilistic distribution. For instance, as figure 11.19 shows, if the agent takes action A_1 at state S_1, it will end up in state S_2 with a probability of 0.5 and in state S_3 with a probability of 0.5. The rewards associated with the two state transitions are different. In such stochastic *MDPs*, the agent must take into account the randomness by calculating the *expected* future reward. The expected future reward is a weighted average of all possible rewards, with weights being the probabilities. Can you apply this probabilistic approach and estimate the Q-values for a_1 and a_2 at s_1 in the figure? Based on the answer, is a_1 or a_2 the better action at state s1?

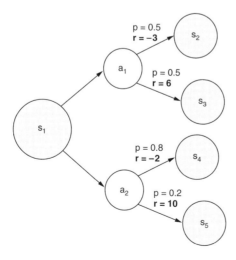

Figure 11.19 The diagram for the MDP in the first part of exercise 3

Now let's look at a slightly more complicated stochastic MDP, one that involves more than one step (see figure 11.20). In this slightly more complex case, you need to apply the recursive Bellman equation in order to take into account the best possible future rewards after the first action, which are themselves stochastic. Note that sometimes the episode ends after the first step, and sometimes it will last another step. Can you decide which action is better at s_1? For this problem, you can use a reward discount factor of 0.9.

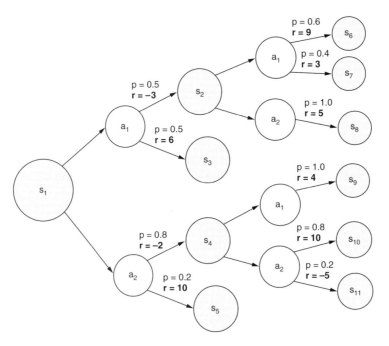

Figure 11.20   The diagram for the MDP in the second part of exercise 3

4   In the snake-dqn example, we used the epsilon-greedy policy to balance the needs for exploration and exploitation. The default setting decreases epsilon from an initial value of 0.5 to a final value of 0.01 and holds it there. Try changing the final epsilon value to a large value (such as 0.1) or a smaller one (such as 0), and observe the effects on how well the snake agent learns. Can you explain the resulting difference in terms of the role epsilon plays?

Summary

- As a type of machine learning, RL is about learning to make optimal decisions. In an RL problem, an agent learns to select actions in an environment to maximize a metric called the *cumulative reward*.

- Unlike supervised learning, there are no labeled training datasets in RL. Instead, the agent must learn what actions are good under different circumstances by trying out random actions.

- We explored two commonly used types of RL algorithms: policy-based methods (using the cart-pole example) and Q-value-based methods (using the snake example).

- A policy is an algorithm by which the agent picks an action based on the current state observation. A policy can be encapsulated in a neural network that takes state observation as its input and produces an action selection as its output. Such a neural network is called a *policy network*. In the cart-pole problem, we used policy gradients and the REINFORCEMENT method to update and train a policy network.

- Unlike the policy-based methods, Q-learning uses a model called *Q-network* to estimate the values of actions under a given observed state. In the snake-dqn example, we demonstrated how a deep convnet can serve as the Q-network and how it can be trained by using the MDP assumption, the Bellman equation, and a construct called *replay memory*.

Part 4

Summary and closing words

The final part of this book consists of two chapters. Chapter 12 addresses concerns that TensorFlow.js users may have when deploying models into production environments. It discusses best practices that help developers gain higher confidence in model correctness, techniques that make models smaller and help them run more efficiently, and the range of deployment environments that TensorFlow.js models support. Chapter 13 is a summary of the entire book, providing a review of the key concepts, workflows, and techniques.

Testing, optimizing, and deploying models

—WITH CONTRIBUTIONS FROM
YANNICK ASSOGBA, PING YU,
AND NICK KREEGER

This chapter covers

- The importance of and practical guidelines for testing and monitoring machine-learning code
- How to optimize models trained in TensorFlow.js or converted to TensorFlow.js for faster loading and inference
- How to deploy TensorFlow.js models to various platforms and environments, ranging from browser extensions to mobile apps, and from desktop apps to single-board computers

As we mentioned in chapter 1, machine learning differs from traditional software engineering in that it automates the discovery of rules and heuristics. The previous chapters of the book should have given you a solid understanding of this uniqueness of machine learning. However, machine-learning models and the code surrounding them are still code; they run as a part of your overall software system. In order to make sure that machine-learning models run reliably and efficiently, practitioners need to take similar precautions as they do when managing non-machine-learning code.

This chapter is devoted to the practical aspects of using TensorFlow.js for machine learning as a part of your software stack. The first section explores the all-important but oft-neglected topic of testing and monitoring machine-learning code and models. The second section presents tools and tricks that help you reduce the size and computation footprint of your trained models, accelerating downloading and execution, which is a critical consideration for both client- and server-side model deployment. In the final section, we will give you a tour of the various environments in which models created with TensorFlow.js can be deployed. In doing so, we will discuss the unique benefits, constraints, and strategies that each of the deployment options involves.

By the end of this chapter, you will be familiar with the best practices surrounding the testing, optimization, and deployment of deep-learning models in TensorFlow.js.

12.1 Testing TensorFlow.js models

So far, we've talked about how to design, build, and train machine-learning models. Now we're going to dive into some of the topics that arise when you deploy your trained models, starting with testing—of both the machine-learning code and the related non-machine-learning code. Some of the key challenges you face when you're seeking to surround your model and its training process with tests are the size of the model, the time required to train, and nondeterministic behavior that happens during training (such as randomness in the initialization of weights and certain neural network operations such as dropout). As we expand from an individual model to a complete application, you'll also run across various types of skew or drift between training and inference code paths, model versioning issues, and population changes in your data. You'll see that testing needs to be complemented by a robust monitoring solution in order to achieve the reliability and confidence that you want in your entire machine-learning system.

One key consideration is, "How is your model version controlled?" In most cases, the model is tuned and trained until a satisfactory evaluation accuracy is reached, and then the model needs no further tweaking. The model is not rebuilt or retrained as part of the normal build process. Instead, the model topology and trained weights should be checked into your version-control system, more similar to a binary large object (BLOB) than a text/code artifact. Changing the surrounding code should not cause an update of your model version number. Likewise, retraining a model and checking it in shouldn't require changing the non-model source code.

What aspect of a machine-learning system should be covered by tests? In our opinion, the answer is "every part." Figure 12.1 explains this answer. A typical system that goes from raw input data to a trained model ready for deployment consists of multiple key components. Some of them look similar to non-machine-learning code and are amenable to coverage by traditional unit testing, while others show more machine-learning-specific characteristics and hence require specially tailored testing or monitoring treatments. But the important take-home message here is never to ignore or underestimate the importance of testing just because you are dealing with a machine-learning system. Instead, we'd argue that unit testing is all the more important for machine-learning code, perhaps even more so than testing is for traditional software development, because machine-learning algorithms are typically more opaque and harder to understand than non-machine-learning ones. They can fail silently in the face of bad inputs, leading to issues that are hard to notice and debug, and the defense against such issues is testing and monitoring. In the following subsections, we will expand on various parts of figure 12.1.

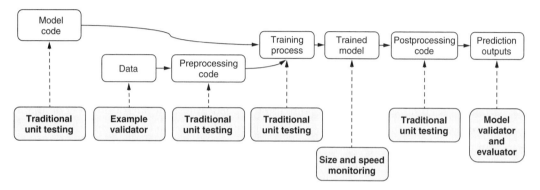

Figure 12.1   The coverage of a production-ready machine-learning system by testing and monitoring. The top half of the diagram includes the key components of a typical pipeline for machine-learning model creation and training. The bottom half shows the testing practice that can be applied to each of the components. Some of the components are amenable to traditional unit testing practice: the code that creates and trains the code, and the code that performs pre- and postprocessing of the model's input data and output results. Other components require more machine-learning-specific testing and monitoring practice. These include the example validation for the quality of data, the monitoring of the byte size and inference speed of the trained model, and the fine-grained validation and evaluation of the predictions made by the trained model.

12.1.1 Traditional unit testing

Just as with non-machine-learning projects, reliable and lightweight unit tests should form the foundation of your test suites. However, special considerations are required to set up unit tests around machine-learning models. As you've seen in previous chapters, metrics such as accuracy on an evaluation dataset are often used to quantify the final quality of the model after successful hyperparameter tuning and training. Such evaluation metrics are important for monitoring by human engineers but are not suitable for automated testing. It is tempting to add a test that asserts that a certain evaluation metric is better than a certain threshold (for example, AUC for a binary-classification task is greater than 0.95, or MSE for a regression task is less than 0.2). However, these types of threshold-based assertions should be used with caution, if not completely avoided, because they tend to be fragile. The model's training process contains multiple sources of randomness, including the initialization of weights and the shuffling of training examples. This leads to the fact that the result of model training varies slightly from run to run. If your datasets change (for instance, due to new data being added regularly), this will form an additional source of variability. As such, picking the threshold is a difficult task. Too lenient a threshold wouldn't catch real problems when they occur. Too stringent a threshold would lead to a flaky test—that is, one that fails frequently without a genuine underlying issue.

The randomness in a TensorFlow.js program can usually be disabled by calling the `Math.seedrandom()` function prior to creating and running the model. For example, the following line will seed the random state of weight initializers, data shuffler, and dropout layers with a determined seed so that subsequent model training will yield deterministic results:

```
Math.seedrandom(42);   ◁————
```
> 42 is just an arbitrarily-selected, fixed random seed.

This is a useful trick in case you need to write tests that make assertions about the loss or metric values.

However, even with deterministic seeding, testing only `model.fit()` or similar calls is not sufficient for good coverage of your machine-learning code. Like other hard-to-unit-test sections of code, you should aim to fully unit test the surrounding code that is easy to unit test and explore alternative solutions for the model portion. All your code for data loading, data preprocessing, postprocessing of model outputs, and other utility methods should be amenable to normal testing practices. Additionally, some non-stringent tests on the model itself—its input and output shapes, for instance—along with an "ensure model does not throw an exception when trained one step" style test can provide the bare minimum of a test harness around the model that allows confidence during refactoring. (As you might have noticed when playing with the example code from the previous chapters, we use the Jasmine testing framework for testing in tfjs-examples, but you should feel free to use whatever unit test framework and runner you and your team prefer.)

For an example of this in practice, we can look at the tests for the sentiment-analysis examples we explored in chapter 9. As you look through the code, you should see data_test.js, embedding_test.js, sequence_utils_test.js, and train_test.js. The first three of these files are covering the non-model code, and they look just like normal unit tests. Their presence gives us heightened confidence that the data that goes into the model during training and inference is in the expected source format, and our manipulations on it are valid.

The final file in that list concerns the machine-learning model and deserves a bit more of our attention. The following listing is an excerpt from it.

Listing 12.1   **Unit tests of a model's API—its input-output shapes and trainability**

```
describe('buildModel', () => {
 it('flatten training and inference', async () => {
    const maxLen = 5;
    const vocabSize = 3;
    const embeddingSize = 8;
    const model = buildModel('flatten', maxLen, vocabSize, embeddingSize);
    expect(model.inputs.length).toEqual(1);
    expect(model.inputs[0].shape).toEqual([null, maxLen]);
    expect(model.outputs.length).toEqual(1);
    expect(model.outputs[0].shape).toEqual([null, 1]);
```
> Ensures that the input and output of the model have the expected shape

```
model.compile({
  loss: 'binaryCrossentropy',
  optimizer: 'rmsprop',
  metrics: ['acc']
});
const xs = tf.ones([2, maxLen])
const ys = tf.ones([2, 1]);
const history = await model.fit(xs, ys, {
  epochs: 2,
  batchSize: 2
});
expect(history.history.loss.length).toEqual(2);
expect(history.history.acc.length).toEqual(2);

const predictOuts = model.predict(xs);
expect(predictOuts.shape).toEqual([2, 1]);
const values = predictOuts.arraySync();
expect(values[0][0]).toBeGreaterThanOrEqual(0);
expect(values[0][0]).toBeLessThanOrEqual(1);
expect(values[1][0]).toBeGreaterThanOrEqual(0);
expect(values[1][0]).toBeLessThanOrEqual(1);
});
});
```

Trains the model very briefly; this should be fast, but it won't be accurate.

Checks that training is reporting metrics for each training step as a signal that training occurred

Makes sure the prediction is in the range of possible answers; we don't want to check for the actual value, as the training was exceptionally brief and might be unstable.

Runs a prediction through the model focused on verifying the API is as expected

This test is covering a lot of ground, so let's break it down a little bit. We first build a model using a helper function. For this test, we don't care about the structure of the model and will treat it like a black box. We then make assertions on the shape of the inputs and outputs:

```
expect(model.inputs.length).toEqual(1);
expect(model.inputs[0].shape).toEqual([null, maxLen]);
expect(model.outputs.length).toEqual(1);
expect(model.outputs[0].shape).toEqual([null, 1]);
```

These tests can catch problems in terms of misidentifying the batch dimension—regression versus classification, output shape, and so on. Next, we compile and train the model on a very small number of steps. Our goal is simply to ensure that the model is trainable—we're not worried about accuracy, stability, or convergence at this point:

```
const history = await model.fit(xs, ys, {epochs: 2, batchSize: 2})
expect(history.history.loss.length).toEqual(2);
expect(history.history.acc.length).toEqual(2);
```

This snippet also checks that training reported the required metrics for analysis: if we trained for real, would we be able to inspect the progress of the training and the accuracy of the resulting model? Finally, we try a simple:

```
const predictOuts = model.predict(xs);
expect(predictOuts.shape).toEqual([2, 1]);
const values = predictOuts.arraySync();
expect(values[0][0]).toBeGreaterThanOrEqual(0);
expect(values[0][0]).toBeLessThanOrEqual(1);
```

```
expect(values[1][0]).toBeGreaterThanOrEqual(0);
expect(values[1][0]).toBeLessThanOrEqual(1);
```

We're not checking for any particular prediction result, as that might change based on the random initialization of weight values or possible future revisions to the model architecture. What we do check is that we get a prediction and that the prediction is in the expected range, in this case, between 0 and 1.

The most important lesson here is noticing that no matter how we change the inside of the model's architecture, as long we don't change its input or its output API, this test should always pass. If the test is failing, we have a problem in our model. These remain lightweight and fast tests that provide a strong degree of API correctness, and they are suitable for inclusion in whatever commonly run test hooks you use.

12.1.2 *Testing with golden values*

In the previous section, we talked about the unit testing we can do without asserting on a threshold metric value or requiring a stable or convergent training. Now let's explore the types of testing people often want to run with a fully trained model, starting with checking predictions of particular data points. Perhaps there are some "obvious" examples that you want to test. For instance, for an object detector, an input image with a nice big cat in it should be labeled as such; for a sentiment analyzer, a text snippet that's clearly a negative customer review should be classified as such. These correct answers for given model inputs are what we refer to as *golden values*. If you follow the mindset of traditional unit testing blindly, it is easy to fall into the trap of testing trained machine-learning models with golden values. After all, we want a well-trained object detector to always label the cat in an image with a cat in it, right? Not quite. Golden-value-based testing can be problematic in a machine-learning setting because we're usurping our training, validation, and evaluation data split.

Assuming you had a representative sample for your validation and test datasets, and you set an appropriate target metric (accuracy, recall, and so on), why is any one example required to be right more than another? The training of a machine-learning model is concerned with accuracy on the entire validation and test sets. The predictions for individual examples may vary with the selection of hyperparameters and initial weight values. If there are some examples that must be classified correctly and are easy to identify, why not detect them before asking the machine-learning model to classify them and instead use a non-machine-learning code to handle them? Such examples are used occasionally in natural language processing systems, where a subset of query inputs (such as frequently encountered and easily identifiable ones) are automatically routed to a non-machine-learning module for handling, while the remaining queries are handled by a machine-learning model. You'll save on compute time, and that portion of the code is easier to test with traditional unit testing. While adding a business-logic layer before (or after) the machine-learning predictor might seem like extra work, it gives you the hooks to control overrides of predictions. It's also a place where you can add monitoring or logging, which you'll probably want as your tool becomes more widely used. With that preamble, let's explore the three common desires for golden values separately.

One common motivation of this type of golden-value test is in service to a full end-to-end test—given an unprocessed user input, what does the system output? The machine-learning system is trained, and a prediction is requested through the normal end-user code flow, with an answer being returned to the user. This is similar to our unit test in listing 12.1, but the machine-learning system is in context with the rest of the application. We could write a test similar to listing 12.1 that doesn't care about the actual value of the prediction, and, in fact, that would be a more stable test. However, it's very tempting to combine it with an example/prediction pair that makes sense and is easily understood when developers revisit the test.

This is when the trouble enters—we need an example whose prediction is known and guaranteed to be correct or else the end-to-end test fails. So, we add a smaller-scale test that tests that prediction through a subset of the pipeline covered by the end-to-end test. Now if the end-to-end test fails, and the smaller test passes, we've isolated the error to interactions between the core machine-learning model and other parts of the pipeline (such as data ingestion or postprocessing). If both fail in unison, we know our example/prediction invariant is broken. In this case, it's more of a diagnostic tool, but the likely result of the paired failure is picking a new example to encode, not retraining the model entirely.

The next most common source is some form of business requirement. Some identifiable set of examples must be more accurate than the rest. As mentioned previously, this is the perfect setting for adding a pre- or post-model business-logic layer to handle these predictions. However, you can experiment with *example weighting*, in which some examples count for more than others when calculating the overall quality metrics. It won't guarantee correctness, but it will bias the model toward getting those correct. If a business-logic layer is difficult because you can't easily pre-identify the properties of the input that trigger the special case, you might need to explore a second model—one that is purely used to determine if override is needed. In this case, you're using an ensemble of models, and your business logic is combining the predictions from two layers to do the correct action.

The last case here is when you have a bug report with a user-provided example that gave the wrong result. If it's wrong for business reasons, we're back in the immediately preceding case. If it's wrong just because it falls into the failing percent of the model's performance curve, there's not a lot that we should do. It's within the accepted performance of the trained algorithm; all models are expected to make some mistakes. You can add the example/correct prediction pair to your train/test/eval sets as appropriate to hopefully generate a better model in the future, but it's not appropriate to use the golden values for unit testing.

An exception to this is if you're keeping the model constant—you have the model weights and architecture checked into version control and are not regenerating them in the tests. Then it can be appropriate to use golden values to test the outputs of an inference system that uses the model as its core, as neither the model nor the examples are subject to change. Such an inference system contains parts other than the model, such as parts that preprocess the input data before feeding it to the model and ones that take the model's outputs and transform them into forms more suitable for use by downstream systems. Such unit tests ensure the correctness of such pre- and postprocessing logic.

Another legitimate use of golden values is outside unit testing: the monitoring of the quality of a model (but not as unit testing) as it evolves. We will expand on this when we discuss the model validator and evaluator in the next section.

12.1.3 *Considerations around continuous training*

In many machine-learning systems, you get new training data at fairly regular intervals (every week or every day). Perhaps you're able to use your logs for the previous day to generate new, more timely training data. In such systems, the model needs to be retrained frequently, using the latest data available. In these cases, there is a belief that the age or staleness of the model affects its power. As time goes on, the inputs to the model drift to a different distribution than it was trained on, so the quality characteristics will get worse. As an example, you might have a clothing-recommendation tool that was trained in the winter but is making predictions in the summer.

Given the basic idea, as you begin to explore systems that require continuous training, you'll have a wide variety of extra components that create your pipeline. A full discussion of these is outside the scope of this book, but TensorFlow Extended (TFX)[1] is an infrastructure to look at for more ideas. The pipeline components it lists that have the most relevance in a testing arena are the *example validator, model validator,* and *model evaluator*. The diagram in figure 12.1 contains boxes that correspond to these components.

The example validator is about testing the data, an easy-to-overlook aspect of testing a machine-learning system. There is a famous saying among machine-learning practitioners: "garbage in, garbage out." The quality of a trained machine-learning model is limited by the quality of the data that goes into it. Examples with invalid feature values or incorrect labels will likely hurt the accuracy of the trained model when deployed for use (that is, if the model-training job doesn't fail because of the bad examples first!). The example validator is used to ensure that properties of the data that go into model training and evaluation always meet certain requirements: that you have enough data, that its distribution appears valid, and that you don't have any odd outliers. For instance, if you have a set of medical data, the body height (in centimeters) should be a positive number no larger than 280; the patient age should be a positive number between 0 and 130; the oral temperature (in degrees Celsius) should be a positive number between roughly 30 and 45, and so forth. If certain data examples contain features that fall outside such ranges or have placeholder values such as "None" or NaN, we know something is wrong with those examples, and they should be treated accordingly—in most cases, excluded from the training and evaluation.

---

[1] Denis Baylor et al., "TFX: A TensorFlow-Based Production-Scale Machine Learning Platform," KDD 2017, www.kdd.org/kdd2017/papers/view/tfx-a-tensorflow-based-production-scale-machine-learning-platform.

Typically, errors here indicate either a failure of the data-collection process or that the "world has changed" in ways incompatible with the assumptions you held when building the system. Normally, this is more analogous to monitoring and alerting than integration testing.

A component like an example validator is also useful for detecting *training-serving skew*, a particularly nasty type of bug that can arise in machine-learning systems. The two main causes are 1) training and serving data that belongs to different distributions and 2) data preprocessing involving code paths that behave differently during training and serving. An example validator deployed to both the training and serving environments has the potential to catch bugs introduced via either path.

The model validator plays the role of the person building the model in deciding if the model is "good enough" to use in serving. You configure it with the quality metrics you care about, and then it either "blesses" the model or rejects it. Again, like the example validator, this is more of a monitor-and-alert-style interaction. You'll also typically want to log and chart your quality metrics over time (accuracy and so on) in order to see if you're having small-scale, systematic degradations that might not trigger an alert by themselves but might still be useful for diagnosing long-term trends and isolating their causes.

The model evaluator is a sort of deeper dive into the quality statistics of the model, slicing and dicing the quality along a user-defined axis. Often, this is used to probe if the model is behaving fairly for different user populations—age bands, education bands, geographic, and so on. A simple example would be looking at the iris-flower examples we used in section 3.3 and checking if our classification accuracy is roughly similar among the three iris species. If our test or evaluation sets are unusually biased toward one of the populations, it is possible we are always wrong on the smallest population without it showing up as a top-level accuracy problem. As with the model validator, the trends over time are often as useful as the individual point-in-time measurement.

12.2 *Model optimization*

Once you have painstakingly created, trained, and tested your model, it is time to put it to use. This process, called *model deployment,* is no less important than the previous steps of model development. Whether the model is to be shipped to the client side for inference or executed at the backend for serving, we always want the model to be fast and efficient. Specifically, we want the model to

- Be small in size and hence fast to load over the web or from disk
- Consume as little time, compute, and memory as possible when its `predict()` method is called

This section describes techniques available in TensorFlow.js for optimizing the size and inference speed of trained models before they are released for deployment.

The meaning of the word *optimization* is overloaded. In the context of this section, *optimization* refers to improvements including model-size reduction and computation acceleration. This is not to be confused with weight-parameter optimization techniques such as gradient descent in the context of model training and optimizers. This distinction is sometimes referred to as model *quality* versus model *performance*. Performance refers to how much time and resources the model consumes to do its task. Quality refers to how close the results are to an ideal.

12.2.1 *Model-size optimization through post-training weight quantization*

The need to have small files that are swift to load over the internet should be abundantly clear to web developers. It is especially important if your website targets a very large user base or users with slow internet connections.[2] In addition, if your model is stored on a mobile device (see section 12.3.4 for a discussion of mobile deployment with TensorFlow.js), the size of the model is often constrained by limited storage space. As a challenge for model deployment, neural networks are large and still getting larger. The capacity (that is, predictive power) of deep neural networks often comes at the cost of increased layer count and larger layer sizes. At the time of this writing, state-of-the-art image-recognition,[3] speech-recognition,[4] natural language processing,[5] and generative models[6] often exceed 1 GB in the size of their weights. Due to the tension between the need for models to be both small and powerful, a highly active area of research in deep learning is model-size optimization, or how to design a neural network with a size as small as possible that can still perform its tasks with an accuracy close to that of a larger neural network. Two general approaches are available. In the first approach, researchers design a neural network with the aim of minimizing model size from the outset. Second, there are techniques through which existing neural networks can be shrunk to a smaller size.

MobileNetV2, which we visited in the chapters on convnets, is produced by the first line of research.[7] It is a small, lightweight image model suitable for deployment on

---

[2] In March 2019, Google launched a Doodle featuring a neural network that can compose music in Johann Sebastian Bach's style (http://mng.bz/MOQW). The neural network runs in the browser, powered by TensorFlow.js. The model is quantized as 8-bit integers with the method described in this section, which cuts the model's over-the-wire size by several times, down to about 380 KB. Without this quantization, it would be impossible to serve the model to an audience as wide as that of Google's homepage (where Google Doodles appear).

[3] Kaiming He et al., "Deep Residual Learning for Image Recognition," submitted 10 Dec. 2015, https://arxiv.org/abs/1512.03385.

[4] Johan Schalkwyk, "An All-Neural On-Device Speech Recognizer," Google AI Blog, 12 Mar. 2019, http://mng.bz/ad67.

[5] Jacob Devlin et al., "BERT: Pre-training of Deep Bidirectional Transformers for Language Understanding," submitted 11 Oct. 2018, https://arxiv.org/abs/1810.04805.

[6] Tero Karras, Samuli Laine, and Timo Aila, "A Style-Based Generator Architecture for Generative Adversarial Networks," submitted 12 Dec. 2018, https://arxiv.org/abs/1812.04948.

[7] Mark Sandler et al., "MobileNetV2: Inverted Residuals and Linear Bottlenecks," IEEE Conference on Computer Vision and Pattern Recognition (CVPR), 2018, pp. 4510–4520, http://mng.bz/NeP7.

resource-restricted environments such as web browsers and mobile devices. The accuracy of MobileNetV2 is slightly worse compared to that of a larger image trained on the same tasks, such as ResNet50. But its size (14 MB) is a few times smaller in comparison (ResNet50 is about 100 MB in size), which makes the slight reduction in accuracy a worthy trade-off.

Even with its built-in size-squeezing, MobileNetV2 is still a little too large for most JavaScript applications. Consider the fact that its size (14 MB) is about eight times the size of an average web page.[8] MobileNetV2 offers a width parameter, which, if set to a value smaller than 1, reduces the size of all convolutional layers and hence provides further shrinkage in the size (and further loss in accuracy). For example, the version of MobileNetV2 with its width set to 0.25 is approximately a quarter of the size of the full model (3.5 MB). But even that may be unacceptable to high-traffic websites that are sensitive to increases in page weight and load time.

Is there a way to further reduce the size of such models? Luckily, the answer is yes. This brings us to the second approach mentioned, model-independent size optimization. The techniques in this category are more generic in that they do not require changes to the model architecture itself and hence should be applicable to a wide variety of existing deep neural networks. The technique we will specifically focus on here is called *post-training weight quantization*. The idea is simple: after a model is trained, store its weight parameters at a lower numeric precision. Info box 12.1 describes how this is done for readers who are interested in the underlying mathematics.

> **INFO BOX 12.1   The mathematics behind post-training weight quantization**
>
> The weight parameters of a neural network are represented as 32-bit floating-point (float32) numbers during training. This is true not only in TensorFlow.js but also in other deep-learning frameworks such as TensorFlow and PyTorch. This relatively expensive representation is usually okay because model training typically happens in environments with unrestricted resources (for example, the backend environment of a workstation equipped with ample memory, fast CPUs, and CUDA GPUs). However, empirical findings indicate that for many inference use cases, we can lower the precision of weights without causing a substantial decrease in accuracy. To reduce the representation precision, we map each float32 value onto an 8-bit or 16-bit integer value that represents the discretized location of the value within the range of all values in the same weight. This process is what we call *quantization*.

---

[8]   According to HTTP Archive, the average page weight (total transfer size of HTML, CSS, JavaScript, images, and other static files) is about 1,828 KB for desktop and 1,682 KB for mobile as of May 2019: https://httparchive .org/reports/page-weight.

(continued)

In TensorFlow.js, weight quantization is performed on a weight-by-weight basis. For example, if a neural network consists of four weight variables (such as the weights and biases of two dense layers), each of the weights will undergo quantization as a whole. The equation that governs quantization of a weight is

$$quantize(w) = floor((w - w_{Min})/w_{Scale} \times 2^B)$$ **(Equation 12.1)**

In this equation, B is the number of bits that the quantization result will be stored in. It can be either 8 or 16, as currently supported by TensorFlow.js. w_{Min} is the minimum value of the parameters of the weight. w_{Scale} is the range of the parameters (the difference between the minimum and the maximum). The equation is valid, of course, only when w_{Scale} is nonzero. In the special cases where w_{Scale} is zero—that is, when all parameters of the weight have the same value—quantize(w) will return 0 for all w's.

The two auxiliary values w_{Min} and w_{Scale} are saved together with the quantized weight values to support recovery of the weights (a process we refer to as *dequantization*) during model loading. The equation that governs dequantization is as follows:

$$dequantize(v) = v/2^B \times w_{Scale} + w_{Min}$$ **(Equation 12.2)**

This equation is valid whether or not w_{Scale} is zero.

Post-training quantization provides considerable reduction in model size: 16-bit quantization cuts the model size by approximately 50%, 8-bit quantization by 75%. These percentages are approximate for two reasons. First, a fraction of the model's size is devoted to the model's topology, as encoded in the JSON file. Second, as stated in the info box, quantization requires the storage of two additional floating-number values (w_{Min} and w_{Scale}), along with a new integer value (the bits of quantization). However, these are usually minor compared to the reduction in the number of bits used to represent the weight parameters.

Quantization is a lossy transformation. Some information in the original weight values is lost as a result of the decreased precision. It is analogous to reducing the bit depth of a 24-bit color image to an 8-bit one (the kind you may have seen on Nintendo's game consoles from the 1980s), the effect of which is easily visible to human eyes. Figure 12.2 provides intuitive comparisons of the degree of discretization that 16-bit and 8-bit quantization lead to. As you might expect, 8-bit quantization leads to a more coarse-grained representation of the original weights. Under 8-bit quantization, there are only 256 possible values over the entire range of a weight's parameters, as compared with 65,536 possible values under 16-bit quantization. Both are dramatic reductions in precision compared to the 32-bit float representation.

Practically, does the loss of precision in weight parameters really matter? When it comes to the deployment of a neural network, what matters is its accuracy on test data.

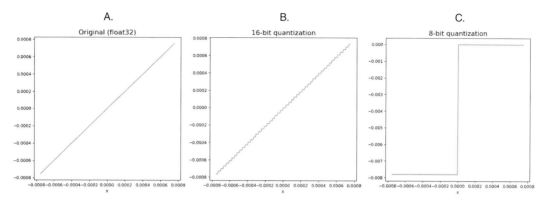

Figure 12.2 **Examples of 16-bit and 8-bit weight quantization. An original identity function (y = x, panel A) is reduced in size with 16-bit and 8-bit quantization; the results are shown in panels B and C, respectively. In order to make the quantization effects visible on the page, we zoom in on a small section of the identity function in the vicinity of *x* = 0.**

To answer this question, we compiled a number of models covering different types of tasks in the quantization example of tfjs-examples. You can run the quantization experiments there and see the effects for yourself. To check out the example, use

```
git clone https://github.com/tensorflow/tfjs-examples.git
cd tfjs-examples/quantization
yarn
```

The example contains four scenarios, each showcasing a unique combination of a dataset and the model applied on the dataset. The first scenario involves predicting average housing prices in geographic regions of California by using numeric features such as median age of the properties, total number of rooms, and so forth. The model is a five-layer network that includes dropout layers for the mitigation of overfitting. To train and save the original (nonquantized model), use this command:

```
yarn train-housing
```

The following command performs 16- and 8-bit quantization on the saved model and evaluates how the two levels of quantization affect the model's accuracy on a test set (a subset of the data unseen during the model's training):

```
yarn quantize-and-evaluate-housing
```

This command wraps a lot of actions inside for ease of use. However, the key step that actually quantizes the model can be seen in the shell script at quantization/quantize_evaluate.sh. In the script, you can see the following shell command that quantizes a model at the path MODEL_JSON_PATH with 16-bit quantization. You can follow the example of this command to quantize your own TensorFlow.js-saved models. If the option flag --quantization_bytes is set to 1 instead, 8-bit quantization will be performed:

```
tensorflowjs_converter \
      --input_format tfjs_layers_model \
```

```
   --output_format tfjs_layers_model \
   --quantization_bytes 2 \
"${MODEL_JSON_PATH}" "${MODEL_PATH_16BIT}"
```

The previous command shows how to perform weight quantization on a model trained in JavaScript. `tensorflowjs_converter` also supports weight quantization when converting models from Python to JavaScript, the details of which are shown in info box 12.2.

INFO BOX 12.2 Weight quantization and models from Python

In chapter 5, we showed how models from Keras (Python) can be converted to a format that can be loaded and used by TensorFlow.js. During such Python-to-JavaScript conversion, you can apply weight quantization. To do that, use the same `--quantization_bytes` flag as described in the main text. For example, to convert a model in the HDF5 (.h5) format saved by Keras with 16-bit quantization, use the following command:

```
tensorflowjs_converter \
      --input_format keras \
      --output_format tfjs_layers_model \
      --quantization_bytes 2 \
      "${KERAS_MODEL_H5_PATH}" "${TFJS_MODEL_PATH}"
```

In this command, `KERAS_MODEL_H5_PATH` is the path to the model exported by Keras, while `TFJS_MODEL_PATH` is the path to which the converted and weight-quantized model will be generated.

The detailed accuracy values you get will vary slightly from run to run due to the random initialization of weights and the random shuffling of data batches during training. However, the general conclusion should always hold: as shown by the first row of table 12.1, 16-bit quantization on weights leads to miniscule changes in the MAE of the housing-price prediction, while 8-bit quantization leads to a relatively larger (but still tiny in absolute terms) increase in the MAE.

Table 12.1 Evaluation accuracies for four different models with post-training weight quantization

Dataset and model	Evaluation loss and accuracy under no-quantization and different levels of quantization		
	32-bit full precision (no quantization)	16-bit quantization	8-bit quantization
California housing: MLP regressor	MAE[a] = 0.311984	MAE = 0.311983	MAE = 0.312780
MNIST: convnet	Accuracy = 0.9952	Accuracy = 0.9952	Accuracy = 0.9952
Fashion-MNIST: convnet	Accuracy = 0.922	Accuracy = 0.922	Accuracy = 0.9211
ImageNet subset of 1,000: MobileNetV2	Top-1 accuracy = 0.618 Top-5 accuracy = 0.788	Top-1 accuracy = 0.624 Top-5 accuracy = 0.789	Top-1 accuracy = 0.280 Top-5 accuracy = 0.490

a. The MAE loss function is used on the California-housing model. Lower is better for MAE, unlike accuracy.

The second scenario in the quantization example is based on the familiar MNIST dataset and deep convnet architecture. Similar to the housing experiment, you can train the original model and perform evaluation on quantized versions of it by using the following commands:

```
yarn train-mnistyarn quantize-and-evaluate-mnist
```

As the second row of table 12.1 shows, neither the 16-bit nor 8-bit quantization leads to any observable change in the model's test accuracy. This reflects the fact that the convnet is a multiclass classifier, so small deviations in its layer output values may not alter the final classification result, which is obtained with an `argMax()` operation.

Is this finding representative of image-oriented multiclass classifiers? Keep in mind that MNIST is a relatively easy classification problem. Even a simple convnet like the one used in this example achieves near-perfect accuracy. How does quantization affect accuracies when we are faced with a harder image-classification problem? To answer this question, look at the two other scenarios in the quantization example.

Fashion-MNIST, which you encountered in the section on variational autoencoders in chapter 10, is a harder problem that MNIST. By using the following commands, you can train a model on the Fashion-MNIST dataset and examine how 16- and 8-bit quantization affects its test accuracy:

```
yarn train-fashion-mnist
yarn quantize-and-evaluate-fashion-mnist
```

The result, which is shown in the third row of table 12.1, indicates that there is a small decrease in the test accuracy (from 92.2% to 92.1%) caused by 8-bit quantization of the weights, although 16-bit quantization still leads to no observable change.

An even harder image-classification problem is the ImageNet classification problem, which involves 1,000 output classes. In this case, we download a pretrained MobileNetV2 instead of training one from scratch, like we do in the other three scenarios in this example. The pretrained model is evaluated on a sample of 1,000 images from the ImageNet dataset, in its nonquantized and quantized forms. We opted not to evaluate the entire ImageNet dataset because the dataset itself is huge (with millions of images), and the conclusion we'd draw from that wouldn't be much different.

To evaluate the model's accuracy on the ImageNet problem in a more comprehensive fashion, we calculate both the top-1 and top-5 accuracies. Top-1 accuracy is the ratio of correct predictions when only the highest single logit output of the model is considered, while top-5 accuracy counts a prediction as right if any of the highest five logits includes the correct label. This is a standard approach in evaluating model accuracies on ImageNet because—due to the large number of class labels, some of which are very close to each other—models often show the correct label not in the top logit, but in one of the top-5 logits. To see the MobileNetV2 + ImageNet experiment in action, use

```
yarn quantize-and-evaluate-MobileNetV2
```

Unlike the previous three scenarios, this experiment shows a substantial impact of 8-bit on the test accuracy (see the fourth row of table 12.1). Both the top-1 and top-5 accuracies of the 8-bit quantized MobileNet are way below the original model, making 8-bit quantization an unacceptable size-optimization option for MobileNet. However, 16-bit quantized MobileNet still shows accuracies comparable to the nonquantized model.[9] We can see that the effect of quantization on accuracy depends on the model and the data. For some models and tasks (such as our MNIST convnet), neither 16-bit nor 8-bit quantization leads to any observable reduction in test accuracy. In these cases, we should by all means use the 8-bit quantized model during deployment to enjoy the reduced download time. For some models, such as our Fashion-MNIST convnet and our housing-price regression model, 16-bit quantization leads to no observed deterioration in accuracy, but 8-bit quantization does lead to a slight worsening of accuracy. In such cases, use your judgment as to whether the additional 25% reduction in model size outweighs the decrease in accuracy. Finally, for some types of models and tasks (such as our MobileNetV2 classification of ImageNet images), 8-bit quantization causes a large decrease in accuracy, which is probably unacceptable in most cases. For such problems, you need to stick with the original model or the 16-bit quantized version of it.

The cases in the quantization example are stock problems that may be somewhat simplistic. The problem you have at hand may be more complex and very different from those cases. The take-home message is that whether to quantize your model before deploying it and to what bit depth you should quantize it are empirical questions and can be answered only on a case-by-case basis. You need to try out the quantization and test the resulting models on real test data before making a decision. Exercise 1 at the end of this chapter lets you try your hand on the MNIST ACGAN we trained in chapter 10 and decide whether 16-bit or 8-bit quantization is the right decision for such a generative model.

WEIGHT QUANTIZATION AND GZIP COMPRESSION

An additional benefit of 8-bit quantization that should be taken into account is the additional over-the-wire model-size reduction it provides under data-compression techniques such as gzip. gzip is widely used to deliver large files over the web. You should always enable gzip when serving TensorFlow.js model files over the web. The nonquantized float32 weights of a neural network are usually not very amenable to such compression due to the noise-like variation in the parameter values, which contains few repeating patterns. It is our observation that gzip typically can't get more than 10–20% size reduction out of nonquantized weights for models. The same is true for models with 16-bit weight quantization. However, once a model's weights undergo 8-bit quantization, there is often a considerable jump in the ratio of compression (up to 30–40% for small models and about 20–30% for larger ones; see table 12.2).

---

[9] In fact, we can see small *increases* in accuracy, which are attributable to the random fluctuation on the relatively small test set that consists of only 1,000 examples.

This is due to the small number of bins available under the drastically reduced precision (only 256), which causes many values (such as the ones around 0) to fall into the same bin, and hence leads to more repeating patterns in the weight's binary representation. This is an additional reason to favor 8-bit quantization in cases where it doesn't lead to unacceptable deterioration in test accuracy.

Table 12.2 The gzip compression ratios of model artifacts under different levels of quantization

Dataset and model	gzip compression ratio[a]		
	32-bit full precision (no quantization)	16-bit quantization	8-bit quantization
California-housing: MLP regressor	1.121	1.161	1.388
MNIST: convnet	1.082	1.037	1.184
Fashion-MNIST: convnet	1.078	1.048	1.229
ImageNet subset of 1,000: MobileNetV2	1.085	1.063	1.271

a. (total size of the model.json and weight file)/(size of gzipped tar ball)

In summary, with post-training weight quantization, we can substantially reduce the size of the TensorFlow.js models transferred over the wire and stored on disk, especially with help from data-compression techniques such as gzip. This benefit of improved compression ratios requires no code change on the part of the developer, as the browser performs the unzipping transparently for you when it downloads the model files. However, it doesn't change the amount of computation involved in executing the model's inference calls. Neither does it change the amount of CPU or GPU memory consumption for such calls. This is because the weights are dequantized after they are loaded (see equation 12.2 in info box 12.1). As regards the operations that are run and the data types and shapes of the tensors output by the operations, there is no difference between a nonquantized model and a quantized model. However, for model deployment, an equally important concern is how to make a model that runs as fast as possible, as well as make it consume as little memory as possible when it's running, because that improves user experience and reduces power consumption. Are there ways to make an existing TensorFlow.js model run faster when deployed, without loss of prediction accuracy and on top of model-size optimization? Luckily, the answer is yes. In the next section, we will focus on inference-speed optimization techniques that TensorFlow.js provides.

12.2.2 *Inference-speed optimization using GraphModel conversion*

This section is organized as follows. We will first present the steps involved in optimizing the inference speed of a TensorFlow.js model using the `GraphModel` conversion. We will then list detailed performance measurements that quantify the speed gain provided by this approach. Finally, we will explain how the `GraphModel` conversion approach works under the hood.

Suppose you have a TensorFlow.js model saved at the path my/layers-model; you can use the following command to convert it to a `tf.GraphModel`:

```
tensorflowjs_converter \
    --input_format tfjs_layers_model \
    --output_format tfjs_graph_model \
    my/layers-model my/graph-
    model
```

This command creates a model.json file under the output directory my/graph-model (the directory will be created if it doesn't exist), along with a number of binary weight files. Superficially, this set of files may appear to be identical in format to the files in the input directory that contains the serialized `tf.LayersModel`. However, the output files encode a different kind of model called `tf.GraphModel` (the namesake of this optimization method). In order to load the converted model in the browser or Node.js, use the TensorFlow.js method `tf.loadGraphModel()` instead of the familiar `tf.loadLayersModel()`. Once the `tf.GraphModel` object is loaded, you can perform inference in exactly the same way as a `tf.LayersModel` by invoking the object's `predict()` method. For example,

```
const model = await tf.loadGraphModel('file://./my/graph-model/model.json');
    const ys = model.predict(xs);
```

Or use an http:// or https:// URL if loading the model in the browser.

Perform inference using input data 'xs'.

The enhanced inference speed comes with two limitations:

- At the time of this writing, the latest version of TensorFlow.js (1.1.2) does not support recurrent layers such as `tf.layers.simpleRNN()`, `tf.layers.gru()`, and `tf.layers.lstm()` (see chapter 9) for `GraphModel` conversion.
- The loaded `tf.GraphModel` object doesn't have a `fit()` method and hence does not support further training (for example, transfer learning).

Table 12.3 compares the inference speed of the two types of models with and without `GraphModel` conversion. Since `GraphModel` conversion does not support recurrent layers yet, only the results from an MLP and a convnet (MobileNetV2) are presented. To cover different deployment environments, the table presents results from both the web browser and tfjs-node running in the backend environment. From this table, we can see that `GraphModel` conversion invariably speeds up inference. However, the ratio of the speedup depends on model type and deployment environment. For the browser (WebGL) deployment environment, `GraphModel` conversion leads to a 20–30% speedup, while the speedup is more dramatic (70–90%) if the deployment environment is Node.js. Next, we will discuss why `GraphModel` conversion speeds up inference, as well as the reason why it speeds up the inference more for Node.js than for the browser environment.

Table 12.3 Comparing the inference speed of two model types (an MLP and MobileNetV2) with and without `GraphModel` conversion optimization, and in different deployment environments[a]

Model name and topology	predict() time (ms; lower is better) (Average over 30 predict() calls preceded by 20 warm-up calls)					
	Browser WebGL		tfjs-node (CPU only)		tfjs-node-gpu	
	LayersModel	GraphModel	LayersModel	GraphModel	LayersModel	GraphModel
MLP[b]	13	10 (1.3x)	18	10 (1.8x)	3	1.6 (1.9x)
Mobile-NetV2 (width = 1.0)	68	57 (1.2x)	187	111 (1.7x)	66	39 (1.7x)

a. The code with which these results were obtained is available at https://github.com/tensorflow/tfjs/tree/master/tfjs/integration_tests/.
b. The MLP consists of dense layers with unit counts: 4,000, 1,000, 5,000, and 1. The first three layers have relu activation; the last has linear activation.

HOW GRAPHMODEL CONVERSION SPEEDS UP MODEL INFERENCE

How does `GraphModel` conversion boost TensorFlow.js models' inference speed? It's achieved by leveraging TensorFlow (Python)'s ahead-of-time analysis of the model's computation graph at a fine granularity. The computation-graph analysis is followed by modifications to the graph that reduce the amount of computation while preserving the numeric correctness of the graph's output result. Don't be intimidated by terms such as *ahead-of-time analysis* and *fine granularity*. We will explain them in a bit.

To give a concrete example of the sort of graph modification we are talking about, let's consider how a BatchNormalization layer works in a `tf.LayersModel` and a `tf.GraphModel`. Recall that BatchNormalization is a type of layer that improves convergence and reduces overfitting during training. It is available in the TensorFlow.js API as `tf.layers.batchNormalization()` and is used by popular pretrained models such as MobileNetV2. When a BatchNormalization layer runs as a part of a `tf.LayersModel`, the computation follows the mathematical definition of batch normalization closely:

$$\text{output} = (x - \text{mean}) / (\text{sqrt}(\text{var}) + \text{epsilon}) \times \text{gamma} + \text{beta}$$

(Equation 12.3)

Six operations (or ops) are needed in order to generate the output from the input (x), in the rough order of

1 `sqrt`, with `var` as input
2 `add`, with `epsilon` and the result of step 1 as inputs

3 sub, with x and means as inputs

4 div, with the results of steps 2 and 3 as inputs

5 mul, with gamma and the result of step 4 as inputs

6 add, with beta and the result of step 5 as inputs

Based on simple arithmetic rules, it can be seen that equation 12.3 can be simplified significantly, as long as the values of mean, var, epsilon, gamma, and beta are constant (do not change with the input or with how many times the layer has been invoked). After a model comprising a BatchNormalization layer is trained, all these variables indeed become constant. This is exactly what GraphModel conversion does: it "folds" the constants and simplifies the arithmetic, which leads to the following mathematically equivalent equation:

$$output = x * k + b \qquad \text{(Equation 12.4)}$$

The values of k and b are calculated during GraphModel conversion, not during inference:

$$k = \mathrm{gamma}/(\mathrm{sqrt}(\mathrm{var}) + \mathrm{epsilon}) \qquad \text{(Equation 12.5)}$$

$$b = -\mathrm{mean}/(\mathrm{sqrt}(\mathrm{var}) + \mathrm{epsilon}) \times \mathrm{gamma} + \mathrm{beta} \qquad \text{(Equation 12.6)}$$

Therefore, equations 12.5 and 12.6 do *not* factor into the amount of computation during inference; only equation 12.4 does. Contrasting equations 12.3 and 12.4, you can see that the constant folding and arithmetic simplification cut the number of operations from six to two (a mul op between x and k and an add op between b and the result of that mul operation), which leads to considerable speedup of this layer's execution. But why does tf.LayersModel not perform this optimization? It's because it needs to support training of the BatchNormalization layer, during which the values of mean, var, gamma, and beta are updated at every step of the training. GraphModel conversion takes advantage of the fact that these updated values are no longer required once the model training is complete.

The type of optimization seen in the BatchNormalization example is only possible if two requirements are met. First, the computation must be represented at a sufficiently *fine granularity*—that is, at the level of basic mathematical operations such as add and mul, instead of the coarser, layer-by-layer granularity at which the Layers API of TensorFlow.js resides. Second, all the computation is known ahead of time, before the calls to the model's predict() method are executed. GraphModel conversion goes through TensorFlow (Python), which has access to a graph representation of the model that meets both criteria.

Apart from the constant-folding and arithmetic optimization discussed previously, GraphModel conversion is capable of performing another type of optimization called *op fusion*. Take the frequently used dense layer type (tf.layers.dense()), for example. A dense layer involves three operations: a matrix multiplication (matMul) between the input x and the kernel W, a broadcasting addition between the result of the `matMul` and the bias (*b*), and the element-wise relu activation function (figure 12.3, panel A). The op fusion optimization replaces the three separate operations with a single operation that carries out all the equivalent steps (figure 12.3, panel B). This replacement may seem trivial, but it leads to faster computation due to 1) the reduced overhead of launching ops (yes, launching an op always involves a certain amount of overhead, regardless of the compute backend), and 2) more opportunity to perform smart tricks for speed optimization within the implementation of the fused op itself.

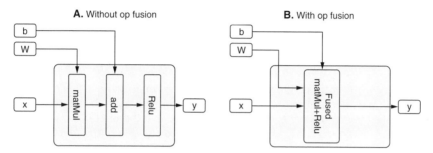

Figure 12.3   Schematic illustration of the internal operations in a dense layer, with (panel A) and without (panel B) op fusion

How is op fusion optimization different from the constant folding and arithmetic simplification we just saw? Op fusion requires that the special fused op (`Fused matMul+relu`, in this case) be defined and available for the compute backend being used, while constant folding doesn't. These special fused ops may be available only for certain compute backends and deployment environments. This is the reason why we saw a greater amount of inference speedup in the Node.js environment than in the browser (see table 12.3). The Node.js compute backend, which uses libtensorflow written in C++ and CUDA, is equipped with a richer set of ops than TensorFlow.js's WebGL backend in the browser.

Apart from constant folding, arithmetic simplification, and op fusion, TensorFlow (Python)'s graph-optimization system Grappler is capable of a number of other kinds of optimizations, some of which may be relevant to how TensorFlow.js models are optimized through `GraphModel` conversion. However, we won't cover those due to space limits. If you are interested in finding out more about this topic, you can read the informative slides by Rasmus Larsen and Tatiana Shpeisman listed at the end of this chapter.

In summary, `GraphModel` conversion is a technique provided by `tensorflowjs_converter`. It utilizes TensorFlow (Python)'s ahead-of-time graph-optimization capability to simplify computation graphs and reduce the amount of computation required for model inference. Although the detailed amount of inference speedup varies with model type and compute backend, it usually provides a speedup ratio of 20% or more, and hence is an advisable step to perform on your TensorFlow.js models before their deployment.

INFO BOX 12.3   How to properly measure a TensorFlow.js model's inference time

Both `tf.LayersModel` and `tf.GraphModel` provide the unified `predict()` method to support inference. This method takes one or more tensors as input and returns one or more tensors as the inference result. However, it is important to note that in the context of WebGL-based inference in the web browser, the `predict()` method only *schedules* operations to be executed on the GPU; it does not await the completion of their execution. As a result, if you naively time a `predict()` call in the following fashion, the result of the timing measurement will be wrong:

```
console.time('TFjs inference');
const outputTensor = model.predict(inputTensor);      Incorrect way of measuring
console.timeEnd('TFjs inference');    ◁──────────────  inference time!
```

When `predict()` returns, the scheduled operations may not have finished executing. Therefore, the prior example will lead to a time measurement shorter than the actual time it takes to complete the inference. To ensure that the operations are completed before `console.timeEnd()` is called, you need to call one of the following methods of the returned tensor object: `array()` or `data()`. Both methods download the texture values that hold the elements of the output tensor from GPU to CPU. In order to do so, they must wait for the output tensor's computation to finish. So, the correct way to measure the timing looks like the following:

```
console.time('TFjs inference');
const outputTensor = model.predict(inputTensor);
await outputTensor.array();        ◁──  The array() call won't return until the
console.timeEnd('TFjs inference');      scheduled computation of outputTensor has
                                        completed, hence ensuring the correctness of
                                        the inference-time measurement.
```

Another important thing to bear in mind is that like all other JavaScript programs, the execution time of a TensorFlow.js model's inference is variable. In order to obtain a reliable estimate of the inference time, the code in the previous snippet should be put in a `for` loop so that the measurement can be performed multiple times (for example, 50 times), and the average time can be calculated based on the accumulated individual measurements. The first few executions are usually slower than the subsequent ones due to the need to compile new WebGL shader programs and set up initial states. So, performance-measuring code often omits the first few (such as the first five) runs, which are referred to as *burn-in* or *warm-up* runs.

If you are interested in a deeper understanding of these performance-benchmarking techniques, work through exercise 3 at the end of this chapter.

12.3 Deploying TensorFlow.js models on various platforms and environments

You've optimized your model, it's fast and lightweight, and all your tests are green. You're good to go! Hooray! But before you pop that champagne, there's a bit more work to do.

It's time to put your model into your application and get it out in front of your user base. In this section, we will cover a few deployment platforms. Deploying to the web and deploying to a Node.js service are well-known paths, but we'll also cover a few more exotic deployment scenarios, like deploying to a browser extension or a single-board embedded hardware application. We will point to simple examples and discuss special considerations important for the platforms.

12.3.1 Additional considerations when deploying to the web

Let's begin by revisiting the most common deployment scenario for TensorFlow.js models, deploying to the web as part of a web page. In this scenario, our trained, and possibly optimized, model is loaded via JavaScript from some hosting location, and then the model makes predictions using the JavaScript engine within the user's browser. A good example of this pattern is the MobileNet image-classification example from chapter 5. The example is also available to download from tfjs-examples/mobilenet. As a reminder, the relevant code for loading a model and making a prediction can be summarized as follows:

```
const MOBILENET_MODEL_PATH =
    'https://storage.googleapis.com/tfjs-
    models/tfjs/mobilenet_v1_0.25_224/model.json';
const mobilenet = await tf.loadLayersModel(MOBILENET_MODEL_PATH);
const response = mobilenet.predict(userQueryAsTensor);
```

This model is hosted from a Google Cloud Platform (GCP) bucket. For low-traffic, static applications like this one, it is easy to host the model statically alongside the rest of the site content. Larger, higher-traffic applications may choose to host the model through a content delivery network (CDN) alongside the other heavy assets. One common development mistake is to forget to account for Cross-Origin Resource Sharing (CORS) when setting up a bucket in GCP, Amazon S3, or other cloud services. If CORS is set incorrectly, the model will fail to load, and you should get a CORS-related error message delivered to the console. This is something to watch out for if your web application works fine locally but fails when pushed to your distribution platform.

After the user's browser loads the HTML and JavaScript, the JavaScript interpreter will issue the call to load our model. The process of loading a small model takes a few hundred milliseconds on a modern browser with a good internet connection, but after the initial load, the model can be loaded much faster from the browser cache. The serialization format ensures that the model is sharded into small enough pieces to support the standard browser cache limit.

One nice property of web deployment is that prediction happens directly within the browser. Any data passed to the model is never sent over the wire, which is good for latency and great for privacy. Imagine a text-input prediction scenario where the model is predicting the next word for assistive typing, something that we see all the time in, for example, Gmail. If we need to send the typed text to servers in the cloud and wait for a response from those remote servers, then prediction will be delayed, and the input predictions will be much less useful. Furthermore, some users might consider sending their incomplete keystrokes to a remote computer an invasion of their privacy. Making predictions locally in their own browser is much more secure and privacy sensitive.

A downside of making predictions within the browser is model security. Sending the model to the user makes it easy for the user to keep the model and use it for other purposes. TensorFlow.js currently (as of 2019) does not have a solution for model security in the browser. Some other deployment scenarios make it harder for the user to use the model for purposes the developer didn't intend. The distribution path with the greatest model security is to keep the model on servers you control and serve prediction requests from there. Of course, this comes at the cost of latency and data privacy. Balancing these concerns is a product decision.

12.3.2 *Deployment to cloud serving*

Many existing production systems provide machine-learning-trained prediction as a service, such as Google Cloud Vision AI (https://cloud.google.com/vision) or Microsoft Cognitive Services (https://azure.microsoft.com/en-us/services/ cognitive-services). The end user of such a service makes HTTP requests containing the input values to the prediction, such as an image for an object-detection task, and the response encodes the output of the prediction, such as the labels and positions of objects in the image.

As of 2019, there are two routes to serving a TensorFlow.js model from a server. The first route has the server running Node.js and performing the prediction using the native JavaScript runtime. Because TensorFlow.js is so new, we are not aware of production use cases that have chosen this approach, but proofs of concept are simple to build.

The second route is to convert the model from TensorFlow.js into a format that can be served from a known existing server technology, such as the standard TensorFlow Serving system. From the documentation at www.tensorflow.org/tfx/guide/serving:

> *TensorFlow Serving is a flexible, high-performance serving system for machine-learning models, designed for production environments. TensorFlow Serving makes it easy to deploy new algorithms and experiments, while keeping the same server architecture and APIs. TensorFlow Serving provides out-of-the-box integration with TensorFlow models, but can be easily extended to serve other types of models and data.*

The TensorFlow.js models we have serialized so far have been stored in a JavaScript-specific format. TensorFlow Serving expects models to be packaged in the TensorFlow standard SavedModel format. Fortunately, the tfjs-converter project makes it easy to convert to the necessary format.

In chapter 5 (transfer learning) we showed how SavedModels built with the Python implementation of TensorFlow could be used in TensorFlow.js. To do the reverse, first install the tensorflowjs pip package:

```
pip install tensorflowjs
```

Next, you must run the converter binary, specifying the input:

```
tensorflowjs_converter \
    --input_format=tfjs_layers_model \
    --output_format=keras_saved_model \
    /path/to/your/js/model.json \
    /path/to/your/new/saved-model
```

This will create a new saved-model directory, which will contain the required topology and weights in a format that TensorFlow Serving understands. You should then be able to follow the instructions for building the TensorFlow Serving server and make gRPC prediction requests against the running model. Managed solutions also exist. For instance, Google Cloud Machine Learning Engine provides a path for you to upload your saved model to Cloud Storage and then set up serving as a service, without needing to maintain the server or the machine. You can learn more from the documentation at https://cloud.google.com/ml-engine/docs/tensorflow/deploying-models.

The advantage of serving your model from the cloud is that you are in complete control of the model. It is easy to perform telemetry on what sorts of queries are being performed and to quickly detect problems. If it is discovered that there is some unforeseen problem with a model, it can be quickly removed or upgraded, and there is little risk of other copies on machines outside of your control. The downside is the additional latency and data privacy concerns, as mentioned. There is also the additional cost—both in monetary outlay and maintenance costs—in operating a cloud service, as you are in control of the system configuration.

12.3.3 *Deploying to a browser extension, like Chrome Extension*

Some client-side applications may require your application to be able to work across many different websites. Browser extension frameworks are available for all the major desktop browsers, including Chrome, Safari, and FireFox, among others. These frameworks enable developers to create experiences that modify or enhance the browsing experience itself by adding new JavaScript and manipulating the DOM of websites.

Since the extension is operating on top of JavaScript and HTML within the browser's execution engine, what you can do with TensorFlow.js in a browser extension is similar to what is possible in a standard web page deployment. The model security story and data privacy story are identical to the web page deployment. By performing prediction directly within the browser, the users' data is relatively secure. The model security story is also similar to that of web deployment.

As an example of what is possible using a browser extension, see the chrome-extension example within tfjs-examples. This extension loads a MobileNetV2 model and applies it to images on the web, selected by the user. Installing and using the extension is a little different from the other examples we have seen, since it is an extension, not a hosted website. This example requires the Chrome browser.[10]

First, you must download and build the extension, similar to how you might build one of the other examples:

```
git clone https://github.com/tensorflow/tfjs-examples.git
cd tfjs-examples/chrome-extension
yarn
yarn build
```

After the extension has finished building, it is possible to load the unpacked extension in Chrome. To do so, you must navigate to chrome://extensions, enable developer mode, and then click Load Unpacked, as shown in figure 12.4. This will bring up a file-selection dialog, where you must select the dist directory created under the chrome-extension directory. That's the directory containing manifest.json.

Once the extension is installed, you should be able to classify images in the browser. To do so, navigate to some site with images, such as the Google image search page for the term *tiger* used here. Then right-click the image you wish to classify. You should see a menu option for Classify Image with TensorFlow.js. Clicking that menu option should cause the extension to execute the MobileNet model on the image and then add some text over the image, indicating the prediction (see figure 12.5.)

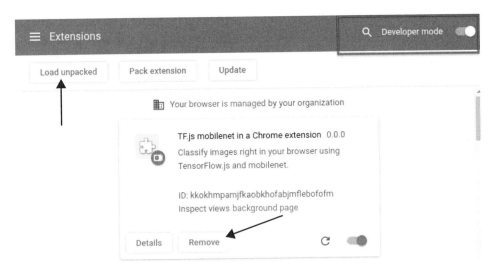

Figure 12.4   Loading the TensorFlow.js MobileNet Chrome extension in developer mode

---

[10] Newer versions of Microsoft Edge also offer some support for cross-browser extension loading.

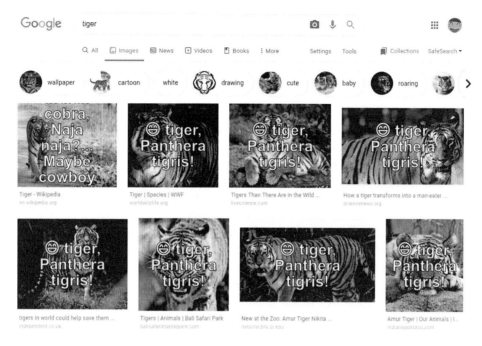

Figure 12.5   The TensorFlow.js MobileNet Chrome extension helps classify images in a web page.

To remove the extension, click Remove on the Extensions page (see figure 12.4), or use the Remove from Chrome menu option when right-clicking the extension icon at top-right.

Note that the model running in the browser extension has access to the same hardware acceleration as the model running in the web page and, indeed, uses much of the same code. The model is loaded with a call to `tf.loadGraphModel(...)` using a suitable URL, and predictions are made using the same `model.predict(...)` API we've seen. Migrating technology or a proof of concept from a web page deployment into a browser extension is relatively easy.

12.3.4   *Deploying TensorFlow.js models in JavaScript-based mobile applications*

For many products, the desktop browser does not provide enough reach, and the mobile browser does not provide the smoothly animated customized product experience that customers have come to expect. Teams working on these sorts of projects are often faced with the dilemma of how to manage the codebase for their web app alongside repositories for (typically) both Android (Java or Kotlin) and iOS (Objective C or Swift) native apps. While very large groups can support such an outlay, many developers are increasingly choosing to reuse much of their code across these deployments by leveraging hybrid cross-platform development frameworks.

Cross-platform app frameworks, like React Native, Ionic, Flutter, and Progressive Web-Apps, enable you to write the bulk of an application once in a common language and then compile that core functionality to create native experiences with the look, feel, and performance that users expect. The cross-platform language/runtime handles much of the business logic and layout, and connects to native platform bindings for the standardized affordance visuals and feel. How to select the right hybrid app development framework is the topic of countless blogs and videos on the web, so we will not revisit that discussion here, but will rather focus on just one popular framework, React Native. Figure 12.6 illustrates a minimal React Native app running a MobileNet model. Notice the lack of any browser top bar. Though this simple app doesn't have UI elements, if it did, you would see that they match the native Android look and feel. The same app built for iOS would match *those* elements.

Happily, the JavaScript runtime within React Native supports TensorFlow.js natively without any special work. The tfjs-react-native package is still in alpha release (as of December 2019) but provides GPU support with WebGL via expo-gl. The user code looks like the following:

Figure 12.6   A screenshot from a sample native Android app built with React Native. Here, we are running a TensorFlow.js MobileNet model within the native app.

```
import * as tf from '@tensorflow/tfjs';
import '@tensorflow/tfjs-react-native';
```

The package also provides a special API for assisting with loading and saving model assets within the mobile app.

Listing 12.2   Loading and saving a model within a mobile app built with React-Native

```
import * as tf from '@tensorflow/tfjs';
import {asyncStorageIO} from '@tensorflow/tfjs-react-native';

async trainSaveAndLoad() {
    const model = await train();
    await model.save(asyncStorageIO(           Saves the model to AsyncStorage—a simple
        'custom-model-test'))                  key-value storage system global to the app
    model.predict(tf.tensor2d([5], [1, 1])).print();
```

```
const loadedModel =
  await tf.loadLayersModel(asyncStorageIO(      Loads the model
      'custom-model-test'));                    from AsyncStorage
loadedModel.predict(tf.tensor2d([5], [1, 1])).print();
}
```

While native app development through React Native still requires learning a few new tools, such as Android Studio for Android and XCode for iOS, the learning curve is shallower than diving straight into native development. That these hybrid app development frameworks support TensorFlow.js means that the machine-learning logic can live in a single codebase rather than requiring us to develop, maintain, and test a separate version for each hardware surface—a clear win for developers who wish to support the native app experience! But what about the native desktop experience?

12.3.5 *Deploying TensorFlow.js models in JavaScript-based cross-platform desktop applications*

JavaScript frameworks such as Electron.js allow desktop applications to be written in a cross-platform manner reminiscent of cross-platform mobile applications written in React Native. With such frameworks, you need to write your code only once, and it can be deployed and run on mainstream desktop operating systems, including macOS, Windows, and major distributions of Linux. This greatly simplifies the traditional development workflow of maintaining separate codebases for largely incompatible desktop operating systems. Take Electron.js, the leading framework in this category, for example. It uses Node.js as the virtual machine that undergirds the application's main process; for the GUI portion of the app, it uses Chromium, a full-blown and yet lightweight web browser that shares much of its code with Google Chrome.

TensorFlow.js is compatible with Electron.js, as is demonstrated by the simple example in the tfjs-examples repository. This example, found in the electron directory, illustrates how to deploy a TensorFlow.js model for inference in an Electron.js-based desktop app. The app allows users to search the filesystem for image files that visually match one or more keywords (see the screenshot in figure 12.7). This search process involves applying a TensorFlow.js MobileNet model for inference on a directory of images.

Despite its simplicity, this example app illustrates an important consideration in deploying TensorFlow.js models to Electron.js: the choice of the compute backend. An Electron.js application runs on a Node.js-based backend process as well as a Chromium-based frontend process. TensorFlow.js can run in either of those environments. As a result, the same model can run in either the application's node-like backend process or the browser-like frontend process. In the case of backend deployment, the @tensorflow/tfjs-node package is used, while the @tensorflow/tfjs package is used for the frontend case (figure 12.8). A check box in the example application's GUI allows you to switch between the backend and frontend inference modes (figure 12.7), although in an actual application powered by Electron.js and TensorFlow.js, you

Figure 12.7   A screenshot from the example Electron.js-based desktop application that utilizes a TensorFlow.js model, from tfjs-examples/electron

would normally decide on one environment for your model beforehand. We will next briefly discuss the pros and cons of the options.

As figure 12.8 shows, different choices of the compute backend cause the deep-learning computation to happen on different computation hardware. Backend deployment based on @tensorflow/tfjs-node assigns the workload to the CPU, leveraging the multithreaded and SIMD-enabled libtensorflow library. This Node.js-based model-deployment option is usually faster than the frontend option and can accommodate larger models due to the fact that the backend environment is free of resource restrictions. However, their major downside is the large package size, which is a result of the large size of libtensorflow (for tfjs-node, approximately 50 MB with compression).

The frontend deployment dispatches deep-learning workloads to WebGL. For small-to-medium-sized models, and in cases where the latency of inference is not of major concern, this is an acceptable option. This option leads to a smaller package size, and it works out of the box for a wide range of GPUs, thanks to the wide support for WebGL.

As figure 12.8 also illustrates, the choice of compute backend is a largely separate concern from the JavaScript code that loads and runs your model. The same API works for all three options. This is clearly demonstrated in the example app, where the same module (ImageClassifier in electron/image_classifier.js) subserves the

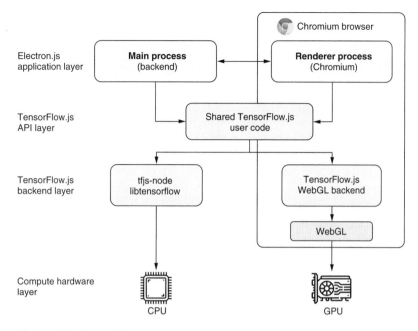

Figure 12.8　The architecture of an Electron.js-based desktop application that utilizes TensorFlow.js for accelerated deep learning. Different compute backends of TensorFlow.js can be invoked, from either the main backend process or the in-browser renderer process. Different compute backends cause models to be run on different underlying hardware. Regardless of the choice of compute backend, the code that loads, defines, and runs deep-learning models in TensorFlow.js is largely the same. The arrowheads in this diagram indicate invocation of library functions and other callable routines.

inference task in both the backend and frontend environments. We should also point out that although the tfjs-examples/electron example shows only inference, you can certainly use TensorFlow.js for other deep-learning workflows, such as model creation and training (for example, transfer learning) in Electron.js apps equally well.

12.3.6 Deploying TensorFlow.js models on WeChat and other JavaScript-based mobile app plugin systems

There are some places where the main mobile-app-distribution platform is neither Android's Play Store nor Apple's App Store, but rather a small number of "super mobile apps" that allow for third-party extensions within their own first-party curated experience.

A few of these super mobile apps come from Chinese tech giants, notably Tencent's WeChat, Alibaba's Alipay, and Baidu. These use JavaScript as their main technology to enable the creation of third-party extensions, making TensorFlow.js a natural fit for deploying machine learning on their platform. The set of APIs available within these mobile app plugin systems is not the same as the set available in native JavaScript, however, so some additional knowledge and work is required to deploy there.

Let's use WeChat as an example. WeChat is the most widely used social media app in China, with over 1 billion monthly active users. In 2017, WeChat launched Mini Program, a platform for application developers to create JavaScript mini-programs within the WeChat system. Users can share and install these mini-programs inside the WeChat app on-the-fly, and it's been a tremendous success. By Q2 2018, WeChat had more than 1 million mini-programs and over 600 million daily active mini-program users. There are also more than 1.5 million developers who are developing applications on this platform, partly because of the popularity of JavaScript.

WeChat mini-program APIs are designed to provide developers easy access to mobile device sensors (the camera, microphone, accelerometer, gyroscope, GPS, and so on). However, the native API provides very limited machine-learning functionality built into the platform. TensorFlow.js brings several advantages as a machine-learning solution for mini-programs. Previously, if developers wanted to embed machine learning in their applications, they needed to work outside the mini-program development environment with a server-side or cloud-based machine-learning stack. Doing so makes the barrier high for the large number of mini-program developers to build and use machine learning. Standing up an external serving infrastructure is outside of the scope of possibilities for most mini-program developers. With TensorFlow.js, machine-learning development happens right within the native environment. Furthermore, since it is a client-side solution, it helps reduce network traffic and improves latency, and it takes advantage of GPU acceleration using WebGL.

The team behind TensorFlow.js has created a WeChat mini-program you can use to enable TensorFlow.js for your mini-program (see https://github.com/tensorflow/tfjs-wechat). The repository also contains an example mini-program that uses PoseNet to annotate the positions and postures of people sensed by the mobile device's camera. It uses TensorFlow.js accelerated by a newly added WebGL API from WeChat. Without access to the GPU, the model would run too slowly to be useful for most applications. With this plugin, a WeChat mini-program can have the same model execution performance as a JavaScript app running inside mobile browsers. In fact, we have observed that the WeChat sensor API typically *outperforms* the counterpart in the browser.

As of late 2019, developing machine-learning experiences for super app plugins is still very new territory. Getting high performance may require some help from the platform maintainers. Still, it is the best way to deploy your app in front of the hundreds of millions of people for whom the super mobile app *is* the internet.

12.3.7 *Deploying TensorFlow.js models on single-board computers*

For many web developers, deploying to a headless single-board computer sounds very technical and foreign. However, thanks to the success of the Raspberry Pi, developing and building simple hardware devices has never been easier. Single-board computers provide a platform to inexpensively deploy intelligence without depending on network connections to cloud servers or bulky, costly computers. Single-board computers can be used to back security applications, moderate internet traffic, control irrigation—the sky's the limit.

Many of these single-board computers provide general-purpose input-output (GPIO) pins to make it easy to connect to physical control systems, and include a full Linux install to allow educators, developers, and hackers to develop a wide range of interactive devices. JavaScript has quickly become a popular language for building on these types of devices. Developers can use node libraries such as rpi-gpio to interact electronically at the lowest level, all in JavaScript.

To help support these users, TensorFlow.js currently has two runtimes on these embedded ARM devices: tfjs-node (CPU[11]) and tfjs-headless-nodegl (GPU). The entire TensorFlow.js library runs on these devices through those two backends. Developers can run inference using off-the-shelf models or train their own, all on the device hardware!

The release of recent devices such as the NVIDIA Jetson Nano and Raspberry Pi 4 brings a system-on-chip (SoC) with a modern graphics stack. The GPU on these devices can be leveraged by the underlying WebGL code used in core TensorFlow.js. The headless WebGL package (tfjs-backend-nodegl) allows users to run TensorFlow.js on Node.js purely accelerated by the GPU on these devices (see figure 12.9). By delegating the execution of TensorFlow.js to the GPU, developers can continue to utilize the CPU for controlling other parts of their devices.

Figure 12.9   TensorFLow.js executing MobileNet using headless WebGL on a Raspberry Pi 4

---

[11] If you are looking to utilize the CPU with ARM NEON acceleration, you should use the tfjs-node package on these devices. This package ships support for both ARM32 and ARM64 architectures.

Model security and data security are very strong for the single-board computer deployment. Computation and actuation are handled directly on the device, meaning data does not need to go to a device outside of the owner's control. Encryption can be used to guard the model even if the physical device is compromised.

Deployment to single-board computers is still a very new area for JavaScript in general, and TensorFlow.js in particular, but it unlocks a wide range of applications that other deployment areas are unsuitable for.

12.3.8 *Summary of deployments*

In this section, we've covered several different ways to get your TensorFlow.js machine-learning system out in front of the user base (table 12.4 summarizes them). We hope we've kindled your imagination and helped you dream about radical applications of the technology! The JavaScript ecosystem is vast and wide, and in the future, machine-learning-enabled systems will be running in areas we couldn't even dream of today.

Table 12.4 Target environments to which TensorFlow.js models can be deployed, and the hardware accelerator each environment can use

Deployment	Hardware accelerator support
Browser	WebGL
Node.js server	CPU with multithreading and SIMD support; CUDA-enabled GPU
Browser plugin	WebGL
Cross-platform desktop app (such as Electron)	WebGL, CPU with multithreading and SIMD support, or CUDA-enabled GPU
Cross-platform mobile app (such as React Native)	WebGL
Mobile-app plugin (such as WeChat)	Mobile WebGL
Single-board computer (such as Raspberry Pi)	GPU or ARM NEON

Materials for further reading

- Denis Baylor et al., "TFX: A TensorFlow-Based Production-Scale Machine Learning Platform," KDD 2017, www.kdd.org/kdd2017/papers/view/tfx-a-tensorflow-based-production-scale-machine-learning-platform.
- Raghuraman Krishnamoorthi, "Quantizing Deep Convolutional Networks for Efficient Inference: A Whitepaper," June 2018, https://arxiv.org/pdf/1806.08342.pdf.
- Rasmus Munk Larsen and Tatiana Shpeisman, "TensorFlow Graph Optimization," https://ai.google/research/pubs/pub48051.

Exercises

1 Back in chapter 10, we trained an Auxiliary Class GAN (ACGAN) on the MNIST dataset to generate fake MNIST digit images by class. Specifically, the example we used is in the mnist-acgan directory of the tfjs-examples repository. The generator part of the trained model has a total size of about 10 MB, most of which is occupied by the weights stored as 32-bit floats. It's tempting to perform post-training weight quantization on this model to speed up the page loading. However, before doing so, we need to make sure that no significant deterioration in the quality of the generated images results from such quantization. Test 16- and 8-bit quantization and determine whether either or both of them is an acceptable option. Use the `tensorflowjs_converter` workflow described in section 12.2.1. What criteria will you use to evaluate the quality of the generated MNIST images in this case?

2 Tensorflow models that run as Chrome extensions have the advantage of being able to control Chrome itself. In the speech-commands example in chapter 4, we showed how to use a convolutional model to recognize spoken words. The Chrome extension API gives you the ability to query and change tabs. Try embedding the speech-commands model into an extension, and tune it to recognize the phrases "next tab" and "previous tab." Use the results of the classifier to control the browser tab focus.

3 Info box 12.3 describes the correct way to measure the time that a TensorFlow.js model's `predict()` call (inference call) takes and the cautionary points it involves. In this exercise, load a MobileNetV2 model in TensorFlow.js (see the simple-object-detection example in section 5.2 if you need a reminder of how to do that) and time its `predict()` call:

   a As the first step, generate a randomly valued image tensor of shape [1, 224, 224, 3] and the model's inference on it by following the steps laid out in info box 12.3. Compare the timing result with and without the `array()` or `data()` call on the output tensor. Which one is shorter? Which one is the correct time measurement?

   b When the correct measurement is done 50 times in a loop, plot the individual timing numbers using the tfjs-vis line chart (chapter 7) and get an intuitive appreciation of the variability. Can you see clearly that the first few measurements are significantly different from the rest? Given this observation, discuss the importance of performing burn-in or warm-up runs during performance benchmarking.

   c Unlike tasks a and b, replace the randomly generated input tensor with a real image tensor (such as one obtained from an `img` element using `tf.browser.fromPixels()`), and then repeat the measurements in step b. Does the content of the input tensor affect the timing measurements in any significant way?

    d Instead of running inference on a single example (batch size = 1), try increasing the batch size to 2, 3, 4, and so forth until you reach a relatively large number, such as 32. Is the relation between the average inference time and batch size a monotonically increasing one? A linear one?

Summary

- Good engineering discipline around testing is as important to your machine-learning code as it is to your non-machine-learning code. However, avoid the temptation to focus strongly on "special" examples or make assertions on "golden" model predictions. Instead, rely on testing the fundamental properties of your model, such as its input and output specifications. Furthermore, remember that all the data-preprocessing code before your machine-learning system is just "normal" code and should be tested accordingly.

- Optimizing the speed of downloading and inference is an important factor to the success of client-side deployment of TensorFlow.js models. Using the post-training weight quantization feature of the `tensorflowjs_converter` binary, you can reduce the total size of a model, in some cases without observable loss of inference accuracy. The graph-model conversion feature of `tensorflowjs_ converter` helps to speed up model inference through graph transformations such as op fusion. You are highly encouraged to test and employ both model-optimization techniques when deploying your TensorFlow.js models to production.

- A trained, optimized model is not the end of the story for your machine-learning application. You must find some way to integrate it with an actual product. The most common way for TensorFlow.js applications to be deployed is within web pages, but this is just one of a wide variety of deployment scenarios, each with its own strengths. TensorFlow.js models can run as browser extensions, within native mobile apps, as native desktop applications, and even on single-board hardware like the Raspberry Pi.

Summary, conclusions, and beyond

This chapter covers

- Looking back at the high-level concepts and ideas about AI and deep learning

- A quick overview of the different types of deep-learning algorithms we've visited in this book, when they are useful, and how to implement them in TensorFlow.js

- Pretrained models from the ecosystem of TensorFlow.js

- Limitations of deep learning as it currently stands; and an educated prediction for trends in deep learning that we will see in the coming years

- Guidance for how to further advance your deep-learning knowledge and stay up-to-date with the fast-moving field

This is the final chapter of this book. Previous chapters have been a grand tour of the current landscape of deep learning, enabled by the vehicles of TensorFlow.js and your own hard work. Through this journey, you have hopefully gained quite a few new concepts and skills. It is time to step back and look at the big picture again, as well as get a refresher on some of the most important concepts you've learned. This last chapter will summarize and review core concepts while expanding your horizons beyond the relatively basic notions you've learned so far. We want to make sure you realize this and are properly equipped to take the next steps of the journey on your own.

We'll start with a bird's-eye view of what you should take away from this book. This should refresh your memory regarding some of the concepts you've learned. Next, we'll present an overview of some key limitations of deep learning. To use a tool properly, you should not only know what it *can* do but also what it *can't* do. The chapter ends with a list of resources and strategies for furthering your knowledge and skills about deep learning and AI in the JavaScript ecosystem and staying up-to-date with new developments.

13.1 *Key concepts in review*

This section briefly synthesizes the key takeaways from this book. We will start from the overall landscape of the AI field and end with why bringing deep learning and Java-Script together introduces unique and exciting opportunities.

13.1.1 *Various approaches to AI*

First of all, deep learning is not synonymous with AI or even with machine learning. *Artificial intelligence* is a broad field with a long history. It can generally be defined as "all attempts to automate the cognitive process"—in other words, the automation of thought. This can range from very basic tasks, such as an Excel spreadsheet, to very advanced endeavors, such as a humanoid robot that can walk and talk.

Machine learning is one of the many subfields of AI. It aims at automatically developing programs (called *models*) purely from exposure to training data. This process of turning data into a program (the model) is called *learning*. Although machine learning has been around for a long time (at least several decades), it only started to take off in practical applications in the 1990s.

Deep learning is one of many forms of machine learning. In deep learning, models consist of many steps of representation transformation, applied one after another (hence the adjective "deep"). These operations are structured into modules called *layers*. Deep-learning models are typically stacks of many layers or, more generally, graphs of many layers. These layers are parameterized by *weights*, numeric values that help transform a layer's input into its output and are updated during the training process. The "knowledge" learned by a model during training is embodied in its weights. The training process is primarily about finding a good set of values for these weights.

Even though deep learning is just one among many approaches to machine learning, it has proven to be a breakout success compared to other approaches. Let's quickly review the reasons behind deep learning's success.

13.1.2 *What makes deep learning stand out among the subfields of machine learning*

In the span of only a few years, deep learning has achieved tremendous break-throughs in multiple tasks that have been historically thought of as extremely difficult for computers, especially in the area of machine perception—namely, extracting useful information from images, audio, video, and similar modalities of perceptual data with a sufficiently high accuracy. Given sufficient training data (in particular, *labeled* training data), it is now possible to extract from perceptual data almost anything that humans can extract, sometimes with an accuracy that exceeds that of humans. Hence, it is sometimes said that deep learning has largely "solved perception," although this is true only for a fairly narrow definition of perception (see section 13.2.5 for the limitations of deep learning).

Due to its unprecedented technical success, deep learning has single-handedly brought about the third and by far the largest-so-far *AI summer*, also referred to as the *deep-learning revolution*, which is a period of intense interest, investment, and hype in the field of AI. Whether this period will end in the near future, and what happens to it afterward, are topics of speculation and debate. But one thing is certain: in stark contrast with previous AI summers, deep learning has provided enormous value to a large number of technology companies, enabling human-level image classification, object detection, speech recognition, smart assistants, natural language processing, machine translation, recommendation systems, self-driving cars, and more. The hype may recede (rightfully), but the sustained technological impact and economic value of deep learning will remain. In that sense, deep learning could be analogous to the internet: it may be overly hyped for a few years, causing unreasonable expectations and overinvestment, but in the long term, it will remain a major revolution that will impact many areas of technology and transform our lives.

We are particularly optimistic about deep learning because even if we were to make no further academic progress in it in the next decade, putting the existing deep-learning techniques to every applicable practical problem would still be a game changer for many industries (online advertisement, finance, industrial automation, and assistive technologies for people with disabilities, just to list a few). Deep learning is nothing short of a revolution, and progress is currently happening at an incredibly fast pace due to an exponential investment in resources and headcount. From where we stand, the future looks bright, although short-term expectations may be somewhat overly optimistic; deploying deep learning to the full extent of its potential will take well over a decade.

13.1.3 *How to think about deep learning at a high level*

One of the most surprising aspects of deep learning is how simple it is, given how well it works and how more complicated machine-learning techniques that came before it didn't work quite as well. Ten years ago, nobody expected that we could achieve such amazing results on machine-perception problems by using only parametric models trained with gradient descent. Now it turns out that all you need is sufficiently large parametric models trained with gradient descent and sufficiently many labeled examples. As Richard Feynman once said about his understanding of the universe, "It's not complicated, it's just a lot of it."[1]

In deep learning, everything is represented as a series of numbers—in other words, a *vector*. A vector can be viewed as a *point* in a *geometric space*. Model inputs (tabular data, images, text, and so on) are first vectorized, or turned into a set of points in the input vector space. In a similar way, the targets (labels) are also vectorized and turned into their corresponding set of points in the target vector space. Then, each layer in a deep neural network performs one simple geometric transformation on the data that goes through it. Together, the chain of layers in the neural network forms a complex geometric transformation, made of a series of simple geometric transformations. This complex transformation attempts to map the points in the input vector space to those in the target vector space. This transformation is parameterized by the weights of the layers, which are iteratively updated based on how good the transformation currently is. A key characteristic of this geometric transformation is that it is *differentiable:* this is what makes gradient descent possible.

13.1.4 *Key enabling technologies of deep learning*

The deep-learning revolution that's currently unfolding didn't start overnight. Instead, like any other revolution, it's the product of an accumulation of several enabling factors—slowly at first, and then suddenly accelerating once critical mass is reached. In the case of deep learning, we can point out the following key factors:

- Incremental algorithmic innovations, first spread over two decades[2] and then accelerating as more research effort was poured into deep learning after 2012.[3]
- The availability of large amounts of labeled data, spanning many data modalities, including perceptual (images, audio, and video), numeric, and text, which enables large models to be trained on sufficient amounts of data. This is a byproduct of the rise of the consumer internet, spurred by the popularization of mobile devices, as well as Moore's law applied to storage media.
- The availability of fast, highly parallelized computation hardware at a low cost, especially the GPUs produced by NVIDIA—first gaming GPUs repurposed for parallel computing and then chips designed ground-up for deep learning.
- A complex stack of open source software that makes this computational power available to many human developers and learners, while hiding the enormous amount of complexity underneath: the CUDA language, the web browser's

---

[1] Richard Feynman, interview, "The World from Another Point of View," Yorkshire Television, 1972.
[2] Starting with the invention of backpropagation by Rumelhart, Hinton, and Williams, convolutional layers by LeCun and Bengio, and recurrent networks by Graves and Schmidthuber.
[3] For example, improved weight initialization methods, new activation functions, dropout, batch normalization, residual connections.

WebGL shader languages, and frameworks such as TensorFlow.js, TensorFlow, and Keras, which perform automatic differentiation and provide easy-to-use, high-level building blocks such as layers, loss functions, and optimizers. Deep learning is changing from the exclusive domain of specialists (researchers, graduate students in AI, and engineers with an academic background) into a tool for every programmer. TensorFlow.js is an exemplary framework in this front. It brings two rich and vibrant ecosystems together: the cross-platform ecosystem of JavaScript and the fast-advancing deep-learning ecosystem.

A manifestation of the wide and deep impact of the deep-learning revolution is its fusion with technological stacks different from the one in which it originated (the C++ and Python ecosystem and the numeric computation field). Its cross-pollination with the JavaScript ecosystem, the main theme of the book, is a prime example of that. In the next section, we will review the key reasons why bringing deep learning to the world of JavaScript unlocks exciting new opportunities and possibilities.

13.1.5 *Applications and opportunities unlocked by deep learning in JavaScript*

The main purpose of training a deep-learning model is to make it available for users to use. For many types of input modalities, such as images from the webcam, sounds from the microphone, and text and gesture input by the user, the data is generated and directly available on the client. JavaScript is perhaps the most mature and ubiquitous language and ecosystem for client-side programming. The same code written in JavaScript can be deployed as web pages and UIs on a wide range of devices and platforms. The web browser's WebGL API enables cross-platform parallel computation on a variety of GPUs, which is leveraged by TensorFlow.js. These factors make JavaScript an attractive option for the deployment of deep-learning models. TensorFlow.js offers a converter tool that allows you to convert models trained with popular Python frameworks such as TensorFlow and Keras into a web-friendly format and deploy them into web pages for inference and transfer learning.

Apart from the ease of deployment, there are also a number of additional advantages to serving and fine-tuning deep-learning models using JavaScript:

- Compared to server-side inference, client-side inference foregoes the latency of two-way data transfer, benefiting availability and leading to a smoother user experience.
- By performing computation at the edge using on-device GPU acceleration, client-side deep learning removes the need to manage server-side GPU resources, significantly reducing the complexity and maintenance costs of your technology stack.
- By virtue of keeping the data and inference results on the client, the user's data privacy is protected. This is important for domains such as healthcare and fashion.

- The visual and interactive nature of the browser and other JavaScript-based UI environments provides unique opportunities for visualization, aided understanding, and teaching of neural networks.
- TensorFlow.js supports not only inference but also training. This opens the door to client-side transfer learning and fine-tuning, which leads to better personalization of machine-learning models.
- In the web browser, JavaScript provides a platform-independent API for access to on-device sensors, such as webcams and microphones, which accelerates the development of cross-platform applications that use inputs from these sensors.

In addition to its client-side eminence, JavaScript extends its prowess to the server side. In particular, Node.js is a highly popular framework for server-side applications in JavaScript. Using the Node.js version of TensorFlow.js (tfjs-node), you can train and serve deep-learning models outside the web browser and hence without resource constraints. This taps into the vast ecosystem of Node.js and simplifies the tech stack for members of the community. All of this can be achieved by using essentially the same TensorFlow.js code that you write for the client side, which brings you closer to the vision of "write once, run everywhere," as has been demonstrated by several examples throughout the book.

13.2 Quick overview of the deep-learning workflow and algorithms in TensorFlow.js

With the historical overview out of the way, let's now visit the technical aspects of TensorFlow.js. In this section, we will review the general workflow you should follow when approaching a machine-learning problem and highlight some of the most important considerations and common pitfalls. We will then go over the various neural network building blocks (layers) that we've covered in the book. In addition, we'll survey the pretrained models in the TensorFlow.js ecosystem, which you can use to accelerate your development cycle. To wrap up this section, we will present the range of machine-learning problems you can potentially address by using these building blocks, stimulating you to imagine how deep neural networks written in TensorFlow.js can assist you in addressing your own machine-learning problems.

13.2.1 The universal workflow of supervised deep learning

Deep learning is a powerful tool. But perhaps somewhat surprisingly, the most difficult and time-consuming part of the machine-learning workflow is often everything that comes before designing and training such models (and for models deployed to production, what comes after it, too). These difficult steps include understanding the problem domain well enough to be able to determine what sort of data is needed, what sort of predictions can be made with reasonable accuracy and generalization power, how the machine-learning model fits into the overall solution that addresses a practical problem, and how to measure the degree to which the model succeeds at doing its job. Although these are prerequisites for any successful application of machine learning, they aren't something that a software library such as TensorFlow.js can automate for you. As a reminder, what follows is a quick summary of the typical supervised-learning workflow:

1 *Determine if machine learning is the right approach.* First, consider if machine learning is the right approach to your problem, and proceed with the following steps only if the answer is yes. In some cases, a non-machine-learning approach will work equally well or perhaps even better, at a lower cost.

2 *Define the machine-learning problem.* Determine what sort of data is available and what you are trying to predict using the data.

3 *Check if your data is sufficient.* Determine if the amount of data you already have is sufficient for model training. You may need to collect more data or hire people to manually label an unlabeled dataset.

4 *Identify a way to reliably measure the success of a trained model on your goal.* For simple tasks, this may be just prediction accuracy, but in many cases, it will require more sophisticated, domain-specific metrics.

5 *Prepare the evaluation process.* Design the validation process that you'll use to evaluate your models. In particular, you should split your data into three homogeneous yet nonoverlapping sets: a training set, a validation set, and a test set. The validation- and test-set labels ought not to leak into the training data. For instance, with temporal prediction, the validation and test data should come from time intervals after the training data. Your data-preprocessing code should be covered by tests to guard against bugs (section 12.1).

6 *Vectorize the data.* Turn your data into tensors, or n-dimensional arrays—the lingua franca of machine-learning models in frameworks such as TensorFlow.js and TensorFlow. You often need to preprocess the tensorized data in order to make it more amenable to your models (for example, through normalization).

7 *Beat the commonsense baseline.* Develop a model that beats a non-machine-learning baseline (such as predicting the population average for a regression problem or predicting the last datapoint in a time-series prediction problem), thereby demonstrating that machine learning can truly add value to your solution. This may not always be the case (see step 1).

8 *Develop a model with sufficient capacity.* Gradually refine your model architecture by tuning hyperparameters and adding regularization. Make changes based on the prediction accuracy on the validation set only, not the training set or the test set. Remember that you should get your model to overfit the problem (achieve a better prediction accuracy on the training set than on the validation set), thus identifying a model capacity that's greater than what you need. Only then should you begin to use regularization and other approaches to reduce overfitting.

9 *Tune hyperparameters.* Beware of validation-set overfitting when tuning hyperparameters. Because hyperparameters are determined based on the performance

on the validation set, their values will be overspecialized for the validation set and therefore may not generalize well to other data. It is the purpose of the test set to obtain an unbiased estimate of the model's accuracy after hyperparameter tuning. So, you shouldn't use the test set when tuning the hyperparameters.

10 *Validate and evaluate the trained model.* As we discussed in section 12.1, test your model with an up-to-date evaluation dataset, and decide if the prediction accuracy meets a predetermined criterion for serving actual users. In addition, perform a deeper analysis of the model's quality on different slices (subsets) of the data, aiming at detecting any unfair behaviors (such as vastly different accuracies on different slices of the data) or unwanted biases.[4] Proceed to the final step only if the model passes these evaluation criteria.

11 *Optimize and deploy the model.* Perform model optimization in order to shrink its size and boost its inference speed. Then deploy the model into the serving environment, such as a web page, a mobile app, or an HTTP service endpoint (section 12.3).

This recipe is for supervised learning, which is encountered in many practical problems. Other types of machine-learning workflows covered in this book include (supervised) transfer learning, RL (reinforcement learning), and generative deep learning. Supervised transfer learning (chapter 5) shares the same workflow as nontransfer supervised learning, with the slight difference that the model design and training steps build on a pretrained model and may require a smaller amount of training data than training a model from scratch. Generative deep learning has a different type of goal from supervised learning—that is, to create fake examples that look as real as possible. In practice, there are techniques that turn the training of generative models into supervised learning, as we saw in the VAE and GAN examples in chapter 9. RL, on the other hand, involves a fundamentally different problem formulation and consequently a dramatically different workflow—one in which the primary players are the environment, the agent, the actions, the reward structure, and the algorithm or model types employed to solve the problem. Chapter 11 provided a quick overview of the basic concepts and algorithms in RL.

13.2.2 *Reviewing model and layer types in TensorFlow.js: A quick reference*

All the numerous neural networks covered in this book can be divided into three families: densely connected networks (also referred to as MLPs, or multilayer perceptrons), convnets (convolutional networks), and recurrent networks. These are the three basic families of networks that every deep-learning practitioner should be familiar with. Each type of network is suitable for a specific type of input: a network architecture (MLP, convolutional, or recurrent) encodes assumptions about the structure of the input data—a hypothesis space within which the search for a good model via

---

[4] Fairness in machine learning is a nascent field of study; see the following link for more discussion http://mng.bz/eD4Q.

backpropagation and hyperparameter tuning occurs. Whether a given architecture will work for a given problem depends entirely on how well the structure in the data matches the assumption of the network architecture.

These different network types can easily be combined in a LEGO-like fashion to form more complex and multimodal networks. In a way, deep-learning layers are LEGO bricks for differentiable information processing. We provide a quick overview of the mapping between the modality of input data and the appropriate network architecture:

- Vector data (without temporal or serial order)—MLPs (dense layers)
- Image data (black-and-white, grayscale, or color)—2D convnets
- Audio data as spectrograms—2D convnets or RNNs
- Text data—1D convnets or RNNs
- Time-series data—1D convnets or RNNs
- Volumetric data (such as 3D medical images)—3D convnets
- Video data (sequence of images)—either 3D convnets (if you need to capture motion effects) or a combination of a frame-by-frame 2D convnet for feature extraction followed by either an RNN or a 1D convnet to process the resulting feature sequence

Now let's dive a little deeper into each of the three major architecture families, the tasks they are good at, and how to use them through TensorFlow.js.

DENSELY CONNECTED NETWORKS AND MULTILAYER PERCEPTRONS

The terms *densely connected networks* and *multilayer perceptron* are largely exchangeable, with the caveat that a densely connected network can contain as little as one layer, while an MLP must consist of at least a hidden layer and an output layer. We will use the term *MLP* to refer to all models built primarily with dense layers for the sake of succinctness. Such networks are specialized for unordered vector data (for example, the numeric features in the phishing-website-detection problem and the housing-price-prediction problem). Each dense layer attempts to model the relation between all possible pairs of input features and the layer's output activations. This is achieved through a matrix multiplication between the dense layer's kernel and the input vector (followed by addition with a bias vector and an activation function). The fact that every output activation is affected by every input feature is the reason such layers and the networks built on them are referred to as *densely connected* (or referred to as *fully connected* by some authors). This is in contrast to other types of architecture (convnets and RNNs) in which an output element depends only on a subset of the elements in the input data.

MLPs are most commonly used for categorical data (for example, where the input features are a list of attributes, such as in the phishing-website-detection problem). They are also often used as the final output stages of most neural networks for classification and regression, which may contain convolutional or recurrent layers as feature extractors that feed feature inputs to such MLPs. For instance, the 2D convnets we covered in chapters 4 and 5 all end with one or two dense layers, and so do the recurrent networks we visited in chapter 9.

Let's briefly review how to select the activation of the output layer of an MLP for different types of tasks in supervised learning. To perform binary classification, the final dense layer of your MLP should have exactly one unit and use the sigmoid activation. The `binaryCrossentropy` loss function should be used as the loss function during the training of such a binary-classifier MLP. The examples in your training data should have binary labels (labels of 0 or 1). Specifically, the TensorFlow.js code looks like

```
import * as tf from '@tensorflow/tfjs';

const model = tf.sequential();
model.add(tf.layers.dense({units: 32, activation: 'relu', inputShape:
    [numInputFeatures]}));
model.add(tf.layers.dense({units: 32, activation: 'relu'}));
model.add(tf.layers.dense({units: 1: activation: 'sigmoid'}));
model.compile({loss: 'binaryCrossentropy', optimizer: 'adam'});
```

To perform single-label multiclass classification (where each example has exactly one class among multiple candidate classes), end your stack of layers with a dense layer that contains a softmax activation and a number of units equal to the number of classes. If your targets are one-hot encoded, use `categoricalCrossentropy` as the loss function; if they are integer indices, use `sparseCategoricalCrossentropy`. For instance,

```
const model = tf.sequential();
model.add(tf.layers.dense({units: 32, activation: 'relu', inputShape:
    [numInputFeatures]});
model.add(tf.layers.dense({units: 32, activation: 'relu'});
model.add(tf.layers.dense({units: numClasses: activation: 'softmax'});
model.compile({loss: 'categoricalCrossentropy', optimizer: 'adam'});
```

To perform multilabel multiclass classification (where each example can have several correct classes), end your stack of layers with a dense layer that contains a sigmoid activation and a number of units equal to the number of all candidate classes. Use `binaryCrossentropy` for the loss function. Your targets should be k-hot encoded:

```
const model = tf.sequential();
model.add(tf.layers.dense({units: 32, activation: 'relu', inputShape:
    [numInputFeatures]}));
model.add(tf.layers.dense({units: 32, activation: 'relu'}));
model.add(tf.layers.dense({units: numClasses: activation: 'sigmoid'}));
model.compile({loss: 'binaryCrossentropy', optimizer: 'adam'});
```

To perform regression toward a vector of continuous values, end your stack of layers with a dense layer with the number of units equal to the number of values you are trying to predict (often only one number, such as the price of housing or a temperature value) and the default linear activation. Several loss functions can be suitable for regression. The most commonly used ones are `meanSquaredError` and `meanAbsolute-Error`:

```
const model = tf.sequential();
model.add(tf.layers.dense({units: 32, activation: 'relu', inputShape:
    [numInputFeatures]}));
model.add(tf.layers.dense({units: 32, activation: 'relu'}));
model.add(tf.layers.dense({units: numClasses}));
model.compile({loss: 'meanSquaredError', optimizer: 'adam'});
```

CONVOLUTIONAL NETWORKS

Convolutional layers look at local spatial patterns by applying the same geometric transformation to different spatial locations (patches) in an input tensor. This results in representations that are translation-invariant, making convolutional layers highly data efficient and modular. This idea is applicable to spaces of any dimensionality: 1D (sequences), 2D (images or similar representation of nonimage quantities, such as sound spectrograms), 3D (volumes), and so forth. You can use the `tf.layers.conv1d` layer to process sequences, the conv2d layer to process images, and the conv3d layer to process volumes.

Convnets consist of stacks of convolutional and pooling layers. The pooling layers let you spatially downsample the data, which is required to keep feature maps to a reasonable size as the number of features grows, and to allow subsequent layers to "see" a greater spatial extent of the convnet's input images. Convnets are often terminated with a flatten layer or a global pooling layer, turning spatial feature maps into vectors, which can in turn be processed by a stack of dense layers (an MLP) to achieve classification or regression outputs.

It is highly likely that regular convolution will soon be mostly (or completely) replaced by an equivalent but faster and more efficient alternative: depthwise separable convolution (`tf.layers.separableConv2d` layers). When you are building a network from scratch, using depthwise separable convolution is highly recommended. The separableConv2d layer can be used as a drop-in replacement for `tf.layers.conv2d`, resulting in a smaller and faster network that performs equally well or better on its task. Following is a typical image-classification network (single-label multiclass classification, in this case). Its topology contains repeating patterns of convolution-pooling layer groups:

```
const model = tf.sequential();
model.add(tf.layers.separableConv2d({
    filters: 32, kernelSize: 3, activation: 'relu',
    inputShape: [height, width, channels]}));
model.add(tf.layers.separableConv2d({
        filters: 64, kernelSize: 3, activation: 'relu'}));
model.add(tf.layers.maxPooling2d({poolSize: 2}));

model.add(tf.layers.separableConv2d({
        filters: 64, kernelSize: 3, activation: 'relu'}));
model.add(tf.layers.separableConv2d({
        filters: 128, kernelSize: 3, activation: 'relu'}));
```

```
model.add(tf.layers.maxPooling2d({poolSize: 2}));

model.add(tf.layers.separableConv2d({
    filters: 64, kernelSize: 3, activation: 'relu'}));
model.add(tf.layers.separableConv2d({
    filters: 128, kernelSize: 3, activation: 'relu'}));
model.add(tf.layers.globalAveragePooling2d());
model.add(tf.layers.dense({units: 32, activation: 'relu'}));
model.add(tf.layers.dense({units: numClasses, activation: 'softmax'}));

model.compile({loss: 'categoricalCrossentropy', optimizer: 'adam'});
```

RECURRENT NETWORKS

RNNs work by processing sequences of inputs one timestamp at a time and maintaining a state throughout. A state is typically a vector or a set of vectors (a point in a geometric space). RNNs should be used preferentially over 1D convnets in the case of sequences in which the patterns of interest are not temporally invariant (for instance, time-series data in which the recent past is more important than the distant past).

Three RNN layer types are available in TensorFlow.js: simpleRNN, GRU, and LSTM. For most practical purposes, you should use either GRU or LSTM. LSTM is the more powerful of the two, but it is also computationally more expensive. You can think of GRU as a simpler and cheaper alternative to LSTM.

In order to stack multiple RNN layers on top of each other, every layer except the last one needs to be configured to return the full sequence of its outputs (each input timestep will correspond to an output timestep). If no stacking of RNN layers is required, usually the RNN layer needs to return only the last output, which in itself contains information about the entire sequence.

The following is an example of using a single RNN layer together with a dense layer to perform binary classification of a vector sequence:

```
const model = tf.sequential();
model.add(tf.layers.lstm({
  units: 32,
  inputShape: [numTimesteps, numFeatures]
}));
model.add(tf.layers.dense({units: 1, activation: 'sigmoid'}));
model.compile({loss: 'binaryCrossentropy', optimizer: 'rmsprop'});
```

Next is a model with a stack of RNN layers for single-label multiclass classification of a vector sequence:

```
const model = tf.sequential();
model.add(tf.layers.lstm({
  units: 32,
  returnSequences: true,
  inputShape: [numTimesteps, numFeatures]
}));
model.add(tf.layers.lstm({units: 32, returnSequences: true}));
model.add(tf.layers.lstm({units: 32}));
model.add(tf.layers.dense({units: numClasses, activation: 'softmax'}));
model.compile({loss: 'categoricalCrossentropy', optimizer: 'rmsprop'});
```

LAYERS AND REGULARIZERS THAT HELP MITIGATE OVERFITTING AND IMPROVE CONVERGENCE

Apart from the aforementioned mainstay layer types, some other types of layers are applicable across a wide range of model and problem types and assist the training process. Without these layers, the state-of-the-art accuracies on many machine-learning tasks wouldn't be as high as they are today. For instance, the dropout and batch-Normalization layers are often inserted in MLPs, convnets, and RNNs to help the model converge faster during training and to reduce overfitting. The following example shows a regression MLP with dropout layers included:

```
const model = tf.sequential();
model.add(tf.layers.dense({
  units: 32,
  activation: 'relu',
  inputShape: [numFeatures]
}));
model.add(tf.layers.dropout({rate: 0.25}));
model.add(tf.layers.dense({units: 64, activation: 'relu'}));
model.add(tf.layers.dropout({rate: 0.25}));
model.add(tf.layers.dense({units: 64, activation: 'relu'}));
model.add(tf.layers.dropout({rate: 0.25}));
model.add(tf.layers.dense({
  units: numClasses,
  activation: 'categoricalCrossentropy'
}));
model.compile({loss: 'categoricalCrossentropy', optimizer: 'rmsprop'});
```

13.2.3 *Using pretrained models from TensorFlow.js*

When the machine-learning problem you aim to solve is specific to your application or dataset, building and training a model from scratch is the right way to go, and TensorFlow.js empowers you to do that. However, in some cases, the problem you face is a generic one for which there exist pretrained models that either match your requirement exactly or can satisfy your needs with only minor tweaking. A collection of pretrained models is available from TensorFlow.js and third-party developers who build on them. Such models provide clean and easy-to-use APIs. They are also packaged nicely as npm packages that you can conveniently depend on in your JavaScript applications (including web apps and Node.js projects).

Using such pretrained models in appropriate use cases can substantially accelerate your development. Since it's impossible to list all the TensorFlow.js-based pretrained models out there, we will survey only the most popular ones that we are aware of. The packages with the name prefix @tensorflow-models/ are first-party and maintained by the TensorFlow.js team, while the rest are the work of third-party developers.

@tensorflow-models/mobilenet is a lightweight image-classification model. It outputs the probability scores for the 1,000 ImageNet classes given an input image. It is useful for labeling images in web pages and for detecting specific contents from the webcam input stream, as well as for transfer-learning tasks involving image inputs. While @tensorflow-models/mobilenet is concerned with generic image classes, there are third-party packages for more domain-specific image classification. For instance, nsfwjs classifies images into those that contain pornographic and other inappropriate content versus safe content, which is useful for parental control, safe browsing, and similar applications.

As we discussed in chapter 5, object detection differs from image classification in that it outputs not only *what* objects an image contains but also *where* they are in the coordinate system of the image. @tensorflow-models/coco-ssd is an object-detection model capable of detecting 90 classes of objects. For each input image, it can detect multiple target objects with potentially overlapping bounding boxes, if they exist (figure 13.1, panel A).

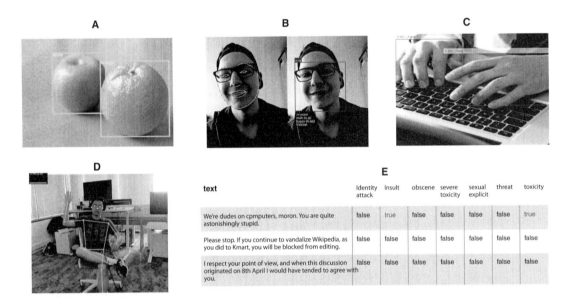

Figure 13.1 Screenshots from several pretrained, npm-package models built with TensorFlow.js. Panel A: @tensorflow-models/coco-ssd is a multitarget object detector. Panel B: face-api.js is for real-time face and facial-key-point detection (reproduced from https://github.com/justadudewhohacks/face-api.js with permission by Vincent Mühler). Panel C: handtrack.js tracks the location of one or both hands in real time (reproduced from https://github.com/victordibia/handtrack.js/ with permission by Victor Dibia). Panel D: @tensorflow-models/posenet detects skeletal key points of the human body using image input in real time. Panel E: @tensorflow-models/toxicity detects and labels seven types of inappropriate content in any English text input.

For web applications, certain types of objects are of especially high interest due to their potential for enabling novel and fun computer-human interactions. These include the human face, the hands, and the whole body. For each of the three, there are specialized third-party models based on TensorFlow.js. For the face, face-api.js and handsfree both support real-time face tracking and detection of facial landmarks (such as the eyes or mouth; figure 13.1, panel B). For the hands, handtrack.js can track the location of one or both hands in real time (figure 13.1, panel C). For the whole body, @tensorflow-models/posenet enables high-precision, real-time detection of skeletal key points (such as shoulders, elbows, hips, and knees; figure 13.1, panel D).

For the audio input modality, @tensorflow-models/speech-commands offers a pretrained model that detects 18 English words in real time, directly utilizing the browser's WebAudio API. Although this is not as powerful as large-vocabulary continuous speech recognition, it nonetheless enables a range of voice-based user interactions in the browser.

There are also pretrained models for text input. For instance, the model from @tensorflow-models/toxicity determines how toxic given English input texts are along several dimensions (for example, threatening, insulting, or obscene), which is useful for aided content moderation (figure 13.1, panel E). The toxicity model is built on top of a more generic natural language processing model called @tensorflow-models/ universal-sentence-encoder, which maps any given English sentence into a vector that can then be used for a wide range of natural language processing tasks, such as intent classification, topic classification, sentiment analysis, and question answering.

It needs to be emphasized that some of the models mentioned not only support simple inference but also can form the basis for transfer learning or downstream machine learning, which lets you apply the power of these pretrained models to your domain-specific data without a lengthy model-building or training process. This is partly due to the LEGO-like composability of layers and models. For example, the output of the universal sentence encoder is primarily intended to be used by a downstream model. The speech-commands model has built-in support for you to collect voice samples for new word classes and train a new classifier based on the samples, which is useful for voice-command applications that require custom vocabulary or user-specific voice adaptation. In addition, outputs from models such as PoseNet and face-api.js regarding the moment-by-moment location of the head, hands, or body posture can be fed into a downstream model that detects specific gestures or movement sequences, which is useful for many applications, such as alternative communication for accessibility use cases.

Apart from the input modality-oriented models mentioned previously, there are also TensorFlow.js-based third-party pretrained models oriented toward artistic creativity. For instance, ml5.js includes a model for fast style transfer between images and a model that can draw sketches automatically. @magenta/music features a model that can transcribe piano music ("audio-to-score") and MusicRNN, a "language model for melodies" that can "write" melodies based on a few seeding notes, along with other intriguing pretrained models.

The collection of pretrained models is large and continues to grow. The JavaScript community and the deep-learning community both have an open culture and sharing spirit. As you go further on your deep-learning journey, you may come across interesting new ideas that are potentially useful to other developers, at which point you are encouraged to train, package, and upload your models to npm in the form of the pretrained models we've mentioned, followed by interaction with users and making iterative improvements to your package. Then you'll truly become a contributing member of the JavaScript deep-learning community.

13.2.4   *The space of possibilities*

With all these layers and pretrained modules as building blocks, what useful and fun models can you build? Remember, building deep-learning models is like playing with LEGO bricks: layers and modules can be plugged together to map essentially anything to anything, as long as the inputs and outputs are represented as tensors, and the layers have compatible input and output tensor shapes. The resulting stack of layers that is the model performs a differentiable geometric transformation, which can learn the mapping relation between the input and the output as long as the relation is not overly complex given the model's capacity. In this paradigm, the space of possibilities is infinite. This section offers a few examples to inspire you to think beyond the basic classification and regression tasks that we've emphasized in this book.

We have sorted the suggestions by input and output modalities. Note that quite a few of them stretch the limits of what is possible. Although a model could be trained on any of the tasks, given that a sufficient amount of training data is available, in some cases, such a model probably wouldn't generalize well far from its training data:

- Mapping vector to vector
  - *Predictive healthcare*—Mapping patient medical records to predicted treatment outcomes
  - *Behavioral targeting*—Mapping a set of website attributes to a potential viewer's behavior on the website (including page views, clicks, and other engagements)
  - *Product quality control*—Mapping a set of attributes related to a manufactured product to predictions about how well the product will perform on the market (sales and profits in different areas of the market)
- Mapping image to vector
  - *Medical image AI*—Mapping medical images (such as X-rays) to diagnostic results
  - *Automatic vehicle steering*—Mapping images from cameras to vehicle control signals, such as wheel-steering actions
  - *Diet helper*—Mapping images of foods and dishes to predicted health effects (for example, calorie counts or allergy warnings)
  - *Cosmetic product recommendation*—Mapping selfie images to recommended cosmetic products
- Mapping time-series data to vector
  - *Brain-computer interfaces*—Mapping electroencephalogram (EEG) signals to user intentions

- *Behavioral targeting*—Mapping past history of product purchases (such as movie or book purchases) to probabilities of purchasing other products in the future
- *Prediction of earthquakes and aftershocks*—Mapping seismic instrument data sequences to the predicted likelihoods of earthquakes and ensuing after-shocks

- Mapping text to vector
  - *Email sorter*—Mapping email content to generic or user-defined labels (for example, work-related, family-related, and spam)
  - *Grammar scorer*—Mapping student writing samples to writing-quality scores
  - *Speech-based medical triaging*—Mapping a patient's description of illness to the medical department that the patient should be referred to

- Mapping text to text
  - *Reply-message suggestion*—Mapping emails to a set of possible response messages
  - *Domain-specific question answering*—Mapping customer questions to automated reply texts
  - *Summarization*—Mapping a long article to a short summary

- Mapping images to text
  - *Automated alt-text generation*—Given an image, generating a short snippet of text that captures the essence of the content
  - *Mobility aids for the visually impaired*—Mapping images of interior or exterior surroundings to spoken guidance and warnings about potential mobility hazards (for example, locations of exits and obstacles)

- Mapping images to images
  - *Image super-resolution*—Mapping low-resolution images to higher-resolution ones
  - *Image-based 3D reconstruction*—Mapping ordinary images to images of the same object but viewed from a different angle

- Mapping image and time-series data to vector
  - *Doctor's multimodal assistant*—Mapping a patient's medical image (such as an MRI) and history of vital signs (blood pressure, heart rate, and so on) to predictions of treatment outcomes

- Mapping image and text to text
  - *Image-based question answering*—Mapping an image and a question related to it (for instance, an image of a used car and a question about its make and year) to an answer

- Mapping image and vector to image
  - *Virtual try-on for clothes and cosmetic products*—Mapping a user's selfie and a vector representation of a cosmetic or garment to an image of the user wearing that product

- Mapping time-series data and vector to time-series data
  - *Musical style transfer*—Mapping a musical score (such as a classical piece represented as a timeseries of notes) and a description of the desired style (for example, jazz) to a new musical score in the desired style

As you may have noticed, the last four categories in this list involve mixed modalities in input data. At this point in our technological history, where most things in life have been digitized and can hence be represented as tensors, what you can potentially achieve with deep learning is limited only by your own imagination and the availability of training data. Although almost any mapping is possible, not every mapping is. We'll discuss in the next section what deep learning *cannot* do yet.

13.2.5   *Limitations of deep learning*

The space of applications that can be implemented with deep learning is nearly infinite. As a result, it is easy to overestimate the power of deep neural networks and be overly optimistic about what problems they can solve. This section briefly talks about some of the limitations that they still have.

NEURAL NETWORKS DO NOT SEE THE WORLD IN THE SAME WAY HUMANS DO

A risk we face when trying to understand deep learning is *anthropomorphization*—that is, the tendency to misinterpret deep neural networks as mimicking perception and cognition in humans. Anthropomorphizing deep neural networks is demonstrably wrong in a few regards. First, when humans perceive a sensory stimulus (such as an image with a girl's face in it or an image with a toothbrush), they not only perceive the brightness and color patterns of the input but also extract the deeper and more important concepts represented by those superficial patterns (for example, the face of a young, female individual or a dental hygiene product, and the relation between the two). Deep neural networks, on the other hand, don't work this way. When you've trained an image-captioning model to map images to text output, it is wrong to believe that the model understands the image in a human sense. In some cases, even the slightest departure from the sort of images present in the training data can cause the model to generate absurd captions (as in figure 13.2).

In particular, the peculiar, nonhuman way in which deep neural networks process their inputs is highlighted by *adversarial examples*, which are samples purposefully designed to trick a machine-learning model into making classification mistakes. As we demonstrated by finding the maximally activating images for convnet filters in section 7.2, it's possible to do gradient ascent in the input space to maximize the activation of a convnet filter. The idea can be extended to output probabilities, so we can perform gradient ascent in the input space to maximize the model's predicted probability for any given output class. By taking a picture of a panda and adding a "gibbon gradient" to it, we can cause a model to misclassify the image as a gibbon (figure 13.3). This is despite the fact that the gibbon gradient is noise-like and small in magnitude, so that the resulting adversarial image looks indistinguishable from the original panda image to humans.

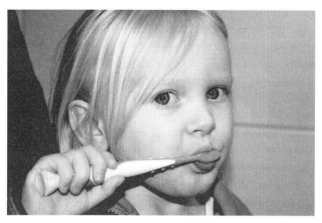

"The boy is holding a baseball bat."

Figure 13.2 Failure of an image-captioning model trained with deep learning

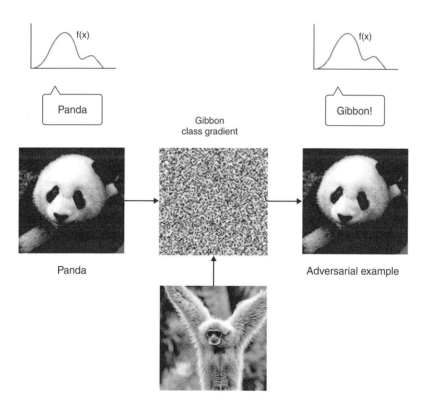

Figure 13.3 Adversarial example: changes imperceptible to human eyes can throw off a deep convnet's classification result. See more discussion on adversarial attacks of deep neural networks at http://mng.bz/pyGz.

So, deep neural networks for computer vision don't possess a real understanding of images—at least not in a human sense. Another area in which human learning stands in sharp contrast with deep learning is how the two types of learning generalize from a limited number of training examples. Deep neural networks can do what can be called *local generalization*. Figure 13.4 illustrates a scenario in which a deep neural network and a human are tasked to learn the boundary of a single class in a 2D parametric space by using only a small number of (say, eight) training examples. The human realizes that the shape of the class boundary should be smooth and the region should be connected, and quickly draws a single closed curve as the "guesstimated" boundary. A neural network, on the other hand, suffers from a lack of abstraction and prior knowledge. Therefore, it may end up with an ad hoc irregular boundary severely overfit to the few training samples. The trained model will generalize very poorly beyond the training samples. Adding more samples can help the neural network but is not always practically possible. The main problem is that the neural network is created from scratch, just for this particular problem. Unlike a human individual, it doesn't have any prior knowledge to rely on and hence doesn't know what to "expect."[5] This is the fundamental reason behind a major limitation of current deep-learning algorithms: namely, a large number of human-labeled training data is usually required to train a deep neural network to decent generalization accuracy.

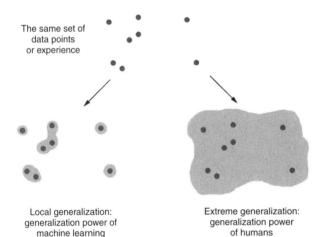

The same set of data points or experience

Local generalization: generalization power of machine learning

Extreme generalization: generalization power of humans

Figure 13.4   Local generalization in deep-learning models vs. extreme generalization in human intelligence

---

[5]   There are research efforts to train a single deep neural network on many different and seemingly unrelated tasks to facilitate cross-domain knowledge sharing (see, for example, Lukasz Kaiser et al., "One Model To Learn Them All," submitted 16 Jun. 2017, https://arxiv.org/abs/1706.05137). But such multitask models have not received wide adoption yet.

13.3 *Trends in deep learning*

As we've discussed, deep learning has made amazing progress in recent years, but it still suffers from some limitations. But the field is not static; it keeps advancing at a breathtaking velocity, so it's likely that some of the limitations will be ameliorated in the near future. This section contains a set of educated guesses about what important breakthroughs in deep learning we'll witness in the coming years:

- First, unsupervised or semisupervised learning could see significant advancements. This will have a profound impact on all forms of deep learning because even though labeled datasets are costly to construct and hard to come across, there is an abundance of unlabeled datasets in all sorts of business domains. If we can invent a way to use a small amount of labeled data to guide the learning from a vast amount of unlabeled data, it will unlock many new applications for deep learning.

- Second, hardware for deep learning may continue to be improved, ushering in more and more powerful neural network accelerators (such as the future generations of the Tensor Processing Unit[6]). This will allow researchers to train ever more powerful networks with ever larger datasets and thereby continue to push forward the state-of-the-art accuracy on many machine-learning tasks, such as computer vision, speech recognition, natural language processing, and generative models.

- Designing model architecture and tuning model hyperparameters will likely become more and more automated. We are already seeing a trend in this area, as exemplified by technologies such as AutoML[7] and Google Vizier.[8]

- The sharing and reuse of neural network components will likely continue to grow. Transfer learning based on pretrained models will gain further momentum. State-of-the-art deep-learning models are getting increasingly powerful and generic by the day. They are increasingly trained on larger and larger datasets, sometimes with huge amounts of computation power for the sake of automated architectural search and hyperparameter tuning (see the first and second predictions). As a consequence, it's becoming more sensible and economical to reuse such pretrained models, for either direct inference or transfer learning, than to train them from scratch over and over again. In a way, this makes the field of deep learning more similar to traditional software engineering, in which high-quality libraries are depended on and reused regularly, to the benefit of standardization and the development velocity of the field as a whole.

---

[6] Norman P. Jouppi et al., "In-Datacenter Performance Analysis of a Tensor Processing Unit™," 2017, https://arxiv.org/pdf/1704.04760.pdf.

[7] Barret Zoph and Quoc V. Le, "Neural Architecture Search with Reinforcement Learning," submitted 5 Nov. 2016, https://arxiv.org/abs/1611.01578.

[8] Daniel Golovin, "Google Vizier: A Service for Black-Box Optimization," Proc. 23rd ACM SIGKDD International Conference on Knowledge Discovery and Data Mining, 2017, pp. 1487–1495, http://mng.bz/O9yE.

- Deep learning may be deployed to new areas of application, improving many existing solutions and opening up new practical use cases. In our opinion, the potential areas of application are truly limitless. Fields including agriculture, finance, education, transportation, healthcare, fashion, sports, and entertainment present countless opportunities waiting to be explored for deep-learning practitioners.
- As deep learning penetrates more application domains, there will likely be a growing emphasis on deep learning at the edge because edge devices are closest to where the users are. As a result, the field will likely invent smaller and more power-efficient neural network architectures that achieve the same prediction accuracy and speed as existing, larger models.

All these predictions will affect deep learning in JavaScript, but the last three predictions are especially relevant. Expect more powerful and efficient models to become available to TensorFlow.js in the future.

13.4 *Pointers for further exploration*

As final parting words, we want to give you some pointers about how to keep learning and updating your knowledge and skills after you've turned the last page of this book. The field of modern deep learning as we know it today is only a few years old, despite a long, slow prehistory stretching back decades. With an exponential increase in financial resources and research headcount since 2013, the field as a whole is now moving at a frenetic pace. Many of the things you learned in this book won't stay relevant for very long. It is the core ideas of deep learning (learning from data, reducing manual feature engineering, layer-by-layer transformation of representation) that will likely stick around for a longer time. More importantly, the foundation of knowledge you developed by reading this book will hopefully prepare you to learn about new developments and trends in the field of deep learning on your own. Fortunately, the field has an open culture in which most cutting-edge advances (including many datasets!) are published in the form of openly accessible and free preprints, accompanied by public blog posts and tweets. Here are a few top resources you should be familiar with.

13.4.1 *Practice real-world machine-learning problems on Kaggle*

An effective way to acquire real-world experience in machine learning (and especially deep learning) is to try your hand at competitions on Kaggle (https://kaggle.com). The only real way to learn machine learning is through actual coding, model building, and tuning. That's the philosophy of the book, as reflected in its numerous code examples ready for you to study, tweak, and hack. But nothing is as effective in teaching you how to do machine learning as building your models and machine-learning systems in a ground-up fashion, using a library such as TensorFlow.js. On Kaggle, you can find an array of constantly renewed data-science competitions and datasets, many of which involve deep learning.

Although most Kaggle users use Python tools (such as TensorFlow and Keras) to solve the competitions, most of the datasets on Kaggle are language-agnostic. So, it is entirely feasible to solve most Kaggle problems using a non-Python deep-learning framework like TensorFlow.js. By participating in a few competitions, maybe as a part of a team, you'll become familiar with the practical side of some of the advanced best practices described in this book, especially hyperparameter tuning and avoiding validation-set overfitting.

13.4.2 Read about the latest developments on arXiv

Deep-learning research, in contrast with some other academic fields, takes place almost completely in the open. Papers are made publicly and freely accessible as soon as they are finalized and pass review, and a lot of related software is open source. ArXiv (https://arxiv.org)—pronounced "archive" (the X stands for the Greek letter *chi*)—is an open-access preprint server for mathematics, physics, and computer science papers. It has become the de facto way to publish cutting-edge work in the field of machine learning and deep learning, and hence is also the de facto way to stay up-to-date with the field. This allows the field to move extremely fast: all new findings and inventions are instantly available for all to see, to critique, and to build on.

An important downside of ArXiv is the sheer quantity of new papers posted every day, which makes it impossible to skim them all. The fact that many of the papers on ArXiv aren't peer-reviewed makes it difficult to identify which ones are important and of high quality. The community has built tools to help with these challenges. For example, a website called ArXiv Sanity Preserver (arxiv-sanity.com) serves as a recommendation engine for new ArXiv papers and can help you keep track of new developments in specific vertical domains of deep learning (such as natural language processing or object detection). Additionally, you can use Google Scholar to keep track of publications in your areas of interest and by your favorite authors.

13.4.3 Explore the TensorFlow.js Ecosystem

TensorFlow.js has a vibrant and growing ecosystem of documentation, guides, tutorials, blogosphere, and open source projects:

- Your main reference for working with TensorFlow.js is the official online documentation at www.tensorflow.org/js/. The detailed, up-to-date API documentation is available at https://js.tensorflow.org/api/latest/.
- You can ask questions about TensorFlow.js on Stack Overflow using the tag "tensorflow.js": https://stackoverflow.com/questions/tagged/tensorflow.js.
- For general discussion about the library, use the Google Group: https://groups.google.com/a/tensorflow.org/forum/#!forum/tfjs.
- You can also follow members of the TensorFlow.js team who have an active presence on Twitter, including
  - https://twitter.com/sqcai
  - https://twitter.com/nsthorat

– https://twitter.com/dsmilkov
– https://twitter.com/tensorflow

Final words

This is the end of *Deep Learning with JavaScript*! We hope you've learned a thing or two about AI, deep learning, and how to perform some basic deep-learning tasks in Java-Script using TensorFlow.js. Like any interesting and useful topic, learning about AI and deep learning is a life-long journey. The same can be said for the application of AI and deep learning to practical problems. This is true for professionals and amateurs alike. For all the progress made in deep learning so far, most of the fundamental questions remain unanswered, and most of the practical potential of deep learning has barely been tapped. Please keep learning, questioning, researching, imaging, hacking, building, and sharing! We look forward to seeing what you build using deep learning and JavaScript!

appendix A
Installing tfjs-node-gpu
and its dependencies

To use the GPU-accelerated version of TensorFlow.js (tfjs-node-gpu) in Node.js, you need to have CUDA and CuDNN installed on your machine. First of all, the machine should be equipped with a CUDA-enabled NVIDIA GPU. To check whether the GPU in your machine meets that requirement, visit https://developer.nvidia.com/cuda-gpus.

Next, we list the detailed steps of the driver and library installation for Linux and Windows, as these are the two operating systems on which tfjs-node-gpu is currently supported.

A.1   Installing tfjs-node-gpu on Linux

1. We assume you have installed Node.js and npm on your system and that the paths to node and npm are included in your system path. If not, see https://nodejs.org/en/download/ for downloadable installers.

2. Download the CUDA Toolkit from https://developer.nvidia.com/cuda-downloads. Be sure to choose the suitable version for the version of tfjs-node-gpu you intend to use. At the time of this writing, the latest version of tfjs-node-gpu is 1.2.10, which works with CUDA Toolkit version 10.0. In addition, be sure to select the correct operating system (Linux), architecture (for example, x86_64 for machines with mainstream Intel CPUs), Linux distribution, and version of the distribution. You will have the option to download several types of installers. Here, we assume you download the "runfile (local)" file (as opposed to, for example, the local .deb package) for use in the subsequent steps.

3. In your downloads folder, make the just-downloaded runfile executable. For example,

   ```
   chmod +x cuda_10.0.130_410.48_linux.run
   ```

477

4 Use `sudo` to run the runfile. Note that the CUDA Toolkit installation process may need to install or upgrade the NVIDIA driver if the version of the NVIDIA driver already installed on your machine is too old or if no such driver has been installed. If this is the case, you need to stop the X server by dropping to the shell-only model. On Ubuntu and Debian distributions, you can enter the shell-only model with the shortcut key Ctrl-Alt-F1.

Follow the prompts on the screen to install the CUDA Toolkit installation, followed by a reboot of the machine. If you are in shell-only mode, you can reboot back to the normal GUI mode.

5 If step 3 completed correctly, the `nvidia-smi` command should now be available on your path. You can use it to check the status of your GPUs. It provides information such as the name, temperature-sensor reading, fan speed, processor, and memory usage of the NVIDIA GPUs installed on your machine, in addition to the current NVIDIA driver version. It is a handy tool for real-time monitoring of your GPU when you are using tfjs-node-gpu to train deep neural networks. A typical printed message from `nvidia-smi` looks like the following (note this machine has two NVIDIA GPUs):

```
+-----------------------------------------------------------------------------+
| NVIDIA-SMI 384.111                   Driver Version: 384.111                |
|-------------------------------+----------------------+----------------------+
| GPU  Name        Persistence-M| Bus-Id        Disp.A | Volatile Uncorr. ECC |
| Fan  Temp  Perf  Pwr:Usage/Cap|         Memory-Usage | GPU-Util  Compute M. |
|===============================+======================+======================|
|   0  Quadro P1000        Off  | 00000000:65:00.0  On |                  N/A |
| 41%   53C    P0    ERR! /  N/A |   620MiB /  4035MiB |      0%      Default |
+-------------------------------+----------------------+----------------------+
|   1  Quadro M4000        Off  | 00000000:B3:00.0 Off |                  N/A |
| 46%   30C    P8    11W / 120W |     2MiB /  8121MiB |      0%      Default |
+-------------------------------+----------------------+----------------------+

+-----------------------------------------------------------------------------+
| Processes:                                                       GPU Memory |
|  GPU       PID   Type   Process name                             Usage      |
|=============================================================================|
|    0      3876      G   /usr/lib/xorg/Xorg                           283MiB |
+-----------------------------------------------------------------------------+
```

6 Add the path to the 64-bit CUDA library files to your `LD_LIBRARY_PATH` environment variable. Assuming that you are using the bash shell, you can add the following line to your .bashrc file:

```
export LD_LIBRARY_PATH="/usr/local/cuda/lib64:${PATH}"
```

tfjs-node-gpu uses the `LD_LIBRARY_PATH` environment variable to find the required dynamic library files when starting up.

7 Download CuDNN from https://developer.nvidia.com/cudnn. Why do you need CuDNN in addition to CUDA? This is because CUDA is a generic computation library with uses in fields other than deep learning (for example, fluid

dynamics). CuDNN is NVIDIA's library for accelerated deep neural network operations built on top of CUDA.

NVIDIA may require you to create a login account and answer some survey questions in order to download CuDNN. Be sure to download the version of CuDNN that matches the version of CUDA Toolkit installed in the previous steps. For example, CuDNN 7.6 goes with CUDA Toolkit 10.0.

8 Unlike CUDA Toolkit, the downloaded CuDNN doesn't come with an executable installer. Instead, it is a compressed tarball that contains a number of dynamic library files and C/C++ headers. These files should be extracted and copied into the appropriate destination folders. You can use a sequence of commands like the following to achieve this:

```
tar xzvf cudnn-10.0-linux-x64-v7.6.4.38.tgz
cp cuda/lib64/* /usr/local/cuda/lib64
cp cuda/include/* /usr/local/cuda/include
```

9 Now that all the required drivers and libraries have been installed, you can quickly verify CUDA and CuDNN by importing tfjs-node-gpu in node:

```
npm i @tensorflow/tfjs @tensorflow/tfjs-node-gpu
node
```

Then, at the Node.js command-line interface,

```
> const tf = require('@tensorflow/tfjs');
> require('@tensorflow/tfjs-node-gpu');
```

If everything went well, you should see a number of logging lines confirming the discovery of a GPU (or multiple GPUs, depending on your system configuration) ready for use by tfjs-node-gpu:

```
2018-09-04 13:08:17.602543: I
tensorflow/core/common_runtime/gpu/gpu_device.cc:1405] Found device 0
with properties:
 name: Quadro M4000 major: 5 minor: 2 memoryClockRate(GHz): 0.7725
 pciBusID: 0000:b3:00.0
 totalMemory: 7.93GiB freeMemory: 7.86GiB
 2018-09-04 13:08:17.602571: I
tensorflow/core/common_runtime/gpu/gpu_device.cc:1484] Adding visible
gpu devices: 0
 2018-09-04 13:08:18.157029: I
tensorflow/core/common_runtime/gpu/gpu_device.cc:965] Device
interconnect StreamExecutor with strength 1 edge matrix:
 2018-09-04 13:08:18.157054: I
tensorflow/core/common_runtime/gpu/gpu_device.cc:971]      0
 2018-09-04 13:08:18.157061: I
tensorflow/core/common_runtime/gpu/gpu_device.cc:984] 0:   N
 2018-09-04 13:08:18.157213: I
tensorflow/core/common_runtime/gpu/gpu_device.cc:1097] Created
TensorFlow device (/job:localhost/replica:0/task:0/device:GPU:0 with
7584 MB memory) -> physical GPU (device: 0, name: Quadro M4000, pci bus
id: 0000:b3:00.0, compute capability: 5.2)
```

10 Now you are all set to use the full features of tfjs-node-gpu. Just make sure you include the following dependencies in your package.json (or their later versions):

```
...
"dependencies": {
  "@tensorflow/tfjs": "^0.12.6",
  "@tensorflow/tfjs-node": "^0.1.14",
  ...
}
...
```

In your main .js file, make sure you import the basic dependencies, including `@tensorflow/tfjs` and `@tensorflow/tfjs-node-gpu`. The former gives you the general API of TensorFlow.js, while the latter wires TensorFlow.js operations to the high-performance computation kernels implemented on CUDA and CuDNN:

```
const tf = require('@tensorflow/tfjs');
require('@tensorflow/tfjs-node-gpu');
```

A.2   Installing tfjs-node-gpu on Windows

1 Make sure that your Windows meets the system requirements of CUDA Toolkit. Certain Windows releases and 32-bit machine architectures are not supported by CUDA Toolkit. See https://docs.nvidia.com/cuda/cuda-installation-guide-microsoft-windows/index.html#system-requirements for more details.

2 We assume you have installed Node.js and npm on your system and that the paths of Node.js and npm are available in your system's environment variable `Path`. If not, see https://nodejs.org/en/download/ for downloadable installers.

3 Install Microsoft Visual Studio, as it is required by the installation of CUDA Toolkit. See the same link as in step 1 for which version of Visual Studio to install.

4 Download and install CUDA Toolkit for Windows. At the time of this writing, CUDA 10.0 is required for running tfjs-node-gpu (latest version: 1.2.10). Be sure to select the correct installer for your Windows release. Installers for Windows 7 and Windows 10 are available. The step requires administrator privileges.

5 Download CuDNN. Make sure that the version of CuDNN matches the version of CUDA. For example, CuDNN 7.6 matches CUDA Toolkit 10.0. NVIDIA may require you to create a login for its website and answer some survey questions before you can download CuDNN.

6 Unlike the CUDA Toolkit installer, the CuDNN you just downloaded is a zip file. Extract it, and you will see three folders within: cuda/bin, cuda/include, and cuda/lib/x64. Locate the directory in which your CUDA Toolkit is installed (by default, it is something like C:/Program Files/NVIDIA CUDA Toolkit 10.0/cuda). Copy the extracted files to the corresponding subfolders with the same name there. For example, the files in cuda/bin of the extracted zip archive should be copied to C:/Program Files/NVIDIA CUDA Toolkit 10.0/cuda/bin. This step may also require administrator privileges.

7 After installing CUDA Toolkit and CuDNN, restart your Windows system. We found this to be necessary for all the newly installed libraries to be properly loaded for tfjs-node-gpu use.

8 Install the npm package `window-build-tools`. This is necessary for the installation of the npm package `@tensorflow/tfjs-node-gpu` in the next step:

```
npm install --add-python-to-path='true' --global windows-build-tools
```

9 Install the packages `@tensorflow/tfjs` and `@tensorflow/tfjs-node-gpu` with npm:

```
npm -i @tensorflow/tfjs @tensorflow/tfjs-node-gpu
```

10 To verify that the installation succeeded, open the node command line and run

```
> const tf = require('@tensorflow/tfjs');
> require('@tensorflow/tfjs-node-gpu');
```

See that both commands finish without errors. After the second command, you should see some logging lines in the console printed by the TensorFlow GPU shared library. Those lines will list details of the CUDA-enabled GPUs that tfjs-node-gpu has recognized and will use in subsequent deep-learning programs.

appendix B
A quick tutorial of tensors and operations in TensorFlow.js

This appendix focuses on the parts of the TensorFlow.js API that are not `tf.Model`. Although `tf.Model` provides a complete set of methods for training and evaluating models and using them for inference, you often need to use non-`tf.Model` parts of TensorFlow.js in order to work with `tf.Model` objects. The most common cases are

- Converting your data into tensors that can be fed to `tf.Model` objects
- Marshalling the data out of the predictions made by `tf.Model`, which are in the format of tensors, so they can be used by other parts of your program

As you will see, getting data into and out of tensors is not hard, but there are some customary patterns and cautionary points worth pointing out.

B.1 Tensor creation and tensor axis conventions

Remember that a *tensor* is simply a data container. Every tensor has two fundamental properties: data type (dtype) and shape. *dtype* controls what kinds of values are stored within the tensor. A given tensor can store only one kind of value. At the time of this writing (version 0.13.5), the supported dtypes are float32, int32, and bool.

The *shape* is an array of integers indicating how many elements are in the tensor and how they are organized. It can be thought of as the "shape and size" of the container that is the tensor (see figure B.1).

The length of the shape is known as the tensor's *rank*. For example, a 1D tensor, also known as a *vector*, has rank 1. The shape of a 1D tensor is an array containing one number, and that number tells us how long the 1D tensor is. Increasing rank

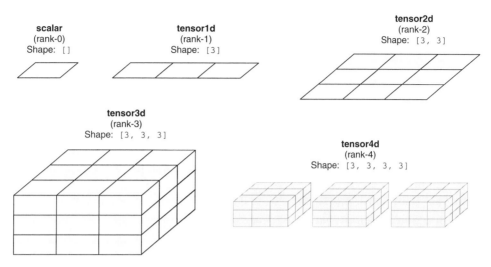

Figure B.1 Examples of tensors of rank 0, 1, 2, 3, and 4

by one, we get a 2D tensor, which can be visualized as a grid of numbers in a 2D plane (like a grayscale image). The shape of a 2D tensor has two numbers, which tell us how tall and how wide the grid is. Further increasing the rank by one, we get a 3D tensor. As shown in the example in figure B.1, you can visualize a 3D tensor as a 3D grid of numbers. The shape of a 3D tensor consists of three integers; they tell us the size of the 3D grid along the three dimensions. So, you see the pattern. Tensors of rank 4 (4D tensors) are harder to visualize directly because the world we live in has only three spatial dimensions. 4D tensors are frequently used in many models, such as deep convnets. TensorFlow.js supports tensors up to rank 6. In practice, rank-5 tensors are used only in some niche cases (for example, those involving video data), while rank-6 tensors are encountered even more rarely.

B.1.1 Scalar (rank-0 tensor)

A scalar is a tensor whose shape is an empty array ([]). It has no axes and always contains exactly one value. You can create a new scalar using the tf.scalar() function. At the JavaScript console (again, assuming TensorFlow.js is loaded and available at the tf symbol), do the following:

```
> const myScalar = tf.scalar(2018);[1]
> myScalar.print();
Tensor
    2018
> myScalar.dtype;
"float32"
> myScalar.shape;
```

---

[1] Note that for space and clarity, we will skip the JavaScript console output lines that result from assignments, as they are not illustrative to the issue at hand.

```
[]
> myScalar.rank;
0
```

We have created a scalar tensor holding just the value 2018. Its shape is the empty list, as expected. It has the default dtype (`"float32"`). To force the dtype to be an integer, provide `'int32'` as an additional argument when calling `tf.scalar()`:

```
> const myIntegerScalar = tf.scalar(2018, 'int32');
> myIntegerScalar.dtype;
"int32"
```

To get the data back out of the tensor, we can use the async method `data()`. The method is async because, in general, the tensor may be hosted out of the main memory, such as on GPUs, as a WebGL texture. Retrieving the value of such tensors involves operations that are not guaranteed to resolve immediately, and we don't want those operations to block the main JavaScript thread. This is why the `data()` method is async. There is also a synchronous function that retrieves the values of tensors through polling: `dataSync()`. This method is convenient but blocks the main JavaScript thread, so it should be used sparingly (for example, during debugging). Prefer the async `data()` method whenever possible:

```
> arr = await myScalar.data();
Float32Array [2018]
> arr.length
1
> arr[0]
2018
```

To use `dataSync()`:

```
> arr = myScalar.dataSync();
Float32Array [2018]
> arr.length
1
> arr[0]
2018
```

We see that for float32-type tensors, the `data()` and `dataSync()` methods return the values as a JavaScript `Float32Array` primitive. This may be a little surprising if you expected a plain old number, but it makes more sense when considering that tensors of other shapes may need to return a container of multiple numbers. For int32-type and bool-type tensors, `data()` and `dataSync()` return `Int32Array` and `Uint8Array`, respectively.

Note that even though a scalar always contains exactly one element, the converse is not true. A tensor whose rank is greater than 0 may have exactly one element as well, as long as the product of the numbers in its shape is 1. For example, a 2D tensor of shape [1, 1] has only one element, but it has two axes.

B.1.2 *tensor1d (rank-1 tensor)*

A 1D tensor is sometimes called a rank-1 tensor or a vector. A 1D tensor has exactly one axis, and its shape is a length-1 array. The following code will create a vector at the console:

```
> const myVector = tf.tensor1d([-1.2, 0, 19, 78]);
> myVector.shape;
[4]
> myVector.rank;
1
> await myVector.data();
Float32Array(4) [-1.2, 0, 19, 78]
```

This 1D tensor has four elements and can be called a 4-dimensional vector. Don't confuse a 4D *vector* with a 4D *tensor*! A 4D vector is a 1D tensor that has one axis and contains exactly four values, whereas a 4D tensor has four axes (and may have any number of dimensions along each axis). Dimensionality can denote either the number of elements along a specific axis (as in our 4D vector) or the number of axes in a tensor (for example, a 4D tensor), which can be confusing at times. It's technically more correct and less ambiguous to refer to a rank-4 tensor, but the ambiguous notation 4D tensor is common regardless. In most cases, this shouldn't be a problem, as it can be disambiguated based on the context.

As in the case of scalar tensors, you can use the data() and dataSync() methods to access the values of the 1D tensor's elements; for example,

```
> await myVector.data()
Float32Array(4) [-1.2000000476837158, 0, 19, 78]
```

Alternatively, you can use the synchronous version of data()—namely, dataSync()—but be aware that dataSync() may block the UI thread and should be avoided if possible:

```
> myVector.dataSync()
Float32Array(4) [-1.2000000476837158, 0, 19, 78]
```

In order to access the value of a specific element of the 1D tensor, you can simply index into the TypedArray returned by data() or dataSync(); for example,

```
> [await myVector.data()][2]
19
```

B.1.3 *tensor2d (rank-2 tensor)*

A 2D tensor has two axes. In some cases, a 2D tensor is referred to as a *matrix*, and its two axes can be interpreted as the row and column indices of the matrix, respectively. You can visually interpret a matrix as a rectangular grid of elements (see the third panel of figure B.1). In TensorFlow.js,

```
> const myMatrix = tf.tensor2d([[1, 2, 3], [40, 50, 60]]);
> myMatrix.shape;
[2, 3]
> myMatrix.rank;
2
```

The entries from the first axis are called the *rows*, and the entries from the second axis are the *columns*. In the previous example, [1, 2, 3] is the first row, and [1, 40] is the first column. It is important to know that when returning the data, using data() or dataSync(), the data will come as a flat array in *row-major* order. In other words, the elements of the first row will appear in the Float32Array first, followed by elements of the second row, and so forth:[2]

```
> await myMatrix.data();
Float32Array(6) [1, 2, 3, 40, 50, 60]
```

Previously, we mentioned that the data() and dataSync() methods, when followed by indexing, can be used to access the value of any element of a 1D tensor. When used on 2D tensors, the indexing operation becomes tedious because the TypedArray returned by data() and dataSync() *flattens* the elements of the 2D tensor. For instance, in order to determine the element of the TypedArray that corresponds to the element in the second row and second column of the 2D tensor, you'd have to perform arithmetic like the following:

```
> (await myMatrix.data())[1 * 3 + 1];
50
```

Fortunately, TensorFlow.js provides another set of methods to download values from tensors into plain JavaScript data structures: array() and arraySync(). Unlike data() and dataSync(), these methods return nested JavaScript arrays that properly preserve the rank and shape of the original tensors. For example,

```
> JSON.stringify(await myMatrix.array())
 "[[1,2,3],[40,50,60]]"
```

To access an element at the second row and second column, we can simply perform indexing into the nested array twice:

```
> (await myMatrix.array())[1][1]
 50
```

This gets rid of the need to perform index arithmetic and will be especially convenient for higher-dimensional tensors. arraySync() is the synchronous version of array(). Like dataSync(), arraySync() may block the UI thread and should be used with caution.

In the tf.tensor2d() call, we provided a nested JavaScript array as the argument. The argument consists of rows of arrays nested within another array. This nesting structure is used by tf.tensor2d() to infer the shape of the 2D tensor—that is, how many rows and how many columns there are, respectively. An alternative way to create the same 2D tensor with tf.tensor2d() is to provide the elements as a flat (non-nested) JavaScript array and accompany it by a second argument that specifies the shape of the 2D tensor:

---

[2] This is different from the column-major ordering seen in some other numerical frameworks such as MATLAB and R.

```
> const myMatrix = tf.tensor2d([1, 2, 3, 40, 50, 60], [2, 3]);
> myMatrix.shape;
[2, 3]
> myMatrix.rank;
2
```

In this approach, the product of all the numbers in the shape argument must match the number of elements in the float array, or else an error will be thrown during the tf.tensor2d() call. For tensors of ranks higher than 2, there are also two analogous approaches to tensor creation: using either a single nested array as the argument or a flat array accompanied by a shape argument. You will see both approaches used in different examples throughout this book.

B.1.4   *Rank-3 and higher-dimensional tensors*

If you pack several 2D tensors into a new array, you will get a 3D tensor, which you can imagine as a cube of elements (the fourth panel in figure B.1). Rank-3 tensors can be created in TensorFlow.js following the same pattern as previously:

```
> const myRank3Tensor = tf.tensor3d([[[1, 2, 3],
                                       [4, 5, 6]],
                                      [[10, 20, 30],
                                       [40, 50, 60]]]);
> myRank3Tensor.shape;
[2, 2, 3]
> myRank3Tensor.rank;
3
```

Another way to do the same thing is to provide a flat (non-nested) array of values, together with an explicit shape:

```
> const anotherRank3Tensor = tf.tensor3d(
    [1, 2, 3, 4, 5, 6, 7, 8, 9, 10, 11, 12],
    [2, 2, 3]);
```

The tf.tensor3d() function in this example can be replaced with the more generic tf.tensor() function. This allows you to generate tensors of any rank up to 6. In the following, we create a rank-3 and a rank-6 tensor:

```
> anotherRank3Tensor = tf.tensor(
    [1, 2, 3, 4, 5, 6, 7, 8, 9, 10, 11, 12],
    [2, 2, 3]);
> anotherRank3Tensor.shape;
[2, 2, 3]
> anotherRank3Tensor.rank;
3

> tinyRank6Tensor = tf.tensor([13], [1, 1, 1, 1, 1, 1]);
> tinyRank6Tensor.shape;
[1, 1, 1, 1, 1, 1]
> tinyRank6Tensor.rank;
6
```

B.1.5   *The notion of data batches*

In practice, the first axis (axis 0, because indexing starts at 0) in all tensors you'll come across in deep learning will almost always be the *batch axis* (sometimes called the *samples axis* or *batch dimension*). Therefore, an actual tensor taken by a model as input has a rank that exceeds the rank of an individual input feature by 1. This is true throughout the TensorFlow.js models in this book. The size of the first dimension equals the number of examples in the batch, known as *batch size*. For instance, in the iris-flower-classification example in chapter 3 (listing 3.9), the input feature of every example consists of four numbers represented as a length-4 vector (a 1D tensor of shape [4]). Hence the input to the iris-classification model is 2D and has a shape [null, 4], where the first null value indicates a batch size that will be determined at the model's runtime (see figure B.2). This batching convention also applies to the output of models. For example, the iris-classification model outputs a one-hot encoding for the three possible types of iris for every individual input example, which is a 1D tensor of shape [3]. However, the model's actual output shape is 2D and has a shape of [null, 3], where the null-valued first dimension is the to-be-determined batch size.

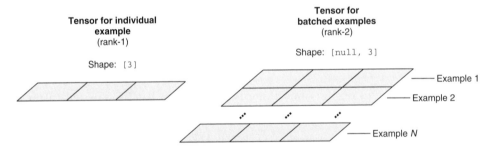

Figure B.2   Tensor shapes for individual examples (left) and batched examples (right). The tensor for batched examples has a rank one greater than the tensor for an individual example and is the format accepted by the `predict()`, `fit()`, and `evaluate()` methods of `tf.Model` objects. The `null` in the shape of the tensor for batch examples indicates that the first dimension of the tensor has an undetermined size, which can be every positive integer during actual calls to the aforementioned methods.

B.1.6   *Real-world examples of tensors*

Let's make tensors more concrete with a few examples similar to what you'll encounter in the book. The data you'll manipulate will almost always fall into one of the following categories. In the previous discussion, we follow the batching convention and always included the number of examples in the batch (numExamples) as the first axis:

- *Vector data*—2D tensors with shape [numExamples, features]
- *Time-series (sequence) data*—3D tensors with shape [numExamples, timesteps, features]

- *Images*—4D tensors with shape [numExamples, height, width, channels]
- *Video*—5D tensors with shape [numExamples, frame, height, width, channels]

VECTOR DATA

This is the most common case. In such a dataset, each single data sample can be encoded as a vector, and thus a batch of data will be encoded as a rank-2 tensor, where the first axis is the samples axis, and the second axis is the features axis.

Let's take a look at two examples:

- An actuarial dataset of people, in which we consider each person's age, ZIP code, and income. Each person can be characterized as a vector of 3 values, and thus an entire dataset of 100,000 people can be stored in a 2D tensor with shape [100000, 3].
- A dataset of text documents, where we represent each document by the counts of how many times each word appears in it (for example, out of an English dictionary of the 20,000 most common words). Each document can be encoded as a vector of 20,000 values (one count per word in the dictionary), and thus a batch of 500 documents can be stored in a tensor of shape [500, 20000].

TIME-SERIES OR SEQUENCE DATA

Whenever time matters in your data (or the notion of sequence order), it makes sense to store it in a 3D tensor with an explicit time axis. Each sample is encoded as a sequence of vectors (a 2D tensor), and thus a batch of samples will be encoded as a 3D tensor (see figure B.3).

The time axis is almost always the second axis (axis of index 1) by convention, as in the following examples:

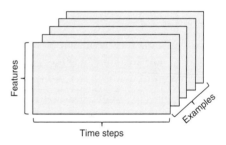

Figure B.3 A 3D time-series data tensor

- A dataset of stock prices. Every minute we store the current price of the stock, the highest price in the past minute, and the lowest price in the past minute. Thus, each minute is encoded as a vector of three values. Since there are 60 minutes in an hour, an hour of trading is encoded as a 2D tensor of shape [60, 3]. If we have a dataset of 250 independent hours of sequences, the shape of the dataset will be [250, 60, 3].
- A dataset of tweets in which we encode each tweet as a sequence of 280 characters out of an alphabet of 128 unique characters. In this setting, each character can be encoded as a binary vector of size 128 (all zeros except a 1 entry at the index corresponding to the character). Then each can be considered as a rank-2 tensor of shape [280, 128]. A dataset of 1 million tweets can be stored in a tensor of shape [1000000, 280, 128].

IMAGE DATA

The data of an image typically has three dimensions: height, width, and color depth. Although grayscale images have only a single color channel, by convention, image tensors are always rank 3, with a 1-dimensional color channel for grayscale images. A batch of 128 grayscale images of size 256×256 would thus be stored in a tensor of shape [128, 256, 256, 1], and a batch of 128 color images would be stored in a tensor of shape [128, 256, 256, 3] (see figure B.4). This is called the NHWC convention (see chapter 4 for more details).

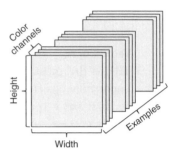

Figure B.4   A 4D image data tensor

Some frameworks put the channels dimension before the height and width, using the NCHW convention. We don't use this convention in this book, but don't be surprised to see an image tensor of a shape such as [128, 3, 256, 256] elsewhere.

VIDEO DATA

Raw video data is one of the few types of common real-world data for which you'll need rank-5 tensors. A video can be understood as a sequence of frames, each frame being a color image. Since each frame can be stored in a rank-3 tensor [height, width, colorChannel], a sequence of frames can be stored in a 4D tensor [frames, height, width, colorChannel], and thus a batch of different videos would be stored in a 5D tensor of shape [samples, frames, height, width, colorChannel].

For instance, a 60-second, 144×256 YouTube video clip sampled at 4 frames per second would have 240 frames. A batch of four such video clips would be stored in a tensor of shape [4, 240, 144, 256, 3]. That's a total of 106,168,320 values! If the dtype of the tensor were 'float32', then each value would be stored in 32 bits, so the tensor would represent 405 MB. This is a heavy amount of data! Videos you encounter in real life are much lighter because they aren't stored in float32, and they're typically compressed by a large factor (such as in the MPEG format).

B.1.7   *Creating tensors from tensor buffers*

We've shown how to create tensors from JavaScript arrays using functions such as tf.tensor2d() and tf.tensor(). To do so, you must have determined the values of all the elements and set them in the JavaScript arrays beforehand. In some cases, however, it is somewhat tedious to create such a JavaScript array from scratch. For instance, suppose you want to create a 5×5 matrix in which all the off-diagonal elements are zero, and the diagonal elements form an increasing series that equals the row or column index plus 1:

```
[[1, 0, 0, 0, 0],
 [0, 2, 0, 0, 0],
 [0, 0, 3, 0, 0],
 [0, 0, 0, 4, 0],
 [0, 0, 0, 0, 5]]
```

If you were to create a nested JavaScript array to meet this requirement, the code would look something like the following:

```
const n = 5;
const matrixArray = [];
for (let i = 0; i < 5; ++i) {
  const row = [];
  for (let j = 0; j < 5; ++j) {
    row.push(j === i ? i + 1 : 0);
  }
  matrixArray.push(row);
}
```

Finally, you can convert the nested JavaScript array `matrixArray` into a 2D tensor:

```
> const matrix = tf.tensor2d(matrixArray);
```

This code looks a little tedious. It involves two nested `for` loops. Is there a way to simplify it? The answer is yes: we can use the `tf.tensorBuffer()` method to create a `TensorBuffer`. A `TensorBuffer` object allows you to specify its elements by indices and change their values by using the `set()` method. This is different from a tensor object in TensorFlow.js, whose element values are *immutable*. When you have finished setting the values of all the elements of a `TensorBuffer` you wish to set, the `TensorBuffer` can be conveniently converted to an actual tensor object through its `toTensor()` method. Hence, if we use `tf.tensorBuffer()` to achieve the same tensor-creation task as the previous code, the new code will look like

```
const buffer = tf.tensorBuffer([5, 5]);     ◁─────   Specifies the tensor shape when
for (let i = 0; i < 5; ++i) {                        creating a TensorBuffer. A TensorBuffer
  buffer.set(i +  1, i, i);          ◁──────         has all-zero values after creation.
}
const matrix = buffer.toTensor();     ◁──────   The first arg is the desired values,
                                                while the remaining args are the
              Gets an actual tensor object      indices of the element to be set.
              from the TensorBuffer
```

Therefore, by using `tf.tensorBuffer()`, we reduced the lines of code from 10 to 5.

B.1.8 *Creating all-zero and all-one tensors*

It is often desirable to create a tensor of a given shape with all elements equal to zero. You can use the `tf.zeros()` function to achieve this. To call the function, provide the desired shape as the input argument; for example,

```
> const x = tf.zeros([2, 3, 3]);
> x.print();
Tensor
    [[[0, 0, 0],
      [0, 0, 0],
      [0, 0, 0]],
     [[0, 0, 0],
      [0, 0, 0],
      [0, 0, 0]]]
```

The tensor created has the default dtype (float32). To create all-zero tensors of other dtypes, specify the dtype as the second argument to `tf.zeros()`.

A related function is `tf.zerosLike()`, which lets you create an all-zero tensor of the same shape and dtype as an existing tensor. For example,

```
> const y = tf.zerosLike(x);
```

is equivalent to

```
> const y = tf.zeros(x.shape, x.dtype);
```

but is more succinct.

Analogous methods allow you to create tensors of which all elements are equal to one: `tf.ones()` and `tf.onesLike()`.

B.1.9 *Creating randomly valued tensors*

Creating randomly valued tensors is useful in many cases, such as the initialization of weights. The most frequently used functions for creating randomly valued tensors are `tf.randomNormal()` and `tf.randomUniform()`. The two functions have similar syntax but lead to different distributions in element values. As its name suggests, `tf.random-Normal()` returns tensors in which the element values follow a normal (Gaussian) distribution.[3] If you invoke the function with only a shape argument, you will get a tensor whose elements follow the *unit* normal distribution: a normal distribution with mean = 0 and standard deviation (SD) = 1. For example,

```
> const x = tf.randomNormal([2, 3]);
> x.print():
Tensor
    [[-0.2772508, 0.63506  , 0.3080665],
     [0.7655841 , 2.5264773, 1.142776 ]]
```

If you want the normal distribution to have a no-default mean or SD, you may provide them as the second and third input arguments, respectively. For instance, the following call creates a tensor in which the elements follow a normal distribution of mean = -20 and SD = 0.6:

```
> const x = tf.randomNormal([2, 3], -20, 0.6);
> x.print();
Tensor
    [[-19.0392246, -21.2259483, -21.2892818],
     [-20.6935596, -20.3722878, -20.1997948]]
```

`tf.randomUniform()` lets you create random tensors with uniformly distributed element values. By default, the uniform distribution is a unit one—that is, with lower bound 0 and upper bound 1:

```
> const x = tf.randomUniform([3, 3]);
> x.print();
Tensor
```

---

[3] For readers familiar with statistics, the element values are independent from each other.

```
    [[0.8303654, 0.3996494, 0.3808384],
     [0.0751046, 0.4425731, 0.2357403],
     [0.4682371, 0.0980235, 0.7004037]]
```

If you want to let the element value follow a non-unit uniform distribution, you can specify the lower and upper bounds as the second and third arguments to tf.random-Uniform(), respectively. For example,

```
> const x = tf.randomUniform([3, 3], -10, 10);
```

creates a tensor with values randomly distributed in the [-10, 10) interval:

```
> x.print();
Tensor
    [[-7.4774652, -4.3274679, 5.5345411 ],
     [-6.767087 , -3.8834026, -3.2619202],
     [-8.0232048, 7.0986223 , -1.3350322]]
```

tf.randomUniform() can be used to create randomly valued int32-type tensors. This is useful for cases in which you want to generate random labels. For example, the following code creates a length-10 vector in which the values are randomly drawn from the integers 0 through 100 (the interval [0, 100)):

```
> const x = tf.randomUniform([10], 0, 100, 'int32');
> x.print();
Tensor
    [92, 16, 65, 60, 62, 16, 77, 24, 2, 66]
```

Note that the 'int32' argument is the key in this example. Without it, the tensor you get will contain float32 values instead of int32 ones.

B.2   *Basic tensor operations*

Tensors wouldn't be of much use if we couldn't perform operations on them. Tensor-Flow.js supports a large number of tensor operations. You can see a list of them, along with their documentation, at https://js.tensorflow.org/api/latest. Describing every single one of them would be tedious and redundant. Therefore, we will highlight some of the most frequently used operations as examples. Frequently used operations can be categorized into two types: unary and binary. A *unary* operation takes one tensor as input and returns a new tensor, while a *binary* operation takes two tensors as its inputs and returns a new tensor.

B.2.1   *Unary operations*

Let's consider the operation of taking the negative of a tensor—that is, using the negative value of every element of the input tensor—and forming a new tensor of the same shape and dtype. This can be done with tf.neg():

```
> const x = tf.tensor1d([-1, 3, 7]);
> const y = tf.neg(x);
> y.print();
Tensor
    [1, -3, -7]
```

FUNCTIONAL API VS. CHAINING API

In the previous example, we invoked the function `tf.neg()` with the tensor x as the input argument. TensorFlow.js provides a more concise way to perform the mathematically equivalent operation: using the `neg()` method, which is a method of the tensor object itself, instead of a function under the `tf.*` namespace:

```
> const y = x.neg();
```

In this simple example, the amount of saved typing due to the new API may not seem that impressive. However, in cases where a number of operations need to be applied one after another, the second API will show considerable advantages over the first one. For instance, consider a hypothetical algorithm in which you want to take the negative of x, calculate the reciprocal (1 divided by every element), and apply the relu activation function on it. This is the code it takes to implement the algorithm in the first API:

```
> const y = tf.relu(tf.reciprocal(tf.neg(x)));
```

By contrast, in the second API, the implementing code looks like

```
> const y = x.neg().reciprocal().relu();
```

The second implementation outshines the first one in these aspects:

- There are fewer characters, less typing, and hence a smaller chance of making mistakes.
- There is no need to balance the nested pairs of opening and closing parentheses (although most modern code editors will help you do this).
- More importantly, the order in which the methods appear in the code matches the order in which the underlying mathematical operations happen. (Notice that in the first implementation, the order is reversed.) This leads to better code readability in the second implementation.

We will refer to the first API as the *functional* API because it is based on calling functions under the `tf.*` namespace. The second API will be referred to as the *chaining* API, owing to the fact that operations appear in a sequence like a chain (as you can see in the previous example). Most operations in TensorFlow.js are accessible as both the functional version under the `tf.*` namespace and the chaining version as a method of tensor objects. You can choose between the two APIs based on your needs. Throughout this book, we use both APIs in different places, with a preference for the chaining API for cases that involve serial operations.

ELEMENT-WISE VS. REDUCTION OPERATIONS

The examples of unary operations we mentioned (`tf.neg()`, `tf.reciprocal()`, and `tf.relu()`) have the common property that the operation happens on individual elements of the input tensor independently. As a result, the returned tensor of such an operation preserves the shape of the input tensor. However, other unary operations in TensorFlow.js lead to a tensor shape smaller than the original one. What does "smaller" mean in the context of tensor shape? In some cases, it means a lower rank. For example, a unary operation may return a scalar (rank-0) tensor given a 3D (rank-3) tensor. In other cases, it means the size of a certain dimension is smaller than the original one. For instance, a unary operation may return a tensor of shape [3, 1] given an input of shape [3, 20]. Regardless of how the shape shrinks, these operations are referred to as *reduction operations.*

tf.mean() is one of the most frequently used reduction operations. It appears as the mean() method of the Tensor class in the chaining API. When invoked without any additional arguments, it computes the arithmetic mean of all elements of the input tensor, regardless of its shape, and returns a scalar. Its usage in the chaining API looks like

```
> const x = tf.tensor2d([[0, 10], [20, 30]]);
> x.mean().print();
Tensor
    15
```

Sometimes, we require the mean to be calculated separately over the rows of the 2D tensor (matrix) instead of over the whole tensor. This can be achieved by providing an additional argument to the mean() method:

```
> x.mean(-1).print();
Tensor
    [5, 25]
```

The argument -1 indicates that the mean() method should calculate the arithmetic means along the last dimension of the tensor.[4] This dimension is referred to as the *reduction dimension,* as it will be "reduced away" in the output tensor, which becomes a rank-1 tensor. An alternative way to specify the reduction dimension is to use the actual index of the dimension:

```
> x.mean(1).print();
```

Note that mean() also supports multiple reduction dimensions. For example, if you have a 3D tensor of shape [10, 6, 3], and you want the arithmetic mean to be calculated over the last two dimensions, yielding a 1D tensor of shape [10], you can call mean() as x.mean([-2, -1]) or x.mean([1, 2]). We leave this as an exercise at the end of this appendix.

Other frequently used reduction unary operations include

- tf.sum(), which is almost identical to tf.mean(), but it computes the sum, instead of the arithmetic mean, over elements.
- tf.norm(), which computes the norm over elements. There are different kinds of norms. For example, a 1-norm is a sum of the absolute values of elements. A 2-norm is calculated by taking the square root of the sum over the squared elements. In other words, it is the length of a vector in a Euclidean space.

---

[4] This follows the indexing convention of Python.

tf.norm() can be used to calculate the variance or the standard deviation of a list of numbers.

- tf.min() and tf.max(), which calculate the minimum and maximum value over elements, respectively.
- tf.argMax(), which returns the index of the maximum element over a reduction axis. This operation is frequently used to convert the probability output of a classification mode into the winning class's index (for example, see the iris-flower classification problem in section 3.3.2). tf.argMin() provides similar functionality for finding the minimum value.

We mentioned that element-wise operations preserve the shape of the input tensor. But the converse is not true. Some shape-preserving operations are not element-wise. For instance, the tf.transpose() operation can perform matrix transpose, in which the element at indices [i, j] in the input 2D tensor is mapped onto the indices [j, i] in the output 2D tensor. The input and output shapes of tf.transpose() will be identical if the input is a square matrix, but this is not an element-wise operation, as the value at [i, j] of the output tensor does not depend only on the value at [i, j] in the input tensor, but instead depends on values at other indices.

B.2.2   *Binary operations*

Unlike unary operations, a binary operation requires two input arguments. tf.add() is perhaps the most frequently used binary operation. It is perhaps also the simplest, as it simply adds two tensors together. For example,

```
> const x = tf.tensor2d([[0, 2], [4, 6]]);
> const y = tf.tensor2d([[10, 20], [30, 46]]);
> tf.add(x, y).print();
Tensor
    [[10, 22],
     [34, 52]]
```

Similar binary operations include

- tf.sub() for subtracting two tensors
- tf.mul() for multiplying two tensors
- tf.matMul() for computing the matrix product between two tensors
- tf.logicalAnd(), tf.logicalOr(), and tf.logicaXor() for performing AND, OR, and XOR operations on bool-type tensors, respectively.

Some binary operations support *broadcasting*, or operating on two input tensors of different shapes and applying an element in the input of a smaller shape over multiple elements in the other input according to a certain rule. See info box 2.4 in chapter 2 for a detailed discussion.

B.2.3 *Concatenation and slicing of tensors*

Unary and binary operations are tensor-in-tensor-out (TITO), in the sense that they take one or more tensors as the input and return a tensor as the output. Some frequently used operations in TensorFlow.js are not TITO because they take a tensor, along with another nontensor argument, as their inputs. tf.concat() is perhaps the most frequently used function in this category. It allows you to concatenate multiple tensors of compatible shape into a single tensor. Concatenation is possible only if the shape of the tensors satisfies certain constraints. For example, it is possible to combine a [5, 3] tensor and a [4, 3] tensor along the first axis to get a [9, 3] tensor, but it isn't possible to combine the tensors if their shapes are [5, 3] and [4, 2]! Given shape compatibility, you can use the tf.concat() function to concatenate tensors. For example, the following code concatenates an all-zero [2, 2] tensor with an all-one [2, 2] tensor along the first axis, which gives a [4, 2] tensor in which the "top" half is all-zero and the "bottom" half is all-one:

```
> const x = tf.zeros([2, 2]);
> const y = tf.ones([2, 2]);
> tf.concat([x, y]).print();
Tensor
    [[0, 0],
     [0, 0],
     [1, 1],
     [1, 1]]
```

Because the shapes of the two input tensors are identical, it is possible to concatenate them differently: that is, along the second axis. The axis can be specified as the second input argument to tf.concat(). This will give us a [2, 4] tensor in which the left half is all-zero and the right half is all-one:

```
> tf.concat([x, y], 1).print();
Tensor
    [[0, 0, 1, 1],
     [0, 0, 1, 1]]
```

Apart from concatenating multiple tensors into one, sometimes we want to perform the "reverse" operation, retrieving a part of a tensor. For example, suppose you have created a 2D tensor (matrix) of shape [3, 2],

```
> const x = tf.randomNormal([3, 2]);
> x.print();
Tensor
    [[1.2366893 , 0.6011682 ],
     [-1.0172369, -0.5025602],
     [-0.6265425, -0.0009868]]
```

and you would like to get the second row of the matrix. For that, you can use the chaining version of tf.slice():

```
> x.slice([1, 0], [1, 2]).print();
Tensor
    [[-1.0172369, -0.5025602],]
```

The first argument to slice() indicates that the part of the input tensor we want starts at index 1 along the first dimension and index 0 of the second dimension. In other words, it should start from the second row and the first column, since the 2D tensor we are dealing with here is a matrix. The second argument specifies the shape of the desired output: [1, 2] or, in matrix language, 1 row and 2 columns.

As you can verify by looking at the printed values, we have successfully retrieved the second row of the 3 × 2 matrix. The shape of the output has the same rank as the input (2), but the size of the first dimension is 1. In this case, we are retrieving the entirety of the second dimension (all columns) and a subset of the first dimension (a subset of the rows). This is a special case that allows us to achieve the same effect with a simpler syntax:

```
> x.slice(1, 1).print();
Tensor
    [[-1.0172369, -0.5025602],]
```

In this simpler syntax, we just need to specify the starting index and the size of the requested chunk along the first dimension. If 2 is passed instead of 1 as the second input argument, the output will contain the second and third rows of the matrix:

```
> x.slice(1, 2).print();
Tensor
    [[-1.0172369, -0.5025602],
     [-0.6265425, -0.0009868]]
```

As you may have guessed, this simpler syntax is related to the batching convention. It makes it easier to get the data for individual examples out of a batched tensor.

But what if we want to access *columns* of the matrix instead of rows? In this case, we would have to use the more complex syntax. For example, suppose we want the second column of the matrix. It can be achieved by

```
> x.slice([0, 1], [-1, 1]).print();
Tensor
    [[0.6011682 ],
     [-0.5025602],
     [-0.0009868]]
```

Here, the first argument ([0, 1]) is an array representing the beginning indices of the slice we want. It is the first index along the first dimension and the second index along the second dimension. Put more simply, we want our slice to begin at the first row and the second column. The second argument ([-1, 1]) specifies the size of the slice we want. The first number (–1) indicates that we want all indices along the first dimension (we want all rows starting), while the second number (1) means we want only one index along the second dimension (we want only one column). The result is the second column of the matrix.

Looking at the syntax of slice(), you may have realized that slice() is not limited to retrieving just rows or columns. In fact, it is flexible enough to let you retrieve any "submatrix" of the input 2D tensor (any consecutive rectangular area within the matrix), if the beginning indices and size array are specified properly. More generally, for tensors of any rank greater than 0, `slice()` allows you to retrieve any consecutive subtensor of the same rank inside the input tensor. We leave this as an exercise for you at the end of this appendix.

Apart from `tf.slice()` and `tf.concat()`, two other frequently used operations that split a tensor into parts or combine multiple tensors into one are `tf.unstack()` and `tf.stack()`. `tf.unstack()` splits a tensor into multiple "pieces" along the first dimension. Each of those pieces has a size of 1 along the first dimension. For example, we can use the chaining API of `tf.unstack()`:

```
> const x = tf.tensor2d([[1, 2], [3, 4], [5, 6]]);
> x.print();
Tensor
    [[1, 2],
     [3, 4],
     [5, 6]]
> const pieces = x.unstack();
> console.log(pieces.length);
  3
> pieces[0].print();
Tensor
    [1, 2]
> pieces[1].print();
Tensor
    [3, 4]
> pieces[2].print();
Tensor
    [5, 6]
```

As you can notice, the "pieces" returned by `unstack()` have a rank one less than that of the input tensor.

`tf.stack()` is the reverse of `tf.unstack()`. As its name suggests, it "stacks" a number of tensors with identical shapes into a new tensor. Following the prior example code snippet, we stack the pieces back together:

```
> tf.stack(pieces).print();
Tensor
    [[1, 2],
     [3, 4],
     [5, 6]]
```

`tf.unstack()` is useful for getting the data corresponding to individual examples from a batched tensor; `tf.stack()` is useful for combining the data for individual examples into a batched tensor.

B.3   Memory management in TensorFlow.js: tf.dispose() and tf.tidy()

In TensorFlow.js, if you deal directly with tensor objects, you need to perform memory management on them. In particular, a tensor needs to be disposed after creation and use, or it will continue to occupy the memory allocated for it. If undisposed tensors become too many in number or too large in their total size, they will eventually cause the browser tab to run out of WebGL memory or cause the Node.js process to run out of system or GPU memory (depending on whether the CPU or GPU version of tfjs-node is being used). TensorFlow.js does not perform automatic garbage collection of user-created tensors.[5] This is because JavaScript does not support object finalization. TensorFlow.js provides two functions for memory management: `tf.dispose()` and `tf.tidy()`.

For example, consider an example in which you perform repeated inference on a TensorFlow.js model using a `for` loop:

```
const model = await tf.loadLayersModel(
    'https://storage.googleapis.com/tfjs-models/tfjs/iris_v1/model.json');
const x = tf.randomUniform([1, 4]);
for (let i = 0; i < 3; ++i) {
  const y = model.predict(x);
  y.print();
  console.log(`# of tensors: ${tf.memory().numTensors}` );
}
```

Creates a dummy input tensor

Loads a pretrained model from the web

Checks the number of currently allocated tensors

The output will look like

```
Tensor
     [[0.4286409, 0.4692867, 0.1020722],]
# of tensors: 14
Tensor
     [[0.4286409, 0.4692867, 0.1020722],]
# of tensors: 15
Tensor
     [[0.4286409, 0.4692867, 0.1020722],]
# of tensors: 16
```

As you can see in the console log, every time `model.predict()` is called, it generates an additional tensor, which doesn't get disposed after the iteration ends. If the `for` loop is allowed to run for enough iterations, it will eventually cause an out-of-memory error. This is because the output tensor `y` is not disposed properly, leading to a tensor memory leak. There are two ways to fix this memory leak.

In the first approach, you can call `tf.dispose()` on the output tensor when it is no longer needed:

```
for (let i = 0; i < 3; ++i) {
  const y = model.predict(x);
  y.print();
  tf.dispose(y);
  console.log(`# of tensors: ${tf.memory().numTensors}` );
}
```

Disposes the output tensor after its use

In the second approach, you can wrap the body of the `for` loop with `tf.tidy()`:

---

[5] However, the tensors created inside TensorFlow.js functions and object methods are managed by the library itself, so you don't need to worry about wrapping calls to such functions or methods in `tf.tidy()`. Examples of such functions include `tf.confusionMatrix()`, `tf.Model.predict()`, and `tf.Model.fit()`.

```
for (let i = 0; i < 3; ++i) {
  tf.tidy(() => {          ←─────────────
    const y = model.predict(x);
    y.print();
    console.log(`# of tensors: ${tf.memory().numTensors}` );
  });
}
```

> **tf.tidy() automatically disposes all tensors created within the function passed to it except the tensors that are returned by the function.**

With either approach, you should see the number of allocated tensors become constant over the iterations, indicating that there is no tensor memory leak anymore. Which approach should you prefer? In general, you should use `tf.tidy()` (the second approach), because it gets rid of the need to keep track of what tensors to dispose. `tf.tidy()` is a smart function that disposes all tensors created within the anonymous function passed to it as the argument (except those that are returned by the function—more on that later), even for the tensors not bound to any JavaScript objects. For example, suppose we modify the previous inference code slightly in order to obtain the index of the winning class using `argMax()`:

```
const model = await tf.loadLayersModel(
    'https://storage.googleapis.com/tfjs-models/tfjs/iris_v1/model.json');
const x = tf.randomUniform([1, 4]);
for (let i = 0; i < 3; ++i) {
  const winningIndex =
        model.predict(x).argMax().dataSync()[0];
  console.log(`winning index: ${winningIndex}`);
  console.log(`# of tensors: ${tf.memory().numTensors}` );
}
```

When this code runs, you will see that instead of leaking one tensor per iteration, it leaks two:

```
winning index: 0
# of tensors: 15
winning index: 0
# of tensors: 17
winning index: 0
# of tensors: 19
```

Why are two tensors leaked per iteration? Well, the line

```
    const winningIndex =
        model.predict(x).argMax().dataSync()[0];
```

generates two new tensors. The first is the output of `model.predict()`, and the second is the return value of `argMax()`. Neither of the tensors is bound to any JavaScript object. They are used immediately after creation. The two tensors are "lost" in the sense that there are no JavaScript objects you can use to refer to them. Hence, `tf.dispose()` cannot be used to clean up the two tensors. However, `tf.tidy()` can still be used to fix the memory leak, as it performs bookkeeping on new tensors regardless of whether they are bound to JavaScript objects:

```
const model = await tf.loadLayersModel(
    'https://storage.googleapis.com/tfjs-models/tfjs/iris_v1/model.json');
```

```
const x = tf.randomUniform([1, 4]);
for (let i = 0; i < 3; ++i) {
  tf.tidy(() => {
    const winningIndex = model.predict(x).argMax().dataSync()[0];
    console.log(`winning index: ${winningIndex}`);
    console.log(`# of tensors: ${tf.memory().numTensors}` );
  });
}
```

**tf.tidy() automatically disposes tensors created in the body
of an anonymous function passed to it as the argument, even
when those tensors are not bound to JavaScript objects.**

The example usages of tf.tidy() operate on functions that do not return any tensors. If the function returns tensors, you do not want them to be disposed because they need to be used afterward. This situation is encountered frequently when you write custom tensor operations by using the basic tensor operations provided by TensorFlow.js. For example, suppose we want to write a function that calculates the normalized value of the input tensor—that is, a tensor with the mean subtracted and the standard deviation scaled to 1:

```
function normalize(x) {
  const mean = x.mean();
  const sd = x.norm(2);
  return x.sub(mean).div(sd);
}
```

What is the problem with this implementation?[6] In terms of memory management, it leaks a total of three tensors: 1) the mean, 2) the SD, and 3) a more subtle one: the return value of the sub() call. To fix the memory leak, we wrap the body of the function with tf.tidy():

```
function normalize(x) {
  return tf.tidy(() => {
    const mean = x.mean();
    const sd = x.norm(2);
    return x.sub(mean).div(sd);
      });
}
```

Here, tf.tidy() does three things for us:

- It automatically disposes the tensors that are created in the anonymous function but not returned by it, including all three leaks mentioned. We have seen this in the previous examples.
- It detects that the output of the div() call is returned by the anonymous function and hence will forward it to its own return value.
- In the meantime, it will avoid disposing that particular tensor, so it can be used outside the tf.tidy() call.

---

[6] There are other problems with this implementation. For instance, it doesn't perform sanity checks on the input tensor to make sure it has at least two elements so SD won't be zero, which would lead to division by zero and infinite results. But those problems are not directly related to the discussion here.

As we can see, `tf.tidy()` is a smart and powerful function for memory management. It is used extensively in the TensorFlow.js code base itself. You will also see it many times throughout the examples in this book. However, it has the following important limitation: the anonymous function passed to `tf.tidy()` as the argument must *not* be async. If you have some async code that requires memory management, you should use `tf.dispose()` and keep track of the to-be-disposed tensors manually instead. In such cases, you can use `tf.memory().numTensor` to check the number of leaked tensors. A good practice is to write unit tests that assert on the absence of memory leaks.

B.4   *Calculating gradients*

This section is for readers who are interested in performing derivative and gradient calculation in TensorFlow.js. For most deep-learning models in this book, the calculation of derivatives and gradients is taken care of under the hood by `model.fit()` and `model.fitDataset()`. However, for certain problem types, such as finding maximally activating images for convolution filters in chapter 7 and RL in chapter 11, it is necessary to calculate derivatives and gradients explicitly. TensorFlow.js provides APIs to support such use cases. Let's start from the simplest scenario—namely, a function that takes a single input tensor and returns a single output tensor:

```
const f = x => tf.atan(x);
```

In order to calculate the derivative of the function (`f`) with respect to the input (`x`), we use the `tf.grad()` function:

```
const df = tf.grad(f);
```

Note that `tf.grad()` doesn't give you the derivative's value right away. Instead, it gives you a *function* that is the derivative of the original function (`f`). You can invoke that function (`df`) with a concrete value of x, and that's when you get the value of `df`/dx. For example,

```
const x = tf.tensor([-4, -2, 0, 2, 4]);
df(x).print();
```

which gives you an output that correctly reflects the derivative of the `atan()` function at x-values of –4, –2, 0, 2, and 4 (see figure B.5):

```
Tensor
    [0.0588235, 0.2, 1, 0.2, 0.0588235]
```

`tf.grad()` is limited to a function with only one input tensor. What if you have a function with multiple inputs? Let's consider an example of `h(x, y)`, which is simply the product of two tensors:

```
const h = (x, y) => x.mul(y);
```

`tf.grads()` (with the "s" in the name) generates a function that returns the partial derivative of the input function with respect to all the arguments:

```
const dh = tf.grads(h);
const dhValues = dh([tf.tensor1d([1, 2]), tf.tensor1d([-1, -2])]);
dhValues[0].print();
dhValues[1].print();
```

which gives the results

```
Tensor
    [-1, -2]
Tensor
    [1, 2]
```

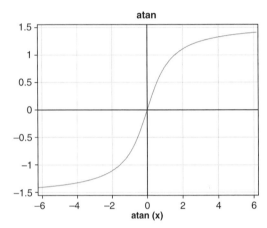

Figure B.5   A plot of the function atan(x)

These results are correct because the partial derivative of $x * y$ with respect to x is y and that with respect to y is x.

The functions generated by tf.grad() and tf.grads() give you only the derivatives, not the return value of the original function. In the example of $h(x, y)$, what if we want to get not only the derivatives but also the value of h? For that, you can use the tf.valueAndGrads() function:

```
const vdh = tf.valueAndGrads(h);
const out = vdh([tf.tensor1d([1, 2]), tf.tensor1d([-1, -2])]);
```

The output (out) is an object with two fields: value, which is the value of h given the input values, and grads, which has the same format as the return value of the function generated by tf.grads()—namely, an array of partial-derivative tensors:

```
out.value.print();
out.grads[0].print();
out.grads[1].print();
```

```
Tensor
    [-1, -4]
Tensor
    [-1, -2]
Tensor
    [1, 2]
```

The APIs discussed are all about calculating the derivatives of functions with respect to their explicit arguments. However, a common scenario in deep learning involves functions that use weights in their calculation. Those weights are represented as `tf.Variable` objects and are *not* explicitly passed to the functions as arguments. For such functions, we often need to calculate their derivatives with respect to the weights during training. This workflow is served by the `tf.variableGrads()` function, which keeps track of what trainable variables are accessed by the function being differentiated and automatically calculates the derivatives with respect to them. Consider the following example:

```
const trainable = true;
const a = tf.variable(tf.tensor1d([3, 4]), trainable, 'a');
const b = tf.variable(tf.tensor1d([5, 6]), trainable, 'b');
const x = tf.tensor1d([1, 2]);

const f = () => a.mul(x.square()).add(b.mul(x)).sum();
const {value, grads} = tf.variableGrads(f);
```

$f(a, b) = a * x \char`\^ 2 + b * x.$ The sum() method is called because tf.variableGrads() requires the function being differentiated to return a scalar.

The `value` field of `tf.variableGrads()`'s output is the return value of f given the current values of a, b, and x. The `grads` field is a JavaScript object that carries the derivatives with respect to the two variables (a and b) under the corresponding key names. For example, the derivative of `f(a, b)` with respect to a is $x \char`\^ 2$, and the derivative of `f(a, b)` with respect to b is x,

```
grads.a.print();
grads.b.print();
```

which correctly gives

```
Tensor
    [1, 4]
Tensor
    [1, 2]
```

Exercises

1 Use `tf.tensorBuffer()` to create an "identity 4D tensor" satisfying the following properties. Its shape should be `[5, 5, 5, 5]`. It should have 0 values everywhere, except for the elements whose indices are four identical numbers (for example, `[2, 2, 2, 2]`), which should have the value 1.

2 Create a 3D tensor of shape `[2, 4, 5]` using `tf.randomUniform()` and the default `[0, 1)` interval. Using `tf.sum()`, write a line of code to perform a reduce-sum over the second and third dimensions. Examine the output. It should have a shape of `[2]`. What do you expect the values of the elements to be, approximately? Does the output match your expectations?

(Hint: what is the expected value of a number distributed randomly in the `[0, 1)` interval? What is the expected value of the sum of two such values, given statistical independence?)

3   Use `tf.randomUniform()` to create a 4 × 4 matrix (a 2D tensor of shape `[4, 4]`). Get the 2 × 2 submatrix located at the center using `tf.slice()`.

4   Use `tf.ones()`, `tf.mul()`, and `tf.concat()` to create such a 3D tensor: its shape should be `[5, 4, 3]`. The first slice along the first axis (the tensor of shape `[1, 4, 3]`) should have element values that are all 1; the second slice along the first axis should have element values that are all 2; and so forth.

   a   Extra points: The tensor has many elements, so it is hard to test its correctness just by looking at the text output of `print()`. How can you write a unit test to check its correctness? (Hint: use `data()`, `dataSync()`, or `arraySync()`).

5   Write a JavaScript function that performs the following operations on two input 2D tensors (matrices) of identical shapes. First, sum the two matrices. Second, the resultant matrix is divided by 2, element by element. Third, the matrix is transposed. The result of the transpose operation is returned by the function.

   a   What TensorFlow.js functions do you use to write this function?

   b   Can you implement the function twice, once using the functional API and once using the chaining API? Which implementation looks cleaner and more readable?

   c   Which steps involve broadcasting?

   d   How do you ensure that this function doesn't leak memory?

   e   Can you write a unit test (using the Jasmine library at https://jasmine.github.io/) to assert on the absence of memory leak?

glossary

Activation function   The function at the last stage of a neural network layer. For example, a rectified linear unit (relu) function may be applied on the result of the matrix multiplication to generate the final output of a dense layer. An activation function can be linear or nonlinear. Nonlinear activation functions can be used to increase the representational power (or capacity) of a neural network. Examples of nonlinear activations include sigmoid, hyperbolic tangent (tanh), and the aforementioned relu.

Area under the curve (AUC)   A single number used to quantify the shape of an ROC curve. It is defined as the definite integral under the ROC curve, from false positive rate 0 to 1. See *ROC curve*.

Axis   In the context of TensorFlow.js, when we talk about a *tensor*, an axis (plural *axes*) is one of the independent keys indexing into the tensor. For example, a rank-3 tensor has three axes; an element of a rank-3 tensor is identified by three integers that correspond to the three axes. Also known as a *dimension*.

Backpropagation   The algorithm that traces back from the loss value of a differentiable machine-learning model to the gradients on the weight parameters. It is based on the chain rule of differentiation and forms the basis of training for most neural networks in this book.

Backpropagation through time (BPTT)   A special form of backpropagation in which the steps are not over the operations for the successive layers of a model, but instead over the operations for the successive time steps. It underlies the training of recurrent neural networks (RNNs).

Balance (dataset)   A quality of a dataset with categorical labels. The more equal the numbers of examples from different categories are, the more balanced a dataset is.

Batch   During the training of neural networks, multiple input examples are often aggregated to form a single tensor, which is used to calculate the gradients and updates to the network's weights. Such an aggregation is called a *batch*. The number of examples in the batch is called the *batch size*.

Bellman equation   In reinforcement learning, a recursive equation that quantifies the value of a state-action pair as a sum of two terms: 1) the reward the agent is expected to get immediately after the action and 2) the best expected reward the agent can get in the next state, discounted by a factor. The second term assumes optimal selection of action in the next state. It forms the basis of reinforcement-learning algorithms such as deep Q-learning.

Binary classification   A classification task in which the target is the answer to a yes/no question, such as whether a certain X-ray image indicates pneumonia or whether a credit card transaction is legitimate or fraudulent.

Broadcasting   TensorFlow allows for pairwise operations between tensors with different but compatible shapes. For instance, it is possible to add a tensor of shape [5] to a tensor of shape [13, 5]. In effect, the smaller tensor will be repeated 13 times to compute the output. The details for the rules of when broadcasting is allowed are in info box 2.4 in chapter 2.

Capacity   The range of input-output relations that a machine-learning model is capable of learning. For example, a neural network with a hidden layer with a nonlinear activation function has a greater capacity than a linear-regression model.

Class activation map   An algorithm that can visualize the relative importance of different parts of an input image for the classification output of a convolutional neural network. It is based on computing the gradient of the final probability score of the winning class with respect to the output of the last internal convolutional layer of the network. It is discussed in detail in section 7.2.3.

Computer vision   The study of how computers can understand images and videos. It is an important part of machine learning. In the context of machine learning, common computer-vision tasks include image recognition, segmentation, captioning, and object detection.

Confusion matrix   A square matrix (a 2D tensor) of the shape [numClasses, numClasses]. In multiclass classification, a confusion matrix is used to quantify how many times examples of a given truth class are classified as each of the possible classes. The element at indices [i, j] is the number of times examples from the true class i are classified as class j. The elements on the diagonal line correspond to correct classification results.

Constant folding   A type of computation-graph optimization in which a subgraph that contains only predetermined constant nodes and deterministic operations among them is reduced to a single constant node. The GraphModel conversion technique in TensorFlow.js leverages constant folding.

Convolutional kernel   In convolution operations, a tensor that operates on the input tensor to generate the output tensor. Take image tensors, for example: the kernel is usually smaller in its height and width dimensions compared to the input image. It is "slid" over the height and width dimensions of the input image and undergoes a dot product (multiply and add) at every sliding position. For a convolutional layer of TensorFlow.js (such as conv2d), the kernel is its key weight.

Data augmentation   The process of generating more training data from existing training samples (x, y) by creating mutations of the training samples via a family of programmatic transformations that yield valid inputs x' without changing the target. This helps expose the model to more aspects of the data and thus generalize better without the engineer having to manually build invariance to these types of transformations into the model.

Deep learning   The study and application of deep neural networks (that is, using a large number of successive representational transformations to solve machine-learning problems).

Deep neural network   A neural network with a large number (anywhere between two and thousands) of layers.

Dimension   In the context of a tensor, synonymous with *axis*. See *axis*.

Dot product   See *inner product*.

Embedding   In deep learning, a representation of a certain piece of data in an *n*-dimensional vector space (*n* being a positive integer). In other words, it is a representation of a piece of data as an ordered, length-*n* array of floating-point numbers. Embedding representations can be created for many types of data: images, sounds, words, and items from a closed set. An embedding is usually from an intermediate layer of a trained neural network.

Ensemble learning   The practice of training a number of individual machine-learning models and using them together for inference on the same problem. Even though each individual model may not be very accurate, the ensemble model can have a much higher accuracy. Ensemble models are often used by the winning entries of data science competitions, such as Kaggle competitions.

Epoch   When training a model, one complete pass through the training data.

Epsilon-greedy policy   In reinforcement learning, an action-selection method that parametrizes the balance between random exploratory behavior and optimal behavior on the part of the agent. The value of epsilon is constrained between 0 and 1. The higher it is, the more likely the agent is to select random actions.

Example   In the context of machine learning, an individual instance of input data (for example, an image of the appropriate size for a computer-vision model), for which a machine-learning model will generate an output prediction (such as a label for the image).

Feature   One aspect of the input data for a machine-learning model. A feature can be in any of the following forms:

- A number (for example, the monetary amount of a credit card transaction)
- A string from an open set (name of transaction)
- A piece of categorical information (such as the brand name of the credit card)
- A one- or multidimensional array of numbers (for instance, a grayscale image of the credit card customer's signature represented as a 2D array)
- Other types of information (for example, date-time)

An input example can consist of one or multiple features.

Feature engineering   The process of transforming the original features in input data into a representation more amenable to solving the machine-learning problem. Before deep learning, feature engineering was performed by engineers with domain-specific knowledge through trial and error. It was often a labor-intensive and brittle process, without any guarantee of finding the optimal solution. Deep learning has largely automated feature engineering.

Fine-tuning   In transfer learning, a phase of model training during which the weights in some layers of the base model are allowed to be updated. It usually follows an initial phase of model training during which all weights in the base model are frozen to prevent large initial gradients from perturbing the pretrained weights too much. When used properly, fine-tuning can boost the capacity of the transfer-learning model, thereby achieving superior accuracy while consuming significantly less computation resources than training an entire model from scratch.

Generative adversarial network (GAN)   A type of generative machine-learning model that involves two parts called the *discriminator* and the *generator*. The discriminator is trained to distinguish real examples from a training set from fake ones, while the generator is trained to output examples that cause the discriminator to output high realness scores (that is, to "fool" the discriminator into "thinking" that the fake examples are real). After proper training, the generator is capable of outputting highly realistic fake examples.

Golden value   In the context of testing a machine-learning system, the correct output a model should generate for a given input. An example is the "classical" label for a neural network that classifies audio recordings into genres of music when given a recording of Beethoven's Fifth Symphony.

Gradient descent   The process of minimizing the numerical output value of a system by iteratively changing the parameters of the system along the direction of the gradients (that is, derivatives of the parameters with respect to the output value). It is the primary way in which neural networks are trained. In the context of neural network training, the system is formed by the neural network and a loss function selected by the engineer. The parameters of the system are the weights of the neural network's layers. The iteration process happens batch-by-batch over the training data.

Graphics processing unit (GPU)   Parallel-computing chips equipped with a much larger number (hundreds or thousands) of cores than typical CPUs. GPUs were originally designed to accelerate the computation and rendering of 2D and 3D graphics. But they turned out to be useful for the kind of parallel computing involved in running deep neural networks as well. GPUs are an important contributing factor to the deep-learning revolution and continue to play critical roles in the research and applications of deep learning today. TensorFlow.js harnesses the parallel-computing power of GPUs through two conduits: 1) the WebGL API of the web browser and 2) binding to the TensorFlow CUDA kernels in Node.js.

GraphModel   In TensorFlow.js, a model converted from TensorFlow (Python) and loaded into JavaScript. `GraphModel` has the potential to undergo TensorFlow-internal performance optimizations such as Grappler's arithmetic optimization and op fusion (see section 12.2.2 for details).

Hidden layer   A neural network that consists of a layer whose output is not exposed as an output of the network but is instead consumed only by other layers of the network. For example, in a neural network defined as a TensorFlow.js sequential model, all layers except the last one are hidden layers.

Hyperparameter optimization   Sometimes also called *hyperparameter tuning*; the process of searching for the set of hyperparameters that gives the lowest validation loss on a given machine-learning task.

Hyperparameters   Tunable parameters of the model and optimizer that are not tunable with backpropagation. Typically, the learning rate and model structure are common example hyperparameters. Hyperparameters may be tuned by grid search or more sophisticated hyperparameter-tuning algorithms.

Hypothesis space   In the context of machine learning, the set of possible solutions to a machine-learning problem. The training process involves searching for a good solution in such a space. The hypothesis space is determined by the type and the architecture of the machine-learning model chosen to solve the problem.

ImageNet   A large-scale public dataset of labeled colored images. It is an important training set and benchmark for computer-vision-oriented deep neural networks. ImageNet was instrumental in ushering in the beginning of the deep-learning revolution.

Imputation   A technique for filling in missing values from a dataset. For instance, if we had a dataset of cars, and some cars were missing their "weight" feature, we might simply guess the average weight for those features. More sophisticated imputation techniques are also possible.

Inception   A type of deep convolutional neural network featuring a large number of layers and a complex network structure.

Independent and identically distributed (IID)   A statistical property of data samples. If we assume that data is sampled from an underlying distribution, then the samples are identically distributed if each sample comes from the same distribution. Samples are independent if knowing the value of one sample gives you no additional information about the next sample.

   A sample of dice rolls is an example of an IID collection of samples. If the dice rolls are sorted, the samples are identically distributed but not independent. Training data should be IID, or there is likely to be convergence or other issues during training.

Inference   Using a machine-learning model on input data to generate an output. It is the ultimate purpose of training the model.

Inner product   Also known as *dot product*; a mathematical operation on two vectors of equivalent shape, yielding a single scalar value. To calculate the inner product between vectors a and b, sum up all a[i] * b[i] for all valid values of i. In geometric terms, the inner product of two vectors is equal to the product of their magnitudes and the cosine of the angle between them.

Keras   A popular library for deep learning. Today, it is the most frequently used deep-learning library in Kaggle competitions. François Chollet, currently a software engineer at Google, is its original author. Keras is a Python library. The high-level API of TensorFlow.js, which is a main focus of this book, is modeled after and compatible with Keras.

Label   The desired answer for an input example given the task at hand. A label can be a Boolean (yes/no) answer, a number, a text string, a category among a number of possible categories, a sequence of numbers, or more complex data types. In supervised machine learning, a model aims at generating outputs that closely match the labels.

Layer   In the context of neural networks, a transformation of the data representation. It behaves like a mathematical function: given an input, it emits an output. A layer can have state captured by its weights. The weights can be altered during the training of the neural network.

LayersModel   A model built using the Keras-like high-level API of TensorFlow.js. It can also be loaded from a converted Keras (Python) model. A LayersModel supports inference (with its predict() method) and training (with its fit() and fitDataset() methods).

Learning rate   During gradient descent, model weights are modified to reduce loss. The exact change in the weights is a function not only of the gradient of the loss but also of a parameter. In the standard gradient-descent algorithm, the weight update is calculated by multiplying the gradient by the learning rate, which is typically a small positive constant. The default learning rate for the 'sgd' optimizer in tensorflow.js is 0.01.

Local minimum   When optimizing the parameters of a model, a setting of the parameters for which any sufficiently small change in the parameters always increases the loss. Similar to a marble at the bottom of a bowl, there is no small movement that is even lower. A local minimum is distinguished from a *global minimum* in that a local minimum is the lowest point in the local neighborhood, but the global minimum is the lowest point overall.

Logit   In machine learning, an unnormalized probability value. Unlike probabilities, logits are not limited to the [0, 1] interval or required to sum to 1. Hence, they can be more easily output by a neural network layer. A set of logits can be normalized to probability values through an operation called *softmax*.

Machine learning   A subfield of artificial intelligence (AI) that automates the discovery of rules for solving complex problems by using data labeled with the desired answers. It differs from classical programming in that no handcrafting of the rules is involved.

Markov decision process (MDP)   In reinforcement learning, a decision process in which the current state and the action selected by the agent completely determine the next state that the agent will end up with and the reward the agent will receive at the step. It is an important simplification that enables learning algorithms such as Q-learning.

Model In machine learning and deep learning, an object that transforms input data (such as an image) into the desired output (such as a text label for the image) through a number of successive mathematical operations. A model has parameters (called *weights*) that can be tuned during training.

Model adaptation The process of training a pretrained model or a part of it in order to make the model achieve better accuracy during inference on the input data from a specific user or specific use case. It is a type of transfer learning, one in which the types of the input features and the type of the target don't differ from the original model.

Model deployment The process of packaging a trained model to the place where it can be used for making predictions. Similar to "pushing to production" for other software stacks, deployment is how users can get to use models "for real."

MobileNet A pretrained deep convolutional neural network. It is typically trained on the ImageNet image-classification dataset and can be used for transfer learning. Among similar pretrained convolutional neural networks, it has a relatively small size and involves less computation to perform inference, and is therefore more suitable to run in a resource-restricted environment such as the web browser, with TensorFlow.js.

Multiclass classification A classification problem in which the target may take more than two discrete labels. Examples are what kind of animal a picture contains or what (natural) language a web page is in given its content.

Multi-hot encoding A way to represent the words in a sentence (or, in general, the items in a sequence) as a vector by setting the elements that correspond to the words to 1 and leaving the rest as 0. This can be viewed as a generalization of *one-hot encoding*. It discards the information regarding the order of the words.

Multilayer perceptron (MLP) A neural network consisting of feedforward topology and at least one hidden layer.

Natural language processing The subfield of computer science that studies how to use computers to process and understand natural language, most prominently text and speech. Deep learning finds many applications in natural language processing.

Neural network A category of machine-learning models inspired by the layered organization seen in biological neural systems. The layers of a neural network perform multistep, separable transformations of the data representation.

Nonlinearity An input-output relation that does not meet the definition of linearity (linear combinations of inputs lead to a linear combination of the outputs, up to a constant-term difference). In neural networks, nonlinear relations (such as sigmoid and relu activations in layers) and the cascading of multiple such relations can increase the capacity of the neural networks.

Object detection   A computer-vision task that involves detecting certain classes of objects and their location in an image.

One-hot encoding   The scheme of encoding categorical data as a vector of length N consisting of all zeros except at the index that corresponds to the actual class.

Op fusion   A computation-graph optimization technique in which multiple operations (or ops) are replaced with a single equivalent op. Op fusion reduces the op-dispatching overhead and can lead to more opportunities for further intra-op memory and performance optimization.

Out-of-vocabulary (OOV)   In the context of deep learning, when a *vocabulary* is used on a set of discrete items, the vocabulary sometimes doesn't include all possible items. When an item outside the vocabulary is encountered, it is mapped to a special index called out-of-vocabulary, which can then be mapped to a special element in the one-hot encoding or embedding representation. See *vocabulary*.

Overfitting   When a model is fit to the training data in such a way that the model has sufficient capacity to memorize the training data, we see the training loss continue to go down, but the testing or validation loss starts to rise. Models with this property begin to lose their ability to generalize and perform well only on the exact samples in the training data. We say models in this circumstance are overfit.

Policy gradients   A type of reinforcement-learning algorithm that computes and utilizes the gradients of certain measures (such as logits) of selected actions with respect to the weights of a policy network in order to cause the policy network to gradually select better actions.

Precision   A metric of a binary classifier, defined as the ratio of the examples labeled by the classifier as positive that are actually positive. See *recall*.

Pseudo examples   Additional examples based on known valid mutations of input training examples, used to supplement the training data. For instance, we might take the MNIST digits and apply small rotations and skews. These transformations do not change the image label.

Q-network   In reinforcement learning, a neural network that predicts the Q-values of all possible actions given the current state observation. The Q-learning algorithm is about training a Q-network using data from the agent's experience.

Q-value   In reinforcement learning, the expected total future cumulative reward for taking an action at a given state. Hence a Q-value is a function of action and state. It guides the selection of actions in Q-learning.

Random initialization   Before a model is fit, the process of assigning the weights an initial value as a starting point. There is much literature on what, exactly, are good distributions to choose from for the initial values based on the layer type, size, and task.

Recall   A metric of a binary classifier, defined as the ratio of the actual examples that are labeled by the classifier as positive. See *precision*.

Regression   A type of learning problem where the desired output (or label) is a number or list of numbers. Making predictions that are numerically closer to the expected output is better.

Regularization   In machine learning, the process of imposing various modifications to the loss function or the training process in order to counteract overfitting. There are several ways to perform regularization, the most frequently used of which are L1 and L2 regularization of weights.

Reinforcement learning (RL)   A type of machine learning that involves learning optimal decisions that maximize a metric called a *reward* through interacting with an environment. Chapter 11 of this book covers the basics of RL and how to solve simple RL problems using deep-learning techniques.

ResNet   Short for *residual network*; a popular convolutional network widely used in computer vision, featuring residual connections—that is, connections that skip layers.

ROC curve   A way to visualize the trade-off between the true positive rate (recall) and the false positive rate (false-alarm rate) of a binary classifier. The name of the curve (the *receiver operating characteristics curve*) originated from the early days of radar technology. See *area under the curve* (AUC).

Spectrogram   An image-like 2D representation of 1D time signals such as sounds. A spectrogram has two dimensions: time and frequency. Each element represents the intensity or power the sound contains in a given frequency range at a given moment in time.

Supervised learning   The paradigm of training a machine-learning model using labeled examples. The internal parameters of the model are altered in a way that minimizes the difference between the model's output for the examples and the corresponding actual labels.

Symbolic tensor   In TensorFlow.js, an object of the `SymbolicTensor` class that is a specification for the shape and data type (dtype) of a tensor. Unlike a tensor, a `SymbolicTensor` object is not associated with concrete values. Instead, it is used as a placeholder for the input or output of a layer or a model.

Tensor   A data structure for holding data elements, usually numbers. Tensors can be thought of as *n*-dimensional grids, where each position in the grid holds exactly one element. The number of dimensions and size of each dimension is called the tensor's *shape*. For instance, a 3×4 matrix is a tensor with shape [3, 4]. A vector of length 10 is a 1D tensor with shape [10]. Each tensor instance holds only one type of element. Tensors are designed this way because it allows for convenient, highly efficient implementations of common operations necessary for deep learning: for instance, matrix dot products.

TensorBoard   A monitoring and visualization tool for TensorFlow. It allows users to visualize model structure and training performance in the browser. TensorFlow.js can write training logs in a data format compatible with TensorBoard.

TensorFlow   An open source Python library for accelerated machine learning, with a focus on deep neural networks. It was released by Google's Brain team in November 2015. Its API forms a blueprint for that of TensorFlow.js.

Training   The process of altering a machine-learning model's internal parameters (weights) to make the model's outputs more closely match the desired answers.

Training data   The data that is used to train a machine-learning model. Training data consists of individual examples. Each example is structured information (for example, images, audio, or text) in conjunction with the expected answer (the label).

Transfer learning   The practice of taking a machine-learning model previously trained for one task, retraining it with a relatively small amount of data (compared to the original training dataset) for a new task, and using it for inference on the new task.

Underfitting   When a model is trained for too few optimization steps, or a model has an insufficient representational power (capacity) to learn the patterns in the training data, which results in a model that does not reach a decent level of quality, we say that the model is underfit.

Unsupervised learning   The paradigm of machine learning that uses unlabeled data. It is opposed to supervised learning, which uses labeled data. Examples of unsupervised learning include clustering (discovering distinct subsets of examples in the dataset) and anomaly detection (determining if a given example is sufficiently different from the examples in the training set).

Validation data   Data that is set apart from training data for the tuning of hyperparameters, such as the learning rate or the number of units in a dense layer. Validation data allows us to tune our learning algorithm, possibly running training many times. Since validation data is also separate from testing data, we can still rely on the result from the test data to give us an unbiased estimate of how our model will perform on new, unseen data.

Vanishing-gradient problem   A classic problem in training deep neural networks in which the gradients on the weight parameter get increasingly smaller as the number of layers gets larger, and the weight parameters get farther and farther apart from the loss function as a result. In modern deep learning, this problem is mitigated through improved activation functions, proper initialization of weights, and other tricks.

Vectorization   The process of turning a piece of nonnumerical data into a representation as an array of numbers (such as a vector). For example, text vectorization involves turning characters, words, or sentences into vectors.

Visor   In tfjs-vis (a visualization library tightly integrated with TensorFlow.js), a collapsible region that can be created with a single function call on the side of the web page to hold surfaces for visualization. Multiple tabs can be created within a visor to organize the surfaces. See section 8.1 for details.

Vocabulary   In the context of deep learning, a set of discrete, unique items that may be used as the input to or output from a neural network. Typically, each item of the vocabulary can be mapped to an integer index, which can then be turned into a one-hot or embedding-based representation.

Weight   A tunable parameter of a neural network layer. Changing the weights changes the numerical details of how the input is transformed into the output. The training of a neural network is primarily about updating weight values in a systematic way.

Weight quantization   A technique for reducing the serialized and on-the-wire size of a model. It involves storing the weight parameters of the model at a lower numeric precision.

Word embedding   One way to vectorize words in text-related neural networks. A word is mapped onto a 1D tensor (or vector) via an embedding lookup process. Unlike one-hot encoding, the word embedding involves nonsparse vectors in which the element values are continuous-varying numbers instead of 0s and 1s.

index

Numerics

RELATED MANNING TITLES

Deep Learning with Python
by François Chollet

ISBN: 9781617294433
384 pages, $24.99
November 2017

Grokking Deep Learning
by Andrew W. Trask

ISBN: 9781617293702
336 pages, $49.99
January 2019

Deep Learning and the Game of Go
by Max Pumperla and Kevin Ferguson

ISBN: 9781617295324
384 pages, $54.99
January 2019

Deep Learning for Search
by Tommaso Teofili

ISBN: 9781617294792
328 pages, $59.99
June 2019

For ordering information go to www.manning.com